Selections from
The Girl's Own Paper,
1880–1907

The Girl's Own Paper, founded in 1880, both shaped and reflected tensions between traditional domestic ideologies of the period and New Woman values in the context of the figure of the New Girl. These selections from the journal demonstrate the efforts of its publisher (the Religious Tract Society) to combat the negative moral influence of sensational popular literature while at the same time addressing the desires of its audience for exciting reading material and information about topics mothers could not or would not discuss.

Selected fiction gives a rich sense of the conventions and the domestic ideology of the time; the nonfiction prose ranges from essays on conduct and household management to articles on new opportunities in education and work.

Terri Doughty is a Professor at Malaspina University College in Nanaimo, British Columbia. She has published on New Woman fiction as well as on gender issues in children's literature.

Selections from *The Girl's Own Paper,* 1880–1907

Terri Doughty

EDITOR

broadview reprint edition

National Library of Canada Cataloguing in Publication

Selections from The girl's own paper, 1880-1907 / edited by Terri Doughty. — Broadview reprint ed.

ISBN 1-55111-528-X

1. Teenage girls—England—History—19th century—Sources.
2. Teenage girls—England—History—20th century—Sources.
3. Teenage girls—England—Social conditions—Sources.
I. Doughty, Terri, 1962-

AP201.G57 2004   052'.0835'2   C2004-901524-9

Broadview Press Ltd. is an independent, international publishing house, incorporated in 1985. Broadview believes in shared ownership, both with its employees and with the general public; since the year 2000 Broadview shares have traded publicly on the Toronto Venture Exchange under the symbol BDP.

We welcome comments and suggestions regarding any aspect of our publications–please feel free to contact us at the addresses below or at broadview@broadviewpress.com.

North America
PO Box 1243, Peterborough, Ontario, Canada K9J 7H5
3576 California Road, Orchard Park, NY, USA 14127
Tel: (705) 743-8990; Fax: (705) 743-8353
email: customerservice@broadviewpress.com

UK, Ireland, and continental Europe
NBN Plymbridge
Estover Road, Plymouth PL6 7PY
Tel: +44 (0) 1752 202301; Fax: + 44 (0) 1752 202331; Fax Order Line: +44 (0) 1752 202333
Customer Service: cservs@nbnplymbridge.com; Orders: orders@nbnplymbridge.com

Australia and New Zealand
UNIREPS, University of New South Wales
Sydney, NSW, 2052
Tel: 61 2 9664 0999; Fax: 61 2 9664 5420
email: info.press@unsw.edu.au

www.broadviewpress.com

Broadview Press Ltd. gratefully acknowledges the financial support of the Government of Canada through the Book Publishing Industry Development Program for our publishing activities.

PRINTED IN CANADA

Contents

* Note on dating of volumes: Beginning in its first year of publication, the issues up to the end of September were collected and bound as annuals for the Christmas market. The first volume covers January to September of 1880. Subsequent volumes would cover the period from October to September; thus, the second volume covers October 1880 to September 1881, the third covers October 1881 to September 1882, and so on. Although the annual volumes are customarily identified by the second year covered, I have for accuracy's sake listed above the particular year in which each article was published.

Introduction

*T*he *Girl's Own Paper* was founded in 1880 by the Religious Tract Society as a companion to the successful *Boy's Own Paper*, both designed to counteract the influence of penny dreadfuls and cheap romances increasingly available to a susceptible working- and lower-middle-class audience. According to the editor, Charles Peters, *The Girl's Own Paper* would endeavor to be to girl readers "a Counsellor, Playmate, Guardian, Instructor, Companion, and Friend. It [would] help to train them in the moral and domestic virtues, preparing them for the responsibilities of womanhood and for a heavenly home" (qtd. in Reynolds 139–40). To this end, the magazine consisted of first fourteen, then sixteen pages of serial fiction, short stories, advice on household management (including cookery, housework, and both plain and fancy sewing), rules of etiquette, information on health and recreation, and, increasingly, information on new educational and professional opportunities for women. The weekly issue cost one penny (there was also a monthly edition, which cost sixpence). Letters to correspondents, a few letters published from correspondents, and lists of contest winners indicate that readers ranged from pre-teen girls to women in their fifties (there are even a few answers to male correspondents). In terms of class, readers ranged from servants to members of the upper-middle class. However, although the magazine was intended for working-class as well as middle-class readers, there are more articles on managing servants than on being a servant. The fiction and the material on domestic skills and social responsibilities imply a reader who is out of the schoolroom but not yet married: she should be looking forward to marriage, but until that happy day must learn to make productive use of her time and energies. There is also a persistent focus on economy; clearly readers are expected to be concerned about keeping up appearances on a budget. The magazine was highly successful, as *The Girl's Own Paper* rapidly reached a circulation of over 250,000, ultimately surpassing that of the *Boy's Own Paper* (Forrester 14; Dunae 135).

The Girl's Own was not the first magazine for girls. The earliest periodical addressed specifically to young women was the *Young Ladies' Magazine of Theology* (1838); its brief run suggests that it lacked an audience. However, the 1860s saw the emergence of more successful periodicals for adolescent girls: the *English Girls' Journal and Ladies' Magazine* (1863–64), a weekly penny paper published by Edward Harrison; the *Young Englishwoman* (1864–77), a sixpenny weekly published by Samuel Beeton; and the *Young Ladies' Journal* (1864–1920), started as a sixpenny weekly by Edward Harrison, after he had sold the *English Girls' Journal and Ladies' Magazine*. These magazines established a format of mixed short fiction, serial romances, fashion reviews, and articles on household management. Kirsten Drotner, in her excellent history of *English Children and Their Magazines 1751–1945*, calls the 1860s a period of transition in girls' periodical publishing (119). By the end of the decade, a short-lived sixpenny monthly called the *Girl of the Period Miscellany* (1869), no doubt capitalizing on and perhaps a response to Eliza Lynn Linton's 1868 essay, "The Girl of the Period," a notorious attack on the modern girl, added a new note to the mix: a focus on stronger, more independent heroines in its fiction and a movement toward practical, less high-minded advice in the nonfiction prose. *The Girl's Own Paper* would later refine and popularize this approach.

The Girl's Own attempted to capitalize on the new "girl culture" evolving in the 1880s and 1890s. During this period, "girl" became a contested signifier, creating a problem not only of definition, but, as many writers of the period would suggest, of identity. Generally, "girl" refers to an adolescent, unmarried female, but with many young women remaining unmarried for longer periods (by the early twentieth century, the average age at first marriage for women was 25), and some not marrying at all, age and marital status become decreasingly reliable as defining factors (Mitchell 8). On the one hand, this created a problem for some commentators, attested to by the prevalence of periodical articles with variations on the title, "What Can Our Girls Do?" These articles generally construct girlhood as a dangerous period, implying that if a girl is not safely occupied or contained in either the parental or marital home, she represents a frightening potential for social disorder. On the other hand, fluidity in the definition of girlhood could be liberating, just as the expanding space framed by the schoolroom and the marital home created an opportunity for independence of a sort, whether through formal education or work. As the Answers to Correspondents section of *The Girl's Own* attests, many of the self-identified "girl" readers were hungry for information on education, work, and independent living. The new girl culture, manifested in a range of novels, periodicals (*The Girl's Own* would be joined by magazines like *The Girl's Best Friend* and *Girl's Realm*), sports, and leisure activities, was both a market response to and the producer of a newly self-conscious class of young females who inhabited an evolving period of adolescent opportunity, neither children nor wives and mothers.

These New Girls were uneasily related to the figure of the New Woman. As the heroine of an anonymous 1902 *Girl's Own* story entitled "The New Girl" notes, it is "curious that while we talk so often about the New Woman, no one ever mentions the New Girl. The New Woman must have 'growed' somehow; she must have been a girl once, and yet no one ever thinks of that" (24: 153). The New Woman was not "christened" as such until 1894 (see Jordan); however, she had been developing as a cultural stereotype since the 1870s. The New Woman rode a bicycle and advocated for rational dress; she smoked; she was educated; she wanted to do man's work; and she wanted the vote. In the popular press, the New Woman was usually caricatured as an ugly, often mannish, bitter and unhappy spinster. She was the opposite of the "womanly woman," who embodied the virtues of feminine self-sacrifice and devotion to the family, a true "angel in the house," in the term popular-

ized by Coventry Patmore's famous poem of the same title (written in four volumes published between 1854 and 1861). New Girls interested in new educational and professional opportunities had to negotiate the tensions between these two mythical creatures, the monstrous New Woman and the sweet Angel in the House. How far might a girl carry her independence yet avoid being attacked as unwomanly? How far might a magazine cater to the growing market for information on new opportunities for women yet avoid being attacked for promoting unwomanly desires?

Some critics have found *The Girl's Own Paper's* response to this question to be hopelessly conservative. Even though the magazine was distributed by the innocent sounding Leisure Hour Office, it was published by the Religious Tract Society, which maintained that the magazine should improve the moral and religious character of its readers. Annual reports and minutes of the Religious Tract Society record its concern to balance the paper's secular appeal with its spiritual purpose (Dunae 135; Forrester 16). Certainly the fiction in *The Girl's Own* was reactionary, working to absorb and tame rebellion. There are plenty of "madcaps" and rebels in *Girl's Own* serials, with titles like "Wild Kathleen" (vol. 1, 1880) and "Ethel Rivers' Ambition" (vol. 7, 1885–86). Without exception in these stories, willfulness, ambition, and "unwomanliness" are punished. As a case in point, Ethel Rivers, who declines a perfectly suitable marriage proposal because she wants to become a great writer, finds her work ridiculed by reviewers, and the strain of work makes her go blind. Suitably humbled, she finally marries her magnanimous suitor and regains just enough eyesight to raise her family and write occasional stories for children. Serial summaries make for depressing reading. The nonfiction pieces are much more complex than the fiction, however. There are indeed reactionary elements in the nonfiction, particularly in the advice on household management, conduct, and self-culture. Even in seemingly progressive essays, one can find apologetic or cautionary asides: a hospital nurse, describing her profession in 1888, pauses momentarily to explain, "[d]o not misunderstand me; home duties must ever come first, and, well-performed, are surely the truest outcome of real love. I am far, indeed, from setting up nursing above such duties" (see pp. 106–07 in this volume for the full article). Similarly, a rather spirited defense of "Modern Girls" by Amy S. Woods in 1893 loses some of its vigor as the essay progresses. After extolling how far the modern girl has come, and noting her ability to rival men's educational achievements, the writer abruptly changes her tone: "I do not for one moment desire to question the superiority of man" (14: 500). From this point on, the author's sentiments are utterly conventional. Nonetheless, *The Girl's Own* provided a great deal of progressive information as well, catering to the New Girl's desire for guidance on how to negotiate the changing cultural status and identity of women.

The 1894 cartoon "The Child: How Will She Develop?" (16: 12–13) illustrates perfectly the balance maintained by the magazine. The "good" girl moves from social and academic success at school and college to a happy and productive life as wife and mother. The "bad" girl is disliked at school and wastes her time reading what appears to be a French novel, a standard code for lack of morality since the eighteenth century; she ends up discontented and alone with her cat (some stereotypes have had a long life). The point of the cartoon is twofold: first, it shows that women can pursue education yet remain "womanly"; second, it shows that the New Woman, she who dresses in mannish clothing and engages in sexual warfare (note the placard behind the girl which exhorts women to "arise to suppress the enemy—man"), is not an appropriate role model for *Girl's Own* readers. Readers are given a middle ground to occupy: they may pursue new opportunities, but only so far. The editor of *The Girl's Own*, Charles Peters, was particularly skilled at containing the new girl by providing content that fed into the development of an idealized girl culture while still seeming to direct girl readers away from the more "dangerous" aspects of that culture.

This ability to respond to market demand yet still appear to serve the conservative aims of the Religious Tract Society contributed in no small amount to the success of *The Girl's Own Paper*. Girls could find progressive information and inspiration in its pages, and remain safely wrapped in the paper's cloak of respectability. Although numerous girls' magazines emerged in the late nineteenth century, none had the longevity of *The Girl's Own*. There were cheap weeklies aimed at working-class girls, such as *The Girls' Best Friend* (1898; in 1899 the title changed to *The Girls' Friend*, which ran until 1931), a halfpenny paper published by Alfred Harmsworth, who built a publishing empire from catering to what critics felt was the lowest common denominator. These penny and halfpenny papers focused almost entirely on romance and sensation. They marketed escape rather than self-improvement and did not really compete in *The Girl's Own*'s market. The main rivals to *The Girl's Own* were magazines like *Every Girl's Magazine* (1878–88), *Atalanta* (1887–98), and *Girl's Realm* (1898–1915), sixpenny monthlies that catered predominantly to the middle-class girl, offering the established mix of fiction and nonfiction articles designed to educate and promote personal development. *Atalanta*, edited by the popular novelist L. T. Meade, was particularly noted for the quality of its fiction. It also, as Sally Mitchell notes, celebrated women's achievements and culture (11–13). However, Meade was able to sustain the magazine for only eleven years. *Girl's Realm*, which emphasized sports and recreation, lasted a bit longer, but toward the end of its run, it started to move more in the direction of a traditional women's magazine, with more of a focus on the domestic arts; eventually it merged with *Woman at Home*. *The Girl's Own* experienced some of the same problems with readership shortly before the First World War. After Charles Peters's death in 1907, the magazine was edited by Flora Klickmann. In 1908, she retitled the magazine *The Girl's Own Paper and Woman's Magazine* in an attempt to broaden its readership. She discontinued the weekly penny numbers and made a number of changes to the contents of the magazine, cutting down on the number of serials, focusing more on short fiction and informative essays. The magazine continued to offer advice on professional development, but it also devoted greater attention to matters of fashion and domestic management. In 1929, the magazine was briefly titled *The Woman's Magazine and Girl's Own Paper*, before it split into two separate magazines in 1930 (Klickmann resigned as editor

AT SCHOOL. FRIENDS WITH ALL.

THE CHILD :—
HOW WILL SHE DEVELOP?

AT SCHOOL. DISLIKED BY MOST.

AT COLLEGE. CONGRATULATED.

WASTE OF TIME.

DEVELOPMENT OF HEART.

VARIETIES.

RULES FOR HOUSE-FURNISHING.

The following general principles on house-furnishing have been laid down by a French writer :—

1. The dwelling must be like the dweller.

2. In every house the chief room should correspond to the chief interest of the dweller ; for instance, in an artist's it should be the studio, or in the case of a man of letters the study.

3. Furniture should be bought bit by bit, and never all at once, as it is by degrees that our ideas grow and develop.

4. When buying always be guided by taste only, a sense of fitness and a feeling of need, never by any idea of imitation, nor by vanity, nor by the price.

Whether we agree with all this or not, there is no doubt that the more completely a house represents the character, tastes, and ideas of its inmates, the more original and interesting it is, and the more lovable and home-like, if we care for the people living in it.

AN EXPENSIVE YOUNG LADY.

Estimates of the rate of expenditure of any class of people must be taken with a grain of salt. But no doubt there is some truth in the following attempt made recently by a New York journal to reckon up the cost of the fashionable New York girl.

With £500 a year as a low estimate for her dress, a sum ranging from £180 to £300 a year is set down for " finishing " her education at a really first-class school. And this does not include " music, painting, dancing, modern and dead languages," English and French excepted, which are all extras.

The budget is given approximately thus :— Education, £180 ; dancing, £8 ; riding, £8 ; fencing, £8 ; music, £16 ; athletics, £13 ; baths, £30 ; bonbons, £30. The total is £293. But in this estimate there is no allowance for painting, swimming, bowling, languages, flowers, matinée-tickets, a maid, a groom, a manicure, a hairdresser, gifts, charity, or clothing.

LIFE WORTH LIVING.—Make life a ministry of love, and it will always be worth living.
Browning.

THE FALLING AWAY. WANT OF SYMPATHY.

THE INTRODUCTION. GOOD HABITS AND PLEASANT FRIENDS.

BAD HABITS AND BAD FRIENDS.

WEDDED.

MATERNITY.

HAPPY OLD AGE.

GOVERN YOUR TEMPER.—First study to acquire a composure of mind and body. Avoid agitation of one or the other, especially before and after meals, and whilst the process of digestion is going on. To this end, govern your temper, endeavour to look at the bright side of things, keep down as much as possible the unruly passions, discard envy, hatred, and malice, and lay your head upon your pillow in charity with all mankind. Let not your wants outrun your means. Whatever difficulties you have to encounter, be not perplexed, but only think what is right to do in the sight of Him who seeth all things, and bear without pining the results. When your meals are solitary, let your thoughts be cheerful; when they are social, which is better, avoid disputes, or serious arguments, or unpleasant topics. "Unquiet meals," says Shakspeare, "make ill digestions;" and the contrary is produced by easy conversation, a pleasant project, welcome news, or a lively companion. I advise wives not to entertain their husbands with domestic grievances about children or servants, nor to ask for money, nor propound unreasonable or provoking questions; and advise husbands to keep the cares and vexations of the world to themselves, but to be communicative of whatever is comfortable, cheerful, and amusing. Self-government is the best step to health and happiness.—*Walker.*

HOW TO LOOK OLD AND UGLY.—We are doing a great deal towards making ourselves look old and ugly when we give way to worry and fretfulness.—*Ruskin.*

BEWARE OF PRIDE.—There is no passion which steals into the heart more imperceptibly and covers itself under more disguises than pride.—*Addison.*

MORAL COURAGE.—Have the courage to speak your mind when it is necessary to do so, and to hold your tongue when it is better that you should be silent. Have the courage to speak to a poor friend in a threadbare coat, even in the street, and when a rich one is nigh; the effort is less than many take it to be, and the act is worthy a king. Have the courage to adhere to a first resolution when you cannot change it for a better, and to abandon it at the eleventh hour upon conviction. Have the courage to say you hate the "polka," and prefer an English song to an Italian "piece of music," if such be your taste. Have the courage to wear your old garments till you can pay for new ones. Have the courage to prefer propriety to fashion—one is but the abuse of the other.—*W. Jones, F.S.A.*

READING HER OWN PRINTED PHILOSOPHY.

DISCONTENT.

A MISERABLE END.

A "FAIRY" STORY.

BY MRS. BRIGHTWEN, Author of "Wild Nature Won by Kindness."

I AM often envied as the possessor of one of the most charming bird pets it is possible to imagine.

My "Fairy" is a tiny whitethroat, a sleek, delicate grey-coloured bird with a pure white breast, of lovely form, swift in flight, and of most engaging disposition.

I met with it in this wise. A plaintive little cheeping sound attracted my attention one morning at breakfast-time, and looking outside the window, I saw a tiny half-fledged bird sitting on the ground, looking pitifully up at me; it pleaded its hungry condition with open beak, and seemed to have no fear at my approach. Of course such a poor little motherless waif must be cared for, so I brought it in, and it received very readily the provender I offered it.

I never saw such a tiny quaint-looking piece of bird-life; its little throat feathers were beginning to show on either side like a small white cravat; it had about half an inch of tail, and minute quills all over its body gave token of coming feathers. The delightful thing about it was its exceeding tameness; it would sit on your finger and gaze at you with a considering expression; no noise frightened it; it was quite content with life in a basket, or on the table, and therefore it became my constant companion, and has grown to be very dear to me and a wide circle of friends.

Fairy's advent was in July, and for the first month the early morning feeding was no small care, but love makes all things easy, and at last my small charge could feed itself, and learnt the use of its wings.

Daily baths were taken in my soap dish, which was amply large enough at first, but now Fairy is promoted to the sponge basin, in which she flutters every morning to her heart's content and dries herself afterwards by swift flights about the room. The bath over, the next thing is to search for flies on the window-panes, or on the floor; these are snapped up as great dainties, and in this way Fairy has greatly promoted my comfort all through the heat of August and September (1893) by keeping our rooms free of winged insects.

"The Child: How Will She Develop?" (Volume 16, 6 October 1894, p. 13).

at this point) and *The Girl's Own* once again became a strictly adolescent magazine and experienced a kind of renaissance throughout the 1930s. During the Second World War, *The Girl's Own* suffered under paper shortages and was reduced in format in 1941. The magazine never quite regained its popularity after the war. In 1947 the title changed to *Girl's Own Paper and Heiress*; in 1951 this was shortened simply to *Heiress*, but the magazine lasted only a few more years, ceasing publication in 1956.

The prose selections reproduced here come from the period of Charles Peters's editorship, 1880–1907. It might seem more reasonable to have cut off at either 1901, Queen Victoria's death, or 1914, the beginning of the First World War, but I found 1901 an artificial cut-off point, as the magazine continued its work in girl culture well into the twentieth century. I also did not want to select material from the magazine after Peters's death in 1907, as Flora Klickmann's changes in title and content moved the focus of the magazine away from girl culture specifically. By contrast, under Peters *The Girl's Own* helped to make girl culture. Essays and articles on the following topics illustrate the tensions in late-nineteenth- and early-twentieth-century girl culture: household management, conduct, self-culture, education, work, independent living, and health and sports. Each section is organized chronologically, with pieces presented by date of publication. Because many of the articles were published anonymously or pseudonymously, it is not always possible to identify authors. I have done so wherever I could, but I have not provided author biographies. Each section does, nonetheless, have a brief introduction to set the individual articles in context. *The Girl's Own Paper* is not widely accessible, save in library collections of bound annuals, and most of these are kept in special collections. The facsimile pages reprinted here allow readers to see texts as they appeared in original layouts. This means that in addition to the selected texts, readers will find fragments of non-featured articles, stories, poems, and sundry "varieties" used as "filler" by the editor. Setting aside the filter of editorial selection and introductory contexts, this is as close as readers can come to an unmediated relationship with the original texts. A cartoon supportive of women's education like "The Child: How Will She Develop?" exists side by side with "filler" that emphasizes traditional cautions to women on self-monitoring and self-policing, as well as hints on household management. Readers can experience the tensions and contradictions in the design and content of the magazine that spoke to its conflicted readers. This reprint edition finally brings some of this fascinating material back into general circulation. It also serves as a snapshot of a cultural moment: the emergence of a new girl culture and its challenge to traditional notions of femininity.

Works Cited and Recommended Reading

Beetham, Margaret. *A Magazine of Her Own: Domesticity and Desire in the Woman's Magazine 1800–1914*. London: Routledge, 1996.

————, and Kay Boardman, eds. *Victorian Women's Magazines: An Anthology*. Manchester: Manchester UP, 2001.

Cadogan, Mary, and Patricia Craig. *You're a Brick, Angela!* London: Victor Gollancz, 1976.

"The Child: How Will She Develop?" *Girl's Own Paper* 16 (6 October 1894): 12–13.

Drotner, Kirsten. *English Children and Their Magazines 1751–1945*. New Haven: Yale UP, 1988.

Dunae, Patrick. "*Boy's Own Paper:* Origin and Editorial Policies." *The Private Library*, second series 9.4 (1976): 125–58.

Dyhouse, Carol. *Girls Growing Up in Late Victorian and Edwardian England*. London: Routledge and Kegan Paul, 1981.

Flint, Kate. *The Woman Reader 1837–1914*. Oxford: Oxford UP, 1993.

Forrester, Wendy. *Great-Grandmama's Weekly: A Celebration of the* Girl's Own Paper *1880–1901*. Guildford: Lutterworth Press, 1980.

Galbraith, Gretchen R. *Reading Lives: Reconstructing Childhood, Books, and Schools in Britain, 1870–1920*. New York: St. Martin's, 1997.

Jordan, Ellen. "The Christening of the New Woman: May 1894." *Victorian Newsletter* 63 (1983): 19–21.

Ledger, Sally. *The New Woman: Fiction and Feminism at the* Fin de Siècle. Manchester: Manchester UP, 1997.

Linton, Eliza Lynn. "The Girl of the Period." *Saturday Review* 14 March 1868: 339–40.

McCrone, Kathleen E. *Sport and the Physical Emancipation of English Women, 1870–1914*. London: Routledge, 1988.

Mitchell, Sally. *The New Girl: Girls' Culture in England 1880–1915*. New York: Columbia UP, 1995.

Nelson, Carolyn Christensen, ed. *A New Woman Reader: Fiction, Articles, Drama of the 1890s*. Peterborough: Broadview Press, 2001.

"The New Girl." *Girl's Own Paper* 24 (6 December 1902): 153–55.

Reynolds, Kim. *For Girls Only? Gender and Popular Children's Fiction in Britain 1880–1910*. New York: Harvester-Wheatsheaf, 1990.

Schaffer, Talia. "'Nothing but Foolscap and Ink': Inventing the New Woman." *The New Woman in Fiction and in Fact:* Fin-de-Siècle *Feminisms*. Ed. Angelique Richardson and Chris Willis, pp. 39–52. Houndmills: Palgrave, 2001.

Skelding, Hilary. "Every Girl's Best Friend? The *Girl's Own Paper* and Its Readers." *Feminist Readings of Victorian Popular Texts: Divergent Femininities*. Ed. Emma Liggins and Daniel Duffy. Aldershot: Ashgate, 2001. 35–52.

Vallone, Lynne. *Disciplines of Virtue: Girls' Culture in the Eighteenth and Nineteenth Centuries*. New Haven: Yale UP, 1995.

————, and Claudia Nelson, eds. *The Girls' Own: A Cultural History of the Anglo-American Girl 1830–1915*. Athens: U of Georgia P, 1994.

Vicinus, Martha. *Independent Women: Work and Community for Single Women, 1850–1920*. Chicago: U of Chicago P, 1985.

Woods, Amy S. "Modern Girls." *Girl's Own Paper* 14 (6 May 1893): 499–500.

Acknowledgements

I would like to thank my colleagues Marni Stanley and Helen Brown for their lively interest in and support for this project.

The articles reproduced here were scanned from original annuals of the *Girl's Own Paper* from the editor's own collection and volumes from the libraries at Malaspina University-College and the University of Victoria. I owe particular thanks to Lyn Makepeace, Humanities Librarian at Malaspina, and Joanne Whiting, of Inter-Library Loans at Malaspina. I also must thank the staff of the Centre for Digital Humanities Innovation (CDHI) at Malaspina for technical support. All scanning was done by the editor and CDHI staff.

In particular, I want to acknowledge the assistance of Anne Correia, whose energy and commitment to the project were indispensable.

Household Management

From the first, *The Girl's Own Paper* regularly featured articles on household economy, cooking, needlework, and managing servants. Household hints were also often used as "filler" on pages. A few articles were clearly designed for newlyweds, but most were aimed at unmarried girls, promoting the value of domestic duties. If *The Girl's Own* provided information on educational opportunities for girls, it also provided patterns for girls to sew academic hoods for their brothers. In its first decade, the magazine ran serial stories, such as Dora Hope's "She Couldn't Boil a Potato; or, The Ignorant Housekeeper and How She Acquired Knowledge" (vol. 8, 1886–87), that were thinly disguised lessons in housekeeping. In the 1890s, articles not only continued to preach domestic ideology, but some also began to attack New Girls who might want to grow into New Women. Others, looking forward to the development of domestic "science," tried to appeal to New Girls by emphasizing the intelligence, training, and skill required to manage the household.

Alice King's "Higher Thoughts on Housekeeping" (vol. 5, 1883–84, pp. 235–36) insists on the vital importance of domestic duties, urging girls to resist the seductive lure of new work opportunities. King was a regular contributor to the magazine; she also shared "higher thoughts" on work for girls, emphasizing the traditional feminine virtues of self-denial and self-sacrifice.

The anonymously written "How to Live on £100 a Year" (vol. 7, 1885–86, pp. 228–30) addresses a common problem for those of the lower middle-class: how to afford marriage without sacrificing standard of living. The article is supposedly by a young wife, illustrating her successful economies.

The author of the next piece, Phillis Browne [Sarah Hamer], was a frequent contributor to the magazine in its early years, writing about how to shop for and prepare food economically. "The Bride's First Dinner-Party" (vol. 8, 1886–87, pp. 214–16) uses fictive elements to liven its explanation of how, with the help of servants, to prepare for a dinner-party. Note that this article is followed by a poem about a college-educated girl.

Emma Brewer wrote a series of pieces entitled "Our Friends the Servants" (vol. 14, 1892–93); the segment included here (pp. 402–03) gives advice on managing female servants' social lives, warning mistresses particularly to restrict them from receiving male visitors to avoid domestic disruption.

Queen Victoria is often referred to as a domestic exemplar in *The Girl's Own*. "The Queen at Home" (vol. 15, 1893–94, pp. 337–39) focuses on the Queen's love of home life at Balmoral Castle. It appeared in the same year that the New Woman was christened. Clearly, the "homely" Queen is a more favoured model of femininity for *The Girl's Own*.

Mrs. Orman Cooper's "Queen Baby and Her Wants" (vol. 18, 1896–97, pp. 92–93) covers more than how to prepare a layette for a newborn. The article makes a clear attack on the "unwomanly" New Woman in its opening. Subsequent pages focus on the making of babies' clothing.

By the turn of the century, however, even household management had become a subject for formal study. "London's Future Housewives and Their Teachers" (vol. 20, 1898–99, pp. 737–39) describes classes at one of the London County Council's Schools of Domestic Economy, at the Battersea Polytechnic.

Finally, "Good Mistresses" (vol. 26, 1904–05, pp. 588–89) not only illustrates the magazine's ongoing attention to domestic matters, but also typifies the magazine's shift to a more solidly middle-class market.

might be "good-bye" to all the happy interchange of thought and feeling which had so brightened the past few weeks for him, and that in losing Frida his life would become colourless and grey.

A dead silence was the greeting for the musicians at the end of their performance, and it was not till Frida and Szantó were nearly out of the room that a burst of applause testified to them the stillness had come from sympathy, and not from lack of enthusiasm.

They went back to the terrace, and Frida, seating herself and looking across the river to the opposite bank, where the moon was just rising over the trees, said, simply—

"How lovely your music is, and how it tells my heart the sadness of 'Farewell.'"

"Frida," said Szantó, suddenly, "this shall not be farewell. Do you not feel it cannot be? I love you; why should we part? I shall be no musician now, without your inspiration. We have been so happy; let us make our lives one harmony. Think what we might do, and be, if we were together! Dear Frida, tell me you will be my wife."

Frida raised her great eyes to his; they were swimming with tears, but the happy light in them could not be hidden. No fears of the future beset either of them as they sat beside the flowing river in the still night, and talked, as lovers will, as if the world held no other hopes or joys than theirs.

The evening ended all too soon, and Mrs. Somerset seemed for the first time unpleasing, as she came to tell Frida they must go. Demetri was to see Herr Bund to-morrow morning, and no shadow of doubt arose in the girl's mind as to his reception of Von Szantó's proposal to become his son. As she drove home in the soft air, she did think with something of awe and dread of the mother and sisters in the old castle at Szantó, wondering if she should find it very hard to conquer the stiffness which she knew so well she should encounter; but would not everything be easy, for Demetri would be with her? This thought silenced all doubts, and left her to enjoy the happiness of the few hours before the time when she would see her father at breakfast, and would warn him of Von Szantó's coming.

She often remembered that night in after days; the joy of it, and the waking from short slumber with the blissful sense that something glorious had broken on her life.

At breakfast Frida appeared, looking lovelier than ever, and Herr Bund could not help silently admiring her, as she began to tell him, in her usual way, of the doings of the previous night. He was much interested apparently in his letters, and Frida found it rather hard to be sure he was attending to her sufficiently to make it possible she should mention the subject nearest her heart.

At last she told him of the "Farewell," and of the silence which the audience had kept for the few minutes at the end, and then she said, "We went out on the terrace, and Demetri——"

At this, the first time he had heard her mention Von Szantó's Christian name, Herr Bund looked up and said, "My child, you are speaking of Count von Szantó."

Frida rose, and, going to her father's side, said, softly, "He will always be 'Demetri' to me now, father. He loves me; I have promised to be his wife; he comes this morning to talk with you."

Herr Bund started from his chair, and, confronting the dismayed Frida, with rage in his countenance, exclaimed, "What! you have the assurance to tell me you mean to marry? After all I have done for you: after your education, and the never-ceasing care I have bestowed, you throw up your career, you

desert me, you intend to bury yourself in a mouldy castle with a poverty-stricken slip of nobility, forsooth! and all other claims are disregarded. It shall not be!" He paused from lack of breath, and Frida, pale, trembling, and overwhelmed with the sudden outburst, revealing, as it seemed to do, a baser side to her father's character, tried in vain to calm him and to explain that they had no thought of giving up his profession, but that both would work for him, so he would find his life easier instead of more difficult. It was in vain, he had lost all self-control, and stormed and raged, overpowering Frida with his wordy wrath till they were interrupted by the arrival of Demetri, when Herr Bund was forced to become more calm and to listen to Von Szantó, who, in a few manly words, told him of his love for his daughter and of the hopes he entertained.

He, too, was unprepared for the manner in which his advances were received, for Herr Bund, speaking with a sort of calm contempt, put his proposals aside, and said he had quite other intentions as to the way in which Frida's life should be spent.

Demetri turned with a bewildered air to Frida, and asked her if she, too, agreed to dismiss him.

"No," replied she; "I have consented to nothing. I will wait; my father will change."

"Never!" said Herr Bund, brusquely; "I am determined your talent shall not be wasted thus; you shall become famous as no other woman artist has been, and rich——"

"I hope the riches will be hers even when she is my wife," interposed Demetri, "for I have this morning received a telegram from my agent saying that coal has been discovered on my estate, and begging me at once to go home and arrange about excavating it. This explains his behaviour," he continued, turning to Frida, "and I rejoice, for it relieves me from the feeling that all depended on my professional success. Coal is badly needed in our district, and the place where this is found is not so far from a railway as to make the carriage difficult. Surely, Herr Bund, this will change your determination—if I become wealthy you will alter your views?"

"No," replied the other; "this wealth is but a dream. I will hear nothing of your proposals, and I charge you, Frida, to think no more of this folly."

A painful scene ensued, but at the end Demetri was compelled to depart with very little hope that Bund would forego the handling of present gains for the hope of future happiness for his daughter; and Frida, though she would not consent to give up Demetri, was compelled to promise that she would not let his wishes interfere with her father's plans—at any rate, for the present.

Demetri was obliged to leave her, and the parting was necessarily a sad one, more so for her than for him, as he had the prospect of engrossing occupation during the time he could spare to spend in Hungary, and the consciousness that the discovery was for him a most momentous and valuable one—far more so than Bund, with his ignorance of the country, could estimate. He determined that, things once straight at Szantó, no obstacles should prevent him from bringing Frida there as his wife, and he cared very little for the opposition of the "vulgar little music-seller," as he called Herr Bund.

(To be continued.)

HIGHER THOUGHTS ON HOUSEKEEPING.

By ALICE KING.

As we wander through the woods on a summer evening, who has not paused to admire the little spots of gleaming light which sparkle among the long grass and soft mosses, shining as brightly as if they were stars which have been dropped from the clear blue sky above. What beautiful creatures these must be, we think, which glisten and glitter with such strange radiance; surely they must be some of the brightest-tinted insects which we see in the daytime, flashing hither and thither in the sunlight; they must be resting here after their busy wings have grown weary. We stoop down with this idea strong in our mind, we take one of the tiny lamps of harmless fire in our hand, and carry them home with us and place it carefully under a glass, expecting to-morrow morning to rejoice our eyes in the brilliancy of its hues. The sun rises; we turn, when we wake, with eager gaze towards our radiant treasure which we laid by before we slept. What do we behold? Nothing but the most sober-coloured, modest little worm that ever crept through field or hedgerow.

The girl who has a real talent for housekeeping will generally have something of the glowworm in her nature and character; she will shed around her a soft brightness which will light the whole house and family; yet it will be a brightness which shines on others, and does not make herself shine; and when we come to know her intimately, we often find that she is the quietest, most silent, retiring member of the household.

Some of our readers will, perhaps, smile a little contemptuously to hear the word "talent" applied to what seems to them such a realistic, material thing as housekeeping. We can assure them, however, that there are, among our girls, born housekeepers, just as much as there are born authoresses and born musicians. A talent for housekeeping is, to speak shortly and comprehensively, a strong development in a woman of what are called the administrative faculties. Where these exist naturally in a girl she will generally show at once an inclination and an aptitude for managing and overlooking a household and keeping the whole domestic machinery going at once briskly and smoothly.

When a girl displays decidedly this faculty to the attentive eyes of those who watch over her youth and education, everything should be done to help her to unfold it and bring it into active use. She should be early entrusted with money, and should be allowed to manage her own and perhaps her sisters' dress; she should be encouraged to take an interest in all practical matters, such as the price of various commodities of food, etc.; she should be permitted to employ her power of arranging and settling small household affairs, such as parties or excursions of pleasure, or administrating the funds of small charities; she should attend cookery classes, and be helped to make experiments in the art of cookery itself.

Our girls should not entertain the foolish, erroneous idea that the housekeeper will be the stupid girl of the family; far from that, she who will make a really good, effectual housekeeper, is usually endowed, in her quiet way, with a stock of shrewdness, and plain, practical common sense, and bright clear-sightedness. It requires no weak, scanty intellectual power to rule well the domestic affairs of even a comparatively modest household; the eyes of the mind have to be looking at least twenty ways at once, and the thoughts to be travelling in as many directions. A girl who would be a really good housekeeper must have a clear head, and must avoid nothing so much as muddle and confusion. The untidily-kept account-book; the hazy, incorrect memory which can never remember whether the joint of beef or mutton came first into the larder; the slovenly store-room, where groceries and preserves lie huddled in grand disorder—these things most certainly do not belong to what can be called "good housekeeping."

In these days, when so many young women of gentle birth and nurture are so often in need of some means of gaining a respectable livelihood, it would be well if the prejudice could be got over among us against ladies taking situations as housekeepers in hotels or boarding-houses or large private establishments. On this point we want to do away with much false pride and much false shame; our girls should learn to feel and think that there is nothing low and degrading in such positions in life, if they are filled conscientiously and bravely, and with a high Christian sense of duty. If ladies would show themselves thorough practical workers as housekeepers, no doubt the prejudice against their occupying such situations would rapidly die out among us. It is certain that their lady's manners, and lady's feelings, and lady's culture would, in the long run, be a real help to them in such a calling; they would make them better managers of the inferior servants, would teach them that small economies are not beneath a good housekeeper's notice, would prevent their being above sometimes performing little domestic duties with their own hands. A real lady knows that she is just as much a lady when she sweeps a room as when she plays upon a piano, or sits on a sofa doing crewel work.

If our girls were taught a little more practical housekeeping in their school days, the benefit would certainly be incalculable in many a family of small means and limited income; such instruction would also greatly widen the sphere of usefulness of our girls themselves. It would be utterly ridiculous, if it were not utterly sad, as we pass down some row of houses in a country town, where our middle classes find their homes, to hear ringing forth from every window the tinkle of an inferior piano, or to enter the rooms in the same houses, and see every article of furniture in them clothed in specimens of wool-work, each more nameless and useless than its fellow; and then to reflect how much bright, healthy energy in the minds and fingers of the daughters of the family is wasted in these poor, make-believe counterfeits of real, earnest occupation. If the girl who is making indifferent, not to say bad music, was to be upstairs instead, sweeping and dusting, and making the home fresh and fair; if the girl who is sorting wools, was to be downstairs cooking the dinner, and making the family meal more wholesome and digestible, what a much more reasonable and sensible arrangement it would be, and what a much more useful and important member she would be of society.

It would be well if all those who overlook the education of our girls would impress upon them more, in their system of teaching, the dignity and beauty of all that is useful, and would make a less point of what is ornamental. As we have before said in this series of articles, when a girl has a real talent for any one art—for music, or literature, or painting—it should by all means be allowed a first place in the scheme of her education; but when no such talent exists, how far better it would be for the girl, and for all with whom she comes in contact in life, to make her at home in those branches of knowledge that would be really serviceable to herself and to those around her. We should have classes in our girls' schools for cookery, for plain needle-work, for teaching household management

generally; and in these such girls as have no artistic talent would soon unfold what other powers they have. If such things were more taught in our schools, and if those who excelled in them were to receive from their teachers their due meed of praise and encouragement, our girls would learn to see how foolish it is to look down on such acquirements.

Even the literary woman and the female artist need to know something of housekeeping; it is a branch of knowledge which cannot be left out of any woman's daily life unless under the most peculiar circumstances, and which, therefore, no girl's education can be complete without. The girl, then, who devotes herself to music or literature must certainly give at least a small portion of her time to the study of cookery and of household matters. It is a very wrong and false notion that a literary woman or a female artist cannot make the best of wives and mothers; there is not the smallest reason why she should not stand at the head of the list as both. She should indeed, from the extra refinement and delicacy of her feelings, exceed all other women in the way in which she holds both positions; while her greater breadth of mind should show her that it is no indignity to lay down her pen in order that she may make a pudding, or to employ the hands which have been flying over the keys in cutting out her baby's frocks.

A taste for reading is also quite compatible with being a good housekeeper; it is entirely a woman's own fault if she ever sinks into being a mere household drudge. What is there to hinder her, if she chooses it, from studying a deep book in the morning, and from preparing her husband's dinner in the afternoon? Her brains will not be one bit less clear and strong because her hands know how to be skilful and busy in their own department; she will not make a man the less intelligent and bright companion when he returns of an evening, will not discuss with him with less lively energy the leading topics of the day, because she has made half the dishes which stand between them on the table.

The art of being a good cook does more real excellent work in the world than perhaps our girls may fancy, and contributes more than they are probably aware towards the well-being of society. How many diseases are caused by constant suffering from the evil of indigestion; and even if the health is not permanently injured by it, how many tempers are spoiled by its frequent attacks, and how many lives are clouded by its persistent and relentless visits. Now, the chief cause of much of the indigestion which makes miserable so many English lives, is simply bad, unwholesome cookery. If, however, a woman is really a good, skilful cook, how easily this evil may be kept far from her family. Here is some tangible good at once which our girls may propose to themselves to do by making cookery their study.

One essential part of the duties of a good housekeeper generally consists in the management and guidance of inferiors. Our girls should keep this in mind and should strive to gain a good influence over the servants of their own family; such influence is to be won by a high Christian example, by unalterable sweetness of temper, by the tact which comes of superior mental cultivation. Our girls must strive to be the friends of the young servants of the house, while, at the same time, they must never be familiar with them, and always be leading them on to something nobler and better.

A lady who stands at the head of a large establishment has a vast and wide responsibility in her hands, responsibility which she cannot take upon herself too earnestly and solemnly. God has set her over many

things, and therefore from her much will be required.

The Christian lady who is the mistress of a large establishment will always feel that the moral and spiritual condition of every servant in it, down to the very lowest, is under her care. The conduct of the servants towards each other, their regular attendance at public worship, the religious instruction of the younger ones among them—all these things come within her province. The words just used about the mistress of a large establishment, apply, of course, in equal degree to every housekeeper who has several other people under her charge, and, in some measure, her control. To the manageress of the hotel, with regard to the vast staff of under servants; to the housekeeper in the shop, who superintends the goings in and out of all the young women employed in it; to the matron in charitable institutions, who is set over all the lower dependents belonging to the place; when we look at this side of a housekeeper's duties, we feel that hers is a high office indeed. If the housekeepers of England were to do thoroughly their Christian work in this respect, there would not be so often heard throughout the length and breadth of the land the universal cry about bad servants.

We have just spoken of the most important class of duties which come to the share of a housekeeper in the work of the world; now let us glance for a moment at the mass of small things which falls to her hand to do. Let the Christian woman remember that the very meanest, the very lowest, the most commonplace among them can be gilded and glorified, till it shines like a jewel of light, if only the beams of the Gospel sun fall upon it. It is just as grand and beautiful to sweep a room or polish a saucepan in the Master's name, as it is to write a book or paint a picture, that is, if it is really done thoroughly and to the best of our powers for His dear sake. Our girls need not fear that they shall place themselves on a lower level than their sisters by making housekeeping and household work the study and object of their lives, if they undertake it in a real, conscientious, Christian spirit, resolving to do what they have taken in hand in the very best way that it can possibly be done.

There is more to be said about the smaller employments of a housekeeper than there is room for in a short paper like the present one; such employments might indeed be divided into several different chapters. We may say, however, two things with regard to them all, and these two things are, that they should all be guided by a spirit of regularity and order, and that no extreme should ever be run into in the performance of any of them. A good housekeeper will have the week's work mapped out in her head on Monday morning, as clearly as the confines of each sea and each shore are drawn out on the sailor's chart before he starts on a voyage.

As for the subject of running into extremes, a few special words should perhaps be dedicated to it, as it is an error into which young housekeepers very often fall. Our girls, when they undertake housekeeping, must be careful, above all things, to keep a middle course in all they do. There must be no waste, but there must be no niggardly narrowness. Good housekeeping does not consist in having more cooked in a day than the whole family could consume in a week; but neither does it consist in weighing out every ounce of tea and counting every lump of sugar. Everything should be made the most and best use of that it can; in this respect the English housekeeper may learn much from her French sister, who makes the very utmost that can be made out of every bone and every vegetable in the garden.

Alice King, "Higher Thoughts on Housekeeping" (Volume 5, 12 January 1884, p. 236).

THE SYMBOL.

By HORACE G. GROSER.

NOT thrice the silver summer moon
  Had sphered her crescent dimly grey;
The harvest month was nigh, and soon
  Brown hands at Ceres' feet would lay
White oaten sheaves and poppies red,
  From sun-lit acres far away;

When first to me young Marcius sighed
  His tale of love, with vows sincere,
And wooed me for his virgin bride
  By tender words and names most dear;—
But ah! the myrtle wreaths are dead,
  My sun is set, and night is near.

The bond is severed—he is gone!
  But still I feel his hand's impress,
And see the angry eyes that shone—
  Those eyes once lit with tenderness—
And hear the stern impeachment fall
  From lips yet moist with love's caress.

'Twas in the gardens, when the light
  Fell slant the cypress spires between,
Where, winding from the gazer's sight,
  A pathway curved betwixt the green;
A favourite haunt for lovers all,
  Where many a soft-paced foot had been.

And there he found me, as he came
  From bending at Apollo's shrine,
Stern-browed, as though the Pythian flame
  Had fired his heart with zeal divine,
And, as we kissed, a glance betrayed
  The pendant cross, the hated sign.

I looked into his angry eyes,
  And silent stood, and silent he.
Red cloudlets drifted down the skies,
  The air of every sound was free,
And Pan with stony fingers played,
  Hard by, his silent minstrelsy.

Then came, in cruel tones and clear,
  The mocking words: "I little dreamed
To find the accurséd token here,
  Where all so fair and faultless seemed;
Whereby hath Jove thy favour lost,
  So lightly thus to be esteemed?

" By this I know why unreplaced
  The roses and the myrtles lay,
Wherewith thy stainless fingers graced
  The Paphian's image, day by day;
And why the ungathered apples toss'd,
  Sun-mellowed, o'er the orchard way.

" By this I know why paled thy cheek,
  When, gazing on the arena sands,
Thou trembledst at the dying shriek
  That shrilled above the applauding hands,
Weeping when beast and Christian met
  And crimson splash'd the Dacian brands.

" For this was thine averted glance,
  When, in the gardens, yesternight,
We saw the lurid shadows dance
  Where living torches cast their light,
Uprear'd where they their eyes might set
  Upon the racing chariot's flight.

" Oh, faithless to the mighty gods!
  Cast in thy lot with those that brave
The lions and the lictors' rods,
  And bid your Master seek and save!
Go learn, by tasting death and shame,
  What life remains beyond the grave!"

He ceased; and I am left alone,
  To cry for strength, Oh Christ, to Thee,
Against the awful hour unknown,
  When foes will rage and friends will flee;
Yet, through the clouds of leaping flame,
  These mortal eyes Thy face shall see.

HOW TO LIVE ON £100 A YEAR.

PRACTICAL EXPERIENCES, BY THE HEAD OF A HOUSE.

CONSIDERABLE interest was shown awhile ago in an order of the directors of a certain bank, that in the future none of their staff were to marry, except under special circumstances, on a lower salary than £150 a year, this being considered the minimum upon which such responsibility should be undertaken. There was evident good sense in the order; but when one realises that the majority of those who marry do not obtain this income, and still a large proportion live respectably and in moderate comfort, it is clear that there are more things in household life than are dreamt of in the philosophy of a bank director.

Now the object of this article is decidedly not to recommend the grave step of marrying on £100 a year, which certainly involves the necessity of continual frugality and watchfulness; but since, after all, this is an everyday undertaking, I hope the following hints may be of interest and practical help to many readers of this paper, indicating how affairs may be managed so as to avoid the overcare which we know is not the better part of life.

In determining on prudential grounds, the first step, the great factor is of course the good sense of those directly concerned and the judgment of their advisers. All will agree with me that it would be the height of unwisdom for anyone to adopt household cares unless suitable means of residence—furniture, etc.—are provided, and both parties financially unencumbered; and unless, also, previously contracted habits of extravagance are laid aside, and, in their place, substituted a mutual recognition that in this dual control every effort should be made to husband resources, deeming trifling savings neither inconsequential nor sordid.

To illustrate how a small house should be managed, let me give you my own experience. I will endeavour not to tire you. Before I married I was respectably placed, my income £100. My fiancée lived in a comfortable home; but she was ready in household matters, and deft with her needle. With mutual help we have fully sustained our old status, while our friends have all been retained, and I can at any time invite a friend home; nor have invitations to be declined through our not being *tien mis*.

H., "How to Live on £100 a Year" (Volume 7, 9 January 1886, p. 228).

I had in hand sufficient to furnish the house, while wedding gifts added much to its beauty, and so did the work of a pair of loving busy hands. In choosing a house, I found rents high near my place of employment, but a little over a mile away, just in the country, I found a pleasant six-roomed house with a small garden in front and a large one behind, for £16 a year. I considered this high, when rates were reckoned, for my income; but, as the situation was good, I took it. The walk was by no means a disadvantage. Now came the time for the exercise of forethought, and I strongly recommend you to bear in mind the following conclusions, to make the best of your circumstances.

In starting housekeeping, the amount you have in hand should never be fully expended, as some requirements are certain to be at first overlooked, and will only be noticed after the lapse of a short time.

It is important to always have in hand as much money as will suffice until the next instalment of salary is due, and a pound or so over. To be always holding the last shilling is highly indicative of mismanagement. It is very humiliating to have to borrow small sums; it is equally so to have to ask the gas or rate collector to call again; and you should always be in a position to secure any passing opportunity of making a favourable purchase of anything you may require.

Never, on any account, run a bill or get into debt. You have no right to draw on the future, even for a week. It was the system of cash payments which gave the stores so great an advantage over the shops; but in most towns there are now tradesmen in all branches who for similar payment will place you on similar terms to these stores. For cash, the simplest orders are readily executed at the lowest prices. I emphasise this, as credit is obtained with such fatal facility that a little determination is sometimes necessary to avoid it. Once start running bills, and you will almost certainly overrun your income, and land in a mire of debt from which escape is difficult.

The great secret of managing a small income to its greatest advantage is the proper apportioning of the different items of expenditure, assigning to them the limits beyond which they should not pass, providing for the regular payments for food, rent, clothes,—reserving sufficient for the tailor or bootmaker in their turn, and keeping an eye to possible sickness or accidents. "But," many may say, "we have managed well enough without that trouble. We hardly ever have a bill owing, and we can easily screw a little when one does come, and get it done with." True; but is this the best way? This is the way friction commences which may easily throw the whole machine out of order. A thoughtless way of getting what you want and paying "when convenient" breaks down at the first serious obstacle: a month's illness, an enforced holiday, and you are ankle-deep in debt; and then, besides having this to recover, you are having to pay higher to the different tradesmen than heretofore. In fact, your freedom is lost. A little system is really a great saving of trouble when the habit is once established. When you have ascertained a fair limit to each expense, let that guide you; when you come short of it, you can devote the small spare amounts to any other object without consciousness of doing more than you ought to afford; or you can, more prudently, if you will, add them to your reserve.

To illustrate this fully I append a list of expenditure, by no means an experimental one. The early years of housekeeping require rather fewer expenses; there are no renewals or breakages either, and if well-equipped there are very few expenses indeed, and a decided start ought to be made to lay aside a "nest egg" upon which you can fall back

in case of any reverse. The following list is a tried one, the family numbering three children besides their parents, but as time goes on further alterations will come.

	s.	d.	
Groceries	4	5	per week.
Flour, 1½ stone (sometimes whole meal) ..	2	3	,, ,,
Eggs, 1s., butter 1lb, 1s. 4d.	2	4	,, ,,
Milk 3d. per day	1	9	,, ,,
Butcher	5	0	,, ,,
Bacon, 1s., cheese, 6d. ..	1	6	,, ,,
Vegetables and fruit ..	1	3	,, ,,
Charwoman, etc.	1	6	,, ,,
Books	0	6	,, ,,
	£1	0	6

	£	s.	d.
At £1 0s. 6d. per week these expenses per year amount to	53	6	0
Add rent per year	16	0	0
Rates and taxes	2	5	0
Water, 16s. gas, £1	1	16	0
Clothing for children ..	2	5	0
,, for mistress ..	5	5	0
Suit, boots, and sundries, self ..	5	15	0
Coals, 3 tons at 16s., coke, 1½ tons at 10s.	3	3	0
Household renewals, including linen	1	15	0
Collections or charity	1	0	0
Miscellaneous	1	5	0
Total for the year ..	£93	15	0

We have not reached the hundred here, but have spent quite as large a proportion as is prudent. There is no doctor's bill, insurance, nor holiday allowance, nor is any provision specified for such possibilities as loss of work, removals, or even more serious events, to which all households are liable. If you are relying upon your own resources, and for the first year or two place a £10 note to the credit of a banking account, and afterwards add regularly a few pounds yearly, you place yourself in a far more secure and independent position than otherwise. To neglect to make some reserve, whatever the income, at least in the early years of a household, is shortsighted, if not positively wrong. As to insurance, a systematic habit of depositing in your bank is probably as profitable a method as any of insuring those around you against desolation, if you will only resolutely make the deposits.

To make the best of your income it is necessary to place some limit upon the different headings; and although this list has been proved by experience to be practicable, it is, of course, not necessary that it should be followed literally, provided the decision exists to keep within such bounds as will really enable you to pay your way, and a little over. But, lest you should incline to challenge the list, let us look over it together.

The allowance for groceries appears small, but you see here how greatly the purchasing power of money has increased in the country. There is hardly an article named which, forty years ago, would not have cost fully three times as much for worse quality. It is more convenient to us to obtain supplies fortnightly, and the following is an example of an order for two weeks:—

	s.	d.
½lb. tea	1	3
¼lb. coffee	1	0
6lb. moist sugar	1	3
1lb. lump sugar	0	4
1lb. sago or tapioca	0	4
Currants, sultanas, or carraways	0	4
Lemon peel	0	3
Cocoa	0	6
2lbs. treacle	0	6
4lb. oatmeal	0	4
Mustard, pepper, etc.	0	6
Baking powder, yeast, etc. ..	0	8

	s.	d.
Toilet soap	0	4
Washing materials	1	3
	8	10

Common things at these prices, do you say? Decidedly not. Your cash payment places you on similar terms to the stores, where you would not consider these prices at all indicative of inferiority.

I enter more for milk, butter, and eggs than for grocer's food. There is nothing so wholesome or so perfect a food as dairy produce. Skimmed milk, when it can be obtained good, is much cheaper than new, so can be used more freely for cooking purposes. It contains a really larger proportion of flesh-forming material than new milk. In early summer the best farm lump butter can be obtained very cheap indeed; and it is a good plan then to obtain about a couple of stones, and press down in stone jars with a little salt, and keep in a cool place until winter, when it is double the price.

For vegetables and fruit, it rests upon how your marketing is done whether this sum suffices. You cannot obtain the earliest vegetables or fruit, but a very little management will procure an ample and well-varied supply of garden produce. I find in my own garden —besides amusement—a good supply of fruit; also early green peas and beans, and sufficient flowers to always render the house beautiful; so in this I obtain a distinct advantage over urban residence.

A butcher would tell you I did not allow enough for him. It is, however, a truism that in most families too much meat is eaten; and we have a fair allowance of dairy produce. It is not an economical method to lay out the whole of your portion in one purchase, and, when the middle of the week arrives, to provide meagre dinners or else make another levy on your cash box. A very little experience will guide you in the purchase of suitable pieces of meat, and you find here, as everywhere else, your ready money is a magic wand to reveal the best purchases.

The item for charwoman will allow of her coming for your fortnight's washing, and a day occasionally to clean. A very little more would provide you a little maid.

Sixpence weekly provides occasional newspapers, a monthly or two, and a new book occasionally. Books, even the best, are now so cheap that this trifling sum will bring within your reach the thoughts of the greatest men of all times.

I don't pretend the allowance I make myself for clothes is liberal, but it is sufficient. I generally get a suit of tough black cloth, such as is largely worn by country professional men. If well fitting, a suit will last over a year, and as I was well clad when a bachelor, I make occasional changes with the clothes of other days. By always brushing and folding those not in use, I keep them presentable. My dress suit promises to last a lifetime, through ordinary care. My old tweeds will, in time, I expect, be reduced, and clothe the limbs of my son.

As to the other dress items let my wife speak:—"It requires some management, of course, to keep everything tidy, but I make all the clothes myself, so there is only the cost of the materials. I should apportion a year's allowance as follows:—

	£	s.	d.
Dress materials, 23s. and 14s. ..	1	17	0
2 pairs boots	0	15	6
Jacket material	0	10	0
Hat	0	8	0
Linen, etc.	1	0	0
Gloves	0	7	6
Children's boots	1	5	0
,, clothing	1	0	0
	£7	10	0

" The following year would be rather different.

" It is a good plan to get a dress every year of good cashmere or other similar material, and, if your older dresses are wearing, a second of serge (if cold weather), or a pompadour or cambric for summer. I make my older dresses last a great deal longer than they would otherwise by wearing a polonaise of print, sateen, or indeed almost any material I have on hand, over them. It is needless to say that a good large apron with a bib is necessary when working about the house. A good felt hat, plainly trimmed, is cheap and effective, and lasts a very long time. For summer wear, straws or your old chips retrimmed are the best, and I think that women who lead busy lives always appear to the greatest advantage with as little trimming as possible. For a jacket or mantle I purchase such material as is suitable—not the most expensive, of course. In making it up I find the paper patterns very useful; indeed, I could hardly do without them. I do not go out very much in cold weather, so one jacket now lasts me two years, being altered a little the second year. The items for linen includes hose; and I may say how much better it is to sustain the stockings by suspenders than the old-fashioned method which doctors so rightly condemn.

" When my cashmeres are worn they come in for the bairns. I wish my old boots would also, for boots are the most costly point in a little one's attire. It requires very little money to clothe them, as they have the reversion of their parents' wardrobe.

" My friends sometimes wonder how I manage to get through so much dressmaking as well as to attend to the household; but they find me in good health and spirits, and rightly conclude that to be busy is by no means to be unhappy. If I bought ready-made clothing, it would cost double, and something else in the house would have to go short. The sewing-machine is a great help; I could not manage without it. Of course I am up betimes in the morning and busy until afternoon; but I get out with the children pretty often, and if I do not go out I do a little gardening, as I make the flowers my own special care."

May you all, dear girls, possess the contented spirit of my wife !

A word or two more as to my expense list. I need hardly say how greatly coke saves the coal bill. The ashes should be sifted and the dust thrown away; the remainder should be used again. I need only mention, also, the necessity of renewing breakages in the house and worn linen, using worn sheets by cutting them up the middle and joining the sides, etc.

A very small item is that set aside for Christian purposes ; but you will doubtless supplement it by occasional acts of charity around you (not, mind you, the easy random bestowal of alms on whomever your fancy

dictates), for, though your lot is not high, you are better off than the majority of the earth's inhabitants, and you are under distinct obligations towards those who are less fortunate.

The miscellaneous item includes jams and pickles (both of which are far better homemade than bought). Many little requirements which you would expect to provide from this, you will probably supply from small profits from other items where you find your limit has not been reached.

So much for our list. It is needless for me to point out the many ways in which a thrifty housekeeper will find opportunity to reduce the cost of living, and avoid waste or expense while maintaining the health and comfort of the precious charges in the home.

I invite my friends home quite as freely as I once took them to rooms, prudently avoiding washing days. My experience has always been that a real friend, such only as one ought to bring to one's hearth, cares but little for feeding. Of course, if the visit is planned beforehand, a little supper is really desirable ; and it has often been a matter of surprise to me how little money a really nice supper costs. I need not speak here of the necessity of faultless linen and table appointments. I never hesitate to bring home a friend without pre-arrangement. A little music, chess, an item of science, art, a book, or a hundred other subjects, besides the run of conversation, with a cup of coffee and a sandwich is pleasurable in the highest degree. My friends come with me readily, too ; so I hope the delight is not all on one side.

Wine or beer I consider I cannot afford, so on that ground, as well as for example to the little ones, I banish them from consideration. My cigars, too, were knocked off long ago.

If your finances are satisfactory, and you are in good health, finding your life happy and interesting, your battle is won. I do not need to speak of the necessity of mutual forbearance and help in ever-recurring weakness, without which the greatest plenty is famine ; nor, I hope, to urge that though thrifty management is the keynote to prosperity in life, and an essential to success, it is only a means to another end ; and that health and prosperity are of little worth unless accompanied by higher aims of purity and nobleness and godliness of life, as stepping-stones to a greater hereafter.

A word as to the children. I do not intend to say much, but I would remark how foolish it is to clothe tender children, who are exposed to continual changes of temperature and draughts in breakfast-room or kitchen, in little low-necked dresses which barely cover half their bodies. Many little ones are sacrificed in this way. High-necked, long-sleeved, long dresses, such as Miss Fashion would cry " horror " upon, and grandmother smile over as " sensible "—these are the dresses your little ones should wear as soon as they walk.

Flannel shirts in winter, warm knickerbockers, strong boots, and warm stockings are the only kind of clothes a poor man can afford. They will save many a doctor's bill. The children should go out every morning ; if they can't go a good walk, let them romp well in the garden.

As to their diet, children generally get too much meat and potatoes—both of which can easily be given too freely, on account of the little trouble in preparing along with one's own meals. But their requirements are different from ours, and they should have more than they usually get of oatmeal porridge, milk, brown bread, and milk puddings. If fruit is hard, it is better to cook it. Many bairns thrive rather in spite of their diet than upon it. If children ask for food between meal times, should they have it ? In small houses, it is so convenient for mother to accede that it is generally done, to the injury of the child, for its stomach cannot deal with such rapid supplies. When it asks, it is a good plan to give it a little dry bread ; if really hungry, and requiring food, it will eat it with relish—if not, its appetite will be spared until the next meal-time.

Many of my readers may ask how the children are to be educated on our income. I could, without any effort, provide them with an elementary education—far better, in many ways, by the way, than was given in much higher schools a very few years ago—or I could, by making a modest call on the reserve, provide a larger sum. But there is an item of receipt of which I have not spoken. I suppose there are few with a " fixed " income who have not at times an extra receipt of a few pounds. It is, unfortunately, too commonly the case that such receipts are frittered away without any commensurate benefit. I have, I am glad to say, not unfrequently an extra, though not sufficiently regular that I can anticipate it, and I give myself the pleasure of banking it to an "education fund" for the youngsters. I consider that it is the duty of a parent to give his children the best education he can afford. He then gives them a fortune of greater value than many hundreds a year, and if, with health and religious training, the children have the boon of the best educational teaching, " growing up as the young plants, and becoming as the polished corners of the Temple," there are few parents who will consider trifling self-denials on their own part as worthy of even a passing thought.

In conclusion, if my income never increases, I believe I shall be able to manage to go through the world independent of any other man's money. I consider, however, that in time the way will become more easy, and my experiences will, in that case, show me clearly how to make the most of my income. May it be the same with you ! H.

COURTLEROY.

By ANNE BEALE.

CHAPTER III.
A BORN SOLDIER.

IMPORTANT business letters, and still more publicly important political news in the *Times*, occupied Mr. Prettyman so engrossingly the following morning that he appeared to forget the intruder altogether. Mrs. Prettyman did not remind him of him, knowing that " time and the hour " operated wonders with her husband.

Soon after he had left home for the city, Jones, the policeman, arrived, with a woman

whom he had arrested on suspicion. Sampson told Mrs. Prettyman that the policeman wished to confront the woman with the boy before proceeding farther. Mrs. Prettyman was in a terrible fuss, as may be imagined. She ordered Ada to bring down the child, which she did with much difficulty. The policeman and his charge stood inside the hall door, and they opposite. No sign of recognition passed between the woman and child.

" Do you know her ? " whispered Ada, and Master George shook his head.

She had made some slight inroad into his confidence. Not so Jones ; for when he stepped cautiously forward towards him, he bolted through the nearest open door.

" May I be struck dead, my lady, if ever I see that child before," said the woman. " I m a poor hardworkin', strivin' soul, as have lost half a day's work all along of being took up by this gentleman. And he've lost half a day's work, and the public have to pay all the same, for meddlin' wi' what don't concern him. That's what the p'lice is for. I wish they'd

---

THE BRIDE'S FIRST DINNER PARTY.

By PHILLIS BROWNE, Author of "The Girl's Own Cookery Book."

A CERTAIN young lady, a member of The Girl's Own Cookery Class (in other words, an individual who has educated herself in cookery, with the assistance of articles published in this journal), was married a few weeks ago. Her husband is an exceedingly good fellow, and holds a salaried position in a mercantile establishment. He has plenty of common sense and energy, and, if all goes well, he will make his way; but at the present moment he is not very well off. He has, however, managed to save enough to furnish the small home very prettily and very well, while his wife has received from her father a handsome trousseau, a good supply of house linen of every sort and kind, and a good many odds and ends of things. Besides this, the young couple, having a large circle of friends, have been presented with a considerable number of wedding presents.

Young beginners in these days are really very fortunate; for they get so much friendly help in starting life. It very much simplifies matters if, just as one has arrived at the conclusion that a dinner service is imperatively required, but that the money for purchasing the same is not immediately forthcoming, a knock is heard at the door, and a box is brought in containing a handsome dinner service of the newest pattern and latest fashion, as a small proof of the affection of a friend. The young people now referred to have been most lucky in this way. They must have received scores of presents, all useful, all judiciously chosen, and with only two duplicates, which were speedily exchanged for something else. That delightful Parcel Post has been a messenger of good fortune to them. Pretty things for the table have arrived in profusion; ornaments, pictures, silver, glass, china, cutlery have appeared upon the scene as if by magic; and the result of it all is that the home of this newly-wedded pair is as thoroughly well appointed all the way through as anyone need wish a home to be.

The routine of married-life in these days is first the wedding day, then the honeymoon, and then any amount of visiting—dinner parties and supper parties without limit. Old-fashioned individuals may disapprove of this, and say that it would be better for the newly-wedded to settle down quietly, look at life from a serious standpoint, read improving books aloud to each other in the evenings, and save up every available halfpenny for a future rainy day. Without doubt, the old-fashioned individuals are right; but, unfortunately, few young married people see as they do. Experience is the great teacher, and its lessons can never be learnt by proxy. These young people have not yet been to that school. They have their charming home, their many friends, their limited income, and their pretty table appliances; and the question has now arisen—How shall they entertain their friends? They plume themselves on being prudent; they have no wish to run into extravagance, and they have no thought of entertaining everyone whom they know; but they are hospitably inclined, and they have deliberately arrived at the conclusion that there are one or two special friends whom they must invite, and whom they must make a little fuss over. The result of it all has been the bride's first dinner party.

When first the subject of an entertainment was mooted, the young bride, whom we will call Mabel, was much exercised as to whether it would be wiser to have high tea or dinner. There was much to be said in favour of both.

With high tea it was possible to have everything cold, and put on the table all at once, and this would enable the mistress to see the table laid, and be sure that everything was right before the guests arrived, a consideration not to be disregarded where there was only one little maid, and that one only eighteen, though clever for her age. The bride thought of the anxiety which she would have to go through if there were to be an awful pause between the courses, and then Emma were to come to her side and say, "Please, mum, the pudding won't turn out!" What should she do? Then, too, high tea was quieter, and less pretentious, and the young housekeeper had no desire to make a display beyond her means. On the other hand, dinner would be pleasanter; and, best of all, it would furnish an occasion for bringing out all the pretty presents, the bright silver, the exquisite glass, the artistic table ornaments, the elegant dinner and dessert services. Where was the good of being possessed of all these treasures if they were always to be kept locked up in a cupboard? With these presents a dinner-table could be laid out so effectively that the food would be quite a minor detail. Besides, "the master" preferred dinner. In his bachelor days he had been accustomed to dine on leaving business, and had learnt to regard high tea as a nondescript sort of meal, only to be accepted as a painful discipline when it could not well be avoided. Of course, the master's likes and dislikes counted for a good deal with the mistress, and dinner was almost decided upon. But then came the question, "Which meal would be the more expensive of the two?" Expense was the chief consideration after all. Everything had to be paid for with ready money, and a committee of two of ways and means had decided that a sovereign must cover all expenses apart from beverages. There were to be six guests, eight in all with master and mistress; could the thing be done for £1 sterling? The young lady was doubtful.

At this stage of the cogitation, a double knock was heard, and in a minute or two the maid, young but clever for her age, came up and announced that Mrs. Jones had called to see Mrs. Smith. Amy Jones! exactly the person to consult. Amy was an old school-mate of the bride's, had been married a couple of years ago, enjoyed almost the same yearly income, and deserved the reputation of having arrived at Dora Greenwell's idea of perfection; that is, she had, up to this point, not merely made both ends meet, but made them tie over in a handsome bow. Yet she had been hospitable, too. A person of such abundant experience would be sure to know what was best.

"Amy, if you were in my place, which should you decide upon, a high tea or a small dinner?"

"You have begun to consider the claims of hospitality, have you, Mabel! What is your maid like?"

"She is a very good little girl, and she does her best, but she is very slow. If all goes on quietly, she manages excellently; but if she were to be flurried, I do not know what would happen."

"That's bad," remarked experienced Amy Jones.

"Yet she means well, and really does her best," continued the young mistress, anxiously eager to defend her first domestic. "She can cook plain dishes fairly, and is interested in her work. If I tell her a thing, she never forgets."

"That's good; almost good enough to make up for the slowness. Can she wait?"

"Not properly. She can bring dishes and plates into the room and take them out again quickly, but that is almost the extent of her power; she could not hand round dishes or remain in the room during a dinner to be a credit or help. If we were to decide on dinner, don't you think you would hire a waitress if you were me?"

"If you want my advice, dear, I should say, decidedly, do nothing of the kind. It would be an exhibition of effort which would involve pretence, and the slightest pretence would be a mistake. Whatever you do, don't go beyond the resources of your own modest establishment. At present, all your friends know exactly what your position is; they will respect you if you make the best of it, but if you seem to wish to go beyond it they will begin to criticise, while the people you care for most will blame you."

"Then you would give up all thought of dinner?"

"I don't say so. Why should you not have a small dinner? Prepare everything yourself, altogether dispense with regular waiting, show Emma exactly what she has to do, and let her do her best. Supposing there should be a little *contretemps*, never mind; laugh at it, and your friends will laugh with you. They will only say that you are inexperienced. If all should go well, how pleased your husband will be! You are sure you don't mind the trouble?"

"Mind the trouble! I like it. I think it is fun. I am only uneasy about the expense."

"Well, dear, I should say that high tea, though less troublesome, is quite as expensive as dinner. We can easily ascertain the truth, however. Let us take paper and pencil, and draw up a statement of the cost of both. We will begin with the high tea. I suppose we are to take it for granted that you must have something extra? It would not do to have a thoroughly simple meal."

"Oh, no. If we ask six people on such an occasion, we must make a sort of feast. Let me think. You put the items down as I decide on them. We might have a lobster salad, a couple of boiled fowls with egg sauce, a beefsteak and oyster pie, a strawberry cream, a jelly of some sort, a few tarts and cheesecakes, some fruit and fancy biscuits. Then, of course, tea and coffee and thin bread and butter, brown and white. That would do well enough. We could not well have less."

"A very excellent menu, indeed," said Amy, while a rather amused look passed over her face. "What do you suppose it will cost?"

"I don't know," said Mabel. "You cast it out and see. You understand prices better than I do."

For a while there was silence, and nothing was heard but the scratching of a pencil. Then Amy read aloud:—"Lobster salad, 3s. 3d.; boiled fowls and egg sauce, 7s. 11d."

"Oh, dear!" said Mabel.

"Well, you see, it is spring, and fowls are dear in the spring. I do not suppose you could get a fine pair for less than 3s. 6d. each. Beefsteak and oyster pie, 5s.; strawberry cream (made with your own jam), 1s. 8d.; orange jelly, 1s. 4d.; tarts and cheesecakes we will calculate roughly at 1s. 4d.; a little fruit, 2s.; tea and coffee (say 2d. per person), 1s. 4d.; bread and butter, 2s. Altogether say £1 5s. 10d."

Phillis Browne, "The Bride's First Dinner Party" (Volume 8, 1 January 1887, p. 214).

"That will never do," said Mabel. "We must take something away."

"For one thing, you might take the tarts and cheesecakes. Surely they are not necessary."

"One wants a little trifle of the sort to conclude the meal," said Mabel.

"Then make jam sandwich. I can give you a simple recipe, by following which you can produce a dishful for less than sixpence."

"Thanks. But that will not make matters right. We must reduce much more than that."

"Suppose that before doing so we draw up a dinner, and see what we can make of that. I will furnish the menu this time."

"Very good. Only remember to take into consideration Emma's limited capacity," said Mabel.

Again there was silence. After a few minutes Amy read aloud once more :—

MENU.

Potato Soup.
Tomatoes Farcies.
Rolled Loin of Mutton and Sour Plums.
Mashed Potatoes, with Brown Potatoes round. Stewed Celery.
Ready-made Pudding. Orange Jelly.
Macaroni Cheese.
Dessert.
Coffee.

ESTIMATE.

Potato soup, 11d.; tomatoes farcies, 1s.; mutton, forcemeat, gravy, &c., 6s. 9d.; potatoes and celery, 6d.; orange jelly, 1s. 4d.; ready-made pudding, 1s. 3d.; macaroni cheese, 9d.; dessert, 3s.; coffee, 10d. Altogether, 16s. 4d.

Mabel was silent for a moment from amazement. Then she said—

"That is very extraordinary. I would not have believed it."

"Yes, dear. But you must take into account that you drew up rather a luxurious tea; and my dinner is a very simple and homely one. Therefore you were scarcely fair to yourself."

"I only described the sort of high tea we should have had at home before I was married."

"And you forgot that your mother did not need to make a sovereign cover all expenses."

"And yet your dinner sounds more satisfactory than my tea, and I am sure it would look more. I wonder if Emma could manage a dinner like that; she is not entirely ignorant. She can roast a joint, and boil potatoes very well, and she can bake a pudding——"

"Then I am sure she could manage, for everything else you could yourself prepare beforehand. Of course, if she were more of a cook, you might have a little fish, or perhaps a trifle of game after the mutton, and still keep within the sovereign."

"I feel that I should be wiser to experiment first in a small way," said Mabel.

"Very well. The potato soup you know well. It is good, and cheap; you can get it really beforehand, so that Emma will only have to make it hot. The mutton you can get the butcher to bone, and then stuff it with veal forcemeat, and roll it early in the day, leaving Emma to roast it. The gravy, also, you can make ready, and put, nicely seasoned and free from fat, in a cup, so that Emma will need only to put it in a saucepan to get hot when she begins to dish the meat. The tomatoes you can prepare. The celery and potatoes you may leave with her, I should think."

"Decidedly; she boils vegetables very well, and she can mash potatoes, and put browned potatoes round quite easily. I had better make the sauce for the celery, though."

"You might make it, and put it in a gallipot in a saucepan with boiling water round, to keep hot. Then surely if you make the soup, if you prepare the meat, and make the gravy, make the sauce, get the tomatoes ready, make the jelly, mix the pudding, three parts cook the macaroni, dish the dessert, and altogether make the coffee, there can be no danger."

"I shall be rather tired by the time our friends arrive," said Amy, looking a little grave as she realised the responsibilities which she was proposing to take upon herself.

"Oh, yes; you will have to be very quick, and to do all the head-work. But you said you did not mind the trouble. And besides, remember this, if once you can succeed in your attempt you will find that you are not at all more tired with providing dinner than you are with providing high tea. But there are just two things you would do well to try for, in my opinion."

"What are they?"

"One is to make Emma well acquainted with every dish beforehand. Let her understand how things ought to be and to look when properly cooked ; on no account let the final touches be the product of her imagination as exercised in carrying out your descriptive order."

"No, that would scarcely do," said Mabel, laughing.

"Well, the only way to prevent it is to make the most of the time between now and the important day. Have potato soup one day, rolled mutton another, tomatoes farcies, and ready-made pudding a third, and macaroni cheese a fourth, and so make her familiar with what is coming."

"And the second point?"

"I was going to suggest that if you have anything served in a style superior to your ordinary mode, you should try to keep Emma up to the better way as a regular thing. This will really be a great kindness to her. It will make her more skilful, and fit her for taking a better situation afterwards, and, strange to say, she will be all the happier for it. Right-minded girls (and I should quite think Emma is one) are glad to be shown refined ways, and they respect a mistress who understands and insists upon the best modes of doing things far more than they respect a mistress who lets things go, and puts up with slipshod fashions just for the sake of peace and quiet. And really you will find that when Emma knows what ought to be, all you will need to impress upon her is the time required for the various dishes."

"That is it precisely," said Mabel, who had been listening very quietly to her friend's remarks, but who was evidently giving all her thoughts to the subject in hand. "I can see now exactly what I shall have to do. I shall make out a list of every ingredient, and have everything where it will be close to my hand, the day but one before the dinner. The day before I shall make the jelly and, with Emma's help, brighten all the glass and silver, and look out any pretty ornaments and services. Then quite early on the eventful morning I shall make the soup, and put it ready for making hot; yes, I shall even fry and dish the sippets and chop the parsley, which will have to be sprinkled in at the last moment. I shall stuff and roll the mutton, dish the sour plums (those delightful sour plums ! they were there without needing to be in the estimate; how good it was of Frau Bergmann to give them to me). I shall stuff the tomatoes, turn out the jelly, dish the dessert, arrange the coffee cups and saucers—but, oh, the coffee, what shall I do for that ? Emma never makes it properly."

"Few servants do; and if I were you I should look after it yourself in this case. The coffee is so very important. Really good coffee, served at the close even of an unsuccessful dinner, almost atones for disaster, while inferior coffee spoils the most *recherché* repast. Why should you not steal away for a minute or two when your friends leave the dining-room, make the coffee, and send Emma in with it. Then all is sure to be right."

"Yes, that will be best. Well, as I was saying, I must be as busy as possible before luncheon. Then, after luncheon——"

"After luncheon I should lie down for an hour," said Amy.

"Oh !" said Mabel, dubiously.

"Yes. It would be unfortunate if the dinner were a success, and the hostess laid up next day through fatigue."

"May be. Yes, I will certainly rest awhile after luncheon. Then, while Emma prepares her vegetables, tidies the kitchen, and attends to the roast, I will lay the table ; and I know I can make it beautiful."

"What shall you do for flowers ? We did not allow for them in our estimate."

"I planted some corn a week ago in a large fancy bowl, and it will be lovely. Have you never done that ? You get a few ears of corn, pack them in a bowl full of water, so that the ears are close together and are partially covered with the water. Put the bowl in a warm room, and in about a fortnight the delicate blades will peep out and grow to be very pretty. There could not be anything more effective for the middle of the table, and the grass lasts five or six weeks, and it is a most convenient decoration when flowers are scarce. We always used to provide ourselves with corn in harvest time for this purpose."

"I will remember to do the same," said Amy. "I never heard of growing corn in a bowl."

"I can give you a little meanwhile to experiment with. Then, when the table is laid, I will dress, and when I come down will present Emma first with a written menu, giving a list of what is to go in with each course, and a few notes of reminder—something of this sort :—

"REMEMBER—

"To put the pudding and tomatoes in the oven, also to pour the sauce over the macaroni and set it to brown, as soon as the last guest arrives.

"To put the plates for soup, meat, tomatoes, ready-made pudding, and cheese to heat half an hour before the dinner hour.

"To make the milk boil before stirring it into the boiling soup, and to sprinkle in the chopped parsley at the last moment.

"To shut the dining-room door after taking in or removing dishes, &c., and to move about as quietly as possible.

"To begin to dish the meat and vegetables and make the gravy hot the moment soup is in, so that everything may be quite ready when the bell rings.

"To put the coffee (left ready ground on the dresser) into the oven, to get hot, as soon as dessert is in, and at the same time to set a jug of milk in a saucepan of boiling water."

"What is that for ?" said Amy.

"It is to scald the milk. Coffee tastes so much more delicious when the milk is scalded, not boiled. There, I think that is all. I will write the notes early, and then, if anything else occurs to me, I can put it down. But, Amy, for safety's sake would you mind giving me the recipes for the dishes in your menu. I have one or two, but they may be mislaid, and I should not like there to be a mistake."

"There is not much fear of a mistake, if you take all that trouble. But I will give you the recipes with pleasure. In return, will you give me the recipe for the sour plums ? I should like to have it, for I intend to make some when plums are in season."

The arrangements thus laid down were implicitly carried out, and the "Bride's First Dinner Party" was a great success—so much so that every guest remarked, when the evening was over, "What a clever little woman Mrs. Smith is ! How fortunate her husband is to have a wife thus domesticated." Then,

---

Phillis Browne, "The Bride's First Dinner Party" (Volume 8, 1 January 1887, p. 215).

in a moment, "What lovely wedding presents!"

For the benefit of those who may care to have them, I subjoin a copy of the recipes which were exchanged between Amy and Mabel.

Potato Soup.—Melt a piece of butter the size of an egg in a stewpan. Throw in two pounds of potatoes, weighed after they have been peeled, the white parts of two leeks, and a stick of celery, all cut up. Sweat for a few minutes without browning. Pour on a quart of cold stock or water; boil gently till the vegetables are tender, and pass through a sieve. When wanted, make hot in a clean stewpan, and add salt and pepper. Boil separately half a pint of milk; stir this into the boiling soup. At the last moment sprinkle on the top of the soup a dessertspoonful of chopped parsley. If cream is allowed, the soup will be greatly improved.

Tomatoes Farcies.—Take eight smooth red tomatoes; cut the stalks off evenly, and slice off the part that adheres to them; scoop out the seeds from the centre without breaking the sides. Melt an ounce of butter in a stewpan. Put in two tablespoonfuls of cooked ham chopped, two tablespoonfuls of chopped mushrooms, two shalots, two teaspoonfuls of chopped parsley, pepper and salt, and two ounces of grated Parmesan. Mix thoroughly over the fire, fill the tomatoes with the mixture, and bake on a greased baking tin in a moderate oven for ten or fifteen minutes. The tomatoes should be tender, but not broken. If the ingredients for this forcemeat are not at hand, a little ordinary veal forcemeat may be used, but the taste will be inferior.

Rolled Loin of Mutton.—Get the butcher from whom the meat is bought to bone the loin; spread veal stuffing inside, roll it up, bind it with tape, and bake in the usual way. Thick, smooth gravy should be served with it. This may be made of the bones.

Mashed and Browned Potatoes.—Mash potatoes in the usual way. Prepare beforehand six or eight good sized potatoes of uniform size. Parboil them, then put them into the dripping-tin round the meat for about three-quarters of an hour—less, if small—and baste them every now and then till brown. Pile the mashed potatoes in the middle of the tureen, put browned potatoes round, and sprinkle chopped parsley on the white centre.

Stewed Celery.—Wash the celery carefully, and boil it till tender in milk and water, to which salt and a little butter have been added. The time required will depend on the quality. Young, tender portions will be ready in half an hour or less; the coarse outer stalks will need to boil a long time. Drain thoroughly, dish on toast, and pour white sauce over.

Sour Plums (a substitute for red currant jelly served with meat; to be made in the autumn).—Take three pounds of the long, blue autumn plums, almost the last to come into the market, called in Germany zwetschen. Rub off the bloom and prick each one with a needle. Boil a pint of vinegar for a quarter of an hour with a pound and a-half of sugar, a teaspoonful of cloves, three blades of mace, and half an ounce of cinnamon. Pour the vinegar through a strainer over the plums, and let them stand for twenty-four hours. Next day boil the vinegar, and again pour it over the fruit. Put all over the fire together to simmer for a few minutes until the plums are tender and cracked without falling to pieces. Tie down while hot.

Ready-Made Pudding.—Mix two tablespoonfuls of flour, an ounce of sugar, and a very little grated nutmeg, with a spoonful of cold milk to make a smooth paste, then add boiling milk to make a pint. When cold, beat two eggs with a glass of sherry, mix and bake in a buttered dish for half an hour.

Orange Jelly.—Soak an ounce of gelatine in water to cover it for an hour, and put with the gelatine the very thin rind of three oranges. Squeeze the juice from some sweet oranges to make half a pint, then add the juice of two lemons, and strain to get out all pips, etc. Take as much water as there is fruit juice, put this into a stewpan with the gelatine, and a quarter of a pound of loaf sugar, and simmer for a few minutes till the gelatine is entirely dissolved. Remove any scum that may rise, then add the juice; boil up once, and strain into a damp mould. This jelly has a delicious taste, and is not supposed to be clear.

Macaroni Cheese.—Wash half a pound of Naples macaroni, break it up and throw it into boiling water with a lump of butter in it, and boil it for about half an hour, till the macaroni is tender. Drain it well. Melt an ounce of butter in a stewpan, stir in one ounce of flour, and, when smooth, half a pint of cold milk. Stir the sauce till it boils, add salt and pepper, an ounce of grated Parmesan, and the macaroni drained dry. Pour all upon a dish, sprinkle an ounce of macaroni over, and brown in the oven or before the fire.

Simple Jam Sandwich.—Beat three eggs, and add a breakfastcupful of flour, to which has been added a teaspoonful of cream of tartar. Beat the mixture till it bubbles. Add a scant breakfastcupful of sifted sugar. Beat again, and add half a teaspoonful of carbonate of soda. Turn into a shallow baking tin, greased, and bake for a few minutes in a quick oven. With the oven ready, this cake can be made and baked in half an hour.

A GIRTON GIRL.

By CATHERINE GRANT FURLEY.

"WHY, sir, should you seem so startled
　　When you chance to come on me
Talking silly baby-language
　　To the child upon my knee—
To this happy, crowing urchin,
　　While his peasant mother stands
Watching us, while she is wiping
　　Thick-flaked soapsuds from her hands?

"When you met me first, at dinner,
　　At the Hall the other night,
You were seated on my left hand,
　　The professor on my right;
And you saw I cared to listen—
　　Saw it with a scornful mirth—
To the facts that he was telling
　　Of the strata of the earth.

"And again, when of the Iliad
　　My companion chanced to speak,
You were less pleased than astounded
　　That I quoted Homer's Greek.
And beneath my half-closed eyelids
　　I observed your covert smile,
When our hostess spoke of Ruskin,
　　And I answered with Carlyle.

"Then you thought you read me fully—
　　'Woman in her latest phase,
Following with feebler footsteps
　　In far-reaching manhood's ways.
A half-taught, conceited creature,
　　Something neither wise nor good;
Losing for a vain chimera
　　All the grace of womanhood.

"'Failing in her mad endeavour,
　　Though in every languid vein
Love-warmed heart-blood she replaces
　　With cold ichor from the brain.
Woman striving to be manlike,
　　Making him her enemy,
Fighting where she best had yielded'—
　　This was what you saw in me.

"Sir, I claim to be a woman:
　　Nothing less and nothing more;
Laughing when my heart is joyful,
　　Weeping when my heart is sore;
Loving all things good and tender,
　　Nor so coldly over-wise
As to scorn a lover's kisses,
　　Or the light of children's eyes.

"Over-wise! Nay, it were folly
　　If I cherished in my mind
One poor fancy, one ambition
　　That could part me from my kind—
From the maiden's hopes and longings,
　　From the mother's joy and care,
From the gladness, labour, sorrow,
　　That is every woman's share.

"Not for all life's garb of duty
　　In the self-same tint is dyed;
I must walk alone, another
　　Shelters at a husband's side.
Yet I claim her for my sister,
　　While—though I must stand apart—
All her hopes, her fears, her wishes
　　Find an echo in my heart.

Phillis Browne, "The Bride's First Dinner Party" (Volume 8, 1 January 1887, p. 216).

OUR FRIENDS THE SERVANTS.

By EMMA BREWER.

CHAPTER V.

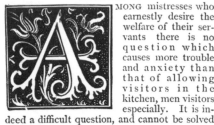

AMONG mistresses who earnestly desire the welfare of their servants there is no question which causes more trouble and anxiety than that of allowing visitors in the kitchen, men visitors especially. It is indeed a difficult question, and cannot be solved for every one alike.

I know several ladies who have thought it right that such of their maids as were engaged should be permitted to receive their sweethearts from time to time in the kitchen; but in every case where this has been granted that has come under my notice, the results have been so disastrous as to necessitate the withdrawal of the privilege. It was found utterly destructive of harmony in the kitchen, and gave no real pleasure to any one. In some cases the fickle men forsook their old love in favour of some younger and more attractive of the fellow-servants, and it is not difficult to imagine the bitterness, anger, and sharp words which became the fashion after such faithlessness.

In others the sweethearts borrowed money of all the foolish girls in order to lay it upon horses in which they were interested; in others, where more stimulant had been taken than was good for them, they have boasted among other men of the beautiful silver, etc., in the houses where their young women lived, with what results may be guessed.

In simple fairness the privilege cannot be granted to one without extending it to all; this, in many houses, would fill the kitchens of an evening; for no maid would acknowledge that she had no young man, and would get one on the spot without considering his character, and such a one would scarcely add to the safety or morality of the kitchen.

To illustrate the evil of receiving men visitors without the knowledge of master or mistress, I am going to tell a true story; but before relating it, I want to beg of our friends the servants not to think themselves badly used because the rule is strict against young men being admitted into the kitchen, while at the same time the young ladies' sweethearts are received upstairs. The comparison does not hold good here, because there is a mother or father in the drawing-room, whereas it often happens that there are only young girls downstairs, without any staid or responsible person to look after them and guard them from evil.

Neither should it be expected that women visitors may come when and how they please. In many instances they are servants out of place through their own folly, and in this case are bad friends and advisers for girls who desire to be good and steady. It is always better to mention to the mistress or housekeeper that such a person has come to see you, and may you ask them in ? it makes all things so much easier and safer, and it is no more loss of self-respect to go to the mistress in such a matter, than it would be to consult the mother at home; and my experience is, that no good mistress ever withholds a favour from her maids if she can possibly grant it. And now for my story—

We were sent for one evening, just as we had settled down for a quiet hour or two with books and work, by a dying woman, whose home, if such it could be called, was in one of the worst parts of London, inhabited mostly by criminals.

We started off at once, and at length found ourselves in a court with a row of squalid-looking houses on both sides. We had difficulty in discovering the one we wanted, for all looked much alike, and the numbers were partly or wholly obliterated from the doors. We were successful at last, and stumbled up the dark filthy staircase. Receiving no answer to our knock, we pushed open the door. The room was cold, wretched, desolate, and lighted by one small candle; a rickety table and a broken chair were the only articles visible, and these were occupied by a ferocious-looking unkempt man. He evidently expected us, for he got up, and without speaking took up the candle and led the way into the next room; he drew down the sheet, and there in a corner of the room, on a few rags, lay a woman and her baby dead. The flaxen curls hung limp about her head, and lent a strange kind of gilded framework to the picture of want, exhaustion, and misery of all sorts, which, even yet, kept hold of the dead mother. There was something about the face which was familiar and puzzling, but our utterance was choked by emotion, and we could not ask a question.

The man replaced the sheet, and we went back to the room adjoining. At length he said, " She wanted you badly just at the last. I don't know why, except perhaps you knew her years ago, for she comes of a better sort." He was right; memory came back, bringing with it a picture of a bright intelligent girl, daughter of tenant-farmers, who were very proud of her, and who, having given her a good education, sent her to be nursemaid in a family of good position in London. " Was her name Mary Fleming ?—and did she come from near Norwich ? " we asked. He nodded. It seems that for a time she was happy and respected in her situation. Unfortunately, among her fellow-servants was one who had made the acquaintance of a civil-spoken, well-dressed man, whom she knew nothing about, on one of her Sundays out. This man followed her up, showed her many attentions, and at length easily gained admittance to the house one Sunday morning, when the family were all at church, except this girl and Mary Fleming. The latter was so distressed at what she knew to be wrong, that she remonstrated seriously with her fellow-servant. The only result of this was that on the following Sunday the man brought a friend with him to engage Mary's attention. The two ticket-of-leave men, for such they were, induced the girls to go with them the following Sunday afternoon as far as Epping Forest, to hear, as they said, " some famous ranter."

Mary had wit and courage enough to slip away from her evil companions and reach home by the proper hour ; the other girl was not so fortunate. A few days subsequent to this Sunday outing the house was robbed, and some of the stolen property found upon the man who first came to the house, and he was transported. The second man, who for this time escaped punishment, so frightened and threatened poor Mary that she was afraid to speak and say what she knew to the mistress ; and when a second attempt was made to rob the house she was in some way suspected and dismissed from her situation. With loss of character and self-respect she could not face her kind parents, and when this man, Elihu Palmer, offered to marry her she consented. Ill-usage, association with criminals, and starvation had been her lot from that day to this on which we saw her lying dead with her baby beside her. Poor Mary ! she might have been happy and loved but for the reckless way servants have of making acquaintances and disregarding rules which are made for their safety.

We were too late to help her, poor thing, but we did what she so earnestly desired, viz., see her parents and tell them she had not been a thief, and that she had suffered bitterly for the wrong she had done ; and secondly, to see that she was not buried in a pauper's grave. She had written a few of the above facts on a soiled piece of paper, which the husband had promised the dying woman to give us, and he told us the rest. This is not a solitary case by any means, but it was one in which we felt deep interest and compassion.

While writing these articles I have received several letters and various communications from masters, mistresses, and servants, and one received yesterday is such an exceedingly good, thoughtful letter, that I give one or two quotations from it.

" The servants we have," says the writer, " are nearly always beginners, and our experience is that their greatest enemies are their relations and friends, who are always worrying them to ' better themselves ' before they are in any way fitted for a better place. The consequence is that if they do get the better place, they are simply dismissed after being there a week or a fortnight, and this sort of thing, often repeated, makes them lose heart and go to the bad.

" My sister-in-law went the other day to see one of these poor girls who was dying in the Brompton consumption hospital. She said, ' Oh, ma'am, if I had only listened to you and remained in your house it would never have come to this. It was my friends who were always worrying me to go in for higher wages, but I could never keep a place more than a week or two, and you can't think the misery I have gone through ; and when I told my friends what bad advice they had given me they only laughed and gave me still worse advice.'

" Servants who have done badly themselves are not good companions to steady, well-intentioned girls, to whom they do a pitiful amount of mischief. In all cases where servants who formerly lived with us turned out badly, the cause was to be traced to the influence of unworthy *female* acquaintances."

The last quotation I give is, " The want of training and the impatience while undergoing instruction is at the root of a good deal of the evil." The writer then gives an example of the opposite :—" We once had a girl who was rather stupid and slow, but patient. She remained with us for three years and slowly learned all that could be taught in such a house as ours. She called upon us a few days since and told us that she was in a place as cook and getting £45 a year. This girl had no brains, but she was so patient, respectful, and anxious to do her best that in the end she quite succeeded in making up for the want of them."

There are a few things in the relationship between mistress and maid which distress me greatly, because I know they are utterly destructive of home-peace and comfort; one is a mistress reproving her servant in public, another is a maid answering her mistress rudely, and a third is a mistress finding fault with servants out of the room to one who is waiting in the room.

No good servant would endure the first nor

be guilty of the second, but one and all are evil in their result, and it is easy to see that, let the fault be what it may, it cannot be remedied in this fashion.

Servants have feelings to be wounded and rights to be respected, and when these are ignored they feel that their occupation is compromising to their respectability and freedom.

We lose many good servants in this way, and get in their place large importations of very inferior ones from the Continent. It gives one a feeling of sadness that while the mother country stands in increased need of good and trustworthy servants, she cannot retain them or make friends of them, but has to look on while her Colonies attract those she herself would so gladly keep.

I do not know if all are aware that every month ships leave England with a number of servants on board; indeed, as many as fourteen vessels go over to Queensland alone, carrying on an average, two hundred servants on each ship. Any young woman with good health and good character can get a free passage to Queensland if she is under thirty-five years of age. This colony, even above others, values highly our friends the servants, whose success is undoubted. They try to live up to the high opinion formed of them, but it is grievous to see them leaving the old country which wants them even more than the Colonies.

It is a curious thing that now, when many of our servants are under-rating their position, gentlewomen are turning their attention to domestic service as a means of earning their living, and up to this have been very successful. They go systematically to work, apprenticing themselves for a certain number of years to the Aid Home, Zeals, Bath, or like teaching institutions, and go through a thorough course of training in the special branch they select, so that at the end of the term they can enter the ranks of domestic servants as "duly qualified." They go out as "aids," or as permanent servants, and very good and reliable ones they are. I have visited in houses where they have served, so can speak with knowledge. This training has turned out very happily in cases where whole families of what are called a superior class have, through misfortune, had to emigrate. The women and girls used to be of no real service in the home, but now with this training they are valuable and steady helpers to the fathers and brothers; and where there are too many girls to find occupation at home, they hire themselves out as domestic servants to other families in the Colonies, often getting very high wages, and naturally, later on, make thoroughly good wives. The way some of our general servants, who were snubbed here in the Old Country, have prospered in the Colonies savours more of romance than reality.

There are good positions waiting to be filled not only in London, but in all parts of England in one branch of domestic work, and that is laundry work. I hear there is the greatest difficulty in obtaining laundry matrons in many of the great institutions. Miss Steer,* a great authority, says:—"The post of laundry matron is one of great importance in an institution, and there is often difficulty in obtaining women of the right stamp; hearts as well as heads must be thoroughly in the work, and I cannot understand why, with the great desire expressed on all hands for Christian work, women with ordinary health should not get themselves properly trained as laundry superintendents. In their daily work, and while earning a fair salary, they would have many opportunities of influencing and guiding those under their care. It seems a matter of surprise to me that women should cast about them to find a field for their services when here is a splendid work waiting to be done."

I thought this announcement might prove of service to every class of domestic servant; it is something to know of an occupation still calling for workers.

There is scarcely any subject which one touches in the relationship between mistress and maid that does not bristle with difficulties, and for the reason that no two cases are the same—that which would be quite correct in the one would be a serious evil in the other; take, for example, that of rigid locking up from the servants. It is one of their great grievances, and one of which they speak in no measured terms. One said to me the other day, "I do not think I can stay in my situation, but I will try." "Why?" I asked. "Mistress takes out her keys to give me even a little salt from the cupboard, and locks it up again; there is not a thing in the house that is not tightly locked. Why, ma'am, it makes a servant feel ashamed. If I am a thief I ought not to be in her house at all; I am not trusted a bit."

---
* Bridge of Hope Mission, Ratcliff Highway.

I myself never lock up from the servants, but trust them entirely, and I do not think I am robbed of the smallest particle of anything. They are on their honour, and would resent a breach of trust on the part of any one of their number. Still, I am quite aware that in many houses this would be folly.

I remember two instances in which my plan of leaving things open acted in a curious manner, and which I ought to mention. The one occurred during my absence from home. My husband bought a small quantity of very choice tea, put it into my tea-caddy, and *locked it up*, intending to make his own tea (bachelor fashion) while I was away. This so roused the anger of our old cook, who had been with us many years, that she gave him a bad time, and was as nearly as possible dismissed from her service by him. She wrote me a long letter complaining of the master's want of trust in her, and it was long before she forgot what she was pleased to call a "slur upon her honour." The second was curious. My child's cabinet, which contained all the pretty pieces of jewellery she had had given her, was, and is always, kept locked by her. We had an under-servant who had been with us a year, and who was, on the whole, a very good girl. Judge of my astonishment when she came up to me in charge of an upper-servant, who said, "Annie has something to say to you, ma'am," and left her with me. "What is the matter?" I inquired; but it was long before I could get an answer. At length it came out that the one thing persistently locked up had been to her a veritable Blue Beard's chamber, and she had been trying all the keys in order to unfasten the cabinet, and had broken one of them in the lock. "But, indeed—indeed, ma'am, I did not want to steal anything, only to look at what was inside." And I believed her; and after a serious talk she went downstairs a happier and a wiser girl. She remained with us three years after this incident, and now fills a very important situation, and she is reckoned quite among our friends.

Hard-and-fast rules which may apply to everyone alike cannot be made or kept with regard to domestic service. Everything depends upon the relationship between mistress and maid; and where faith and trust bridge over the gulf between the one and the other, the difficulties of housekeeping will be minimised.

VARIETIES.

HOW TO ARRANGE WILD FLOWERS.

The prettiest arrangement that girls can make of wild flowers is to secure a thick piece of bright green moss, and fit it into a dish with a little water under it. Then make little holes down through it with a skewer, and thrust down the stems of the flowers—hepaticas, anemones, dog-tooth violets, etc.—pressing the moss around them again to hold them in place.

Do not put them too thick, but just as they might grow on a mossy bank, and they will keep fresh, and continue to bloom for a week or two, if you have secured any buds, and will delight everyone who sees them by their delicate fragrance and beauty.

HIGH AND LOW NOTES.—Fine high or low notes produce a very good effect if used with discretion, but if abused, to the detriment of the rest of the voice, they are better left alone, for good singing does not depend on extraordinary notes, but on the proper use of the ordinary ones.—*Charles Santley.*

A WRONG READING.

"May I kiss you?"
It was in the orchard.
She answered him not. Picking a leaf from a pear tree near by, she handed it to him.
He thought he read her answer—"Leave."
Turning, he went his way.
She gazed at him in astonishment, for she meant her answer to be, "You have leaf."
And so it all ended.

A CHINESE COMPLIMENT.—In China, where fans are carried by men and women of every rank, it is a compliment to invite a friend or distinguished guest to write some sentiment on your fan as a memento of any special occasion.

THE GRADUATING GIRL.

'Twas not her essay we admired,
    Though 'twas of "Earth's perfection;"
But how the way she was attired
    Just suited her complexion.

HAPPINESS.—Happiness is not an easy thing; it is very difficult to find it in ourselves, and it is impossible to find it elsewhere.—*Chamfort.*

ANSWER TO ACROSTIC I. (p. 291).

```
          G
        S I X
      E R R O R
    B O I L E A U
  A S S E S S O R S
M E R I T O R I O U S
G I R L S O W N P A P E R
  P E R S O N A T I O N
    T R A M P L I N G
    P A R A S O L
    H A P P Y
      T E N
        R
```

Emma Brewer, "Our Friends the Servants" (Volume 14, 25 March 1893, p. 403).

VOL. XV.—No. 740.]   MARCH 3, 1894.   [PRICE ONE PENNY.

THE QUEEN AT HOME.

THE fact that our Sovereign is what her people understand as a homely woman has in no small measure contributed to her well-deserved popularity. It was the *Times* which once said that the English people were a nation who found their pleasures chiefly at their own firesides. When the present Queen came to the throne, the time was, in more respects than one, the opening of a new era. The old order of things, which had held on from the eighteenth century, was passing away, and all at once, as it were, the people were charmed when the royal palace became a pattern home. Though George III. and Queen Charlotte had been worthy characters, the English Court had generally shown no very favourable contrast to those of the Continent. The Queen has ever found her chief joy in domestic life; but, while at Windsor, Osborne, and London, she has, perforce, lived more or less in state, becoming the Sovereign of Great Britain, she has been most at home at Balmoral.

Probably that fact is explained not only by the charmingly romantic surroundings of the Highland castle, but also through the estate having been the private property of the late Prince Consort, who erected the house. He first leased the estate in 1848, and finally made the purchase for £32,000. The property extends over about 10,000 acres, in addition to certain hills, and, being on the right bank of the Dee, is fifty miles from Aberdeen and nine from Ballater. The estate formerly belonged to the Farquharsons of Inverary, who sold it to the Earl of Fife. For persons seeking rest and change from the strain and hurry of London life there is no more attractive spot in the British Isles.

To see the Queen really at home, therefore, we have to follow her to Balmoral, where the surroundings are more in keeping with the royal taste than anywhere else. This fact gives additional charm or interest to the little book on the Sovereign's residence in the far North, which one apparently well acquainted with the circumstances has just issued.* Balmoral is the only place where the Queen can unbend from her royal state to enjoy the friendship and

* *The Queen at Balmoral*, by Frank Pope Humphrey (London: T. Fisher Unwin, 1893).

THE QUEEN IN HER CORONATION ROBES.
(*From the painting by Sir George Hayter.*)

G. H. P., "The Queen at Home" (Volume 15, 3 March 1894, p. 337).

sympathy of the common people. Being about 900 feet above sea-level, the spot was recommended by Sir James Clark as unrivalled in Scotland for its dryness and general healthiness. Mr. Humphrey says, " It is a beautiful district, whether in spring, when the birches are in tender leaf and the broom bursting into yellow bloom ; or in summer, when the hills are pink with heather ; or in autumn—the Queen's favourite season here—when there is an indescribable glory upon hill and valley of golden birch, purpling heather, scarlet rowan, and brown bracken."

When the Queen and Prince Albert first visited Balmoral about forty-six years ago, the charm of the solitude and peace of the neighbourhood, in comparison with the fatigue and excitement of life in London, was irresistible. With the estate of Abergeldie, which is leased from the Gordon family, and the forest of Balloch Buie, the land comprises a total of 40,000 acres. On the occasion of their first visit the royal couple went from London to Aberdeen by sea, whence they had to take a carriage drive of fifty miles. An Act of Parliament stopped the railway from coming nearer than Ballater. The old-time castle—originally a farm-house—which was found on the estate half a century ago, gave place to the present palace in 1855. The site was selected by Prince Albert as one which would receive the sun's rays during the greater part of each day when it was shining. About 130 persons can be lodged in the castle. The contractor for the building encountered some difficulty when materials rose in price on account of the Crimean War, but the Prince made good the deficiency. After he had watched the builders' progress with interest, and had himself superintended the laying out of the grounds, Balmoral became the Prince's favourite residence, and at his death he bequeathed it to the Queen, who regards the house and its surroundings with ever-increasing favour.

Visitors may inspect the house when the Queen is not in residence, and on entering the hall one is confronted by stags' heads, and among them is the head of a boar which Prince Albert killed in the Fatherland. Then a bust of the Queen, as she was in 1867, confronts you in one direction, while in a recess is a life-size statue of King Malcolm of Scotland, 1057-1093. In the hall, under glass, the colours of the 79th Highlanders, which did service in the Crimean War and in the Indian Mutiny, are to be seen. The hall fire-irons were presented to the Queen by the Marchioness of Lorne, and with such good implements, showing the national thistle, " the sturdy fire-dogs" beneath the chimney are said to be " well fitted to bear up the logs of which the fire is always made." Beneath the life-size statue of the Prince Consort in the arch of the staircase is the inscription :—

" His life sprang from a deep inner sympathy with God's will, and therefore with all that is true, beautiful, and good."

Somewhat higher up the stairs is a bronze bust of the late Emperor Frederick who was betrothed to the Princess Royal at Balmoral. Busts of others who are gone also attract notice, for cut in marble you recognise the likeness of the Grand Duke of Hesse, husband of the Princess Alice, Prince Leopold, Dr. Macleod, and Principal Tulloch.

The principal rooms have carpets of royal Stuart tartan pattern, and the pictures are all engravings. Everything in the way of furniture is comfortable and well-arranged ; but those who go there expecting to see anything like royal state will come away disappointed. " Splendours are reserved for the royal palaces," Mr. Humphrey reminds us ; " Balmoral is a home." The ornaments on the walls as well as the bust of Sir Walter Scott in the smoking-room all remind the visitor

that it is a Scottish house, while the glorious views from the windows show that it is in the Highlands.

Since the Queen has discontinued attending the little parish church, just rebuilt, divine service is held in what is called the service room, the Presbyterian order being observed. The apartment strikes the visitor as having an interest of its own, the material for its panels being brought from Balloch Buie wood, the wood itself being described as dark and handsome and having many knots. " The chairs are of the same wood, seated with dark leather," adds Mr. Humphrey. " The seat of the Queen's large armchair is embroidered with the Scotch thistle, a small table stands beside it with silk cushions for Bible and hymnal. Against the walls are seats or settles of dark carved wood." A princess or a lady-in-waiting will play the organ, while the minister's desk is on a platform in one corner of the room.

Loving as she did the simplicity of the service at the little parish church, the royal pew being in the gallery and not differing from the others, the Queen was for long disinclined to make any change ; but circumstances left her no choice in the matter. The services at Crathie church were attended until the shoals of visitors attracted to the little sanctuary became an annoyance ; horses waiting outside for a long distance on either side, the church itself being crowded to the last standing-place. " But the overcrowding was not the worst of the infliction," we are told. " Unmindful of the sacredness of the place and day, as well as of the respect due to Her Majesty, they persistently stared at her straight through the service, even bringing opera-glasses for the purpose." One attraction for sightseers in the church was the two stained-glass windows put up by the Queen in memory of her favourite chaplain, Dr. Norman Macleod. These will be replaced in the church being re-erected to supersede the old one, the Queen herself giving five hundred pounds to the building fund.

Abergeldie Castle, the house of the neighbouring estate now allied with Balmoral, stands on a picturesque site over two miles away ; and on the ground floor of its old square tower is marked the spot where was chained the last witch of Deeside, and who was burned at Craig-na-ban, now included in the royal estate.

A bewitchment of another kind took place on that same spot in 1856, when the then Crown Prince of Prussia presented a piece of white heather to the Princess Royal as a preliminary to the serious question of asking her to become his wife. The Duchess of Kent, as mother of the Queen, was accustomed to pass the autumn at Abergeldie. The ex-empress Eugenie passed some time here after the death of her son in 1879, and the Prince of Wales with his family has often stayed there.

One pleasing characteristic of Balmoral and other royal estates is, as Mr. Humphrey tells us, you never see posted up " threats of prosecution for trespass," the intimation being, if there is any board at all, that the path or road is " strictly private," and such a notice would seem to be more effective than the harsher and more common words.

Balmoral has many memorials, reminding the visitor of various Highland customs which the Queen finds pleasure in perpetuating. The oldest of these is the Queen's cairn, put up on a memorable day in the fall of 1852 to commemorate the buying of the estate ; the Sovereign placed the first stone, the Prince the second, and then others added to the pile, the Prince Consort placing the topmost stone. Each marriage that has since taken place in the royal family has been commemorated by a cairn.

It was the late Lord Beaconsfield who said that the Queen worked harder than most of her subjects ; and whether this is literally true or not, she undoubtedly leads a busy life for one who is midway between seventy and eighty years of age. She appears to attend to the management of her estates at Osborne and Balmoral, while as regards other matters we find it remarked that, " No living statesman is so thoroughly conversant with the workings of every department—of every log one may say—in the vast governmental department as the Queen."

The Sovereign is a comparatively early riser, and will frequently breakfast at a small cottage a short distance from the castle, where she will remain at work during the morning, nothing being more congenial to royal taste than some secluded and romantic spot where the open air can be fully enjoyed without fear of intrusion. " At Osborne she has a summer-house, and at Windsor she resorts to a tent upon the lawn of Frogmore House," we are told. " And even when she has been temporarily at a place, as at Holyrood Palace, Edinburgh, which stands in anything but a secluded spot, she has contrived, with the help of screens and umbrellas, a place to write in the open air." It is on account of their perfect seclusion that the shiels, or cottage hunting-lodges, built among the woods of the Balmoral estate are in such high favour. In addition to these, however, the Queen has a portable room which can at once be erected anywhere like a tent, open or enclosed according to taste. In former days this love of the open air prompted the Queen to take extensive walks about the estate, and even to make the ascent of the great hills in company with Prince Albert. Now that she has to walk with a stick, however, the Queen has to be content with her morning and afternoon drive, while the tour of the castle grounds has to be made in a bath-chair. Mr. Humphrey tells a pretty little story relating to the early days at Balmoral which may be called—

THE CHILDREN AND THE COWS.

" She, little Mary, in company with her brother Kenneth, was helping her neighbour Maggie to herd the cows. Their business was to see that the cows did not get at the corn ; but they being intent on play, the cows were soon left to Kenneth's herding, who was a little lad of five. When at last the cows were discovered feeding upon the corn, Maggie, true to that instinct which impels every son and daughter of Adam to look about for a scapegoat for his or her own sins, fell upon Kenneth, scolding him volubly for neglecting to look after the cows. In the midst of her tirade she heard a voice call Maggie, and looking up saw the Queen and Prince Albert in a path upon the hillside above. Maggie hesitated, but again the clear voice of the Queen called Maggie, and reluctantly Maggie went forward. ' Maggie,' she said kindly, ' you should remember that Kenneth is a little boy and does not understand about keeping the cows off the corn. It would be a better way to put up a string so that they cannot get at it.' The children were inwardly amused at the idea of a string being a sufficient guard ; but, mindful of what was due to the Queen, did not smile. Not so Prince Albert, who laughed heartily at her, and the two walked merrily off together."

With advancing years the Queen cannot do at Balmoral as she formerly could. The all-day drives across the country have been given up, and she cannot alight from her carriage to call upon cottagers as was her wont in former years. The old folks she favours do not want for attention, however. One or another may be summoned to the castle if the Queen cannot visit them.

G. H. P., *"The Queen at Home" (Volume 15, 3 March 1894, p. 338).*

The royal mistress of Balmoral also manifests great interest in the quaint or picturesque customs of the Highlands which come down from ancient times. One of these is Hallowe'en, when the torches and the dancing remind one of superstitions which have come down from the days of the old fire-worshippers. Centuries ago the day's celebration might hardly have been considered complete without the burning of a witch at eventide; but as material for such a bonfire cannot now be obtained, a more simple programme is prepared—

"The Queen going out for her evening drive is met on her return by a crowd of servants, keepers, gillies, children, each bearing a torch made of splints of fir tied together. They escort the Queen to the door, and then they march round and round the castle, the glare of their torches illuminating wall, and turret, and tower." The excitement culminates in the great bonfire at night, when in solemn procession "the witch" appears in a cart to be consigned to the flames, which in the good old times might have been considered her native element.

It was a happy day for the poorer sort of people of Deeside when Prince Albert purchased the Balmoral estate. The shanties, hardly better than the cabins of Ireland, though made of stone, were such as had served Highland peasants from time immemorial; but these were at once superseded by neat cottages of an approved pattern. The cottagers are thus not only well cared for, but each is known by sight and by name, and when accident or sickness occurs the royal sympathy appears to be never wanting. Thus, one old lady on the estate met with an accident, and a telegram was sent from Windsor to say that she was to have whatever was necessary sent from the castle. In regard to the ailments of her tenants, the Queen has a good memory. "She does not confuse your neuralgia with rheumatism," it is said; "nor inquire as to the welfare of your broken arm when you have had a fever." Many of the cottagers have gifts which, they will tell a visitor, they received from the Queen's own hands: it may be the material for a gown, some trinket which will become an heirloom, a statuette or flower-pot from the Continent. When abroad, the Queen is said "to buy of the special industries of the place where she is staying," and many things appear to be purchased expressly for the Balmoral cottars.

In the season they also receive gifts of venison and beef at Christmas, while from the Christmas-tree at Osborne unforgotten friends in the distant Highlands will invariably receive their gifts. Better than this was the establishment of schools before the days of national education, and, as is well known, the profits of the royal books on *Life in the Highlands* were devoted to the founding of bursaries or scholarships. Mr. Campbell, parish minister of Crathie, is one of the royal chaplains, and his manse contains many presents from his Sovereign: "pottery from Mentone, an exquisite group

THE QUEEN SMILING.
(*From an instantaneous photograph by permission.*)

of Fra Angelico's angels from Florence, . . . a pair of vases, with pale pink roses and leaves in high relief." There was a former mistress of Crathie manse who confessed to feeling a little embarrassed when, in the midst of her household work, the Queen would be announced as coming; but embarrassment vanished as soon as the royal visitor opened her lips. Some of the old peasant-women also felt under some restraint, but, as one of them remarked, "The Queen said she did na want us to feel like that, for she was just a woman like oursels."

Of the Queen's servants John Brown will probably be the most famous in history; but his contemporary Grant, and his successor, as attendant on the Queen, Francie Clarke, will also be remembered. It was Prince Albert who first discovered the good qualities of John Brown when the latter was a stable-boy, and he soon got promoted until he was the Queen's chief attendant. Perhaps there never was a more faithful servant, so that, without exaggeration, one has ventured to say of him, "I believe he would have stood between the Queen and a bullet any day." Everybody does not seem to be aware that the Queen's Indian empire is represented in the royal household by an Indian secretary, a personal Indian attendant, and the native Indian cook.

There are four shiels on the Balmoral estate —hunting - lodges, in which any holiday-makers from London might think themselves fortunate in being permitted to pass a month. The nearest of these, named after the Queen, is three miles from the castle. The Danzig Shiel, in the wood, is surrounded by what is a remnant of the ancient forest. "Everything indicates that we are entering the heart of a great forest. No sight or sound of an outer world greets us. Great Scotch firs shut us in on every hand; the atmosphere is loaded with their resinous fragrance. When the beams of the low-running sun strike them, their red bark glows like the decaying embers of an ingle-nook. In cooler lights it is a reddish purple. Their tall, straight trunks have a columnar aspect, and on a hillside, as you look up, you fancy you are gazing through vast porticoes into the mysterious depths of prodigious halls, wherein once dwelt pre-historic giants. In fact, you may fancy anything you like, as you find yourself seized upon, taken possession of by the spirits of the Balloch Buie. Now and then an ancient birch, gnarled, crooked, and patched with black moss, breaks the uniformity of the pines."

Thus Balmoral is one of the most interesting spots in England, and in the future will have memories which will eclipse those of Hampton Court, Kensington, and Holyrood, though the rooms at the last-named palace are said to be the most interesting suite in Europe. Mr. Humphrey's book is extremely readable; he is somewhat of an enthusiast in the matter of royalty, and he seems to have explored for himself the wide and enchanting domain of Balmoral.

G. H. P.

G. H. P., *"The Queen at Home"* (Volume 15, 3 March 1894, p. 339).

"QUEEN BABY AND HER WANTS."

By Mrs. ORMAN COOPER, Author of "We Wives," etc.

PART I.

Her Clothes.—Perhaps there is no subject more fascinating to the ordinary woman than that of baby-clothes! Of course "the new woman" finds no charm therein. I am not writing for that modern production, only for those sweet, womanly souls who have the instincts of motherhood implanted in them. To such—whether she be mother, sister, cousin, or aunt—those wee, dainty garments which we fashion for "the trailing clouds of glory," that come "out of the nowhere into the here," are a wonderful source of pleasure. The tiny frills and tucks, the delicate laces, the fine-drawn work, the invisible hems, are

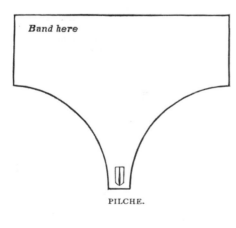

Band here

PILCHE.

each dwelt on with a kind of awe. So much love is tucked into each fold, so much pleasure run into each gusset.

Now in this paper I shall try to recommend only those things which I have personally found most convenient. There may be many other garments thought necessary by some. But I am an old-fashioned woman in most ways, and have tried no new-fangled notions. My one aim has been to have garments that will not try the temper of my babies too much, that will give the minimum of weight with the maximum of warmth, and that will make my treasures look like little bundles of daintiness, purity, and comfort.

I will begin by saying that the outfit for babies is generally too large. The tiny queen —who when she comes rules the household with a rod of iron—needs at first a very moderate *trousseau*. She will require, at the most, four nightgowns, four day-gowns, or monthly robes, four long flannel petticoats, four flannel binders, four little vests, or six wee shirts, two or three robes, twelve dribblers, or bibs, three dozen diapers, six pilches, and several soft fleecy shawls and flannel squares.

We will begin at the very beginning, as we would dress Queen Baby on her natal day.

The Binders.—These may be made of strips of soft flannel, with raw edges. They should be about six inches in depth, and the

full width of ordinary flannel. Do not hem them, they are softer without it, and the nurse can double them if necessary when putting on. Every woman should realise that binders are used for warmth, not for support. So many old nurses put the roller on as tightly as possible " to support the spine." It should do nothing of the sort. The binder is to keep baby from catching cold in stomach or chest. There should not at first be any way of fastening, save with needle and thread. (Pins, even safety ones, should never be tolerated.) After awhile some soft linen buttons at the proper place, and neatly-worked buttonholes at one end will be a comfort.

Over this binder I should advise a soft wool vest, instead of the ordinary linen shirt. It should not be hand-knit. Nothing but a machine can produce web of sufficient gossamer-make to suit our little queen's tender skin. At the shops they can be bought for 1s. 1d. apiece.

If the shirt is thought to look nicer, let it be made of soft pongee silk instead of linen. Why torture a helpless infant with starch and cotton lace. The silk may have a tiny frill of Valenciennes sewn on at the armholes. This will not rub and fray the wee arms; and can be washed out in one's hand-basin. These silk shirts look very dainty, wash like a rag, and wear well.

The flannel pilche is our baby's next garment. It holds the diaper in place. I have found that ordinary fine birdseye squares that are sold, are not so nice for the wee one as hygroscopic or swansdown ones. These are very cleanly and absorbent besides being delightfully thick and warm. They cost about 7d. each.

The pilche itself is made in three different ways. Some women use only a simple square of flannel, held together with a safety pin. I

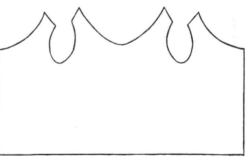

SHAPE OF PETTICOAT BODICE.

prefer one yard of flannel, folded corner-wise and split in two. The edges I bind together with silk ribbon and full the top into a band of calico two inches wide. Sometimes the inner point is bound separately and only attached to the outer one by the band. But, whichever way it is made, the pilche should be of double flannel. A thin tape must be run through the band and should pass through a loop sewn at the point. This point is drawn up between the little feet and keeps all this part of baby's costume neatly together.

We now come to a garment which is very pleasant to make and admits of much decoration if we wish, viz., the barrow or flannel petticoat.

Choose a soft, white, Saxony flannel as fine as possible. It will take nine yards for the necessary four petticoats. But as these are worn day and night a less number would not do. They will cost about 3s. apiece, including silk, etc.

Join together one width and a half of the flannel and hem all round with fine herringbone. The length should be twenty-seven inches long. This is the skirt. For the bodice take a strip of flannel from the end of the roll about seven inches deep. Mitre the two ends, and fold in three. Armholes are hollowed at the two folds. At the back, quilt on a diamond of extra flannel to cover the delicate lungs. Under one arm cut a slit and buttonhole it thickly with silk. Now take a coin and mark out all round the upper part of the strip in scallops. Or better still, get a couple of yards of Briggs' edging and iron off the pattern. Buttonhole each scallop with white silk and put a dot of the same embroidery in each round. Bind the armhole with sarcenet ribbon and cross each with a strap of the same.

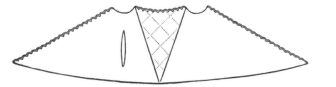

BODICE FOR FLANNEL BARROW.

The way to put on this barrow is as follows. The baby is laid on the quilted back, her arms brought through the holes, one point (fitted with a piece of ribbon) is drawn through the slit under the right arm, and brought to meet the other in front. Here it is tied.

By this arrangement the petticoat (which of course is pleated on to the bodice and bound neatly in place) falls in a double pleat over the little toes, and needs no strings sewn on it.

Except when Queen Baby is going to wear a robe, immediately on the top of this barrow comes the gown. It is well, however, to have two white petticoats at least. For those we need four and a half yards of Nainsook muslin or very fine long cloth, and three yards of narrow lace for edging the bodice. Divide your material in two equal parts, and take off a strip from the end of each ten inches wide. These strips are for the two little bodices and must be cut as diagram. Allow an inch hem at either end of the bodice and make a tiny one round the neck. It and the armholes should be trimmed with lace put on slightly full.

Sleeve

Cuff.

The skirts will measure thirty-three inches in length. This includes a two-inch hem and two and a half in tucks. It must be fulled on to the bodice, through the false hem of which a narrow draw-string is passed.

I have recommended neat lace instead of embroidery in this paper, as it is so much softer and falls in more artistic folds than any cut work can do. Besides the starched points and whirligigs in Madeira work are apt to irritate a baby's neck and arms. But, of course, if preferred embroidery can always be substituted for lace.

Now we are come to the daintiest part of our wee maiden's first *trousseau*. In elaboration it will in no way compare with the white robe she may don some future day—for these tiny gowns cannot be too simple in make. They should owe their fascination to the delicate sewing and fine materials employed on them.

My little queen has eight of these garments. But six are usually sufficient. Four of them, those worn at night, are made from eight yards of fine cambric. They are thirty-two inches long and two breadths wide. Fold each length down the centre and cut out as shown in the diagram. The pieces left in shaping will cut sleeves ten and a half inches long. Cuffs are included in this measurement, and are simply the ends hemmed, bordered with Cash's narrowest frilling, and turned back. They are cut in one piece. For these little monthly gowns I always make a breastplate of tiny tucks covering the bosom. Each one is feather-stitched with fine crochet cotton. Our queen, at this period of her existence, is better without dribblers, so this thickness on the chest is welcome. A band—also thickly feather-stitched—meets these tucks at the waist, viz., six inches from the neck. It is finished with long sash ends of the cambric. These keep the dress in position when tied in a bow, and the frock is finished with a frill and a draw-string at the neck.

Baby's daygowns are made of Nainsook or striped cambric sometimes. Mine are always fashioned from the deep tucked cambric one buys by the yard. It has generally groups of three tiny tucks with spaces between which I fill with one inch Valenciennes. It is made long enough for the skirt (thirty-six inches), but the bodice, cut after the pattern given above, must be cut from plain cambric. Then, round the neck put a frill of the antique Valenciennes—or better still—of pillow handmade lace or Maltese, and fill up to a point at the waist with the same. This makes a charming soft frame for the tiny face, and gives the shoulders a sturdy square look. The sleeves are ornamented with the same lace as the "plastron," and, if wished, the skirt may be lengthened with an edging slightly wider.

My readers must understand that these last garments do not pretend to the grandeur of robes. But Queen Baby seldom wears anything more elaborate during the first month of her existence. I have never made a genuine "robe," spelt in capitals if one trusts nurse's pronunciation, so I cannot tell how to frame its intricate ornamentation. I should advise such being bought. They can be procured from 5s. to £5 5s.

Queen Baby is nearly ready. But our little monarch's head needs a crown. Give it a soft, fleecy shawl, crocheted by granny's patient fingers, I advise you. It is more cosy than even the flannel silk-mitred squares one so often sees. By-the-bye, we have forgotten booties and monkey jackets, and if baby comes in the winter she will need both. I cannot knit, so I can only advise my readers on two points concerning these woollies. Let them be pure white and never put up with crochet work in them. These latter are frauds. They look well until introduced to the hand-basin. Then they harden and stretch in the most exasperating way. Whereas, plain knitted booties will wear and wash to the end. There are three articles required by Queen Baby every day that I would not advise an amateur to meddle with.

One is dribblers. They are so inexpensive to buy and so troublesome to make. I have found silk ones far more satisfactory than the usual padded things; they can be bought for 4s. the half dozen and are made of soft Surah and trimmed with fine torchon. They can be rinsed out in baby's bath, and require neither starching nor ironing, so one needs to invest in fewer at a time. Baby's neck can never be frayed with them, and the creamy tint they eventually acquire is beautiful compared to the yellow hue of badly-made up cambric.

In fact in these days of cheap silk that word may be interpolated wherever I have put cotton. For shirtees and dribblers I would recommend nothing else.

I mentioned three things as "taboo" to an amateur. The two last are cap and cloak. Even the most dainty of untrained fingers cannot turn out millinery equal to what can be bought at any good shop. So I would advise these to be left alone; only premising they should both be made of washing silk, trimmed (if possible) with thick silk cord and real lace.

I am afraid the editor of The Girl's Own Paper will frown if I lengthen this paper much further. But at least I must ask for space just to talk about Queen Baby's bed. Of course all kinds of handsome ones can be bought ready trimmed. I will just tell you how to prepare a dainty inexpensive nest for the birdie.

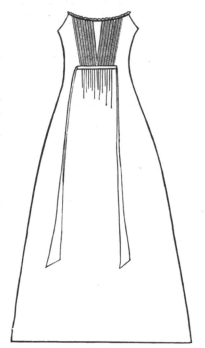

Get an ordinary wicker cradle; it will cost about 3s. 6d. Take off the canes destined to hedge in the tiny head. We shall not need them. Enamel it with Aspinall's ivory white. Get a carpenter to make an ordinary stand of inch square slater's laths. Let the two ends form separate X shape supports and lay the cradle therein. Screw on tiny rollers at each foot. Tie wicker and wood together with ivory ribbons, line the basket with ivory silk, edge it with a frill of soft lace, and you have the daintiest cradle for next to nothing. Of course this way of making baby's bed equal in height with mother's does away with rockers. "And a good thing too," as Dr. Pye Chevasse would say in his learned treatises on this subject.

(To be continued.)

Mrs. Orman Cooper, "Queen Baby and Her Wants" (Volume 18, 7 November 1896, p. 93).

Vol. XX.—No. 1025.]　　　　　AUGUST 19, 1899.　　　　　[Price One Penny.

LONDON'S FUTURE HOUSEWIVES AND THEIR TEACHERS.

If one stands at the entrance of a large Board school either at dinner or tea-time and watches the pupils trooping out, one often wonders what will become of all these lively children in a few years' time, what they will make of their lives, and how enough work is to be found for them all. Has it ever struck any of my readers that, whatever the boys may do in the way of work, sooner or later that of the girls is certain? They are going to be the wives or housekeepers of these or other boys. They will be dressmakers, tailoresses, servants, factory girls or what not for a time, but their final business will be housekeeping, and housekeeping too on small means, so that a great deal of skill, care and knowledge will be needed if they are to do it well.

How are the girls to be trained for this very important work of theirs? Their school life

is very short; the time they will have to spare after leaving school will be very little, their leisure hours in the evening being wanted for rest and recreation as well as for learning; it will be small wonder if many of them marry without any knowledge of household management and if the comfort and happiness of their home is ruined in consequence.

The question is so serious that people interested in education have given it a great deal of thought. There is little doubt that, if it were possible, the best plan would be to give a year's training in housekeeping to every girl when she leaves school; but alas! since most girls from elementary schools are obliged to earn money as early as possible, this plan cannot be carried out. The only thing that can be done by the managers of elementary schools is to proceed on the principle that " half a loaf

is better than no bread," to give the girls, while still at school, weekly lessons for a certain number of weeks each year, in cookery and laundry-work, and sometimes in housewifery generally, and to encourage then to attend evening classes after they have left school. A great deal of good has been done in this way, but the children are so young and the lessons necessarily so few, so far between and so fragmentary, that the result is very far from being all that could be wished.

Seeing this, the Technical Education Board of the London County Council five years ago began to establish, one after another, Schools of Domestic Economy to which girls should go for five months at a time after leaving the ordinary schools, and where they should be occupied for the whole school hours five days a week in household work, thus giving them

A HOUSEWIFERY CLASS AT BATTERSEA POLYTECHNIC.

Anon., "London's Future Housewives and Their Teachers" (Volume 20, 19 August 1899, p. 737).

an opportunity of really understanding their future duties as housewives. The question of enabling poor people to afford this five months' extra teaching for their girls was a difficult one to meet, but as far as it could be done it has been done by giving free scholarships at these schools and by providing the scholars with their dinner and tea free of cost, and providing also the material required by each girl for making herself a dress, an apron and some under-garment during her time at the school. With only two exceptions, these schools, which are nine in number, are held in the polytechnics or in technical institutes, a capital arrangement whereby the rooms needed for evening classes for adults are used also during the day-time.

Let us look in at one of the schools and see of what a day's work consists. We will choose the school at the Battersea Polytechnic, because a Training School for Teachers is held there as well as a school for girls, and we shall have a double interest in the work. The Polytechnic is a great building standing back from Battersea Park Road, and at about nine o'clock in the morning we shall find a stream of teachers and pupils hurrying into it, masters and mistresses of the Science School, the Domestic Economy School, and the Training School for Teachers of Domestic Economy; boys and girls of the Science School; girls and women students of the two Domestic Economy Schools; and a few minutes later we shall find these all gathered in a large hall for "call over" and prayers, and then filing off to their separate departments.

Let us ask Miss Mitchell, the head of the Domestic Economy Schools, to spare us a little of her time and explain the work to us. We follow the women and girls to a separate wing of the building, and as they divide off into the different class-rooms we enter the large cookery school and watch the students in training settling down to their morning's work, fetching their pots and pans from cupboards and shelves, looking up the list of their work on the blackboard, weighing out ingredients, and so on. We look round the room, a little confused at first with all the movement, and see that it is large and well lighted with coal-stoves at one end and gas-stoves fixed into two large tables in the centre, with a lift, up which provisions for the day are still being sent, and down which, as we find later, the dinner is to go to the dining-room punctually at one o'clock; large sinks and plate-racks are fitted in one corner, low cupboards with shelves over them run far along the walls, and at the end of the room opposite the stoves is a stepped gallery, where forty or fifty pupils can sit for demonstration lessons. The head cookery teacher is busily engaged inspecting the food materials bought in by the student-housekeeper, criticising the quality and hearing the prices given, and Miss Mitchell explains to us that the students take it in turns to be housekeepers, and have to buy in materials for dinners for some sixty people every day; they are given lists of what will be wanted by the teachers, but the whole responsibility of choosing and buying the food rests with them, and so out they go every day into the neighbouring streets, taking with them two or three girls from the Domestic Economy School, to choose fish, meat and vegetables from the shops and stalls of the neighbourhood, for they are to learn how to choose and make the best of such provisions as the working people of the neighbourhood are accustomed to buy, and capital training this is for them.

"Do the students here cook dinners for sixty people?" we ask in wonder; and in answer, Miss Mitchell takes us next door into a smaller cookery room, where fifteen girls are at work under the charge of a teacher and a student, also busy on dishes which are to be ready by dinner-time. Everything left from one day's dinner, we are told, is brought up to the cookery schools again by the "house-keeper" to be re-cooked and made into dainty dishes — no waste of any kind is allowed.

Crossing the corridor we find two rooms given up to dressmaking and needlework; here again both students-in-training and girls are working in separate classes. One of the students, who has nearly completed her course of training, is helping a teacher with a class of girls (fifteen in number again we notice), and the other students, under the head dress-making teacher, are busy on their own work— this morning they are drafting bodice patterns for various types of figures, but that their work is not confined to pattern-making is evident when the cupboards are opened and dresses taken out for our inspection — dresses made by each student to fit herself, funds being provided as in the case of the girls by the Technical Education Board. Very neatly made the dresses are, and proud the students seem to be of them, though their pride is tempered by anxiety as to what the examiner's opinion of them may be when the time of examination for their diplomas comes. Each student has to make two dresses, that is, sample garments to show her plain needle-work, and to learn to patch and mend old dresses and under-garments, her pride culminating in a sampler of patches, darns, and drawnthread work, such as that hanging in a show cupboard on the wall. The girls, we are told, in their shorter course make them-selves one dress, one apron, and an under-garment each, and spend one lesson of two hours each week in practical mending of worn garments.

We ask why it is that every class we have seen consists of fifteen pupils only, and are told that in all classes for practical work for which funds are supplied by the Technical Education Board the number of pupils is limited to fifteen, so that the teacher may be able to attend thoroughly to the practical work of each pupil, instead of having to teach her class somewhat in the manner of a drill ser-geant, as must inevitably be the case when dealing with large numbers.

But the morning is getting on, and we hurry downstairs to the laundry, perhaps the most striking of all the class-rooms, a glass partition shutting off the washing-room, with its large teak troughs where a busy set of girls are at work, from the ironing-room, fitted with long solid tables on which blouses of many shapes and colours are being ironed into crisp fresh-ness. A special feature of the room is the white-tiled screen keeping the heat of the ironing stove, with its dozens of irons, from the rest of the room, while the height and good ventilation keep the room fresh and pleasant even in hot weather. We turn away from this vision of dainty whiteness to be in time to see the last class we are to visit this morning, the "housewifery" class, which is conducting a "spring-cleaning" in one of the social rooms of the polytechnic, which lends itself admirably for the purpose of teaching the girls how to turn out a well-furnished sitting-room. The housewifery lessons are a great feature of the Domestic Economy Schools,

we hear, and include the whole routine of household work apart from actual cooking, washing, and dressmaking, these being, as we have seen, taught separately, so that girls who have gone through the course ought not to find themselves at a loss in any department of housekeeping, the whole series of lessons in each department being made to dovetail one into the other.

It is nearly one o'clock now, and Miss Mitchell asks us to come into the dining-room, where the tables are just laid for dinner, and we find the housekeeping-student in charge, lifting dishes on to "hot-plates" as they come down from the cookery schools, with the group of girls who are told off to help her giving final touches to the tables, these being laid with pretty blue and white crockery, and with here and there bunches of flowers which have been brought by one or other of the pupils. The teachers aim at having the tables laid as nicely as possible and at giving the girls a high standard of neatness and daintiness to take back with them to their own homes.

Presently a bell rings and the girls file in and take their places at three long tables, with a teacher and a student at the head and foot of each, the other students-in-training having a table to themselves. We feel rather in-trusive as we watch them take their places, and, turning out of the room, ask Miss Mitchell to spare us yet a few minutes to answer some of the questions that are in our minds.

"How many of such schools are there? Where are the others, and how do the girls get their scholarships? Can we help girls we know to get such a chance, and specially how are the scholarships for training teachers to be obtained, and what chance is there for these teachers at the end of their two years' train-ing?" Miss Mitchell tells us laughingly that to answer all this fully would take much more than a few minutes, but this much she can say: that at present, though the number of schools is far from enough to give as many scholarships as are needed for all London, they are steadily increasing in number; there are such schools at the Borough, Chelsea, Woolwich, Clerken-well, St. John's Wood, Bloomsbury, Wands-worth and Norwood, while others will be opened in Holloway, at Globe Road, Bow, and at Deptford next term: that the girls' scholarships are given on their being nominated by their school mistresses for the approval of the Technical Education Board, and that there-fore anyone interested in getting such a scholar-ship for a working girl should write to the offices of the Technical Education Board of the London County Council for information, and then get the girl to apply to her mistress for a nomination for next term. As regards the training scholarships, they have to be won by passing an examination, not in itself very stiff, but sufficient to ensure that the teachers of domestic economy trained in the school shall possess a fairly good general education. All particulars can be obtained from the offices of the Technical Education Board. As to the chance of employment, the experience of teachers holding good diplomas from the Battersea Training School has been very happy, few of them having had to wait long for work. And so she wishes us good-bye, and we leave the building feeling that we have had a glance into a new world, one full of energy and hopefulness, and giving promise of happier conditions of life for future generations of citizens in our great city.

Anon., "London's Future Housewives and Their Teachers" (Volume 20, 19 August 1899, p. 738).

A NEEDLEWORK CLASS, BATTERSEA POLYTECHNIC.

THE HOUSE WITH THE VERANDAH.

By ISABELLA FYVIE MAYO, Author of "Other People's Stairs," "Her Object in Life," etc.

CHAPTER XXI.

THE TELEGRAM FROM THE NORTH.

THE days went on: the mysterious "knocks" did not recur, and as the police inspector made no more inquiries, and the Marvels attempted no further intercourse with the little house with the verandah, the very memory of them readily faded from the minds of the little household there, and especially from that of its mistress, ever becoming more pre-occupied with the prolonged delay of letters from Charlie, or indeed of any news from the *Slains Castle*.

Lucy's brother-in-law, Mr. Brand, went down to Bath to attend Mr. Bray's funeral, and his wife Florence accompanied him "to be with the dear old lady in her sorrow." Indeed, Mr. Brand left his wife with the widow while he went to and fro between Bath and London, looking after his own business and winding up Mr. Bray's affairs. Lucy would have liked to visit the old lady in the early days of bereavement, but, of course, in her circumstances any such expression of sympathy was out of the question. Still, every evening, no matter how tired and despondent she felt she wrote a loving little note to her mother's old friend, so that every morning she might find it on her breakfast-table. Also, Lucy copied a little picture of the Surrey village where she knew Mrs. Bray had first met her dead husband, and she

sent it to the widow as a tender sign of sympathy. Lucy did not wonder that Mrs. Bray herself never acknowledged these tokens of love, for she knew the lady was old and feeble, and that deep grief is sometimes very silent. She knew that Mrs. Bray received all her remembrances, for Florence wrote delivering the old lady's "thanks for all kindnesses," and adding how grateful she also was for Florence's companionship, and for all the arrangements "Jem" was making for her welfare.

"There is not so much property left as one might have supposed, considering that Mr. Bray has earned such a large income for so many years," wrote Florence. "But then the Brays have always lived among people of rank and wealth, and naturally they got into the habit of spending as their friends did."

"Ah," said Miss Latimer, as Lucy read the letter to her. "In that way, earned incomes, however big, soon break up and vanish, as did the clay jar in the fable, when it raced with the iron pot!"

Lucy resumed her reading. "Florence goes on: 'Never mind; they have both enjoyed the best of everything, and have had many advantages which they might not have had, if people had not believed them to be rich. Jem is always saying that there's nothing so expensive as poverty. Therefore, though there is not much property left, it won't matter

much, for in many ways Mrs. Bray's spending days are necessarily over. Jem is managing so cleverly that she will scarcely know she is poorer than she used to be. She will even be able to afford to go on living in the same house, when she returns to London. It would be a great trial to her if she could not hope to do that—and it can be managed, for, you see, she is old and can't live long. She trusts Jem implicitly and leaves everything to him. She always says, "I don't want to know anything about money matters; I never have known and I don't wish to begin now. I ask for nothing but my little comforts and Rachel to look after me." And then Jem assures her that is quite easy, and so she is satisfied. I can't think what Mrs. Bray would do without Rachel. She is more devoted to her mistress than ninety-nine daughters out of a hundred are to their mothers. I don't anticipate that my girls will be half so kind to me when my dismal days come—and of course, I hope they'll be married and gone off long before I'm an old woman. I should not like to be the mother of ungathered wall-flowers! But where am I likely to find a Rachel? I'll just have to go and stay at an "hydropathic" when I'm an old woman. But old age is a long way off yet—and I devoutly trust that I'll be dead before it comes.'"

Those last words struck Lucy. She

her eyes. "God bless you! You ask very little of me, but yet it is the hardest thing of all," he said as he turned to go.

Bryde suddenly remembered the money that was such a burden to her. "Stay," she said. "Will you take this for me, Captain Estcourt? It is the last thing I shall ask of you. Will you find out from whom my father won this last night, and return it quietly?"

He took the bag from her, warm from its resting-place

upon her breast. "I will do it as a sacred duty," he said simply. "I think you will be glad to know that part of the money was won from young Sevett of ours. He is in terrible trouble to-day, poor fellow."

"I am—very glad."

Bryde kept up bravely until the door was closed behind him and she was alone, and then she flung herself face downwards on the sofa in bitter tears.

(*To be continued.*)

GOOD MISTRESSES.

THE question of servants, with their numerous faults, and the worries attendant upon them, is one which has frequently been discussed. Let us turn to the subject of mistresses, good, bad and indifferent, for on somewhat the same principle that a man is what a woman makes him, so also the behaviour of servants, whether meritorious or otherwise, depends in no small degree upon how they are governed by those who sit in the seat of authority over them.

The ordering of a woman's household is one of the chief responsibilities of her married life, and if she wishes the domestic wheels to run on velvet, she must see to it that they are oiled by skilful management and forethought.

The minds and bodies of men, and women too for that matter, are inseparably connected, and react upon each other; consequently the fact of his material comforts being attended to, and his home rendered a pleasant place to him, will undoubtedly exercise a very sweetening effect upon a man's temper and character generally.

When everything goes by clockwork, and there is apparently no flaw in the household arrangements, it does not invariably follow that there is a good mistress at the head of affairs.

Perfectly trained and skilled servants may leave her very little to do, and the real test of merit lies in the capability for keeping things nice with badly trained or indifferent ones. There are some women, fair weather mistresses we should call them, who manage very well when the wheels run smoothly of their own accord, but who find themselves hopelessly at a loss when their servants are inefficient or make mistakes.

One of the first things essential for the mistress of a household is that she should possess practical knowledge of domestic affairs. Before she can teach others she must know herself what ought to be done, and the manner of doing it, and if she is lacking in this respect, she must make it her business to find out. Good mistresses, as a rule, are born, not made, but they can be developed by dint of perseverance.

There are many women who, from their cradles, so to speak, show signs of a veritable talent for housekeeping and household management, and whose childish souls are centred in their doll's kitchen to the exclusion of other toys. What we like doing we mostly do well, and this preference, which grows with their years, helps them considerably when they have houses of their own to manage, and renders their duties a real labour of love.

There are others, however, also a large class, who detest domesticity and its attendant cares and responsibilities, and find, to their cost, that the taste is not one easily to be acquired.

If they are rich, they leave everything in the hands of their housekeeper, and if they are fortunate enough to engage an honest and capable woman, so much the better for them. But if, as often happens, they combine this distaste with a slender income and a husband who likes to be made as comfortable in his modest *ménage* as circumstances permit, it is a somewhat dreary prospect for both the parties concerned.

Whether it is a congenial occupation or not, the duties of a household must nevertheless be attended to, and even in those cases where all the practical details fall upon the housekeeper's shoulders, an establishment is always the better for a little occasional personal supervision from the mistress herself.

It is not, however, those households where everything is on a large scale, and the mistresses' *rôle* merely a nominal one, which we are discussing at present, but those more unassuming ones where only two or at the most three servants are kept.

A general rule to be observed when dealing with our inferiors in station is that they should be treated with consideration and kindness, and that the fact of their being human beings like their masters and mistresses should never be lost sight of, but it must also be remembered that firmness is necessary in our dealings with those under us.

A woman should make a study of her servants' characteristics, so as to be able to discriminate as to the amount of praise and blame which it will be beneficial to bestow.

Some natures require a little judicious severity, while with others a few timely words of encouragement will, if rightly earned, bring out and foster their best qualities. These may seem somewhat superfluous considerations to some people concerning those who serve us, but there would be fewer complaints from both drawing-room and kitchen if they were more frequently put in practice. A mistress should never be afraid of reiterating a given order. This is not a point where silence is golden, and it is better to speak too much than too little when it is a question of teaching servants their duty.

She should also not be content with having given an order, but should see that it is carried out, and if not, promptly demand the reason.

It is a mistake that is often made on first engaging a servant, to overlook any carelessness, or slovenly habits, on the score of her inexperience, or "not knowing our ways."

It is better far to begin as you mean to continue, for later on any fresh suggestions on the mistress's part will be looked on in the light of new ideas, and rebelled at accordingly. Tidiness and cleanliness are, of course, essentials, and most especially so when only one general servant is kept, whose appearance is often apt to suffer, on account of the extra amount of work she has to get through.

In the case of new parlourmaids or page-boys, a mistress should see that the table arrangements are as carefully attended to, and the waiting as ceremoniously performed, when she and her husband are alone, as on the occasions when they are entertaining guests at luncheon or dinner. This is not only good training for the servant, but also relieves the mistress's mind from the fear that any mistakes may be made when strangers are present.

G. C., "Good Mistresses" (Volume 26, 10 June 1905, p. 588).

It is sometimes rather a disadvantage to a woman, as far as her domestic education is concerned, to possess an easygoing husband, who is either oblivious to or tolerant of trifling defects. Naturally, under these circumstances, unless the wife is methodically inclined, and has a talent for government, she lets things slide, and does not aspire to perfection.

Her husband is content with matters as they are, so this and that omission or mistake is allowed to pass unnoticed and unreproved. This should not be. A mistress should not rest until everything in her department is as well ordered as possible, at all times, and nothing should be slurred over because it is not likely to be noticed by the master's eye.

Again, there are women who, either from natural indolence of character, or a dislike to taking their servants to task, allow things to drift on as they like, until their husbands protest, when they rouse themselves, and make strenuous and generally futile efforts at a wholesale reformation. The ideal mistress of a house is one who keeps all her domestic affairs perpetually and perfectly in train, so that if her lord and master complains, she can have the satisfaction of putting it down to his mood, or his liver— which is quite the same thing—and be able to lay the soothing unction to her soul, that it is *that* which is in fault, and not her housekeeping.

On behalf of the husbands, we must first remark that, as a rule, they have, at any rate, what they consider a reason for their complaints, and it is only occasionally that they grumble when anything is perfect.

A mistress should be able to rise to emergencies, such as the advent of an unexpected guest, or a household at sixes and sevens, at a moment's notice. She must remember that she is the governing power, for although the master is the head of the house, it is from the mistress that the servants usually take their orders. She is therefore the one to whom the entire household will consider they have a right to look for help and guidance in any difficulty, and she must be prepared with clear decisive orders, and, if necessary, explicit instructions as to how they can best be carried out.

Even to the domestic woman, whose happiest moments are those in which she is looking after her home and her servants, the management of a household is not always a bed of roses.

There are many crumpled leaves here and there, and occasionally a few sharp thorns lurking in unexpected places. A fit of the sulks, or a strongly developed taste for stimulants on the part of the cook, innumerable breakages and general stupidity from the housemaid, or dishonesty from the page-boy, all these, trifling as they may perhaps appear to lookers-on, are distinct and very real grievances to a mistress. They should not, however, be allowed to depress her unduly, but, on the contrary, put her on her mettle to make things go smoothly again. Just as adversity brings out either the best or the worst qualities in human nature, so do the pin-pricks of life—which often irritate more than the sword-thrusts—the little disappointments and daily worries, help to prove of what stuff a woman is made.

A great deal more could be said on this subject did space permit, for it would be hardly exaggeration to call it an inexhaustible one.

In conclusion, we would impress upon young mistresses who have not quite settled down into the domestic groove, that they should avoid the error of allowing their household duties to fritter themselves over the entire day. Let them devote an hour or two in the mornings to orders, accounts, supervision, and perhaps a study of the cookery book by way of adding a little novelty and originality to their husbands' dinners, and then they will be at liberty for the performance of social and family duties.

There is no real reason why a woman should not be an admirable mistress of a house, and yet play her part in Society as well, and if the two *rôles* are ever found to clash, she will have only herself and her bad management to blame for it.

G. C.

AUNT PATTY'S PAYING GUESTS.

By ÆGLANTON THORNE.

CHAPTER XI.

THE UNFORESEEN BEFALLS.

In spite of the fears she had exhibited on her arrival, Paulina Dicks was apparently content with her life at Gay Bowers. As she appeared cheerful, and was never one to disguise her feelings, we could safely conclude that she was not dull. Of a highly nervous, energetic temperament, she was for ever planning new enterprises, and whatever she took in hand she accomplished most thoroughly.

When she wearied of cycling, she took to driving about the country roads in Aunt Patty's little old-fashioned chaise. Sometimes her father and sometimes Miss Cottrell accompanied her. Aunt was much afraid that she overdrove the fat little pony, that had grown accustomed to an easy life; but Paulina declared that he was far too fat, and she was doing him good by rousing him from the silly jog-trot which was the pace he preferred.

She played croquet occasionally under protest to please her father; but she was indefatigable at tennis until she heard Alan Faulkner say that the common was just the place for golf, and drew from him an admission that he was extremely fond of this game. Then nothing would do but she must learn golf. It was in vain that anyone raised objections. She made light of every difficulty suggested, and would not rest till she had coaxed Mr. Faulkner into helping her to arrange a course and get the requisites for the game.

"What Pollie Dicks wants she'll have," said her

Conduct

The inclusion of articles on etiquette in the early years of *The Girl's Own Paper* indicates the editor's sense of his audience: lower middle-class, would-be socially mobile readers eager to know how to present themselves. As the magazine developed a wider circulation, however, it began to feature fewer articles on etiquette and conduct. Presumably, judging from the Answers to Correspondents at the end of each issue, readers still had an interest in both subjects, but the editor seems to have decided to relegate advice on social relationships, courtship, and general behaviour to the back pages. At the beginning of the twentieth century, articles on etiquette made a bit of a comeback, perhaps in response to the perceived end of an era and sense of social changes following Victoria's death and Edward VII's ascension. By this point the magazine was also well established in the middle-class market, so articles on conduct and etiquette served to reinforce class markers. Throughout its first decades, though, at regular intervals *The Girl's Own Paper* offered guidance to girls on matters of conduct.

Ardern Holt's "Etiquette for Ladies and Girls" (vol. 1, 1880, pp. 211–12, 407) is a good example of the early advice on how to avoid social embarrassment. S. F. A. Caulfeild, a frequent contributor to the *Girl's Own*, indicates the magazine's sense of mission in her subsequent article "Etiquette for All Classes" (vol. 3, 1881–82, pp. 90–91) which, as the title suggests, addresses the working-class girl as well as the middle-class girl, encouraging the former to adhere to a higher standard of conduct.

"Unpopular Girls" (vol. 7, 1885–86, pp. 484–86) takes a motherly approach to matters of conduct. The anonymous author, identified only as a middle-aged woman, teaches by negative example. She promotes traditional feminine codes of behaviour.

The Girl's Own also addressed conduct for wives. In the late 1880s and into the 1890s, the periodical press conducted a heated discussion of the status and worth of marriage. However, *The Girl's Own* begs the question of whether or not marriage is worthwhile. Instead, the Countess de Boerio, in "Some Marriage Thorns, and How to Avoid Them" (vol. 14, 1892–93, pp. 659–60, 763–65) teaches girls that submission to one's husband is the only guarantee of marital bliss. If young women were unhappy in marriage, they apparently had only themselves to blame.

Margaret Bateson's "Paying Visits" (vol. 24, 1902–03, pp. 150–51) is a sample of the renewed interest in social etiquette in the beginning of the twentieth century. It offers commonsense advice on how to be a good guest.

Gordon Stables, a retired naval doctor, also wrote for *The Girl's Own* on health and beauty under the pseudonym "Medicus." "To Girls in Their 'Teens'" (vol. 26, 1904–05, pp. 106–08) is typical of the advice he offered girls. No fan of the New Girl, he praises traditional feminine virtues.

velled backwards through the past and glanced at the future, finding no rest.

Presently he felt a gloved hand softly touching his fingers, that were still closed over his eyes.

"Are you feeling better, sir?" Zara whispered.

He caught her hand in both his with an eager grasp, and looked at her with pleading eyes.

"We are friends, are we not, Zara? Promise we shall always be friends. You must forgive me, my poor child!"

"I have nothing to forgive, sir; and there's no reason I know of why we shouldn't be friends."

Paul rose slowly from his leaning place on the rock.

"No reason at all. We *are* friends, remember."

"All right. Now I must go home; for Miss White will wonder what in the world has happened to me. I am coming out in a new song to-night. I wonder if you will like it, sir?"

"I shall not hear it, Zara."

"Won't you be at the 'Music Hall'?"

"No; I have paid my last visit there."

"Oh, sir! I didn't expect that from you!" Her face grew haughty as she spoke.

"Can't you see why I ever went to the place? To meet you, Zara. Now we have met and spoken, and are friends, I have no wish to enter the doors again."

Her flush of anger changed to a smile of gratified vanity. She looked round at Paul, but met only a grave face and thoughtful eyes.

"I hope you also will soon bid adieu to the 'Harmony Music Hall.'"

"Me, sir!"—a start of surprise.

"Yes, child. But don't call me 'sir' any more. Friends do not use such terms; and we are friends who must help each other—bear with each other, and perhaps pity each other."

Paul spoke from his own view of things, Zara listened from hers; and it must be confessed she set down in her own mind that something very flattering was intended.

Like many untrained girls of seventeen she had a high opinion of the power of her attractions. She had known something of triumph in her power from the applause in the "Music Hall," and had already decided Paul Tench was another admirer on her list—another of her slaves.

True, his looks and words puzzled her, but London fashions were different from country fashions, and it must be his way of showing admiration. He was speaking now very gravely and earnestly.

"Zara, as a proof of the confidence I place in you, I hope to bring a lady to call on you to-morrow, for I suppose I shall never gain admission to Miss White's 'sanctum' unless I am thus accompanied."

"A lady to call on me! Is she young?"

"Yes, and lovely. She is the daughter of a London clergyman."

"But a clergyman's daughter won't want to know me, Mr. Tench, unless she comes to bring good books, and to lecture

me about singing in public, and the like of that. I don't care for such visits; and I hold there is some merit even in trying to amuse people who haven't very much pleasure in their lives. 'All work and no play makes Jack a dull boy,' the old saying tells us. And those who have the art of amusing deserve to be paid. The vicar's daughter will not agree with my opinions, so she had better not come."

(*To be continued.*)

ETIQUETTE FOR LADIES AND GIRLS.*

IF "manners make the man" they even more decidedly make the woman, and few gifts ensure greater happiness and affection to their possessor than a good manner.

Now, while all good manners are the off-shoot of a good heart, and while kindly courteousness and thought for others are the very kernel of the matter, still there are certain laws laid down which it is necessary to thoroughly understand, and I purpose to set these before my readers. For etiquette and good breeding are not identical though they are twin sisters; for example, it is possible for a foreigner to be perfectly well bred and yet show an ignorance of some details of etiquette.

All the niceties of personal behaviour in regard to eating, drinking, and cleanly habits are learnt imperceptibly by children from their parents and guardians, hence it is most necessary that mothers who are unable to have their children constantly with them should ensure innate refinement in the teachers and attendants who surround them.

It is when a girl is old enough to "come out," as the phrase is, and to take a recognised position in the social world, that a knowledge of the code that rules good society becomes necessary. For there is but one recognised code in really good society, although some old-fashioned modes may prevail in country places,

* The importance of attention to rules of etiquette will be admitted even by those whose pressing duties or higher avocations hinder from rigid observance of them. For example, no one would expect the cere-monies of formal visiting from hospital nurses, though some of these are of high and noble families. They are better employed. No one is surprised at their disregard of etiquette, any more than at their not wearing gloves, which they never do. Such excep-tions are very different from those made without excuse of duty. We have known good people who, from ignorance or neglect of rules and usages of social life, cause religion itself to be evil spoken of. They think such things to be "conformity to the world." But the true principle is to be in the world, yet not of the world. The Christian precept, "Be courteous," covers all the innocent usages of society in our time, as it did in the days when Divine illustra-tions were drawn from the usages of the Jews in their feasts and marriages and other social institutions.— EDITOR.

and with old-fashioned people. "Coming out" means introduction to society, either at a party at home or by being presented at Her Majesty's Drawing-room, or by merely accept-ing the invitations of friends. When a young lady is "out" her name appears on her mother's visiting card, immediately below her mother's name; or with those of her sister's as one of the Misses ——. An unmarried lady, unless she has arrived at a certain age, does not have a card of her own, nor does she make calls on her own account, as she should certainly not have acquaintances who are un-known to her parents.

Visiting cards should be printed on thin un-glazed cards, in as plain letterings as possible in text hand, with no flourishes or any remark-able style of printing, the gentlemen's about half the depth of the ladies', but in cases where there is no mother the daughters have their father's name printed on cards of the usual ladies' size, with their own beneath. Some ladies put their husband's name on their cards as well as their daughters, Mr. and Mrs. S —— in one line. This is not a solecism, but is somewhat old-fashioned.

The plan of card-leaving is regulated by very plainly-defined laws of etiquette. Cards were originally introduced so that people on whom the calls were made might be aware of the fact even should the servant be forget-ful, and when a personal call is made they are never sent in, excepting in cases of business visits where there is no acquaintance, as, for example, in calling for the character of a servant.

If an acquaintance is not at home when she calls, a lady leaves her own card with the names of her daughters upon it, and two of her husbands cards, one for the master and one for the mistress, with occasionally an additional one for the sons. If the mistress is at home, on leaving she deposits two of her husband's cards on the hall table. She must neither give them to the servant nor to the hostess. As a rule, the wives do the card-leaving for married men, who rarely call in person.

The right-hand corner of a lady's card turned down means that she intends the call to be on the young ladies as well as their mother. Cards should bear the prefix of their owner—Mrs. Miss, Lady (if a knight or baronet's wife), Countess, or any other title. The only one never used on a card is "Honour-able." The Christian name without a prefix is simply a barbarism unheard of in good society—such as "Jane Brown," though young gentlemen, at college and elsewhere, put the name without "Mr."

With card-leaving comes the question of calling. Calling hours are from three to six. First calls should be returned within the week. Calls should be made also within the week after every entertainment, whether it be a dinner, or an "At Home," held either in the evening or afternoon, always assuming that the "At Home" is a party for which invitations have been issued. Many people in London, and large towns, though not, perhaps, the ultra fashionable people of London, have certain days in the week on which they receive their friends, and as the friends who put in an appearance are in fact paying a call, a subsequent call in con-sequence of being present at such an "At Home" is, therefore, unnecessary. After a dinner-party it is best to go in if the lady is at home, leaving cards, if preferred after other entertainments. Most people on coming to town call on all their friends by merely leaving cards; it is etiquette for those who come to town to take the initiative, for, of course, it would be almost impossible for their acquaint-ance to ascertain when they came. If, when a call is made simply cards are left at the door and there is no inquiry as to whether the mistress is at home, the same plan should be adopted in returning the call. Servants should be trained to remember the distinction. It is a vulgarity under any circumstances whatever to send visiting cards by post. If after an entertainment the distance is too great for a call, it would be best, if you are very punctilious, to write a polite note ; but to send cards by post to save the trouble of calling is a breach of good manners.

On leaving a neighbourhood, and sometimes at the end of the season, or going abroad, cards are left with P.P.C., viz., *pour prendre congé*, or *pour dire adieu* written upon them. If young ladies are away from home, and have been accepting hospitalities in the way of dinners and other parties their names should be written in pencil on the card of their *chaperone*.

In the country old residents call on new-comers, but in London and in towns generally this plan does not hold good, and an introduction is necessary before a call is made. When a call has been made the receivers can continue the acquaintance or not as they please, but first calls are generally followed by invitations from those who make them. Cards left in the case of illness should have the words "to inquire" in pencil on the top. To very young ladies a morning call is often an ordeal they would fain avoid ; but this should not be encouraged. If admitted, they, with their mother, would be announced by the servant, and should take a part in the conversation without in any way monopolising it. Supposing other callers were present they can, if they please, enter into conversation with them ; their so doing does not require an introduction nor necessitate an acquaintance. A quarter of an hour is enough for a ceremonious call. Neither when other visitors come or go do those present rise ; they can, if they please, bend slightly, but it is not necessary.

If the call is made about five o'clock, tea is generally served, and, as a rule, poured out by the lady of the house without ceremony.

When calls are received at home more devolves upon the young ladies of the house ; then they are expected to help their mothers in the conversation and in dispensing tea, etc. They can, if they please, receive lady visitors in their mother's absence, but it depends on her approval whether gentlemen are admitted, and this is not often allowed if there is but one daughter.

A young lady visiting at a house must use her discretion with regard to remaining in the room when visitors call. It depends whether she thinks her hostess would wish her to do so, and unless she happens to be herself acquainted with the people who come, it would be better, after a short interval, to retire. If visitors call upon her who are unknown to the hostess, as a young lady it would be right for her to introduce them, her chaperone taking the place of her mother for the time being.

A young girl with all the freshness of her youth and the sweet dignity of womanhood has a sure passport into society which secures her a warmth of welcome ; it depends on herself whether this grows or is early nipped in the bud.

Fastness and prim sedateness are equally to be avoided ; a calm, frank, unembarrassed manner, a sympathetic interest in and thought for others, a habit of saying the right thing in the right place, the power of being a good listener, and of letting the conversation take any turn most agreeable to the speaker—these are some of the component parts of good and pleasing manners. The fault of the age rather runs towards young people assuming too much, being too confident and self-assertive and too thoughtless with regard to their elders— all essentially bad manners.

People who have at all a large acquaintance should keep a visiting book with the names and addresses of those on whom they are on visiting terms, and a correct alphabetical list of the several members of their family who, in case of an entertainment being given, would be invited. Without this a hostess is apt to forget the number of sons or daughters. A supplementary list in a small note-book kept in or with the card-case saves a great deal of trouble when visits are paid.

Twice a year as a broad rule is sufficient

"ALL HAVE THEIR TASKS TO DO."

number of times to call on acquaintances, unless they have given entertainments which necessitate card-leaving.

On hearing of the death of an acquaintance, cards should be at once left at the house, and when the relatives feel able to see their friends again they send by hand or post either specially printed cards or their own, " with thanks for kind enquiries," which are acknowledged by a call.

Ladies do not leave cards on gentlemen, unless they have been entertained. After a dinner given to ladies by a bachelor a wife would leave her card with her husband's. Common sense should be exercised in all these matters. The wife of a naval officer would hardly leave her husband's cards on mutual acquaintances when he was at sea.

ARDERN HOLT.

WORK FOR ALL.

'TIS not a single bird
  That makes the forest ring ;
A thousand joyous notes are heard,
  A thousand warblers sing.

'Tis not a lonely flower,
  Though it may glad the sight,
That makes the earth one summer bower,
  All beautiful and bright.

But each thing brings its share
  Amidst the mingled throng ;
Some cadence, or some treasure rare,
  Of beauty, or of song.

All have their tasks to do,
  All have their work assigned,
And carry out in order true
  The plan their God designed.

The chorus grand rings forth
  From things both great and small :
" On the broad circle of the earth
  God giveth work for all."

            M. M. P.

A CANADIAN HEROINE.

IT was towards the end of June that one afternoon a clergyman was riding through the forest in the neighbourhood of the Beaver Dams, near the town of Thorold —a place which received its name from the remarkable constructions of the industrious animal which has been adopted as the national emblem of Upper Canada —where there was a small force of British troops posted. In the twilight he observed a travel-worn woman approaching upon the forest pathway, with an air of bodily weariness, yet of mental alertness and anxiety. As she drew near he recognised a worthy Canadian matron, whom he had more than once seen in his congregation in the schoolhouse in the village of Chippewa.

" Why, Mrs. Secord," he exclaimed, reining in his horse as she attempted to pass him, furtively trying to conceal her face, " are you not afraid to be so far from home on foot, when the country is so disturbed ? "

" Thank God it is you, Mr. Trueman !" she earnestly replied. " I was afraid it might be one of the American scouts. ' Home, did you say ? I have no home," she added, in a tone of bitterness.

" Can't I be of service to you ? Where is your husband ? " Neville asked, wondering at her distraught air.

" Haven't you heard ? " she replied. " He was sore wounded at Queenston Heights, and will never be a well man again ; and our house was pillaged and burned. But we're wasting time; what reck my private wrongs when the country is overrun by the King's enemies ? How far is it to the camp ? "

" Farther than you can walk without resting," he answered. " You seem almost worn out."

" Nineteen miles I've walked this day through woods and thicket, without bit or sup, to warn the King's troops of their danger."

" What danger ? " asked Neville, wondering if her grief had somewhat affected her mind

" The enemy are on the move—hundreds of them—with cannon and horses. I saw them marching past my cottage this very morning, and I vowed to warn the King's soldiers or die in the attempt. I slipped unseen into the woods and ran like a deer, through

ETIQUETTE FOR LADIES AND GIRLS.—II.

ANY young girls conceive a dislike for society simply because they experience a *mauvais honte*, brought about by an ignorance of how to act under the various circumstances which arise in their intercourse with other people. They are too shy, too ashamed of their own ignorance to ask for information, and indeed often do not realise exactly what it is they want to know. Now I would counsel them to have no false shame in the matter; knowledge does not come by intuition, and we are all learning up to the last day of our lives.

Knowledge brings confidence and helps to banish shyness and self-consciousness. They would do well to think as little of themselves as they can, of how they look, and what others think of them. It should be the object of their elders by their own perfect self-possession to set them as much as possible at their ease. The higher the social scale the more courtesy and the more ease of manner prevail.

One of the difficulties which young people experience is in knowing when to bow. In England a lady by right takes the initiative, and bows first; abroad this is reversed, and English women should then follow the custom which prevails.

A young lady would do right to bow to a gentleman by whom she had been taken in to dinner, or had been introduced to in any other way, but she would not bow if she had merely talked to him when casually meeting him with friends, or at a friend's house. She would naturally not go out of her way to bow even when by etiquette she was entitled so to do, but it would be *gauche* to avoid doing so when the opportunity naturally occurred.

A true lady should, more than all other things, take the greatest care not to wound the feelings of anybody. We meet in society for our mutual pleasure, but want of thought and good feeling often cause mortification and pain to others. Men are even more sensitive about trifles than women imagine, though a certain free-and-easiness of manner has crept in of late between the sexes, which occasionally leads to a lack of deference that it would perhaps be stilted to call a want of respect. A woman has in her own hands the power of making men treat her with friendly kindness and simple courtesy, which honours them in giving and she in receiving. If a young lady walking with her father or brother meet a gentleman known to them whom they recognise, in returning their salutation he would raise his hat to her without knowing her, which she would acknowledge by the slightest possible motion of the head, but this would not constitute an acquaintance. Supposing she bowed to a gentleman of her acquaintance who was accompanied by a friend, he would raise his hat as well as her acquaintance. As a rule men do not take off their hats to each other, but to ladies only.

Women bowing to each other mostly do so simultaneously, but according to the strict etiquette a married lady or the one of the higher rank bows first. It is not necessary to rise when an introduction is made, unless it be to a lady of much higher social rank, and it is more courteous when introduced to an older lady for the younger one to half-rise.

A gentleman is introduced to a lady, a young lady to an old one, one of inferior rank to one of higher and not *vice versa*, and it is not usual to shake hands on an introduction, but in saying good-bye, after an introduction, it would be correct.

The question of whether to introduce or not is a fruitful source of difficulty in social life. Among quite the upper ten thousand it is rarely necessary to do so, as they are mostly acquainted. In general society it requires tact and knowledge of the world to know when it is advisable to make people acquainted. In the small circles in the country it can be rarely done to advantage; but in London, if it is calculated to lead to the personal enjoyment of friends and guests at any social gathering, it is well-bred to do so, and it is a matter of choice whether such introductions lead to any real acquaintance. It is best where practicable to consult the wishes of those concerned before introducing them.

Luncheon parties are perhaps the most informal mode of entertainment. The time is from 1 to 2. The guests generally keep on their bonnets and lay their cloaks aside in the drawing-room. They proceed to the dining-room without any ceremony, and not in twos and twos as for dinner. In large establishments the servants wait throughout; but it is quite usual for them to leave after the vegetables are handed round, for the chief viands, sweets, cake, and fruit, if any, are all on the table. Should the people present not know each other they can enter into general conversation without introductions.

Five o'clock tea parties are of many kinds. If only a few friends are expected, it is served on a small tea-table placed in front of the hostess, the young ladies or the gentlemen present dispensing the cups, bread and butter, and cake. Everybody joins in the general conversation, and the entertainment is thoroughly without *gêne*. A friendly note would be the most ordinary style of invitation, and its purport would be the best guide as to answering it. But, as a rule, it would require an answer only in case of not being able to accept it. If the party be more numerous tea would be dispensed on a larger table in the corner of the room, the urn being set with plenty of cups and saucers, cakes, and bread and butter on a cloth embroidered round, or trimmed with lace. Many fantastic styles of adorning such cloths prevail, and change from time to time. Plates and d'oyleys are out of date.

For an afternoon party the invitations are sent out on the ordinary visiting card or on cards specially printed thus:—

Mr. and Mrs. Brown.

Mrs. Smith.

At Home.

Tuesday Afternoon, 4 to 7.

Laurel Hall.   Music.

The "music" can, of course, be dispensed with. "R.S.V.P." must be added if an answer is requested, otherwise the guests do not reply, unless they are unable to come. Tea, coffee, and light refreshments are served in the dining-room.

The hostess receives her guests at the door of the drawing-room, into which they pass at once, taking vacant seats if there are any, and talking to their friends, the hostess occasionally introducing a gentleman to take a lady down for refreshments, or two people seated together, in order to secure a little pleasant conversation. But all appearance of fussiness must be avoided by the hostess, and her daughters can materially assist her. Musical parties given in the afternoon may be only amateur, or with first-rate professional artists, in which case programmes are circulated among the guests, who are expected not to indulge in conversation while singing is going on.

Garden parties held in the country and in the suburbs of London are of many kinds. At present they take most generally the form of lawn tennis parties, and the guests are often ushered at once into the gardens. The refreshments, which consist of tea, coffee, ices, fruit, cakes, biscuits, and occasionally game sandwiches, are laid either in a tent or in the dining-room. The invitations are the same as for ordinary afternoon parties, though they often have "weather permitting" in addition. More ambitious garden parties are extended to 10, 11, or 12 o'clock, a substantial cold repast being served about 7 o'clock, and a variety of entertainments arranged to amuse the guests, such as Tyrolese minstrels, performing dogs, or anything that happens to be the fashion of the moment. There should be plenty of seats and garden chairs dispersed about, and several different places indoors and out where refreshments are served. Ladies generally leave some light wraps in a room set apart for them. At the least ceremonious of afternoon parties gentlemen when they make a call take their hats into the drawing-room, but leave them in the hall in the case of a garden party or if *invited* to an afternoon party.

Whether to an afternoon or to any other kind of party, it is rude and bad-mannered to take friends uninvited, unless, as in the case of some country invitations, the wording of the invitation is "Mrs. —— *and party.*" Much judgment should be exercised at all times in asking for invitations for friends. As a rule, people have a large circle of their own, which they do not desire to extend, and in asking for such invitations it should be always made clear that the hostess will not be affronting the asker by refusing. Mothers with large families should not take more than two daughters if the invitation is for "The Misses ——," and some hostesses ask but one.

Evening parties are also of various kinds, but the invitations take the same form as for the afternoon, except where the hostess prefers to send friendly notes. They need not be answered unless "R.S.V.P." is upon them, and then as quickly as possible.

An "at-home" may mean merely conversation, when the hours are from 8 or 9. Light refreshments are served down-stairs, and sometimes a supper, sometimes a concert, is given. Then it behoves a guest to be punctual.

It is not necessary to say good-night to the hostess before leaving, as it tends sometimes to break up the party.

For dinner parties it behoves the guests to be punctual, that is to come to the hour or half-hour, whether the invitation be for the quarter to or for the time exactly. The gentlemen are introduced to the ladies they take down, and they proceed to the dining-room, the host with the lady of highest rank going first, the hostess last with the gentleman of highest rank. The guests are seated according to a pre-arranged plan, the ladies removing their gloves as soon as they are seated; gentlemen do not wear them at dinner parties. It is usual, whether introduced or not, to talk to people seated on either side. Dinner parties are now universally served *à la Russe*, so that, being well taken care of in the matter of food, which is in the hand of the servants, the host does not press his guests to partake of anything.   ARDERN HOLT.

Ardern Holt, "Etiquette for Ladies and Girls" (Volume 1, 26 June 1880, p. 407).

truth, she was still more afraid to think of facing Miss Nelly with the admission that she had made no attempt to accomplish the object of her errand. She made a desperate effort to fight down her nervousness. Walking forward to the counter, she hastily lifted her bag on to it, and, with trembling fingers, undid the clasps. She next proceeded to undo the paper coverings of the doll's bedstead, which had been carried separately for its greater safety.

Meantime, Mrs. Budgen returned to the shop, and stood looking on with a countenance more mystified than before. She was not used to such nervous customers.

"Is it anything of matching that you've come about, miss?" she asked at last, doubtfully.

"Matching!" repeated Maggie, in an absent tone, and as if she did not know what the word meant.

"Aye, miss, matching!" was the snappish answer. "I suppose you're after wanting to match some silks, or wools, or tassels, to some of the things you've got there—isn't that it?"

"Oh, no," exclaimed Margaret, with sudden energy at the idea that some imputation of incompleteness had been cast upon her goods. "No, indeed! they are all finished off beautifully, I am sure you will find, if you will only kindly just look at them, please."

It was Mrs. Budgen's turn to repeat words now.

"Look at them! look at them!" she said twice over, while her companion hurriedly pulled out of the bag parcel after parcel, and displayed the contents before her astonished eyes. "And pray, miss," she almost gasped at length—"and pray, miss, if I may make so bold as to ask, why may it be that I, of all people, am to look at all these fal-lals here?"

"Oh!" answered Margaret Hill, in tones of gentle assurance, her courage and confidence reviving as her eyes rested on the really pretty collection she had set out. "Oh! I should like you, please, to look at them before you buy them, and I know my sister would too, to make sure that they are all right and perfect."

Her voice was perfectly decided in spite of the slightly nervous tremor still lingering in it. Nelly making her calculations at home did not feel more innocently certain that their merchandise had only to be offered to be accepted than did Maggie. Poor Maggie!

Having finished her little speech, Margaret Hill was about to raise her eyes to her listener's face, to receive the expected gracious assent to her reasonable proposal, but the next moment she started back from the counter as if she had been shot.

The woman gazed at her for an instant with eyes that literally blazed with anger, and then let loose her indignation in words.

"Before I buy them! Before I buy them!" she shouted, in shriller accents than her listener had ever had to submit to before. "Do you mean to say that you've kept me all this while from my dinner, and dawdling here, to look at your trumpery rubbish because you thought that I'd buy it! I wouldn't give you a shilling, no, nor a paper of pins, for the lot, so there."

With those last words, happily for poor, young, inexperienced Margaret Hill, Mrs. Budgen turned sharp round, and once more retired to her sitting-room, and her half-cold dinner. Had she remained in the shop most decidedly the startled and terrified girl would have run out of it, and left all the tasteful little affairs made by her sister and herself at the shopkeeper's disposal, even without so much payment for them as a paper of pins. As it was, the packing was the most difficult task that Maggie had ever performed in her life, and the elegant bedstead was huddled into its wrappings with an utter want of the admiring care that had so shortly before been bestowed upon it by Elinor.

(To be continued.)

ETIQUETTE FOR ALL CLASSES.

So many are the queries put to the Editor of this Magazine on the above-named subject—as may be observed by readers of the correspondence columns—that it may not be offering "too much" of a good thing to collect together fugitive remarks, and answers already made, and to supplement them in the form of a separate article.

The word "Etiquette" signifies a "Ticket," and owes its origin to the ancient custom of presenting a card, containing a list of directions and regulations connected with attendance at Court, to those about to be admitted. As employed by us, it therefore denotes the whole collection of laws by which, in all countries, though customs may vary in each respectively, "polite society" is inexorably governed.

Much that has reference to etiquette may be found, not merely under the title of "The Foundation of all Good Breeding," but likewise in "The Art of Letter-Writing," "The Art of Conversing Agreeably," and "Dinners in Society." But as multitudes who read this paper never dine "in society"—as we understand the expression—and to whom much advice that has been already given must be altogether superfluous, I gather up a few ideas, partly suggested by the correspondence, which may meet the position and circumstances of this class, as well as the better informed.

In the article entitled "The Foundation of all Good Breeding" I endeavoured to demonstrate that certain rules which may appear very trifling are the natural offspring of the highest and noblest feelings. In the present article I wish to point out the fact that amongst these rules of etiquette there are some which belong as much to the young girls of the working class as to those in a higher position. Furthermore, that they are positively essential to their morals and preservation, not alone from the gross evils to which their more or less unprotected situation may often expose them, but also from making most unfortunate marriages, plunging them in pecuniary difficulties and distress. From these remarks it will at once be apparent that the point from which I now regard the question of good manners is that which has reference to the deportment of our girls towards those, of all ranks and ages, not of their own sex.

In common with others, I have been amused, yet even more shocked, with the strange questions raised as to the conduct of young girls and women with reference to young men. Hitherto an extraordinary amount of freedom, and reckless want of caution, as well as of self-respect, has been winked at by the parents of respectable girls of the middle and lower classes, simply because many of them were brought up, or, as I have heard it graphically described, "dragged up," in the same utter disregard or ignorance of the risks run, by infringing the common laws of female self-restraint, tact, and propriety.

At this moment, as I write, my thoughts have been interrupted by loud laughter outside my open window. I looked up to see three well-dressed, fine-looking girls—two of about seventeen years of age, and one rather younger—and, as the habit is of many young people, they accompanied their laughter by rolling about, like boats in a swell, first on one side, then on the other, and tumbling up against one another in a very ungraceful way. I enjoy hearing the happy sounds of merriment amongst the young, and can sympathise in the freedom from care, and the keen sense of the ridiculous, which result in laughter at almost an inappreciable joke—for I was one of that class myself, in

" . . . the days that are no more!"

But such *abandon* and complete freedom of action are inadmissible elsewhere than within the precincts of home, or in that of an intimate friend, when all around are on familiar terms; with the merry-makers within some garden enclosure; in a country field, and amongst familiar associates; or at some comic entertainment. But even under such circumstances as these there should be an ever-abiding self-recollection, and slight self-restraint, when in the company of young men; and loud laughter and rolling about are by no means what may be commonly understood as "ladylike," under any circumstances, and outrageously the reverse in the streets.

"Why so?" I think I hear some readers inquire.

Because such utter disregard of propriety, such a public and uninvited display of your feelings and emotions, such an attraction of notice to yourself—directing all eyes to you, even of the "street Arabs"—invites the intrusion of men into your party of merry-makers, naturally disposing them to join you, to learn the nature of the joke. And in thus forcing their acquaintance upon yourself, remember that it is not with feelings of deferential attraction, but with a full appreciation of your lack of proper dignity, and of that amount of maidenly reserve which a girl should always maintain when in the company of acquaintances of the other sex, and even more so in the presence of utter strangers.

Perhaps some may wonder that I should dwell so long on this point. But their surprise will cease when I direct attention to a query recently made, by certain evidently respectable and well-meaning girls, in the correspondence columns, who inquire "how they should act in reference to the strange men who continually address them in the street, and sometimes make an excuse of asking the time, and then join them in their walk, as they (the girls) do not wish to be rude and impolite to them"! The answer given was that such impertinence is generally the result of some lack of dignity of demeanour in themselves—some ill-timed and unseemly laughter or loud talking, inviting the attention of strangers—or from looking in a man's face as he passes. A girl's conduct is thus very often misunderstood, and she has to pay the penalty. Acquaintances are continually formed in this way that may be most unsuitable, and lead to grave and disastrous results. Besides this, they are formed clandestinely, and might be highly objected to by the parents.

I know, from information obtained from domestic servants of my own family, that it is permissible in their class to allow a man to address them without any introduction; and, if found agreeable by the girl, she consents to his "keeping company" with her, should he desire it.

Now, to you, my young friends who belong to this class, I more especially address myself, and tell you that of which you are now quite unaware—that etiquette forbids any man presuming to introduce himself to you; that it is a gross act of impertinence, and shows that he thinks you of little account, and free to be "taken up" and dropped as quickly as if you were nobody, and no one cared into whose hands you might chance to fall. Just, for example, as they might pat a stray dog in the street, and throw him a bone, without asking anyone's leave ; treating you, in fact, as if you were a poor "waif or stray," to whom he paid a compliment by offering to take a walk with her !

Should respectable young women become so cheap and common as this ? Turn over, I pray you, a new leaf. Etiquette requires the introduction of a man to a woman, whether she be what is called a "lady," or a working girl. Your characters, the comfort of your future homes, and the happiness of your lives mainly depend on the acquaintances you form with persons of the opposite sex. You are perpetually asking about the same rules of etiquette in reference to them ; and I trust that a proper knowledge of them will prove a valuable and efficient safeguard to you in your much exposed and unguarded condition of life.

From this class of my readers I now turn to one raised a little higher in the social scale : those who belong to what is called the "middle class," the youthful members of which appear to be as equally anxious to learn all that THE GIRL'S OWN PAPER can tell them respecting the rules which should guide their behaviour towards the other sex.

The etiquette to be observed in meeting an acquaintance requires the lady to bow first, as she has the right to look another way, and avoid meeting his eyes (if, for any motives of prudence, and to escape from unacceptable intrusion, she should prefer to ignore his presence, and avoid an interview). In this case, again, the above-named code of rules provides for a woman's defence. At the same time she must beware of appearing to "cut" anyone by allowing them to see that passing them without a bow of recognition was intentional. This would be an act of exceedingly bad taste, and actual rudeness.

Should a stranger be walking with your gentleman friend, when you bow to the latter it is the duty of that stranger to raise his hat to you likewise, but while so doing he should look down, and not meet your eyes during that bow, because such a formal act of respect does not involve you in any acquaintance with him, nor should it lead you to think he means to intrude himself on any subsequent meeting, when no bow on either side should be made. Of course, however, as the instance that your friend raises his hat, in acknowledgment of your recognition of him, you should extend your bow, and look towards his friend (if he raise his hat) in return for his salutation.

A foreigner, and an English highly-bred man, will raise his hat on meeting a lady in a hall or passage, or in a narrow path, bringing him closer to her than otherwise he needed to be. This he does merely to set her at ease, and prove that she is in the company of a man who knows how to show her all due respect. But, as in the former case named—if a bow from a stranger--a gentleman should not look at the lady when so raising his hat ; but there should be a marked gravity and reserve in his manner and his general bearing.

Again. It is against all rule for a girl to give or receive presents, unless the recipient or giver be one of her own sex. I do not, of course, name this as a rule of universal appli-cation ; for your first-cousin, with whom you may have grown up on terms of the greatest brotherly intimacy, or your uncle ; or a middle-aged man, who is an old family or personal friend, might give or receive any little token of friendship, first premising that these mutual gifts be openly given, and with the full knowledge of his wife, and your own people. "Your good must not be evil spoken

of" ; in other words—what you may do honestly and innocently is not to bear the smallest appearance derogatory to your pro-priety of feeling, nor be permitted to bear the least misconstruction.

Of course, when once you have plighted your faith to a man, the case is quite other-wise. Gifts may pass between persons betrothed to each other without fear of mis-construction, and with perfect propriety.

Excepting in reference to business matters, the rule which forbids the exchange of gifts holds good in reference to correspondence.

In meeting an acquaintance out of doors, it would be ill-bred on a man's part to stop you for conversation. It is incumbent on him to turn and walk your way for a few paces, to communicate what he has to say. But this rule does not extend to old gentlemen, nor to near relatives.

In taking a carriage-drive accompanied by gentlemen, whether relatives, old friends, or strangers, except in the case of a very aged man, they should never take the back seat, facing the horses ; nor should you offer to resign your place in their (a man's) favour, as that would imply that they did not know the most common rules of good breeding in refer-ence to one of the gentler sex. But suppose the case of your driving with ladies only. If the carriage be your own, request your guests or family to enter first, and assign the best seats to them ; at the same time inquiring whether, to escape a cold wind, any of them would prefer to drive backwards ; or, whether any young person, who would naturally take a seat with her back to the horses, would suffer from giddiness or sickness from going backwards. If a guest yourself, offer to sit backwards by placing yourself in that posi-tion ; but yield to the wishes of the hostess, if she appear decided in her desire that you should take the other seat. It would be ill-bred on your part to keep her waiting to seat herself, while you were arguing with her about the occupation of her own carriage ! To "do as you are desired" is a golden rule in all cases connected with etiquette.

While on the subject of your conduct in a carriage, I must remind you to sit well into a corner, so as to throw back the shoulders and elbow on the inner side. Perhaps you will ask, "Why sit crooked in a carriage, when you tell us that it is a vulgar habit to do so on a chair ?" It is simply because on a chair it has an appearance of discomfort and insecurity which are unpleasant to others ; whereas in a carriage the appearance is one of comfort, ease, and security ; and, above all, it is to give more room to your next neighbour ; and to show respect and politeness, by turning your-self facing more towards them, instead of turning your shoulder to them, and so by sitting square occupying too much space, and thus selfishly incommoding them.

Though comparatively a trifling matter, I may tell you *en passant* that by well-bred people—or at least those persons of this class who have been carefully taught, and have been observant of the modes of speech employed by those very conversant with such matters —the word "ride" is never employed with reference to a carriage, coach, or sleigh. It is always substituted by the word "drive." The latter word does not merely denote the act of holding the reins and managing the horses ; it equally signifies that you are being conveyed after this manner, and you drive by proxy. If, for instance, you said (to be con-sistent), "I took a ride," or "I have been out riding," it would be understood to mean that you had been on horseback. When you go out in any kind of vehicle, you must say you are going to "take a drive," or have been driving ; for the horses that conveyed you along were not "ridden," but "driven." To say you were going "to take a ride" in any

vehicle would be to stamp you, if not as a vulgar person, at least as a well-bred one whose training in etiquette had been neglected, or who had not had the advantage of associa-ting much with highly-bred persons of their own station in society.

There are certain other applications of words that are quite inadmissible in society, although used by many whose position and good breeding in all other respects are unquestionable ; for instance, the word "parlour" in lieu of "dining-room," unless employed in speaking of the small apartment doing duty in the double capacity of drawing and dining-room in a very small house or cottage. In schools the term "parlour boarder" is employed ; but then there is much to be learnt on leaving the best school by young people going into society as they can all testify themselves.

Again, a custom obtains in Germany of extending the official title of a husband to his wife ; but while I have heard persons of undoubtedly good position, and living in upper circles of society, speak of women by the professional rank of their husbands, I have likewise heard the strange incongruity commented upon of hearing such expressions from such persons. Thus, you should never say Mrs. Dr. Dash, or Mrs. Commodore Blank, or Mrs. Major So-and-So, or Mrs. General, and Mrs. Archdeacon "Chose."

Again, do not ask for "a drink of water," say "a glass of water," nor ask for a "bit" or a "slice" of anything. To say "be seated" or "take a chair" are likewise vulgar ways of asking a friend to "sit down." And I may here observe that on paying a visit, if the lady of the house, or whoever may represent her, be out of the room when you arrive, you must stand until she appear ; or, at all events, if fatigued and obliged to sit down, take care to rise before her entrance.

Should a gentleman call on you, or come invited to any meal at your house, it shows great ignorance of the usages of society to take his hat from him, which he is bound to bring into the drawing-room with him ; unless he be a medical man, who, when paying pro-fessional visits, must, by the rules of his pro-fession, leave his hat and stick in the hall. Half-bred people usually torment a man about his hat, and will sometimes even place it in the middle of the table as a mark, I suppose, of respect !

To go out of doors in the act of finishing the arrangement of your out-of-door toilet, and before your gloves are put on, is very objectionable ; but nevertheless it is, perhaps, one of the most usual of small misdemeanours.

I have observed that "our girls" are much in the habit of saying, "Kindly *pass* your opinion on my writing," instead of "kindly oblige me with," or "give me," or "would you be so good as to criticise ?" or "pronounce an opinion ?" all of which modes of expression would be correct.

But the limits of a single article forbid the further multiplication of examples of under - bred expressions and inelegancies. Any further hints for your guidance on the subject of a suitable selection of words and course of conduct must be reserved for a second paper on the rules of etiquette. In the latter I propose to enter fully into the question of complimentary and family mourn-ing, giving the relative degrees of its depth, the style and nature of the costumes, and the term of duration allotted for its wear.

SOPHIA F. A. CAULFEILD.

Just at that moment I heard the tanyard gate swing back, and turning saw my father standing there with a gentleman, who, of course, must have seen me embracing my old nurse.

"What, children, are you here already?" said my father, coming forward in his shabby office coat ; a grey-haired, grey-bearded man, stooping somewhat, and looking worn and weary in the bright sunlight. "It seems but a few minutes since I heard the train passing at the bottom of the meadows."

Mabel had already alighted from the dog cart, and she stepped forward, and in her pretty way asked father how he was, and put up her face to be kissed. I saw the stranger, who, I felt sure, must be Mr. Howard Steinthorpe, look at her with interest as she did so.

Perhaps it was because his companion's exceedingly well-to-do appearance acted as a foil that I thought my father looking so much more grey and worn than usual. Mr. Steinthorpe was a man in the prime of life, with a healthy, vigorous, well-satisfied air, of middle height, and by no means slim of figure, yet hardly to be called stout. He was considered a very handsome man by most persons at Burford, but this was not the impression which his appearance made on me as Mabel and I were now introduced to him, though I gradually became aware that his features were well cut and regular, that his cold blue eyes were all that could be desired in size and shape, and that his fine auburn moustache was in itself a distinction. He was irreproachably dressed, in a style quite superior to anything to which we were accustomed at Burford, and was altogether so well groomed, if I may be allowed to use such a horsey expression, that my poor father, always careless of his personal appearance, looked deplorably shabby by his side. His manners, too, had a finish that Burford manners lacked, but which Mabel and I, fresh from our London boarding school, felt to be the correct thing. Mabel actually coloured with gratification as he bowed low before her. I was less elated by his courtesy, for I was not conscious of deserving admiration, and I fancied I detected a sardonic gleam in his eyes as they met mine.

We exchanged a few polite commonplaces, and then, gracefully expressing a hope that he should see more of us, Mr. Steinthorpe bowed again and went on his way. We entered the house with our father, I with a lurking sense of irritation, which I could hardly have explained.

"Father, dear, it is time I came home to look after you," Mabel said, as she laid her hand caressingly on his arm. "What a shocking coat ! You must hand that over to Luke."

"Oh, it is good enough for me," said my father, wearily, as he hung up his hat in the passage. "But I am glad to have you home again, children."

"So that is Mr. Steinthorpe !" Mabel said to me as we went upstairs together. "What a perfect gentleman he is ! But I was vexed that he should see us all dusty and untidy from our journey."

"You mean that you are vexed he saw me so untidy," I said. "You looked most proper, as you always do." For I had felt some pride in Mabel as she talked to Mr. Steinthorpe. Although I had not taken to him myself, I was pleased that he should see what a charming little lady my sister was. Mabel appeared gratified by my words.

"He is very good-looking," she observed, as she surveyed her neat little person in the glass.

"Oh, I can't bear his looks," I burst out ; "I think he has a dreadful expression. Depend upon it, he is not a man to be trusted."

"You don't mean to say that you have taken one of your unreasonable dislikes ?" said Mabel, with an air of patiently enduring my perversity. "I never knew anyone like you for jumping to wild conclusions. You always set yourself against nice people."

"Someone else is jumping to conclusions now," I observed. "How do you know that Mr. Steinthorpe is nice ?"

But Mabel vouchsafed me no reply to this question.

(*To be continued.*)

UNPOPULAR GIRLS.

By A MIDDLE AGED WOMAN.

IRLS have their hopes and ambitions in beginning life as well as their brothers. Some, in these days of Girton and Newnham, aim at fame and intellectual progress ; in others the instinct of motherhood is strongly developed. I remember a poor, hardworking girl of eighteen once saying to me, with indescribable earnestness, "The greatest happiness in life must be to have a dear little baby of one's very own. If I had a darling child all to myself to work for and love, I don't think I should care for anything else in the whole world." Her eyes positively sparkled and her cheeks glowed with the imagined delight of a tiny creature to pet and cherish, and, as she said, "to live for."

The commonest ambition of all is, or course, to be married, and have a home of one's own. With some girls, perhaps, the home occupies a larger space in the mental vision than the husband ; with others, especially if they happen to have fixed on the hero of their day-dreams, the home falls so far into the background as scarcely to be recognised as a necessity at all. One hope, however, is shared by everyone—the hope of being liked. Admiration and love are, of course, more highly prized than popularity, but they can only be expected from a few, while any girl may reasonably aspire to be liked by the whole circle of her acquaintances. Indeed, probably all young people start in life with the expectation of seeing this aspiration fulfilled. As time goes on many quick-witted young women perceive that they are not liked, and wonder why. They are conscious of meaning well, and often of doing well, but they see that they are less attractive than many of their acquaintances whose virtues, talents, and accomplishments, so far as they can discover, by no means exceed their own. Now, some people, men as well as women, have a natural charm about them which is inexplicable. They fascinate ; no one can tell why exactly, but they do. This kind of thing cannot be imitated or acquired ; like beauty or genius, it is born with its fortunate possessors, and often stands them in good stead when health, fortune, and character are gone, and their lives wrecked by folly, self-indulgence, or vice.

It is a common practice to tell little children, "If you are good, people will love you." Perhaps this is true—to a certain extent it must be so ; but it certainly does not follow when you are grown up that if you are good, people will like you. It must be confessed that morals have much less to do with popularity than manners. Think over your acquaintances. Are the most agreeable persons in all cases those you consider the best, those for whom you have the highest respect ? You know very well that they are not. You may regret the fact, but a fact it remains. It is surely, then, worth your while to study to avoid those little ways which make even good people disagreeable, before they become stereotyped into habits. We cannot undertake to teach you to be agreeable, but we may give you a few hints how to escape being disagreeable. To this end keep a strict watch over your tongue. Of conversation it is especially true that

"Evil is wrought
By want of thought
As well as want of heart."

Talk as little as possible about yourself. To you, self is naturally a deeply-interesting subject, but it by no means follows that your friends will find it so. Of course, boasting and direct self-commendation will be eschewed by everyone with any pretensions to good manners. Whatever people think, they do not often say, as I once heard a very worthy woman remark at a charity working party, "I'm the most charitable and unselfishest person that can be."

But many persons, nevertheless, particularly young ones, manage perpetually to bring themselves on the *tapis*. Whatever the subject in hand may be, it is always brought round to themselves—*their* opinion, *their* experience, *their* expectations, what people said about *them*. Or they tell little stories in which they appear to advantage, or repeat compliments which have been paid them, in a deprecatory manner, of course, but still repeating them. Others go on quite a different tack ;

A Middle Aged Woman, "Unpopular Girls" (Volume 7, 1 May 1886, p. 484).

they dwell perpetually on their defects, mental or physical. Politeness prevents their hearers showing their utter want of interest. They cannot say, what they feel, "At your age, neither your opinion nor experience can be of importance to anyone but yourself," or, "Yes, your temper is bad, your eyes are green, you are very indolent; it is a pity you do not try to improve." If they are conscientious they cannot endorse the compliments and deny the defects, which would be the shortest and pleasantest way out of the difficulty. Nothing remains but to take the earliest opportunity of escaping the infliction with a determination to keep out of the way of it for the future. All egotism is offensive, but that springing from " the pride that apes humility " is perhaps one of its most irritating manifestations.

The next thing to talking about yourself is talking about your relations. Young mothers are famous for teasing their friends with baby talk, but some girls are quite as great offenders. "My brother at college," "My uncle the Dean," or "My sister who paints," are perpetually in their mouths. Family affection is a pleasant thing to see, and a right thing to encourage, but it is possible to give outsiders too much of what "my people" think and say. On the other hand, take care how you speak of your friends' relatives. People often have a low opinion themselves of their parents, husbands, brothers or sisters, but they do not like to hear others echo this opinion. It may be illogical and inconsistent, but so it is. Family quarrels are generally made up sooner or later, and more or less forgotten, when no one is more unwelcome than the intimate friend who shows by her conversation that she remembers all about the disputes which have now sunk into oblivion. Avoid patronising or slighting expressions in referring to your friends' relatives. You may think this hint superfluous, but I assure you I have heard girls, who consider themselves well-bred, say such things as this: " Your mother was in here this morning; the poor old lady seemed quite in spirits." " Your father? Oh, let the poor old man have what he fancies." An affectionate child does not care to be reminded that her parents are old, and to a dutiful one the half-pitying, half-patronising tone is most offensive, innocent as the person using it may be of any wish or intention of giving offence.

Another unpleasant habit to which some young people are prone is that of giving advice unasked. Older persons, as a rule, are much too prudent to commit themselves in this way. Most people have their own ideas and methods, and dislike being interfered with. A young lady has devised a new costume with her dressmaker; it is nearly finished, perhaps quite, and she is pleased with the effect. A friend comes in and assures her that she ought to add a bow here and rosette there, turn the front to the side and remodel the drapery, and it will be exactly right.

What wonder if the girl and the dressmaker feel something approaching detestation for the well-intentioned friend who has spoiled their pleasure at the very moment of success? A married lady of some standing, who prides herself on her housekeeping, makes the acquaintance of a lively young matron, who has scarcely kept house as many weeks as she has years. The girl, full of her own experiments, assures her friend that her ways are old-fashioned, her tradesmen expensive, and kindly points out how much better and more cheaply things may be done. It does not matter from my point of view, whether she is right or wrong, in either case the elder lady will be hurt if not offended, and will certainly exercise a careful reticence as to her domestic affairs in the younger one's presence for the future, if she does not avoid her altogether. I have met with girls, pleasant

and praiseworthy in other respects, who are almost insufferable as companions, in consequence of their mania for advising. Whatever subject may be under discussion—needlework, gardening, cookery, dress or mental improvement—a young lady of the sort I mean is always ready with "I can show you a better way of doing it," "We always do so and so," "My way is much quicker," and so on. This kind of thing may be borne with patience from a senior, though annoying, but from a junior, or even an equal, it is unendurable. Always remember that if people wish for your advice they will ask it; if they refrain from doing so keep it to yourself, however valuable it may be.

One way in which girls often thoughtlessly offend against good taste and good manners is by asking questions. Very few like to be examined as to their feelings, affairs, or intentions. I believe young people frequently ask questions simply for the sake of making conversation, without caring at all for the answers. Many, however, who are inquisitive and prying when young, develop into gossips and mischief-makers, with the natural result that they are dreaded and kept at arm's length by all sensible people. Habits formed in youth are rarely broken through afterwards, and, believe me, no habit is more likely to render you unpopular than that of asking questions. "Where have you been?" " Where are you going ? " "How much did you pay for it ? " "Where did you get this ? " "Who told you that ? " frequently reiterated, will assuredly lead your acquaintances to shun you as an ill-bred, troublesome meddler. Mind your own business and leave your neighbours to mind theirs. It is impossible to say how much harm has been done by inopportune questioning. Habits of deceit have been induced and fostered, hopeful prospects have been permanently destroyed, waverers have been driven into wrong doing, and sensitive persons have been set against their best friends by this objectionable climax.

As far as you can, avoid personal remarks altogether. They are seldom acceptable, and give offence oftener than not. Shy people are made uncomfortable by compliments or critical observations on their appearance. Nervous and self-conscious individuals are rendered absolutely miserable by having their little awkwardnesses and peculiarities of manner laughed at or remarked on. It is scarcely necessary to warn you against touching on sore points. You will not, of course, talk of "old maids" or "elderly young ladies" in the presence of women "of a certain age." Neither must you comment on the ugliness of large feet, red hands, a coarse complexion, a squint or any personal defects before people who have the misfortune to suffer from them. Do not be too ready to tell your friends they look ill or well; timid people are frightened by the former, and people who think it "interesting" to look delicate are annoyed by the latter. It is really provoking to a person whose face is flushed by toothache or some other of the so-called minor maladies of life to be met by a hearty congratulation on her blooming looks. Never grumble if you can help it. I quite admit that it is a relief for the time. You feel decidedly better after having aired your grievance, but you have bored your friend, who has, no doubt, plenty of grievances of her own and takes but a limited interest in yours. Do not be a wet blanket either. Who can help disliking the company of a person who always thinks it will rain if you have a special reason for wishing it to be fine; is convinced you will miss your train if the cab comes a minute or two late; predicts certain failure if you are trying an experiment; discovers faults in your newest toy; and, in

short, looks persistently on the dark side of things? If you wish your society to be sought after and appreciated, cultivate a hopeful frame of mind and a cheerful exterior, suppress your own troubles, and sympathise heartily in the pleasures of others.

Some girls, few I hope, have a morbid liking for painful subjects, physical or moral. Without absolutely indulging in "improper" conversation, they hover on its borders. Any coarse or nasty story has an attraction for them. Disgusting symptoms in illness, horrible crimes, distressing operations, are favourite topics. To refined women, and still more to refined men, this style of conversation in a young woman is peculiarly repugnant. Better be too fastidious than continually dabbling in the foul pools that must collect in this world of sin and shame.

I have only two more hints to give about the use of the tongue. One is, Do not contradict. If possible, agree with your friend; if not, say nothing. Opposition is always disagreeable; the feeling, " So-and-so is sure to think the opposite of what I do," has checked in the bud many a promising friendship. Of course, there are cases, where principle is concerned, when it is our duty to speak out, whether we are offensive or not, but they do not very often occur, and if we speak moderately, kindly, and politely, we rarely suffer for it in the estimation of our friends if they are worth preserving. This is quite different from continually contradicting about trifling and unimportant matters in everyday life, a common and very reprehensible practice.

Lastly, and this is very important—Do not talk too much. The most brilliant of talkers, such as Macaulay and Rogers, have become wearisome at times, because they did not know when to stop. Sydney Smith on one occasion said Macaulay had been more agreeable than usual because he had had " several brilliant flashes of silence." Think, then, what an intolerable bore perpetual chatter must be which has neither genius nor wit to recommend it. I have seen the youngest and most uninteresting member of a party entirely spoil what might have been a pleasant evening by monopolising the conversation, and consequently reducing to silence those who had something to say worth listening to. A good listener, responsive and appreciative, is often a more valuable acquisition in society than even a fairly good talker. Observe the word "responsive." A listener who sits stolidly silent, never smiling at a joke or assenting to a proposition, showing no sign of hearing what you say, possibly not even answering a question till it is repeated a second time, is by no means a pleasing addition to any company.

I will mention two more habits which, though unconnected with conversation, tend to make some worthy and excellent people unpopular. They may be considered trifling, but in many cases they are a real bar to happy intimacy. The first is a habit of borrowing. This is often troublesome to the lender. Some girls seem invariably short of change; you scarcely ever take a walk with them without a request for a small sum, which they probably forget to return. To remind a friend of a debt is at best a delicate operation, and many girls would rather sustain a slight pecuniary loss than attempt it. Besides, the transaction often escapes the lender's memory as well as the borrower's, and leads to vexations and hopeless confusion in accounts. Persons whose income is strictly "limited," and who can only just make both ends meet, may be put to serious inconvenience in this way.

But other things may be borrowed besides money—books, for instance. We all know how apt we are to borrow books and keep them (by accident of course!) for weeks, months, and even years. Sometimes valuable works are spoiled by the loss of one volume, or when a book is wanted for reference a space is found where it ought to be, and the owner has no guide to its whereabouts beyond a vague idea that it was "lent to somebody." I have known people so unscrupulous as to borrow a new, brightly bound volume, warp its covers over the fire or in the sun, lend it to their friends without the owner's permission, and at last return it, shabby, faded, and old.

Some women are fond of borrowing bags, portmanteaus, waterproofs, umbrellas, and articles of wearing apparel, forgetful apparently of the fact that these things do not last for ever, and wear out quite soon enough in their owner's service. Bad housekeepers have been known to plague their neighbours by continual requests for small quantities of tea, sugar, flour, coals, and the like "till they can get in their own." It will be remembered that poor Mrs. Carlyle in her letters complains bitterly of Mrs. Leigh Hunt, her next door neighbour, who seems to have carried the practice to abnormal lengths. Few girls, however, are likely to have the

opportunity of offending in this way. They do, however, sometimes venture to ask the loan of jewellery and curiosities of value which are lent with many anxious fears for their safety by amiable people, who are too kind and polite to refuse, but who would much prefer to keep their treasures under their own eyes. Of course these observations do not apply when your friends offer to lend without any hints or suggestions from yourselves, but even then, except to relations and very old friends, it is better as a rule to avoid incurring the obligation.

Unpunctuality is a sad drawback in a companion. A girl agrees to call for her friend at a specified time. The friend keeps her waiting just long enough to make her late at church or for class, or to compel her to run all the way to the station to catch the train. This happens not once merely but frequently. Who can be surprised that after a time the girl prefers to walk alone or finds a fresh companion? The causes which lead to unpunctuality are threefold—trying to squeeze too much work into a given time; careless

forgetfulness, which makes girls oblivious altogether of engagements; and a habit of dawdling procrastination, which is easily acquired and very difficult to shake off. Whatever the cause may be, the effect is generally fatal to a girl's popularity.

I have but just touched the borders of many important subjects. I have passed by some altogether which are perhaps even more important. Do not imagine that I have set up a warning at every pitfall that lies in your way. Far from this, I have but selected a few that seemed most likely to escape notice. "Little things," you may say, "mere trifles, hardly looking for!" Not so; life is made up of little things. It is but a fly that spoils the pot of ointment, a little blot disfigures the fairest page, and a little failing may so obscure the good points of a girl's disposition in the eyes of her neighbours as to render her a bugbear to be shunned, instead of a treasure to be sought after. And it should never be forgotten that we are bidden by Divine authority to strive after "Whatsoever things are lovely, whatsoever things are of good report."

COURTLEROY.

By ANNE BEALE.

CHAPTER XXIV.
DRIVEN TO BAY.

BARBER looked sadly crestfallen when he answered Mr. Le Roy's summons. He received his orders like a mute. He was told to see that everything was prepared for the autocrat—dinner, his room, and sundry other matters.

"I will do my best, sir," he said, at last. "But Mr. Sellon would be glad to see you at once. Searle is anxious to be off."

"Ask them to come here, and send refreshments for Mr. Sellon and me." "How can I go through with it?" mused Le Roy. "This place will kill me. I wish I had read the letters and attended more to George Hope; but Searle must be honest."

Mr. Sellon came in alone. He began upon business at once.

"I find that all your papers are either at Mr. Searle's house or with the Prestbury firm," he said. "I propose to return with him and look into the affairs to-night; to-morrow morning we can all three proceed to Prestbury and see after the Units. I have asked Mr. Searle to give me a bed, as your establishment here is not—well, not quite—equal to your London one, and Miss Marmont is not accustomed to chance visitors. I fear Searle is a scoundrel, and we must not lose sight of him for a moment. I have left him under your man's special care at present lest he escape us. The scene at the farm was ominous, and I think you must be prepared for the worst, since it is impossible to say what excesses he may have been guilty of in your name. Of course, I do not know what you have actually ordered and approved of, but it seems scarcely probable that you can have willingly let your property go to rack and ruin."

"I trusted Searle, and I trust him still!" said Mr. Le Roy, coldly and majestically.

"We shall discover to-morrow whether your confidence has been misplaced or not; to-day you can remain in happy ignorance. I had no idea that you had been living in the dark for the best part of twenty years. The little I have gathered from Miss Marmont proves that a system of extortion and neglect has been carried on here during that period on the plea that money must be secured for Mr. Le Roy's needs at all costs. Excuse my speaking plainly, but you must face it at last."

"I shall return to town to-morrow and leave the affairs between you and Searle," returned Le Roy.

"We shall see," added Sellon, significantly.

"I have ordered—dinner. You will stay?" asked Le Roy, pausing long and doubtfully on the name of the proffered repast.

"No, thank you; I dare not leave the lion's provider, alias the jackall, Searle. He will hunt up food for me, I daresay, knowing that he is in my power, in the same way that he cannot refuse to find me a lair. I wish you a good appetite and a good night's rest."

Mr. Le Roy was offended at Sellon's ironical tone, scarcely understanding that the lawyer was worked up into a state of indignation at what he saw and heard. He rose, however, and opened for him the door which led into the passage.

"You know your way to—to—the library, the business-room, the——Where is Searle?" he asked, with affected indifference.

Barber appeared, his lugubrious face longer and more melancholy than ever.

"Those rooms are no longer habitable, sir; but Mr. Searle won't wait, he is off by the path across the park. There he is, sir! You will catch him if you make haste," he added to Sellon.

"Send my portmanteau in the fly!" cried Sellon, and rushed out of the hall door.

Mr. Le Roy looked after him with some show of interest, but when he saw him overtake Searle he turned from the window. In the centre of the room he saw an elderly woman leaning on a stick. He made a sort of bow, for with all his faults he was a gentleman; but did not recognise her.

"I am right glad to welcome you home again, master," she said, with an attempt at a curtsey. "I'm thankful to a' lived to see this day. You don't remember me, sir, and no wonder, for I'm near seventy now, and when you saw me last I wasn't much over—— I beg your pardon, sir, I didn't mean to speak of that time—indeed, I made a solemn vow not—but rheumatism do make one so forgetful!"

"Mrs. Stone! I beg your pardon," said Le Roy, going towards her, and shaking hands with her, as if some sudden memory impelled him.

He had never so honoured her before, and the good woman's stick slipped, and the rheumatic hip gave way in her attempt at a second curtsey, so that she nearly fell. He was obliged to support her, and the kind act brought tears to her eyes. He helped her to a seat near the table, seeing that she had difficulty in standing.

"Thank you kindly, sir. The doctor says my rheumatism's crownick, and sure enough like an old crow I am. But the offices are damp, and the rain comes into my bedroom. There now, I come to ask about dinner and I'm a talking about myself. I am afraid, sir, that we're not prepared as we ought to be, seeing you were not expected; but if you'll be so good as to make a 'igh tea with the ladies to-night we'll manage better to-morrow. Miss Marmont says we can lay it here, sir, instead of in the schoolroom."

"Why not in the dining-room?" interrupted Mr. Le Roy.

"Well, sir, it's damp, and there's no fire; and if I may make so bold, this 'all is more comfortable. Miss Marmont has made a porter to draw right across the windows so that it's the 'ottest place in the house in winter, and, as you may remember, sir, the coolest in summer. There now, I'm forgetting again."

He remembered but too well.

"Settle it as you will, only let me have something to eat and drink," he said, between irritation and a sort of desire not to be exacting under the circumstances.

"Yes, sir. There are spring chickens, and early vegetables, and blancmange, and tea or coffee, or both."

"Wine if you please. I hate tea and coffee with meat."

---

but one that invariably excited interest in women's minds, and won for him countless social invitations which his busy studious life compelled him to decline.

But Auriol's joy was very short-lived. Telling her that Herr Frickenstein, naming a great German celebrity, was very anxious to be introduced to her, Claude Havilland led her very reluctantly, it must be confessed, up to a hairy-faced foreigner, and then left her, saying in a low voice, "I will try and get a few quiet moments with you later on." Auriol listened absently to the German's flattering comments on her writings, expressed in broken English, and tried to smile and look gratified as she told him how honoured she felt; but a tumult of happiness was surging in her breast. Those "few quiet moments," when were they coming? Did he mean—? Could he mean—? And he had looked so agitated. Surely he would come to take her down to supper! But as no Claude Havilland appeared, the task devolved on Mr. Walter Rowlands, the genial novelist, whose delightful works of fiction have made his name a household word. On entering the room there was a temporary block at the door, and Auriol and her companion were kept waiting a few moments outside. Suddenly

Auriol gave a start, and Mr. Rowlands glancing down at her saw her face had become deadly white, whiter than the dress she wore. Wondering a little at the sudden transformation he led her to a less crowded part of the corridor, and began vigorously fanning her.

"If you will stay here, I will go and get you something," as he saw she was beginning to revive.

"No, thank you, I would rather go into the room. I was only a little faint. The evening is so warm."

What had Auriol seen? Only Claude Havilland gazing down with all his heart in his eyes at a slender childish figure leaning confidingly on his arm, her golden head touching his shoulder, and her melting blue eyes lifted up appealingly to his. What had she heard? Only two or three whispered words that she thought—alack! alack! should have been hers, and hers alone. But after the first violence of the shock had passed off pride came to the rescue. No one should guess she had been wounded. With a mighty effort she pulled herself together again, and for the rest of the evening was if possible brighter, and talked with more animation than before

People said they had never known Auriol Walgrave so witty and brilliant. Even the Duchess was heard to exclaim, "What has the child been doing to herself? I never saw her look so radiant. Genius ought always to be dressed in gold and white."

During the drive home Auriol amused her friend by her graphic account of the evening's experiences. There was a certain dash of recklessness in her speech which her chaperon attributed to over-excitement, thinking in the simplicity of her heart that the young author's head had been slightly turned by all the adulation she had received. She did not see the spasm of pain that passed over the girl's face when Claude Havilland's name was casually mentioned.

"Did you happen to hear who that young girl was to whom he was talking so much?"

"Some one told me she belonged to the house-party, but I didn't hear her name," Auriol answered, with what she was pleased to think was consummate indifference. And they parted at Auriol's door with a cheery "Good-bye; I shall see you again to-morrow, or rather this evening I ought to say."

(To be concluded.)

SOME MARRIAGE THORNS, AND HOW TO AVOID THEM.

By the COUNTESS DE BOERIO.

PART. I.

THE lot of eight girls out of ten is marriage, and maternity. These states are their natural sphere, and comprise the chief duty of women, duty distinctly marked out, and in spite of many and great difficulties containing no real complications.

Saint Paul says: "Wives submit yourselves unto your own husbands, as unto the Lord." And again: "Let the wife see that she reverence her husband."

Saint Peter says: "Ye wives be in subjection to your own husbands; that if any obey not the Word, they also may without the Word be won by the conversation of the wives; while they behold your chaste conversation coupled with fear."

Follow these broad lines of the duty of woman to her husband in spirit and in detail, and it certainly would never be the fault of the wife that matrimony so often turns out a fiasco; but alas! women are frequently so capricious, so exacting, so tactless in their treatment of the man they have married that they drive him into ways and habits which, although in themselves wrong, are in reality the outcome of the wife's conduct. Thus things gradually go from bad to worse, and the happiness of two lives is ruined, all perhaps for want of a little tact in the first place on the part of the woman.

Let us look into this matter from the beginning, and try to discover some of the more general thorns amongst the flowers of married life.

During the engagement both sides are generally seen at their best. The man is, figuratively speaking, at the feet of the woman; he sees her through rose-coloured glasses; she is to him the embodiment of every grace and virtue; he is blind to her every fault, and

probably agrees with every preposterous thing she may say. Now woman, being woman, enjoys this immensely; she uses her power but in a pretty gracious way which enchants her adorer. She herself perhaps is yet a little diffident, and can scarcely realise that her power is absolute. There may be quarrels sometimes, tears, despair, and thoughts of an early grave, but we all know that lovers' quarrels are but the renewal of love, and are in reality more or less enjoyed by both parties as giving a little exciting touch to what is perhaps otherwise rather a smooth and monotonous courtship. Thus the engagement continues until the wedding-day, when, amid a shower of rice and old slippers, the happy couple start off on their honeymoon. Whilst talking of weddings let me say a few words about this custom of throwing rice and old shoes after the newly-married couple. The old shoes are decidedly disagreeable, and I do not think many people indulge in the pleasure of throwing them, but rice is still a very general habit, and a very dangerous one too, besides making the newly-married pair the object of attention and often ridicule to every cabman, porter and waiter they speak to, for these little grains of rice have a horrible habit of hiding in the folds of the dress, or veil, or on the top of the bonnet and falling out just at the wrong moment. As regards the danger, amongst other stories of the sort this is perhaps the saddest. A young couple most deeply attached to one another, after an engagement of nine years, during which time they suffered all the sorrows of separation and opposition to their marriage, were at length joined together in holy matrimony. The wedding took place in a small Irish village far from the railroad, so that after the breakfast the young couple started in a dog-cart for the station some ten miles distant amidst a shower of rice and good wishes. The horse, which was young and fresh, became rather restive during the shower of rice, but at last started off calmly enough. A few grains of rice had however fallen into his ears, and this at last so maddened him that he ran away, and finally upset the dog-cart in a ditch, and spiked himself on the shaft. The bridegroom was killed

on the spot, the bride injured for life, and the groom very badly hurt. Can you imagine anything more sad than this end to nine years' fidelity, and all for the foolish gratification of throwing a few handfuls of rice.

Well! the young couple have started on their honeymoon, the period of blissful mooning about together and seeing sights which sooner or later pall terribly. It is understood that during the honeymoon the young couple live and spend money in a way quite incompatible with their rent-roll and future way of living. When a man finds himself spending in a three weeks' holiday the sum which must suffice for three months for his whole household, it is no wonder that he feels somewhat like a fish out of water, and that after a while this existence apart from all duties and cares, this butterfly life, charming though it be, begins to pall and even weary him. His thoughts in spite of himself go back to his daily life and occupation. He asks himself if this young soul linked to his will be a true "helpmeet" in the more serious business of life, or whether she will still desire to live this life of pleasure and *sans souci;* and so it happens that from time to time he will snub some pleasure-trip she has planned, or answer impatiently, or maintain an attitude of indifference and *ennui.* These things, so new and full of delight to her, are not so to him, and her continual enjoyment of them at last exasperates him. Man, there is no doubt about it, is more or less selfish, he cannot well help himself, it is a fault which to a certain degree is compatible with his position as a "lord of creation." He is the master, the head of his wife and household; his word is, or should be law, and the wife's duty is to submit and carry out his will. The temptation to real selfishness is great, and one hardly knows where to draw the line. This moment of satiety on the man's side during the honeymoon is the moment for the wife to show her tact, her desire to put self aside and be a real "helpmeet" to her husband; but alas, it is too often the moment for the first little rift, the first crease in the rose-leaf to be felt and seen. Instead of, with ready tact, understanding her husband's feelings and thoughts, and herself proposing that they shall leave these scenes of thoughtless pleasure and idling, and return home to begin seriously the life they are to spend together, that dear life which she will smooth for him by her care, her thought, her love, the young wife flies off at a tangent ; she listens to her imagination rather than her common-sense, declares he is already tired of her, that she is the most miserable woman on the face of the earth, that she has married a man who has wearied of her as of a toy, in fact she makes a regular scene and drives her poor husband, who is also young and probably inexperienced in women's ways, perfectly frantic.

Now this is the first critical moment in married life.

And now much depends on the husband and his delicacy of treatment and comprehension of his wife. With some women the gentle reasoning course is the best, with others firm displeasure, but in either case the result must be the same, that the wife be made to understand her error as regards her husband's love, and that she be taken into his full confidence, and allowed to feel that though he cannot pass his life in idle adoration, that she is to him his one real thought, and that he looks to her to give him that consolation and peacefulness which shall make his home a very Eden. Some men, who have married sensible girls, succeed in making them understand this at once, and the first scene is the last ; some take months, perhaps a whole year, whilst with others it becomes such a cause of dissension and misunderstanding that love takes wing and both go their own way in life. I know some very funny stories of such scenes between young people ; but really, though one laughs heartily after, one cannot help wondering how so many husbands put up as they do with such scenes, and how so many intelligent, loving women can behave so unreasonably, so illogically, or bring themselves to give such trouble and anxiety to a husband they really care for, and it is a fact that the more a woman loves her husband the more likely she is during these first days to allow her imagination to run away with her on this subject. The truth of it is that after marriage each see the other in a new light, many little faults and failings become evident, many little habits annoy and

aggravate which could not possibly do so beforehand simply because circumstances did not bring them into evidence. However much an engaged couple may meet, they cannot possibly see as much of each other as when married. The very hours of their meeting change their normal life ; they give themselves up to the joy of being together, and for the time being the ordinary things of life are forgotten. But after marriage it is different ; picture for instance a man who is the pink of neatness and order discovering the wife he loves to be just the contrary. At first he will expostulate gently, if without producing any effect he will grow impatient ; later, when time and habit have accustomed him to her, he will probably grow angry. If she is a woman who answers back or makes weak excuses without trying to mend her ways, quarrels will be the result. Or suppose a man to be very punctual, his wife the contrary, he will naturally at last become exasperated ; should she reproach him by stating that " he never used to be like that before they were married," he may well reply that what he then took to be girlish coquetry which amused him, or even bashfulness which charmed him, he now finds to be a habit, and a habit with which he will not put up.

One of the faults most objected to by men is the habit of nagging. A nagging woman is their pet aversion, and to find that the wife of his bosom is one of this sort must indeed be a sore trial to a man. Avoid nagging, girls ; if you have a grievance out with it frankly and have done with it ; also, do not hint and insinuate and refer constantly to the subject in a martyr-like tone, and then declare with resignation if asked for an explanation, that you mean nothing, that you are quite happy and have nothing, oh ! nothing whatever to complain of ! You may have the petty triumph of seeing your husband look utterly helpless and nonplused ; but oh ! what a very small satisfaction it is, and how very far are you from being the " helpmeet " you should be, and making your home the little Eden of calm and joy your perhaps hard-working husband dreamt of. Another little fault which is most frequent in women and most aggravating to men, especially to some men, is the habit of jeering at them when you are right and they are wrong, and saying with mocking triumph,

" I told you so, but you would not believe me." How many serious quarrels have arisen out of that " told you so," given in a certain tone of voice.

" Well, but have men no faults ? " I hear you say ; " is it all on the women's side—the fault of division in a household ? "

Yes, men have many and great faults, and some men, I agree with you, are perfectly impossible creatures ; but for the most part men's faults are perfectly amenable to a wife's gentle influence, and little by little with time and tact will grow so beautifully less that they will cease to annoy others, and they themselves derive benefit without knowing the cause of the change.

A woman's gentleness and patience with her husband's faults should never flag, nor should she make her submission to his will too evident a favour ; her submission should be graceful and dignified, given freely and willingly to please him, not sulkily and grumblingly because she supposes she must.

The sacrifices of self that a woman makes to keep the wheels of domestic life smoothly rolling should be known only to herself ; outsiders should never be taken into her confidence, neither should her husband ; it is her duty, and that should be her recompense, together with the increasing of her domestic happiness, and the joy of making her husband love his home. A woman should never seek to make a man happy after her manner, by taking advantage of his love to impose on him her tastes, her preferences, her opinions ; these she must keep in the background, and so ordain their life, and study what pleases her husband that she will find everything arranged naturally according to his tastes and ready to his hand without any ostentation. When a man comes home from work, whatever it may be, and in whatever class he is, the picture of a woman waiting for him whose sole thought is to be agreeable to him, will make his home seem, not only a house arranged according to his own ideas, but a sort of enchanted place where every want, every delicate desire of his soul is ministered to ; the wife is the angel of this refuge from the outside world and its troubles, and as such and through his gratitude becomes the greatest influence in his life.

(To be concluded.)

THE FLAGS OF OUR EMPIRE.

WHAT THEY ARE, AND HOW TO MAKE THEM.

PART I.

THE subject of flags may be very naturally divided into three distinct departments. First, they may be considered historically ; secondly, as at present in use ; and lastly, with a view to practical work in their manufacture.

The history of the past is rich in interesting stories connected with the ensigns of all nations, and especially remarkable as regards that of our own empire, dating back to the

early days of our first civilisation. But what is the antiquity of those times, compared with the era, in the history of the world, when the use of flags was first inaugurated ? The earliest records to which we can refer are those supplied by Holy Writ, and the first is accompanied by a Divine command (see Numbers ii.). Besides this, there are no less than thirteen allusions to banners and standards, and eight to ensigns, in the sacred writings.

Most of our readers have seen representations of the ancient Roman standards which were surmounted by an eagle, a pole support-

ing a cross-piece from which the drapery depended. The Assyrians and Egyptians carried standards consisting of poles surmounted with figures, but no drapery ; so did the Persians and the very early Greeks. But later on they displayed a red flag at sea as the insignia of battle ; and they hoisted a purple garment on a spear-head for the same purpose on land, this idea being copied by Clovis I. of France, who hoisted the blue cape of St. Martin as the royal banner. And so it held its place till A.D. 630, when it was superseded and enveloped by a red flag with a green fringe, terminating in five tongue-like streamers, called

SOME MARRIAGE THORNS, AND HOW TO AVOID THEM.

By the COUNTESS DE BOERIO.

PART II.

NEVER insist on getting your own way. Most husbands are only too pleased to accede to their wives' desires if reasonable ; in any case there is but little real pleasure in getting your own way by force, and making your husband give in for the sake of peace. Instead of an agreeable companion, you have probably one whose face is a mile long, who has nothing to say for himself, simply because he is utterly bored. Do you not think you would have had double the enjoyment if, putting self aside, you cheerfully agreed to do as your husband wished, directly you saw that your plan was not a pleasing one ? Why should wives always be those to give in ? I hear you ask. Well! it is a difficult question to answer, except because they ought, because God ordained it so, and ordained that by gentleness and tact and patient submission, woman should gain and keep her influence ; and woman's influence is great, perhaps one of the greatest influences in the world. Men listen and reflect over an intelligent woman's gentle advice, they weigh well her words, and finding them wise, follow them. If the same woman were to give the same advice in an opinionated, superior, nagging way, she would immediately rouse the spirit of the "lord of creation," who does not like to be dictated to, and her words would fall on idle ears. Many wives of my acquaintance have tried this system, and always with success. Indeed the wife the most spoilt that I know is the most submissive. She never tries to force her husband to give way in any instance, she invariably tries to like to do what he likes to do. If there is a choice to be made between two things, and their opinions differ, she gives way quietly and does her best to hide any disappointment she may feel. He is a man of iron will, too, and has not the least idea of allowing anyone, much less his wife, to revolt against his rule. This young woman rebelled during the first year of her marriage, but, as she has often told me, she might just as well have tried to knock a hole in the wall with her head, her husband never gave way in any one little matter. She changed her tactics, she resolved to be a model wife, to submit gracefully to every desire of her husband ; she did not succeed quite at first, for her character is naturally independent, and her temper quick, but after a time she found it easier, and what is the result now ? She has so entirely studied her husband's tastes that her own are almost identical, she has so won him by her cheerful submission to his will that he refuses her nothing he can possibly give her. His nay is still nay, and his yea yea, but she

is so sure of his desire to please her, that when he does say nay, she knows quite well that he must have a very good reason, and, therefore, does not even discuss the matter with him. Now if this young wife had continued her first system, she would probably by now be a most unhappy woman, and instead of being the sunshine of her husband's life, she would have become a worry and anxiety to him, for she would never have got the better of him, however hard she may have tried ; he would always be master, as every true man should be.

Let us now study a little the cause and result of these first quarrels ; by first quarrels, I do not mean those little disputes between bride and bridegroom, which, like lovers' quarrels, are the renewal of love, but those more serious ones, which although they may begin out of nothing, increase in severity, so that words are said by both which wound like sharp swords, and leave their mark for many a day after.

The most perfect confidence and free exchange of ideas and feelings should exist between husband and wife. From the moment that they, and in particular the wife, keep silence, and nurse their little grievances, these last assume enormous proportions, until they burst forth in one tremendous storm which does double the damage a quiet little grumble would have done. Under these circumstances, we can safely say woman shows herself in a most unfavourable light. She appears to be a creature who has neither reason nor logic, nor even any idea of truth. She allows her heated imagination to run away with her, and says the most utterly preposterous things she can lay her tongue to, and what is worse, she thoroughly believes them for the moment. This belief gives an appearance of reality to her words, which strikes as a funeral knell of happiness on the young husband's ears, inexperienced as he is in women's ways.

Woman is not at times mistress of her words, and most certainly seldom attaches the same importance to them as her unfortunate audience ; thus, an hour, nay, sometimes half an hour after, she will utterly deny having said such and such a thing ; calm and reason have resumed their sway, and she either cannot really remember what she said in her wrath, or she is ashamed to remember.

The husband requires all his tact and delicacy at this moment. If he, alas ! has also lost his temper, the result of these first great quarrels is, that they become the point of departure of a permanent yet secret hostility, which ends in a sort of moral divorce, and sometimes in separation.

If he, taking advantage of these strong expressions and words, reproaches her with them, after peace has been made, and insists on her owning to them instead of quietly accepting her denial, he risks starting her off again worse than ever ; for woman is apt when thus pushed into a corner, during or directly after one of these nervous attacks of temper, to turn round on her husband and say, " Well, yes ! I did say so, and I meant it," etc., followed by perhaps still more cruel words.

Neither should the husband remain utterly silent and passive during the torrent of unkind words with which his wife assails him ; instead of conciliating her, it will probably make her doubly furious. She will imagine he does not consider her worth answering, and will in consequence stab him morally with the sharpest swords she can think of. She will paint him in the blackest colours, and end probably by declaring that she can never look on him with affection again. Oh ! a great deal of patience and kindness do these poor husbands need to bear with the sometimes terrible waywardness of their young wives. But once a husband thoroughly understands his wife, and knows that this excess of language is but the outcome of a nervous condition she is perhaps hardly mistress of, his task becomes comparatively easy. He no longer criticises her cruel words, nor does he ask himself if she is right or wrong ; he sees, and understands that she suffers, that her woman's vivid imagination has run away with her, and made her imaginary grievances really exist for the time being, and so there is a general air of anxiety and tenderness about his manner, pleasing to the exacting and difficult character at such times of woman ; she softens, gives way to her feelings in tears, and then smiles and gentle words appear as readily as May flowers after April showers.

Whatever the subject of dispute between husband and wife is, it almost always changes its character as soon as the wife takes refuge in tears. Her husband's one idea now is to comfort her, not to show her where she is wrong and he right. Their reconciliation is complete, and whether their respective opinions are changed on the subject of the quarrel or not, no further mention of it should be made just now. The husband who holds his tongue soon reaps the fruit of his wisdom. The less he says and appears to think of his wife's conduct, the more she remembers it to her own disadvantage, and the greater her humility and sorrow. When a woman is not forced to defend her conduct, or blush for it by allusions and reproaches, she as a rule judges it very

---

rightly and severely. These rules apply to the great majority of women, but some there are who deserve nothing better than a jug of cold water poured over them, and then to be left to come to their senses at their leisure. This style of woman is perhaps less violent; but she is a thousand times more aggravating, being such a peculiar mixture of sulkiness and violence, and taking so very long to regain possession of herself that her husband requires to be almost more than human to bear with her.

Woman, the weaker vessel, is however not the only one to give way to angry violence. Man also often forgets himself, and man, the "king of creation" in a temper is a sight which, although it may sometimes alarm a woman at the time, is certain to rouse in her feelings of contempt for his weakness. An explosion of temper does not end with man as with woman, in tears which relieve and leave her in full and calm possession of herself; on the contrary he feels humiliated, worn-out not only physically, but what is more serious, morally; his will seems to have deserted him for the time being, and he is thus entirely at the mercy of his wife. Never is woman more mistress of the situation than now, and oh, girls! how very delicate should be her treatment of the husband who presents a very pitiable spectacle, shorn of his will and manly dignity. While I think of it let me remind "our girls" that a good woman, a kind and true woman, will never, however weak-minded and incapable her husband may be, allow outsiders to see that she is master. She will always appear to be subservient, she will even persuade her husband that his will is law, and so great will be her tact and gentle thoughtfulness for the man she has promised to "love, honour, and obey," that he as well as others will never suspect that she is the mainspring of their common life. Some women seem to think it grand to show off their power, to air their independence of their husbands. These I think have missed their vocation and were never born to be wives.

Some women (indeed I am afraid most have a touch of it), having learnt by experience that this violence suddenly transfers the power from their husbands to themselves, do not hesitate to take advantage of it in a way which is very mean, but alas! essentially feminine. She knows his faults, his weaknesses well enough to hold him as it were in her hand. She knows what words, what gesticulations, what tone of voice even will annoy him and provoke an explosion of anger strong enough to leave him powerless and destroy the resistance he has opposed to her too often unreasonable demands. Is this loyal, think you? Is it worthy of man's "helpmeet"?

A wife should tenderly bear with her husband's faults and weaknesses, as he with hers. She should know how to put him at peace with himself. Soothe him as a mother a fretful child, with a patience which has no condescension or pity in it, only an infinite tenderness.

There is another type of wife of whom I have not yet spoken, and this is the woman who, when a discussion arises in the *ménage* and there is a resolution to be taken, submits her opinion to her husband's with seeming good grace, though it may be against her most entire conviction. She renounces doing whatever she wished to do, she puts aside her greatest preferences, she sacrifices her dearest plans, and thus shows herself in the most exemplary light, *vis-à-vis* her husband. Only, for there is an only, she wishes it to be well-known and acknowledged that her sacrifices are sacrifices, that she is the more reasonable of the two. She submits to each exigence, only she insists that her husband admits that it is an exigence. In fact, she must be

publicly given her "victim's" diploma, and it is only on this condition that she consents to immolate herself. Now this is one of the most powerful means of aggravating a man. His masculine pride insists on his authority being recognised and bowed down to, he loves to feel that his will is paramount, that when he speaks "let no dog bark." But he hates to be made to feel that he is a tyrant, that morally his wife is no more convinced than if he had never spoken. When she thus submits it is a more cruel blow to his pride than if she resisted him. He is materially the victor, having obtained his desire, but morally he is vanquished, her conviction having escaped beyond his control. So instead of being grateful to her for her sacrifice, he feels injured and all his satisfaction disappears. A man very much dislikes to feel that "a woman convinced against her will is of the same opinion still." Learn by this, girls, to submit yourselves gracefully, cheerfully, as though it were a pleasure to you, or don't submit at all. You will find that in the long-run you will gain by it.

Woman has naturally a temperament given to occasional fits of bad temper; man has them less by nature than by habit. How many young wives would avoid useless disputes with their husbands, if, when they feel this nervous irritability coming on, they would go frankly to him, and say simply, "I feel so cross and peevish to-day, I shall grow quarrelsome for nothing; will you be careful what you say and do, and help me to overcome it?" What husband could resist such an appeal? A young couple, friends of mine, who had frequent "scenes" the first year of their married life, which made them both very unhappy, have employed this method, and I doubt if you would ever hear them quarrel now. An impatient word is the nearest approach to such a thing. This avowal of inferiority, this petition for his help, cannot fail to please man's vanity (and he has plenty); the patience he has now to exercise towards his wife is no longer a sacrifice obligatory, but a protection, and he therefore experiences a certain satisfaction born of this tribute to his manly superiority. This is the surest way for woman to surmount her natural nervous peevishness—to thus acknowledge her bad temper before her husband has suffered from it is simply to have the sense to fight it *à deux* instead of alone. Matrimony shows itself in this as in every other case a visible and sure advantage. The same system may be practised by the husband. From the moment he confides to his wife his worries and anxieties and seeks consolation, his bad temper changes its character in her eyes; instead of resenting it as an injustice to herself, and a discomfort to endure, she looks on it as a burden to bear with him and to lighten if possible (or she should do), and this sympathy in these little daily trials serves to draw them still closer instead of separating them.

Sulkiness is also a fault of some women, very detrimental to married happiness. I am personally acquainted with some young wives who think nothing of sulking for days at a time, and refusing to say more than "yes" or "no" to their husbands. They generally make themselves more than usually amiable to any other man who may be present, and indulge in an exaggerated gaiety of manner when others are present in order that their silence may be the more felt when alone with their husbands. This is a most dangerous enemy of married happiness. The wife begins —it succeeds, her young husband is miserable, it is pleasing to her vanity to see him suffer thus—next time she keeps it up longer, thus it grows and grows until at last it becomes so prolonged that she does not know how to return, as it were, to her natural manner. The young husband too, after a while, tires of trying to make those eyes soften, those lips

smile and speak, so that when the wife does come round, she finds her husband has taken her place, and that he now refuses to speak, to "kiss and make friends." I do not advise, as you know, violence, but violence and angry disputing is a thousand times less dangerous and undermining to married happiness than sulkiness.

Capriciousness is another woman's fault little calculated to render her man's "helpmeet." Everything goes wrong in the house of a capricious woman; her husband is often at his wits' end to know what she really wants, the servants likewise, so often are the orders given and countermanded, until at last they act like the aide-de-camp, who having received an order from his general, still held in his impatient horse. "What do you wait for?" cried the general impatiently.

"The counter-order which will follow," was the unhesitating answer.

Thus you see, girls, marriage is a state not to be entered into lightly, just for the sake of being called Mrs., and having a house of your own; and that reminds me of a warning I have not given you. Do not, when your husband comes home, tired, worried, perhaps a little cross, meet him with complaints of your servants, and your own little insignificant household troubles. Your first thought should be to chase away the frown on his brow, and the shadow in his eyes, not add to them. If you are forced to ask his advice, do so later on; when calmed and tranquillised by the brightness and charm of home, and his wife's loving welcome, he can listen to you patiently, and not feel that you are adding to his worries, without in the least considering his quiet and comfort. "Oh," but I hear you say, "men themselves are selfish enough, and even the best of them are often inconsiderate."

Well, yes, I know they are, but that is neither here nor there. Men, as I think I have said before, are born selfish. Their position entails more or less selfishness; they are masters, and have to insist on certain things in order to keep their place as director of their household, and then, when they come home from their duties, perhaps worried, and with reason, they expect, and, as the bread-winners, merit every attention; they do not know what little things during the day are the cause of the household machinery going wrong, what bother their wife has had; it is in all probability very insignificant in comparison with their own, and so they grumble and growl as their right, and their wives consider themselves very hardly treated, and their husbands selfish cross-patches, and thus the harmony of a whole evening is turned into a discord.

Then again, I know of wives who insist on dragging their hard-working husbands out to ball, and concert, and dinner, night after night. The poor man goes out of good-nature, or perhaps because he considers it his duty as his wife's protector. He is very likely not a dancing man, or is too weary to dance, so he looks on at the whirling couples and listens to the deafening brass band, and thinks what idiots they all look. Who is the selfish one, think you? The weary-eyed husband, or the frivolous wife, laughing and talking inane nonsense to inane youths.

A dear little baby comes to bless the union of husband and wife. The former has desired and awaited the happy event with the same ardour and impatience as the latter. They look on each other with different eyes, they see themselves father and mother, and the authority of the husband seems doubled; and the young wife clothed with a greater dignity and grace. This dainty cradle becomes for a short time the centre of gravitation to the fond father; he comes home earlier, and stays out less, now that the cradle is filled by that strange little creature, the sight of whom stirs

Countess de Boerio, "Some Marriage Thorns, and How to Avoid Them" (Volume 14, 26 August 1893, p. 764).

his whole being. As he watches the young mother attending her babe, he feels that earth contains for him a no more beautiful sight than this; his heart is filled with a greater tenderness for his wife who has given him this treasure; he loves her the more for the child's sake; she is not only his wife, she is now the mother of his child.

Many a man's love and reverence for his "helpmeet" is kept warm by this fact. The little hands join the two together more firmly, there is no escaping them, and the sound of childish voices saying papa, mamma, has an irresistible charm for most men, and the lisping of these two words brings more completely before the husband's eye the union between himself and his wife, and out of gratitude for these loving little souls she has given him, does he cherish her the more tenderly, the more readily forgiving and forgetting faults which otherwise might perhaps estrange him from her.

A man may love his babies quite as much as his wife, but for all that he cannot give up his usual occupations, pleasures, and habits, as she does, and she must not expect it. Indeed, sad as it is to relate, from the arrival of the long-desired first-born often dates the estrangement of husband and wife. Taken up by the care of her baby, the young wife is apt to forget, as it were, the existence of her husband. She is never free to do anything he asks her, as formerly; he finds himself suddenly quite a secondary object. Those delightfully cosy evenings they used to spend together, talking or reading, are at an end; he sits alone now, she is in her room attending to "my baby." If he follows her there, he is either hushed up, and not allowed to speak or move, because "baby" sleeps, or he is the spectator of caresses, denied him, lavished on this unthinking object, and the listener of baby-language, of which a little at first strikes him as charming, but later on as arrant bosh.

What is the result of this conduct on the wife's part? He has patience for weeks, perhaps months. Then one night he suggests to his wife that he shall look in at the club. "Yes, do, dear, certainly," is the answer, perfectly indifferent as to whether he goes or stays. That man's thoughts as he walks to the club, if he is truly in love, as the saying goes, with his wife, are apt to be very bitter against her and his child, who has been made his rival. This is the beginning. Later on, when, as is sometimes the case, the new broom sweeps less clean, and the young wife turns from his child to her husband for companionship, he is no longer there. She abandoned him, now he abandons her. His rival and supplanter was his own child, hers are the club, gambling, theatres, what you will. She has lost her friend and companion, and often all her tears and reproaches are useless to bring him back; she has only herself to blame, as perhaps he will tell her bitterly, "As she has made her bed, so must she lie on it." He is accustomed to his present life, his taste for home has gone, and she may thank God if this is all, and he has not begun to tread the downward path to ruin.

Is this right, think you? Is this what God meant by holy matrimony? No! a thousand times no. It is written "It is not good that man should be alone." Is he not worse than alone, when after having tasted of home-life, after having enjoyed the companionship of the woman he loves, his "helpmeet," he finds himself suddenly put out in the cold and darkness, which is all the more dreary, because he has lately basked in sweet smiles, heard gentle, loving words, and been surrounded by every comfort fond attention could give him.

No, this is my principle, and I will uphold it against every challenger: husband first, children after. A woman need be no less a

good mother because she studies her husband's comfort and wishes before her children's. They are not likely to suffer from it as he does when he is put second, for he has thought for them and their pleasures as it is not possible they, always put first, can ever have for him.

Rejoicing in his wife's love and society, his children are his friends and companions, not his rivals; and thus every one in the family circle derive a benefit from the wife's tact and consideration for her husband. There is no isolation, only union as complete and as perfect as can be had on this earth.

Believe this, girls, take for once in your lives the advice of an old married woman, who has talked to you thus out of her own personal experience and observation. The first months of married life are more frequently than not the hardest, and much, nearly all, in fact, in ordinary cases, depends on the young wife's tact. Women don't need to be extraordinarily clever to make a man happy; an ordinary intelligence, backed up by tact, delicacy of sentiment, and patience, is quite enough. Indeed, if you want any more general rules as to your conduct as married women, read the last chapter of Proverbs.

The saying goes, "There is no rose without a thorn," and another, "A thornless rose has no perfume," * but neither are true. There is a thornless rose, and it has a faint yet subtle odour; pure white it is, and such, girls, let your married lives be. The white rose of a spotless life, fragrant with kind words and actions, and innocent as the white rose of thorns, of spite, and meanness, and impatience.

Act up to this, and you may be sure that your husbands will indeed find you precious, "far above rubies."

_____

* *Rose sans épines, n'a pas d'odeur.*

BLANCHARDYN AND EGLANTINE.

A ROMANCE OF THE MIDDLE AGES.

Transcribed by LILY WATSON.

CHAPTER IX.

WHILE the fortunes related in the last chapter were befalling Blanchardyn, Darius, the son of Alymodes, was waiting in his city of Cassidonie for tidings of those who had started with his prisoner on the journey to the King of Salamandry. But he waited in vain, since all but Blanchardyn were drowned in the sea, as has been told. When no tidings came, Darius could not understand it. He caused a great fleet to be made ready, and furnished with soldiers and artillery, that he might go back to help his father in the siege. He committed the charge of his city to his sister Beatrice, and sailed away with a favourable wind; but when the ships were near the realm of Tourmaday a

terrible storm came on, and the winds and the sea arose in such fury that Darius and all his folk feared instant death. They were driven far away from land, and tossed about until they were cast upon a little island, fair and fruitful, belonging to the kingdom of Friesland. So beautiful was this island that the King of Friesland, Blanchardyn's father, was wont to go there three or four times in the year for change and diversion, hoping to forget a little the great sorrow that abode at his heart for the loss of his son, of whom he had never heard since his departure. The Queen also had fallen into such melancholy on account of her absent Blanchardyn that no one living could rouse her and give her any comfort. This grieved her hus-

band greatly, and so, with a few of his people, he would come to the island to seek relaxation in a beautiful palace he had caused to be built.

It befell that he was staying there just at the time when the fleet from Cassidonie was driven into the haven nearest to the palace. Darius and all his men landed very early one morning, in great joy that they had escaped the perils of the deep, not knowing to what country they had come. They made their way to the palace, where they found three of the King of Friesland's servants. "To whom does this palace belong, and what is the name of the island?" they demanded.

With fear and trembling the men replied that the palace and island

_____

" But surely you don't mean to say that you have constituted yourself their guardian ? " cried the young man in astonishment.

" I cannot—I must not leave them at present, Charles," said Ella piteously.

" Come into the park for a few minutes. I will be responsible for your late appearance at the shop," said Charles Brierley ; and taking Ella's arm he led her to a seat under the trees in a park close at hand.

" Now, let us look this matter fairly and squarely in the face," he said. " I am not going to lose you for the sake of a chimera. If, as you told me some time ago, your salary is necessary to the comfort of those at home, surely out of my increased income, Ella, you and I can allow Mrs. Derwent and the children enough to keep them in comfort. We will do that instead of saving ourselves for the next few years ; at any rate, until the children are educated and able to support their mother."

" You are very generous, Charles," said Ella, with tears in her eyes. " But I must not impose such a burden upon you. We know not what the future may bring. There is nothing else for it. I feel that I must release you from your engagement."

" Nonsense, Ella. I cannot, I will not give you up ! "

" Need you go to South Africa, Charlie ? " broke out the girl impulsively.

A cloud came over the young man's face, and he said—

" Would you have me be a milksop, Ella ? "

" I did not mean that. I ought not to have said it. I am selfish," she faltered. " God will give us strength to bear this separation."

" But it is such an unnecessary separation," he retorted. " If I am willing to bear the responsibility of the maintenance of Minnie and the children, why should you invent unnecessary scruples respecting the matter."

" Money is not everything, Charlie," returned Ella, softly.

" No, it is not. I suppose love is something, though you seem to value it at a low rate," was the moody response. Then with a quick repentance he added, " I ought not to have said that, Ella, but you try me sorely. Think of all the loneliness of the future, dearest, of the long weary months without a sight of each other's face. Think of all that, Ella, and then send me away from you—alone."

The girl dropped her head in her hands, and the young man continued—

" God made us for each other, Ella. He gave us the power to love. Do you think He intended our lives to grow together, and then to be cruelly torn asunder ? "

Still Ella was silent with covered face and bowed head, and as he looked at her a sense of awe came over him. He knew by intuition that she was praying. Then a feeling of despair seized him, for he loved Ella Derwent with all the love of a strong, true, ambitious nature.

Presently the girl uncovered her face, and as he looked into her eyes he experienced a feeling of contrition. How could he press one who was evidently suffering so keenly ! Leaning towards her, he said—

" Ella, forgive me, you are braver than I ! "

Then he took the hand that lay limply upon her lap, and raising it to his lips pressed a kiss upon it, and was gone.

For a few moments Ella sat under the trees perfectly motionless. The sun was still shining overhead, and the leaves still whispered softly in the summer breeze ; but for Ella the aspect of nature had changed. She gazed across the park with bewildered eyes. Surely she would awake to find that the last half-hour had been a hideous dream—a vision of the night. But the dream would not be banished, and, rising from the seat, she hurried across the park.

Whether Charles Brierley had interposed on Ella's behalf she never knew, but no word was said respecting her late appearance, and as though guessing from her altered looks that something serious was amiss, her companions seemed to vie with each other in paying her little attentions.

(*To be continued.*)

PAYING VISITS.

By MARGARET BATESON (Mrs. W. E. Heitland).

PAYING visits is one of the special pleasures of girlhood. I do not mean to say that visiting is the exclusive privilege of girls, for, of course, it is not. Everyone stays with everyone, and it probably never was more the practice than now for people to visit about the country, spending a few days at one house, and a few at another. But middle-aged people, though they often greatly enjoy staying with their friends, do not set out to pay visits in quite the same spirit as does a girl. The time which they can spare from their home and business is limited, and reminders of their own affairs, in the form of correspondence, pursue them wherever they are.

But to a young girl paying visits is an occupation and an amusement in itself. To be staying in another house than her own is always somewhat of an adventure ; the habits and ways of other people are all new to her, and everything unfamiliar is noted by her fresh and observant mind. But a girl gains peculiar advantages from a visit, inasmuch as she usually becomes much more like a member of her host's family than an older guest, or even a young man, can do. She finds a place for herself in the family circle, and shares in all the occupations of the daughters of the house, gaining in this way a knowledge of the inner life of the household which is all the more valuable if up to this time she has seen little of the world outside her own home.

Visiting then may be regarded as a useful part of a girl's education, and it is certainly a very pleasant one. It has its own little difficulties, however, but these can usually be obviated if a girl understands what she is expected to do. The relations between host and guest are governed by common-sense, kindliness and good feeling ; and the rules which some writers on etiquette lay down with much precision are really of no great consequence. The general principle for the girl-visitor to bear in mind is that she

Margaret Bateson, "Paying Visits" (Volume 24, 6 December 1902, p. 150).

must adapt herself and her wishes to the convenience of her hosts. It ought hardly to be needful to remind a visitor that a friend's house is not an hotel. Nevertheless, there are persons who seem to forget this fact, and who inflict upon their friends all the inconsiderateness and selfishness of which unfortunate hotel and boarding-house keepers are the victims. Young visitors, however, commonly err more from ignorance of social customs than from any idea of making their friends' convenience subservient to their own.

One cause of possible difficulty is generally removed by the host, or rather the hostess, who, in writing to invite the visitor, should give some tolerably clear indication of the length of stay which she wishes her guest to make. If she says "a week-end," "a few days," "a week or ten days," the visitor will understand pretty well what is meant. I would only hint that the longer periods indicated should not be interpreted to mean the maximum in each case. An invitation for "a week or ten days" might be accepted for a week or the inside of a week; "some weeks" might be taken to mean a fortnight, and so on. But the important point is that dates, once fixed, should be adhered to. Only under most exceptional circumstances may visits be prolonged beyond the time originally agreed upon. I have heard of a visitor who came for a week-end and remained for years. Such persistency in staying must, to say the least, have upset his host's arrangements. For it is needful to remember, though the host may keep silence about the matter, that other guests have often been invited to succeed the present visitor, and that the host, in any case, has probably made some arrangements on the assumption that the guest would have left his house at the time fixed.

As the date of the visit draws near, the girl-visitor naturally writes to tell her hostess by what train she will arrive. She should try so to arrange the plan of her journey as to reach her destination some time between four and seven o'clock. This again simply means that she studies the convenience of her hostess by not letting her arrival interrupt the plans of the day. It is not necessary to make an iron rule upon the subject. Supposing a girl to be travelling straight through from Ireland or the Continent, it may be necessary to arrive in the morning. But a girl should bear in mind the fact that the arrival of a tired visitor during the business hours of the day is not likely to be convenient, and should therefore do all in her power to mitigate any trouble she may cause. The inexperienced visitor may also like to be reminded that she should be firm on the subject of paying for the cabs which take her to and from the station, whatever may be urged to the contrary by her entertainers. And while I am on the subject of conveyances, I may say that, supposing her hosts take her for a drive in a hired carriage, the visitor need not offer to pay her share of the expense, though she may do so—her hosts, however, probably not allowing it—if the taking of railway tickets for some expedition is involved. In general, a girl is on the safe side when she says, "I hope you will allow me to pay for my ticket," or whatever it may be. Young girls are sometimes rather severely criticised by people for mistakes that only arise from want of social knowledge, and many a hostess has censured a guest with "I think so-and-so takes all one does for her very much as a matter of course," when the hapless visitor has simply done nothing because she had no idea what she was expected to do. On the whole girls should try to show that they appreciate the kindness they receive, though the visitor who gushes all the while and invariably finds everything "too delightful" can be almost as wearisome as the silent girl who suggests that she is utterly bored throughout her visit. Girls should remember that rather more effort to please should be made by them than by older visitors, because they are not, as a rule, able to contribute so much to the general conversation.

Our visitor, having arrived, will probably be given some tea and then shown to her room. In the houses of wealthy people a servant generally offers to unpack for her. A girl whose wardrobe is somewhat limited finds this attention occasionally inconvenient. The one evening dress which she thought grand enough for a big party may be laid out for the first evening when nobody is expected; and never

do shabby petticoats and doubtful shoes look so humble as when the visitor feels that they have been exposed to the withering glance of a superior lady's maid. Young visitors, therefore, who have any misgivings about the completeness of their appointments had better decline to be unpacked for. The visitor, if she has arrived late, should remain in her room till dinner-time, and then go down into the drawing-room. That the guest should make every endeavour to be punctual at meal-times we ought hardly to need to say, yet there are persons who throw an air of fashion over their own selfishness by coming down persistently long after the bell or gong has sounded; while there are others, still more tiresome, who require breakfast and many intermediate repasts in the form of glasses of milk, biscuits, etc., to be taken to their rooms. Such persons put a great strain upon households with few servants.

A girl is often puzzled to know how much time she ought to spend in her own room. This is a matter upon which no law can be made. A girl who retires constantly to a cold bedroom may only make her hostess feel uncomfortable about her and show a misplaced politeness. But the visitor should always be able to efface herself during some of the morning hours at all events; and she can do this either by writing letters, or making a piece of fancy-work, or carrying on any occupation in one of the sitting-rooms, by which she relieves her hostess of the trouble of amusing her.

And she should always have some piece of lighter needlework to take up in the evening when there is only the home party. The hostess does not then feel that she must keep up an incessant conversation. Bedtime brings the question, "Who is to make the first move?" "The visitor" is the reply of strict etiquette. But in practice the hostess usually says on the first evening, "I do not know what time you are in the habit of going to bed, but you must not sit up later than you like," and the visitor can presently, on this hint, say good night.

One more visitor's puzzle is connected with her own private friends in the neighbourhood where she is staying. The common-sense rule is that the visitor consults her hostess before making any plans of her own. Friends may call upon the visitor without asking for the hostess; but the visitor should generally ask her hostess whether she may introduce these strangers to her. It often happens that a lady does not care to add to an already large acquaintance, and she may then make some excuse for not appearing in the drawing-room on occasions of this kind; but otherwise she will just make the acquaintance of the callers and exchange a few words with them.

As the visit nears its end, the visitor sometimes racks her brain on the subject of tips. But she really need not, for very little expenditure of this kind is looked for from quite young girls. Two shillings or half-a-crown given to the housemaid will be a sufficient acknowledgment of services during an ordinary visit, and a girl who has only stayed a night or maybe two nights may content herself with giving a shilling. Servants recognise that the majority of young visitors only have a small allowance, and they do not expect much from them.

Girls who are well off and are in the habit of staying in large houses may fittingly give with more liberality. Visitors of this class will give not less than half-a-crown to their host's coachman, if a private carriage has been placed at their disposal, and they may also give something to the lady's maid, if she has helped them in packing or dressing. In conclusion, the visitor should leave in the morning, for the same reason that she arrived in the evening, so that the day may be left clear for her hosts. And, of course, as soon after her return home as possible, she sends a little note of thanks in which she expresses gratitude for the hospitality she has received, but she need not say she "can never forget her hosts' kindness," that the visit has been "the happiest time of her life," or indulge in any of those excessive phrases which some uncandid guests employ.

Such are the chief rules to be remembered by her who sets out to pay visits. Yet if they are not strictly observed it is no great matter. There is only one rule that does matter, and this is to try to please and be pleased.

Margaret Bateson, "Paying Visits" (Volume 24, 6 December 1902, p. 151).

measurer "—and an examination of a thermometer made for outdoor use will show that a certain point or degree is labelled " freezing," and another " dew-point."

Now, although we speak of dry air or damp air, perfectly dry air is inconceivable under natural atmospheric conditions. As long as the atmosphere surrounding our earth can come in contact with a water surface, or a damp surface of any kind, the " air " cannot be dry, for evaporation is continually taking place between those surfaces and the surrounding atmosphere. Evaporation means that a part of the water is changing from the liquid into the gaseous form called vapour, and this vapour mixes with the air. A special machine, not unlike the thermometer in appearance and principle, has been invented to determine the relative amount of vapour in the air of a given place at a given time, and this is called a hygrometer. But the air cannot keep this water-vapour for an unlimited time or in unlimited quantities. The atmosphere is continually returning it to the earth from which it was received, and the return is made as dew, fog, mist, hoar-frost, rain, or snow, according to the temperature and other atmospheric conditions prevailing at the time of return.

Although air can be compelled to assume a liquid form under the double influence of extreme cold and extreme pressure, it does not naturally have any " substance." It cannot be grasped like a solid, or tangibly felt like a liquid. You cannot tread upon air or float upon it, and its power of supporting alien bodies is therefore very slight. Nevertheless, air has a certain power of supporting alien substances having weight, such as particles of dust or masses of water-vapour. But when the proportion of water-vapour held in suspension in the atmosphere reaches a certain point, the burden of it becomes too heavy and is returned to earth. The quantity of water-vapour which a given portion of space can contain at a given temperature varies with the temperature, and when this point is reached that portion of space is said to be " saturated." A saturated atmosphere immediately returns, that is, deposits, part of the vapour which it contains as soon as the temperature falls, and this deposit only ceases when the new point of saturation proper to the lower temperature is reached. This occurs because a part of the vapour " condenses " when the temperature falls, and thus becomes relatively more heavy as compared with the smaller space of atmosphere which it then occupies.

The form in which this condensation occurs naturally varies with the amount of the fall in temperature, and the rate of that fall. If a current of cold air comes in contact with a section of saturated and warmer atmosphere, the moisture in this is condensed, and becomes visible in the form of cloud or mist. But when a section of saturated atmosphere touches earth which is at a lower temperature, the condensed vapour is deposited in the form of dew, if the temperature of the earth is only low enough to cause simple condensation ; as hoar-frost, when the temperature of the earth is so low as to stand at the point which causes

the vapour to assume the solid form. After a warm day the land loses its heat more rapidly than the surrounding atmosphere, and thus we get the copious dew-fall of summer evenings. On frosty nights, however, the temperature of the earth falls below dew-point and reaches freezing-point, so that the vapour solidifies as it falls, and is seen next morning as hoar-frost.

Hoar-frost is the suspended atmospheric vapour deposited on the earth because the temperature of the earth is at or below freezing-point. Snow is formed for an identical reason. A cold air-current causes a cloud when it enters a part of space which is saturated with vapour at a slightly warmer temperature. When it is cold enough to condense yet more vapour, we get a fall of rain. When the cold air-current is at the temperature of freezing-point, or below it, the condensed vapour falls as snow.

Ice is formed when water in its natural liquid state is subjected to a temperature at or below the point at which water, or its vapour, congeals—becomes solid.

Snow and ice and hoar-frost are not, at first sight, identical. They are none the less both the same thing and due to the same causes.

Let us now turn to the first picture, representing the twig of a tree covered with hoar-frost. Seen thus closely, the dazzling white appearance, familiar to all who have seen trees on a frosty morning, explains itself. The twig is covered with a multitude of white crystals, so closely packed that on the edges alone can we see that the covering is no solid dress, but a composite garment formed of infinite small feather-like particles. A glance at the third picture shows one of these particles in isolation, and we at once see that it is no formless mass, but a most complex and very beautiful growth having the appearance of a fern. It is, in fact, not one crystal, but a vast agglomeration, or joining together, of minute crystals, and picture four adds yet further to our knowledge, showing us a " frost-flower " which must be of almost record size, since it measured more than twelve inches across.

How these crystals " grow " cannot be seen very well on the branch of a tree, where the space which can be covered is limited, and the crystals are consequently pressed close one against another. Thus no single " flower " can grow to its fullest possible extent without coming in contact with the petals of another " flower " ; and remember that these " flowers " are not single crystals, but an infinite number of crystals piled one upon another until they assume the flower form which we know, in a flattened state, as the " ferns " upon a frosty window-pane. Picture two was taken from a group upon a flat sheet of ice, where the " flowers " had " ample room and verge enough, the characters " of their nature " to trace." We see a perfect " flower," others in various stages of formation, and also many minute white dots. These dots are single crystals which, in time, will grow into full " flowers " by the addition of other like particles.

J. S.

TO GIRLS IN THEIR " TEENS."

By GORDON STABLES, M.D., R.N. (" MEDICUS").

THE very fact that you are a reader of THE GIRL'S OWN PAPER proves you to be a sensible girl in the main. That much praise at the very least is due to you. I should like also to believe that most of my innumerable girl-readers are thinking girls, and that they devote a portion of each day to quiet meditation. Though I do not expect them to be as serious as little nuns, still I could not have much respect for a girl who never gives her future in this world a single anxious thought. The world of her womanhood will come, when she may be a wife and a mother, or at all events have the care of a household. Whether or not happiness is to be her lot therein depends to a very great extent on what she does and what she learns while still in her younger teens.

If, then, girls, you spend your idle moments in reading

novels, nearly all of which give pictures of social life which are as unreal as the scenes in a modern drama, and if you base your notions of your coming life on these, I can only say, God pity and help you !

LIFE IS A VOYAGE.

Life is a voyage, and I hope it will be a long and pleasant one for all who read these pages. But much, oh, so very much, depends upon how your barque of life is built and ballasted, fitted and found. What would you think of the captain of a ship who should leave harbour and put out to sea without having everything right and ready, taut and trim alow and aloft, without having the best of sails and rigging, the best of provisions, and plenty of them, without

---

Gordon Stables, "To Girls in Their 'Teens'" (Volume 26, 5 November 1904, p. 106).

having a perfect rudder with which to steer, and well-adjusted compasses by which he might find his way with unerring certainty across the trackless ocean? You would think such a man very unwise, to say the least. Nor is a girl any wiser who, while young, neglects to lay up a store of precisely that kind of knowledge which shall best fit her to encounter the storms and squalls that shall rage around her, and to withstand the buffeting of the wildest waves that may threaten her barque with destruction.

While still in dock or in harbour, the captain of a ship that is soon to sail is the busiest of busy men, and his crew must be busy also. For on what is done then depend the comfort, the health, happiness and the very lives of himself and his people, as well as the success of the voyage. And mark this, the captain works with a will and with whole-heartedness, and he is really happy while so engaged. He is so impressed with the necessity of the duties that devolve upon him, that he needs no guiding hand to direct him, no word of encouragement to stimulate him, and so he sails away at last in peace and with the assurance of safety in his heart.

A MARKED CONTRAST.

Between such an officer as this and the more thoughtless of girls in their teens what a marked contrast there is! To lounge and to laze seem to be the chief objects of the lives of the latter. Their school hours, or those spent in learning useful home duties, are looked upon by them as the most tiresome and irksome of all the weary day. If their own wishes were to be consulted they would do absolutely nothing except read and play. Such a girl lives in a fool's paradise, comforting herself with the thought that some day some gallant hero will appear upon the scene, coming from somewhere and somehow, to throw his heart and fortune at her feet, and that she will live happy ever after that joyful day. But even should this hero heave in sight over the horizon, beauty alone—if such a girl can possess any—is but little likely to allure him. Men are chary nowadays of entering into the "holy bonds," and are apt to seek for something else than mere good looks. If a girl has money, even without other attractions, she may get a husband, but ten to one the marriage will be a very unhappy one as far as she is concerned; for from his point of view it has been one of convenience, or, I might say, commerce. I do not mean, however, to let this health sermon degenerate into an essay on marriage or love either, although I know a little about both.

But I must say this, that marriages of convenience have been the curse of France and are rapidly becoming the ruin of our own land. No happiness in married life is possible unless, as fishermen say, "love beats up the creel."

"Marry for love and work for siller (money)" is the one motto that has made Scotland so great and noble a nation as it is, and it is well known that her statesmen and soldiers and great engineers not only "run" England, but are to be found on the highest seats of honour in almost every country under the sun.

But, girls, don't lay yourselves out by dress and coquetry to attract men. I can assure you that men do not go by looks nowadays. As to dress, a man never knows what you wear—just the *tout ensemble*, just the general effect, perhaps, but no more. A man, if he be worth calling a man, is repelled by advances, and I must add, whether you like it or not, that he has small respect for girls who make them.

THE NEW GIRL.

There has arisen in this country of ours, and very recently, the new girl. Of course, she is but a second edition of the new woman. Just an imbecile off-shoot. But these new girls—and Heaven forbid that you, dear reader, should be one of them—foolishly imagine that they can go anywhere and do anything that young men do. To some extent the bicycle began it. But the idea of parental control or chaperoning is most distasteful to them. They imagine they can take care of themselves, and live a kind of "half-he" life without losing either caste or character. As a student of Sociology I can boldly affirm that they lose both.

A tom-girl up to the age of twelve or even thirteen is easily forgiven, but nine men out of every ten would fight shy, as far as matrimony is concerned, of tom-girls in their later teens or their sweet-and-twenties. A young man who wants to get married is, as a rule, a thinking individual, and he will think of his future, and take good care not to wed a flirt. For a flirt, or woman who adores flattery or high-flown compliments of the greasy French sort, which come but from the teeth forwards, will flirt after marriage as well as before; she would soon therefore lose the trust and therefore the love of her husband, and, after that, he would prefer male friends to her; he will spend longer evenings at his club, and become generally reckless. I am telling the truth, girls, in my own simple, sailor way. Of course you may know better, but really there are some things that even young people don't know.

LOOKING FORWARD TO HAVING A HOME.

"Be it ever so humble, there's no place like home." That is, if love dwells therein. But is love all? I think not, and, whatever the rich may do, the middle-class man cannot be long happy with a wife who knows nothing about household affairs. The girl will never make a proper wife who has not acquired a knowledge of all that is useful in a home long before she is married.

Some people will tell you that marriage is all a lottery. Not so much, say I, as one generally imagines. Married life will be like a placid river winding slowly through beautiful scenery under the rays of a summer's sun, if man and maid have both been ready for all its duties before the nuptial knot was tied.

Both husband and wife must be healthy. If they lack strength or have seeds of disease in their bodies, to marry were a crime.

They must be healthy and strong, and they must be good-natured and willing to bear and forbear, and help to carry each other's burdens.

But rest is essential sometimes, and the summer or autumn holiday should come like a blessing to both, and a good husband won't forget this.

HINTS FROM OTHER LANDS.

Although we—the "G.O.P."—have princesses who read our paper every month, it is not for them I write, nor for the wealthy either. As a rule, our princesses are humble, and, therefore, "ladies" in the sweetest sense of the word. The very wealthy, on the other hand, especially among the *nouveaux riches*, will go on their own little way in spite of anything I may preach. Don't envy them for their fine dresses, their French hats and made-up faces, not even for their motor-cars. It is not all gold that glitters, I can assure you. Many of them are mere weaklings, and even our old aristocracy—our sword aristocracy—would soon die out entirely if their ranks were not being constantly recruited by the strong and healthy among the middle-classes.

You girls have to look to yourselves, and you won't find that your face will be your fortune either, if you have no sterling worth to back it up with. Men-fools are, owing to the steady advance of education, getting fewer every year, and therefore marriages are becoming fewer also. A bonnie face is not such fine bait as it used to be. The young man on the outlook for a wife, unless he falls into his calf-love, and marries then, looks behind the scenes. Is the young lady with the bonnie face kind to her parents? Is she nice towards her little brothers and sisters? Does the star of honour shine in her heart even above that of love?

And, to come down a peg, does she know anything about housekeeping, anything about cooking, anything about sewing? In Norway, Sweden and Scotland no girl who has been brought up well would dream about entering into the holy bonds of matrimony who had not first acquired these useful arts. She is not fitted to be a wife until she has. She ought also to be able to nurse a sick person and be an adept in little matters of surgery.

Gordon Stables, "To Girls in Their 'Teens'" (Volume 26, 5 November 1904, p. 107).

MANNERISMS.

Nothing is so objectionable in a girl in her teens or sweet-and-twenties as little mannerisms visible in her gait or face. If I am walking behind a girl on the village highway, one whom probably I have never seen before, I can tell, before I pass her and cast a sly glance with the tail of my eagle eye at her face, whether or not she is a lady. However humble in circumstances a girl may be, mind you, she can be a lady in the truest sense of the word.

But concerning this lass behind whom I am walking, there are little pedantic movements about her body, little sways and jerks that show me, prove to me that she is self-conscious, proud in a manner, confident that she is a beauty, though she may not be. A lady walks gracefully and easily and calmly.

But bad and silly as mannerisms of body are, those of voice and face are ten times worse. Few girls can open their mouths in company without giving themselves away. No, nor look at you. Suppose a lassie's eye is sweet, soft and brown, or heavenly blue, is that any reason why she should roll them about like a duck in thunder, or like a snail that wears its eyes on the end of stalks? A lady's eyes are placid eyes, their motions involuntary.

Yes, you may have rosy lips and a mouth that isn't a bit too big, but, o'i, for beauty's sake keep it still! Smile if you like, but don't work your pretty mouth, nor purse it, nor screw it. This is abominable, and if you do, you'll soon have wrinkles all down your upper lip like the meridian lines on a map that converge towards the pole. Keep your eyebrows still. Don't wrinkle your brow. Be calm, be placid. Never laugh when you speak or read, be the yarn ever so funny, else you show your teeth too much and utterly spoil your beauty.

IDLENESS.

If my gentle readers only were aware what an amount of injury accrues to youthful bodies and youthful minds from idleness, they would avoid it as they would poison. Take the body first. A girl who idles and never takes pleasant happy exercise in the sunshine, or who reads the trashy love-serials of the every-day magazines, sitting and poring over them till her neck becomes cramped, soon gets deformed. Her spine gets bent forward like a raspberry cane, and her head refuses after a time to poise well. Her face wrinkles early, and she loses complexion because important organs of the body are all huddled together, as if in a tub. She gets stout about the waist, loses figure and never grows, or if she does grow, it is to lankiness and scragginess.

The mind suffers; it becomes languid and lax. In a word, body and soul go to the wall, and she becomes a mere weed in the world, in which she might be a thing of brightness and a joy to look upon.

Don't be idle. Time is short and there is much to do.

PHOTOGRAPHY.

By GEORGE W. HASTINGS.

PART II.

EXPOSURE.

THE next thing is to get ready for the actual taking of the photograph. For this it will be necessary to obtain some plates and insert them in the camera. Plates are made in varying speeds; some are more quickly acted upon by light than others, and so require a shorter exposure. The former are generally known as rapid plates, the latter as ordinary plates. For snapshots fast plates are essential, but for most purposes ordinary ones will do.

It will be well for the beginner to obtain a box of ordinary plates of the proper size for the camera. These will be found to be labelled " Only to be opened in a dark room or ruby light," and so it will be needful to choose some place which can be converted into a dark room. For the putting in of plates any room will do, provided daylight can be excluded. If preferred, plates can be put in at night; moonlight has little effect, especially if direct rays are not allowed to fall on the plate. Later on it will be of advantage to have a dark room fitted with a cupboard for chemicals, etc., and with a sink and tap. For the present purpose any small room or cupboard will do. As it is difficult to work in the dark, a red lamp may be employed; one with a big red chimney will do very well. If preferred, the window may be covered with red paper, or fitted with a sheet of red glass. In any case all daylight must be strictly excluded, or the plates will be ruined.

Before closing the door, the dark slides should be put ready, or the back of the camera opened for the insertion of the plates. With dark slides the business is quite simple. A plate is taken from the box and looked at by the light of the red lamp. It will be seen that one surface is shiny and the other dull. The dark slide should then be opened and the plate inserted with its face outwards, i.e., towards the shutter of the dark slide. If the slide is a double one, another plate is put in similarly and the slide closed up.

With a camera of the magazine kind, wherein several plates are carried, the case is different. Inside the camera will be found a number of metal sheaths which work in a groove. In each of these a plate must be put face outwards, and the sheath put into its place in the camera. Film cameras again have spools of film, or packs of cut films; nearly all cameras of this kind have a different system, usually very simple, whereby the spools or packs are inserted. Instructions as to their use are always given with the cameras.

When putting in plates it is well to lightly dust the film of each with a soft camel-hair brush. This often saves pinholes and such worries from occurring at a later stage.

As soon as the camera is charged, or the slides filled, the box of plates should be shut carefully, and the door may then be opened. The advice as to shutting the box may appear unnecessary, but beginners are inclined to forget this, and consequently the opening of the door results in the ruin of a number of the plates left in the box.

Now comes the actual taking of the picture, and this should be a matter of care, not a mere snapping of the first object that comes into sight. In the first place it is well to start on an inanimate object; not only is the

Self-Culture

Since the implied reader of *The Girl's Own Paper* is an unmarried "girl" between the late teens and early twenties, a good portion of the magazine was devoted to providing its readers with ideas for ways to occupy themselves profitably in the years between the schoolroom and marriage. A prominent focus was on self-culture. The magazine provided guides for reading, sheet music for instruments and vocals, and competitions for writing and fancy needlework, among other activities. Eventually, the magazine sponsored clubs for girls: for instance, the Erinna Club for girls interested in literature, and the Fidelio Club for musicians. The emphasis on self-culture was rarely progressive; the pursuit of self-culture was most often presented as preparation for matrimony and motherhood. It was a girl's duty to ensure that she would be a graceful and interesting companion for her husband as well as an intelligent teacher of her children.

"How to Form a Small Library" (vol. 2, 1880–81, pp. 7–8, 122–23), by James Mason, not only addresses the mechanics of building a library, but also presents a recommended reading list on a variety of subjects. In a bit of puffery it also recommends that girls read and collect *The Girl's Own*.

J. P. Mears's "How to Improve One's Education" (vol. 2, 1880–81, pp. 794–96) discusses reading for girls, filling gaps in a girl's education in English studies, arithmetic, English history, foreign languages and literature, music and drawing, and needlework and housework.

"Between School and Marriage" (vol. 7, 1885–86, pp. 769–70), by the Author of How to Be Happy Though Married, a telling title, notes that this time in a girl's life can be a difficult one. During the latter decades of the nineteenth century, the time for most girls between sexual maturity and marriage was expanding. This article encourages girls to continue to see marriage as their destiny and to develop their domestic skills.

The Girl's Own was fairly conservative in its recommendation of fiction. A number of essays warned against the dangers of bad fiction and against misreading. Mary Louisa Molesworth, a popular children's writer best known today for her fantasy *The Cuckoo Clock* (1877), tries to present a balanced view in "On the Uses and Abuses of Fiction" (vol. 13, 1891–92, pp. 452–54).

Dora de Blaquière's "Magazine and Book Clubs, and How to Manage Them" (vol. 13, 1891–92, pp. 710–11) typifies *The Girl's Own*'s encouragement of clubs for self-improvement. It always promoted the productive use of leisure hours.

"Self-Culture for Girls" (vol. 20, 1898–99, pp. 225–26) is the first part of a rather lengthy series, which includes detailed appreciations of particular poets and other authors. Space does not permit inclusion of the entire piece, but this first section is perhaps the most interesting. Lily Watson, a frequent contributor to the magazine, presents a detailed definition of self-culture and a rather high-minded argument why it is a necessary pursuit for all girls.

Lady Dunboyne's "Study" (vol. 26, 1904–05, pp. 312–13) is a good companion piece to Watson's. It shares a sensibility with the earlier piece, but focuses more on the personal benefit of study.

HOW TO FORM A SMALL LIBRARY.

" Books, we know,
Are a substantial world, both pure and good."
—Wordsworth.

IT would be easy to fill a whole number of this magazine with the good things that have been said from time to time about books and reading. Some of these have been far-fetched, no doubt, just as we find man's expressions inclined to extravagance when he speaks of her he cares for most, but in the main they are no more enthusiastic than the subject deserves.

In books, be it remembered, we have the best products of the best minds, and in such a form, too, that we can conveniently appropriate them for our own use. Through books we enjoy the companionship of the most noble spirits, not only of the present but of the past. Think of this, and you will be inclined to re-echo the words of Sir John Herschel, " If I were to pray for a taste which should stand me in stead under every variety of circumstances, and be a source of happiness and cheerfulness to me through life and a shield against its ills, however things might go amiss and the world frown upon me, it would be a taste for reading."

We must be fully alive to all the advantages of reading or we are not likely to be much interested in anything that can be said on the formation of a small library. Unfortunately, ignorance with its narrow views gives bad counsel in many a home, and the reading of books is often regarded as a refined species of trifling, instead of being, as it is, the most economical pleasure, and the most profitable of employments.

Those in the habit of observing what goes on in the circle of their friends will readily acknowledge that reading good books, if it does no more, at any rate does this, it raises the tone of the mind and purifies the morals in much the same way as the frequenting of good society. No one, it has been said, can write in a vulgar style who is in the frequent habit of reading the Bible, and the remark may be applied, though in a less degree, to all books. A girl becomes a reflection of the graces of her favourite authors, and though she may have no wealthy or aristocratic friends, if she moves at home in the society of Shakspeare and Milton she can never be commonplace, and will always make herself respected.

By reading, too, we learn how best to make our way in the world. Almost everything worth our knowing is to be found in books, and if a girl has to earn her own living, let her read till she makes herself mistress of all connected with the business in which she is engaged. This is a way to succeed that will seldom be found to fail.

The study of books, to mention another advantage, enables us to take our place with credit in society. When people meet together it should be to exchange ideas, and the trifling conversation one hears nowadays, in the company of otherwise very charming women, arises in a great measure from the fact that they have never acquired a taste for reading.

But one of the greatest charms connected with books is that by their aid we can support loneliness with tranquility. Take the case of a girl away from home, and working every day for her living amongst strangers. How invaluable books are to her, supplying her with the most friendly counsel, the most wholesome instruction, the most rational amusement, and the best of companionship. There are thousands of young women in London and other large towns, who, if they could only be induced to form a small library, would find in it the surest safeguard against the perils which surround their solitary condition.

We might show, also, how reading puts us in the best possible position for doing good in the world, and how the formation of a taste for it is one of the best preparations for the old age that will insist on coming all too soon. But the subject is one which you girls can work out for yourselves; so think it over, and you are all so sensible, that I anticipate your coming to the conclusion that every one who can afford anything beyond the necessaries of life should set apart a definite sum at regular intervals for books, and form the habit of always looking out for new ones.

You may have it cast in your teeth that you are nothing but a book-worm. Never mind ; have the answer ready, that a book-worm is one of the most respectable of worms, and that you are in company to be proud of. There is certainly one class of book-worm which I hope you will never be like ; to it belong all those who love nothing but books, and are so absorbed in them that they forget their duties in real life. But this sort of book-worm in our busy age is fast becoming an extinct animal.

A well-chosen library, growing larger year by year, is an honourable part of a girl's history. No one whose opinion is worth having, but will love and esteem her the more for it.

To all girls I say, never marry a husband who has not a collection of books of more general interest than his cash-book and ledger. The reading young man makes a stay-at-home fireside-loving husband. Like to like. Unhappily, it is not always so. The book-lover marries, and is linked for life to one who thinks books an encumbrance, and the money spent on them a waste. When he comes home with a newly-bought treasure he has perhaps—it is no overdrawn picture—to slink through the shrubbery, and drop his book in at the library window, before he goes round to his own front door to ring the bell.

Alas! It is a difficult thing to convince some people that there is any necessity for buying and owning books. They point out how many circulating libraries there are in the country, and how there are public libraries and free libraries everywhere for the express benefit of earnest students and those of voracious literary appetite.

Now the value of these institutions no one can deny. But the fact remains that to get real benefit from the best books we must buy them and keep them always beside us. Think of sending to a circulating library for a copy of Spenser, or Milton, or Dante, to be read and returned in fourteen days. No ; books like these are not to be run through as you would a volume of travels or a popular story. Books of reference, also—dictionaries, commentaries, and such like—we should own. Asking at the library for the loan of a dictionary would show about as ill-furnished a house as begging your next-door neighbour to lend you a teapot or a frying-pan.

However, though it cannot be stated too emphatically that no one who really loves books should abandon the pleasure of possessing them, and that, however small, everyone should have a collection of her own, we do not advise the neglect of circulating libraries. In them we find the literature of the day, and with that it is the duty of everyone to be more or less acquainted. We live in the present, not in the past, and if we are to be of any use in our time we must understand what is going on.

How many books should our small library contain ?

This is a question of considerable difficulty, but as we are bound to name some number, suppose we say fifty. Fifty volumes of good books form a respectable library, and they may be so selected as to contain a vast fund of beauty, wisdom, and information.

Of course, compared with the number of books that have been published, fifty is but a millionth part of a drop in a bucket. You might, if your tastes lay that way, gather together over a thousand volumes on the subject of chess alone, and  a fully-appointed library in theology must contain far over 30,000 volumes. But it is impossible to buy all literary works, and it is perhaps not desirable even to buy a great many, unless you wish your room to be like that of one of my friends, in which you cannot sit down for the books piled up on the chairs. Fifty will do very well to start with.

Fifty, then, be it. It will be a matter of great surprise if you stop at fifty. In book buying the appetite increases with every purchase. I began—if by way of illustration one may be permitted a scrap of autobiography —not so many years ago with modest notions and a handful of half a dozen books. Now I have considerably over four thousand volumes, and the modest notions have given place to extravagant visions of additional spoil. But none of you girls are ever likely to be in such a bad way. The famous founders of libraries have for the most part been old bachelors.

Now what will be the cost of our small library of fifty ? The purse of the fairy tales that was always full of gold and silver has either been lost, or the present possessor keeps it all to herself; otherwise, we might speak of cost with perfect indifference. But as it is, we must look the question in the face, and in times when people are reluctant to spend because money is hard to obtain, we shall do our best to be economical.

At one time books could only be obtained at great expense, but things have changed since then, and the best literature is to be had

TRUST

o you remember ? Yesterday was bright,
And fresh and fair ;
The sea was sunny blue—and rippled o'er
By soft sweet air.

" But look how those wild waves, foam-tipped and
Roll in to-day ;   [dark,
Listen how sadly those great restless winds
Howl round the bay.

" Their moan and roar *will* strike upon my heart
With sudden pain ;
Oh ! will my boy—my bonny sailor boy
Come back again ? ''

*   *   *   *   *   *   *

" O faithless heart ! be still. For God is God
As much to-day
As when the world and sea and sky were fair
And bright and gay.

" Are not the winds His messengers of Love,
Doing His will ?
' His path is in the sea,' and His dear voice
Has said, ' Be still.'

" And He can say it now. Trust then, O heart !
And be at rest ;
Your sailor boy is in His Father's hands,
And *must* be blest.   G. M.

pleted her fifty books for eight years, but she will know them in the end quite as thoroughly as it she had bought them in two, and that is the great matter.

It is impossible to gather together a library, however small, without making some sacrifice for it. And the books are all the dearer if to purchase them we have denied ourselves something. Reduce the amount you spend in dress, if that can be done without ceasing to be tidy and respectable, and your library is already gained and an incalculable addition made to your chances of happiness and usefulness.

There is no reason why we should not buy almost all our books second-hand ; it makes a great difference in the expense, and the books are often none the worse for having previously formed part of another's library. Avoid, however, forming a ragged regiment. There is a joy in thumbing one's own books out of existence for oneself, but none in using books half thumbed out of existence by other people.

The best plan in buying second-hand books is to make the acquaintance of some large dealer who has a general stock which he is frequently turning over, not one who deals in any particular class of books. Tell him the books you wish to buy, and if you have any skill in the art of management, you will not be long in making his experience of material service to your inexperience.

You cannot buy expensive editions; that is understood. But, after all, we want books to read, not to look at, and they will serve our turn if they are so clearly printed as not to try the eyes. At the same time, it must be acknowledged that there is a real enjoyment in reading a fine edition, and it would be affectation to say that we would not invariably buy the best copies if money were always at command.

Neither can you indulge in extravagant bindings. Dictionaries and books that are frequently handled should have strong leather binding ; for all others the ordinary cloth is good enough. Some people who have only a half-hearted interest in paper and print, recommend that we should never bind up our magazines. On the other hand, bind up everything, say I, magazines, pamphlets, prospectuses, and programmes. You have no idea of what interest a few such odd volumes will become in the course of a few years.

While on the subject of magazine literature, we might mention that every girl should by this time have had the numbers or parts of the first volume of the GIRLS' OWN PAPER bound up, so that they may not become dirty and untidy-looking. Every girl who is not extravagant, and who wishes to make the best use of her paper, should have the " Annual " already on her bookshelf, so that, with the aid of the index, she might be able to refer to any information that has already been printed relating to matters requiring immediate attention. This is the more important to a wise girl, as it is the editor's intention to decline to repeat any assistance or instruction that has already been imparted in the first volume.

Now we can speak about the bookcase—the house in which our family of books is to be lodged. About it there is no great difficulty, for fifty books do not require much space. Between sixty and seventy inches of shelf-room will be quite enough for that number. We must, however, provide extra accommodation for library books, and for books borrowed from friends, as

at a figure which it is no exaggeration to say is no cost at all. The fifty books will cost, on an average, two shillings apiece ; thus five pounds will cover the whole library. It might even be done for less, but in giving a quotation it is better to err on the safe side. Should it cost quite five pounds, it will, I hope and believe, prove the best investment of that sum you ever made or can make.

The five pounds need not be paid out all at once ; indeed, ought not. The accumulation of your library should be spread over a long time, or it is not likely to do you much good. Besides, what is the pleasure of going into a bookseller's shop and ordering fifty books to be sent home in a box, compared with the delight of paying the bookseller visit after visit, looking over his shelves, picking out treasure after treasure, and carrying them home in your hand ?

You might begin by laying aside for the purposes of your library, say a shilling a week. What would be the result ? A shilling a week makes fifty-two shillings in a year, and amounts up to a hundred and four shillings—more than the five pounds you require by four shillings—in two years. If a shilling a week is too much, say sixpence, and if a girl cannot spare sixpence, there is no reason in the world why she should not set aside threepence. True, she will not have com-

well as for magazines and other periodicals, so I think we would not make quite a satisfactory start unless we had at least nine feet of shelving. This would not be a tight fit.

But beware of having too much space. Nature abhors a vacuum, and so does every well-regulated mind detest a bookshelf with nothing on it. Many a one has been seized by all the symptoms of bibliomania just from possessing a bookcase a few feet larger than he actually required.

The material of which the bookcase is made should, according to the laws of artistic furnishing, be the same as the principal furniture of the room in which it is to stand. Circumstances, however, must be our guide, and as I am always in favour of economy, especially in starting a new pursuit, my advice is in favour of a bookcase at first of the cheapest wood that looks respectable.

There is not much choice in the matter of form. The hanging bookshelves and the dwarf bookcase shown in the illustrations on the previous page are very neat, and will be found to answer admirably, whilst they are so simple in construction that a girl's brother, if accustomed to the use of tools, might put them together in a few spare hours.

We have now discussed the accommodation for our books. Next, about the books themselves. What are the fifty to be ?   JAMES MASON.

James Mason, "How to Form a Small Library" (Volume 2, 2 October 1880, p. 8).

HOW TO FORM A SMALL LIBRARY.—II.

WE agreed, you may remember, to aim at accumulating a library of fifty books. Now what these fifty are to be is a nice question, for a great deal depends on the character and education of the people who are to read them.

The poet Southey once drew out a " list of a gentleman's necessary library," and the works he put in it were the Bible, Shakespeare, Spenser's " Faerie Queen," Sidney's " Arcadia," the works of Sir Thomas Browne, the works of the Rev. Cyril Jackson, Walton's " Complete Angler," Clarendon's History, Milton, Chaucer, Jeremy Taylor, South's Sermons, and Fuller's " Church History." These are all good books, and one of Southey's scholarly tastes might think his bookshelves completely furnished with nothing else ; but it is doubtful whether we, who are less sedate, would care for five books out of the whole thirteen.

Perhaps the poet would have been as little satisfied with the following " list of a girl's library ;" but if you, girls, are pleased that is enough.

The longer I think about the fifty, the smaller the number seems to be. Let none of you run away with the impression that a little book-case can contain all the literature of worth in the world. Even had you ten times that number you might well heave a sigh at the consideration of the number of works of beauty and glory of which you have not so much as turned over the leaves.

Many of our books will be necessary ones, but others I shall mention only "on approval." They are recommended, certainly, with all the enthusiasm with which one introduces his best friends : but if a girl desires to read other books, then those others are likely to do her most good, so let her buy them, after taking counsel with some friend whose judgment she respects.

In selecting the fifty I have tried to put it to myself in this way : Suppose I were Mary, or Kate, or Alice, and banished— of course for nothing at all — to a desert island, what books would I carry with me of a useful and fairly representative kind, so that the time might be pleasantly and profitably spent till remorse attacked my oppressors and urged my recall ? Here they are :—

The first is the Bible, the best of books and a library in itself. " Turn it, and turn it again," says an old writer, " for everything is in it." The Bible should form the keynote of every collection, and all the rest should be in harmony with it. Get a good edition, with notes, and strongly bound, so that it may stand constant handling.

Whoever sets a high value on the Bible will welcome every aid to the understanding of its sacred pages. The best of all helps in this way is " Cruden's Concordance," of which there are several cheap and serviceable editions to be had.

Of other religious books to be placed beside the Bible and the Concordance, we shall choose five. The first is the " Pilgrim's Progress," the work of the " prince of dreamers." No other book in the English language, the Bible alone excepted, has, as everyone knows, obtained so constant and so wide a sale.

Besides prayer-book and hymn-book, you should have a good manual of daily devotional reading. Bogatzky's " Golden Treasure " is an old favourite, and one of the best of those recently published is " The Daily Round." The " Book of Praise," edited by Lord Selborne, is one of the best collections of sacred poetry. With the concordance, I ought to have mentioned the new Companion to the Bible, published at 56, Paternoster-row, a little book, with much information on scriptural subjects. The Bible Handbook of Dr. Angus is also of great value.

We have now decided on seven books, but perhaps we have gone ahead too fast. We should, maybe, have begun by speaking of what are strictly utility books, books not for reading but for reference. These form a good solid foundation for a library.

There must be a Dictionary of your own language, of course, and let it be the best you can afford to buy. When you get it, too, use it, and never fall into the lazy habit of making a guess at a word whose meaning you do not know. As a supplement to the dictionary, you must have a good work on English Grammar ; including, if possible, a sketch of the history of the language. When on the look out for this at your second-hand bookseller's, do not buy the first that offers merely because you have not patience to wait till another turns up. The best and most satisfactory purchases are often only to be made by waiting.

Next comes a Dictionary of Dates, which will give you in a disjointed fashion the history of the world. To this should be added the " Elements of History," and from it you will gain a correct idea of the orderly progress of events.

A Dictionary of Biography cannot be done without ; neither can a Gazetteer, and we can as little dispense with an Atlas. Let these books be of recent date ; give the cold shoulder indeed on every occasion to antiquated books of reference. They are little better than waste paper.

You must now narrow your views, and having what will represent in a general way the places, the biography, and the notable events of the whole world, invest in a History of your own country ; it must be the best your purse can afford. But stay, we said that when speaking of the dictionary. It is, indeed, a rule applicable to every book bought for your library.

Whose history should it be ? Why, my friend, if I were to name an author for this, or for many another of these books, it would be of small use. If we had started with the understanding that you were going to buy them all new it would have been different. As it is, you must take the best that present themselves, and may fortune send you a happy choice !

A Handbook of English Literature will come in nicely now, giving short notices and specimens of all the famous authors who have adorned the past. This is a most interesting branch of study, one rich in everything that can enlarge the mind and improve the heart. There is none better than the Handbook of Dr. Angus, and its companion volume, " Specimens of English Literature."

An Atlas and Geography you must possess ; Milner's Geography, new edition, by Keith Johnston, is the best. Add next a Guide to your own town or county, so that you may take an intelligent interest in your own immediate neighbourhood.

In Biography there is an immense number of books one would like to have, and all the more so because in biography we have one of the most valuable aids in the formation of character ; but we must be satisfied with three. There is Plutarch's " Lives " to start with, a readable, medicinal, invigorating book, which is not to be spared from the smallest library. When I name it I always remember how Alfieri, the great tragic poet of Italy, read it with such enthusiasm that he was afraid the people in the next house would think he was mad. The second is Boswell's " Life of Johnson," and let the third be some collection of the lives of eminent women.

Amongst volumes of Essays we may select as many as we did of biographies. The first are those of Lord Bacon, a book containing a great fund of useful knowledge and displaying a more intimate acquaintance with human life and manners than perhaps any other. " It may be read," says the great Scotch philosopher, Dugald Stewart, " from beginning to end in a few hours, and yet, after the twentieth perusal, one seldom fails to remark in it something overlooked before." Then there is the " Spectator " of Addison and Steele, an inexhaustible mine of humour, invention, and good counsel ; last of all, we must have the Essays of Lord Macaulay.

What about Poetry ? Now we feel pinched, indeed, for room, and filled with alarm lest we should not be compelled to make another shelf. Let us begin by getting a good general Collection of English Poetry. There are several good ones to be had, books which will familiarise us with the names and highest efforts the chief writers of verse of our land.

We must next make the acquaintance of the ancient heroic world by purchasing and reading Pope's translation of Homer. The defects of this translation have often been pointed out, but its merits, too, are great. The only objection which you who are so gentle-minded are likely to find with it is one that belongs to the subject, and not to either the poet or his translator ; the Iliad, at any rate, has rather much fighting in it.

The next whose works you must buy is Shakespeare, the greatest dramatic poet of the world. Then comes Dante, in whom the Middle Ages found a voice, and of Dante the most readable translation is Cary's. We must not forget the gentle Spenser either, or Milton, and these are all the poets I shall insist upon. They are five of the greatest of the great. Read them, and as you do so thank heaven for having sent such genius to brighten, elevate, and purify the lives of men.

But you may wish to add other poets, for one is sometimes most in love with lesser lights. Choose, therefore, three others, whom you please. Cowper, Wordsworth, Tennyson, Longfellow, and Scott might be suggested, and pray don't forget the " holy George Herbert."

How are we getting on now ? We have named thirty-five books in all, and after enumerating fifteen more shall be at the end of our tether.

To fiction we shall devote five books. One will be " The Vicar of Wakefield," and this, by the way, you may meet with bound up in the same volume with Goldsmith's Poems, and some of his dramatic and miscellaneous works. Thus you will increase your collection without infringing the rule as to the fifty. The remaining four should be one story by Scott, one by Dickens, and one by Thackeray— say "Pendennis," "David Copperfield," and "Vanity Fair," and one favourite —you will yourself name who he is to be. What! no? You ask me to choose, do you? Then, I say, a good translation of Grimm's "Fairy Tales," for the enjoyment of which all happy people can never grow too old. These will supply more nourishment to the imagination than half the novels in Christendom.

This will be a delightful corner of our library, but we must not be too much taken up with it. The rule, as somebody says, should be this—"Mix light reading with serious reading, so that the one shall not engross nor the other weary."

Good Letter-writing is a rare accomplishment, and one book may be named as a model in this department. Critics of most opposite tastes, Southey, Jeffrey, Robert Hall, have all pronounced the poet Cowper the most charming of letter-writers. An edition of his selected letters, with memoir, and notices of his correspondents, is published at the office of this paper.

In Science we must have something, and the most charming work in this line I know is White's "Natural History of Selborne." Get it by all means, and it will teach you, as it has already taught many, to be a close observer of nature and an enthusiast for rural life. Add to this one work of a thoroughgoing character on any science for which you have a decided taste: botany, zoology, astronomy, or anything else.

Now we come to miscellaneous books, and of these you would do well to have three at least: a Dictionary of Quotations, a Book of English Proverbs, and a Collection of Anecdotes. These are all food for thought, and most valuable for such as know how to use them.

Of "home books" you must have three also. Let one be a sensible work on Cookery, another a book on Domestic Management, and the third a Guide to the Preservation of Health and the cure of simple ailments. These all treat of subjects belonging to the sphere of woman, and you will relish the poets none the less for knowing the best way to boil potatoes, lay the fire, or bind up your little brother's cut finger.

An almanack is hardly to be reckoned in our list, being usually of pocket size; but if a book, let it be "Whitaker's Almanack," the completest and best.

You are musical, of course; so your forty-ninth book — for we have really come to the forty-ninth — should be a thorough-going treatise on the Theory of Music, another special subject for girls.

And the fiftieth; what is that to be? What should it be but THE GIRL'S OWN ANNUAL? Modesty makes the Editor insist that I should put it last, but we all know how high a place it deserves to hold. It is true that all our other books differ from THE GIRL'S OWN ANNUAL in this, that they may be had in one volume, whereas, in the course of time, there is no saying to how many volumes our magazine may grow. "But," says Mary, "never mind that; we shall shut our eyes to the peculiarity you have mentioned, and, whatever number of volumes we possess, we shall always reckon them just as one book." Thank you, Mary; you are a very nice example of woman's ingenuity.

Now our library is complete. Complete, at least, for the present; for, as I said before, the appetite for books grows by what it feeds on. In these fifty books you have a little collection representing the best thought of all

time, and containing an immense store of the most useful information, and no one who possesses it and uses it can fail to lead a happy intellectual life—a life, too, that may exercise some good influence in the world.

But never forget that many of the books just named are not of necessity the right ones for you. I hope you will in the end let them all rank with your best friends; but never, no, never, form a library on a plan suggested by somebody else without regard to your own inclinations. If a library is worth anything, it should faithfully represent the tastes and aspirations of its owner. It should be such that a stranger coming in and looking at it might say with confidence either, "There are many points of contact between that girl's mind and mine;" or, "I am sure that girl and I will never get on, for she cares for nothing that I like and likes nothing I am keen upon."

You may say that we have made our library hold more books than we can ever hope to read. I do not think so; but what matter if we have? To own more books than we can read, is one of the conditions of intellectual growth. Our minds expand even by the contemplation of the subjects we cannot master and the authors with whom we can never hope to grow familiar.

Having started your collection, keep it in good order. Keep everything in order, but especially your books. Have them neatly arranged according to size, placing the biggest on the bottom shelf as ballast. Were your library larger, I would recommend placing the books by subjects; but you will be able to run over the whole fifty in a minute, so it is not necessary, and I expect you to handle them so often that you will be able to pick them out blindfolded or in the dark.

Keep a catalogue, and whenever you bring home a book enter it; and whenever you lend one enter it also, with the date and the name of the friend who has borrowed it.

On the subject of lending, do not cease from indulging in this kindly practice because of some unhappy experiences. I sometimes think there is a great deal of false delicacy shown in not asking the borrower to return a book when one thinks she has had it long enough. It has been suggested that at Christmas one should devote some time to searching for borrowed books and returning them to the owners. This would certainly add another charm to the festive season.

Enter all the books you borrow in an appendix to your catalogue. This is a useful practice, and in the course of time you thus secure an interesting record of all the books which have passed through your hands.

BITS ABOUT ANIMALS.

JOHNNY AND PEACOCK.—These were a pretty little pair of horses, that ran together in a carriage. They were merry little things, full of tricks and capers; but as docile and free from vice as possible. Very often, when out together, it was noticed that Johnny would give Peacock a sly kick, not enough to hurt him, but certain to be followed by a start forward and more rapid trot. This was observed again and again, and at last the coachman was asked what Johnny meant by thus assaulting his companion. "Peacock is a little bit lazy sometimes," said the man, "and does not take his honest share of work; but Johnny is a cute little fellow, and not to be done; so he just gives him a slight kick whenever he catches him lagging. Peacock knows what he means quite well, and starts off at a proper pace to keep alongside his mate, or he would soon get another and harder kick."

POLLY, THE BLIND MARE.

WHEN returning home in a cab, one day, I was much pleased with the kind and gentle manner in which the cabman treated his little mare. No whip was called into use; but now and then he cheered her on with a chirrup, a little shake of the reins, or a "Come up, Polly," which she responded to by a brisk toss of the head and more rapid trot. There seemed to be a positive friendship, as well as a perfect understanding, between the mare and her master; and, as I took out my purse to pay the man, I could not help expressing my pleasure at seeing the humane manner in which he treated her.

"No need of a whip for Polly, ma'am," said he, his face quite lighting up as he patted her sleek sides. "She's as gentle and loving as a little dog, and I should be sorry for her to have a smart of my causing. Have you noticed, ma'am, that Polly is stone blind?"

I certainly had not; and when I thought of the manner in which the mare had threaded her way, in and out, amongst all the horses and vehicles in the busiest part of Manchester, I was astonished to find that Polly had never been able to see.

"She's the best little thing that ever was," said the cabman, "and so sure footed she never slips. Many of my lady customers would rather have Polly in the shafts than any horse going, and ask for her to take them to the city. She's quite a pet, too, and often gets a piece of bread from the ladies. If we go to a house where she has once had it, she knows as well as I do, and she turns her head to the door and waits and listens for somebody to bring her a bit again. Polly's very fond of bread."

I took the hint, and brought out some bread, which the pretty creature took from my hand as gently as a child—I mean a polite child—would do. While she was munching it she kept turning her sightless eyes towards her master, and, guided by his voice, moved near enough to let her now and then place her head over his shoulder with a caressing touch, to which he always responded with a "Poor old Polly," or a pat.

I observed this scene with great pleasure, and my sympathy encouraged the man to tell me still more about Polly.

"She is just petted like a dog by the children," he said; "and when we are at dinner in the kitchen, which opens right into the yard, she will come and pop her head in and then step towards the table to be fed from their hands.

"I've a little thing, only a twelvemonth old, and she always will give Polly some broth or milk out of her spoon, and it looks so funny to see Polly taking it. Then baby gives her such small pieces of bread out of her little hand, that you would wonder she could take them without hurting the child; but she never does. She would rather drop the nicest bit than hurt the baby. We are never afraid, and the mare goes about the place like a dog; we never fasten her.

"Polly will never forget this place, ma'am. You have talked to her and given her bread, and she will know your voice as well as possible whenever she may hear it."

The mare had by this time finished her lunch, and the master, with a "Good morning, ma'am, and thank you for Polly," started on his way. Not on the box, though. He only said "Come on, old girl," and the pretty mare, guided by his voice alone, walked after her master, never deviating from the path or stepping on the edge of the lawn, until they passed the entrance gates and were lost to sight.

I always remember Polly and her kind master with peculiar pleasure, and wish that every one who had to do with horses displayed as much humanity towards them as did the kind-hearted cabman towards his little mare.

James Mason, "How to Form a Small Library" (Volume 2, 2 November 1880, p. 123).

HOW TO IMPROVE ONE'S EDUCATION.—II.

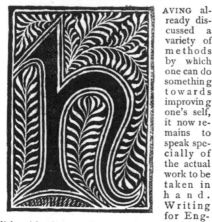

AVING already discussed a variety of methods by which one can do something towards improving one's self, it now remains to speak specially of the actual work to be taken in hand. Writing for English girls, it scarcely seems necessary to remind them that they should know their own language well, and that excellence in English studies should be our *first*, though not our only, aim.

I. ENGLISH STUDIES.

To be a fair English scholar it is necessary *to be able to speak and write in a clear and correct manner*. Elegance and grace of style may be added to these, but though they charm us much they are not absolutely essential, while clearness and accuracy are altogether indispensable. To procure these qualities one requires a good sound knowledge of *English grammar and analysis of sentences*. When one always associates with well-educated people, one naturally acquires the habit of good speaking; nevertheless it is really essential that one should know and be able to apply the laws of language. Unfortunately, the study of English grammar has not always been made as easy and clear as it might be, and it is more than probable that many readers of this paper have decided that grammar is "very dry"; to these especially we would say that the subject is most interesting, and will not only repay you for any labour you may bestow upon it, but will give you much pleasure. Of the most clear and useful books on this subject, and most to be depended upon, the following may be named: "English Grammar and Analysis, arranged in a series of lessons for home use," by George Gill, price 2d.; "English Grammar," by Dr. Morris, 1s., published by Macmillan in the Primer Series; "Mason's English Grammar," published by Bell and Daldy; "Morell's English Grammar and Analysis," published by Longmans, London; "The Handbook of the English Tongue," by Dr. Angus, published by the Religious Tract Society, 56, Paternoster row. The two first of these are quite easy books, anyone may understand them; the last is for more advanced students, and "Craik's History of the English Language" is a useful book to study with it. All these books may be consulted with advantage; but it is not necessary to use them all to attain to a satisfactory degree of proficiency, while it is possible that many of our readers already possess some of them without actually knowing their worth. Having studied well the use of every word, and acquired the power of applying the rules of syntax, the next phase of our work lies in reproducing our own thoughts, of putting down for the eye to see what the mind has taken in. This is really what we call *composition*. No one who has studied her grammar well can write incorrectly, though it is not equally easy to all persons to find words to express their thoughts at once. A few hints here: Make up your mind what you want to say, and say it in the simplest

manner possible. Never use a long hard word when a short easy one answers exactly the same purpose. Never use a word of the meaning of which you are not quite sure (look in the dictionary if you have a doubt). Avoid long sentences. In writing letters be perfectly natural, and write as you would speak if the person to whom you are writing were present.

Style in composition depends largely on the command of language that one has, that is, the number of words that come readily to one, as well as one's power of imagination. A good style may be best obtained by the careful reading of well-written books, and by trying to write from memory abstracts of what one has read. A good rule, too, to be observed in speaking is to avoid careless and inelegant speeches, and to speak as if what were being said were going to be put into print at once. The habit of exact, methodical speech, and of writing, in the most choice language, may be acquired by all who will take the pains to do so. Of the art of composition, Angus gives much help in the book already mentioned, and there is a composition primer in Macmillan's Series. A book on "English Composition," by Johnson, for pupils preparing for examination, and published by Longmans, also contains a good deal of useful information, put in a simple manner, and the specimens of exercises or short essays written by pupils is encouraging, and shows what can be done by ordinary people in this way. Of course it is not expected that these should all be perfect, and many girls doubtless will be inclined on reading some of them to say that they are not very good. Some at least will be encouraged by the use of this book.

Before proceeding further, it would be well here to remind the reader that though several books will be named on each subject of study, it is not in the least intended that they should all be consulted at the same time. The intention is rather to help the *many*, which must include students in various stages of mental growth; as well as to cover the ground of the various books which may already be in the hands of those who read this, and therefore to save expense in buying what is necessary.

To the student who works alone we will advise the use of one or two books at a time, and these mastered first, then a wider reading. The case is quite different where a good teacher is at hand to reconcile and explain the apparent differences which exist in different books on the same subject.

2. Of ARITHMETIC every girl should have some *practical* knowledge. One must keep up the practice of bills of parcels, the use of weights and measures, the working out of sums for wall-papering and carpeting, as well as know something of interest and stocks. All bills should be tested, and no girl who has the full charge either of her own or another's money should think of spending it without keeping a strict account. It should be easy also to calculate how much the odd ounces of the meat should come to, as well as the quarters of yards of dress material, &c.

3. ENGLISH LITERATURE, too, is a necessary part of a complete education, and much may be added to the store of knowledge on this subject during the *whole of life*. A knowledge of the chief writers of our country, with the time in which they lived, and the kind of work they wrote, should be perfectly familiar to us; and of the most important among them one should know something from direct reading of their style. The powers of observation and comparison should be sufficiently trained to help each one to form an opinion for herself, in preference to repeating the opinion of another, though much deference should be given to the opinions of well-read

people. "Chaucer's Prologue," at least, should be well studied among the old writers; Spenser's "Faëry Queen," should not be a stranger to us; and Sir Philip Sydney's book on "Criticism," Bacon's "Essays," and some other writings of those times, should be quite mastered. Of course, Shakespeare will be widely read. The separate plays published in the Clarendon Press Series, with notes, are very useful for those who *study* Shakespeare, a work which gives immense pleasure and profit. Some of Milton's prose works, as well as his poetry, the poems of Dryden and Pope, and Johnson's "Lives of the Poets," should be read. One should also know something of the works of Addison, Defoe, Scott, Wordsworth, Coleridge, Southey, Charles Lamb, Burke, Cowper, Jane Austen, Lord Brougham, Tennyson, Thackeray, Dickens, Miss Mulock, Maria Edgeworth, Macaulay, and many others too numerous to mention here. It is of mental culture only that we are now treating, and we therefore do not specially name religious books, doctrinal or devotional, which have their own higher claims.

To study carefully English literature, Stopford Brooke's "Primer," in Macmillan's Series, will be found a great help, both to those who know very little and to more advanced pupils. "Chaucer to Wordsworth," by T. Arnold, published by Murby, is a larger and most useful work. "The "Biographical History of English Literature," in Morell's Series, published by Longmans, is prepared specially for students who are not very advanced, and has many helps in the form of questions and notes. Angus's "Specimens of English Literature," a companion volume to his "Handbook of English Literature," also will be found most valuable. Nothing, however, should deter students from reading *some* of the best works of our great authors for themselves; the common practice of reading some other person's view of a book, and of giving it out as one's own, is by no means to be admired. Honesty in this, as in every other work of life, will bring its own reward.

4. ENGLISH HISTORY, like English literature, forms a wide field of study; but intelligent reading in a systematic manner will abundantly repay all who will make up their minds to read up this subject for one or two hours a week. For those who feel they know very little on the subject, Edith Thompson's little book will be a pleasant teacher; but there are so many good books on English history that it is difficult to say which is best. It is only right, however, that no one should expect any single book to be perfect. "The Student's Hume" is one of the long-established histories, and those who *know it well* maintain that it is too useful to be set aside for more modern works. "Green's History of the English People" is a most enjoyable book, but unless the reader is fairly well informed on history, she will find after reading it that she does not *retain* a clear and comprehensive view of the subject. This book should most decidedly be read; but it should be used as the companion of "Student's Hume," which is quite different in style. "Bright's Public School History of England" is certainly one of the best books that can be used; but there are three volumes, costing respectively 4s. 6d., 5s., and 7s. 6d.

In studying history it is a very good plan to fix upon a certain period, a reign, or a dynasty for instance, and get up very thoroughly all its details. The lives of the chief men taking a prominent part in the history of their time should be read from another source where not sufficiently related in history; the literature of the time should be read where possible with the history of the time in which it appeared; Shakespeare's historical plays should be read side by side with the history which they represent, and so on. The "Epochs of History" (Longmans) will here be of great use.

Every student of history should read Dr. Arnold's "Lectures on Modern History," as well as those of Professor Smyth : they could be obtained from any good library, and are valuable as showing what great teachers of history think to be necessary, and also in helping us to form judgments on historical events. For the few who are already well informed, and require deeper or more general historical reading, we would recommend that some acquaintance be made with White's "Nineteen Christian Centuries," Collier's "Great Events of History," Macaulay's "Essays, Biographies, and History," Hallam's "Constitutional History," and the works of Froude, Freeman, Stubbs, and Erskine May.

5. GEOGRAPHY as a study is so closely connected with history that it is scarcely possible to be well informed on the one subject without having a fair knowledge of the other. Geography may be studied in a variety of ways; it is possible to reduce it to a dry series of hard words ; but it is also possible to make it one of the most delightful and enjoyable of studies. Much may be learned through the *eye ;* indeed, a railway journey may be made intensely interesting (and far less fatiguing than it sometimes becomes) by following from time to time on a good railway map the stations, rivers crossed, &c., and deciding the county in which they are situated, noticing the direction (winding or otherwise) the river follows, the nature of the district, whether flat or hilly, whether pasture or cultivated land, whether the crops look good or poor, what the crops consist of, &c. In passing through railw y cuttings the nature of the underlayers of the earth will be shown, and those who know a little geology will here find much to interest them. A boat journey on a fine day may be equally instructive. Few people will deny that a journey by rail through the Peak district, or from Exeter to Penzance, or by steamer through the Kyles of Bute, or from London to Plymouth, may not be made extremely instructive.

There are many good books on geography, but a good atlas is absolutely indispensable to an intelligent study of geography, no matter how good the book may be. Much is also to be learnt from good-guide books, such as Black, Murray, Baedecker, and more than most people seem to realise, from "Whitaker's Almanack." To work well at geography the student should accustom herself to *draw* maps (not *trace* them) in which she fixes exactly the things which she knows something about, whether mountains, rivers, lakes, or towns. Books of travels will be found to give excellent geography lessons, and they should in all cases be read with the map in hand, every place should be found, and this remark also applies to historical reading.

Every English girl should know well the geography of the British Isles (some charming descriptions of scenery by Wordsworth and other poets, as well as Scott's "Lady of the Lake," give a charm in this) and of the colonies and dependencies of Great Britain. The history of the latter should also be known; this would greatly add to the interest which attaches to the questions of the day, such as the war at the Cape, the occupation of Candahar, &c. Then we ought to know something of the countries which supply us with food. Does every girl realise that the food raised in our own country would only maintain the inhabitants of the country two days in the week, and that for the remaining five days we depend upon other countries ? Then we should also know the countries which buy our manufactured goods, and those which supply us with raw materials, &c. We ought also to

be familiar with the countries near us, those which we may probably visit some day, if we have not already visited them.

Some of the best books for the study of geography are Hughes's "Manual of Geography" (Longmans), Clyde's "School Geography" (Simpkin and Marshall), "The World of Waters, and Recreations in Physical Geography," by R. Zorulin (Parker and Son), Milner's Geography, edited by Keith Johnstone (56, Paternoster-row), an i the most comprehensive book, published by Stanford, is called, "Geography : Physical, Historical, and Descriptive." It is a charming book, but rather expensive.

6. ELEMENTARY SCIENCE should also find a place in the studies of all girls of the present day. The present has rightly been called the " age of science," and there are so many good books on the subject that every girl could fairly well teach herself something of such subjects as botany, physiology, geology, &c. The pleasure of a country walk is increased tenfold to all those who have made even small progress in the study of botany or geology, and all the pleasures of a visit to the country, or a holiday at the seaside, may be recalled by looking over one's collection of plants and stones made during these times. Railway cuttings, sea-cliffs, and other places of disregard to many people become objects of intense interest to the young geologist, while of the practical advantages to health accruing from a knowledge of physiology one could write for some time.

"Macmillan's Science Primers," 1s. each, are capital books on special subjects, but will require a good deal of industry on the part of the student.

II. ON THE STUDY OF FOREIGN LANGUAGE AND LITERATURE.—Of foreign languages *French* is the most universally-studied, though German is much more generally learnt now than formerly. As the only sure method of acquiring any proficiency in any language depends upon a thorough knowledge of its grammar, we begin at once to discuss the question of the French grammars. Of these, none is better than *Baume's*, published by Simpkin and Marshall (1st volume, 3s. 6d.). It contains neither too little nor too much. Its rules are simple, and the exercises eminently practical, while the 2nd volume (4s.) containing the syntax, is invaluable. To all those who are familiar with Smith's "Principia Latina," the French books on the same principles are likely to be acceptable; and "Household French," by Havet (Sampson and Low), is a very practical French grammar. For those who have much time to give to French and wish to learn the conversational style, we recommend the complete French course by Havet. The familiar phrases, however, used in daily life, as well as accurate accent, cannot be obtained from books, and can only be acquired by colloquial lessons from a teacher possessing skill to guide conversation and to correct errors.

As reading books, Cassal and Karcher's "Modern French Readers" (Trübner) are very good. The junior course commences with anecdotes and short tales, and concludes with longer and very interesting stories. The second part contains extracts from the best contemporary writers, and is especially useful as showing the real idiomatic style of the most distinguished authors of modern France.

Having mastered the grammar, and acquired a good stock of idiomatic expressions by these means, the student should now begin to translate from the English into French, in order to acquire facility of expression, and the application of the rules already learnt. The first book for this purpose should be Neven's "Letters and Conversations," for translation into French (Williams and Norgate). It contains extracts from French authors translated

into English, to be re-translated into French. The Key contains the original French. This arrangement lightens considerably the work of the student, by arranging the English in a more easy manner for putting into French. "The English into French," by Van Laun (Public School Series), may be used in a similar manner to this book. It has three volumes, but these three together are cheaper than Neven's book, and, moreover, each volume contains a good vocabulary. "Half-hours of French Translation," by Mariette, is a good book, but rather difficult. In making a special study of idioms, "First Steps in French Idioms," by Bué (Hachette), will be found very useful ; but the book which every student who wishes to know French thoroughly should use is " Le Questionnaire Français," by Karcher (Trübner). It contains questions upon all the niceties of the language, and its systematic use must of necessity produce a thorough knowledge of French.

In reading French we would say that instead of devoting one's time to extracts from different authors one should read short original tales, such as those of Souvestre, viz. : " Au coin de feu," " Récits et souvenirs," " Sous la tonnelle," &c. After this we should recommend Erckman and Chatrian's stories, as " Madame Thérèse," " Le Conscrit de 1813," " Waterloo," " L'histoire d'un paysan," &c. The reader cannot fail to be interested in these works, and their natural, simple, and conversational styles make them extremely useful.

Hachette and Co. have published some very good reading books for advanced students, with explanatory notes, and biographies of authors, &c. The volumes devoted to About, Musset, and Töppfer are excellent ; Colomba, by Mérimée, is a most valuable book, the notes, explanations of difficult passages, idioms, &c., being beautifully rendered.

French poetry may now be studied, and no better books for this can be found than Cassal and Karcher's "Anthology of French Poetry" (Longmans) and "Staaf's Littérature Française," especially the fifth volume.

Classic French authors may now be studied, such as Molière's "L'Avare," " Le Misanthrope," " Les Précieuses Ridicules," Racine's " Athalie " and " Esther," and " Le Cid " by Corneille. " Hernani," by Victor Hugo, may be studied for the purpose of comparing classic and modern tragedy.

For those who are beginning or are not far advanced in the study of *German*, " Schmid's Tales," 1s., published by Nutt, will be found useful. They are extremely simple. They have no vocabulary, but steady use of the dictionary is an advantage sometimes. For comparison of English and German words few books will be found as useful as Neuhofer's " German Vocabulary " (Norgate) ; and Aue's " Elementary Grammar," published by Chambers, 1s. 6d., will clear up most difficulties, as well as Meyer's "Grammar" (Collins), which is 2s.

For the second stage of study in German, Buchheim's "Deutsches Theater," with notes and vocabulary (Norgate), 2s. 6d., will be found a very useful work, while more advanced students will find "Prose Compositions f r Translation into German," by Buchheim, extremely serviceable

As such full directions have been given for the study of French, it is not considered necessary to enter into further details on German, but no student should consider herself proficient in German till she can read Schiller's " Wilhelm Tell."

III. MUSIC AND DRAWING are generally classed as "accomplishments," and formerly so much time was devoted to them (especially to music) by some girls that they scarcely had time to do anything else. Now, however, music with most people takes its place

J. P. Mears, "How to Improve One's Education" (Volume 2, 10 September 1881, p. 795).

as one of the required subjects of education. There cannot be a doubt about music being a universally favourite subject, and one which gives very much pleasure to most people. With a few exceptions we may say that people of all ages and all ranks love music; and music often has the most soothing effect on the sick and suffering. There are many inducements to urge one, then, to persevere in the study of music, and every girl who does not live en irely for *self* will strive to do her very best in cultivating her voice, and in improving her playing. To those who are unable to take lessons from a good teacher, we would say that a *daily* practice of scales and excercises for at least twenty minutes (not necessarily together), is absolutely necessary. No one who really follows this out will find herself at a loss to appreciate the help of an occasional lesson, which we should strongly recommend. One other point: be most strict with yourself as to *time*: always count in your daily practices. The best excercise books to use are Carl Engel's "Piano School," and Bertini's "Petits Morceaux et Préludes," both published by Augener and Co. Clementi's Sonatines, and Kuhlau's Sonatas, also published by Augener and Co., afford excellent practice, giving good work to the left hand as well as the right.

As a study-book we recommend most highly "A Plan for Teaching Music to a Child," by Mrs. Frederick Inman, published by Simpkin and Marshall (1s. 6d.). It gives a great deal of very valuable instruction to those who teach themselves as well as to those who teach others. Mrs. Inman has a musical soul, and is perfect as a teacher of music. She has done and continues to do much good in helping to establish a love of good music.

The fourteen lessons in harmony, by J. E. P., published in the *English Mechanic and World of Science* from June 26 to Oct. 14, 1874, will more than reward every student who will carefully study them. By all means get them if possible.

To those who have only the use of the harmonium, as well as to others, we would remark that the practice of playing hymn tunes is one of the best chord exercises, setting aside the extreme usefulness of being able to play hymns well. Girls living in the country are often liable to be called upon to play the harmonium in church, and only those who have undertaken to do so without sufficient practice will realise the importance of giving some attention to this subject, while those who regret the want of a piano may console themselves with the knowledge of being able to "manage" the harmonium. Sunday music at home too, especially in country houses, is a source of real pleasure when the family join in psalms and hymns and spiritual songs, making melody in the heart.

To all who play we would advise strongly the cultivation of the power to accompany songs. To accompany well requires a special training, a sympathy must be established between the song and the instrument, and the pianist does much towards making or marring a song. There must be a gentleness, a power of adaptation, and a certain forgetfulness of self in a good accompanyist; no desire to exhibit great execution, but the greatest grace in giving utterance to the most gentle sounds in order to add charm and effectiveness to the voice. All girls with brothers will find themselves wonderfully repaid for the efforts they make in doing their best when playing songs for them, and many a happy evening may be spent in practising together such an elevated form of self-improvement. Everyone is more or less familiar with songs, but there are one or two books we would recommend for family and social use. "Kinderfreund," parts I. and II., and "The Garland Song Book" (with piano accompaniment) published by Boosey and Co.,

are among these; also the "German Song Book" (the family singing book), by F. Weber (Augener and Co.), and Murby's "New Tunes to Choice Words," Parts I and II. Some progress in music may be made by every person, though all cannot become great musicians. Milton tells us that "music hath charms to soothe the savage breast," while Shakespeare says that "The man who has no music in himself, nor is not moved with concord of sweet sounds is fit for treason, stratagems, and spoils."

Of drawing there is much to be said. It too has a refining influence on the mind, and is a very able educator of the eye, the hand, the ta te, &c., besides having a very effective use in making ourselves understood when we come face to face with people who do not understand our language, and we are reduced to representing our wants in rough sketches, or when one wishes to make one's self understood in giving suggestions or directions to workmen. All people cannot draw, but all people could be taught to draw, and it is not too much to say that, with proper teaching, drawing would be as easy and familiar to most people as writing is.

Among the higher influences of drawing we wish specially to speak of the cultivation of taste in form and in colour, in proportion, and in combination, &c. Mr. Ruskin says that "Perfect taste is the faculty for receiving the greatest possible pleasure from those material sources which are attractive to our moral nature in its purity and perfection. He who receives little pleasure from these sources wants taste; he who receives pleasure from any other sources has false or bad taste." We should strive, then, to cultivate this true taste and not be led away by the varying tastes of fashion.

With regard to improving one's drawing, the means seem greater than in many things. With a careful eye, a patient hand, and a diligent study of the object before us, we can do much by ourselves. One thing will be well to remember, not to be too ambitious, then we shall give sufficient time to secure success in our work step by step. Much help may be got by watching others draw, and only those who draw themselves will note all the little details which are secret springs of success, such as manner of holding pencil, of fixing light and shade, of sketching roughly, and lining in, of laying on washes, &c., &c. It is wonderful how much more interest one takes in drawings generally when one draws one's self, and with how much more real benefit and pleasure one visits a picture-gallery or art collection when one knows even a very little of art work.

The Science and Art Department, South Kensington Museum, has done much to advance the teaching of drawing in England, and more especially among designers and artizans, and they have issued many excellent copies and models, besides which, they test the proficiency in drawing of every grade of persons, and grant certificates. No better lesson could probably be given to anyone striving to improve in drawing than would be obtained by inspection of the drawings annually exhibited in the Museum, and no greater encouragement. Vere Foster, too, has done much in the same direction, and his books on drawing and on writing are well known throughout the country. A series of papers on sketching from nature has already appeared in THE GIRL'S OWN PAPER, and "The Handbook of Drawing," by W. Walker (Seeley, Jackson, and Halliday, Fleet-street), is certainly one of the most helpful of books that could fall into the hands of those who simply want guidance and counsel in their great work of self-help.

IV. NEEDLEWORK AND HOUSEKEEPING are the special and sole duties of women, and

those who are ignorant on these subjects are much to be pitied. The happiness of life depends on the home, and the housekeeper has much to reproach herself with if discomfort and misery result from any neglect or ignorance on her part. In these days of cooking lessons, ambulance lectures, lectures on health and physiology, &c., and in the face of innumerable books which exist on the subjects of household interests, it seems scarcely possible that anyone could be quite ignorant. To our reader, we recommend the use of "Home Comfort," by J. Stoker (Stewart and Co.), "The Chemistry of Common Things," by Macadam (Nelson), "Home Duties" (Thomas Laurie), and careful study of the papers on "The Difficulties of a Young Housekeeper, and How She Overcame Them," by D. Hope.

Improvement in needlework is so thoroughly within the means of every girl that it seems scarcely necessary to mention them. Of course, practice, and patience, and determination not to be satisfied unless one does the *best* that can be done, are among the secrets of success. For those who are not obliged to work for themselves, the dressing of dolls for children's hospitals, and the making of garments as charity gifts, are good inducements to call forth earnest work. To those to whom the making and mending of their clothes is a necessity, we repeat "try, try, try again." If you have a garment that fits you well, take the pattern of it to make others from, and never be above asking someone to show you how to work; there always will be ready at hand kind and generous people who delight in helping those who help themselves.　　　　　J. P. MEARS.

BOTH IN THE WRONG.

CHAPTER III.

"So that is your 'gentle, docile little girl,' Arthur?" said Evelyn a little later, when Sophy's absence was first discovered. "She does not strike me as being special y docile. I do not mean to *me*; that would be too much to expect. But to *you* ——"

"I do not understand, my love," her husband replied, helplessly, and a little wistfully. "Something seems to have come over the child which I cannot make out. But try and be patient with her, will you? She will soon—very soon—grow to love and honour you; as who could help doing? I suppose she fancies, foolish child, that she is not quite the same to me as when I had only her."

"She is jealous, and looks upon me as an interloper," the young wife said to herself. But she did not breathe the thought to her husband, who was evidently so anxious to see her and his daughter on truly affectionate terms with one another; and to please him she exerted herself next morning to be even more than usually kind and conciliatory to poor Sophy, who came down to the breakfast table cold, silent, and, it must be confessed, rather sulky.

But her well-meant advances met with no better return than they had done on the previous evening. There was the slightest suspicion of patronage in her manner which stirred up every ill feeling in the girl's heart, though Evelyn herself was entirely ignorant of offence. But to be patronised by a stranger! She, who had reigned supreme hitherto at the Towers; she, who had been her father's own darling until supplanted by an intruder, should she submit to be patronised by her? Never!

Besides, to admit this stranger, with her beauty and her winning ways—for beautiful and winning she was in spite of all—was treason to the dead mother; and was *she* to

Vol. VII.—No. 349.]　　　　　SEPTEMBER 4, 1886.　　　　　[Price One Penny.

BETWEEN SCHOOL AND MARRIAGE.

By the Author of "How to be Happy Though Married."

THIS time in a girl's life corresponds to that in a man's which is passed in a university, or in learning the work of his profession. Too many girls look on it as a *mauvais quart d'heure*, which may be dawdled through in an irresponsible way until they have a house of their own. Marriage represents a home, a position; sometimes even less than that—a trousseau, or a wedding tour. So they hasten through the years of adolescence as well as may be in order to reach the end of a wearisome task.

And yet if the girl is mother to the woman—that is to say, if the woman will be what the girl now is, this time, which is essentially one for settling habits, cannot be anything less than the most important in life. If the girl spend it in thoughtless idleness and discontented trifling, the result will be seen in the character of the woman. It is well for any of us when our work is cut out for us, so to speak, and we have not to look about for a profitable way of passing the time; but this last is the miserable condition of many girls belonging to daughter-full houses in easy circumstances. What can they do between school and marriage?

When the financial resources of her father are slender, a girl is quite right to seek for some employment by which she may earn her own living, and perhaps help her brothers and sisters; but when this is not the case, let no feeling of quixotic restlessness induce her to rashly leave home. It may be her plain duty to remain at home, and she may be independent and pay her way quite as much as one who earns and pays current coin. She can pay her way by filling in the little spaces in home life as only a dear daughter can, by lifting the weight of care from her mother, and by slipping in a soft word or a smile where it is like oil on the troubled waters of a father's spirit. What better remuneration can a father have for his ex-

A HOMELY LASSIE.

penditure upon his daughters than their laughter, good humour, and sympathy? "The laughter of girls," says De Quincey, "is, and ever was, among the delightful sounds of earth," and most fathers will agree with me that their grief-dispelling wiles are far better than gold and silver.

Those girls soon slide into uselessness, and drift aimlessly through their golden girlhood, who have no system in the ordering of their lives. We ought not to be chained to our system, but we should arrange our time so as to improve every precious moment, and find facility in the performance of our respective duties. Especially valuable are the hours between ten o'clock and one. These should be occupied with study, music (if you really have a taste for it), or the learning of some useful art by which you could earn your living if required to do so. Would anybody be worse, and would not everybody be much better, if girls of all ranks were taught to do something so well that they could earn money if necessary? Habits of attention, method, and dispatch, acquired in the study of any fine handicraft or art, lay a better basis for the character of a noble house-mother than the idle sauntering of common girl existence. The daughters of wealthy families need not rush into the labour market simply because they have the power to do so. Because they can engrave they need not be engravers, any more than they need become servants because they can dust a room or cook a potato.

Usefulness of any kind may be kept in store, as well as used as current coin. There is such a thing as adult education, and we may learn from everybody and everything until the day of our death, so that nothing is more ridiculous than to speak of a girl's education being "finished" when she leaves school. She need not keep up the routine of school work, but she may at least try to keep what she has learnt with much difficulty and drudgery. "It is less pain to learn in youth than to be ignorant in age;" and, indeed, it is only the first steps to the Temple of Wisdom that are the painful ones. Every girl ought to "make the most of herself," and gain accurate and general information on the subjects that interest intelligent people. Why should she give up study at eighteen, just at a time when, having got beyond the rudiments, the work of teaching herself would after some time become so enjoyable that it would in many cases be continued even after marriage? When books are looked upon by a girl on leaving school as instruments of mental torture, she is stopping her education just when she has reached its most interesting phase.

But mind and body are co-partners, and while cultivating the one a girl must not injure the other. In after life she will require all the health and vigour of body she can obtain from riding, swimming, tennis, rowing, and the gymnastic exercises which have now been made to suit girls. These games, if practised in moderation, and in suitable clothes without lung-compressing corsage, will give a firm hand, a trained eye, a clear complexion, and the light-heartedness which comes of a body unclogged in its machinery. They will confirm health and perfect beauty.

Girls who have been well brought up dress with simplicity; they are occupied, but not preoccupied, with dress. Two young men, the other day, were heard commenting, *sotto voce*, upon a girl who was attracting attention. "Yes; very pretty," said one, "but entirely spoilt by that terrible hat trimmed with giblets!" The head-covering thus alluded to was decorated with an arrangement of a bird's head, feathered neck, and claws. It is a great help to papa's pocket when daughters make their own dresses and hats—as it is, too, when they undertake the elementary teaching of younger brothers and sisters.

"What can I do to help mother?" This should be a question with all girls. In a large and well-ordered home, the daughters supervise different departments. One becomes responsible for the arrangement of the kitchen and dining-room, and sees that the table is properly furnished with viands and the economy of everything downstairs administered wisely. Another takes charge of the drawing-room or bedrooms. The next week, perhaps, they change employments; and in this way their mother has time to read, to go out, to receive friends, and to take a well-earned holiday.

We agree with Mrs. Warren in thinking that there is no household work such that a girl should deem it beneath her position to know how to do it. To scrub floors, scour saucepans, blacklead and clean grates, to black boots, to clean plate, to wash and iron —all these things may be done in a right or a wrong way, and it is only by learning how they ought to be done that a woman can teach others. Whether her destiny lies in the old country or in the colonies, her knowledge of home matters will be the greatest of blessings to herself and to others. Every day a young lady should do a little bit of household work thoroughly, so as to be a pattern of perfection to the servants, who are only too ready to be satisfied with half-done work or "That'll do."

Daughter (home from school): "Now, father, are you satisfied? Just look at my testimonial. Political economy, satisfactory; fine art and music, very good; logic, excellent!"

Father: "Very much so, my dear, especially as regards your future. If your husband should understand anything of housekeeping, cooking, mending, and the use of a sewing-machine, your married life will indeed be happy."

All girls cannot marry moneyed men, nor can they be sure, in the uncertain conditions of modern life, but that men who are rich to-day may be poor and struggling in a short year or two; and, surely, these men have a right to expect that the women they place at the head of the homes they have, in many cases, toiled hard to make shall be able to teach servants to carry out their plans, or, if need be, to throw themselves into the breach, and, unassisted, carry on the household machinery without a jar.

Nor is this incompatible with culture and accomplishments. Writing of university life for women in *Cassell's Family Magazine*, a scholar of Newnham College says: "Nowhere have I heard it more consistently and reverently asserted that a woman's true sphere is the home. Most of the ladies rather pride themselves on their domestic accomplishments. Among my own contemporaries were some whose nimble fingers could wield the needle as well as the pen, and produce with equal ease a copy of Latin verses or a fashionable bonnet. Others could send up a dinner not to be despised by the most fastidious of College Fellows."

As soon as a girl comprehends what duty really means, and attempts to do it, she first tries to do her work at home, and then looks out for work abroad. She does her best to relieve the indigent, to teach the ignorant, and to bring joy to the sad. There are benevolent societies established in every district to carry out these benevolent enterprises, and the directors are very glad to receive offers of help, and willingly give work to those who will undertake it.

But all work and no play will make Jill, as well as Jack, dull and dispirited. There are "between-times" when serious work does not call for us, or when we are weary of it, and for health's sake must indulge in recreation and light employment. Because a life of pleasure is a life of pain, that is no reason why we should have no pleasure in our lives. Is not happiness indeed a duty as well as self-denial? A girl could not have a better guide on the subject of amusement than Mr. Ruskin, who says: "Never seek for amusement, but be always ready to be amused. The least thing has play in it—the slightest word wit, when your hands are busy and your heart is free. But if you make the aim of your life amusement, the day will come when all the agonies of a pantomime will not bring you an honest laugh."

We have heard of an Eastern custom which enjoined that on the day of her marriage the bride should sit all the afternoon with her face to the wall. If any one spoke she was not to answer. This was supposed to typify her grief at leaving the state of single blessedness. An English girl may not feel this poignant grief at getting married, but if she can make her girlhood happy by putting it to a good account, she will be able to wait in dignified tranquillity until the right man comes to claim her, instead of throwing herself away upon the first worthless person who desires to marry and make a woman miserable.

When Mr. Wilberforce, years ago, was a candidate for Hull, his sister, an amiable and witty young lady, offered a new dress to each of the wives of those freemen who voted for her brother. When saluted with "Miss Wilberforce for ever!" she pleasantly observed, "I thank you, gentlemen, but I cannot agree with you, for really I do not wish to be *Miss* Wilberforce for ever."

We do not blame Miss Wilberforce or any other young lady for not wishing to be a "Miss" for ever, but she ought not to disturb herself if other girls have been preferred before her, and she remain unsought in marriage. As to what she can do to make herself more attractive, it depends on the kind of man she wishes to attract. If, however, she desire a good, worthy husband, she had better use no art, but simply be her own natural self. Let her cultivate the powers of her mind, engage in good and useful work, both within and without the home, study to acquire practical knowledge of domestic affairs, and trust that, if it is most expedient for her, God, the best Maker of marriages, will send a husband worthy of her choice.

Author of How to Be Happy Though Married, "Between School and Marriage" (Volume 7, 4 September 1886, p. 770).

In an instant the woman started to her feet. The fire had begun to send up a cheery blaze, and did more to light the room than did the sputtering candle which was sinking in the socket.

"It's well there is no more light," murmured Sue. "The place is like my thoughts—it won't bear looking into. The more light, the more rubbish is shown that wants clearing away. Here goes for the outside business."

Sue's capable hands began the work of tidying with a vigour that told little of a long day's work in the rag-cellar. Cleaning materials at her disposal were of the scantiest; but she made the best of them, and in a short time produced a wonderful change in the look of the room.

"I'll do better next time," she said; then turned to a low shelf, on which crockery, saucepan, and frying-pan rested side by side. No wash-basin or soap-dish was visible. There was a brown earthenware bowl that did duty for many purposes, but was rarely used as a wash-basin. "I'll make shift with it," thought Sue. "Warm water will

be best;" and she poured half the contents of the now boiling kettle into the bowl, then took a battered tin can to the outside tap in the court. With its contents she replenished her kettle, cooled the water in the bowl, and prepared for the much-needed wash. But another want had to be faced. "No soap, of course; and no washing clean without that."

There was a hard scrap sticking fast to the shelf; but Susan decided that it would be worse than nothing for the work to be accomplished. She was about to throw a shawl over her head and shoulders and go to the nearest shop, when she noticed the little packet given her by "Uncle Mat."

"I've never looked at my present yet," thought Sue. "I may as well see what it is before I go."

Perhaps she had a presentiment of its contents, and thought they might render a journey needless. At any rate, she found what she wanted—a square of soap. No fancy article, but just plain yellow, of excellent quality.

"Thank you, Uncle Mat. You saved me a step by giving this, and I've no doubt you would be very pleased if you could know that I'm going to use it to move the veil from my face. You're a plain-spoken one, but you mean well. If I had been told this morning that I would stand such a talking to from anybody living, I wouldn't have believed it. I'd have said, 'Let anybody try it on, that's all; and before they are five minutes older they'll wish they had kept a civil tongue in their heads.' I shouldn't have thought twice about pushing a good mouthful of this soap between the teeth of any woman at the cellar that had been impudent enough to offer it straight off. But the ugly man with his pleasant voice and kind ways made me look at myself inside and out as one may say—not at him. And an ugly sight he showed me. If ever we meet again, I'll thank him both for his talk and his present. He shall see for himself that neither of them was lost on me."

(To be continued.)

ON THE USE AND ABUSE OF FICTION.

By Mrs. MOLESWORTH.

ICTION, as we all know, in the sense in which we use it in the present day, is a new growth. One does not need to go very far back into the social life of the past, or to read up much in any history, to be satisfied as to this; and like all influences, new and old, it has its good side and its bad—its use, but also its grave possibilities of abuse and misuse. I have more than once heard it said that it would be by no means a matter for regret, but in many ways the reverse, if during one whole year no new books were to be written. I certainly think it would be a great cause for congratulation if for some such given time no new *novels* were to appear! There would be leisure then for a thorough weeding out of those already in existence, which would, I think, be salutary for authors as well as for readers. Weeding out always *is* effected in time, it is true, but the ever-increasing mass of publications renders it more and more difficult. And meantime, it is melancholy to reflect on the enormous waste of time and energy on books that are even less worth reading than writing. For, after all, though I would be the last to encourage or urge young people with no special gift, or no special reason for imagining they may have such a gift, though dormant, to rush into print; still, the doing so is sometimes a very wholesome lesson. No

book can be written without a good deal of patience and toil; and except in wrong-doing, patience and toil are never altogether thrown away. And nothing tests the reality of literary power like seeing one's productions in print—unless it may be the humiliation of finding the result of one's labours ruthlessly cut to pieces, or, still worse, altogether ignored. For where there is real talent, these trials often serve but as a spur to renewed effort.

This increase of books of fiction—tales and stories of every kind, more especially novels, not to mention children's books—with which just now we are scarcely concerned—is almost incredible. Even forty or fifty years ago, when the three-volume novel was already fairly launched, and circulating libraries on a small scale had been for some time in existence, the number of tales and stories was infinitesimal compared with to-day. And in another way fiction was of much less importance as a factor in social life. Novels, as a rule, at that time were so poor. With the exception of the works of a very few leading authors, the run of them was both dull and uninteresting, exceedingly untrue to nature, badly written, and *terribly* sentimental. The word "romance," which tells its own tale, had not yet altogether gone out of fashion. I do not think many of these second- or third-rate—no rate at all we should now dub them—productions would find much favour with the girls of the present day. There is no doubt whatever that the whole level of fiction—the higher ground having been first sighted by some great pioneers such as Charlotte Brontë, Dickens, Thackeray, Harriet Martineau; a little further back by Sir Walter Scott, Miss Austen, Miss Edgeworth (whose *Helen*, a novel of almost typical excellence, is far less known than it should be); a little later on by Mrs. Gaskell, Anthony Trollope, Charles Kingsley, Miss Thackeray, Charles Reade, Miss Mulock, Miss Yonge, Mrs. Oliphant, Dr. Macdonald, and by that time already many others—the whole level has risen incalculably. Nowadays it would take nearly all the space at my disposal merely

to enumerate the *names* of existing novels of unquestionable merit, both English and American, and among these, I may remark parenthetically, not a few good judges place women writers, led by George Eliot, in the foremost rank. These greater authors are followed by an innumerable crowd of smaller ones, many a one of whose productions would, earlier in this century, have been looked upon, and rightly, as a masterpiece. And it is just *because* the level has so risen; just because there are so very many books of fiction worth reading; that the subject requires such serious consideration;—that it behoves us out of much that is good to choose the best, and not only the best in the abstract, but to find out what is the best for *us*, and that we are left without excuse if ever we are guilty of reading a book that is in any sense *bad*—for of course the bad has come with the good. With the improvement both in matter and literary skill has crept in a great wave of false cleverness; of writing for effect and notoriety instead of from any higher motive or true love of art; of pandering to public taste, already satiated with too much light and ephemeral literature, and ever seeking for new excitement—in a word, what has been called the "sensational school" in fiction, though in using this well-worn expression I do so only in its objectionable sense; for it covers a wide field, and I should be very sorry to be supposed to refer to the many wholesome and harmless, as well as clever, novels which yet, as is rather to be regretted, must, technically speaking so to say, be classed as belonging to that school.

There are a great many things I should like to impress upon girls with regard to novel or story-book reading. I can only touch upon the most important; and first of all comes a very commonplace piece of advice—almost, indeed, a truism—never forget that reading fiction is to be looked upon as *recreation*. There are, it is true, some novels—among them I might mention Mr. Pater's *Marius, the Epicurean*, perhaps Mr. Shorthouse's *John Inglesant*—which are *hardly* to be ranked as such. They are certainly not "light" reading, however beautiful. Such books are the product of immense learning and research, and profound scholarship: to be read, understood, and admired as they deserve, they must be *studied*. But as regards fiction in general, if it is to fall into its right place as an influence for good on a girl, it should be looked upon as among the sweetmeats of her life; otherwise it not only unfits one for graver reading, and most probably interferes practically with duties not to be set aside; but it actually loses its own charm if indulged in too much, or at unseasonable hours. First thing in the morning and last at night seem to me very prominent among these unsuitable times. Not only do we owe our very first and last waking thoughts to the best and highest interests of all; but besides this, novel reading in the forenoon leaves one in a curiously unready and desultory condition for the day's work; and sitting up late at night over an interesting or exciting tale is equally sure to make one's brain unhealthy, tired, and listless.

As to *what* fiction to read, I would, to start with, strongly advise a girl, on first beginning to feel her own way a little in Bookland, to read some of the best *older* novels. Sir Walter Scott is sadly out of fashion, I know. Young people find him woefully dull; but I cannot believe that young human nature has changed so extraordinarily as all that in half a century or less. I fear the mischief is almost entirely due to premature, and perhaps indiscriminate, indulgence in novels while still very young; even in some cases before childhood is really past. If girls had as few books as their grandmothers in *their* youth, fresh from school-work and with unspoilt taste, I think most of them would be as susceptible to the wonderful charm of the great northern wizard as were these grandmothers in their day. Indeed, I have seen it tested. Some young people I know were brought up on the Continent under rather "old-fashionedly" strict surveillance. Story-books of any kind were rare; novels unknown. Just as they were growing up, a return to England opened out a wide field to them; and as they were wisely directed, the Waverley novels were almost their first pasture ground. I can scarcely exaggerate, and shall never forget, the delight and enjoyment these boys and girls found in them. Nor has this freshness of taste ever been altogether lost. I think the restricted story-reading of their earlier youth has not proved a subject of regret.

And close upon the Waverleys come others, varying so widely that no one can complain of monotony in our older fiction, though its amount may be limited. Dear Miss Austen for one; *The Newcomes*; *Pendennis*, the almost embarrassing wealth of Charles Dickens's books, leading us on gradually to the later novelists of this century, who one by one have been canonised by the slow but sure decision of time as "Standard authors, whose works will live." Along with this reading, or interspersed with it, it may be well to divert yourself now and then, in anticipation, as it were, with a present-day novel. But when you begin with these, I would earnestly advise you to ask advice and direction. Do not be in a hurry to read a book just because "everybody" is reading it; do not feel ashamed *not* to have seen "*the* book of the season." It may sometimes prove a very blessed thing for you never to see it at all. Far better miss altogether the reading the cleverest book that ever was written, than soil your mind and memory in *the very least*: far better even to be laughed at as prudish, or behind the day, than risk any contact with the mental or moral pitch which is so *very* hard quite to rub off again. For though, taken in the mass, our English fiction is not often, thank God, open to the terrible verdict that must be passed on that of some other nations, there are a great many novels that are not *good*, where no real belief or nobility of principle underlies the cleverness, which leave a young mind confused as to what *is* "good," or what the writer means one to think so; or, worse still, insinuates a strange chaotic distress as to whether right *is* right any longer, or wrong, wrong.

I think, though they may not be obtrusively so, we who are Christians *must* call such books "bad." For, remember, it is not writing about bad things that is necessarily bad.

As girls grow older they have to face evil in many forms in real life, and even sometimes its delineation in fiction. But it should be recognised *as* evil, as the powerful yet miserable thing we have to do battle with while life lasts; never as a skilfully-draped and dressed-up figure, which is to be misnamed *good*. Nor, even when *recognised* as evil, should its deformities be unnecessarily dwelt upon; the doing so is one of the worst of the morbid tendencies of present-day fiction, and can do *us* no good. It may possibly, in some cases, bring home his own degradation to the hardened and stupified conscience of a drunkard to see it portrayed in its terrible reality, though even this is an open question; but supposing it were ever our painful task to help any such unhappy ones, I do not think we should do it any the better from having studied some morbidly accurate picture of this terrible vice in a novel, French or English. For, to my sorrow, I could name some recent English novels, written, I am assured, with the best motives, and supposed to be suited to young readers, which I should shrink from putting into the hands of such almost more than an honestly coarse mediæval romance.

But having sought and received wise, and at the same time sympathetic, counsel as to your choice of books, do not keep yourself too much in leading-strings. Do not be afraid to form and to hold, while always open to correction, or suggestions, or re-adjustment of your views, *your own opinion*. You have several things to consider—not only what is good in the abstract, but, as I said before, what is good for *you ;* what you really enjoy; what you feel you profit by. Nothing is more pitiful or absurd than to hear a young person, parrot-like, praising or trying to be enthusiastic about some book he or she neither admires nor understands, just because it seems the thing to do. One of the very cleverest and most cultivated women I know is not ashamed to own, when the subject comes up, that she has never been able to derive any kind of pleasure from the writings of Charles Dickens. And, to me personally still more astonishing, I *have* met people who found *Pride and Prejudice*, and *Northanger Abbey*, very flat. I myself feel the same want of attraction in some American novelists whose genius is incontestable. We are not all made alike; and even if one's own want of appreciation of books that *should* be appreciated is somewhat humiliating, it is better to be humiliated than not to be honest, though at the same time good taste and true humility should prevent one's *obtruding* these eccentricities of taste—another little danger of which I could warn young readers. For mental powers and perceptions change as well as develop. "*Fontaine, je ne boirai jamais de tes eaux*, is a rash declaration; the very books you cannot like now, may become your greatest friends in later years. Say you do not care for them if your opinion is called for, but beware of inferring that they are unworthy of being cared for.

Then you have to find out what books have the best effect on you. Some people cannot stand very exciting or thrilling stories, just as some people are better without any wine. If you find it so with you; if certain novels so engross your mind and imagination that real life becomes dreamland, and you go about your duties in a sort of sleep-walking, then give them up, or indulge in them but rarely, and at judicious times; unless, indeed, you can train yourself to sufficient self-control resolutely to keep their fascination under mental lock and key—a grand piece of self-discipline in itself.

Many people object to reading stories that appear in serials. I think there is a good deal to be said in their favour, unless of course one reads too many at a time, which cannot but lead to confusion. I have often noticed that the tales one reads in parts are those that remain the longest in one's memory; they mellow there, as it were. During the intervals one seems to live with the characters, to get to know them, to distrust some, to feel increasing affection and admiration for others. We wonder how they are getting on, what will be the next news of them, and so on; almost as if they were real acquaintances at a distance. And it is often a pleasant and not unprofitable subject of conversation to discuss the incidents of a serial story between times with others who are following the gradual unfolding of its plan, much in the same way that one of the good results of reading aloud is the common interests it brings into family or friendly life. I wish reading aloud were more in fashion. I am always sorry when I hear girls say they "hate" it, or declare ungraciously that they have never been able to read aloud well. I know it calls often for patience and unselfishness—on the part of the listeners sometimes as well as the reader; but is that any real objection? Are not pleasures shared the truest? And from another point of view as regards the reader, who can tell what may be before any of us in the unseen years to come? If not darkened vision, enfeebled physical powers of some kind are the lot of most before the end: you may come to be very thankful to have acquired the art—for a real art it is—of reading a story aloud well, before there was actual call for doing so. And later on still, when the time comes that you yourselves may be dependent on the kindliness of others for anything to cheer or lighten monotonous days, will it not be pleasant to remember that when your eyes were keen and your voice clear, you grudged neither in this often welcome service?

To return to the choice of books of fiction. I should like to say a word or two about *foreign* literature of this class, notably French or German. It is most advisable not to limit your light reading to English. Most girls nowadays can read both French and German, the former especially, with ease and pleasure; but even in the rare cases where it is not so, I should recommend good translations. For it is not only of self-improvement as a linguist that one should think. The variety, the *newness* to you of the life of other countries, when well depicted, are most wholesome and widening in their influence. Nothing, next to actual foreign travel, takes one more out of oneself than a story of which the scene and characters are entirely unlike one's ordinary surroundings, provided of course that the essence of *all* good fiction, the magic "touch of nature," be not wanting. And one of the greatest services fiction can render us all—brain-weary men and women as well as young girls—is this *taking us out of ourselves*. It is one of the reasons why historical novels, or stories of long ago, are often so refreshing. It is a great part of the secret of the charm of fairy-tales. I remember not long ago asking a woman who is really a deeply-read scholar, what kind of fiction she enjoyed the most. Her reply was—"Well, on the whole, I think I would choose a good rollicking story of adventure, such as Mr. Stevenson's *Treasure Island*. It is such a *change*."

And as regards foreign fiction, do not be surprised at my recommending some French as well as the many excellent German tales. It is a great mistake to imagine that *all* French novels are objectionable or unwholesome. There are some already "standard" ones, besides the two or three—*Paul and Virginia*, and *The Exiles of Siberia*—which our grandmothers were restricted to; a few of George Sand's, one or two of Balzac's, and some others, which I really think everybody who reads at all should read; and a fair number of modern ones, pre-eminent among them perhaps those of Mrs. Craven—whose death her many friends are still mourning—no mother need object to a daughter's reading, though of course they must be chosen with care and knowledge. As works of art, too, as models of literary skill, French novels stand unrivalled. There is no such thing as slovenly or slip-shod writing in French. The exigencies of the language, its poverty of *words* as compared with our own, necessitating extreme variety and delicacy of *expressions* or combinations of words, and partly from the same cause, the much greater precision of grammar, make it impossible for uneducated or half-educated authors to exist. It is to be regretted that our own standard in such directions is so much less stringent.

In closing, I should like to say a little more about what seems to me one of the great dangers of fiction for the young, one of the shoals to be avoided. I have already alluded to it in speaking strongly of the advantage of those tales which take us out of ourselves. These need not necessarily be laid in far-away places or long-ago days. Such a book, for instance, as Miss Lawless's admirable Irish tale, *Hurrish*, a story not only of present day events, but of, in one sense, actually our own countrymen and women, transports us to

scenes as unfamiliar to many as those of the Middle Ages; thereby not only refreshing our imagination, but marvellously widening our sympathies. But still, after all, when all is said and done, I fancy girls, as girls, prefer stories of the life they themselves are actors in. And this is natural, and to some extent, when one takes into account the eager anticipations, the vivid hopes, the vague wonderment as to the unfolding of the drama of your own future, without all of which youth would no longer be youth—to some extent this preference is not to be objected to. But keep it well in hand; beware of reading yourselves into all you read; try to avoid sentimentalism, as distinct from true sentiment, in every form; while sympathising with your heroine let it be with *her*, not with yourself under her name; try to treat her objectively, so to say. Nothing is more dwarfing and enervating than to make all you read into a sort of looking-glass—and often a most misleading one!—to measure and judge and criticise solely by your own personal feelings and experience.

And even with regard to the very best works of fiction, remember they *are* fiction. It is highly improbable that your own life, taken as a whole, will resemble the most life-like story in three volumes. Art must *be* art; to restrict it to literalness would be to destroy it. Thoroughly to enter into the explanation of this would lead us into very abstruse regions, and would be, on my part, presumption to attempt. I can but hint at it. Fiction cannot be biography; an oil-painting cannot be a photograph. In the former the *characters* must be true to life; the situations and action never (in ordinary story-telling that is to say) *impossible*, and but rarely improbable; but more than this one cannot ask. Into all

fiction, if it is to serve its purpose, must be infused a breath of the ideal; it must be touched by the wand of Hans Andersen's *Spirit of Fairy-tale*. It is the attempt at literalness, the exaggeration of the "realism" we hear so much about, that is degrading and distorting art in so many directions. Pictures, on canvas or in books, must be "composed"; subjects striking and beautiful selected; all must be grouped, harmonised, re-cast by the poetic genius of the artist, the "maker." For poetry, in the widest acceptation of the word, is the soul of all art. We must see with the artist's eyes; it is his power of seeing as others do not, and of partially communicating this power, which makes him what he is.

And, after all, as regards our own experience, I doubt if any human being, even at the close of the longest life, really feels at the end of the third volume. Not only do we live again in the interests, the hopes, and fears of those around us, but we feel our own life still. We are not *meant* to close the book of ourselves, it seems to me, for surely all that *makes* us will live on; not only our few good deeds, our two or three completed tasks, but, better still, the teaching of our failures, the clear vision of our mistakes, of the fitfulness of our best efforts, of the scantiness of our self-renunciation—the influence of all this training on our characters, which *are* ourselves, and must last. And above all, the love for God and for each other, which, however imperfect now, is yet the germ and mainspring of true living—all these will be found—"continued" in the Book of Golden Letters waiting for us to read when this poor stained *first* volume is done—in that new life "whose portals we call Death."

MISS FANNY; A STORY OF YOUTHFUL LIFE.

ADAPTED FROM THE DANISH.

By ANNE BEALE.

PART I.

MISS FANNY'S ACQUAINTANCES.

AN elegant young lady left Copenhagen by steamer to pay a visit to the honest Jutlanders, while a melancholy midshipmite stood on the pier watching the smoke. She had been ill, and the doctor had told her parents that if she were ever to get well again she must take a trip to the country. Now her father was a rich merchant and her mother an invalid, and between business and illness they were unable to accompany her.

They were at their wits' end, when, just in the nick of time, there arrived from Jutland the baron, brother of Miss Fanny's mamma, and owner of Söholm. No sooner did he hear how matters stood than he exclaimed, with native boldness—

"Let me take the little maiden to Söholm. Peter shall be her *cavaliere servente*, and I will bring her back in a month, frisky as a bird, and with cheeks like red tulips."

Although Miss Fanny wrinkled up her nose at the prospect of this Jutland cavalier, the offer was accepted; and thus it came about that the melancholy midshipmite stood gazing at the smoke while she went off on her adventures with the baron.

Little Miss Fanny was a much-admired damsel, and she held up her curly head as if she knew it. She had two brown eyes, which shone so brightly that you would think a tear could never darken them; and a clever little

nose, slightly turned up, as much as to say, that we are not all on the same level in this motley world. She was smartness itself, and her dress might have been modelled from a fashion-book. Her little feet seemed formed for tripping up and down Œstergade,† and she was altogether the most elegant eight-year-old lady to be found within the walls of Copenhagen.

While Miss Fanny and the baron were steering towards the Jutland coast, grand old Söholm was decking herself in all her summer garments in preparation for their reception; for the wind had been there, flying in and out of every nook, and whispering that distinguished guests were on their way. And dame Söholm did not look amiss when in full dress.

This was an old manor house, which, though of staid and sober air, looked as if life and mirth might flourish beneath its careful tendence. The walls had been whitewashed and smartened; a whole regiment of storks kept guard on the roof; and swallows and sparrows flew and twittered everywhere. A green framework of forest, shaped like a crescent, sheltered it at the back; while in front, rich waving cornfields sloped down to the clear water of one of the inlets that cut the coast of Jutland. This little bay was separated from the main sea by a bare, high-ridged, homely isthmus, which looked like a huge boat, bottom upwards, enjoying repose on dry land, after having fought the battles of life on the ocean wave.

Amid these rural surroundings wandered, in all the glee of careless youth, a brave, cheerful little fellow about Miss Fanny's age. This was Peter, the future lord of Söholm, and the joy and pride of the baron. His heart was light as the spring breeze; his cheek round as a summer apple; but, alas! no one could say he was elegant, like Miss Fanny and the midshipmite. Still, he was too well-bred to adopt the manners of his intimate friend, the coachman; but, on the other hand, had too little taste for dress to please Miss Lœrke, the housekeeper. She, who was old and sensible, declared him to be the worst of all the bad Peters who, in this wicked world, tear their trousers and maltreat their clean collars.

The baron was a widower. His wife had died soon after the birth of Peter, and he had loved her so dearly that he could never forget her, as some good men are said to do. He had sought and found consolation in Peter, who became to him henceforth both wife and son. He was a kind man, and such an indulgent father, that he willed that Peter should be allowed to do just as he liked; and the good boy never failed to fulfil his father's loving wish. A rare devotion to horses, dogs, servant-lads, and other wild creatures; a magnanimous indifference to his clothes, and an amiable disposition to give away all he possessed, were amongst the early features of young Peter's character. He was also remarkable for making friends with everybody, high and low, Miss Lœrke, perhaps, excepted. These traits filled the baron's heart with joy and pride.

---

* This story was originally translated by Augusta Plesner, but never before published in English.

† The Regent Street of Copenhagen.

Mrs. Molesworth, "On the Use and Abuse of Fiction" (Volume 13, 16 April 1892, p. 454).

MAGAZINE AND BOOK CLUBS, AND HOW TO MANAGE THEM.

By DORA DE BLAQUIÈRE.

BOOK and magazine clubs are associations formed with the object of buying new books or magazines by adding the members' subscriptions together, so as to constitute a common fund. They were immensely popular about twenty years ago, and did good work in that day; but at present the advance of postal facilities, and the spread of the great circulating libraries, have diminished their usefulness, and they are less needed than they were. Nevertheless, in many parts of the country they are still flourishing, and principally in those places remote from London, and not touched by the railways; and likewise in some of our distant colonies they are in great favour.

They are valuable as enabling one to procure, at a moderate cost, the book wanted; and in the same way to read the best literature at the earliest moment that it is out, if it be desired. They were rarely formed for novel-reading, the aims of their founders being usually of a higher character, and looking towards the best and most solid forms in all branches of art, science, history, and general literature. The kind of books selected would be biographies, essays, philosophy, and poetry; and amongst the authors represented would be Ruskin, Frank Buckland, and Professors Dawson and Tyndall; Whymper and Mrs. Bishop; Tennyson and Longfellow; Thoreau and Richard Jefferies; the Greville Memoirs, Prescott, Motley, and Greene. I have selected these names at random from a list of books shown to me, and should advise the intending secretary of such a club to send for catalogues to Mudie's or Smith's, and thus to get suggestions and ideas—supposing that the members of her club should need them, and have no

ideas of their own. A weekly paper, dealing solely with the reviewing of books—such as the *Athenæum*, the *Academy*, or the *Literary World*—would be of great value to the members, as well as to the secretary, and would be a means of guiding their choice, and drawing attention to the best of the *new* books of the day.

There are two ways of managing them—the most usual being, I think, a yearly subscription of a guinea or more, and at the end of the year the books are disposed of either amongst the members, or to a second-hand bookseller. This seems to be the general way of conducting magazine clubs; and the magazines are divided by the members at the end of the year.

The other way of managing a book club is to allow each member to choose a book, sending in three names in case of someone's selecting the same volume, the book chiefly desired being marked 1, 2, or 3 on the list, according to the member's taste. The price of each, and the name of the publisher, should also be given. Each person pays for her own volume, and generally is entitled by the rules of the society to have the first reading of the same. A book society is generally got up by some enterprising person in society who does not mind trouble; and on her shoulders fall very often the duties of secretary—a rather onerous post, as unpaid ones are often apt to be. A treasurer also is needed to receive and account for the money; and in some clubs members are restricted in price—not below three shillings, nor above half a guinea. Of course where the books are obtained at a reduction of threepence in the shilling, these prices will secure a more expensive set of books than appears on the surface, or the reduction may be used to cover the cost of postage and letter-writing.

Twenty is a very usual number to form a book club, and each member takes the books

she has selected at the end of the year; and the greatest pains are bestowed to preserve the volumes from injury, and keep them clean during the period of their use, so that they may form valuable additions to the library of the future owner. Amongst the most onerous duties of the secretary—unless she be aided by some of the members—is the covering of the books, and pasting into them the names and the rules. The covers are composed of stout brown paper, which no member is allowed to remove, as it is carefully pasted on to preserve the cover and the edges as completely as possible.

When the new books are purchased, a general meeting is held at the house of either the secretary or the treasurer, when the books are inspected and the business of covering is often performed, if there be time to do it carefully. On this occasion each member should pay for his or her book; and if there be a rule to that effect, sixpence also; which small sum is paid by each member towards the expenses of postage, paper, and wrappers. This, as I have also said, may sometimes be paid by the discount obtained on the books when bought. The time for reading each book is a fortnight. Therefore, if you have twenty members in your club, the reading of the twenty books will take nearly ten months. These arrangements all depend on the size of the club; but if too large, the work entailed on the secretary is too much to be pleasant. Members pass the books from one to the other themselves, entering on the list pasted inside the date and name, in order that it may be known that she had incurred no fine by retaining it too long.

I have a dozen lists of different book clubs. The main of them agree as to the amount of fines being fixed at one penny a day for retaining a book too long. The following is a copy of one of them :—

THE WHITEHOUSE BOOK CLUB.

This book to be kept one fortnight only, and to be sent on to the member next on the list.

NAME.	WHEN RECEIVED.	WHEN FORWARDED.
Mrs. James	Dec. 7th	Dec. 21st
Mrs. Smith	Dec. 21st	..
Mrs. Hall	..	..
Mrs. Clark	..	..
Captain Lane ..	..	..
General Birch ..	..	..
Mr. John Mayen ..	..	..
Mr. Forster	..	..
etc.		

Fines to be entered by the offender on this list, and paid in to Treasurer.
This book, after circulation, is to be retained by GENERAL BIRCH.

The order of circulation is sometimes very puzzling indeed to arrange, and needs time and thought; for members find it more convenient to exchange the nearer they are together, of course; and care should be taken to avoid the expense of carriage on all occasions when possible.

A magazine club is conducted in much the same manner. My half-dozen lists vary one from another, some being mostly reviews, others only magazines ranging from sixpence to one shilling and sixpence. In most of them the American magazines are included, with two or three half-crown reviews, three shilling magazines, and several sixpenny ones. The members send in a list, which is then voted upon; or each member sends in the name of a review or magazine. The W—— Magazine Club consists of eight members, one guinea a year being the fee paid by each, and one dozen magazines are taken, the price of the twelve being £7—£1 8s. is thus left for postage, etc., as well as the discount taken off the magazines when purchased. The list contains one review, seven sixpenny and three shilling magazines, and two at one and six-pence each. But I only give this as a speci-men. I find that it is considered best to have fewer members in a magazine club than in a book society, as the former are circulated oftener and much more trouble is entailed, the magazines being kept only one week. Magazine club rules are a little different. The following come to me from Scotland :—

MAGAZINE CLUB RULES.

To be kept six days—Sundays excepted—and returned to the secretary by the member who last received it. If received any day after Tuesday may be retained till the next Saturday week. Day of transfer for all maga-zines, Saturday. One penny a day fine if kept beyond six days, unless as above. No fine to exceed sixpence. Any member wishing to see a magazine a second time, to put a cross opposite his or her name on list and apply for it to the secretary on the completion of the circulation. The magazines are allotted by ballot at the end of each year. Subscrip-tion £1 1s. yearly.

The list pasted in each magazine.

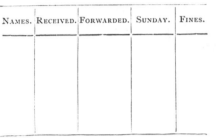

NAMES.	RECEIVED.	FORWARDED.	SUNDAY.	FINES.

The magazine club may, of course, be much smaller. Indeed, I often find that in the country it takes the shape of two or three ladies arranging to take in a certain magazine each, and exchanging them, when read, with each other. In the case of three ladies, each has a magazine for ten days, and pays for her own. Of course, in this case, there are no fines. It has been a little difficult to write so as to make myself understood; but I shall be very glad if my description of these useful little clubs incites any of my readers to start one among their own circles of friends. The magazine club is specially delightful; and now that so many of our best and most able maga-zines are sold at sixpence, there is no difficulty in the way of those with very slender purses. In the case of families joining, I should recom-mend a selection of Sunday monthlies being put in; and also that illustrations should be thought of, as young people learn much through them, I think, and through their means take more interest in what they read.

There is no doubt that the newest, freshest work goes into our reviews and magazines to-day; and we shall find our zest in life will be enhanced, and the happiness of our home-circle increased, by the appearance of our monthly visitors in their dresses of blue or yellow, or vested only in sober brown and drab. The advent of all new ideas is calcu-lated to keep us young in thought, and, what is still better, youthful and fresh at heart. So shall our love be larger for all good, and our sympathies wider, with every effort towards the higher ideals of life.

FRAGRANT LEGACIES.

CHAPTER II.

THE CRYSTALLISING OF FRUITS AND FLOWERS.

THE poetic industry of extracting the sweet-ness of flowers appeals more especially to the grown-up and refined classes of society; but who among all ages and conditions would refuse or fail to appreciate the products of Mons. Négre's industry if they were given a chance of accepting? In fact, I felt quite mean, as I walked through his factory, when I thought of the thousands of young people who would like to have been in my place.

The fruit which grows in and about Grasse is specially beautiful; some of it will grow only in a warm and clear atmosphere such as obtains here. Among these are the fig, the mandarin orange, the lemon, and the Japanese medlar. These and the commoner kinds are a treat when eaten fresh; but when they have passed into their new form under the hands of Mons. and Madame Négre they are simply irresistible.

In addition to these fruits, incredible as it may seem, the magicians dish up for us *fairy food* such as real violets, orange-flowers, and rose-leaves, which are as agreeable to the taste as, when fresh, to the smell.

For nearly three quarters of a century this firm has been engaged in its charming work, and has gained a reputation not only for the taste and beauty, but for the wholesomeness, of its sweets.

Naturally, the work in this factory is much more simple and easy to describe than the perfumery manufacture of Bruno Court, for the reason that no elaborate machinery is used here, and only two kinds of processes.

The house in which this work of crystallising is carried on is in itself a real curiosity, and well worth seeing. It is entered on one side through a small door in a narrow and sombre street, and one is quite unprepared for the magnificent prospect which opens out to view on the opposite side.

Both fruits and flowers are first of all cooked slowly in sugar and water, the latter being exceptionally good in this district, and helps to give the fruits their delicate, transparent look. They are then slowly cooled off in syrup in order to glaze them; and we noticed that the syrup used for cooking was not available for the process known as glazing.

Passing through the store-room, where a few people were engaged in packing the finished stock for export, we came into the cooking room, or kitchen, as it might really be called, where a low range occupied one end, and the greater portion of the remaining space was taken up by rows and piles of red earthenware pans filled with every variety of fruit, violets, orange-flower, and rose-leaves all cooling down in syrup, and presenting such a tempting dis-play as fairly made one's mouth water.

We asked Madame Négre, who kindly ac-companied us, as to the quantities of fruit and flowers consumed by them; but she could give us no information on this point beyond saying that eight or nine thousand kilos of apricots and plums are preserved every season, and about the same quantity of other fruits, such as figs and strawberries, etc., making in all about eighteen thousand kilos, or, roughly speaking, nearly forty thousand pounds.

All fruits must first be cooked, as I have said, slowly in sugar and water; and it is necessary that the sugar be of the very best quality. This being done, the man-cook ladles the fruit slowly out on to a wire netting over a table, where it is carefully examined by girls, who remove every imperfect one, no matter how slight the imperfection, leaving only those without crack or blemish to cool and drain. After this they are glazed or crystallised; and as two syrups are used both for fruits and flowers, the process is somewhat long.

When the glaze is dry, and does not come off on being touched, it is a sign that the fruit is ready for use, and it will be found that in the process to which the fruit has been sub-jected it has suffered no detriment, the juice has not dried up in the least, neither does the most delicate fruit lose its flavour or brilliancy.

Seeing lovely fruit placed on one side owing, perhaps, to a slight crack in the skin, I wanted to know what became of it, and found it was made into *household jam*, with just the same care and ingredients as are used in the crystal-lising of the fruit; indeed, so good is it that it is eagerly sought after and bought up.

The manner of cooking violets for eating is slightly different, these being cooked in sugar only; and great care is needed to have the exact quantity of sugar—just so much and no more; then the violets are taken into an ad-joining room heated by pipes, where they are left twelve hours on a wire-covered table to drain and crystallise.

These gridiron tables enable the workers to detect in a moment any imperfect specimen, which is at once removed. All the violets are brought in from the environs—that is to say, from the gardens of Grasse, Cannes, Nice, and Bordighera, where the culture of the orange, the rose, and the Parma violet has become a very lucrative industry. The peasant flower-farmers contract to give the firm the same quantity every year.

The sweet chestnut, which grows abundantly in and about Grasse, holds quite a prominent place among the crystallised fruits, and having passed through the transformation scene, is known as *marron glacé*. It requires only three days to arrive at perfection, and the same syrup in which it is cooked serves to crystallise it.

There are no duties in England on these fruits, though there are on alcoholic perfumes such as are produced by Bruno Court. As Madame Négre laughingly said, "*Sugar and fruit* seemed a more natural and pleasing com-bination than flowers and fat;" and yet we reminded her of the exquisite result of this apparently incongruous blend.

The home of these magicians is, as I have said, quaint and curious enough to set it apart from ordinary houses; and surely the transfor-mation imposed on every flower and fruit that finds its way within its portal is not to be sur-passed in any fairy story, and the beauty of it all is, that nothing so transformed loses any-thing of its beauty and wholesomeness.

Both here and at Bruno Court's success has been obtained, and a reputation made by thoroughness, skill, and patience, urged to the exercise of these qualities by the incessant need of meeting the ever-increasing demands for their stores.

From Cannes to Grasse is but a short railway journey, and a day spent amid its beauty and quaintness, together with a sight of the poetic industries carried on within it, would be a day to remember always.   EMMA BREWER.

VOL. XX.—No. 993.] JANUARY 7, 1899. [PRICE ONE PENNY.

SELF-CULTURE FOR GIRLS.

PART I.

THERE is, perhaps, no word in the present day which has been more frequently used and abused than "culture." It has come so readily to the lips of modern prophets, that it has acquired a secondary and ironical significance. Some of our readers may have seen a clever University parody (on the *Heathen Chinee*) describing the encounter of two undergraduates in the streets of Oxford. One, in faultless attire, replies proudly to the other's inquiry where he is going—

"I am bound for some tea and tall culture."

ASPIRATION.

Lily Watson, "Self-Culture for Girls" (Volume 20, 7 January 1899, p. 225).

He is, in fact, on the way to a meeting of the Browning Society, and when a Don hurries up to tell him the society has suddenly collapsed, great is the lamentation !

Probably the society in question deserved no satire at all ; but there is a sort of " culture for culture's sake " which does deserve to be held up to ridicule.

We find nothing to laugh at, however, but a very real pathos, in the letters that are reaching us literally from all quarters of the globe ; and we long to help the writers, as well as those who have similar needs and longings unexpressed. " How can I attain self-culture ? " is the question asked in varying terms, but with the same refrain.

Girls, after schooldays are past, wake up to find themselves in a region of vast, dimly-perceived possibilities :

" Moving about in worlds not realised."

More to be pitied is the lot of those who have not had any schooldays at all worth speaking of, and who are awaking to their own mental poverty—poverty, while there is wealth all about them which they cannot make their own. Their case is like that of the heir to some vast estates, who cannot enjoy them, because he cannot prove his title.

What, then, is this much talked-of culture ? There are several things which it is *not*.

To begin with, it is not a superficial smatter-ing of certain accomplishments.

It is not a general readiness to talk about the reviews one has read of new books.

It is not the varnish acquired from as-sociating day by day with well-educated and urbane people.

It is not development to an enormous extent in one direction only.

It is not attending one course of University Extension Lectures.

It is not the knack of cramming for examina-tions, and of passing them with *éclat*.

All these elements may enter into culture, but they are not culture itself.

It is a harder matter to define culture than to say what it is not. As we write these words, our eye falls on the saying of a well-known prelate, reported in the *Times* of the day : " General culture—another name for sympathetic interest in the world of human intelligence." This sounds rather highflown and difficult, but we may add three more definitions—

" Culture is a study of perfection."— *Matthew Arnold.*

" Culture is the passion for sweetness and light, and (what is more) the passion for making them prevail."—*Matthew Arnold.*

" Culture is the process by which a man becomes all that he was created capable of being."—*Carlyle.*

The third of these is, perhaps, the best working definition of culture, for it shows its real importance and significance, and also makes it simpler to understand.

Look at a neglected garden. The grass is long and rank ; the beds are a mere tangle of weeds and of straggling flowers that have run to seed, or deteriorated in size and sweetness until they can hardly be called flowers at all. It is a wilderness.

The garden is taken in hand and cultivated, not by a mechanical ignorant gardener, but by someone who understands the capacities of the soil, and knows what will do well and repay his care. See the transformation in time to come ! There is everything by turn that is beautiful in its season ; the lovely herbaceous border, the standard rose-trees, the sheltered bed of lilies of the valley, the peaches on the warm southern wall, the ferns waving in feathery profusion in the cool corner near the well—all that the garden can produce for delight to the eye or for food is there. The ground is not given over exclusively to one flower, one vegetable ; it is not stocked

mechanically for the summer with geraniums and calceolarias ; but it is, as we say in homely parlance, " made the most of " in every particular, and is a delight to behold.

This may seem a simple illustration, and we are writing not for the erudite, but for the simple reader. The man or woman of culture is the man or woman whose nature has been cultivated in such a way as to develop all its capabilities in the best possible direction ; whose education has been adapted skilfully to taste and capacity, and who has been taught the art of self-instruction.

It is hardly necessary to urge the value of this " cultivation." " Cultivation is as ne-cessary to the mind as food to the body," said a wise man, and this is gradually coming to be believed. Culture is something more by far than mere instruction, though instruction is a means by which it may be attained. Bearing in mind our simile of the garden, we are led on from one thought to another.

It was a very wise man indeed who pointed out that, even as ground will produce some-thing, " herbs or weeds," the mind will not remain empty if it is not cultivated ; it tends to become full of silly or ignorant thoughts like " an unweeded garden."

Again, in a well-ordered, cultivated plot of ground we have what is useful as well as what is lovely. In culture, not only the acquire-ment of " useful knowledge " plays a part, but the storing of the mind with what is beautiful, the development of taste in all directions.

In brief, a woman of real culture is the woman who makes you instinctively feel, when in her company, that she is just what she was meant to be ; harmoniously developed in accordance with her natural capacity. There is nothing startling about her paraded attainments. The extreme simplicity of a person of true culture is one of the most marked traits, and the chief point that distinguishes spurious from real culture is that the former is inclined to " tall talk " and the latter is not.

Charles Dickens can still make us smile at his caricature of an American L. L. (literary lady) and her remarks on her introduction to some great personage. She immediately begins—

" Mind and matter glide swift into the vortex of Immensity. Howls the sublime, and softly sleeps the calm Ideal in the whisper-ing chambers of Imagination. To hear it, sweet it is. But then outlaughs the stern philosopher and saith to the Grotesque : ' What ho ; arrest for me that Agency ! Go, bring it here ! ' And so the vision fadeth."

The woman of culture does not attempt fine talking, and it is only gradually that her power and charm dawn upon her companion. " It is proof of a high culture to say the greatest matters in the simplest way."

In the same manner simplicity is a proof of high breeding. The people who are " some-body " are, as a rule, easy to " get on " with. It is the rich " parvenue " who is disconcerting, and who tries to drag into her conversation the names of great people or great doings that will impress her companion.

When we observe this sort of thing in a woman, we always know she is not " to the manner born." So when we hear people declare, " I am afraid of So-and-so because she is so clever," we feel that, if there is ground for their fear, there is something defective in the clever one's culture.

Why should Culture be Desired ?

It opens the eye and ear to the beauty and greatness of the world, revealing wonders that could not otherwise be understood, and bring-ing with it a wealth of happiness ; and more, it gives an understanding of life in its due proportion. The woman of culture is not the woman who objects to perform necessary tasks at a pinch because they are " menial," or takes offence at imaginary slights, or is for ever

fussing about her domestic duties and her servants, or gets up little quarrels and " storms in a teacup " generally, or delights in ill-natured gossip. She sees how ineffably small such things are, and she sees them in this light because she has the width of vision which enables her to discern the meaning of life as a whole. Those whose eyes have once been opened to the beauty and pathos that lie around their path, even in the common round of daily duty, do not notice the dust that clings to their shoes.

Sympathy is an accompaniment of true culture ; the sympathy that comes of under-standing. Ignorant people are very often hard just because of ignorance. They cannot in the least enter into the feelings of others, nor do they understand that there is a world beyond their own miserable little enclosure.

For instance, what a puzzle a clever, sen-sitive, imaginative child is to people of con-tented matter-of-fact stupidity ! One need not think of Maggie and Mrs. Tulliver, or Aurora Leigh and her aunt, to illustrate this—there are plenty of examples from real life.

The girl does not take to sewing and the baking of bread and puddings ; she is always wanting to get hold of a book—never so happy as when she is reading. Or the boy is always poring over the mysteries of fern and flower—never so happy as when he is afoot to secure some fresh specimen. People of culture would foresee that the one may be a student, the other a botanist, in days to come, and, while of course insisting that practical duty is not selfishly overlooked, they would try to give scope for the individual taste. People without culture would set the whole thing down as laziness and vagabond trifling and " shirking," to be severely repressed. Sym-pathetic insight is one of the most valuable attributes of culture ; valuable all through life, especially when dealing with others.

But we can imagine that the reader may be thinking rather hopelessly, " It is not necessary to preach to me on the advantages of culture ; I am fully convinced of them ; but all you say makes me hopeless of ever attaining such a degree of perfection. In fact, I can see culture is not for me at all, and I must just go on as I am."

The dictionary definition of culture is " the application of labour, or other means, to improve good qualities, or growth." This does not sound quite like the other definitions, and a great deal of confusion has been caused by people forgetting that the word " culture " is used for two things—the " process " of cultivation, and the " result " of that process. Now it is quite true that " culture," in the last and highest sense, is not within the reach of all our readers ; but surely there is no reader who would say she cannot " apply labour or other means " to improve her intelligence, be it in ever so small a degree. It is better to cultivate a garden ever so little than to leave it a wilderness.

Culture, looked upon as a process, may begin and go on almost indefinitely. Goethe well says—

" Woe to every sort of culture which destroys the most effectual means of all true culture, and directs us to the end, instead of rendering us happy on the way."

In other words, it is foolish to strain miserably after " culture for culture's sake," endeavouring to reach an impossible goal, and feeling discontented and wretched because it is too remote. The wise way is to do the best one can with the opportunities that lie within reach. Every girl who reads these pages can do something to render herself a little nearer her ideal of " culture," and in the subsequent papers we shall try to show her how she can best succeed.

LILY WATSON.
(To be continued.)

Lily Watson, "Self-Culture for Girls" (Volume 20, 7 January 1899, p. 226).

STUDY.

By LADY DUNBOYNE.

To study is to appease one of the three great cravings of human nature. The body craves for food, the soul craves for love, and the mind craves for knowledge, which knowledge can only be acquired by study. And for the general well-being of the human organisation this hunger of the mind for knowledge requires satisfying just as much as the hunger of the body for food, or the hunger of the soul for love. We are apt not to think so, because the operations of the mind and their consequences are not directly exposed to the human eye, but they exist none the less and work silently and incessantly within us for good or ill.

Now if we reflect a moment we shall find that the hunger of the mind for knowledge is the only one of these three human cravings which cannot be appeased without conscious effort on our part. We eat mechanically; we love involuntarily, but we cannot acquire knowledge without conscious effort, and, as we are always inclined to postpone making efforts to a more convenient season, our mind-hunger too often remains unfilled. This is an increasing evil amongst the women of the present day. All the new inventions, such as bicycles and motor-cars and telephones, which should simplify life for them and give them more leisure for occupations requiring thought and reflection, seem to add to their restlessness and to the neglect of the regular study which is so essential to their well-being. And their minds become dwarfed for want of proper nourishment, and they themselves, upon whose mental guidance Nature has decreed hangs the fate of future generations, become totally unfit for the high destiny assigned to them.

There are infinite capacities in the human mind. It is so made that nothing but work can satisfy it. Give it wholesome, regular work and its might and strength increases, its Divine origin asserts itself, and in this world of death and mortality it testifies of powers that can never die, of capabilities that can never be limited. But withhold from it its proper food, and it becomes a prey to the moth and rust of corruption, a victim to the inner discord which inevitably follows the violation of Nature's laws. Does not this truth manifest itself on the very features and countenances of human beings? In scenes of gaiety where,

"While fashion's arts decoy,
The heart distrusting asks if this be joy,"

how often does the querulous voice and the bored demeanour speak of the want of harmony and happiness in the inner being: whereas in the lecture or class room, or wherever two or three are gathered together for the purpose of acquiring knowledge, the beaming eyes and animated features speak of inward contentment and conformity to the true and rightful calling.

But to experience the satisfaction study is capable of giving we must not enter upon it without forethought and reflection. For to study, though it may seem a simple task in prospective, is, at first at all events, a difficult one in fulfilment. It involves fixing the mind resolutely for a certain time upon a certain subject, and the mind is the most volatile part of the being. St. Vitus with his jerky dances and incessant movements visits it far oftener than he does the body. We have need to exert our utmost determination and perseverance to banish those innumerable irrelevant thoughts which make their way into the sanctum of the brain when we sit down to study. They are impertinent, unbidden intruders, those thoughts, and they spring upon us so suddenly that we have not time to say "not at home" to them; but our will, whose special prerogative is to help our moral and intellectual powers, can turn them out for us, and their attempts to visit us will become feebler and less frequent in the proportion that our rejection of them becomes more determined and more persistent. Our intellect must be subservient to our will, and our will must be exercised in its full strength in order to study. La Rochefoucauld says, "Nous avons plus de force que de volonté, et c'est souvent pour nous excuser à nous-mêmes que nous imaginons que les choses sont impossibles." We should never imagine anything impossible to our intellectual capabilities. They are Divine gifts, given to us with no mean sparing hand like the gifts we make each other. In measure and in strength they are infinite. The more we draw from them, the greater does their supply become, and study is the means given us to draw from their infallible spring. Doubtless there is a difference in individual mental capacities, but the greatest mind can never bring forth fruit without study, whereas the feeblest may be made capable by study of doing work which will prove a source of usefulness and happiness to all generations. All the great works of art, all the great discoveries of science, have proceeded from germs such as we each possess in our own being, watered and nourished by study. Effort and study were the inexorable price put upon those germs by Nature to render them fit for their mighty work; and we may as well expect the earth to bring forth the necessaries of life without labour as for the mind to bring forth profitable work without study.

But besides the will and the intellect there is yet one other part of our nature, the co-operation of which is necessary to profitable study, and that is the heart. The will must guide the intellect and the heart must guide the will, for study to be of use. Dryden has set before us in a few words the three stages of mental experience which culminate in successful study.

"What the child admired,
The youth endeavoured and the man acquired."

And the second stage is the essential one of the three, for on its fulfilment the other two depend. Without it the first would come to no use, and the third to no fruition. And girls should appropriate it as their guide and watchword when entering upon that period of life in which they are freed from the daily duties of lessons and are as yet untrammelled by the daily duties of practical life. During that period they should listen for the voices of their childhood, for the promptings of their nature while it was yet fair and fresh from the Hand of God, and they should bring their intellects to act in accordance with those voices and those promptings, in other words they should cultivate the talents which stirred their hearts and imaginations as children. Children's predilections are sure augurs of their capabilities. The history of nations and of literature and of art, all three testify to this great truth. Napoleon used to amuse himself with a miniature cannon and playing at battles during his childhood; Nelson with a miniature ship and sailing it on a pond, during his. Charles Kingsley's delight as a child was to make a pulpit in his nursery and to preach sermons in a pinafore to an imaginary congregation. There are still extant some of these youthful bursts of eloquence delivered at four years old. Scott loved to listen to his mother and grandmother reciting poetry long before he could read. And there is a story of a celebrated painter being too poor as a child to buy paint brushes and providing himself with them from the bristles of his cat.

The secret of a happy and a useful life is to find one particular occupation in which we can always become absorbed and in which our efforts and activities must be brought to bear upon the highest part of our nature.

" Every man has two educations, one which he receives from others and one, more important, which he gives himself." And one of the first and most important steps in self-education is to find out the subject for which we have most aptitude and to cultivate it to the utmost of our capabilities. Girls are apt to follow a sudden impulse to work at what happens to be brought before them. They see a sketch painted by one friend, hear a song sung by another, a poem recited by a third, and they immediately devote themselves to painting, singing or reciting, as the case may be. Now this is a great mistake. We each have our special talents, and we are wasting them if we allow ourselves, like the Athenians of old, constantly to spend our time on some new thing. It is all very well to know something about everything, but it is very much better to know everything about something, about that certain something to which our hearts and minds respond and to the cultivation of which distractions of pursuits are fatal. There may be some people capable of mastering many subjects, but they are few and far between, and the geniuses and mental helpers of the world are to be found amongst those whose whole energies have been concentrated on one subject to the exclusion of all others.

The great sculptor, Edgar Boehm, took no sort of interest in politics, but was persuaded on one occasion by a friend to go to the House of Commons to hear Gladstone speak. At the end of the speech he was asked his opinion as to its merits. " If I must tell the truth," he answered, " I was so occupied in studying the orator's face and expression, that I did not listen to a word he said." Such a man was bound to succeed. He looked upon every detail of life with an artist's eye, he treated every trivial circumstance as a means to increase his knowledge and to strengthen his capabilities in his own beloved art.

We cannot all be Edgar Boehms, but we can each follow his method of making one study an object around which all the little events of life will gather and subordinate themselves. But that one study at the outset requires care. We must choose it with thought and reflection, we must enter upon it with faith and trust, and we must persevere in it with thoroughness and earnestness.

Thought and reflection are the first mental exercises we have to use in regard to it. As I said before, we must meditate carefully upon our childhood's experiences, and by means of this process of retrospection we must ascertain the study for which we have most predisposition. And having made quite sure of it, we must enter upon it with faith and trust, thus exercising the Divine part of our nature. Spiritual inspiration lies always about our path and about our bed, if we would but open the eye of faith

to see it and stretch out the hand of trust to grasp it. As Tennyson says—

" Speak to Him thou, for He hears, and Spirit with Spirit can meet,
Closer is He than breathing, and nearer than hands and feet."

God is ever ready to bless our endeavours if we are using them according to His will, and how can we use them more surely in accordance with His will than by improving the special talents with which He has endowed us ? We cannot explain these mysteries but we know them to be true, and we know too that the life of the soul depends upon faith and trust for its very breath, that by means of them it sets up noble aims and high endeavours and becomes a source of blessing to all around it.

And finally we must use practical means to help us in study. Discipline and method must be brought to bear upon it. We must set apart a certain time daily in which we can be undisturbed and alone. Solitude promotes study. The presence of another individual, unless that individual is acting and feeling with us, raises a disturbing influence and in some inexplicable way seems to draw our thoughts from our work on to himself. Having once chosen the time, we must adhere to it in spite of any difficulties which may arise. Outside instructors are engaged for particular hours and are only put off for very special reasons. Self-instructors should follow the same rule. Before we begin we must surround ourselves with books of reference and with any mechanical helps or implements we may require. And then we must set to work diligently, patiently and perseveringly. Above all we must aim at thoroughness. A little thorough study will be of far more use than a great deal superficially got through. It will not only leave a deeper and more lasting impression, but it will necessitate thought and discipline and all experiences that invigorate the mind and strengthen the intellect.

Now I cannot promise you that this course of study which I am urging you to plan out and pursue for yourselves will bring you wealth or fame or distinction, but I can promise you that it will bring you what is far better. I can promise you that it will brighten many a weary hour for you, and that it will help you to steer wisely and cheerfully through all the changes and chances of this mortal life. And what shall I say of it in relation to that immortal life which lies before us all behind the veil ? That which we have sown here we shall reap there. The creations of the mind and of the soul can never die. And it may be that amongst the joys that await us which eye hath not seen nor ear heard, not the least will be the completion and bringing to perfection those studies begun in a world where the best work bears the stamp of imperfection and where the highest aspirations remain unsatisfied.

THE HEART OF UNA SACKVILLE.

By Mrs. GEORGE DE HORNE VAIZEY, Author of " About Peggy Saville," " Pixie O'Shaughnessy," etc.

CHAPTER XX.

June 15th.

O-DAY the first roses have opened in the garden, the rose-garden at the Moat, for we came home two months ago, and are still luxuriating in the old haunts and the new rooms, which are as beautiful as money and mother's beautiful taste can make them. I felt a sort of rush of happiness as I buried my face in the cool, fragrant leaves, and, somehow or other, a longing came over me to unearth this old diary, and write the history of the year.

It has been a long, long winter. We spent three

months in Bournemouth for Vere's sake, taking her to London to see the specialist on our way home. He examined her carefully, and said that spinal troubles were slow affairs, that it was a great thing to keep up the general health, that he was glad we had been to Bournemouth, and that no doubt the change home would also be beneficial. Fresh air, fresh air—live as much in the fresh open air as possible during the summer—— Then he stopped, and Vere looked at him steadily, and said—

" You mean that I am worse ? "

" My dear young lady, you must not be despondent. Hope on, hope ever ! You can do more for yourself than any doctor. These things take time. One never

Education

Although almost all of the fiction and a certain amount of the non-fiction in *The Girl's Own Paper* were fairly conservative, if not reactionary, the magazine was always more progressive in detailing educational opportunities. In part this must have been a response to a clear demand from readers, as there are numerous replies in Answers to Correspondents that address questions regarding admission to particular schools and training for various careers. Initially, the main focus was on secondary and post-secondary education. However, by the turn of the century, the magazine began to focus on newer opportunities in technical and professional training. This seems to have been designed to encourage readers to consider not only nontraditional work, but also professions that might be considered lower class (see the chapter on Work). Also, some of the technical training was promoted as beneficial to girls who were considering emigration.

J. A. Owen's "Girton College" (vol. 1, 1880, pp. 492–93) and E. A. L. K.'s "The North London Collegiate School for Girls" (vol. 3, 1881–82, pp. 494–96) are typical of the early articles that described pioneering educational institutions for girls. Girton College was founded in 1869 at Hitchin, Hertfordshire, by Emily Davies and Barbara Bodichon, both active in the promotion of women's education and suffrage. The college moved to Cambridge in 1873. At the time of this article, women were not yet allowed to sit the Tripos examinations; that would come in the following year. The North London Collegiate School for Girls had been founded in 1850 by the educational pioneer Frances Buss; it was considered a model school for the quality of the education it offered its students.

"The Girls of the World: Facts and Figures" (vol. 7, 1885–86, pp. 198–99, 268–69) is a multi-part series by Emma Brewer that makes use of the new science of statistics. The section reproduced here focuses on education, comparing that of English girls to that of girls around the world. Those who follow current debates on gender and education will be interested in this article's data comparing the abilities of boys and girls in different fields of learning.

An anonymous Lady Graduate shares her feelings of pride and accomplishment in her description of "Presentation Day at London University" (vol. 19, 1897–98, pp. 676–77). The institution described is Bedford College (the first English post-secondary institution for women, founded in 1849 by Elizabeth Jesser Reid), affiliated with the University of London, which was the first English post-secondary institution to offer degrees to women, beginning in 1878 (Oxford did not offer degrees to women until 1920, and although Cambridge offered the title of degrees to women in 1921, it did not grant full degree privileges to women until 1947).

Lily Watson describes "The Battersea Polytechnic" (vol. 25, 1903–04, pp. 628–31), explaining the concept of technical education but focusing mostly on training in domestic economy. Students include teachers in training and young women intending to emigrate.

The anonymously written article on "Pitman's Metropolitan School" (vol. 25, 1903–04, pp. 308–10) emphasizes the benefits of commercial training.

Lena Shepstone's description of the Swanley Horticultural College in "Gardening as a Profession for Girls: How They Are Trained at Swanley" (vol. 26, 1904–05, pp. 424–28, 596) is interesting both for its promotion of physical labour and its concluding discussion of the benefits of this type of training for girls who are planning to emigrate.

GIRTON COLLEGE.

HE higher education of women" is a hackneyed phrase, which has served as a peg to many—who do not stop to consider what the words may mean—whereon to hang anything they may wish to say in ridicule of the general desire of women in the present day to possess for themselves, and to give to others, those educational and intellectual advantages which have so long been denied them.

A little definite information as to how the movement arose, out of which the foundation of Girton College sprang, may be acceptable to some of our readers.

In 1871 Mrs. William Grey, who had long had the more systematic and thorough education of girls at heart, and had endeavoured to promote it in every way, initiated at the meeting of the Social Science Association held at Leeds that year, the union for promoting this "higher education."

The name by which the movement is officially known is "National Union for Improving the Education of Women of all Classes," and its office is at 1, Queen-street, Brompton; the secretary, Miss Louisa Brough. The president is the Princess Louise; and amongst its vice-presidents are Archbishop Trench, the Bishops of London, Exeter, and Manchester, Dowager Lady Stanley of Alderley, Dean Stanley, and other distinguished names. The central committee has as its chairman Captain Douglas Galton.

Out of this union came the girls' public day schools, usually called "High Schools," in which so many of you are being educated. Owing to its efforts, also, the authorities of the Universities of Oxford and Cambridge consented to allow girls to be candidates for the examinations established at different local centres. None over the age of eighteen were to be eligible for these. This was a restriction which was thought by some to be both arbitrary and ungenerous. Why, they said, should women who had the desire and the means for study be limited in this way? In order to meet their needs and wishes an association was formed, having for its object the founding of a college which should stand in relation to girls' schools and home teaching as the Universities do towards the public schools for boys.

According to the report, this association aimed at erecting, maintaining, and conducting a college for the higher education of women (hence the phrase now so common); to take such steps as from time to time may be thought most expedient and effectual to obtain for the students admission to the examinations for degrees of the University of Cambridge, and to place the college in connection with that University.

Religious instruction and services according to the principles of the Church of England are given in the said college, but attendance on these is not required from any student of full age, or whose parents or guardians may object thereto in writing. No person is admitted who has not passed the entrance examination, unless they have passed one of the senior local university examinations.

These examinations are held in London in March and June, the fee being £1; and every candidate must pass the preliminary—arithmetic, English grammar and composition, physical and political geography, English and Scripture (New Testament) history; and, besides these, in any *two* of the following subjects: Latin—translation of easy passages from Latin into English, and the reverse; Greek, French, German, Algebra, geometry, trigonometry (up to and including the solution of triangles), and conic sections. Not all these, remember, but a choice of any two.

Some people imagine that all who enter Girton must try for a University degree. In reference to this, Miss E. Davies, the treasurer of the college, writes: "This impression is entirely contrary to fact, and, as it is calculated to frighten away those who might be glad to become students and also to discourage support on the ground of its being an unreasonable requirement, it is important in the interests of the college that it should be dispelled. No student, as such, apart from special conditions attached to certain scholarships, is, or ever has been, required to take any University examination, or to try for any kind of certificate. They choose their own course. If they choose to try for 'degree examinations' we do our best to obtain the opportunity for them on the same conditions as those which the University imposes on undergraduates."

About half of the students look forward to being teachers; not governesses in private families, but teachers and head mistresses in schools. The rest work without any special career in view, chiefly from the love of study.

The college was opened on October 16, 1869, and a house hired at Hitchin for the temporary reception of students. In October, 1873, the present building at Girton was ready for occupation, with accommodation for twenty-one students and the necessary class-rooms. Since that time considerable enlargements and additions have been made. During last term over forty-two were residing in the college. The Michaelmas term begins about the middle of October, and lasts eight weeks; the Lent term, beginning about the end of January, lasts eight weeks; and the Easter term, beginning in April, lasts eight weeks. The charge for board, lodging, and instruction is £35 per term, to be paid in advance. This sum covers all charges.

For the encouragement of would-be students of limited means several scholarships are attached to the college. Last year Mrs. Russell Gurney presented the sum of £1,000 as the endowment fund of an entrance scholarship, to be called the "Russell Gurney Scholarship" in memory of her husband, and to be awarded upon the results of an examination in history. The Right Hon. Russell Gurney, late Recorder of London, was one of Girton's first and best friends. Lady Goldsmid also presented £1,200, in memory of her husband, Sir Francis Goldsmid, to found the "Sir Francis Goldsmid scholarship." This was awarded for the first time last March. Then there are two scholarships of £60 and £40 each, for three years, given by the Goldsmiths' Company; a scholarship of £35 a year, founded by Mr. F. D. Mocatta; the "Gilchrist scholarship" of £50 a year, for three years; a foundation scholarship of £90 a year, for four years; one formerly of £50, now increased to the value of 80 guineas a year, for three years, founded by the Clothworkers' Company for the benefit of a lady of limited means; Mr. R. S. Wright gave a scholarship of £100 a year, for three years; an entrance exhibition of 50 guineas a year, for three years, to a lady of limited means, who is engaged in or preparing for teaching, is also given by Lady Stanley of Alderley.

The course of study comprises divinity, modern languages, English, French, and German classics, mathematics, moral science, natural science, history, and vocal music. This course is, in a measure, optional. To quote again from Miss Davies: "The entrance examination puts a hindrance in the way of those whose early education has been so defective as to leave them unprepared for advanced studies. The examination is by no means severe, and the candidates who have failed to pass it were certainly not fit to enter upon a course of higher education.

"Then as to the nature of the teaching given at the college, which is, perhaps, its most important distinction. This, though it goes by the name of lectures, is very different from the sort of teaching usually understood by that term. It is given to very small classes, in which the students ask as well as answer questions. We consult the lecturers as to whether the instruction can be best given to a class or individually, and in some subjects, especially in mathematics, the differences in the stage of progress and the manner of working are such as to make it desirable that it should be to a great extent individually."

An old Girton student, an American lady, the founder of a scholarship mentioned above, has given in an American paper an account of student life at Girton, which presents an attractive and pleasant picture. From it we shall draw a little of our description. But first as to the daily routine, which is as follows: 7 a.m., prayers; 8.15 to 9 a.m., breakfast; 12 to 3 p.m., luncheon—which means that these two meals are allowed to remain so long on the tables, and the students come in as convenience serves and help themselves; 6 p.m., dinner. Students must enter their names on the marking roll at some time between the hours of 8 a.m. and 9 a.m., 12 and 3 p.m., and 6 and 7 p.m. Every student must be present at all the lectures belonging to her course, except when leave of absence has been granted by the mistress.

Students can have tea in their rooms at four o'clock, and after dinner up to nine o'clock.

The college gates are closed in winter at 6 p.m.; in summer at dusk; after which students may not be out beyond the grounds. They may accept invitations from families, but not pay visits of any sort to college rooms without permission. They must not be later than 11 p.m., and must not accept evening invitations for more than once a week in any one term. In asking leave of absence the student must say where she is going. The house is closed at 10 p.m. Subject to such regulations as the mistress sees fit to prescribe, visitors may be invited to join in games in the college grounds and in the gymnasium, and may be entertained at luncheon or dinner in hall, or at tea in the private rooms at a fixed charge. The term friend or guest only applies to ladies, except in the case of parent or guardian. There is a public room in which general visitors, subject to the approval of the mistress, may be seen.

A bedroom and a study, or one large room serving as both, is set apart for each student, fitted with every necessary convenience: these are cheerful, airy rooms. In each is a large table, on which the occupant can place her papers, text books, &c. These rooms are made bright-looking, according to the individual character of the student, with photographs, flowering plants, art needlework, &c.

After luncheon, where plenty of good milk is supplied, they go off in pairs for an hour's walk over the fields, through hedge and ditch, rambling at "their own sweet will." If the weather is bad they turn into the gymnasium, which is a covered court separate from the college building. It is used much for "fives." In spring and autumn cricket and lawn tennis

J. A. Owen, "Girton College" (Volume 1, 31 July 1880, p. 492).

are played on the lawns near the building. After lecture many of the students take exercise before dinner. Some of them make riding parties ; those who can afford to hire. Most of the lectures take place in the afternoon, and, on an average, a student has only one lecture a day. The variety of subjects causes the attendance on each course to be rather small as yet. The lecturer reviews the work done by each student since the last lecture ; any questions are answered, and special help needed is given. Then the lecturer gives his lecture proper, without the limitations of class book.

After dinner there is often choral music. After that, the students usually give themselves for a time to their labours, which are only broken by the advent of tea, coffee, or cocoa, in many cases. Others who are sociably inclined receive their friends in their own rooms.

The descriptions one hears from Girton students sound very pleasant, and make some of us older women wish such advantages had been open to us fifteen or twenty years ago. It is amusing in these days to read over again the description of college life, given in Tennyson's "Princess," and pleasant to women to realise what progress in almost everything relating to woman's place in the world has been made since the time when that charming poem was written.

J. A. OWEN.

ON WATERING FLOWERS.

WATERING in gardens requires different rules from watering pot-plants, though both need thought, and must vary with the time of year and weather. In London, or any very smoky town, I should recommend more frequent watering than in the country in dry weather. In the country the water is only wanted for the roots of the plants, but in London it is wanted by the leaves too, or the foliage gets choked and poisoned by the smoke.

Plants breathe through their leaves, as we do through our mouths, so it is necessary to the lives of some, and to the health of all, that their leaves should be kept clean. Otherwise, in watering your garden, you should try to imitate nature. Do not water your garden in a hot sun ; it makes the foliage shrivel and turn colour. Nature takes care about this, for when rain falls the sun is hidden by clouds. So in hot weather do your watering very early, or else in the evening, unless your garden is shady, and then any time will do. You should water as seldom as possible, except when the foliage needs washing, and then you should be very careful to soak the roots thoroughly before any water touches the leaves. A sprinkling of water on the surface of the ground does much more harm than good, as it makes the ground cake, and then the earth below gets both hotter and drier than if the surface were loose, and not a single drop of water will have reached the roots of the plants.—*L. M. Forster.*

From the Painting of SIR THOMAS LAWRENCE.

GAZE on—'tis lovely ! Childhood's lip and cheek,
   Mantling beneath its earnest brow of thought !
Gaze—yet what seest thou in those fair and meek
   And fragile things, as but for sunshine wrought ?
Thou seest what grace must nurture for the sky,
What life must fashion for eternity !

hands, and then concentric rings were formed until the whole green seemed in motion. Another pretty figure was made by the lasses and lads each taking the end of a streamer dependent from the top of the pole, and by skilfully jetting "in and out" plait them all, and then by a backward movement unplait them.

The Robin Hood games made a prominent feature in the day's observance. An ample space, marked off from the crowd by a barrier of rope, was entered first by six young wood-men, bearing axes and garlanded with ivy. Six maidens, clad in blue and crowned with primroses, led in a sleek milch cow profusely decorated, and they were followed by six foresters dressed all in green.

The cream of the procession included Robin Hood, with Little John and Will Stukely; two maidens in orange-coloured kirtles, strewing flowers; Maid Marian, crowned and supported by two bridemaidens in blue, crowned with violets, and followed by four others dressed in green; Friar Tuck bearing a huge quarter-staff, and Much, the miller's son, came next, then the maypole, and at last the hobby horse and the dragon. The villagers were allowed to decorate the pole, which was raised amidst general acclamations, and then the gay party within the barrier danced and sang. The hobby horse frisked, ambled, curvetted, and performed feats of jugglery, the dragon hissed, yelled, and clapped his wings. Much cast meal slily into the faces of the gazing rustics, or rapped their heads with his bladder, and Friar Tuck dropped his staff upon the toes of those who pressed forward too eagerly, bidding them mind their prayers.

At last the horse and dragon becoming weary, Robin Hood and his men practised archery, Robin winning the prize. Then the villagers began dancing.

Among later customs, we read of the Milk-maids' dance even as near our own time as 1795. They formed a garland of silver plate, borrowed from the pawnbrokers, and tastefully arranged on a pyramidal frame with ribbons and knots of flowers. It was borne by two men; and the maids followed, pausing to dance in front of the houses of their customers.

The old customs have almost dwindled down to the practice of carrying garlands common among country children in remote villages, or to rude festivals, which bear the marks of their ancient origin. The May fair of some small towns in Leicestershire has still its juggler and clown, the apologies for the hobby horse and Much, the miller's son; and the song of the Mayers, in its reference to the Spaniards, points to the time of Queen Elizabeth.

It is still customary for the young girls of Edinburgh to rise early on May morning and to repair to Arthur's Seat, there to bathe their faces in the dew. And in the streets of London the chimney-sweeps collect about their Jack-in-the-green—a man concealed in a framework of evergreens and herbs, dancing and soliciting halfpence from the passers-by. As the gratuities thus obtained often provided a rough carousal at the close of the day, the more respectable sweeps have withdrawn from these displays.

Perhaps the most interesting relics of bygone days are the real maypole, still elegant and lofty in a small village near Chester, and the fragment of one which supports the weather-cock of the church at Pendleton, near Man-chester. The old church of St. Andrew's Undershaft on Cornhill indicates the position of one maypole in Tudor times; and Maypole-alley in the Strand, the site of the last planted there in honour of the Restoration, and removed thence to Wanstead by Sir Isaac Newton in 1717 as a support to his large telescope.

At Knutsford, in Cheshire, and at Worsley, in Lancashire, May-day customs have been revived with immense success.

In the former place, the prettiest maid is chosen from the national school, and she is elected May Queen. On May-day she and her maids, all dressed in white and crowned with flowers, head a procession which traverses the town.

Tiny children in waggons follow her, and after them boys dressed appropriately to represent all trades, and maids to personate gipsy girls. A short service is then held in church; and the company proceed to an open space, where the maypole is erected. The queen is escorted to a pavilion, where her maids dispose themselves round her; two courtiers approach; one crowns her, and the other presents the sceptre. Songs and dancing round the pole then take place, and then the queen and her subjects retire for refreshment.

THE NORTH LONDON COLLEGIATE SCHOOL FOR GIRLS.

PERHAPS among the many and various phenomena of nineteenth-century civilisation none is more curious and interesting than the sudden springing into life and rapid vigorous growth, all over the country, of large public schools for girls. Twenty years ago even, if the daughter in an ordinary English household had twice the intellect and capacity of her brother, his head it was that Latin, Greek, and mathematics must at any cost be made to fill, or at least to seem to fill, while if she had aspirations for anything beyond her piano, some acquaintance (often the slightest) with the French and Italian langu-ages, and such knowledge of English history and literature as could be gained from an accurate verbal acquaintance with "Mang-nall's Questions," such unfeminine desires were not to be mentioned in a well-regulated family.

Of course, there were homes in which a girl who longed for higher culture found help and sympathy in a clever father, but even then the daughter's ambition and interest in her work were looked upon by the rest of the family as rather reprehensible eccentricities, and her education had to be conducted quite *sub rosa*. Now, though there are still some who sigh regretfully for those good old times, still the majority of Englishmen and Englishwomen are more than willing to allow their daughters to participate in the new educational life which, in the shape of good public schools for girls, is stretching out to meet them almost at their very doors.

Foremost among these public schools for the maidens of the present day is the North London Collegiate School for Girls, the school-house being a large and handsome building, standing close to the Camden-road Station of the Midland Railway. This school was started in Camden Town as a private undertaking by Miss Frances Mary Buss, the present able head mistress, and her mother, and removed in 1850 to Camden-street, where, under the supervision of the Rev. David Laing, Vicar of Holy Trinity, Haver-stock-hill, it became much more widely known, and in 1870 numbered above two hundred pupils. In 1870, after the report of the Schools Inquiry Commission into the state of girls' education, efforts were made to place this school on a more permanent footing, and it was removed to 202, Camden-road, and placed in the hands of a trust. At the same time, the old house in Camden-street was given up to a new and lower middle-class school, a daughter, as it were, of the original institution. The grand buildings in Sandall-road, which are now the home of the North

London Collegiate School, represent not only almost incredible exertion on the part of the head-mistress and her friends to raise a build-ing fund, but also the generous aid of two City companies, the Brewers and Clothworkers, the former company having most liberally sup-plied the endowment from an Educational Fund belonging to them, and derivable from property in St. Pancras. These new buildings were opened in 1879 by the Prince and Prin-cess of Wales, who, at the same time, distri-buted the prizes in the examination-hall. The Princess of Wales has been for some time the gracious and kindly patron of the school.

Let us go into the school-house. To the right of the entrance is a large, light, and pretty room, known as the office; to the left is a most artistic room, which is Miss Buss's own reception-room. Going straight through the corridor, and leaving on the right the library, already beginning to be well-stocked with the standard works of English and foreign authors, we ascend a small flight of steps and arrive at the examination-hall, the munificent gift of the Clothworkers' Company. In this grand hall, built of oak and red brick, and with its galleries capable of accommodating seven hundred people, prayers are read every morning at 9.15 by the head-mistress before the day's work begins, the organ, on which the hymn-tunes are played by one of the pupils, standing on the raised platform at the end of the hall. This organ is a gift to the school from past and present pupils.

There are three sets of class-rooms—the first, occupied by girls in the higher forms, opening on to the hall; the second, used by girls in the middle of the school, opening on to the gallery of the hall, and the third occupied by the younger children higher still. The class-rooms are supplied with rows of separate desks, each provided with a foot-rest and with a movable chair, having an extra support for the back. On looking round these rooms, one is struck by seeing on several desks dotted about the room what looks almost like a double top to the locker, but what is in reality a piece of wood several inches in thickness stained like the desk and shaped to fit the top of it. This is an appliance to raise the books of the short-sighted pupils, and so to prevent the injurious habit of stooping, so common amongst girls who suffer from myopy.

Beneath the examination-hall is the dining-hall, a cheerful, spacious room, with a panelled dado. In the basement are also cloak-rooms and a drying-room, furnished with hot-air pipes, to which on a rainy day wet garments are taken and returned in half an hour perfectly dry.

A short corridor leads from the dining-hall and cloak-rooms to the gymnasium—a large hall paved with square wooden blocks and furnished with parallel and horizontal bars, ropes and ladders, dumb bells, &c. The gymnastic teaching is in the hands of two ladies from the German Gymnasium, the classes, as well as the general health of the pupils, being under the superintendence of Mrs. Bovell Sturge, M.D. The girls who attend the gymnasium are all dressed alike in short, loose dresses, in colour dark blue, trimmed with light blue. Every now and then the young gymnasts are invited by Miss Buss to what is known as a "gymnasium tea"—that is a merry gathering in the gymnasium, where all appear in their gymnastic dresses, and after tea games of all sorts are carried on with great spirit, and great feats are performed with the gymnastic apparatus, soft mats being placed under the bars and giant stride in case of accident.

Above the examination-hall, in addition to the class-rooms, are a chemical laboratory, with every appliance for the teaching of prac-tical chemistry, and a lecture theatre, with the

---

E. A. L. K., "The North London Collegiate School for Girls" (Volume 3, 29 April 1882, p. 494).

THE GYMNASIUM OF THE NORTH LONDON COLLEGIATE SCHOOL FOR GIRLS.

E. A. L. K., "The North London Collegiate School for Girls" (Volume 3, 29 April 1882).

tier arrangement of seats. This lecture-room is associated in the mind of many a pupil with the little addresses on subjects relative to the moral life and well-being of the school, given by the head mistress once a week to every form. These addresses last about twenty minutes, and are marked throughout with the impress of the deep insight into girl nature, and power of sympathy with the weak as well as with the strong—points of that nature which are widely known as eminent characteristics of the lady now at the head of the school.

The building also contains a work-room, where the cutting-out and stitching of many and various garments are carried on, under the supervision of ladies who attend for the purpose. There is also a drawing-school, with a capital collection of casts, models, and copies; and in this studio, to those who are willing to give the extra time, not only model, ornamental and freehand drawing are taught, but lessons are also given in water-colour painting. Below the Fifth Form drawing is a part of the ordinary school course; in the upper forms it is taken in the afternoon by those who show any talent for it. It is found to be an excellent plan that up to a certain age drawing should form part of the education of every pupil, for drawing trains the eye, giving it, so to speak, a second sense; for it is true in an artistic as well as in other applications, that "the eye only sees what it takes with it the power of seeing."

To use a common, if an ungrammatical, phrase, school begins at 9.15, the school doors being opened at 9, and any stranger walking about that time up the Camden or Sandall-roads must be literally amazed at the streams of girls pouring into these roads from all quarters, and flowing steadily in one direction. Indeed, it is not often that one has the opportunity of seeing so many girls together, for the school numbers four hundred and ninety pupils, and about a hundred other girls, who are waiting admission into the school, assemble at the same time in the morning in the preparatory classes held in the old school-house in the Camden-road.

By 9 15 hats and jackets have been taken off and boots changed by every girl in one or other of the cloak-rooms, and all are sitting silently in their places in the examination-hall when Miss Buss appears on the the platform to read prayers. After prayers, the girls, keeping time to a march played on the organ, pass in files to their respective class-rooms, leaving the hall by two entrances. The school is divided into six forms, these forms being sub-divided into sixteen, so that there are really sixteen classes, each having a separate class-room, each form containing about thirty children. Lessons go on uninterruptedly for an hour and a half. At the end of that time, four of the lower forms go down into the dining-hall to luncheon. Every pupil is obliged to take luncheon during the morning, but she may either bring it with her, or procure it in the dining-hall, where fifteen or sixteen different kinds of buns, biscuits, scones, cakes, bread-and-butter, &c., may be procured, no single article costing more than a halfpenny. Milk, lemonade, and coffee are also to be had at the cost of a penny a cup or glass, and water is supplied for all who wish for it.

After ten minutes, during which time conversation is allowed—and a surprising amount of it has been done in those ten minutes—the four forms who first came down pass into the gymnasium for fifteen minutes' drill, and then upstairs to their class-rooms, their places in the dining-hall having been taken by other forms. And this goes on in rotation until every form has had luncheon and gymnastics, and every class-room has had plenty of time to get rid of its exhausted air, and to take in a fresh supply of oxygen.

Work then goes on without interruption until 1.30, when a bell is rung, and each girl straps up her books, and passes down to her cloak-room. Every girl must be out of the school-house by 1.45, unless she stays for dinner. The ordinary school-work is not carried on in the afternoon, but music and harmony lessons are given, and drawing lessons to the more advanced pupils. Those pupils who stay at school for these lessons are expected to dine. An excellent plain dinner is provided in the dining-hall for the moderate cost of tenpence.

The last Wednesday in every month is what is known as "Dorcas Day,"—that is, the day on which every pupil is expected to attend in the afternoon for needlework. Then from one to two hundred stay to dinner, and the chatter in the dining-hall is almost deafening; but the teachers are many of them so young and all so bright and full of sympathy with the young life around them, that they not only survive, but often seem even to enjoy the confusion of tongues.

A few words must be said about the school course. It comprises Holy Scripture,* mathematics, arithmetic, natural science, Latin, French, and German, history, English language and literature, geography, drawing, economics, and class singing.

The lessons are in form something between the old-fashioned repetition lesson and the modern lecture, and, by a combination of the two methods, escape the disadvantage of both. A history lesson, for instance, would be given in the following way:—The teacher would begin by questioning her pupils upon the work done last lesson, the girls answering in turn, and in the case of the lady taking the lesson not being the ordinary teacher of the class, and, therefore, not familiar with every girls' name, she would be supplied with a box of cards with the name written on them, and each girl would answer as her name was read. Then the teacher, having probably prepared her lesson from two or three histories, would give an interesting sketch of the period, bringing out by judicious questioning any previous information on the subject her pupils might possess. Then, at the end of the lesson, she would give a brief abstract of it, the pupils taking this down in their rough note-books and bringing it in, neatly written out, filled in, and enlarged upon for next lesson. Mathematics are taught as low down as the Fourth Form. This branch of study is entered into by the pupils with a spirit that would certainly be a source of extreme surprise, if not of dissatisfaction, to those who still continue to pronounce the studies of geometry and algebra as "quite unsuited to the female mind." One old pupil of the North London Collegiate School having taken a scholarship of £100 a year for three years at the entrance examination to Girton College, Cambridge, was there examined for the Mathematical Tripos, and the examiners declared that, had she been placed, she would have taken the position of twenty-fourth wrangler!

Greek is taught to those pupils who are studying for the B.A. Examination of the London University, or who intend to go to Girton College. The examinations taken throughout the school are the College of Preceptors, Cambridge, Junior and Senior, and the London University Examinations, and the list of honours gained in them is a long one.

Two of the staff mistresses and two old pupils of the school are amongst the first lady graduates of London University; one lady teacher having taken double honours in the B.S.C. examination, and another being placed in the first class in the B.A. examination, while an old pupil not only took honours

* The school is a Church of England School, with the conscience clause.

in Botany as a B.S.C., but won the first place on the list.

Discipline is as far as possible maintained in the school by means of a healthy public opinion. In each class there are two monitors chosen by ballot, the girls of the form, the headmistress, the staff-mistresses, and some of the visiting teachers having votes. These monitors are responsible for the general conduct of their forms, and in the case of any difficulty arising which is too great for them, they may apply to the prefects, who are elected by ballot from among the members of the Sixth Form. The prefects have the power of summoning before them, as a body, any girl for a repeated breach of the rules which has not come under the notice of a teacher, and if their remonstrance be unheeded, of reporting the matter to the headmistress. Small breaches of the rules are entered by the girl herself in a book called the Appearing Book; and if at the end of the half term the number of appearances against a girl's name be too large, she has to appear in person before Miss Buss. Lessons brought in badly written, or with too many careless faults, are placed on a list called the Default List, where they remain until they have been brought in re-written, when they are struck off. Every lesson on the Default List is also entered in the Appearing Book.

Prizes are given once a year throughout the school to all who obtain a certain proportion of marks in the various subjects of study, and kind friends have founded scholarships and offered several special prizes, so that distinguished merit is not

" —— born to blush unseen,
And waste its sweetness on the desert air."

And on the other hand, if the natural fleetness of the hare is recognised, the steady perseverance of the tortoise is not forgotten.

And outside the well-defined boundaries of school-work, there is plenty of bright vigorous life. Annual plays, characters, and concerts are most heartily enjoyed, both by performers and audience, the parents of many of the young actors being asked by Miss Buss to share the fun. Foundation day, the 4th April, is a great day for the school, and has latterly been observed by an exhibition of toys, made by the girls' own hands, for distribution amongst the children of the workhouses and hospitals, &c. Once a term, the teachers, monitors, and prefects meet for tea and to spend a pleasant evening, and in various other ways, too numerous to mention, abundant proof is given that social life is not necessarily swamped by intellectual activity. Then the school has a magazine, which does its best for her young authors in endeavouring to coax into the publicity of a small world of kindly critics brain-children scarcely vigorous enough for the rough handling of a less lenient public. Courses of cooking lessons given and ambulance classes held from time to time give scope to the talents of those who have dexterous fingers, and like to know how to use them; and if the "Wonderland" Mock-Turtle's anxious question, whether instruction in washing forms a part of the school curriculum, cannot be answered by a North London Collegiate girl in the affirmative, yet she can boast of taking part in a damp lesson, for on summer Saturday mornings a swimming class, with a very skilful lady teacher, meets at the St. Pancras Baths, and at the end of the summer term a prize is awarded by Miss Buss to the swiftest naiad.

And the producing power of all this life and happiness throughout the school is to be found in the headmistress herself, and flows from her to the sweet, gracious, and able women whom she gathers round her to second her in her great work; and many a parent, whose daughters have been educated

E. A. L. K., "The North London Collegiate School for Girls" (Volume 3, 29 April 1882, p. 495).

by Miss Buss, is only too proud to acknowledge that, in coming into contact with a lady of such high intellectual power, such real refinement, and true tenderness, his children have gained a conception of the possible dignity of womanhood, which is of even more value to them than the excellent instruction given in the school. E. A. L. K.

ANSWERS TO CORRESPONDENTS.

EDUCATIONAL.

PEBBLE and THE CHASE (W.).—We advise you to write to Miss Leigh, 77, Avenue Wagram, Paris, France.

LILIUM ROSEUM.—Read "How to Improve the Education," page 794, vol. ii. Think more of others than yourself.

LETHE.—You would find it easier to order foreign books through a foreign bookseller. You can find the addresses in any directory.

GELTRUDA.—The origin of "Simnel," or "mid-Lent" Sunday, will be found at page 480, vol. i. It was also called "Mothering Sunday," from the custom amongst servants and apprentices of going to visit their mothers, and taking them a present. "Palm Sunday" is the Sunday next before Easter, and it is so-called from the entry of our blessed Lord into Jerusalem, and the act of the multitudes who cast branches in the way. The 16th December, 1868, was a Wednesday.

A SPRIG OF THYME.—An account of such lives would be best found in an encyclopædia or a biographical dictionary. You would find Miss Strickland's "Lives of the Queens of England" and "of Scotland" very interesting as a book to read for both pleasure and instruction.

ART.

GIRLS OF GLOUCESTER.—Primroses or lenten lilies would look well.

AVACANORA.—Use a little glycerine with the water-colours, which, perhaps, you are keeping in too warm a place.

WYSALL.—The "Crown-Derby" china was always hand-painted by good artists, but towards the close of the last century white Derby china was sold to be painted by amateurs, which accounts for the tastelessly-decorated specimens frequently met with.

LOTTIE.—Your question is very vague. The earliest-known painters were Cimabue, Ghiotto, Ghirlandajo, &c. We think you mean the first-named, but he was not "French," but Italian. Cervantes was a Spaniard, and wrote "Don Quixote."

TERRA-COTTA.—A full description of terra-cotta painting in oils, water-colours, and in etching is given at page 225, vol. ii. Please refer to it, as, although you beg for an immediate answer, your question is of the vaguest kind.

STUDIOUS.—Use a porte-crayon for crayons or chalks, and erase with crumbs of bread. Boldness of outline and shading is required rather than delicacy of colouring. To fix crayon drawings, see page 415, vol. i.

WORK.

CHARITY must cast on a number of stitches according to the size she requires her petticoat to be in width; this she can do by measuring one in wear. When a quarter of a yard, or less, is done in straight rows, the decrease can be commenced by taking two chain stitches together about every twentieth stitch, and working three or four plain rows after each decrease. If the top is required to be very small it will be necessary to leave a slit in the back part, which is done by working the rows backwards and forwards instead of all round.

ALICE.—Send the articles to Miss Tidd, for the bazaar in aid of the Princess Louise Home. See page 349, vol. iii.

AN ENGLISH SCHOOLGIRL.—If the present must be a sofa cushion, use either serge or oatmeal-cloth. As a ground for the crewel design, you would find cross-stitch on linen very pretty; but why not try to trim a work basket, for which we have given so many hints in "My Work Basket"?

E. M. G.—See the long instructions for square netting in the lawn-tennis net lately given.

FRANCES.—The Ladies' School of Technical Needlework, 15, Dorset-street, Baker-street, W.

S. E. D.—Have your hat dyed and pressed by a proper person. Wear your hair in a thick plait at the back, tied with a ribbon, and hanging down.

JANE EYRE.—Curl the hair on hairpins, making little rings, and pinning them flat to the head. Many thanks for your kind instructions.

E PARKER.—We should doubt the geometrical design being either popular or effective. You had better work the screen in panels, using the designs given on pages 228, 229, and 230, vol. ii. If you do not like them, you could adapt an outline figure-design.

G. R.—For "Guipure on Net," see page 372, vol. ii., where designs and patterns are both given.

MISCELLANEOUS.

ANNIE.—Your writing is very fairly good.

NELLIE.—The following is the explanation of *Scrutin d'Arrondissement*:—Paris, for example, is divided into twenty arrondissements. Each inhabitant of one arrondissement votes for the member of his own arrondissement. By *Scrutin de Liste* is meant that each inhabitant votes for all the twenty members for the whole of Paris.

WORDSWORTH.—The poet after whom you name yourself was married to Mary Hutchinson, who survived him, and died January 17, 1859, at Rydal Mount. They had one daughter, Dora, who married Mr. Edward Quillinau, in 1841, and died in 1847. The life of the poet himself was published in 1851, by his nephew, Dr. Christopher Wordsworth. You would obtain the information from the family.

NUMBER SEVEN.—Be comforted, if you really desire to please God, that desire is the gift of His Holy Spirit, who is "striving" in your heart for your eternal good. It is not necessary to do any particular or great thing outside the walls of your own home. Obedience and dutiful attention to your parents and teachers, and the habit of diligence in the work they give you to do, are part of that work which you "want to do for God." Besides this, suppose you make a few little articles of dress for poor children in your leisure time?

A CONNAUGHT GIRL.—There are two homes for students — Brunswick House, Brunswick-square, W.C.; also Russell House, Russell-square, W.C. The terms vary from 15s. to 33s. per week. Apply for information to the Matron.

B. A. B.—We feel sorry for you, but can only refer you to our answer to "Number Seven." Your writing is fairly good.

"'IT COMETH NOT,' SHE SAID."

TWO IRISH GIRLS.—Cocoa-nut fibre refuse is very excellent for ferns. The English "maidenhair" requires shade and moisture, and decaying fronds should be cut off at once.

PAULINE P.—You appear to need a doctor's advice very much, and we hope you will persuade your relations to obtain it forthwith. He will probably advise change of air for a time, and tonic medicines. We should think from your account that you had outgrown your strength, like many another girl.

A GIRL.—We quite agree with you, and we hope that by means of bathing, swimming, lawn-tennis, and all the new ideas on women's physical training, they will ultimately become as strong and healthy as need be. The great fear is that over-study and competitive examinations will cause many failures of health in immature girls.

HEATHER BELL.—The expression, "Gone to the dogs," is commonly derived from the fact that the ace in dice was called "canis"—dog—by the Romans, and a cast of dice where all was lost was by throwing three aces; hence, "dog" meant ill-luck and loss, and "going to the dogs" to be in ill-luck, or to go to the bad. There are other suggestions as to the origin, but this appears to be the best.

A MOTHER.—Write to the Religious Tract Society, 56, Paternoster-row, E.C., for the leaflets for distribution. They are of various prices. Use the essence, to be obtained at every chemist's.

EDITHA.—For full directions how to preserve seaweed, see vol. ii., page 176.

C. F. S.—Clerkships in post and telegraph offices, see answer to "Henriette," vol. ii., page 112.

NELL.—The squares in the satin quilt are not arranged in any special design, but we advise you to confine yourself to either two or three colours. For instance, either blue and white, or pink and white. For a cradle quilt the squares should not be larger than an eighth of a yard each in size. Dame Durden is the heroine of a popular English song, which begins as follows:—

"Dame Durden kept five serving maids
To carry the milking-pail,
She also kept five serving men
To use the spade and flail."

She is described as a notable housewife in the succeeding verses of the song. Mother Shipton lived in the reign of Henry VIII., and was famous for her prophecies. But those remarkable ones attributed to her are forgeries. We regret to hear of your ill-health, and can well understand and sympathise with you in your longing for the fine spring days.

CLARA HOMFRAY.—Gytha, daughter of our last Saxon king, Harold II., who was killed at the Battle of Hastings. She retired with her brothers to the Court of Denmark, and was subsequently married to Vladimir, czar of Russia, to whom she bore a son, Mistislar Harold, the progenitor of an illustrious race.

TWO SCHOOLGIRLS, LITTLE INSEPARABLE, &c.—Send the text cards, &c., to the East London Hospital for Children, Shadwell, E., but be careful either to mount everything thin on cardboard, or to put them in a scrapbook, or else they will be soon destroyed by use. Rats appear to feed indiscriminately on both animal and vegetable foods, grains, and wheat.

WATTEAU.—We suppose a doll dressed like a Watteau shepherdess is what you mean, which consists of a short quilted skirt, a bunched-up tunic, and a square-cut bodice, laced. This dress may be all of pink, or all of blue, and the hair may be worn flowing, or plaited in long plaits beneath a flat hat, trimmed with ribbon.

ONE WISHING TO BE LOVED.—We are glad that our advice has been of service to you, and hope you will soon win the regard and affection of your schoolfellows. Perhaps your father would like to have a set of handkerchiefs embroidered with his initials.

MILDRED.—All hardy annuals should be sown in April. With reference to your poem, we can only insert one verse—

"In the fields the lambs were frisking,
As if in time to Orpheus' lute,
And all their fleecy tails were whisking
At the glad sound of the shepherd's flute;
And every bird is trilling high,
To see whose song first will reach the sky."

What about the ducks? Not "every bird."

A. P. T.—We thank you for both your letter and your three verses. For a recipe for making chocolate cream, see page 399, vol. i.

KITTY P.—If you have an aunt you had better tell her how ill you feel, and she may arrange to procure you a doctor's advice.

MYRTLE.—The word "pass" is sometimes employed as a substantive, and more frequently as a verb. A mountain pass is, of course, a substantive; and in this sense it appears to be used in the passage which you quote.

PRIMROSE.—If marked before marriage, use the maiden name, but many people now delay marking the trousseau until after the wedding.

SCOTCH THISTLE.—"The day is cold and dark and dreary" are the words of a song by Longfellow. It has been set to music by several people.

A CONSTANT READER.—The words, "Richard's himself again," are not in Shakespeare's *Richard III.*, but were interpolated from Colley Cibber by John Kemble.

LADY HENRIETTA.—The weight of Jumbo, who was supposed to be the largest elephant that ever came to Europe, amounted to upwards of six tons, we believe. Take the scent bottle to a shop where they mend china, and they will probably find you a new stopper.

NELLIE.—The cause of warts, we believe, is not known, and they appear and disappear spontaneously, sometimes defying all treatment. Rubbing them with the inside of the broad bean has been much recommended lately.

PANSIE.—You will probably find the kind of book you need in the general catalogue of the Religious Tract Society, sent post free from 56, Paternoster-row, E.C.

POPPY.—There is no reason why you should not take off your gloves in church if you wish to do so. No rule exists to be observed in the case.

AN APPRECIATIVE READER.—The three golden balls are the cognisance of the Medici family, and are probably a punning device on their name.

EMILY.—Your teeth, probably, require to be stopped, or else you may have taken cold in the jaw. Your writing is fairly good for your age, and your spelling is quite correct, but you should not abbreviate. Write "yours," not "yrs."

DAISIANA.—We maintain that the expression is a provincialism, and as such not to be employed.

*** *The author of "The Other Side of the World" wishes us to insert the following:—Those who have been interested in the fortunes of "Annie Steele" may like to hear that when, after she had gone abroad, the directors of the orphan school where she had been reared heard the story of her bright energy and brave endeavour, they wrote her a letter of encouraging praise, and one of them sent her a gift of ten guineas, as a testimony of his admiring approval.*

E. A. L. K., "The North London Collegiate School for Girls" (Volume 3, 29 April 1882, p. 496).

and among others wrote to ask it from Lord Shaftesbury. Almost by return post came back a handsome donation, enclosed in a most kind letter, apologising for the sum being no larger, and saying how difficult he found it to meet the many such applications for assistance which he would so gladly help, did his income permit. The same kind and ready courtesy was always shown to those who had occasion to ask for his votes for any of the innumerable charities in which he had an interest. Busy as he was to the last, one could not help contrasting the polite promptitude of *his* attention to such matters with the negligent tardiness of much smaller personages.

This is no sketch of his life—only a very, very small memento of our own purely personal knowledge of so great and good a man. But when, three weeks ago, we sat in the gathering-place of England's highest chivalry, and listened to the Dean of Windsor's eloquent description of the departed Christian knight, whose banner must now no longer wave in St. George's Chapel, it was a thrilling remembrance that—just that once—the kind hand and brave heart of that true elder (earl) among his peers had sent us such words of personal greeting and goodwill. They were not written in vain; the letter was laid aside to be kept for after years, and its actual phrases were soon forgotten; but the germ of a good purpose was securely lodged in one childish heart, and the passionate longing to be enlisted in the great army of those who fight against all kinds of wrong and fraud, took root, and grew apace from that hour. And when the echo of those knightly vows, by which all who receive the order of the garter are bound, seems to linger about the beauty, and melody, and glorious worship of that royal shrine—the vows to combat wrong and wage war against evil in the name of Christ—it is a pleasant thought to us that one day yet, when innumerable rescued ones, from ragged schools, mines, factories, give their testimony how Lord Shaftesbury's hand was the one to redress their sorrows and aid them to better things, we too may be allowed to thank him for help given to choose the higher quest— "*to suffer ill rather than do ill,*" to "buy the truth and sell it not."

THE GIRLS OF THE WORLD.

FACTS AND FIGURES.

By EMMA BREWER.

CHAPTER III.

EDUCATION OF THE GIRLS AND WOMEN OF THE WORLD.

"Education is the guardian of liberty and the bulwark of morality."—*De Witt Clinton.*

"The object of education is to develop in the individual all the perfection of which he is capable."—*Kant.*

I SHALL try in this chapter to place before you the result of investigation concerning the education of the population of the various countries of the world, the attainments of girls as compared to those of boys, and the amount of education noticeable in girl criminals.

In these days education is appreciated and sought after by all classes and in all countries. None are thought too young, too old, too rich, or too poor to learn. Individuals and the states to which they belong are alike energetically working for the same end, a highly educated population, in the firm belief that, if education be accompanied by sound religious principles, it will elevate the nation, strengthen the national character, and check vice, intemperance, and pauperism. We owe our happiness, usefulness, and profitableness in after life to the class of education and training we receive in early days.

Our minds do not remain blank nor our nature innocent as when we were born; each day and hour as they fly swiftly by leave their mark upon us for good or for evil; if good seed be not early sown and carefully tended, weeds will grow, and at such a pace as to choke every aspiration after good, every desire for freedom. We shall be bound hand and foot by our own evil habits.

War against ignorance is being waged in all directions, and rightly so, for it is a great power for evil and an obstacle to all improvement. I remember reading many years ago the following lines upon the recklessness of ignorance, but I do not in the least know whose words they are :—"Knowledge certainly is power, but who hath considered or set forth the power of ignorance? Knowledge slowly builds up what Ignorance in an hour pulls down. Knowledge works patiently through long centuries to enlarge discovery, and, at length, makes record of it. Ignorance, wanting its day's dinner, lights a fire with the record, and the work of ages is shrivelled up in blackness."

Education and refinement may have their evils, but they are infinitely less than those which result from ignorance, and we must never forget that not only our own happiness and prosperity, but that of future generations, depend upon our uniting in a crusade against ignorance, which is another name for bondage.

Statistics have been the means, not only of placing before us the giant strength for evil possessed by ignorance, and its power of tyranny over and enslaving those who bend beneath its yoke, but they have at the same time shown us the means of escape. We must, each one in her capacity of good citizen, consider the education of the young a paramount duty; we must publish the necessity of this way out of the difficulty, and show clearly the beneficent results of education in checking vice, and producing freedom, order, and happiness. Perhaps there is no surer test of the real condition of a country than the position of its women and girls, and there is no denying that in these days it is a noble and important one in most of the civilised countries of the world. It remains with us to strengthen this position by every means in our power, and carefully to put aside everything that would tend to foster decay in it.

To us women and girls is allotted the rule and government of the homes of the land. We are the companions of fathers, brothers, and husbands, and it is our privilege to influence them, often to work with and for them, and not rarely to comfort and sustain them.

If we keep these homes of ours pure, refined, and virtuous, we wage war against decay, and occupy the proud place of helping to build up the country, and strengthen the hands of the State. Loving, moral, and religious must be the character of the women and girls of a country if the homes over which they preside are to be pure, restful, attractive, and refined. Wherever the homes of the land fall below this standard, statistics prove that the strength, life, and progress of that country is sapped, notwithstanding its armies, its laws, and its institutions.

A great German writer* says, "It is in the home that the true sphere of woman's greatness lies. It is here that she is called upon to comfort those who suffer, to be content with a little, to do nothing for herself and all for others, and quietly but efficiently give new attractions to the uniformity of home life."

The same writer says, "For house and family the husband is everything; within the family the wife is all; she is the inspiring, embellishing, and controlling power. Home is the central point for all the exertions of the man; for home he traverses, searches, conquers the world; the wife rules by goodness over the sanctuary for which the man has exerted his powers."

Luther, in speaking of the influence and rule of girls and women in the home, seems as though he could not speak too highly of them. He says that good home rule is the basis on which all good governments are formed, and that God ordained it to be the first and most important of all rule—for where the home is well and properly governed all else is well provided for.

You see, then, how noble is our position, how far extending is our influence. There is not one among us, be she ever so poor and lowly, but has the power of forming the thoughts and habits of those among whom she lives,* and through them of contributing to the morality and strength of the country.

Our privileges are great, our position noble, and it must be our care so to educate ourselves that we do not fall short of what is required of us. Until a girl is well educated she does not know what she is or what she is capable of.

By education I do not mean merely reading, writing, and arithmetic, for these are only the implements by means of which we may acquire and communicate knowledge.

By education, I mean the cultivation of the head, the heart, and the hand, so as to enable us to diffuse knowledge, provident habits, morality, piety, and happiness among those with whom we associate. In short, I mean the full and healthy use of all the faculties God has bestowed upon us.

This sort of education has been gradually increasing of late years among the women and girls of all lands, and wherever it has been at work there may be seen clearly a steady progress among the people in social and domestic virtues; there is less crime, less drunkenness, less scandal, less improvidence: a greater power of thinking, a greater desire for improved condition.

If education did nothing more than teach the poor habits of strict cleanliness, it would be a wonderful blessing in the amount of disease it would prevent.

It is not possible to overrate the influence of women and girls for good if they will have it so—for evil if they neglect the duties their privileges entail. The education possible to

---

* Zchokke.

* Do you remember in the story of "Seven Years for Rachel," how the heroine, a poor servant girl, influenced master, mistress, child, and fellow-servant for good?

girls at the beginning of this century and that which is now within their reach is widely different—the one so meagre, the other so liberal. It is stated that one of the reasons of the early emigration of our forefathers was the difficulty of securing an education for their girls in the old country. Even fifty years ago the education of the people was left almost entirely to private industry. There were no good schools in the United Kingdom for girls, and those that existed were as a rule held in ill-ventilated rooms and presided over by very illiterate people—people who were quite incapable of exercising and training the intelligence, and who certainly were not competent to exercise any good moral influence on the girls.

As short a time back as twenty years England ranked last of all the civilised nations of the earth with regard to education. A great statistician, speaking of the education of the English people at that time, said, "The schools are very bad, and yet much more is being done in them than formerly."

In 1872 education was made compulsory in England, and, indeed, it was time for the Government to make a vigorous effort in that direction, seeing that a large proportion of the population of both sexes was unable to read and write, and statistics showed that out of every hundred men who married, thirty-two were unable to sign their names in the register, and out of a hundred women forty-eight were unable to sign it. And this is not all. Ignorance of common words and phrases amongst the girls was quite remarkable. The following is but one example.

I was on a visit at a vicarage about ten miles from London, when one afternoon a respectable-looking girl of about twenty and a young man came to the church vestry to announce their desire of "being asked in church." The clerk, in a business-like manner, with his book before him, addressing the girl, asked—

"Your name?"

"Mary Bean, sir," was the answer.

"Spinster?" he continued.

Receiving no answer, he looked up, and, to his astonishment, found the girl looking very red and angry. At the question being put a second time, she broke out in choked voice and with angry gesture, "Spinster! No, indeed! and I should like to know how you dare to call respectable girls such names, trying to take away their characters. No, sir, I am not a spinster, I am a respectable servant, and my mistress will speak to my character." And turning to her companion, said, "Come away, John, I'd rather not be married at all than be married here, where decent folk are insulted."

And away they went, to the great distress of the clerk, who came to tell the vicar the occurrence.

Ours was not the only country in which the education of girls was neglected. In Italy fifty-three out of every hundred girls and women were unable to write, and thirty seven per cent. could neither read nor write. In Belgium girls' education was almost entirely neglected. In France thirty-seven per cent. of the female population could neither read nor write. In Sardinia the education of girls was not only entirely neglected, but considered superfluous and dangerous. In Russia the little that was done to educate girls was done so badly as to be worse than useless. In the States, south and south-west of New York and New Jersey, notwithstanding the efforts made, nearly all the girls and women were without the commonest education.

In Algiers there were a few boys' schools in which the boys simply learned to read, but there was no provision made for teaching the girls whatever. In China only one woman in a hundred could read. In the West Indies it was forbidden to teach the Negro either to read or write. In India scarcely a girl in ten thousand could read or write, or play any musical instrument. The women were kept in ignorance, some by their poverty, some by the jealous fears of their husbands, and more than all because no provision was made for teaching them. Ignorance was esteemed the safeguard of rank and morality. For the very few who could read the books were too corrupt to place in their hands, and thus it ever is where the women are kept in ignorance and deprived of their influence. In fact, look where you will, with one or two exceptions, such as Holland, Saxony, and Prussia, you will find that fifty years ago scarcely any provision was made for the intellectual improvement of women and girls. The picture is very different now, as you may see by the figures at the end of the chapter.

The cry is not an uncommon one that we are spending too much money on education in this age; but statistics prove that the money so spent is the best outlay the world ever made—that by its means the criminal population under thirty is decreasing rapidly, and much of the sordid poverty and depravity common among some classes are gradually being got rid of. Take, for example, the work of education in London; it has reduced the number of criminals fifty per cent., and so marvellously has it dealt with the habits and manners of the people that the head of the police declares that if things go on as now, there will soon be nothing left for the police to do.

To transform an uneducated population into a well educated, responsible, thinking people is not the work of a moment. It requires years of steady working to develop the physical, intellectual, and moral powers of a people. That this country and many others have made rapid strides in this direction no one doubts for a moment.

The increased opportunities of education and intellectual improvement have had a most beneficial result on the character of the girls of all lands; it may be seen in a hundred ways by the most unobservant of onlookers. They are less idle, less improvident, less depressed, less inclined to turn to frivolous pleasures in order to drown their sorrows, less given to gossiping and scandal. They are better daughters, better wives, and better citizens; their pleasures and recreations are of a higher class; they are more careful to preserve the dignity of woman, because they are awaking to its existence. Even in the poorest homes you may see the effect of the better education, in the struggle to keep up appearances, by a greater cleanliness and neatness, and by a desire to avoid debt. In the higher social position the good result of a better class of education is equally noticeable, and we have the assurance of Mr. Mundella that never in the history of our country has there been so much real and effective religious instruction going on as at present.

It has been a matter of great interest to discover how much power of learning girls have—whether there are any subjects better learned by them than by boys, and what subjects they fail to do as well.

Of course, there are two subjects peculiar to girls' schools, and with which boys have nothing to do, viz., needlework and cooking. The first of these the various Governments of the world encourage in every way, and it is the opinion of examiners that needlework, properly taught, develops in girls moral and intellectual qualities in a very marked degree. Their opinion is that it trains them in habits of observation, precision, patience, neatness, and order; that it teaches forethought, contrivance, and economy.

These are qualities which tend at once to sharpen the wit and strengthen the character, and which prove valuable to girls of every condition of life—indeed, a good practical knowledge of needlework is essential to mothers; the saving it effects is in itself an income.

"No home," says an inspector, "can be attractive to a man where the wife is slatternly and the children in rags; when there is no stitch in time to save the nine, and where the waste caused by unmended clothes is an incessant drain on his slender resources." It is a shallow prejudice which regards needlework as beneath a clever girl's notice.

Cooking is now being taught in many of our schools, and that girls are enjoying and profiting by the lessons may be seen in the fact that last year the Government grants were bestowed on 7,597 girls in England and Wales, and the result may be seen clearly in the agricultural districts, where the food of the poor is much better and more economically cooked than formerly. These two subjects special to girls, if well taught and made practical, will make their mark in many homes and give an increase of comfort and order to a large portion of the population. Everything which tends to increase the comfort, order, and happiness of our homes is worth cultivating.

(*To be continued.*)

OUR LAKE.

By CLARA THWAITES.

EVEN Christmas trees lose their charm in time, and we set our wits to work to find some novelty for the children, some new environment for gifts and toys at Christmastide.

To those who frequent bazaars and sales of work "Our Lake" will be no novelty, perhaps, but to many a quiet country home it may prove a happy thought, as it did in our "home among the hills." Secrecy in preparation is a great matter in our pleasant scheme. Keep doors shut, dear mothers and elder sisters, while you call into existence in some large recess in your home, or in some boudoir, a gleaming lake surrounded with waving ferns, orange trees, or whatever forms of beauty you can find in your own or a neighbour's conservatory. The neatest housewife need not feel uneasy at bringing a lake into her pretty domains, as the materials composing it are dry.

Procure from your ironmonger a large sheet of polished tin (you can probably hire it for a trifle) and a sufficient quantity of Virginian cork to form an irregular border around it. Some stout brown paper, folded double, should be placed around the edge of the tin and surrounding carpet to preserve them from injury by damp pots and ivy. The cork will form a pretty border when placed irregularly and informally among the drooping ferns, *Osmunda regalis*, and other feathery growths, which will cluster around our mimic lake. Hide the pots with wreaths of ivy and evergreens, and on one side of the lake form a rustic bridge, over which the young anglers can cast their lines. (A small bench, with a back to it, from the village school, will answer this purpose, *faute de mieux*, or you will devise something to your mind.)

Our "fish" are candies, bonbons, preserved fruits, or more valuable gifts, folded in papers that are gold, silver, pink, or yellow, and neatly tied up. Each tiny parcel has a loop attached to it, which the hook of the skilful angler will catch up. Put some of your fish in the pond, keeping a reserve which may be thrown in when the pond is empty.

Our fishing-rods—let there be two—may be of the simplest description, with a string and hook attached to each, and the young anglers find it an exciting amusement to catch fish in "Our Lake."

Emma Brewer, "The Girls of the World: Facts and Figures" (Volume 7, 26 December 1885, p. 199).

the sea of sorrow to be crossed. None watched with Him through His hour of agony, but He has declared such loneliness shall never be His children's portion, for has He not said, "I will be with him in trouble"?—He who never slumbers nor sleeps nor grows oblivious of the smallest need of the feeblest of His followers.

The summer wore away; the long, light days were shortening considerably; the air began to grow chilly in the mornings and evenings; the wind now blew gustily at times, scattering showers of dead leaves; there was every sign of autumn having come, and winter would not be long in following.

Little or nothing had occurred during all these months to interrupt the even course of daily life at Ivy Cottage. Everything had gone on as usual, save that Miss Scott had come downstairs less and had remained in her room more. The warm weather this year had not seemed to revive and put new life into her as it had done in other summers, and now, with these chilly days, she had caught a fresh cold which had settled on her lungs.

It did not at first appear a more serious attack than many a former one, but perhaps she had less strength to fight against it. At any rate, the mischief rapidly increased; there came a day or two of anxious nursing and suspense, and then Miss Scott quietly passed away.

It was so sudden, so unexpected—not the less so that her life for years had been a precarious one—that Rosa could scarcely realise that it was true, that her gentle Aunt Mary would never again need her ministrations, having gone to the land where there is no more sickness. She mourned for her sincerely; the house felt emptier and sadder; but this sense of loss caused her to redouble her attentions to the one left, to whom Miss Scott had been everything in this world, and to whom, therefore, the blow was an irreparable one.

In fact, Mrs. Dunn seemed stunned and prostrated by it. She and her sister had been the last remaining members of a once large family, and now she alone was left. She aged rapidly under her sorrow; a few weeks appeared to do the work of years upon her.

She no longer had strength or energy to rise from her bed, and not even the most exciting debates or the best written leading articles could any longer arouse the slightest interest in her. Rosa would gladly now have read on and on by the hour together if it could have cheered her or helped to turn her thoughts for awhile into a different channel; but what had formerly been so absorbing a topic now seemed a weariness: so the papers were put by.

But Rosa succeeded better when she brought out the Bible and read about the "Land which is very far off;" about the heavenly Jerusalem, the City of the King, where they whom He has redeemed shall be with Him and see His glory; and the aged eyes, which were so dim to earthly things, seemed to look with a clearer vision than ever before upon these unseen and eternal realities.

Mrs. Dunn's moods were very variable now. Sometimes the old impatient, hasty nature showed itself, and she was difficult to please; at others she was wonderfully subdued and gentle, and unlike her usual self.

"Thank you, child," she said to Rosa one day, when the latter had been rendering some service. "You are very good to the old woman, and she has often been cross and disagreeable, I know. You've been very patient with all her little ways, and you've been a great comfort to us both."

"Oh, Aunt Hannah! I only wish I could have done more."

"You have done all you could. You have done more than most girls of your age would have done, and I should like to thank you for it all before I go. Kiss me, Rosa."

The girl, astonished at such a request from her undemonstrative aunt, stooped down and pressed her lips to her cheek.

"I sometimes think I am nearing the end of my pilgrimage now, and that perhaps it will not be long before the pearly gates open to admit me, unworthy as I am. But it's Christ's worthiness, not my own, that I trust to. And now, dear, go down to your tea; I feel inclined to doze awhile."

The next day the blinds were all once more drawn down at Ivy Cottage, for death had again entered the dwelling. With early morning the summons had come, and Mrs. Dunn's long earthly life was closed.

(*To be concluded.*)

THE GIRLS OF THE WORLD.

FACTS AND FIGURES.

By EMMA BREWER.

CHAPTER III.—(*continued.*)

NOW, as regards other subjects. Girls, without doubt, read and spell better than boys; their imitative powers are greater, and their imagination is keener. In grammar and analysis also the girls excel, but, unfortunately, as an inspector observes, this excellence has as yet but little power to alter the incorrect speaking of the homes. For example: a bright little girl, who had done her parsing and analysis papers admirably, being asked by him, "What do you mean by '*Invading us?*'" gave her answer at once, "Fighting we."

Girls are more curious than boys, and are not content with the knowledge their text books give them, but search beyond, and even if they are ignorant of the matter asked by the inspector, will be quick and ready to avoid raising a laugh against themselves.

A girl would rarely be found to give answers like the following,—

"Where is Birmingham?"

"In Warwickshire," said the boy.

"Can you tell me some of the things manufactured at Birmingham?"

"Yes, sir, guns and 'eavy goods, sir."

"What do you mean by heavy goods?" was the next question.

"Please, sir, our books don't tell us that."

Or again, the question being asked, "What is the world made of?" the answer given by a boy was "Muck, sir." *

You never get answers like these from girls.

Geography is not as a rule a favourite study of girls, but the various governments are offering every inducement to make it so. Government inspectors, who have a great deal of experience, declare it to be by far the most useful subject, except needlework, that can be taught in girls' schools.

They consider that it widens their sympathies, quickens their power of observation, cultivates their memories, and affords their curiosity abundant scope, interest, and amusement. In Germany girls excel in this branch of knowledge, perhaps because of the admirable manner in which it is taught.

In English literature girls and boys are about equal. Arithmetic is the one subject that girls fail to do so well in as boys. The following three lines will show that girls have the power to learn, and learn well:—

Of boys, 39 per cent. reach the standard "Fair" and "Good." Of girls, 42 per cent. reach the standard "Fair" and "Good."

Of the power of girls to teach we will speak when we come to the employment of girls.

The difficulties the children of the very poor experience in reaching these standards must be much greater than those to be overcome by children of well-to-do parents.

Think of the hundreds who go in the morning to school with little or no breakfast, how weary and faint they must be, and how much courage and determination they must exercise

---

* These answers were given only two years ago.

---

before they can fix any knowledge in their brains. A most pathetic incident which occurred in a very poor district came to my ears a short time ago, and will serve as an example of what I have just said. It is the custom in all schools to say the Grace Before Meat when the children are dismissed at twelve o'clock, and the Grace After Meat when they reassemble at two o'clock. The schoolmistress of the girls' school discovered that the majority of her children never had any dinner at all, and as it seemed to her a mockery to have the Grace said, she discontinued it.

You have seen in an earlier part of this article how strong a prejudice existed against educating the girls and women of India in the beginning of this century; let us now see how these prejudices and difficulties have been overcome.

In the year 1821 a lady deeply interested in the work of education was sent out by the British and Foreign School Society to Calcutta, with directions to make an attack against the dense ignorance, idleness, and superstition which enveloped the girls, and to see if it were possible to teach them the very rudiments of learning.

She went to work full of love, devotion, and vigour, and the result she was permitted to see at the end of five years of incessant toil was the establishment of five schools and 600 girl and women scholars. The work was then undertaken and carried on by a society of ladies, whose self-imposed duty it was to educate the native girls and women, not only of Calcutta but of all India; a gigantic task indeed when you think of the prejudices and idleness of the women to be overcome ere one letter or figure could be taught.

It was not until 1849 that the Government came to their aid, and included girls' schools in their plans for the education of India.

For a long time girls could not be induced to attend school without being paid for it, and those of the higher class could only be reached by consenting to teach them with a screen between teacher and pupil. Up to 1871 the Government thought it unnecessary to educate girls and women of low caste, but I am happy to say that now all tastes are free to attend school, and the desire for education is rapidly spreading among all classes.

As many of us are engaged in zenana work, it may not be uninteresting to mention that the apartments of the women in native houses are called the zenana, and the efforts to instruct married women in India go by the name of zenana work. In and about Calcutta some of the richer Hindus hire lady teachers to come to their homes and instruct their women. This in itself is a great step forward.

Missionary ladies all over India are engaged in this work of carrying learning and the knowledge of the Gospel to the secluded native women, while their husbands carry on the same work with the men.*

One school in India has attracted unusual attention; it is situate at Dehra, at the foot of the Himalaya Mountains, a spot better adapted to develop strength of mind and body than the plains.

This school is for native Christian girls; the five lady teachers are American. There are more than a hundred pupils, who are boarded, taught to read and write their own language, and to speak English well. The instruction is given in English, and the course of education is of a very high class.

The opinion of one of the greatest statisticians is that the progress of education in India since 1858 is one of the causes of the profound transformation it has undergone in the last thirty years. As yet only a little more than one per cent. of the population is receiving instruction, yet the effect upon the masses is most beneficial.

I should like to say a word or two about a part of the world unknown to civilised people a hundred years ago; I mean the Hawaiian Islands. Rather more than half a century ago Christianity and civilisation undertook a work here, and the result is a nation of heathen Christianised, and civilised, and furnished with a rich language of 20,000 words. The education of the people of these islands was undertaken by a few private people sent there by the American Mission. The chiefs soon enrolled themselves as pupils, and the whole nation followed their example. Not only were the men fired with enthusiasm to learn, but the women and girls in an equal degree, and fortunately no obstacle was placed in their way.

As soon as a grown-up person had mastered the wonderful alphabet of twelve letters and its combination of words and syllables, he or she was told off to teach others. From that time to this, the Hawaiian nation has placed the education of its people before all things, and has nobly supported its schools.

Every girl as well as boy is compelled to attend some school, to be instructed in good morals and elementary learning. Of the lady teachers in these islands the Hawaiian minister says that a more laborious and self-denying class of teachers does not exist than the ladies who have the immediate control of the Hawaiian girls. The Board of Education is required by law to render all assistance in its power to the girls' schools in the islands, the nation realising more and more the necessity of faithfully educating the future mothers of its subjects.

I ought to say that there has always been a very earnest desire among the Hawaiian girls to acquire the English language.

Again, in Japan the necessity of educating

* See Barnard's "Bureau of Education."

the women and girls is keenly felt. Schools are established all over the country, and missionary schools are doing a great work in educating the girls and women. The written language of Japan is largely in the Chinese alphabet, and written in Chinese characters, and so the early days of school-life are taken up with learning the meaning of these Chinese characters. It would make this article too long were I to go to any more countries; but enough has been seen to convince us of the power of education among us, and that it is the most important means for effecting the social and moral elevation of women all over the world.

It seems wonderful that half a century ago the question of women's education did not exist, and that now it occupies a position among the public interests of the day in every country of the world.

We will turn now to girl criminals, and see what kind of education they have had; and in this matter we must turn to statistics, which have not only discovered the amount of education they have received, but have likewise brought to light many curious facts about crime.

Criminal women are nearly all of them uneducated; it is very seldom indeed that one well-educated is seen; and this is easy to understand, for uneducated people have no resources for their leisure hours; they cannot read, they know nothing of the softening influence of music, they have no self-respect, no restraining influences at work, and they see no harm in intemperance, which is the fruitful source of crime.

Criminal women and girls are far more hopeless to deal with than men and boys. They have often had no training but in vice, and not unfrequently they are more uncivilised than the savage. Perhaps some who read this may be working among these female criminals; if so, I think they will corroborate what I say, that when one first goes among them a strong feeling of aversion and repugnance is produced, and just as surely a more intimate knowledge of them creates an extreme pity and yearning in the heart, and a desire to do something towards improving their condition.

Nearly all the women and girl criminals are drunkards. To cope with the sin and misery of this class is an attempt almost bewildering in its magnitude.

Mr. Hoyle, who is well known, traces most of the crime committed to drink, and he speaks with authority when he says, "For every reduction in the consumption of drink there is a corresponding decrease in the amount of crime."

To test the educational condition of criminals, we will take a certain number of prisoners, and by the aid of statistics learn something of them.

Out of 192,746 prisoners in the United Kingdom, 66,295 could neither read nor write; 94,871 could read and write a very little; 14,276 could read and write, but had received no other instruction; 957 had received a good education.

Of the remainder it was difficult to speak with accuracy. The proportion of women to men criminals is, I am happy to say, small. Out of 4,413 in France, 733 were women and girls.

In Germany to 12,184 men criminals, there were 2,770 women, 1,059 girls under 18; and of those who had committed misdemeanours there were 126,652 men, 26,930 women, and 9,780 girls. In Italy, out of 7,598 prisoners, 453 were women and girls. In Victoria, 14,948 men and 3,846 women. Whatever country we select for example, the proportions are about the same. One great encouragement to the various governments to persevere in educating the people is that during the last

few years the number of girl criminals under twenty years of age is remarkable for its decrease.

Crime in towns is much more frequent than in the country, showing the country air to be purer than that of cities, and less exposed to temptation. For example, towns furnish 17 prisoners out of every 100,000 of the population; country only 8.

It is a curious fact that crime is much more frequent among the single than among the married people.

The proportion of those guilty of grave crimes is about 33 in 100,000 of single people, and 11 in 100,000 of married people, widows and widowers.

Another curious fact is that the proportion of criminals varies according to sect. For example, the proportion of the accused is—of Protestants, one in 4 475 of the population; of Catholics, one in 3,926; of Jews, one in 3,391.

The statistics of education of prisoners throughout the world show that in the case of women and girls the largest proportion of them are wholly uneducated, viz., three-fifths.

In England and Wales the proportion of girls and women criminals, wholly ignorant, is 39 per cent.; in France, 44 per cent.

A FEW NOTES.

Country.	
Great Britain and Ireland	3,570,423 girls are receiving a good education.
France	During the last fifty years schools have increased 75 per cent., scholars 70 per cent., and girls' schools have quadrupled.
Spain	1,314,353 girls are being well taught.
Portugal	A great deal being done, but in a primitive and inefficient manner.
Saxony	98 per cent. of the girls attend school.
Turkey	Every town and village have their girls' schools.
Italy	Great progress is being made, but still 47 per cent. of the girls remain uneducated.
Queensland	Education for girls of a very high order.
New Zealand	Children of school age, 105,235.
Victoria	Children of school age, 199,150; girls very well educated—94 per cent.
Japan	There are 25,459 elementary schools and above 2,000,000 scholars, of whom 500,000 are girls.
Brazil	Number of girls attending school, 570,000, and the number of illiterate is decreasing rapidly.

(*To be continued.*)

THE PRINCESS LOUISE HOME.

By ANNE BEALE.

WE are once more permitted to ask "our girls" to help on a second bazaar in aid of the Princess Louise Home. The secretary writes that "he shall be most grateful to the readers of THE GIRL'S OWN PAPER if they will do as they did on the last occasion—send in small money contributions towards the bazaar expenses, as well as fancy and useful articles for sale." He also tells us that the Princess Louise has expressed her willingness to open the bazaar, and, under Her Royal been only to dream again of a roseate future. The future had come, and it was chill and grey enough. He could never cease to love Beattie, he imagined, but it was no longer right for him to carry her image in his heart, to think of her as he had done, since she was betrothed to another. But what put her farthest from him was the knowledge that she loved that other.

He sat still for a little while, watching with unseeing eyes the incoming waves on which the summer sunlight no longer danced so gaily. Mrs. Swannington was right, he thought. There was no advantage in his staying on at Crabsley. Yet he would like to see Beattie once more, not necessarily to speak to her, but just to look at her whose face had been before him in so many lonely hours. He remembered what Mrs. Swannington had said as to her where-abouts. She might have returned home by now, but there was just a likelihood that he would catch a glimpse of her, though alas, not alone. He started up suddenly, and began to walk quickly in the direction of the cliffs. One or two people lazily sauntering on the esplanade turned to look at him as he passed. His set face and resolute walk, and his complete unconsciousness of his sur-roundings, seemed out of keeping with the general Crabsley atmosphere. No one was expected on such a summer's day to do anything but flirt and dawdle and kill time with idleness.

But Mike had not gone very far when he saw her, and for a moment his heart almost stopped beating. The sun which was behind him was shining upon her, and she seemed to him like an angelic vision in her radiance and her white robes, with only the sky for a back-ground. At her companion he scarcely looked. What did he matter after all? It was the sight of Beattie for which he hungered. For one moment there came to him the temptation to forget all that he had heard, to go straight to her and greet her as he had often dreamed of doing? But, unfortunately for himself, he did no such thing. He drew to one side, and Beattie, who had been think-ing of him scarcely an hour ago, with feelings which, had he known of them, would have given him power to overcome any difficulties, now passed by in ignor-ance of his propinquity. If Mike had had any reason—and why should he have—for believing that Mrs. Swan-nington was lying to him, it would probably have been dispersed when he saw these two together: the man with his eyes fixed on the girl, and she apparently oblivious of all else but his presence, and looking the picture of happiness and content. And yet, if he had not had a preconceived idea per-haps he would not have seen anything remarkable in this. Why shouldn't Beattie delight in her life on this beau-tiful day, with all things smiling upon her? And was not one of her charms to Michael himself the way in which she threw herself into everything she did, as if at the time there was nothing else worth doing?

So they moved past him, and then he turned and stood watching them till they were out of sight in the winding way, and he went on alone till he came to a lonely spot, and there he stayed and fought a desperate battle with his misery till the light had faded out of the sky and the sea was only a moving darkness.

But when the moon rose and Aunt Ella and her husband and the other two were driving away from Crabsley, Mrs. Swannington full of uneasy gaiety and eager to laugh and talk to her com-panions, he went quietly down the grassy path that led him back to the town. He walked slowly, for he was tired; but there was a great peace at his heart. It is in the hours of trial and weakness that men learn the reality of those truths which they have accepted and tried to live by for many years.

It was from that hour of wrestling on the lonely cliff with none but God to hear his prayers, that Michael dated the beginning of that conscious spiritual life which was henceforth to make the other life worth living. He had gained a deeper knowledge than had yet been his, and its memory would be his most priceless possession.

Early the next morning he went away from Crabsley. "I seem fated to leave you in haste," he said, as he watched from the windows of the train the little village vanish from sight.

That very day Cecil Musgrove pro-posed to Beattie.

(To be continued.)

PRESENTATION DAY AT LONDON UNIVERSITY.

By A LADY GRADUATE.

ESTERDAY beauty, wit, and fashion re-paired to Bucking-ham Palace to make obeisance to the greatest Queen on earth; the Mall was crowded with car-riages, from which looked bright-eyed débutantes, eager to take the first step into the world of fashion. To-day, science and art are in the ascendant, and graduates—girls as well as men—in their Academic robes fill the theatre of London University, awaiting presentation to the chan-cellor of their alma mater.

The theatre—all too small—is crowded. The graduates of the year, with the flush of success still upon them, sit together, the girl "bachelors" for the most part young and pretty, the classic gown with its flowing hood and the stiff college cap, in strange contrast to winsome faces and bright locks.

On the highest tiers are the friends, usually the fathers and mothers, of the graduates. As I sit in the seat reserved for me and look around whilst awaiting the arrival of the chancellor and senate, I mentally contrast this occasion, when we are happy in our success, and the May sunshine streams in upon us and lingers lovingly on bright heads, with that gloomy October day which ushered in the examination. *Then* we were worried and anxious, our faces pale, our hands trembling, as we eagerly took our papers, quickly scanning them with practised eye, searching for ques-tions we could answer easily. *Now* we feel content; we have won. We are even ready to give up ease and pleasure and commence hard work again.

My meditations are interrupted by the arrival of the chancellor and the senate. We all rise as they come in, Lord Herschell (the chancellor) in Court costume, with robe of rich black silk, heavily embroidered in gold, walk-ing at the head with stately step, and we do not resume our seats until he takes the chair of honour and the others sit near him on the narrow platform. Immediately in front of them sit those who present the graduates—Mrs. Garrett Anderson, M.D., in black silk gown and college cap, Mrs. Bryant, D.Sc., in red robe with light silk facings, Frederick Taylor, M.D., Miss Hurlbatt, principal of Bedford College, and many more. The re-gistrar, who sits to the right of the chancellor, then calls out the names of the undergraduates who have won prizes and exhibitions, and these are presented first, then the graduates.

Quickly they come, the men cheering lustily the girls as they leave their places, each in answer to her name. Lord Herschell shakes hands with all as they are presented, giving to each the diploma, daintily tied with green ribbon; in a few cases medals as well. The medical women, in their bright robes, receive the most cheering, though the one lady D.Sc. is greeted with quite a storm of applause, whilst the doctors of law, in scarlet robes with bright blue facings, secure a goodly meed of praise.

It is delightful to see so many women reap honours, and in truth they look sturdy and strong, fitting mothers for the next generation, able to educate their children in the fullest sense of the word.

When the last presentation has been made, the chancellor rises and begins his speech by heartily congratulating all those who have taken degrees and won distinctions. In well-chosen sentences he begs them not to rest satisfied with their present success, but to be spurred on to greater efforts, ever having a higher end before them. Having touched on other matters relating to the university itself, he closes his speech with the fervently-ex-pressed desire that, whatever changes are made, London University will still be as useful and of as high repute as in former days.

Then Sir John Lubbock also offers his congratulations to us, and remarks how difficult were the examinations and how high the standard. Many of them within the theatre would, he said, in the future occupy high places in the world. He encouraged the students of law to work on, telling them that each one must ever keep before him as his model their own chancellor, the Lord Chan-cellor of England. As for the scientists, worlds of undiscovered truths lay before them; it was for them to probe and lay bare the secrets that would place the universe on ever

---

higher planes. Then he again congratulated all on their success, and amidst ringing cheers sat down.

I think in that moment when Sir John Lubbock, the member returned to Parliament by the university, spoke of the fame of our university, its great work and high standard, there was born in the breast of each one of us a feeling of reverence for our alma mater, a hope that we should never do anything which should make her sorry for her "alumni," but rather should add to her glory, and ever remain worthy children of a noble mother.

We all rose as the Lord Chancellor walked from his seat to the exit, followed by the members of the senate, and then we, too, moved from our places and ran hither and thither, seeking out friends, some only made in the examination-room in October. The most ardent opposer of higher education for women could hardly have disapproved of these happy-looking girls, their bright earnest faces glowing with health. Among them one saw no jaded looks or weary eyes, as one sees among girls who have no aim, no ambition, but to shine at a ball or get an eligible *parti*. One hears so much of the injurious effect study has on girls; many men deplore the strides women are making in the pursuit of knowledge; they prognosticate early loss of youth, bright eyes, and good looks; and yet here to-day I see a goodly number of English maidens as healthy, happy, and comely as surely were the women of bygone ages, who watched their brothers' progress, sighing as they ruined their sight over their tapestry.

Study, as Sir John Lubbock wisely remarked, leaves no time for dulness; the girl who has hard brain-work to do every day has not time to feel miserable. Petty worries and small annoyances leave her as she becomes immersed in Greek, mathematics, or whatever particular branch she has taken up. That study does not rob her of her high spirits and merry laughter is amply proved by the joyous sounds that issue from the robing-rooms. The grey old corridors resound with girlish voices; one catches snatches of conversation as each relates how the scene affected her, how much she has hoped for success, and so on.

It is sweet to work and reach the appointed goal—only those who have given up pleasure and sacrificed ease can say *how* sweet. Let us hope amid the joy which is here to-day, some feelings of compassion are raised in our hearts for those who strove like us, but did not win. To my girl-readers I would say: Work, keeping the thought of success ever before you. Cultivate the brain-powers which God has

given you. Read, and widen your knowledge; think, and broaden your views, and I can

safely say dulness will not often trouble you, nor weariness make you its victim.

As we leave the university we talk of the

next exam. we intend to work for. Somehow, the whole ceremony has fired us with zeal.

We long to climb yet higher, and silent vows are registered to work steadily on, not content with what is already won.

HOUSEHOLD HINTS.

MANY town people taking a holiday in the country are distressed at seeing horses tethered in the fields exposed to the swarms of flies which the switching of their tails is powerless to get rid of, but which wound and torment them beyond endurance, and in our drives and walks we are subject to the same annoyance.

The remedy is simple. Tie a bunch of the scented oak-leaved geranium on the heads or bodies of your horses, and wear a few of them in the front of your dress, and do not forget to place some on the tethered animals.

If you want to keep your room free of the flies, put some plants of the scented oak-leaved geranium in your windows. They will hardly venture through them, for they are always scared at the scent of them.

One word more. This is just the time to get the raspberry leaves, fennel, and parsley fresh from the gardens, so do not forget to prepare the remedy I gave in the November numbers for tired eyes.

PICKLED FRENCH BEANS.—Be careful to have them freshly gathered and quite young. Put them into a brine, made strong enough to float an egg, until they turn colour, then drain them and wipe dry with a clean cloth; put them into a jar and stand as near the fire as possible, and pour boiling vinegar over them sufficient to cover, covering it up quickly to prevent the steam from escaping. Continue to do this until they become green by reboiling the vinegar about every other day. They should take about a week.

PICKLED CABBAGE AND CAULIFLOWER.— Slice the cabbage very finely and cut the cauliflower in small pieces on a board or colander (a pastry board I find answers very nicely), and sprinkle each layer with salt and let it stand for twenty-four hours, sloping the board a little that the brine might run away from it. Procure as much ordinary pickling vinegar as you think will be required to

cover the cabbage, and boil a small portion of it with a little ginger and a small quantity of peppercorns, also a small beetroot peeled and cut up to give it a nice colour; after it has boiled pour it in the remaining vinegar, but take out the beetroot. Put the cabbage and cauliflower into a jar and pour over the vinegar and spices; tie down and keep in a dry place. Will be ready for table-use in about a month.

PICKLED NASTURTIUMS.—Gather them when quite young, and let them remain in brine for twelve hours; have sufficient vinegar to cover them, and with a small portion of it boil a little Jamaica and a little black pepper; when it has just boiled, add to the remaining vinegar. Strain the nasturtiums and put them in a bottle or jar and pour over the vinegar and spices, and tie down. These are very nice to use instead of capers for sauce with either boiled beef or mutton.

A Lady Graduate, "Presentation Day at London University" (Volume 19, 23 July 1898, p. 677).

THE BATTERSEA POLYTECHNIC.

COOKERY.

The word Polytechnic, as some of our readers will know, is derived from two Greek terms, πολύς many, and τέχνη art. The name is now given to the educational institutions which of late years have sprung up throughout London. It takes a long time to convince the public mind, and we are not yet quite sure that girls throughout the country realise the enormous advantages offered by such a Polytechnic, for example, as that we are about to describe.

The Battersea Polytechnic is a huge building fronting the Battersea Park Road. A brief article in THE GIRL'S OWN PAPER for August 19th, 1899, entitled "London's Future Housewives and their Teachers," sketched the Training School for Domestic Economy; but since its publication the school has almost trebled its numbers, and a new wing has been added in connection with the Woman's

IT is not probable that many of our readers will remember the associations formerly evoked by the word "Polytechnic." There was, in Regent Street, a building which, on its first foundation in 1838, bore the high-sounding title of "National Gallery of the Arts and Practical Science," or something to that effect. This "Royal Polytechnic" afforded to the children of generations ago instruction blended with amusement. Entertainment so ostensibly qualified would hardly, we think, appeal to the modern child. But for the sum of one shilling our juvenile ancestors were admitted to a marvellous place where they might descend into a tank, fourteen feet deep, by means of a diving-bell, watch the heavy performance of an automatic acrobat, listen to the terrific strains of an organ which combined within itself all the instruments of a brass band, and see many a novel and portentous show.

Public classes were also held here; but after a fire in 1881 the building was sold, and its original purposes were abandoned.

Work—a wing which was opened on February 26th, 1904, by the Prince and Princess of Wales. Therefore we are not afraid of going over old ground, and the necessity of insistence on the opportunities before girls and women is

LAUNDRY TRAINING SCHOOL.—IRONING.

Lily Watson, "The Battersea Polytechnic" (Volume 25, 2 July 1904, p. 628).

HOUSEWIFERY.

obvious. "Line upon line and precept upon precept" is needful in these matters, and we are sure, from the questions that reach us, that much still remains to learn.

On entering the central hall we become aware of many boys and girls hurrying to and fro, giving brightness and life to the long stone corridors. These are the pupils of the Day Schools. There is a Science School for boys and girls (mixed), and a General and Commercial School for Girls. The latter provides a good secondary education, intended to meet the needs of girls who are preparing for commercial or business life, or for the ordinary examinations of the Civil Service. The fee for each girl is only £1 per term, or 10s. per half term. "Admission to the Schools is limited to boys and girls who have obtained entrance scholarships from a Public Elementary School, or who have passed, or are able to pass, the Sixth Standard of the Educational Code or its equivalent, or who shall exhibit such exceptional knowledge as shall warrant the Governing Body in assuming that they will be able to profit by the advanced education offered." Girls must wear the school badge. There are arrangements made for games, and the whole

prospectus of these Schools, from which we have just quoted, reads delightfully.

But we had not intended to allow much space to the young people of the Day Schools, as we think there are other departments of the Polytechnic which may prove more attractive to our readers. And perhaps the most significant of these is the Domestic Economy Training School, which has greatly developed since the date of the article we mentioned. There are now nearly 90 students in attendance, while there were at that time only 30.

Who, then, are these students?

They are, for the main part, girls over eighteen years of age who are preparing to be teachers. And we may say here, as we have said before, that for the High School girl — uncertain as to her career — of practical energy and household tastes, the post of Teacher of Domestic Economy offers many advantages. For one thing, the profession, unlike that of the ordinary governess, is not overstocked. The Superintendent of the Women's Department who showed us round, Miss Marsden, told us that no properly qualified students were at a loss for work. They may obtain

NEEDLEWORK.

rositions in elementary, secondary, technical schools, or in Polytechnics. And many large institutions now employ a lady cook as head of the kitchen.

We entered one and another kitchen, large, spotless, airy, fitted with a variety of stoves. Two or three descriptions of kitchener were here, nor were gas-stoves lacking. One oil-stove attracted admiration by its absolute freedom from any suggestion of its motive power! At the tables girls were engaged in the various operations of cookery, under the supervision of a teacher.

One kitchen was especially to be noted; it was tiled from floor to ceiling with white tiles. Another is to be set apart in future for " high-class cookery." Arrangements have recently been made for " special day courses " for Housewives and Colonial Training to meet the requirements either of ladies living at home or intending to emigrate to the colonies. The length of the course varies from three to twelve months, and the subjects included in the full course are practical housekeeping, including accounts, housewifery, cookery, laundry-work, needlework,

art by their dainty manipulations. In one kitchen, however, we observed a number of younger girls. These, from the day-schools we mentioned, or from voluntary schools outside the Polytechnic, were being instructed by students, in classes of fifteen, and the students in turn were under the supervision of a mistress. A particularly fine cabbage lay before each child; at the word of command it was divided into four; a bowl of water lay close at hand for washing each piece separately. The children seemed to enjoy the process.

We have often said that teachers need to be trained how to teach, and the advantage of having pupils on whom to practise the art is no small part of the advantages of the Battersea Training School.

" What is done with the food prepared ? " we inquire.

For a sufficient answer we are conducted into a large and cheerful dining-hall where tables are laid for 120 persons. Each day the staff, students, and girls of the Practising School dine here on the eatables cooked in the kitchens, and fifty or sixty take tea. The tables, with a

GYMNASIUM.

including upholstery, dressmaking, hygiene, and first aid. The subjects taken will, of course, depend on the requirements of the students, and the fees vary from £3 to £12.

In a former paper on " Girls' Ambitions " we commended the " domestic ambition " to our readers. What could be better for the middle-class girl who is engaged to be married, for example, than to attend such a course ? Economy means the Law of the Home. We cannot help thinking that it would be wise, in certain cases, if money is scarce, to retrench in the cost of wedding festivities, that the bride may enter on her life well equipped. It will save her from having, in after days, to learn in a very costly school.

But we are anticipating a little. This training for housewives stands somewhat apart from the training for teachers, of which we first spoke, though practically the methods are the same. The majority of students are those training in view of the diplomas, which are recognised by the Board of Education, to qualify them for the posts we enumerated.

Students of various classes of society were busy in the admirably-fitted kitchens we entered, making cookery a fine

delicate bunch of azaleas on that prepared for the teachers, looked inviting.

Cookery is only one of the branches of domestic economy that are taught here; but we hold a firm conviction that the preparation of food is to become more and more the work of trained women.

From the kitchen we pass to another department, where laundry-work is in progress. We look around in vain for the atmosphere of hopeless, steaming wretchedness connected with the " family wash." In one room girls are ironing; in another and a smaller room they are washing. A tiled screen keeps the intense heat of the ironing stove from the room. In a glass case against the wall a gentleman's beautifully got-up white shirt and other articles are exhibited.

The needlework department is exceedingly interesting. The students are hard at work, under a qualified mistress, in various ways. Each one is required to complete a dress for herself before she receives her diploma.

But perhaps the most attractive items to us were the novel ones in which small bedsteads and mannikin figures

Lily Watson, "The Battersea Polytechnic" (Volume 25, 2 July 1904, p. 630).

played a prominent part. For the small bed the students are required to make, in miniature, each necessary article, and a young lady with a roll of striped ticking was carefully considering the proportions of a Lilliputian bolster-case. One of the bedsteads is severely plain. Another is fitted for valances and curtains, and the best way of heading and pleating these, with all the upholstery so often required from a housewife, is taught. Wicker chairs, which we had seen with surprise carried along the corridors, were here waiting to be covered by skilful fingers. And the "man-nikin " figures were in process of being fitted. It is no easy task to fit these little personages, but a tailor-made coat we saw, seemed likely to suit the requirements of the most exacting doll.

It is, of course, easy for the student who has to teach classes to carry the small bedstead and the dressed mannikin with her to exhibit to the children. These answer the same end for demonstration as life-size models.

Among the evening students are a certain number of apprentices, sent by Messrs. Sélincourt to learn the prin-ciples of their trade from competent teachers.

In another department pieces of carpet and a carpet-sweeper were awaiting practical handling.

We were much impressed by seeing one room set aside as a model bedroom, with two made-up beds, each exhibit-ing a different way of arranging a bed. This room is to be in the charge of the students. Nothing seems omitted in this wonderful place that can give girls a practical insight into domestic economy.

We have enlarged before on the importance of learning this on the best possible methods. It is often not easy to study it at home as it should be studied. If the servants are good, they do not welcome amateur aid ; while, if they are bad or non-existent, the press of living is often too great to admit of leisurely study " how to do things " in the best possible way. Yet knowledge of domestic arts does not come by nature, and the failure to understand them, as exhibited in half poisoning people and putting them into damp beds, may be extremely serious.

The "commencing salaries" of Domestic Economy teachers who have just finished their training vary from about £70 to £90 with or without partial board, and, as we have said, there is work for all.

It is impossible to be too lucid in an article of this kind, and we therefore recapitulate the divisions of those who undergo the Polytechnic teaching. They are—

1. The students, *i.e.*, girls over eighteen, who intend to become teachers in after years in elementary, secondary, technical schools, in Polytechnics, etc. For them the full course of instruction, including cookery, plain needlework, dress-making, laundry-work and housewifery, lasts two years and one term, and the fees are £55, including materials for cookery and laundry-work, and all fees for first examination and diplomas. Subjects may, however, be taken separately, at proportionate fees, and we invite those who are interested to write to the Principal for a prospectus. High School girls and others will find this training afford them an opening for a prosperous career.

2. Ladies living at home, or those who intend to emi-grate, who wish to obtain an insight into house manage-ment. The course for these lasts from three to twelve months ; they do not receive a diploma, but a certificate is given to them at the close of their training.

3. Girls who attend the Day Schools in the Polytechnic, and who enter the cookery and other schools for instruction by students under the direct supervision of mistresses.

Scholarships are offered yearly by the London County Council to students over eighteen, and to girls of the age of thirteen and fourteen from elementary schools. The scholarships for students training as teachers are valuable, being equivalent to £55 in fees, with additional advantages in meals and in materials for work. An account of these was recently given in THE GIRL'S OWN PAPER (see page 372).

There is a large and well-equipped gymnasium where students can be trained as gymnastic teachers. As we have before stated, the prospect before these is extremely good.

The instructress is a member of the British College of Physical Education. The course of training extends over a period of two years, and includes full preparation in all theoretical work, lectures on anatomy, physiology, hygiene, first aid, instruction in fencing, swimming, etc.

The vast hall, accommodating a thousand people, with its great organ, where all who attend the Polytechnic meet for prayers each morning, is a sight to behold. There is a pleasant library, a common room, and nothing seems lacking.

We have dwelt at length upon the Training School of Domestic Economy, but this is only a small part of the work that goes on here for women. Unfortunately, in a brief article of this kind, it is impossible to do more than mention, in passing, a great deal that deserves notice. We may just say that there appear to be classes in nearly everything a girl can desire to learn. Sick-nursing, milli-nery, photography, are subjects taken at random from the prospectus.

In this wonderful Polytechnic, then, there are evening classes for both sexes in all subjects of Technology, pure and applied Science, Art, Commerce, and Music. There is also a Day School of Art, and special day courses are given in many subjects. Classes are conducted in preparation for the examinations of the London University, and for most of the examinations in science and art subjects of the Science and Art Department of the Board of Education. The list of successes is admirable.

The instruction in the Art Department comprises a thoroughly practical knowledge of designing, drawing, painting, and modelling. Such occupations as book-bind-ing, pattern-designing for wall-papers and fabrics, art needlework, book illustration, design and drawing in black and white for reproduction, are included in the schedule. The prospectus is bewildering and fascinating in its scope. We can only advise intending students to apply at the inquiry office, which is open daily (10 A.M. to 5 P.M.) for the issue of prospectuses and forms.

There is an attractive list of clubs, some of which—*e.g.*, cycling, lawn tennis, swimming, sketching—are open to both men and women. Entertainments and organ recitals are given in the Great Hall on Saturday and Wednesday evenings. And, lastly, we may add that a boarding house, at reasonable rates, is open to students who may come from a distance.

The Battersea Polytechnic has not yet had a very long life. The foundation stone was laid by his Majesty the King, then Prince of Wales, on July 20th, 1891, and the buildings were formally opened by his Majesty on February 24th, 1894. They were built and equipped at a cost of nearly £90,000, the greater part of which was raised by voluntary subscriptions. The record of ten years is a most fruitful one, and our readers should unite in wishing prosperity to a great institution that is already enlarging its bounds for the benefit of girls and women.

LILY WATSON.

Lily Watson, "The Battersea Polytechnic" (Volume 25, 2 July 1904, p. 631).

she looked up from the page, "this is a very silly half-educated article, but I don't see anything to mind, father dearest. This newspaper man can't hurt you."

"Ah, my dear, but it does not end there," said the Vicar ruefully. "There have been letters, many letters, in the same paper, and an agitation is going to be set on foot—I feel sure of it—to deprive me of the post of Curator and to remove the books. I have cut them all out."

He brought Rosemary as he spoke an old ledger, with dated newspaper cuttings carefully pasted in.

Realising the misery that this task had involved, Rosemary glanced at the letters with a swelling heart. They were all to the same effect—about the injury wrought by outworn trusts, by the "Dead Hand," and so on, while glowing descriptions were given of the volumes as housed in some brand-new Mechanics' Institute. The letters were signed by such names as "Vox Populi," "Inquirer," "Iconoclast."

"Someone is at the back of all this," said Rosemary firmly.

"Well, that is what Gervase says; but, you see, my dear, the letters are from different people. No," said the Vicar despondently, "it is the voice of the public speaking through this popular organ. It is not quite fair though," he continued with mild dignity, "to speak of the books being dusty and mildewed. I dust them myself every fortnight. I do not think," said the Vicar meditatively, "that I could neglect a book, any more than I could neglect a child."

Rosemary rushed at him and threw her arms round his neck.

"Cheer up, father dearest!" she cried. "This is all talk, talk! And what does it mean? I don't even believe this *Daily Champion*, though it is a London paper, is at all well thought of. 'They say—— What say they? Let them say'!"

"I much fear, my dear child," said the clergyman sadly, "that in this case we shall find talk is followed by action."

(*To be continued.*)

PITMAN'S METROPOLITAN SCHOOL.

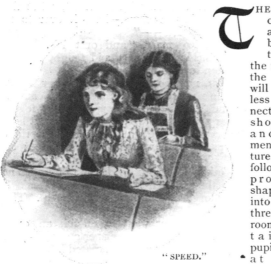

" SPEED."

THE associations aroused by this title in the mind of the reader will doubtless be connected with shorthand, and the mental picture which follows will probably shape itself into two or three dingy rooms, containing pupils hard at work upon that cryptic art. The writer is not ashamed to say that such was the image vaguely existing in her own brain until a close study of the prospectus and a personal visit placed the reality before her.

The School was certainly, on its establishment in 1870, exclusively occupied with shorthand, but it has now become a fully equipped and thoroughly organised Business Training College. Our readers should be specially interested in a description of the place, for, to quote the prospectus, it has made "a new field of enterprise, more especially for girls, who are now able, after six or eight months of study, to command a fair salary in light and congenial employment."

It must be clearly understood that the School stands alone. It is the result of private enterprise, and has nothing whatever to do with the authority under whose auspices the other Technical Schools (enumerated in the list of articles for the present volume of THE GIRL'S OWN PAPER) were founded. The School claims the proud position of being the pioneer of all Commercial Training Institutions in the kingdom, and its list of successes (of which more hereafter) speaks for itself.

The building rears its huge front in Southampton Row, in an open and airy position overlooking the gardens of Russell Square. The light brick of its construction and plenty of windows give it a cheerful appearance. On entering through swing doors (flanked by separate entrances and passages for ladies and gentlemen) we find ourselves in a great airy hall, pleasantly warm on the winter's day. The place, it may here be said, is ventilated on the Sturtevant system, by means of which air is drawn into the building by a large and powerful fan, worked by an engine. The air is cleansed by an air filter, warmed in winter, conducted into every room of the building and changed throughout the corridors and all the rooms at frequent intervals. The fluttering of tapes from the ventilators above the doors shows that ventilation is really going on. None of the pupils wear the heavy-eyed look that comes from used-up air and stuffy warmth.

On the settees against the wall girls are resting; there is a bright, cheery *va-et-vient* throughout the hall, young people of both sexes are ascending and descending the wide stone staircase, while a lift is called into requisition for ourselves. We ascend to the fifth floor

THE PRIVATE SECRETARY.

---

maintained throughout is demonstrated by the fact that over 97 per cent. passed—91 first, 150 second, and only 91 third-class. Prizes of medals and money have been won in shorthand, typewriting, German, English, and précis-writing." There is for year after year a record of "first prize and medal" taken in languages by pupils of this School.

On the floor below we become aware of the click of many typewriting machines, and girls are seen hard at work, with instructors passing from one to another. It is worthy of notice that this was the first School in the kingdom to teach typewriting. Among the machines in use in the School are all the leading makes, and the art of using them appears to be taught in an intelligent manner. No pupil, who has

TYPEWRITING.

GERMAN

CONVERSATION.

and find ourselves, with our escort, on a landing with doors, the upper half of which is of glass, admitting into class-rooms. Here the study of French and German under native professors is in progress. We entered in all four rooms, two being devoted to the study of each language, one to grammar, the other to conversational purposes. The system in the School is that of personal instruction. Instead of one master haranguing a large class, some of whom may be apathetic, others uncomprehending, here are three or four masters in one class-room; going round to the pupils individually, explaining difficulties, talking to each.

We saw tabulated on the walls the extraordinary results of the Society of Arts' examinations. These are best set forth in the words of a printed slip given to us concerning the results in 1903.

"In many respects the School takes first place in the kingdom, notwithstanding the fact that the number of centres has risen to 322, and the total number of papers examined reaches the enormous aggregate of 11,670. 'P.M.S.' awards include 91 first-class certificates (highest in the kingdom), eight prizes, tying for first place with one other centre; first place and first prize in German, in English, and in précis-writing; 30 first-class certificates in shorthand (the next best centre having 20); 14 'firsts' in German (no other centre taking more than 10); 10 'firsts' and medal in typewriting (no other centre having more than five); nine 'firsts' in French (no other institution taking more than six). The total number of papers submitted was 342, and the high standard of excellence

not had abundant practice, is allowed to pass out of this department.

The great feature of the School is undoubtedly the Business Training Hall, to which we now descend, on the third floor. It extends along the whole front of the building, and is, as its name implies, a large hall fitted with office desks, and, in fact, with nearly every appliance that can be met with in an ordinary office. At either end of the hall is a telephone for practical demonstration. The pupils, in telephoning from one end of the hall to the other, observe the registered telephone numbers of the large London firms, and in this way become familiar with information they may afterwards need. There are up-to-date filing cabinets; specimens of the raw materials used in manufacture stand in museum-like cases round the walls, and in some cases the development of the product is clearly shown; the coinage of the different countries is exemplified. But we were most impressed by the fact that in this room the actual books in use are such as would be found in a business office. The student is, in fact, rehearsing his part with thoroughness. The dread of spoiling one of the formidable ledgers

WAITING-ROOM.

usually entrusted to a clerk must be alarming to the novice who has to write in one for the first time in the master's office ; but in this Business Training Hall he or she has to use, not insignificant scraps of paper, but the very books that will be handled later on. Thus the learner grows accustomed to the portentous leather-bound volumes, to the use of the copying-press, and so on. The "letter-book" we saw contained beautifully neat specimens of writing.

In some departments of the school, as in this hall, the students are of both sexes ; in others the sexes are divided. We saw separate rooms for the girl book-keeping students, and then descended to the department which used to be *par excellence* the object of the School ; *i.e.*, the shorthand department. This is divided into two main sections—the one for teaching the theory of the art, the other for training in speed and practical reporting. No girl is allowed to enter the speed section of the shorthand department until an examination, conducted from outside, has certified her to be ready for practical work. When this is accomplished she is led on gradually from the slow to the quickest rate of writing, and the different rooms in which this is done are as follows—

Room No. 11.	Slow :	40, 50, 60 words a minute
,, 10.	Moderate :	70, 80, 90 ,,
,, 12.	Fast :	100–110 ,,
,, 13.	Business :	110–120 ,,
,, 27.	Extra fast :	120 and upward.

We probably all remember that when David Copperfield had learned to write shorthand he was dismayed to find that he was totally unable to read what he had written ! This danger is avoided by the provision of a transcribing and testing room for writing out what has been taken down in shorthand from dictation. Notes taken in the shorthand speed rooms are also transcribed in the typewriting departments under supervision. "In this way," says the prospectus, "the students are from the outset made to feel the interdependence of the 'twin arts,'" shorthand and typewriting. It is worth mentioning that within the past ten years nine members of the School have taken the certificate for writing at the rate of 200 words per minute. At the Society of Arts' Examination, 1902, Pitman's Metropolitan School took 21 first-class certificates, no other, out of the nearly 300 centres, taking more than 10. At the National Union of Teachers' Special Examination for Reporting Honours, 1902, the School took first and second prizes in an examination at 160 words per minute for 10 minutes. At the London Phonetic Society's examination for the gold, silver and bronze medals offered to all London non-professional shorthand writers this School has for the past six years taken all the medals awarded.

Having, ourselves, not the remotest acquaintance with this art, we inquired in awestruck tones how long it would usually take a girl of average ability to acquire a knowledge of shorthand sufficient for business purposes, and were told, to our surprise, "from four to six months only."

As we entered one of the rooms, a pause in the dictation had just occurred, and a master, with the blackboard, was giving practical hints during the interval. "Assassinated ?" asked a voice, and a symbol, which was the equivalent of the word, instantly appeared on the board in explanation. The opportunity of having difficulties cleared up from time to time as they occur is undoubtedly a great advantage. The girls who were sitting at the desks looked cheerful over their work, in spite of the terror with which Charles Dickens has invested it !

But we must hasten on. The shorthand rooms occupy the greater part of two floors. Many other rooms, however, still remained to be visited. In some of these, strangers from various nations were learning English. All seemed bright, busy, interested. The place, with its order and method and hum of business, reminded one of nothing so much as a great hive, and we were struck again and again with the wonderful organisation of the whole.

About 1,600 students attend here daily. The list of studies includes shorthand, typewriting, book-keeping, business methods, arithmetic, longhand, French, German, Spanish, English grammar, composition, orthography, commercial geography, commercial law, mathematics, précis-writing, indexing, science ; preparation for all Civil Service and Professional Preliminary Examinations.

From this list any seven subjects may be chosen by the pupil, one subject being replaced by another when the desired amount of progress has been attained. It is also possible to enter for one subject at a time, or any one group of subjects. The minimum commercial course is regarded as shorthand, typewriting and business methods.

New students may enrol for one, two or three years' courses, having the right to take instruction in any seven subjects on the School's list each year, and of changing four subjects annually.

The following is suggested as a popular Two Years' Course :—

1st Year.—Writing, arithmetic, English grammar and composition, spelling and dictation, shorthand, French and German.

2nd Year.—English grammar, composition, shorthand, French and German (continued), with the addition of book-keeping, business methods and typewriting.

The students are classified as Senior and Junior.

The Seniors are those over 21 years of age and those who are acting on their own resources. The Juniors are those under 21, or those who are sent by parents, guardians or business firms. Each of the Juniors has a log-book, in which the report of the day's work is entered day by day, to be taken home.

These are a few of the distinguishing advantages claimed by the School, to sum up what we have said :—

All pupils are taught by specialists.

Senior students come as often and stay as long as they desire within the School hours ; Juniors as per Time Table.

Students are taught individually.

Great care is taken to see that candidates are making satisfactory progress in all subjects.

Students are frequently examined in the subjects in which they are receiving instruction, and marks are awarded in order that their progress may be clearly ascertained.

We have written enough to give a general idea of the character of this great institution, which is in itself a significant feature of modern times. It is only the empty-headed and foolish who think it grand to despise commerce. They should remember that the need of interchange of commodities laid, in ancient times, the foundation of modern civilisation, of modern thought. It was in the market place (*agora*) that men learned to interchange ideas as well as goods ; it was there that they listened to the words of great philosophers. And the fiscal discussions of modern times may have had a remote prototype in some such episode as the following, exquisitely sketched by Matthew Arnold :—

" As some grave Tyrian trader, from the sea,
   Descried at sunrise an emerging prow
Lifting the cool-haired creepers stealthily,
   The fringes of a southward-facing brow
     Among the Ægæan isles ;
And saw the merry Grecian coaster come,
   Freighted with amber grapes, and Chian wine,
   Green bursting figs, and tunnies steeped in brine,
And knew the intruders on his ancient home,

" The young light-hearted masters of the waves—
   And snatched his rudder, and shook out more sail ;
   And day and night held on indignantly
O'er the blue Midland waters with the gale,
   Between the Syrtes and soft Sicily,
     To where the Atlantic raves
Outside the western straits ; and unbent sails
   There, where down cloudy cliffs, through sheets of foam,
   Shy traffickers, the dark Iberians come ;
     And on the beach undid his corded bales."

Anon., "Pitman's Metropolitan School" (Volume 25, 13 February 1904, p. 310).

THE COLLEGE.

GARDENING AS A PROFESSION FOR GIRLS.

HOW THEY ARE TRAINED AT SWANLEY, AND THE DEMAND FOR COMPETENT STUDENTS.

PART I.

In the sunniest part of Kent, right in the heart of the fruit-growing district, is to be found an up-to-date horticultural college. Here women are trained in all branches of

THE POTTING-SHED.

horticultural work, and when it is stated that scores of young ladies have been turned out from this college, and now hold responsible posts in all parts of the country, and also in the colonies, it is evident that the institution is not only a practical one, but supplies a decided want. Indeed, there is undoubtedly a demand for women gardeners, and in these days, when so many girls are seeking to find some suitable vocation, an account of the college and its work cannot fail to be of interest.

As already stated, it is situated in Kent, about a mile and a half across the fields from Swanley Junction. It was established in 1889, the college building itself consisting of a fine old house, part of it going back to Elizabethan days, standing in forty-three acres of land. "The college aims chiefly," according to the statement in the prospectus, "at giving a thoroughly systematic training to women who wish to become market-growers and gardeners in private places." That it has succeeded and is still succeeding in this desirable object is proved by the number of posts secured last year by Swanley students. Three obtained the position of head gardeners, while five found employment as under-gardeners, and another seven as gardeners. Two students also went as companion gardeners, another as a jobbing gardener, while six obtained situations in schools and institutions, and another three appointments abroad.

The forty-three acres of ground over which the students work is freehold land and belongs to the college. There are twelve acres of kitchen garden, two of flower-garden, seventeen of fruit plantation, the remainder being meadow-land, etc. The main building includes lecture-rooms, class-rooms and laboratories, where most of the science teaching is carried on. Glass-houses for market-work are fifteen in number, each one hundred feet long, and a conservatory, with

HARD WORK ON THE LAND.

UNDER GLASS.

OUT OF DOORS.

Lena Shepstone, "Gardening as a Profession for Girls" (Volume 26, 1 April 1905, p. 425).

DIGGING.

range of glass for private work, has lately been added. There are adjoining stables, a workshop, farm buildings, apiary, dairy, poultry-houses, etc. When the college was first started, only men were taken, but two years later women students appeared on the scene. Now it is devoted exclusively to the training of women. It may be said to have become a college for women since the autumn of 1903, when

THE VINERY.

WARM FRAMES.

it was decided to take only female students.

Whenever you visit Swanley, either in the summer or late in the autumn, you cannot help being struck with the quiet determination with which the young ladies go about their work. There is no excitement, no rush, all is quiet and peace. In all departments of the college it is the same. In the gardens and in the fields, in the glass-houses and conservatories, you come across groups of three, five, and perhaps eight young women, pursuing their labours, paying strict attention to their tutors, and evidently taking the keenest interest in the task set before them.

It was a delightful day when the writer visited this ideal Horticultural College, and requested the Principal to guide her over the grounds. Turning out of a quiet lane, just

Lena Shepstone, "Gardening as a Profession for Girls" (Volume 26, 1 April 1905, p. 426).

beyond the college building, we found ourselves in a large plantation of young fruit-trees, with gooseberry bushes growing between rows of trees alternately with potatoes and other vegetables. It was on the eve of an examination, and here and there, in quiet, shady nooks, might be found a student too much absorbed in books to bestow more than a casual glance at a visitor. Presently we came upon a group of women students busily engaged in picking gooseberries under the supervision of one of the staff of gardeners. To judge by his watchful solicitude and frequent suggestions to the workers, there is more art in picking gooseberries than would at first appear. A few yards from the gooseberry pickers were some lady students skilfully accomplishing the very delicate business of budding young fruit-trees, a task for which feminine fingers are especially adapted.

Near at hand was a pleasant paddock, where numerous coops held indignant hens, who clucked anxiously as we inspected their fluffy little families. The apiary occupied an enclosure near the poultry runs. Some score of hives of the latest pattern stood in rows, and bees in buzzing thousands filled the air with their humming. Two young girls, with their faces hidden behind bee-veils, had opened one of the hives, and had taken out the frame of comb, upon which the bees hung in clustering festoons. The two students were searching for the queen bee, whose loyal subjects seemed to take matters very calmly. After watching the proceedings for a few minutes, we deemed it desirable to pass on, not relishing the prospect of a possible sting from the more excited bees that were flying wildly about.

The flower garden, which is directly opposite the college building, presented a picturesque and even fascinating

MARKING THE LAND.

appearance. Every seasonable flower you could name was to be seen in bloom. Close by were the students' own gardens, little plots where girls can display their own individual tastes to the full. Some of these plots were very charming, both skill and artistic ability being shown in the arrangement of the flowers and shrubs. In the glass-houses all kinds of fruit, such as tomatoes, cucumbers, peaches and the like, are grown. There are also some very fine vineries at Swanley, while a couple of the houses are given over entirely to the production of tropical plants.

GRAPE THINNING.

Lena Shepstone, "Gardening as a Profession for Girls" (Volume 26, 1 April 1905, p. 427).

It has been stated in the Press that anyone visiting Swanley may witness the spectacle of girls ploughing. This is not strictly correct, for ploughing is not included in the curriculum. At the same time, it is true that about two years ago a lady student expressed a wish to learn ploughing and was allowed to do so. The same remarks apply to the scythe. Those who wish to learn how to use this instrument are encouraged to do so. As a rule, too, they make apt pupils, and in a short time can manipulate the unwieldy instrument with remarkable skill.

(*To be concluded.*)

TWO LADIES OF THE STUART PERIOD.

By SARSON C. J. INGHAM, Author of " The White Cross and Dove of Pearls," " Selina's Story," etc.

CHAPTER II.
MRS. PEPYS.

" Is the creature too imperfect, say?
  Would you mend it
  And so end it?
Since not all addition perfects aye!

Or is it of its kind, perhaps,
  Just perfection
  Whence, rejection
Of a grace not to its mind, perhaps?"
Browning.

LIZABETH ST. MICHEL was descended on her father's side from a noble French family, and on her mother's from the Cliffords of Cumberland, recognised as a noble stock. Of her life prior to her marriage there is no record in the Diary.

Pepys' Diary begins 1659–60, when she had been for four years his wife. He does not indulge in retrospect, so we know nothing of their courtship and " parlous " beginning of married life.

The girl of fifteen found herself in London with a husband eight years older than herself, and in some things not as many wiser. He was, however, well able to take care of her, and had the spirit and the will to work for her when an opening was made for him. Indeed, the pair appear to have been extremely well matched. Sam Pepys doted on smart appearance; Elizabeth's beauty was a thing to be proud of, granted and approved wherever he might take her.

If she did not already know, she was not slow to learn that " fine feathers make fine birds." Things had to go very hardly with the Pepys if they did not manage to make a grand show when they walked abroad, went to the theatre or even to church. On holidays and public occasions Pepys was fond of taking his little wife out, and as his circumstances improved he gave her the desire of her heart in many a *chic* article of dress that caught her eye in the shop windows. The Diary shows us how kind he was, and what were Mrs. Pepys' " particular vanities."

April 15*th*, 1662.—" With my wife by coach to the New Exchange, and to buy her some things, where we saw some new-fashioned pettycoats of sarcenett, with a black, broad lace printed round the bottom and before; very handsome, and my wife had a mind to one of them."

May 14*th*, 1665.—" To church, it being Whitsunday. My wife very fine in a new yellow bird's eye hood, as the fashion is now."

Pepys declares on more than one occasion that the sight of fine clothes does him good, we suppose by enlivening his spirits, though we fail to see how the study of Lady Castlemaines' muslin and lace skirts, hung out to dry, could do any man good, if he thought of her as she deserved.

The earlier years of struggle and obscurity ought certainly to be regarded as a touchstone of character. To the credit of the young couple be it spoken then, that when " poverty came in at the door, love did not fly out of the window." Both behaved in a manner that they could recall with pleasure when their ship came in.

Pepys records their conversation in the early hours of a cold morning in February, 1667. The winter was bitter, but its hardships were softened to them. He reminded Elizabeth that she used to get up and make the fires, and stand even at the wash-tub in the days when they lived in a little room at my Lord Sandwich's.

" For which," he adds, " I ought forever to love and admire her, and do; and persuade myself she would do the same thing again, if God should reduce us to it."

So while Elizabeth was performing duties that she perhaps heartily disliked and women with less pretensions to birth and education might have scorned, she was adding to her husband's love fresh justification for the respect and admiration that he always professed to feel for her. It is a thing to reflect upon. Hearts that have sustained each other during the dark days of adversity, are more closely knit than those whose lives have passed like a beautiful succession of summer days.

The pretty custom of St. Valentine's Day was honoured this same year by two of Mrs. Pepys' admirers, little Will Mercer and her husband. We shall see how Pepys consoles himself for the price of his valentine.

Feb. 14*th*.—" This morning come up to my wife's bedside, I being up dressing myself, little Will Mercer to be her valentine, and brought her name writ upon blue paper in gold letters, done by himself, very pretty; and we were both well pleased with it. But I am also this year my wife's valentine, and it will cost me five pounds; but that I must have laid out if we had not been valentines."

The names of valentines were at that time to be drawn for. Two days after date Pepys writes, " I find that Mrs. Pierce's little girl is my valentine, she having drawn me, which I was not sorry for, it easing me of something more that I must have given to others. But here I do first observe the fashion of drawing of mottos as well as names, so that Pierce who drew my wife, did draw also a motto, and this girl drew another for me. What mine was I have forgot, but my wife's was: ' Most courteous and most fair,' which as it may be used or an anagram made upon such name might be very pretty."

The motto made a happy hit in falling to Mrs. Pepys; not only fair, but delicately ladylike if the vignette accompanying Pepys' Diary is to be trusted. So dainty and refined, she might have passed her youth among carpet knights and softly moving dames. The innocent eyes and gentle features do not promise heroic qualities. Only in the hard school of adversity could she have added to (or more correctly chorded with) her womanly dependence, virtue; the power to do and bear; the patience also that can continue in well-doing; suffer and be still. We have seen many such soft and pretty faces as Mrs. Pepys. They are sure of ardent admirers, while the cold critic pronounces them simple, babyish, vain and vapid.

silence. Here on the one hand was offered to her a life of enjoyment and pleasure in the world, while on the other lay a life of difficulty and constant struggle. If she left Malta, she would never see Estcourt or any of her friends again, whereas if she remained with the Gowers, a fair prospect lay before her, with gleams of a golden future filled by love and success. But she had set her hand to the plough, and she must not turn back.

"Thank you a thousand times, dear Mrs. Gower!" she said with a brave smile. "I must stay with my father and make a new home for him. My mother would never have left him when he was in trouble. But I love you for your offer all the same."

Sophy Gower rose and looked into the brave, young face.

"God bless you, my dear," she said heartily. "You are a good girl, and I should like my girls to say the same if the choice was ever set before them."

But after she had gone came Bryde's dark hour of loneliness and desolation. And it was not for many hours that she could turn the cloud of her happiness, and find the silver lining behind it.

(*To be continued.*)

GARDENING AS A PROFESSION FOR GIRLS.

How They are Trained at Swanley, and the Demand for Competent Students.

PART II.

DAIRY-WORK plays a very important part in the students' education, while jam-making and bottling fruit are not neglected. Attention is also paid to table decoration, as well as to packing fruit and flowers for the market. In addition to practical work in the gardens and on the farm, a good share of the students' time is occupied with lectures and with laboratory research. Indeed, the authorities lay great stress on their lectures and an able staff of tutors are engaged for this one purpose. The lectures occupy an average of two hours a day, and after a glance at the syllabus it would seem that no subject or item is omitted. Take, for instance, work in the garden. There are not only lectures on the making of gardens and the formation of paths and lawns, but on the use of garden tools, the propagation of plants by seed, layers, grafts, buds, and cuttings, as well as on the eradication of weeds and insect and fungoid pests. Then there are lectures on botany, geology, entomology, bee-keeping, poultry-keeping and dairy-work. Mention may also be made of the courses in nature-study. The one held at the college in August last, which was termed a "holiday" course, was a decided success. Nearly sixty mistresses from elementary, secondary, and private schools in all parts of the country, from Cornwall to Fife, gathered at Swanley, where they remained for a period of twelve days. During this time they were instructed by experts in horticulture, botany, zoology, and bee-keeping. The aim of this gardening instruction was to qualify the visitors in the planning and management of school-children's gardens.

A description of the work done at Swanley would not be complete without reference to the Colonial Branch. Its object is to train young women for colonial life, so that they may take up positions in our various colonies. A number of young girls have passed through this department of the institution's work and are now doing well. One, a young, uncertificated nursery governess, took up an appointment in South Africa at a salary of £120 per annnm, including board and residence. Another fulfils the duties of gardener on an estate of thirty-two acres in Natal, for which she was offered a salary of £90 rising in the third year to £120 per annum, in addition to a furnished cottage, firewood, vegetables, fruit, and a native servant. Married women, who have taken a course of instruction in the Colonial Branch before proceeding to rejoin their husbands abroad, have written saying how practical and valuable they find the knowledge obtained at Swanley, while unmarried women who have gone out to brothers and friends in South Africa, Canada, Australia, and New Zealand declare that the tuition received at the college has been the making of them.

It must not be imagined that it is easy work at Swanley, and no one should enter the college unless she is fully prepared to do whatever task is set before her. No gardening operation must be regarded as too menial. In the summer the students rise early and work commences in the gardens at 6 A.M. In winter, however, outdoor labour does not begin until 9 A.M. In wet weather students find plenty of occupation in the glass-houses and potting-sheds, or in the carpenter's shop, where women as well as men learn to repair and paint cucumber frames, and other similar work that occasionally falls to the lot of the practical gardener. At first the students work in small groups under a gardener's direction in the different departments in turn. Later on they are allowed to specialise in either private or market work, whichever they intend ultimately to take up.

Anyone may enter the college, provided there is a vacancy, who can give satisfactory references and is over sixteen years of age. There are both in-students and out-students. The former reside either in the college itself, or at South Bank, or at the Colonial Branch House. In each instance the accommodation consists of dining, recreation and bedrooms —either study bedrooms or cubicles. There are two courses, that known as the full Diploma course and the Certificate course. To gain the Diploma or Certificate, which means that the student has satisfied her teachers and examiners on the subjects she has taken up, two years' hard study is demanded, and the fee, which is inclusive, is from £80 per annum. LENA SHEPSTONE.

Lena Shepstone, "Gardening as a Profession for Girls" (Volume 26, 17 June 1905, p. 596).

Work

Along with many requests for information about education and training, *The Girl's Own Paper* received numerous requests for information on opportunities for work. Despite its general focus on marriage as the desirable end of a girl's existence, *The Girl's Own* recognized that many girls needed to earn a living. From the earliest issues, the magazine offered surveys of work opportunities for girls and articles on individual fields of work. Some of the articles tried to focus on matching traditional feminine qualities such as a capacity for nurturance to professions such as teaching and nursing. There was also a tendency to promote women's work in the decorative arts; as late as 1905 one can still find a rather ridiculous recommendation of painting cats on velvet cushions as "A New Profession for Girls" (26: 772–74). However, *The Girl's Own* was generally progressive in noting opportunities in both non-traditional fields for women and new professions. The magazine also published articles by women workers; some of these are reproduced below.

"Female Clerks and Book-Keepers" (vol. 1, 1880, pp. 309–10) is written anonymously, but it was probably by S. F. A. [Sophia] Caulfeild, a frequent contributor who had earlier in this volume written a general article on "Earning One's Living"; an editor's note with it promised more information on specific occupations. The article argues that there is nothing unfeminine about these professions.

A Nursing Sister does her best to debunk idealized images of nursing in "The Unvarnished Side of Hospital Nursing" (vol. 9, 1887–88, pp. 808–09). She also categorizes nursing as "woman's work."

The Girl's Own occasionally addressed articles, often of a cautionary nature, to girls with literary aspirations. The anonymously written "Struggles of a Lady Journalist" (vol. 9, 1887–88, pp. 567, 586–87, 605) purports to share one young woman's difficulties establishing herself in her chosen profession.

In 1896, *The Girl's Own* ran a competition for essays by "girls who work with their hands." The five prize essays were published as "My Daily Round" (vol. 18, pp. 75–77, 115–117, 172–73). The authors followed the popular practice of adopting flower names as pseudonyms. The first prize winner was identified as a "locomotive-tracer"; she worked in an engineering office, tracing designs. The remaining occupations described, in order, were pottery-painter, shirt-maker, lace-maker, and general servant. This competition proved so popular with readers that the magazine ran a "Competition for Professional Girls" and again published the five prize essays (vol. 18, 1896–97, pp. 412–15). The first prize winner, a hospital nurse, appears to have given her own name, Agnes Eugenie Smith. The remaining prize winners, a folklore collector, a musician, a writer, and a post-mistress, all published under pseudonyms. These essays mark a rare and valuable opportunity to hear working women's voices.

The next articles reproduced introduce new opportunities. R. Kathleen Spencer, in "Pharmacy as an Employment for Girls" (vol. 21, 1899–1900, pp. 19–20), outlines how to qualify and where to seek employment as a pharmacist/dispenser. Florence Sophie Davson discusses "Women's Work in Sanitation and Hygiene" (vol. 21, 1899–1900, pp. 29–31), which she describes as a form of "organized district visiting," a formerly charitable undertaking by middle-class women.

By the beginning of the twentieth century, *The Girl's Own* started to address the problem of overcrowded professions. In "Domestic Service as a Profession for Gentlewomen" (vol. 23, 1901–02, pp. 299–300), Alix Joson tries to persuade middle-class readers to reconsider work they might have considered beneath them.

The magazine also offered tips for success in the workplace, such as Margaret Bateson's observations on "Girls and Their Employers" (vol. 24, 1902–03, pp. 69–70). She presents the pros and cons of both male and female employers.

Finally, "House-Decoration: A New and Remunerative Employment for Girls" (vol. 25, 1904–05, p. 24) illustrates the ongoing concern to find new opportunities and create new professions in an ever-more-competitive market for work.

FEMALE CLERKS AND BOOK-KEEPERS.

[EARNING ONE'S LIVING.]

To employment either as a clerk or book-keeper no one can raise any objection on the score of its being unfeminine. It is respectable to work that we may be independent, and a girl may just as well go every day to write letters and keep accounts for some business establishment as sit at home to add up the housekeeping-book or act as her mother's amanuensis.

Already there is a certain demand for women as clerks. When the last census was taken in 1871 there were five hundred and fifty-two of them engaged in connection with commercial business in London alone, and the attention directed of late years to occupations for women must have tended largely to increase their number. Indeed, we may look for some very interesting and encouraging statistics on this head when the new census comes to be taken next year.

One advantage connected with the occupation of a clerk is that it does not require a special education. It is, therefore, particularly suited to those to whom circumstances have denied the careful training required for other pursuits.

What is wanted is a good ordinary education and punctual and orderly habits. Plain neat handwriting is indispensable, and no clerk is anything else than a sorrow to her employers who cannot copy correctly. Accuracy, then, must be made a special study. The ability to write a short letter, saying neatly what we wish to say, is another requisite. An ill-composed, ill-arranged epistle, beginning with a blot and ending with a scribble, will never do for business. It must be clear and to the point, carefully written and neatly folded—there you have in a nutshell the whole art of correspondence.

These, certainly, are not difficult attainments. But in this very ease with which we can qualify ourselves for ordinary clerkships, there is something unsatisfactory. It throws the occupation open to almost everybody, and in consequence we find each vacancy besieged by crowds upon crowds of applicants. Only one can be successful, and all the rest must turn away, often very sick at heart, to try elsewhere.

To meet this difficulty we would suggest to those girls who think of taking their place at an office-desk, that they should try to add to those every-day qualifications enumerated above, some special branch of knowledge. Short-hand, for example, would greatly increase one's chance of obtaining a situation, and a girl knowing French or German would attract favourable notice from all employers worth serving. By knowing French or German, we mean ability to read and write these languages fluently, and not that slipshod knowledge by which we painfully spell out passages by the aid of a dictionary.

A girl possessed of these additional accomplishments would obtain much higher pay than one without them. It is a rule, with few exceptions, that what is easily acquired brings small remuneration, and it is a great encouragement to the industrious to know that in proportion to their labour so will be

their reward. So then, my friends, if we are to be clerks, let us be the best possible clerks, striving to know everything that will make us more useful to ourselves and other people.

The routine of an office is usually simple, and a clerk seldom has any worry or trouble, except what she makes for herself. With pleasant companions to associate with in the intervals of business, she may be very happy, a great deal happier, indeed, than leading an aimless existence at home.

Omitting for the present the postal and telegraph services, there are some establishments in London which employ considerable numbers of young ladies as clerks. Foremost amongst these is a well-known Assurance Company, whose staff may well be referred to as a model of careful organisation.

The young ladies employed by this company must be the daughters of professional men, clergymen, doctors, officers in the army and navy, merchants, and of similar social grade. Their comfort is well attended to, and much kind forethought seems to have been shown in everything connected with them.

Their hours are from ten in the morning till five in the evening, with an hour between one and two for luncheon. Luncheon is provided in the building—and well provided, too—at the exact sum which it costs. When it is over there is time left for a walk. On the streets? Oh, no; on the roof. The roof has been fitted up as a promenade for the young ladies, and there, on a pretty extensive exercising ground, they can enjoy the fresh air and have interesting views of the slate mountains and volcanic chimneys of the neighbourhood, whilst in the distance Hampstead hills may be seen on a clear day.

There is a library filled with interesting books for those who care to read, and for the musical a singing class is provided, meeting at regular intervals. Both are largely taken advantage of. The news of the day should be well understood, for each young lady takes a newspaper home with her every second day, one newspaper being allowed to every two.

And what about the work? That is much the same as falls to the lot of insurance clerks in general. It contains nothing at all intricate, and for its execution requires nothing but ordinary ability and extraordinary accuracy. The examples of accuracy we saw on the occasion of a recent visit were such that if our living depended on our furnishing similar specimens, we would entreat you, girls, to allow of our retiring on a pension into private life.

The salary begins at £32 a-year and rises by stages of £10 till at the end of a few years a young lady finds herself in the enjoyment of £100 or so of annual income, after which she will, no doubt, be content.

There can be no question about the fact that the young ladies like the employment and that the experiment of employing them as clerks has in this instance—thanks, no doubt, to judicious management—been a decided success. This Assurance Company began, in

1872, with the employment of ten young ladies, and their staff now includes no fewer than one hundred and seventy.

Over young men young ladies possess several advantages as clerks. For the same salary you would not get such a respectable class, and it is a doubtful point whether you would get the same amount of steady application. Women, again, as a rule, are more happy and contented; a man must in the nature of things be pushing ahead, and after he has been three or four years at work, he is pretty sure to be marrying and settling down and so requiring a larger income.

A considerable number of young men are employed in the office of which we have been giving an account, but with them the young ladies never come into personal communication. So far as meeting is concerned, they might be a hundred miles apart, the two divisions of clerks even coming into the building by separate entrances.

Another establishment in the metropolis where women are employed as clerks is that of the printers of the Post Office Directories. The experiment of employing young women was begun here quite recently, and the result has been so satisfactory that a handsome room has been built, capable of accommodating forty clerks, and is now quickly filling up.

The success of this experiment, we learn from the Committee of the Society for Promoting the Employment of Women, is in a great measure due to the good sense and earnestness of the lady superintendent and to the good conduct of the two clerks who first learned the work with her in her own private rooms. Everything is done throughout in the most methodical manner; no talking is allowed, and each clerk goes steadily on with her work, which is too varied to become monotonous.

Railway companies have in a few instances engaged young women as clerks, and provided them with occupation at country stations. We are not, however, sure that a railway booking-office is the right place for a girl. On the Continent, no doubt, it is a common field for women's work, but our ideas of modesty and retirement are against it.

Banks present more suitable openings, and we should be glad to see these institutions throwing open their doors to young women of intelligence and capacity. There is a demand for this class of labour also from large warehouses and private counting-houses, and though, as we have said before, every vacancy has a host of applicants, one candidate has as good a chance as another; and to keep from applying because we are not certain of success would be nothing short of ridiculous.

Allied to the occupation we are now speaking about is the business of copying petitions, law copying, and engrossing. "This work," says one authority, "may be taken by the piece, and can be done at home, provided the strictest business habits of neatness, punctuality, and dispatch can be maintained there. I have heard, however, of a single erasure condemning a whole deed, and except in cases of necessity such work is far better done in an office."

We believe there is an office in London where girls may be entered for the study of the art. The apprenticeship should begin whilst they are young, for the special qualification of a clear, round, legal hand is difficult to acquire after the ordinary running hand has been once formed.

For engrossing—which means the writing out of deeds in full and regular form on parchment or paper for signature—good eyesight is required, and one must have a precision and delicacy of touch not unlike that needed for illuminating. In point of remuneration it is not a brilliant occupation. When business is brisk a good writer can earn £2 a week, but there is a slack season, which brings down the average weekly earnings of the year to about seventeen shillings and sixpence.

We come now to speak of book-keeping. To be a good book-keeper requires much more preliminary training and study than would be needed to qualify for a clerkship. Not that the mere mechanical work of book-keeping is at all difficult: it is in thoroughly comprehending why this and that is done that the real difficulty lies.

An adult book-keeping class was started some years since by the Society for Promoting the Employment of Women, the place of meeting being the office of the Society, 22, Berners-street, Oxford-street. The first step towards entering this class is for the student to bring recommendations from two house-holders guaranteeing her thorough steadiness and respectability. In cases where the student has just left school, a letter from the mistress or her latest school report is required. No one can be admitted to the class who does not write clearly and neatly, spell correctly, and work accurately the first four rules of arithmetic, simple and compound.

The course of training ordinarily extends over four or five months. During that time students are instructed in all the mysteries of single and double entry, besides which, every effort is made to fill them with a high sense of responsibility, and teach them to be punctual, orderly, and earnest in the discharge of their duties.

Training over, then comes examination by a competent authority and the granting of certificates. Only those are allowed to go up for examination whose conduct in the class has been satisfactory and who have shown a desire to do their work conscientiously.

During the year 1878-79 this class was joined by fifty students, and certificates were granted to twenty-five candidates, all of whom gained at least seventy-five per cent. of the maximum marks.

After having taken all this preliminary trouble the chances the young book-keeper has of succeeding in the world are just what might have been expected. In the annual report of the Society we are informed that "book-keepers who have gained certificates almost invariably retain their situations with credit. It is often difficult to obtain a first situation, for practical experience is generally required; but in this the certificate is a great help, as it forms a good introduction and is a guarantee of efficiency and respectability. When she has once made a fair start, a certificated book-keeper is seldom unemployed."

The number of book-keepers and clerks for whom the Society was fortunate enough to find permanent employment in 1878-79 was eighteen.

A certificated book-keeper generally receives in her first situation about fifteen shillings a week; after that the remuneration is from about eighteen to twenty-five shillings or its equivalent. If meals are provided, of course less is given, There

are a few exceptional cases in which the pay is higher, but the holders of these situations are usually able to speak or correspond in foreign languages.

The occupation of book-keeping is a highly responsible one. Upon the care and accuracy with which its books are kept depends the the prosperity of many a business establishment. In not a few instances, bankruptcy even has been traced to no other causes than the keeping of an insufficient set of books, and the keeping of these badly.

When the duties of cashier are united with those of book-keeper, the preference is often given to women over men. And why? It has been found by experience that women are, as a rule, more trustworthy than men, and that they are less likely to be found making free with what is not their own. One reason for this is, perhaps, that they are, generally speaking, exposed to fewer temptations in the way of spending; but we hope that a deeper reason will be found in their superior sense of rectitude and their more self-sacrificing devotion to duty.

MORE THAN CORONETS.

By Mrs. G. LINNÆUS BANKS,

Author of "The Manchester Man," &c.

CHAPTER XVII.
DINAH'S NEW MISTRESS.

 ESBA'S ears had not deceived her. Had she and Mercy followed the stranger, who called himself John Rutherford, up New Oxford-street, instead of hurrying along Southampton-street to their lodgings across the square, they might have seen standing before a bookseller's door the self-same carriage which had whirled Dinah away from Euston; and they might have seen the self-same liveried footman carrying a parcel of books to "my lady" in the carriage, and, after placing them with other parcels on the seat, stand back with one hand holding the door and the other touching his forehead, whilst their military friend, marching up, gave a brief order, then joined the lady seated within. They might have seen the footman pass his orders to the coachman, then mount to the rumble; but they would have been no wiser, for there was no Dinah then on the seat, and the man's resplendent purple-and-gold was concealed under a sober overcoat which came to his heels.

We, however, are privileged to follow Major Rutherford to his seat beside his sister, Lady Dynevor, of Dynevor Manor.

He was a man above the middle height, erect, broad-chested, bronzed rather than florid, with a very decided cast of countenance, across which the ploughshare of affliction had drawn its ineffaceable lines, his hair having the nondescript tinge of dark brown on which grey has intruded before its time. Several years his elder was the lady,

but not a thread of white was to be seen in the smooth bands above her brows, not a line on her well kept face, if we except the faint crowfeet at the outer corners of her eyes; her cheek retained something of youth's freshness, something of youthful bloom, and her tall, dignified figure had not lost its graceful curves. Perhaps Dinah knew the secret of her lady's wonderful preservation.

"I have had a little adventure since I left you, Ernestine," said the major as he took his seat.

"Ah! an adventure? An agreeable one, I hope," and the lady smiled, revealing a set of strong white teeth, which did not come from the dentist.

"Partly," was the sober rejoinder. "A young lady and her sister—she *said* she was her sister—both in deep mourning, entered the post-office just as I had given in my telegram, and asked for a letter for Miss Stapleton."

"Miss——" The interruption which began as a startled exclamation dropped into a somewhat languid query, "I—ah—did not catch the name?"

"Stapleton," repeated the major, unobservant that Lady Dynevor had changed colour even beneath the artificial bloom; "the young lady did not seem aware that a charge was made, and I saw she was overwhelmed with shame, having evidently left her purse behind. You may be sure I did not allow her to go back without her letter."

"Ah! just like my simple-minded brother! How do you know the girl was not an impostor?" And up went the lady's eyeglasses, as if to scan unfamiliar features.

"An impostor for *a penny?* Nay, Ernestine, that is an illiberal assumption. She was as much a lady as yourself. 'It was her grandma's letter,' said the younger sister."

"What younger one?" There was a sort of petulant, quickness about the question so foreign to Lady Dynevor, it must have attracted her brother's attention had he been of a suspicious nature.

"That is the point, Ernestine! She was a most lovely girl. I should say thirteen years old—the very counterpart of Blanche! Her rich chestnut hair, her dimpled cheeks, her large brown loving eyes, her nose, her lips — there was scarcely a line memory could not trace. I could not keep my eyes away from the child. I am sure she set me down as rude and impertinent. For my part, I felt as if I could have clasped her in my arms and wept over her! It seemed as if something whispered me, 'The waves have given back your child. Blanche's babe was not lost—she is here!'"

"This is really too absurd," broke from Lady Dynevor, with a faint affectation of supreme indifference.

"You would not have said so, my lady, if you had seen the fair child as I saw her. Indeed, my dream was only partially dispelled when Miss Stapleton replied to my question, 'Yes, sir, she is my sister!' I was compelled to believe her; but if Blanche herself had risen from the dead I could scarcely have had a greater shock;" and the bronzed soldier sighed as he drew his hand across his forehead wearily.

as daintily adorned and hospitably supplied. She had three bridesmaids—Phillis, Laura, and Lucy; her white satin dress fitted her to perfection.

But—rain fell in torrents; a drip from a wet umbrella spotted the bridal robe; invited guests failed to appear; the newly-married Hyltons met them with the bridegroom's party at the church, but neither Miss Pringle, nor Mr. John Crossley, nor his wife came to do them honour. Indeed, the blinds at Pilgrim Place were drawn closely down, as though there had been a funeral, not a wedding in the family, and the sorrowing relative had shut out the sight. People were there who have no place in this history, and presents were many, but when the display came a small box was found marked "A present from Phillis Penelope Pringle to the bride." Within it lay, coiled upon cotton wool, a necklace of mock pearls, labelled clearly, "False as fair."

Yet that was not all. Whilst Mrs. Arthur Rivers was dressing for her honeymoon trip to London, there was an altercation going on between Arthur and his father, which boded ill for all parties concerned.

Stephen Heathfield had promised to give with Mabel four thousand pounds. It turned out one-half the sum had been already advanced to James Rivers, for investment in his business on Arthur's account, and had been otherwise employed; in fact, had gone to make up the sum cautiously settled upon Maud. The handing over by Stephen of his cheque for two thousand only had provoked an explanation, and a final rupture between father and son.

Not a promising beginning for the new year or the newly-married pair

(*To be continued.*)

THE IMMORTAL ROSE.

By EDITH PRINCE.

WHEN the infant eyes awakened
　Mother slept; her silent hand
Might not clasp the tiny fingers,
　But they thought among God's band
She was chosen as the angel
　O'er her baby watch to keep,
And in dreams her love to whisper,
　For the child smiled in her sleep.

Crimson roses sweet they planted
　To the mother's fond heart near,
And with baby's growth the flowers
　Blossomed fresh each dawning year.
Sometimes when the maiden pondered,
　Wondrous deep her blue eyes grew,
As she pictured clear the mother
　That her waking never knew.

Then she said, "Dear God, the flowers
　Planted here bloom in my heart.
Sometimes, dreaming of their beauty,
　Of my life they seem a part.
Oh, then as their fragrance mounting
　On fair angels' wings to Thee,
Grant my prayers their fullest pleading,
　Sending down Thy love on me:

"So when soft my evening cometh,
　And my hair is tinged with snow,
May the crimson rose immortal
　Still in summer beauty glow,
Filling all my life with music,
　And the light of grace divine,
Till I stand before Thy portals
　With my mother's hand in mine."

THE UNVARNISHED SIDE OF HOSPITAL NURSING.

MY article will be no grand intellectual study—merely a few plain facts; but if it should encourage any to work on more bravely in some daily routine, or inspire them with a desire to help their fellow-men in a more practical form, it will not be in vain.

Most people will agree with me in considering that nursing to a large extent comes under woman's work. Though some men are in every way thoroughly good nurses, as a rule women may find a useful work in attending on the sick, and are appreciated by them. Almost everyone thinks herself capable of nursing, except perhaps some few, who shrink from it with a kind of horror, and imagine they could never bear to see or do all that would be required of them.

I am aware that the market, so to speak, is already overstocked with women who have taken up the work of nursing; but are they nurses?

At a course of lectures attended when beginning hospital life, we were informed of the necessary qualifications for a nurse. I will enumerate some of them. Obedience, cheerfulness, patience, conscientiousness, observation, sympathy, judgment, neatness, and order. Hospital nurses are about as mixed a class as you could well conceive; daughters of men in almost every trade or profession, from a general's daughter to the poorly educated lady's maid or servant girl; and if you ask their reasons for becoming nurses, you will find here, too, a strange variety. Young widows and women of good education who are in trouble, imagine (and often find) that caring for others will lighten their own woe. Some from conscientious motives desire to devote their lives to good works; others take to nursing because they must gain a livelihood, and they think it sounds better to be a nurse than a companion, shopwoman, or servant. Some take to it because they think to wear a uniform and be called a sister lends a romance to their lives; and some giddy, thoughtless ones appear to have become nurses for the sake of amusement. It is needless to say these last two do not have quite as easy a time as they expect; but the amount of harm they do to the nursing work is incalculable. Some join because, whilst wishing to earn a livelihood, they truly choose nursing from a love to it; and with such the love for it grows very strong.

Whilst speaking of hospital work, please

remember that the many details—such as salary, hours, and various duties, differ in different hospitals. On an average, I think, a sister will have charge of about thirty-three beds, with two day-nurses, a probationer, and a night-nurse under her; also a woman who comes daily to polish or scrub the floors, clean the grates and windows, carry away the soiled linen, and wash the breakfast and dinner things.

When you think of your one invalid at home, and his many requirements, and remember that these six pairs of hands must supply everything needed for the occupants of these thirty-three beds, besides keeping the wards and all the utensils therein clean, you will see that a nurse cannot have much time to spare.

On first becoming a nurse, it is customary, in most hospitals, to sign an agreement for two or three years. The salary of a nurse (or rather a probationer, as she is at first called) is from £10 to £14 the first year, and from £16 the second year, and from £16 to £20 the third year, with board, washing, and uniform found. A probationer goes on trial for one month. Some leave then because they feel themselves, or are thought to be, physically or otherwise unfitted for the work; others, however, stay on, really unfitted, because they do not care for it, and have not their hearts in it.

At the end of one year, and often much sooner, a probationer is given charge of a ward, under a sister, when she is called nurse; then as a vacancy arises, and she shows herself competent, she is given the post of sister. A regular nurse, after the first two or three years, gets from £20 to £30 yearly; a sister from £30 to £50 yearly. The first year there is a good deal of hard work: scrubbing, sweeping, cleaning, obeying orders (clumsily enough), and being scolded by the nurse, sister, or doctor, and made to do things over and over again. There is, too, the witnessing of suffering and death; very trying to a young nurse, but with which she soon becomes so strangely familiar. Accidents of almost every kind, heartrending stories of cruelty and wrong, friends coming to spend the last few hours with a beloved one, or perhaps arriving too late, when the spirit has returned to its Maker. These are sad scenes, but they come as part of her day's work and her training. A nurse breakfasts at 6.30 a.m., summer and winter, and begins work at 7 a.m., with perhaps eight or ten beds to make, patients to wash, the ward to sweep and dust, besides tables to scour, dressing-trays to be cleaned, and all utensils belonging to the ward to be seen to, medicines and other treatment to be attended to, and all to be in readiness for the doctor's visit at 9 a.m. or 9.30 a.m. From him, through the sister, the nurse receives her daily orders for the treatment of the patients, which, on his leaving the ward, must at once to be carried out. Milk and beef tea must be warmed for luncheon, medicine bottles taken to the surgery to be refilled, fresh prescriptions made up, and fresh diets shown to the cook. In its own turn each ward receives the fresh admissions, and there are patients to be washed and put to bed (not with nice clean hands and faces that a sponge would restore, but with the dirt of hard work, squalor, and misery, that often takes more than hot water, soap, flannel, and a good rub to bring clean); and all this time there are the constant wants on all sides to be supplied.

About 12.30 the dinners come up, and they must be served round, and the helpless ones fed; then the nurse gets her own dinner, which, I am sorry to say, in some hospitals is not very tempting; after which she returns to her ward.

The floor must again be swept, and the dinner things cleared away, the beds tidied, and all put in order for the visiting surgeon or physician, when she may have to stand for the next two hours, going with the doctors and students round the ward; or if there are any operations from her ward, she will be wanted to assist.

Or it may be it is the day for patients to see their friends; and for two hours nurse must act the part of a vigilant detective, and try to stop the intended kindness of ignorant relatives in giving fruits, stimulants, puddings or cakes to her patients.

At 4, or soon after, she must make the tea, cut bread and butter and serve it round, and then she is free to go and get her own. Some nurses get out for an hour and a half once or twice a week, in the afternoon, others from 6 to 8.

Extra hours are often given when asked for, but it must entail a double share of work for some one, and therefore a nurse does not like to be often absent from her ward.

After tea, when she has washed up once more, swept and tidied the ward, there is sometimes an interval in which she can talk and read to her patients before the evening work of dressings, suppers, and preparations for the night begins.

These are supposed to be concluded at 8.30 p.m., when the nurse reads prayers, lowers the lights, and leaves each patient as comfortable as possible, and (even though she loves her work) gladly awaits the coming of the night sister, to whom she must report all the cases before leaving the ward. She then goes to her supper, after which she is free. Do not judge her too hardly, gentle reader, when you hear that instead of improving her mind by reading, she often goes straight to bed, foot-sore and weary.

But courage! the work gets easier as she becomes more accustomed to it, and by morning she will be rested and refreshed.

Those who enter the work thinking life would be a kind of romance; that they could shake a pillow, stroke a forehead, bring flowers, make little dainties, read and cheer the sick, and wander about in a dreamy, listless way, soon see they have got to the wrong place.

Even the giddy ones find it difficult to chatter and attend to their patients, and, discovering that they get into trouble, either reserve their mirth for odd moments or give up the work. Hospital life is not play. I fancy a nurse goes to bed at night (or in the daytime if she be night nurse) as tired as any labourer, often feeling as though she had merely scrambled through her work, and not done half that should have been done. "But only the toilers know the sweetness of rest."

Now let us turn to the bright side. Anyone will own it is a pleasure to find that what he has been at some trouble to do proves a success. So with hospital life. Patients come to be cured, and the trouble and the pains required to attain certain ends are well repaid in finding the result a success; the cripple whole, the suffering eased, the sick made well.

The doctors have a good deal to do with the happiness of a nurse, and a kind cheering word from them is most encouraging. It is one of a nurse's greatest pleasures to satisfy and please the medical man she is working under, and doctor and nurse often get to know each other well.

At the same time, if I wanted a nurse's character I would not go to a medical man for it, if I could get it instead from the patients she had nursed. Though, as I have proved, there is generally but little time for reading or talking to the patients, and, as some may think, caring for their souls, still a life of sympathy and kindness is not wasted. The patients, who are often very quiet in learning from a nurse the many little things to be done in a ward, may learn from her life-lessons also. Certain it is they watch her and get to know her well. She is hardly allowed to let her cheerfulness vanish without a reason. Very soon comes the question, "Why are you looking so cross to-day, nurse?" and she at once rouses and remembers that little vexations and troubles that she may have must not be shown in her ward. There are many opportunities, too, for giving a word of counsel, and expressing sympathy and sorrow whilst nurse is washing her patient, making his bed, dressing wounds or applying treatment, and the bright smile that follows her after a word like this, all the time she is busy in her ward, is most cheering; proving that the little she tried to do was appreciated.

Many a one wants just some little thing done, a pillow shifted or a bandage loosened, for no other reasons than to get a few words with nurse, if he feels he is being neglected; and though she may playfully scold him for wasting her precious time, she does not grudge it, and he knows it. There are numberless little things which the patients love to do to save their nurse; helping each other when able, or, if up and well enough, glad to sweep out the ward, and await her pleasure at finding less to do when she returns.

The children, too, give to their nurse very often the trust and love which before they have so seldom found anyone to appreciate. Many of them have known no homes; the love which makes home has been wanting. They love their nurse, and sometimes shed tears at leaving the hospital.

When nurse has been out in the afternoon, and perhaps returns with a sort of feeling that it would be very pleasant to sit in an armchair and read instead of going back to work, on entering the ward she hears some weary invalid say, "Oh! nurse, I am so glad you are back; it has seemed so long since you went out," the book and the easy chair no longer seem things to be desired. Each has his own little tale to tell, and loves to tell it, and the very knowledge of the trials of the one and the sympathy of the other draw nurse and patient nearer together. Then there are the men and women leaving the hospital, and occasionally even those who are about to take a longer journey, and wish before starting to give their nurse a last farewell. Often it is a pressure of the hand and just an earnest "God bless you, nurse!" but it means a great deal, and gives nurse fresh courage and strength for the future.

I would add one word more. I think a nurse can hardly be a nurse in the highest and best sense unless she feels she is working for her Master in heaven, and realises the truth and solemnity of the words, "Inasmuch as ye did it not," and the joy and comfort of "Inasmuch as ye did it."

I have but very imperfectly set forth the bright side of hospital life. Thoughts and feelings, love and sympathy are very real, but their value cannot be told on paper. Your patients are dependent on you. You feel for their suffering, and you love them, and have their love in return. Reader, if you know what love is, can you say, even amidst its daily cares, its sorrow and pain, that there is not a bright side to our hospital work?

Do not misunderstand me; home duties must ever come first, and, well performed, are surely the truest outcome of real love.

I am far, indeed, from setting up nursing above such duties, or of attaching to it more value than to any other work; only, as we have diversities of gifts, I long that we may really use them; and for those who are free to choose, and possessed of a love for nursing, desire that they may join our ranks, and swell the number of those who may be called real nurses.

A NURSING SISTER, H.M.N.S.

A Nursing Sister, "The Unvarnished Side of Hospital Nursing" (Volume 9, 15 September 1888, p. 809).

THE STRUGGLES OF A LADY JOURNALIST.

THE future of our lives undoubtedly reveals many a hidden secret of the past, accounts for many curious traits of character, bents of mind, which were misunderstood whilst their development was in process, and explains the reason of many a temporary failure by awarding the success which is granted to persevering effort.

So, at least, later experience has taught me to believe.

From my earliest infancy I had a predilection for scribbling. When I was a child I was considered an *enfant terrible* on account of the realistic letters I wrote, the copious diary, upon stray half sheets, which I kept. Being an orphan, I clung to many people from whom circumstances had separated me, and now, in my mature age, I well understand the pain I caused both to those who had the care of me, and to others at a distance, by the vivid description my juvenile pen conveyed of the suffering my lonely lot caused me. But at the time of course I had no idea of this, and only sought the relief of scribbling, as children of different temperaments seek the comfort of shedding tears.

At the age of fifteen my brain was flooded with visions of future greatness as an authoress. My younger brother wrote poetry, and wrote it well; but the solidity of prose was what I aspired to, although at the time religious sentimentality pervaded my whole being, and the result may be imagined!

In the day time my faculties were given up to the conjugation of German verbs, to fragmentary French conversation, hours of pianoforte practice, and those mild excitements which, during the hunting and shooting seasons, even the strictest duenna cannot banish entirely from a country schoolroom. But when night arrived, and I was free to retire to rest, the puppets of my brain held high revel, and at the age of sixteen I wrote a story.

Even now I redden when I think of the terrible twaddle it was, and yet it was accepted by a monthly magazine!

In confidence I read the manuscript to my younger brother, for our surroundings were not literary, and I shrank from my first step upon the ladder of independence becoming known. So, my maiden effort approved by my juvenile critic, I sallied forth to the village post office, and, with a beating heart, dropped it into the letter box. In the course of a week a letter, acknowledging its receipt and offering a low sum for the MS., reached me, and I do not believe anyone guilty of a crime, whose discovery meant penal servitude, could have been more terrified at the prospect in front of them than I was at the idea of my private thoughts—for heart and soul I had thrown myself into the writing of this story—appearing in print. I mention this because my people were well off, and perhaps my very ignorance

of everything connected with literary work may lead to my "Struggles" being of greater use to others who, like myself, have only received an ordinary education qualifying them to fulfil the usual duties of society.

Well, that note of the editor never was answered, for my courage failed me, and my dearest hope was that I never again might hear of the MS. But a year afterwards, when I was going through my first London season, a bulky letter, forwarded on from home, reached me. All unsuspicious, I opened it, and, to my horror, out tumbled the proofs of my tale.

To say that I wished the ground would open and swallow me up would be but to convey a faint idea of my feelings, for unless I had received a guarantee that I was to be hidden away in the centre of our globe, I do not think I should have derived any satisfaction from the escape; a few feet of sod alone would not have felt to be a sufficient covering to my confusion.

What was the meaning of the editor's polite invitation to me to "correct my proofs"? I could not imagine, and my guilty conscience construed it into a tacit reproof for my rudeness in not having replied to his original letter; so I wrote a humble reply, saying I felt sure all he did was right, that I would rather not take any money for my story, and that I was very sorry he had been put to the trouble of sending it to me! In due time a copy of the magazine, containing my story, reached me, and, for all my fright, it was a proud moment when for the first time I saw myself in the glory of print. Fear of ridicule, however, kept me in those days from again contributing to any publication, and for several years I confined my efforts to writing essays, and to character delineation, which latter occupation gave me an unconscious training—so I subsequently found—for writing social and critical articles for the press.

We were in the habit of staying about a great deal during the winter months in large country houses, and whenever we met any noted person, I made myself, by way of an exercise, write down my impression of him or her on retiring to my room at night; and the habits of careful attention to detail, of character analysis and of minute study of peculiarities of speech, and other personal idiosyncrasies which this custom engendered in me, have proved in later times of enforced bread-winning invaluable. Of course there is a danger to amateurs in the method, as it opens out a path for ill nature to tread, but where done conscientiously from the motive of teaching oneself to be accurate in reproducing studies from life in fiction, it is full of advantages.

My literary efforts were, however, still at a dead-lock when circumstances, which do not concern the outside world, led me to undertake the correspondence and to keep the books and accounts of a home, where a large amount of work went on, and a good sum of money was disbursed amongst the poor.

I allude to this episode with intent, because to the nine months' training I received in that institution I trace the development of those powers of organisation which have enabled me to carry on the work which has since fallen to my share. Many may say that I am altogether lowering the professional status of lady journalists by stating it as my firm opinion that no woman will really prove herself successful in this branch of literary work who is not also thoroughly efficient as a woman of business, and well versed in commercial affairs, at least if they aspire to the much-coveted position of editress of a paper.

So many in these days can write, so few, owing to their social positions and similar causes, can put themselves in touch with the City men by whose intellect the vast money-making machinery of our wholesale and retail firms is set in motion! This is why I have it so at heart to tell my own struggles, because I hope, in the near future, we women journalists may band together, and by some concerted action render it possible for women writers to be trained so that, by combining commercial knowledge with literary ability, they may obtain remunerative employment in the field where at present so many labour for nothing.

A few years later on the accident of life brought me into connection with a newspaper which was about to be launched. Its name, its size, its shape, all were of my originating; it owed its creation to me and to one besides, and though, as many another proud young mother has found before me, my devotion to this my first-born has been ill-requited, yet in helping to rear it I have the reward which comes of added knowledge.

The joyous moment when the telegram came from the editor to say that the paper was published—when the morning's post brought me the first number ever turned off the printing press!

The hopes and fears, the excitement and almost delirious happiness of bringing such a venture safely to birth, cannot be described, but many a one can testify to its being a supreme moment in one's life.

All who know anything of this kind of work are aware that the originators of a new journal have much greater need of their faculties of organisation than of their literary ability, there never being any difficulty in getting people to write for a young paper which is believed to be well backed. Authors of note are generous in this way. They give the new venture a chance at first, but later on it must stand or fall according to its merits, and woe betide that paper which lets the good writers slip who rallied round it in the beginning. The public are quick to note this falling off, and the circulation is bound to suffer.

Probably many a lady journalist will bear me out in saying that where you have the interests of a newly-launched paper at heart, a woman on its staff with a large commercial connection can do more to insure its success, if she will, than anyone else connected with it.

But there is a need of generosity, of a willingness to wait until some measure of success is insured; the desire to gain personal advantage at the outset, to grasp commission at the beginning, being a fatal mistake. And also, tact, courtesy, the gracious manner which prompts you to treat all—for the time being—as equals, no matter how inferior to you by birth those you are brought into business contact with may be, are absolutely necessary to the success of such work. Many a lady journalist who possesses the highest literary ability being unfortunately not gifted with these attributes, hence the difficulty of their fulfilling the onerous task of editing a paper. Even the highest born amongst English men is noted for never allowing an inferior to feel his inferiority; but it will take time before the general run of ladies, forced by straitened incomes to take to work which throws them amongst those beneath them in the social scale, will cease ruffling up their feathers, and showing that they dislike having to do with those to whom after all they owe their bread; and on their parts it is a great mistake.

(*To be continued.*)

Anon., "The Struggles of a Lady Journalist" (Volume 9, 2 June 1888, p. 567).

THE STRUGGLES OF A LADY JOURNALIST.

AVING thrown myself into the work of helping on our paper, I developed almost unawares into a fully-fledged lady journalist. I had the advantage of being trained under those well qualified for the work, and no pains were spared to insure me a thoroughly good journalistic education. So that, after gaining the experience which practice alone can give, I grew accustomed to writing to order, and could turn off smart paragraphs, theatrical criticisms, articles on social and other topics of the day, at a moment's notice. Added to this I qualified to publish the paper, and mastered all the intricacies of the advertisement department, for I consider no lady journalist has learnt her trade properly until she has become versed in all the details of editing, printing, and publishing a paper. In these matters we shall be wise to take pattern by the work our sisters on the other side of the Atlantic so ably perform.

Being looked up to as part and parcel of the special organ with which I was so intimately associated, I could have made a very good thing at that time out of a literary career. For, as with everything else in this world, when you are up people will help you on, when you are down they will try and keep you under, and so long as you manage to keep in the literary or journalistic swim, you never have any difficulty in getting plenty of employment. But if for an instant the billows of adversity sweep you under, it will verily be as well if, in times of prosperity, you "made friends "—to quote biblical language—" of the mammon of unrighteousness."

And, all unconsciously, I did this very thing, which has hindered my being borne away ruthlessly on the current of despair.

Mercifully—as things have turned out—I possess an innate and uncomfortable consciousness that most mundane matters are transitory.

Holding the old woman's belief that it is wiser not to carry all your eggs in one basket, I made up my mind to try my hand at writing "a lady's letter." We all know the topics this is supposed to deal with, and the particular one I am now alluding to must have contained very ordinary information, for its news as to the fashions was derived wholly and solely from the shop windows; yet on its being sent in to a well-known lady's journal, it brought forth a request for my address, and led up to my gaining employment on another staff as well. This time my journalistic instruction was supplemented by the acquirement of a good deal of commercial information; and the knowledge I thus obtained induced me to start a series of ladies' letters in the paper which was my "first love."

When I undertook to supply the article, treating on matters of interest to feminine minds, regularly every week, it became necessary, for the sake of my giving the very latest intelligence, and influencing the advertisements connected with the subjects I mentioned, for me to remove to London.

In view of the terrible struggles which I then was in happy ignorance of my having before me, as well as of the deliverance I have met with from them, I tell the little incident which occurred on the occasion.

We—that is my companion, whose knowledge of the City has been since of untold value to me, and I—had agreed to go temporarily into apartments. Not being very strong at the time, the weariness and fatigue which hunting for satisfactory ones brought about rendered me cross; and turning back twice, I irritably vowed I would return from whence we came. The power of foreseeing things, possessed by my friend, enabled her to construe my vacillating conduct into a happy omen. " Turn again, turn again, Whittington ; thrice Lord Mayor of London," she cheerily remarked, quoting the hackneyed words as an encouragement to me to continue our route ; and although in part my "Struggles as a Lady Journalist" may be attributed to my sojourn in London, yet my having overcome them is undoubtedly due to my having followed my companion's advice, and taken up my abode on the scene of my later labours.

Once established in London, as the solitary lady on the staff of the paper whose interests I held perhaps too much at heart, we worked like slaves, and had the reward of the amusement which abounds in such an occupation when it is well carried out.

The curious samples that came for review, and when I was out of town occasionally got opened at the office, it would take up too much space to tell of. Once I remember four wire dress-improvers were sent for me to notice, and being away at the time the editorial staff was greatly exercised as to their use. But tales like this can be told by the score at most newspaper offices. What occasioned me most fun was, I think, the letters I received from correspondents. One girl wrote to me for advice as to how she should dress, and that I might the better enlighten her on the subject, described herself as being " twenty years old, but looking much younger," and went on to inform me that her " dressmaker fell into the mistake of making her a childish dress, instead of one which would heighten the effect of her childish face." Another equally guileless young woman was sorely perplexed as to how to prevent the tip of her nose presenting a shiny appearance during the violent exercise of waltzing in a very hot atmosphere ! Then there were the many many amateurs who thought the world would be the better for knowing what they wore when they sang at a concert held for the benefit of their local charities in the national schoolroom of their parish. Whilst, lastly, not to make the list too long, there were the foolish young men who wished for confidential advice as to the presents they should give their young ladies, treating one to minute accounts of the latters' tastes; and there were the other gilded youths who put "private" on the corners of their envelopes and begged to be told something which would assist them in the cultivation of their moustaches !

These questions have all been asked, and the answers given, and the amusement they have caused has been genuine enough.

But there are difficulties to contend against even in the career of a prosperous lady journalist, and though at the time I never thought to experience the struggles of one, nor to see the darker side of the shield as regards employment in literary work, I yet had many a day in which I did not feel equal to my self-imposed task, grudged the amount of labour I had bound myself to expend on what after all was more or less hack work, and sorely wished, with sighs dedicated to the memory of my first poor little sentimental tale, that I had time to devote to the writing of fiction, and more chance of realising my girlish day-dream of some day becoming an authoress.

With the few, journalism is a profitable pursuit, but it is seldom an elevating one ; women who practise it for bread-winning purposes having to confine their attentions principally to writing on the subjects which will pay, keeping their ideal theories for the benefit of mankind in the background ; and, ill or well, tired or fresh, having to force themselves to write to order upon subjects which after a time become wearisome enough.

No woman should adopt the profession of journalism unless she has a most light-hearted disposition, most sanguine temperament, and is prepared to send in her copy to time, no matter what the physical odds against her doing so may be. Unless you are prepared to spend yourself in the service of the journal on whose staff you are engaged, you will never thrive as a press woman ; but there never was work in which genuine merit was more readily appreciated, and as a rule more fairly paid.

As an instance of what I mean, one year when I had knocked up and gone to the sea for change, the editor—who remained in London—was suddenly taken ill; and, to cover some of his deficiencies, I promised faithfully to post a certain amount of copy to the sub-editor on the eve of their going to press. Work for me on the day my MS. should have been sent up was out of the question, but it was a case of positive necessity ; and, grieved though my companion was to wake me out of the refreshing slumber into which I had fallen, she had to call me at 2 a.m. the following morning, and my task completed shortly before seven o'clock, to leave me exhausted and feverish in order to travel up to London by the 7.30 express, and give my manuscript in at the office in time to save the sub-editor from distraction. Strains such as these upon their strength all women who adopt the profession of journalism must be prepared to encounter.

But this was the halcyon time when I was working for love of the paper I had helped to create.

There came a bitter day when this could no longer be. The uprightness of mere innocence is no safeguard against the wiles of speculators. Having believed in the cajolery of one of the tribe ; having accepted his repeated assurances that " his word was his bond ; " having been led away by his alluring promises of high remuneration for my "invaluable services," I reaped the benefit of my mistaken confidence, and, with poverty staring me in the face, bewailed the broken promises of one who had made use of me only to betray my trust in him.

Women who are forced into business against their wills are very apt to be outwitted by unscrupulous practitioners, and hard though such an experience must necessarily be, sharp though the lesson is, I yet think if it teaches one to listen to one's lawyer and intrust one's business affairs to him ever after, it may yet become, though dearly purchased, a valuable piece of knowledge to carry through life ; and if the experience has the double advantage of being gained early enough in life for your energies to recover from the shock, you may in many respects be the better for it.

If you have any spirit, any strength of character, it must show itself in such a crisis of your fate. Self-reliance came to my rescue, and instead of giving way to a morbid, brooding state of mind, which the treatment I had been subjected to was enough to inculcate, I turned to hard and redoubled work as a panacea for my woes and my salvation from all forms of hysteria. Collecting all my faculties for the task, I determined that what I had drifted into doing for pleasure I would now undertake in real earnest, and that I would become a professional writer.

Anon., "The Struggles of a Lady Journalist" (Volume 9, 9 June 1888, p. 586).

At this period the fungus of poverty struggled so successfully with the pride of birth in me, that I stripped off my social fetters, and, as many a one has had to do before, I went into the arena where all who work for their living meet on the common ground of equality.

My testimonials consisted of two flattering letters from editors of other papers besides our own, a pile of grateful acknowledgments from shops whose novelties I had at various times written up, and copies of all my articles which had ever appeared in print. Armed with these, I intended to commence life over again as a lady journalist.

My first move was to provide myself with a newspaper guide; and I believe I am not exaggerating in saying that I wrote upwards of a hundred and fifty letters to the editors of London and Provincial papers, proprietors of weekly journals, and others, telling them of my varied and all-round experience, and offering them my services in any way they chose, if only they would engage me permanently on their staffs, or failing this, grant me temporary employment.

I must say, from one and all I received the most civil replies, but each answer as it arrived was more discouraging than the last, till at length my heart used literally to sink within me when I heard the postman's knock at our door.

Some editors said they had "no opening at present," others informed me that all their "town gossip and fashionable news came through press agencies," whilst the generality laconically announced that their "staffs were full."

After a time I became convinced there was no opening in these directions, and with the recollection of my one attempt at fiction, which got itself accepted by a sixpenny monthly magazine in the years gone by, I scribbled off a story, which I purposed offering to the editor of some present day periodical.

Need I say that I was again disappointed? That my tale was rejected on all hands, and that in each instance I was informed—although with the utmost courtesy—that the editors were overstocked with matter (some of them still had MSS. lying crowded in the pigeon-holes of their office shelves which had never even been glanced through yet), and it was rather a mark of favour towards me than otherwise that I should be told plain and straight tales of the kind I submitted were simply a drag in the market nowadays. Interest here and there might get one taken, or occasionally a lady with a handle to her name got her stories accepted as she could make their acceptance good; but if you were a nobody, who had never hitherto written anything to attract the notice of the critics and command reviews, you had no chance whatever of getting your stories read, let alone taken.

What was I to do? Journalists are not in the habit of reviewing one another's scissors and paste productions; the most able article, the smartest par, does not live in the memory of press men, in these rapid days, much beyond the week in which it is printed; and the triumph of the greatest leader writer is ephemeral compared to that of the writer of one successful novel.

I was conscious of the need to make money somehow. I knew if only I could tide on, the testimonials I could show, the proofs of my capacity as an experienced journalist which I could produce, would in time enable me to gain a livelihood somehow. But meanwhile? Why, I might starve.

(To be concluded.)

ODD CHARACTERS.

A GALLERY OF ECCENTRIC WOMEN.

By NANETTE MASON.

VI.—LADY HATTON.

ECCENTRICITY in single women is bad enough, but when married women have a turn that way, may providence doubly befriend all who live under the same roof with them! Take the case of the "strange lady," as an old writer calls her, whose story we have now to tell.

About the close of the reign of Queen Elizabeth, one of the interesting figures at Court was a beautiful young widow, about twenty years old, with no children, and possessed of an immense fortune. Her family connections were highly respectable, she being the daughter of Lord Burleigh, afterwards Earl of Exeter. But she was now known as Lady Hatton, her husband having been Sir William Hatton, the nephew of Sir Christopher Hatton, Queen Elizabeth's famous Chancellor. He had died in 1597.

Young, beautiful, and wealthy she certainly was, but it is just as sure that in temper she was a regular vixen. Her "gentle blood," in which she prided herself, never appeared in the softening of her character; she was heartless, overbearing, and vindictive. In the gaieties of the Court—hawking, balls, masques, and such like—she took great pleasure, as was natural at her years, and it was noticed that not only whilst engaging in such amusements, but in everything else, she was greedy of admiration.

The powerful family relations and large fortune of Lady Hatton brought a host of suitors to her feet, all of them so dazzled by her money and good looks that they had no eyes for her mental failings. Amongst them came the illustrious Francis Bacon, then in the beginning of his career, who was assisted in his wooing by his ever faithful friend the unfortunate Earl of Essex.

An old proverb says that "he who would the daughter win must with the mother first begin," so we find Essex exerting his eloquence on Lady Burleigh. "If she were my sister or my daughter," he says in one of his letters, "I protest I would as confidently resolve to further the match as I now persuade you." And in another epistle he adds, "If my faith be anything, I protest if I had one as near me as she is to you, I had rather match her with him than with men of far greater titles."

But Bacon was not to have her. The prize, such as it was, was to fall to Edward Coke, his rival in law as well as in love, who, like him, had cast a longing eye on the widow's great possessions. Coke was one of the most eminent lawyers that ever lived in this country, but he was hardly the husband one would have expected a gay young widow to select. He was fifty years of age, which to twenty usually appears about the number of the years of Methuselah. To his family there was really nothing to object, he being able to trace his ancestors as far back as the twelfth century. But a great deal was to be said against his proving himself a husband who could manage the wayward will of a spoiled, whimsical young woman.

He had an overruling nature to begin with, an arrogant manner, and a bad temper, which showed itself not only at the bar but at his own fireside. For the poetry of life he had no relish, he was seldom enthusiastic about anything, and never showed much sympathy for other people. He was simply a lawyer devoted to his briefs, and heartily detesting all gaiety and expense. His habits were very simple. When the sun set he went to bed, and on most mornings he rose at three o'clock. He took regular exercise, sometimes riding and sometimes walking, and his only amusement was an occasional game at bowls.

This cold-blooded lawyer had been married before. His first wife was an heiress, by whom he had about £30,000, and with her, as she was sensible and affectionate, he had lived happily. She died in 1598, and Coke mourned her loss even more than one would have expected in a man of his peculiar temperament. In a memorandum book kept for his own exclusive use we find this entry on the day of her death :—" Most beloved and most excellent wife, she well and happily lived, and as a true handmaid of the Lord fell asleep in the Lord, and now lives and reigns in heaven." She left ten of a family—seven sons and three daughters.

Before she had been long in the grave her husband set what affections he was possessed of on Lady Hatton, and proposed to enter with her into another matrimonial speculation. How he obtained her consent we do not know, but the probability is she was urged to the match by her relations. No one seemed to see the folly of her marrying a man old enough to be her father and with irreconcilable differences in taste and manners.

The two were married on the 24th of November, 1598. We find an entry of it in the parish register of St. Andrew's, Holborn, as the marriage of Edward Coke, "the Queen's Attorney-General," and "my Lady Elizabeth Hatton." The beginning was singularly unfortunate : for the way in which the wedding ceremony was conducted landed them both in trouble.

Irregular marriages just at that time were being a good deal talked about, but Coke and Lady Hatton, in spite of that, resolved on having the marriage secretly performed. Perhaps it was that they thought themselves above taking notice of such things, or it may be that the lady refused to be paraded in the face of the church as the bride of the wrinkled old Attorney-General. At any rate, they were married in the evening in a private house

THE STRUGGLES OF A LADY JOURNALIST.

THEN a desperate determination took possession of me. I made up my mind to work on till I could turn my experience to a money making account, and achieve success, or, if the Supreme Power willed it so, to die in harness.

Rays of counsel and of comfort came occasionally to cheer me along the rugged uphill path which circumstances obliged me to follow, and a keen sense of the ridiculous acted as my alpenstock.

Two well-known and able critics were good enough to read a lengthy manuscript of mine. One sent me a very favourable verdict, the other told me I was to persevere in writing fiction, neither of them being aware of my long apprenticeship to journalism; and I acted on the latter's advice.

Out of the many short society stories I wrote in consequence of this gentleman's encouragement, a few got taken. In one instance, acting under advice from a manager, I sent in some rather good paragraphs gratis, as a kind of thank-offering for the acceptance of a story —such a sop to the editorial maw having been known on occasion to lead to the donor's obtaining a permanent post on the staff of the paper. In my case it did not do so.

But though the tortures of starvation may be prolonged by these literary odd jobs, life is scarcely rendered enjoyable by their means, and patience is apt to fail one when the weary months roll by without bringing any substantial grist to one's domestic mill.

After hearing by letter from an American author of world-wide repute that though I was "experienced, and fully equipped for varied journalistic work . . . . the New York market was as fully over supplied with writers as our own;" and that for nearly two years he had been "trying in vain to get work and a position for a near friend of his own." And also learning from an English correspondent that one should "always try and get on the new papers, as old stagers have their hands so full of copy," I determined to confine my exertions to the new English journals.

From one I received a most satisfactory reply, acknowledging the receipt of my testimonials, and giving me an effusive promise that so soon as their arrangements permitted of their taking a lady on their staff I should be applied to. I filed this document, and after the lapse of a few months, happening to glance over the paper and see a "lady's letter" appearing in its columns, I took it upon myself to invade the editorial sanctum, with the following result.

"Oh! yes, we remember you perfectly, but you see, to be candid, we cannot afford to pay a professional!"

"But I see you have a lady on your staff."

"Well, not exactly! To be confidential, we had an offer which not another journal has a chance of. *A lady of rank, who moves in the highest circles, has been presented at Court, visits at Buckingham Palace and Marlborough House, and is one of your tip top swells, jots all the news down for us, and sends it in straight.* She can't write a bit, but that's of no consequence; we round her 'pars' into shape, and of course you could not give us such information."

"Then testimonials showing wide experience have no weight with you?"

"We won't say that, madam; but professional writers, even of your fair sex, expect to be paid; whilst titled ladies like to see themselves in print, and give us the news for nothing."

"But supposing any one combined rank with journalistic efficiency, what then?"

"Oh! well, supposing they did, we should be glad of their help!" This latter with the scorn of ineffable unbelief.

The old Adam arose in me. I told the individual, with what dignity I could command, that although I always wrote under a *nom-de-plume*, and had hitherto been impressed with the idea that they required good writers, rather than high-born dames, on the staffs of newspapers, yet that I had the misfortune to combine these two opposite advantages in my own proper person, and would inform the next editor I applied to of the fact. I need not say my informant was in his turn amazed at the information I vouchsafed him; he bowed me out of his office with many assurances that had he only known, etc., etc., he would have asked me to write for him from the first.

After this I took in despair to answering advertisements in the newspapers. I was decoyed by one reply which I received, right down into the heart of the City, and after toiling up to the garret of a large house in one of the principal thoroughfares, found myself in the presence of a miserable little man, a bailiff, and a canary bird. I noticed these items because the walls were whitewashed and the room devoid of all furniture excepting three rush-bottomed chairs and a deal table. I entered with avidity into his plan for developing a paying property out of a halfpenny broadsheet which was piled up in quires before him; for I felt the ghost of Charles Dickens was hovering around us, and pitied the poor wretch from my heart. I solemnly handed him my testimonials, enlarged to him on my wide and various experience, with a sort of comical wonder as to what terms, if any, he would make me; and after minute arrangements for the supply of a series of articles, which would necessitate my going through a considerable amount of reading up at the British Museum, I retired with a solemn promise that I should "hear from him." A promise which, I need hardly say, was never fulfilled.

Again I sent a stamped envelope for reply to an enterprising publisher who invited amateurs with a talent for fiction to enter the ranks of professional writers. As he did not know me, and I did not know him, I declined making his further acquaintance when I received his answer.

These are only picked from literally hundreds of other advertisements of the same class which I answered. I called on publishers; was advised to advertise. I went on to the advertising agents, who seemed to pity me, and was told they did not think I should get a single reply, but at all events it was useless my inserting an advertisement at that time of the year. I had better let them insert mine in about two months time. This was intended as kindness, but it was a kindness which killed, having regard to the slender condition of my finances, to the impossibility of subsisting upon air for the space of eight weeks.

Two more advertisements I answered, about a dozen more letters I wrote, and then—as darkest night is nearest day—there came a happy ending to my difficulties. But my response to these two last advertisements so bears upon my subject, that, at the risk of being lengthy, I must give my experience.

Both came out in the same issue of a fashionable daily paper; one emanated from an agency which undertakes to supply ladies with good situations, and my eye having been attracted by the offer held out in this advertisement to introduce literary workers, amanuenses, etc., into families, I ventured to call upon the lady principal. I was ushered into the presence of a very formidable, flashily dressed person, who apparently regarded fine feathers as the making of fine birds, and, misled by my somewhat dowdy and unfashionable appearance, considered me unworthy of being enrolled upon her books.

Being, however, more accustomed to deal with people of her class than she imagined, I proceeded, with much meekness, to explain my errand to her. I humbly owned to having had my hopes excited by the wording of her advertisement, and proceeded to say that I felt myself qualified to fill either of the posts mentioned in it. But, alas! for my pride, I was informed by this well-bred individual that she only dealt with quite the "upper aristocracy," and could not think of recommending me to them. Then, calling an amiable smile to my aid, I told her I hoped that if in confidence I mentioned my people's position she would be so kind as to do something for me, and producing my testimonials I assured her I should not discredit her establishment. Where was my tact? I might as well have offered a sop to Cerberus. With a flounce and a bounce this omnipotent purveyor of amanuenses jumped out of her chair, and with a sweeping curtsey gave me to understand our interview was concluded. "If you will allow me to say so," was her parting thrust, "you professionals cut the ground from under our feet, and keep us out of the field altogether." Being hit on the cheek when I offered my gentility side, and receiving a nasty slap when, in deference to a high command, I offered the commercial one, I of necessity retired from the flashy presence a sadder but a wiser woman.

The other advertisement informed me that a well-known literary gentleman—whose courtesy I gratefully acknowledge, although he could not see his way to helping me as an unknown stranger—"instructed a few young men in the literary and practical branches of journalism," and it also plainly conveyed the fact to these aforesaid young men that their instruction, even if of the minimum kind, would result in their attaining to a possible income of one thousand a year.

Can I be blamed for going to ask whether some inferior instruction might not be given to a lady, by which she might obtain, by way of a maximum income, to something like five hundred a year?

I did not wish to put the sexes on an equality; but I did wish—in these days when, owing to topsy-turvyism prevailing somewhere, wives have to help husbands to keep the children as well as to bear them—to gain some money; and the reply I received was instructive.

The gentleman who inserted the advertisement I allude to above told me he had refused, only the week before I called on him, seven hundred pounds from a lady, because his business would not allow of his helping on lady journalists as it enabled him to assist, I suppose, journalists proper.

Food for reflection was provided me here.

Subsequently I wrote the round dozen letters I have mentioned to the London managers of various provincial papers, from whom I had, on an earlier occasion, obtained courteous replies.

One of them did me the ineffable service of putting me into communication with a literary agent who is teaching me that the time I have expended in writing fiction has not been wasted; whilst from this connection introductions have come, bringing renewed journalistic work in their train, and I venture to hope my experiences and struggles may comfort, as I trust eventually to make them help, others who have been forced by adverse circumstances to go down into the arena of life and battle by their writing for their daily bread.

[THE END.]

Anon., "The Struggles of a Lady Journalist" (Volume 9, 16 June 1888, p. 605).

MY DAILY ROUND.

A COMPETITION FOR ALL GIRLS WHO WORK WITH THEIR HANDS.

T is not possible to over-rate the interest felt by all classes of society in these competitions for hand workers, or, as one girl quaintly calls it, *hard* workers, and the reason is not far to seek.

The "daily round" of these hundreds of brave courageous girls comes as a revelation to those who, having the good things of life, have no need to work with their hands, it illustrates the ennobling results of enduring hardness, and sows the seed of good deeds; it comes as a help and encouragement to those who have lost heart in the battle of life; it acts as a stimulant to those who are standing shoulder to shoulder in the struggle; and it is a lesson to every one in whatever rank they may be to see what these handworkers get through cheerfully in their twelve or sixteen hours of daily toil.

Every line of the 390 papers just sent in has been read by us with all-engrossing interest. The quiet unostentatious way in which each writer has put before us her daily life, with its struggles, its pains, its pleasures, its self-denials, its aspirations, makes us feel that such lives spent in our midst must influence for good every class with which they come in contact, be they high in the scale or low down, and consequently the world is the better for them.

Studying these "human documents" we see the lives of our working girls and their influence as clearly as though we lived with them. In all these papers written by weavers, teachers, needlewomen, artists, shop-girls, home-workers, farm-labourers, domestic servants, tailors, laundresses and others there is not a vulgar phrase or envious thought, scarcely an expression of discontent, and the only painful part of the whole competition is the selection from these for prizes and Honourable Mention; all are so good and conscientiously written that it is with the utmost difficulty we make selection. We go over them again and again and that we may be sure we are correct. Many a good paper has to be set on one side because the writer has forgotten the rules of the competition; for example, one admirable description of farm-life in Scotland ran into three full sheets of foolscap and had reluctantly to be put out. In another, the writer instead of confining herself to her special daily round took up that of her sister's, which she thought more interesting than her own, and although it was beautifully written could not therefore be accepted.

We should naturally think that the twelve or fourteen hours of compulsory daily toil would be quite enough and even more than enough to satisfy these girls, but if you could read all their papers you would find their evenings as busy as their days. After their evening meal some go off to an evening class and teach dressmaking to poor girls, others to various polytechnics to study languages, science or music. Most of them make their own clothes, some of them have bedridden parents and devote their leisure in reading aloud to them and in making them comfortable; while the majority of them are Sunday-school teachers and members of the church or chapel choirs. If any of their fellow-workers are ill the evenings are spent in visiting them.

This description of our competitors' method of spending their leisure is not confined to those at home, but applies equally to those who earn their daily bread in our far-away Colonies.

It seems to us that these Competitions are doing good service in that they enable us to see and appreciate the daily lives of *those* girls who work with their hands.

PRIZE WINNERS.

FIRST PRIZE (£5 5s.).

"Edelweiss," Locomotive-Tracer, Gorton, nr. Manchester.

SECOND PRIZE (£4 4s.).

"Pansy," Pottery-Painter, Hanford, Stoke-on-Trent.

THIRD PRIZE (£3 3s.).

"Lily of the Valley," Shirt-Maker, Dalston.

FOURTH PRIZE (£2 2s.).

"Primrose," Lace-Maker, Branscombe, near Axminster, Devon.

FIFTH PRIZE (£1 1s.).

"Begonia," General Servant, Mount Pleasant Road, Hastings.

HONOURABLE MENTION.

Nellie Jessiman, Assistant in Shoe Shop, Aberdeenshire.

Mary Ann E. Cue, Dressmaker, Poplar, St. Leonard's Road.

Eleanor White, General Servant, Slough, Bucks.

Mary E. Broadbent, Weaver, Sowerby, York.

Amy Burchett, Farmer, Gippesland, Victoria, Australia.

Kate A. Barnes, Book-Folder, Oxford.

Mary Slade, Parlour-Maid, Asylum Road, King's Langley.

Margaret Isabella Hay, in Publisher's Office, Hamilton, N.B.

Florence Gregson, Maker of Athletic Goods, Ossett, York.

Susan Barrowman, Farmer, Castle Douglas, Kirkcudbright.

Edith Holt, Housemaid, Kentish Town.

Helen Smith Thomson, on a Farm in the Bush, Murmangee, Victoria, Australia.

Janet Joycey, Collar-Maker, Lewisham.

Annie Jones, Compositor, Haberton Road, London.

"Orange Blossom," Nursery Governess, Ceylon.

Ellen Knight, Shoe Girl, Wellingborough.

L. Plaskett, Confectioner, Brierley Hill, Staffordshire.

M. F. Letts, General Servant, West Norwood.

Edith Williams, Dentist's Assistant, Walthamstow.

Hannah Maria Booth, Calico Weaver, Hayfield.

Eleanor Hare, Weaver, Blackburn.

Nellie Trafford, Silk Weaver, Macclesfield.

M. A. Anderson, Crofter's Daughter, Woodhead, Aberdeen.

Laura Bonden, Home Worker, Guernsey.

M. J. Taylor, Fur Tailoress, Lancashire.

M. J. Whiteside, Straw-Hat Cleaner, Clithero, Lancashire.

"Lilies of the Valley," Mantlemaker, Islington.

Florence Emily Parish, Lodging-House Maid, King's Road, Chelsea.

E. Beauchamp, Shirt Finisher, Pentonville.

"Marguerite," Shop-Girl, Great Homer Street, Liverpool.

FIRST PRIZE ESSAY (£5 5s.)

MY DAILY ROUND.*

AMONG the vast amount of useful work, begun, suggested, and carried out by the late Miss Emily Faithful; was the suggestion, some few years ago, to a friend; of the employment, in his large Engineering establishment, of females, to do the work of tracing the Locomotive and other drawings passing through his hands. Undismayed by the example of a large firm, at no great distance from his own, who had tried the experiment, and failed; this gentleman built, in the new Offices, which he was then in the course of erecting, a commodious office, cloak room, etc., for the sole use of a few female tracers; and determined to give the idea a fair and patient trial. The practical carrying out of the notion, might have proved as great a failure as

* This essay is printed exactly as written, without correction or alteration of any kind.—Ed.

the one mentioned above, but for the painstaking care of one of the draughtsmen; to whom the young girls were given in charge; and who tutored, and looked after them, to such purpose, that the idea became a fact accomplished in a very short time: for which I, for one, have cause to be devoutly thankful, as I am one of the aforementioned tracers employed by the Firm in question.

The Office in which we follow this employment—there are not a dozen of us, all told:—is, I am glad to say, a lofty, airy, and well-lighted room; so that we do not work under the unhealthy conditions, which are the,—often unavoidable—accompaniments of so many trades, in these feverish and busy days; nor do we breathe the vitiated atmosphere, in which so many of our bonny English, Scotch, and Irish girls pass the greater part of their lives. We are paid by the hour; and our salaries commence at ten, and rise to fifteen shillings weekly. We commence work at 45 minutes past 8; and continue till 12.45; when we separate for dinner. Those who like, can stay to take this meal in the office, if they prefer it; for, thanks to the kind thought of our employer, we are the rich possessors of an oven and grate, and, beautiful to say, of a nice little tin kettle, and pan; in which we can warm or infuse anything; and have a few cups and saucers, plates, etc, in a cosy cupboard in the corner. We return from dinner at 2.15; so that we have an hour and a half for our mid-day meal; a privilege for which I must say, I think we work all the better. At 5.15. we give up business for the day; our hours being timed so that we do not come or go with the draughtsmen, or the men; of whom, in busy times, the firm employs about 2000.

Our work, which is brought to our department from the drawing offices by one of the younger boys, or, on rare occasions by the foreman draughtsman himself; mainly consists in tracing, through transparent cloth, with instruments, with which our employer provides us; the drawings of the draughtsmen, or the architect; which we afterwards colour: using for the various metals, etc.,—a mixture of Indigo or Prussian Blue, and Crimson Lake, to represent the steel: Indian Yellow, with a little Crimson Lake, for the brass: Crimson Lake, and a little Indian Yellow, for copper: Neutral Tint, for cast iron: Prussian Blue, or Indigo, for wrought iron: Burnt Sienna, and a little Indian Ink, for wood: Burnt Sienna, a little Indian Ink, and Indigo, for fire brick: and etc. The drawings given to us, do not always have to be made a straightforward copy of, but we have at times to put in alterations, and afterthoughts; or to make one tracing from two, three, or more drawings; as different orders may require. Also, in some cases, such as the copying of maps; specially wanted plates etc. from the Engineering Press; or small diagrams, the work is done partly or wholly by hand. And sometimes again, when the work is fine, or is an ill-taken Photograph from some other firm; the aid of a magnifying glass is needed. Our firm, in addition to Tracings, supplies Photographs to those who like the latter better than the former. In case of this, the ink having been first mixed with a little Indian Yellow; a tracing is made, minus the colour; photographed in the Photographic room; and then the photographs thus made, one, two, or three, of each tracing, as the case may be, brought down into our Office by one of the boys, to be coloured by us. If the Photographs have not taken nicely, it is also our duty to fill in the parts wanting; (which we do by drawing in the lines with a mixture of Prussian Blue:) and to leave them in a finished condition, ready to be forwarded to their destination; to which both they, and the Tracings are sent, fastened together, book fashion, and carefully packed inside a wooden box. If there are any red lines, on our drawing requiring to be photographed; (red lines are often shown to represent the bulk of anything, before it goes through that process known to the initiated as "Finishing"; or in other instances, the differently formed portions of a right and left-handed rod,—or anything of which there is one on each side of the Engine, and where one drawing represents both.) These red lines must be copied by us, from the drawing, on to the Photograph, as the sun refuses to do that part of our business for us. The kind of Photographs made by our firm, are those having blue lines on a white ground, which are, it is difficult perhaps to say why, much plainer to see than those which consist of white lines on a blue ground.

We supply our own men with tracings for use in the shops; and one Set of Tracings, or Photographs,—or in some cases two or more,—accompany all the Engines sent out from the Locomotive department of the Works. These represent different parts and sections of the Engine; and are drawn, some the full size of the object represented, and some in 3 inch, or 1½ inch scale: in the former, as I don't think I need tell you, 3 inches signify a foot; in the latter, 1½ inches represent the same. I cannot tell you exactly how long it takes us to complete a set of tracings for one Engine, as we are at work on so many at one time. As a rule, the "General Drawing" of the interior and fittings of the Loco, takes one person from three days, to a week, to complete; according to the fulness of detail given, and the manner in which it is coloured. The smaller drawings take to trace, from that length of time, to about, perhaps, an hour. It is impossible to give the precise time taken by each, as drawings of the same thing vary so much, but last year, we sent out of the office upwards of 2000 tracings, without

counting the photographs; working about five weeks overtime, during that period.

I used to think, when I was younger, that Locomotives were generally made of one design and pattern, for a few years together, at all events;—but now—well! I know different. One finds the continually recurring alterations and variations in interior detail, are simply legion. This Wheeled Mercury, that carries so many of her busy children, to and fro, on the bosom of Ma Earth, is a strange thing in its way. The dear little creature costs a small matter of from two to three thousand pounds; and weighs the paltry trifle of from 38 to 50 tons; according to whether it is a sturdy-looking luggage drawer, or a mere playful little passenger engine. Here I must not let myself be really misunderstood. Strange to say, it is the (to my mind) lighter looking Passenger Engine, which often weighs the heavier of the two. Those in use at present, in the Mersey Tunnel, weighing, I am told, when standing fully equiped for service, 80 tons. Our flame-breathing acquaintance, sometimes carries as much as 3250 gallons of water in his Tender, if he possesses one; or about 1000 gallons if he is a Tank Engine, and bears his own supplies. This he will use, at the rate of, say, 8000 gallons per 200 miles, as he speeds us along. He also, during the same distance, in his busy process of converting each cubic inch of water into a cubic foot of steam,—and so, by the sheer force of expansion ploughing his way onward; gobbles up, monster like, 4 tons of coal. He is supposed to last, without repairs, from eighteen months, to two years, or thereabouts, and from fifteen to twenty years afterwards, according to the distances he is destined to cover. This familiar Monster of the Iron Road, the dear old "Puffing Billy" of our childhood's early recollections, has also a grotesque reflection of the Human about him. There is something *Eccentric*, as well as wonderful, in his anatomy. He wears *Clothing*; (with a *Pocket* in it, too.) He is also possessed of *Stays*; vain creature! and carries *Rings, Collars, Studs, Links*, and such like gew-gaws. Like the dandies of old, he moves along in *Breeches*, and *Buckles*; wears *Braces*; possesses a choice variety of *Pipes*, *Smokes* industriously; and, as is perhaps not surprising, after the announcement of such ways and habits, is often seen in the company of a *Bogie*. He has his individual characteristics, and his moods, like,—there! I had almost said, like any creature of the female sex,—as if *we* stood alone in moods, and whimsicallaties, and such like things; I think our brothers have their fair proportion, and frequently don't know it. But, in real earnestness, that reminds me; it is a curious thing, that no two Engines made, however exactly, to the same pattern, behave themselves alike under the hands of the driver, or show the same characteristics. Time, place, and circumstance; and, yes, even the characters, and moods of the workmen, through whose hands it passes—who knows—may have something to do with it. At all events, they say the thing is so; and it struck me as curious; for they do say, too, that nothing we ever touch, is left quite the same as we found it, and that our character, and present state of temper, influences the very air we breathe.

But enough of "they say"'s. Now let us turn to the "we do,"'s and the "we are "'s. To begin with; we are, then, at our house, a small family quartette; consisting of a father and mother, advanced in years; one elder sister whose sphere of duty lies in the Home-Castle; and myself;—though, as Wordsworth would have put it, we are really eight, all told. —So much for home matters. Now to the work-a-day world once more.

I will just take one "daily round" for a sample of all the others; choosing a time

when we are for the most part busy with the smaller drawings; and after that I will take —my leave of you, dear Editor. First of all then; I rise in good time, to avoid all hurry and flutter; and, it being a rather doubtful looking morning, arm myself with my *para-pluie* and sally forth. I reach the office at about 8.35. Having popped my umbrella in the stand, just inside the door of the cloak room; taken off my hat, cape, &c., and put on my apron and half sleeves, for which a wardrobe, filled with pegs, is provided, together with a whisk for chalky dresses;—the reason for which alarming state of untidiness, though to do us justice it very seldom happens, I will describe presently.—Having, as I was saying, put on my apron, and poured out a goblet of water, I walk into the office; and proceed to take out of my drawer, my duster, and case of instruments.—I happen to be tracing this morning, not colouring. Morning greetings pass between those of us who are already present; and then the ink, a stick of Indian, about five inches long, and a little thicker than your finger, is rubbed, in white metal pallets; we get out our set-squares, straight-edges, and a few curves from one of the drawers in the handsome dresser at the end of the room, lift our drawing boards on our desks; mount on our stools; and business commences in earnest.

This morning, of which I am now speaking, I am at work on a sheet of Bolts, of which I have done the greater part the day before. I now first put in the lines and curves which are still needed; and then, arming myself with a six grooved pallet, and the colour box, proceed to mix and apply the colours; first putting into the water with which I mix them, a little prepared Ox-gall; for the cloth is glazed almost like white satin, and would not take at all kindly to the colour, without it. In about an hour and a quarter I have finished my Bolt Sheet; putting in everything, but the writing, and dimentions; which our forewoman often jots in herself. And now I proceed to take off the cloth, and the drawing, from the board, by prizing up the tacks with which they are fastened down, with a tack-raiser; and carry both down to the ledger; where I enter the date, the number of the drawing, the Engine number, and the name of the drawing; with my own name following. Then I go up to the forewoman for further work. This time it is a Locomotive "Boiler Details" (a 3 inch scale.) which I receive; to make a straightforward copy of. I hasten to find a drawing board to fit my Boiler; and then for a few minutes the office echoes, not to the "music of the spheres," but to the music of the hammer, driving home a few tacks;—though I am not so sure but that the hearty and purposeful stroke of the Hammer, no less than the hum of the Sewing Machine, and the sound of the Dust Shovel, has its allotted, and essential part, in such harmony. Nay! I believe it has.

Having tacked on my drawing as flatly as possible; taking care to have it straight, but not wasting too much time about it; as the tracings, and photographs, are invariably cut square after each set is finished, by two of our number, told off for the purpose; I bring the roll of cloth; which is in this instance 38 inches wide;—our widest is 43 inches, by the way:—and, laying the length of the cloth to the length of the drawing; roll it over it from end to end; fastening it down with tacks, each of which must be pushed through a tiny square of drawing or photograph paper, to keep them from bruising the cloth unnecessarily; and stretching it, in every direction, as much as possible. This process of stretching the cloth, has to be repeated two or three times during tracing, in some states of the weather; and so we must, perforce, be content with doing a little detached view at a time, if we have any little, sweet, obliging detached views, pleading to be traced ; if not, we have to do the best we can ; taking the greatest care to keep the lines in as correct a possition as possible. I am always glad, if I am going to begin anything, to get the cloth tacked on it before the dinner hour, as that gives it a little time to stretch in ; or, if I can manage to get the cloth fastened down over a drawing the last thing at night, I am as pleased as two pins and a half ; for having the night to stretch in, it generally does it thoroughly, and is as good and flat as you please afterwards. Now the surface of this tracing cloth of ours, is very greasy ; and would not take the ink nicely if left in its present condition ; so my next proceeding, is to go to the chalk box under one of the racks ; scrape a little chalk into the duster I find there, and coming back to my desk, rub the chalk well over and *into* the cloth ; after which process the ink should work smoothly and evenly enough. By this time my covering of cloth has stretched, and must be tightened, which I hasten to do. And now I commence to put in, first radial corners, and circles ; by which time the greater part of the morning is gone ; and then the straight lines, curves, etchings, &c. ; working from the right hand corner downwards, as far as I can reach across the board, which, when all within reach is finished, I turn round ; and continue to trace from the other side. The moments pass on. There is a subdued hum of conversation going on all round me. The day is close and sultry. One of the girls says something which I do not catch, which sets everyone laughing. The sunlight, which has been absent the whole of the morning, peeps suddenly in at one of the south windows, changing the whole aspect of things, like a cheerful heart does ; and making everything bright and bonny. Of course we all

have our special private troubles and trials ; I think it is a sign that God is not leaving us alone, but thinks it worth while still, to forge us into shape for up yonder ; but happiness, they say, is always more a creature of mind, and heart, than of circumstances. Parenthetically speaking, I don't know of any recipe for making a discontented and mopesy heart light, and buoyant, better than that of trying to make somebody else happy, and serving them with all your might ; but, referring to circumstances, now,—just while these straight lines, and curves of mine are going in,—we ought, at this Office of ours, to be thankful-hearted girls, when we think what some of our, sometimes weaklier, often worthier, sisters, in the worlds battle-fields of labour, have to go through in one short day ; a day all too long for the flesh and bones of some of them ; though not for that essence of God within the earth-shell, which "breathes sweetness out of woe." My mind, carried up and away, I suppose, on the ladder of the sunlight, is just beginning (not, be it for a moment imagined, to the neglect of present duty.) to wander into the regions, not bounded by time, and space, but by Love, and Majesty ; when I am suddenly brought back to sublunary things, by the voice of my superior officer :— "Time to go home, girls ; " it says. There is a general rustle in the office ; stools are vacated and lifted into place ; instruments are wiped out and put away ; dusters are folded ; aprons and sleeves are quickly laid aside ; and home we go to our mid-day meal.

2.15. We are busy once again ; feeling refreshed and strengthened by the intervening rest. In my case, the process of putting in lines, curves, and penshading, goes on uninterruptedly ; until I, having finished my Boiler, (it happens to be one drawn without

colour ; a thing which, I must say, very seldom occurs.) our forewoman comes down to my place, and brings me two Photographs, showing the alterations in the arrangement of pipes in a Locomotive ; which I am to colour, and fill in. Our method, by the way, of colouring these Photographs, is very much the same as that used with respect to the Tracings ; but that, in the former case, we mix the tintings and shadings very thin, and do not use Ox-gall. And thus the afternoon wears on. The big clock in the Tower strikes four ; and then—five. At length comes the expected—"Time to go home ; " —and we are soon after this out into the street ; speeding our different ways. Then follows the always pleasant home-coming ; tea ; mending, or a little reading aloud ; a little family intercourse ; and to bed. And so another day's tracing is over. Tracing of two sorts ; very different in kind, and durability ; both to be reckoned for ; both done under the same MASTER's eye. But one has been done on Tracing Cloth of Imperial Stamp ; the other has been traced by each thought and action, in the book of the Recording Angel ; and on the hearts and lives of all those with whom we have come in contact. Our thoughts, our tendencies, have traced something on their lives to day ; for good, or for evil. May it be for good.

And thus the days come and go, with all We Humans ; come, and go, with God's light at the heart of them ; until we have finished our training, and education ; and the tasks and duties set us are ended ; and we are ready to " go home," to our Father's house, out of this gymnasium school of a world.

I declare the statements in this paper to be true.
EDELWEISS.
Gorton, near Manchester.

THE GIRL'S OWN GUILD OF SCRIPTURE-READING AND STUDY.

BEING a scheme for studying the Bible day by day for self-culture, with test questions to prove that the reading has not been wasted.

RULES.

Half-an-hour's study and reading each day.

A course of Biblical study will occupy three years and three months.

Ten questions to be published each month in the " G. O. P."

Answers to be sent in by the first week in the following month by readers in Great Britain ; by readers in Greater Britain answers to be sent within a month later.

Books required for the present year's study : —*The Bible Handbook* (Dr. Angus, R. T. S., 5s.) ; *Bible Cyclopædia* (Dr. Eadie, R. T. S.) ; Oxford (or Queen's Printers') *Aids to the Study of the Bible*, 1s. or 3s. 6d. ; the *Revised Version of the Bible.*

Prizes will be given at the close of each year (not of the course).

First Prizes will be given to each student who has obtained the necessary number of marks. Also a certain number of Second Prizes, according to the number of the students, will

be given to the best of those who have reached the required standard. Handwriting and neatness in the MSS. will be considered.

First Prizes to consist of books to the value of One Guinea. Second Prizes to the value of Half-a-Guinea. Students who are prepared to make-up the answers to the questions that have gone before may join at any time during the first six months of the " G. O. P." year, *i.e.* from November to April inclusive. But in all cases the subscription will be 1s. per annum, payable always in advance, and sent by postal note to the Editor of THE GIRL'S OWN PAPER, 56, Paternoster Row, London. Each letter in connection with this work to have written upon the envelope " The Girl's Own Guild." A card of membership will be sent to each member, signed by the Editor.

QUESTIONS FOR THE MONTH.

361. Who was the author of the " Acts of the Apostles ? " How does he designate it, and of what is it a history ?

362. With which of the apostles is this Book mainly concerned ? And in which two cities are its scenes chiefly laid ?

363. Divide the book into two sections, and show which chapters contain, first the acts of St. Peter, and then those of St. Paul.

364. Relate the circumstances of the first apostolic miracle, the first sermon, the first persecution, and give the name of the first martyr.

365. Who was the first recorded Gentile convert ? Give the name of the first place where the Gospel was preached in Europe.

366. When did the first and second general persecutions of the Church take place ?

367. Give the name of the cradle and first metropolis of the Gentile Church. On what river was it situated ? Who first preached there ? By what title were the professors of the new religion called, for the first time in this city ? By whom was the name probably given ?

368. When did the first council of Jerusalem take place ? What were its decrees ?

369. Give a brief account of the three apostolic journeys of St. Paul, and state by whom he was accompanied.

370. What are we told in the sacred writings of the early life and parentage of St. Paul ?

would have said aristocratic-looking, only he disliked the word. A haughtiness of bearing, and a somewhat imperious manner implied a consciousness of superiority which Herbert also disliked, although the fine, intelligent face of his fellow-traveller and its handsome, well-defined features made him anxious to find whether he had a mind in unison with them. Herbert, however, contented himself by addressing such questions as he wished to ask about the objects he passed to the coachman, and as the country was new to him, found enjoyment enough in commenting upon it.

At last the stranger put his newspaper into his pocket, and scanning Herbert rather curiously, as if to discover who he was, asked him if he was bound for Oxford. Herbert replied in the affirmative. The gentleman made another short remark upon the weather. Herbert answered with equal brevity, not liking the tone he assumed. The stranger eyed him more closely, and was, perhaps, struck in turn by his appearance, for Herbert was very good-looking. He inquired whether he were going to Oxford for the first time, but still the haughty tone, which was really innate in the speaker, repelled cordiality, and Herbert's reserve increased. The stranger, whose keen eye seemed to look through the very heart, was interested, and he made an effort to unbend, not only his own pride, but that of his companion. He spoke generally of Oxford, its colleges, and its masters. The subject was too engrossing to be set aside, and Herbert sought to conquer his natural shyness, and to place himself on an equality with the haughty unknown, by conversing freely.

By degrees the young men forgot their reserve, in the pleasure of finding a similarity of thought and taste. The stranger was a man of the world, and was inwardly amused by Herbert's want of knowledge upon points that he had, from childhood, considered essentials; but he was not the less pleased and astonished when he discovered his superiority in literary acquirements. They spoke of books, and Herbert's life of study was soon apparent. His new acquaintance was as much behind him in the lore of the black-letter world, as he was his inferior in that of the concerns of the present day. The one was a scholar, the other a deep-sighted observer of human nature. They became, before they reached Oxford, mutually pleased with one another; but the stranger did not make any advances

towards a further acquaintance, and Herbert felt that his position was too uncertain to permit of his doing so. Besides there was an evident desire on the part of the stranger to avoid any familiarity that might lead to future intimacy.

As they approached Oxford, the conversation gradually flagged. It was twilight when they entered the town, and the ancient buildings looked solemnly grand and mysterious beneath its shadows. A thrill of awe and reverence ran through Herbert, when he found himself actually in the place whither his dreams and hopes had so often led him in imagination, and he seemed to have added years to his existence in the brief space of a few minutes. So much was begun, so much, indeed, consummated in that short interval. He was in a profound reverie, when the coach stopped, and his companion had dismounted before he could thoroughly understand that it was no time for visionary flights, but that he must descend to the task of looking after his luggage. A polite bow, and a "good evening to you," separated him from his coach acquaintance, whilst "Is your name Llewellen," introduced him to a new friend.

Dr. Marsden, one of his grandfather's old college chums, had come to see after him, and with a warm shake of the hand, welcomed him to Oxford, and invited him to his house, where, he said, a bed was prepared for him until his own rooms were ready. Herbert followed him, and was soon seated in a room not unlike his grandfather's study, in which books and papers were the most conspicuous furniture.

Dr. Marsden was unmarried, never having found time to think of a wife, and having been wedded to study ever since his early youth. He was avowedly a silent man, and except on one or two subjects, rarely said more than yes or no. Absent to a degree, his mind never seemed at home, and a sudden question startled him as much as a sudden accident. But he was a good and kind man, and although he never made any professions, a staunch friend when once he became attached. He was predisposed to like Herbert for his grandfather's sake, and before the first evening of their intimacy was over, he liked him for his own, and for a very singular reason; because he did not trouble him with questions, but was contented to let his taciturnity take its course.

They certainly were not loquacious,

but what they said was to the purpose, and Dr. Marsden was pleased with the remarks Herbert made upon his favourite authors, as well as with his desire to set to work at once, and leave no stone unturned to get on at college.

"Persevere, persevere," said the old man; "nothing to be done in the world without perseverance. Talents without it are like gas, easily kindled, but soon extinguished."

"And with it?" asked Herbert.

"Like a good coal fire, that will bear a puff of wind or a poker, and burn the brighter for them."

The following day was spent in visiting the lions of Oxford, and settling Herbert in some very plain rooms that Dr. Marsden helped him to procure. He also introduced him to several of his friends, all men of eminence and ability. Herbert called on his grandfather's other friend, Mr. Silvester, who received him very cordially and gave him a general invitation to his house, which was echoed by his wife, a good-natured woman, who was sitting in awful state at a work-table, surrounded by several grown-up daughters. From these fair damsels Herbert felt it rather a relief to escape, not having yet learnt the art of talking about nothing, in which, to be an agreeable caller, it is necessary to be versed.

It was to Dr. Marsden that he looked for counsel, feeling assured that he should obtain it, for there was in his manner a friendliness that he could not mistake, and an evident desire to be of service to him. Through his means he soon became initiated into the customs of the University, and by following his pithy, but sure advice, gradually saw his way clearly, and began a course of study that he hoped would insure ultimate success. He sought no further acquaintances, and courageously refused many an invitation from the Silvesters, contenting himself with sitting an hour or two, occasionally, with Dr. Marsden, in whose society he always felt himself benefited, even though conversation was carried on by fits and starts and short sentences. But the doctor gradually became more communicative as their acquaintance ripened, and gladdened Mr. Lloyd's heart by a letter, in which his praise of his grandson's talents and good sense was so warm and sincere, that it was evident he regarded his young friend with feelings of esteem and affection, that he was never known to lavish upon an undeserving object.

(To be continued.)

COMPETITION FOR GIRLS WHO WORK WITH THEIR HANDS.

SUBJECT: "MY DAILY ROUND."

Second Prize Essay (£4 4s.)

DEAR MR. EDITOR.—

I have not seen as yet among your many hand workers one whose "Daily Round" is performed in any branch of the "Potting" trade, so I will try to tell you a little about my own. I am employed in one of the largest Manufactories in the Potteries, as a

Paintress, and although it is not the largest Factory it is productive of every kind of earthenware that is made, tea and dinner services, toilet sets, jugs, vases, flower-pots, and sanitary etec: all of which are made in various sizes and shapes, and come in for a share of some kind of decoration, and as all the Decorators have a department of their own each one understands their own particular branch of the work. The kind of decorating

I am engaged in is called "Enameling" which consists of filling in, in all kinds of colours and many different ways the patterns that are already printed for us.

I am twenty-six years of age. I live in a small village just outside the town with my Grandmother. I get up about seven o'clock generally, sometimes earlier but if I should happen to be a little later Grandmother will waken me with the exclaimation "M—— it is

---

"My Daily Round: A Competition for All Girls Who Work with Their Hands" (Volume 18, 21 November 1896, p. 115).

getting late." The first thing on opening my eyes I peep out of the window to see what sort of a morning it is. "Oh! how I love these bright sunny days, and the lovely showers too that makes it so much pleasanter for my long walk to work. I am soon down stairs, never forgetting first to give thanks and ask for guidance of Him in Whom I live and have my being. Then I prepare breakfast, take Grandmother a cup of tea and do a few household duties and on washing days a little washing, when I rise a little earlier. Then after putting my dinner in my bag, I get my breakfast which is very often a hurried one. I start about half past eight generally and in half an hours time I reach the smoky town, another half hours walk brings me to the Factory. This is a large four storey building, I have to climb two flights of steps to the top storey where our branch of the work is carried on. On entering the workshop which is a very large one with white-washed walls and great wooden beams, I am greeted with a very strong smell of turpentine, oil and tar that we use for our work. There are fiftyfour Paintresses and Gilders in the shop each sitting on a three legged stool opposite tables ranged under the windows which stretch the whole length of either side. Then we have a Designer who makes the patterns and colouring, and a Manager who has to see that they are executed accordingly, besides a Lady who we take orders from and counts our work when it is finished.

Our hours generally are from half past nine to six, but when we are very busy from eight till seven, which I do not like at all as it means that I must be up an hour and half earlier and almost bed time before I get home, besides if not there we get sent back for the day, but I am pleased to say this has not occurred yet in my case. I will however take one of our busy days and describe to you " My Daily Round " at the Factory when I arrive there at eight oclock. The first thing I have to do is to prepare my colour which is done by grinding it on a tile with a small knife in as much turpentine as will wet it and when fine enough add a little fat oil (as we

call it) which is already prepared for us, and I may say the finer we grind it the easier it is to work with and our work has a much nicer appearance when it is finished. Now for my pencils, the oil causes them to go hard when dry so I put those that I intend using in my turpentine cup to soak while I am dusting and getting my ware ready, which for instance is four toilet sets called " Camelia " the principal flowers first are what we call " washed in," in pink, this is done with a pencil I keep for the purpose by dipping it in turpentine and fat oil then in my colour as deep a strength as I need it. I have now painted a few flowers and it is nine o'clock which from that to half past is our breakfast time and if we should happen to work a minute after the Manager will pop out of his office and call. " Now you girls do you know what time it is." Which means we must stop work at once because if the Inspector should find us working during meal times we are liable to a very heavy fine. After breakfast and a chat we set to work again, I finish pink, and the remaining flowers are done in mauve and yellow, these I do together and now all the flowers are " washed in." While These are drying I do the leaves in light and dark green. All this time it is very noisy, some hunting after patterns or colours, others carrying up ware out of the warehouse to be painted or gilt, (as we all have to carry our own up two flights of steps which is very heavy work) and the kiln boys tramping up and down with empty boxes on their shoulders asking if the ware is ready for them to carry away to the kiln, as before they can do so, each piece as it leaves our hands has to be counted so that it may be known at the end of the week what work each has done and what wages they have to receive. At half past twelve preparations are being made at the stove for dinner, such as cooking meat, making tea or warming food. From one till two is allowed for this meal. During this time various occupations are engaged in such as needlework, knitting, crotchet, reading and much talking. Many I am sorry to say take much interest in halfpenny Noveletts. I try

to sell as many " Church Army Gazette's " as I can each week both in the shop and elsewhere hoping to be able to do some little to counteract the evil that is wrought through reading bad books. From two oclock till seven I am hard at work again with only a little break (about four oclock) for a cup of tea. I shade on my flowers and leaves (which are now dry) the various colours and tints, to do which I have to take up each piece several times as the colours dry, at seven oclock I have completed my four toilet sets which consists of from six to ten pieces each, the Ewers and Basins being very heavy to hold with one hand while working with the other. For this I earn the sum of two shillings and eightpence, the prices paid for our work varies according to the patterns, some being as low as twopence halfpenny a set. For colouring a dinner set of fifty-two pieces I get sevenpence halfpenny, for flower pots I get from fourpence to two shillings a dozen according to size etec : I have described to you one of my busiest and best days as sometimes I have had as little as one shilling. So ends " My Daily Round " in the workshop. I reach home about eight o'clock very tired and often bring back the food I have taken with me in the morning, as the heat and smell of the shop affects it so much I cannot eat it. I have supper and devote what little time I have after in mending or making my clothes or in doing little jobs for Grandmother, and after reading the portion of Scripture appointed for the day I retire to rest. I often feel " My Daily Round " very wearisome and wish that the Presence of Him Who has hallowed our daily toil by having once toiled Himself could be more fully realized in our workshops for—

Work shall be prayer, if all be wrought
   As Thou wouldst have it done!
And prayer by Thee inspired and taught
   Itself with work be one.

I declare the statements in this paper to be true.

                     " Pansy "
August 29th 1896.   Stoke-on-Trent.

THIRD PRIZE ESSAY (£3 3s.).

My daily round is a very busy and complicated one. I have always longed to be a hospital nurse, but this hope had to be laid aside when my father died five years ago leaving my delicate mother unprovided for with two of us not able to go to work & the eldest of all " my sister " an invalid. I was then at a well known firm of shirt makers in Milk St. City & my earnings were very largely depended upon. Home has been from that time quite a hospital in itself. Nearly a year ago my mother died which greatly increased my work & it is from that time I will write.

I now have my shirt work at home (from the same firm) as my sister is a helpless sufferer from an advanced form of Chronic Rhuematism & requires a great deal of my time Part of my day is spent in (what I like to call) my hospital ward, & my shirt work is squeezed in between times & is the chief support of my " home hospital." I can do 6 in one day & the price varies according to quality, but we will reckon to-day I am doing the better work which will be 6d. each when finished. I am up at 6 A.M. dress & prayers, downstairs, light the fire, call my little sister & brother, (give my patient her breakfast first) & our own will be ready by 7 oclock.

We three sit down together but it is rather a hasty meal for my brother has to start for

work by half past, and before then I must get his food ready for the day which he takes with him. After then I see to my little sisters food (for she has started to work now) & fetch my patients breakfast things away, & make her comfortable to leave until 9 oclock, during which time I do the daily necessary house duties including bedmaking & general tidying, but as the work is equally divided for the week, each morning has its own portion. My little sister goes to work at 8 o.c., & before I go to my patient I must prepare our dinner. At 9 o.c. I must begin to wash my patient, this (with dressing) means an hour's work; as she is so helpless and needs such tender handling, & I think in a general hospital would be considered to bad to set up; but she prefers to get up as long as she is able to bear it. About 10 o.c. I carry her downstairs & after arranging her comfortable & giving her a small lunch I leave her to begin my 6 shirts which will be very close work if I am to be in mothers place in the evening; & who does not know of the many attractions there are to draw young people (boys especially) away from home; Well I dont want my brother to drift away, so home must be attractive too. I do not work in my patients day ward for my work necessitates plenty of space & makes the room look very untidy with white calico scattered all

about & my patient is like all invalids (more or less fastidious) & likes her room tidy, & the noise of the machine would worry her, & I can work quicker alone. When I am wanted my patient rings a small bell, but unless interrupted I work away until 12.30, first: hem the six shirts, seam the sides, put binders round armholes, and yokes on, & prepare fronts (linen) i.e. turn them down ready to put in the bodies. I now leave off for about an hour & half to get our dinner ready & after we have eaten it I wash the dishes &c. & freshen my patient with another little wash & Leave her again for the afternoon when she generally sleeps a little while & I get on well. By 4 o.c. I can put my fronts in & make the sleeves. Visiting time at a hospital is generally from 2 till 4 & my ward is not an exception & sometimes I find my patient has had a very pleasant afternoon & nurse is invited to tea which has been got ready by her visitor. This is only occasionally & I mostly have to get it myself. I rather like visitors for they help to brighten my invalid up & she is not hurried so much for after a hasty cup of tea myself I leave them still happy over theirs & hurry back to finish my work which will take me two hours to put the wristbands & collarbands on (these are made by a different machine & sent to me ready to put on) & put the sleeves into the

---

"My Daily Round: A Competition for All Girls Who Work with Their Hands" (Volume 18, 21 November 1896, p. 116).

shirts. I try to be finished by 7 o.c. that things may be as homelike as possible without mother, for it is mother who makes the home even though she be a great invalid at times & it is when the days work is done that mother is most missed, & I try to make up as well as I can for her loss, in the *numberless little* things which constitute home. There is now a meal to prepare for all after which my patient is ready to be put to bed which is almost as trying as the morning performance ; My brother will carry her upstairs, he likes to feel he can do something for her.

Every day is very much the same except tuesday when I do the washing which I get finished by dinner time & do my shirt work afterwards. Perhaps the next ½ doz. will only be 2/3. & in the busy time which is May, June, July. I have to do more than ½ doz. in a day, and I have to sit up late to do them, but one does not mind this when we think of the winter when for several weeks I shall have very little or nothing. It means very quick work while it is here & everything has to be done to time or I could not get all in, but I can never hurry over my patient as every movement gives her pain. I have no trouble with taking my work in when finished for my little sister brings it home with her at night & takes it in the morning which is a great save of time for me. The button-holes are made by indoor hands after they go from me. Saturday is a general clearing up day & preparing for Sunday, which (as in all hospitals) is just as busy only rather different ; for a nurses life is always busy, for if she has not to do other work to support her hospital she has more than one patient to attend to ; but still I do not have my day off once a week & I have to do night duty as well My patient is still making a downward progress in spite of all the Drs. efforts to stop it, & he with some other friends think it is more than I can manage & even while I write I am expecting that my patient will be taken from me as the Dr is trying to get her into "Freidenheim," Hampstead.

On Sunday I get up at 7.30. give my patient her breakfast & get to church by 8.30. home again and have my breakfast by 9.30. (we are living only about 2 minutes walk from church) After preparing the dinner I am ready to see to my patient & to-day she has the benefit of my extra time in a sponge bath. My little sister is a great help to me on Sunday morning before school time & I have the dinner quite ready by 1 o.c. when service is over. This gives us time to be nicely cleared away by 2 o.c. Now I make my patient cosy for the afternoon & get ready for S. School where I have a class. Lately I have been persuaded to give this up (at least for a time) but doesn't our Master promise "As thy day so shall thy strength be" & I am so thankful for the opportunity to tell others of Him who has done so much for me that I wish I could do more, and I try to live the thankfulness which no words of mine can express, for the priceless gift of health by doing what I can for the weaker ones &

instead of going out to seek for the work I longed for, it is given me within my own home. We who work with our hands have great opportunities of thinking while we are at work over the lesson we shall be giving the next Sunday in school.

I get home by 4.30. this gives 2 hours quiet rest including tea time which is always bright on Sunday when we are all at home & this is when I get a glance at the articles & monthly sermon by Medicus in the favourite G. O. P. leaving the stories until I may have more time for reading. Sometimes my patient will have a visitor to sit with her while I go to the evening service, or perhaps she would rather be alone. There are many little things to be done for an invalid which cannot be written here & when my shirt-work is not so busy I make my own & my sisters clothes dresses included. Amongst other things there is the management of home & spending to the best advantage our small income, which, between my brother & little sister & myself now earing about 25/ a week. I think it is as necessary to be careful "how we spend" as in "what we earn," for if the one is rather a worry at times, the other needs a great deal of forethought & economy, but through mother's ill-health I had a little practical experience in housekeeping, only I had mothers advice to look to, & at 27 (my age then) I did not feel equal to the responsibilities of father, mother, husband,

PHOTOGRAPH COMPETITION : SECOND PRIZE (£3 3s.)—
Edith Mathew, Beckenham.

& wife together with the duties of nurse, but still after nearly a year's trial I am proud of my home hospital & pleased to think I am useful to others, for even if it be only *one* talent with which we are entrusted by the Master & doing what we can with it we can look forward to the time of great rejoicing when we shall hear our Lord say—Well done — because thou hast been faithful over few things I will set thee over many things. What is it that makes work such a pleasure

Labour is sweet for Thou hast toiled
And care is light for Thou hast cared

Some the Master calls aside from active work & it is as important for these to watch & wait, at the same time living very useful lives & the reward is equal according to our abilities May we all make up our minds to do all the good we can even though we pass this way only *once*.

I declare the statement in this paper to be true
"LILY OF THE VALLEY"
Dalston

** *These essays appear exactly as written —without alteration of any kind.*—ED.

PHOTOGRAPH COMPETITION : THIRD PRIZE (£1 1s.)—*J. Nicholson, Lewes.*

THE SECOND COMPETITION FOR GIRLS WHO WORK WITH THEIR HANDS.

FOURTH PRIZE ESSAY (£2 2s.).

MY DAILY ROUND.

DEAR MR. EDITOR

I have been thinking since I read your last Daily Round Competition letters that I should like to let you see a lace workers daily round, which work I have to earn my living by,

The summer is my busy time and I rise very early and get my little oil stove ready and make a cup of tea and ready to sit down to work by 5 oclock sometimes earlier than that. I live quite alone in a little cottage facing the sea and cliffs, and as the days are so hot I like to have the early morning as I have to keep my work very clean so that it does not have to be washed before I sell it. I am to day doing point lace cuffs, and I work for the village shop people who give out the work ready tacked to the pattern they require, which first I draw around with needle and fine cotton in every pinhole of the braid; the pattern is covered with; then if we require a new pattern to work on again I place a sheet of paper over the work drawn and with a piece of heelbore, it is called, rub and the black marks comes on the clean paper, and then we have a new pattern, to begin another time, then I do a lot of buttonhole bars and pretty stitches which we have learnt, then the last stitch is called pearling; which is done with a coarser cotton, on the outside edge then we rip it off the paper; and take it to the shop, where I get things to make use of as we are not paid money there;

I sit to work untill 8 oclock then I get my breakfast and put my house tidy and if I have any dinner to cook I get all ready. I sit to work again by half past nine or ten sometimes then work untill 12 oclock, and if very busy for post as we call it, that is the work we are asked to do by a certain time; I do not stop only for a bread and cheese dinner and a cup of tea or an egg for we cannot afford meat dinners, every day I get fish and things very cheap in our village so it helps one a lot where we have not much money to spare, so after having my bit of dinner if not busy I take my book and sit down in the fields or indoors in my hour we have for dinner, Sometimes there are two of us have a piece of work between us so then I take my piece to a friends house to work alike or they come to mine and it is nice to have company at times so I get to work again and work until 4 oclock and then put on my little kettle on my oil stove which saves coal in Summer; and get my tea then sit to work until 8 o clock then I leave off and if I have not finished my peice; I then take my can to fetch my water and do any odd jobs I find to do; take my little can to a neighbours for her little girl to fetch my milk at the farm in the morning then I fetch other things I may want for my use and if I have time to go to see a dear old woman, who I call granny and who loves to talk to me, and then I go to see how much work my girl friend has done and then go home to my supper and book for living alone I love books they are my friends now I have lost my mother, Then I go to bed and before retiring I thank my Heavenly Father for his mercies which I enjoy which are many I am glad to say then if I am spared I begin my daily round each day but often get weary but glad to be able to get work to do The lace work is very trying to the sight and I am often very glad of an order from Ladies who pay money and a better price than what the shop people do for after working all day as I have said I earn but bare 7d and then only taken out in the shop

Ladies often send their Honiton Lace to be cleaned and put on new net; which is called transferring and then it will look like new lace; and that is real pillow lace which I have learnt; but it went down in price years agone and now if wanted they don't pay the full price for so the Point lace is done quicker and then we get really more for it We used in the village to have schools for teaching children the work but it does not do now they have to keep to the daily school and then they go to service, I have learnt all the different sorts and find it most useful now as I cannot live in service my knee gives out so glad to come home to the lace work.

A pair of cuffs takes two days and we get 1/2 for them or the worth of it in goods, so I hope if ever my daily round should be in print it will help to show the readers how hard some have to work to earn a shilling before they can spend it if we want clothes we have a book at the shop and they buy us what we want and we work on until we have paid for it.

All these statements I declare to be perfectly true—

"PRIMROSE."
Branscombe
Nr. Axminister
August 11th. Devon

FIFTH PRIZE ESSAY (£1 1s.).

MY DAILY ROUND.

DEAR MR. EDITOR,—I thought I should like to take advantage of your competition in, "The Girls Own Paper," for those who work with their hands, and in case you should think my, "Daily Round," is very easy and not worth writing about, I will just mention that I am afflicted with a very bad lameness, and nearly lost the sight of one eye, so perhaps you will understand then that my place is by no means easy to me, whatever it may seem to others, I am a general servant and I have been in my present situation, (indeed I have been in no other) eleven years, I must say; I have a very kind, considerate, mistress, or perhaps I should not have been able to stay so long. My day's work begins at seven in the morning, when I rise from my bed and dress, strip my bed, open the window top and bottom, come downstairs, and clean the kitchen grate, then light the fire, and clear up generally, Then the dining room is to be swept, grate cleaned, and the room then dusted. By that time, my mistress being a great invalid, I get breakfast ready, and take her's up to her in bed. I then come down, and have my breakfast, when I am allowed to sit over it nearly an hour, so as I do not take a quarter of that time to eat, I generally have a book, I like reading my Girls own paper, then, or I do a bit of knitting, or needle-work, after that my time being up I go up-stairs & bring my mistress's tray down, and arrange her room ready for her to rise, wash supper and breakfast things up together, then clean my front steps, After which I go up-stairs again, help my mistress to finish dressing, & then make the beds &c, take up the pieces off the floors (bedrooms) dust the rooms, and then by that time my mistress being downstairs I go into her to see about dinner, when she tells me what we are to have, after that, I commence to turn a room out, and I begin by moving everything I can out of the room, I can sweep so much better when it is clear, after it is swept, I thoroughly clean the grate, fire-irons, windows, & glass, and well dust the venetian blinds, then by that time, as I am rather slow through my lameness, I return to the kitchen and look to see that my oven is getting hot. & pots beginning to boil, I then prepare the vege-tables, and whatever sweets there are to be eaten, and then get my joint into the oven or in the pot, I then go back to the room & return the furniture ornaments &c to there right places, polish up furniture, and finish dusting, then go and see my dinner is getting on alright, take all the lamps out, and pro-perly trim and refill them by that time there are generally some letters ready I slip on my hat and run out to post them & then come back to my next task, which is generally some brass, or bright cooking utensils, to be cleaned, for as I like them always to look nice, but have a great dislike to this particular kind of work, I do a few each day so that I do not notice it so much, as making a morn-ing's work of it as I am supposed to do, or was, when I first came. By that time dinner is ready to be dished up, so I go into the dining room and lay the cloth, take dinner in, and as I have mine at the same time, my mistress cuts it off, & so I have it nice and hot, which I think is very nice, as it is so tan-talising I think after one, as had all the trouble of preparing the food to have it (as I know so many girls do) nearly cold, after the family have had theirs, especially if it is mutton; After dinner of course, there are all the plates, dishes, &c to wash up, knives to clean, what-ever silver, as been used, to rub up, and then clean up the kitchen grate, and tidy up, On Fridays I clean all the passages and stairs, silver, Saturdays is the easiest day of all, (excepting of course Sundays) as I only have my kitchens to well clean out and any little thing to do that I have not done during the week, This is a nine roomed house and there is enough to keep me going always, & then of course when visitors are staying in the house there is more to do, and washing week, to, especially as up to now I have had all the starching, ironing &c to do by my self of course! I am not able to do my work all so smoothly as I have written it down here there are so many interruptions, and answering the door is the worst of all, one as to go every quarter of an hour sometimes oftener & to a lame leg it often means terrible aches. And there are so many little things to do that one scarcely remembers before or after the time they have to be done, Well, after I have tidied up the kitchen I go up to change my dress, and then as we have a large dog, I take him for a run, come home and get tea by 5 o'clock, clear away, wash up, and then if there are any errands I go and do them, When I come home, there is generally some needlework to do or knitting heels to be set or toes to

---

"My Daily Round: A Competition for All Girls Who Work with Their Hands" (Volume 18, 12 December 1896, p. 172).

finish, and as my Mistress is a very charitable Lady, I generally have plenty of that to do, I also do all the cutting out of the Material she gets for that purpose which is a great deal in the course of a year, I also do all my own needlework and make most of my own dresses, as I cannot afford to put them out only about one in two years, I only have fourteen pounds a year, and not that until last year, I also like to do a little on my own account to make up a small parcel by the end of the year for the poor little children, Then at nine o'clock we have a light supper, I then clear away once more, leaving the washing up until morning, We then have prayers, and go up to bed, for which I am quite ready, I expect my, "Daily Round," does not look very hard to my other hard-worked sisters, but it is so hard to me for I have the greatest difficulty to get up and down on my knee (I have only one). I have tried other work, dressmaking, and Furriers before I tried service but sitting so long did not suit me and so I had to try the very work I hated so and never shall like it try as I will, althro I do my best and pray God to help me, and he as been very good to me, making the rough ways smoother, and helping me wonderfully, I hope dear Mr. Editor if you should think this paper worth printing that it will be the means of helping some one else to have courage and work and hope on, who have as great disadvantages to contend with as I have, perhaps greater. And now once more we have got to Sunday, and all is bright and clean, for that beautiful day of rest, what should we do without it, How it freshens one us each up for Monday and, "Our Daily Round," once more.——I declare the statement in this paper to be true.

"BEGONIA"
Mount-Pleasant Road
Hastings.

July 20th. 1896.

*** These essays are printed exactly as written, without correction or alteration of any kind.--ED.

THE WHITE ROSE OF THE MOUNTAIN.

By ANNE BEALE, Author of "The Queen o' the May," "Seven Years for Rachel," etc.

CHAPTER X.

THERE was a tuning of instruments, and a buzz of many voices ; there was a crowd of people of every rank and condition, and there were hearts beating with hope and expectation, and faces beaming with gaiety and excitement. Gwenllean sat in the old hall unconscious of the scene that was passing, and without venturing to uplift her face to the gaze of the stranger. David was beside her, and they were stationed, with the other performers, upon a platform overlooking a large room filled with company. But she heard nothing—saw nothing ; she was scarcely sensible of the grand flourish of trumpets that heralded the performers, and did not even perceive that the hum of voices gradually ceased ; that an old harper began to run over the chords of his instrument with a fearless touch, and to play a piece of music, the air of which she must have known well. Even the welcome burst of applause that greeted him was unheeded. She sat with her head bent low, totally lost in the confusion of her emotions, whilst the musicians, one after another, awoke the strings of their harps with the touching airs of their native land ; some warlike or heroic, others sentimental ; adding to them variations frequently of their own composition. When David's turn came, however, and he whispered to her that he must leave her side, she started, and listened with breathless attention. She had never heard him play that favourite Welsh air, "The march of the men of Harlech," with his own original variations, so well before, and her heart beat when the well-merited "encore" followed, and he repeated the piece.

Still she listened with trembling, for a young girl, about her own age, advanced and seated herself at the harp. She appeared almost as timid as herself, but gradually recovering her self-possession, she executed a piece with some skill. Gwenllean felt conscious of superior powers, and tried to summon courage for her approaching ordeal. She had come unprepared by practice, but at home neither her memory nor her finger ever failed her, therefore she hoped they would still stand her friends. There was one piece that everybody liked. It was an arrangement of Welsh airs that she had made with the assistance of David, some years ago, and to which she had since added variations of her own. Whilst the performers continued to play with more or less success, she was going through this piece in imagination.

At last her turn came, and when David led her forwards, and left her alone a little in advance of the other musicians, she thought she must sink to the earth. Her confusion increased, when, by way of encouragement to one so young, and evidently so unaccustomed to public performance, the company welcomed her by clapping of hands. She sat down by the harp, and the cheek that had been blushing like the rose, became pale as the lily. Her head sunk upon her breast, and her hand refused to produce a sound from the chords over which they were accustomed to run with such wild ease. She would have wholly failed, had not a vision of her mother, pale and anxious, presented itself to her mind's eye, and carried her back to the cottage, recalling, as it did so, the circumstances that had brought her to the Eisteddfod. She made a violent effort, and succeeded in striking a few faint notes of prelude, and then she began the first air of her piece "Nos Galan," or "New Year's Night," which every one present knew well.

It sometimes happens that persons, whose minds are agitated by fear, or any other emotion, perform mechanically the music which they have been used to play. This was something of Gwenllean's case. Oppressive timidity and shame almost deprived her of consciousness ; still her fingers ran over the strings without effort, and when the first difficulty of the commencement was mastered, she went from air to air with great effect and perfect correctness. There was not, perhaps, all the soul and fire of genuine genius that she threw into her notes when playing to her mother at home ; but yet they were so exquisitely thrilling, that she was listened to with mute delight and astonishment by all. Nothing like it had been given before. There were those present who had heard Bochsa, and the other celebrated performers of the day, yet whose very souls were entranced by the simple and expressive music of the young girl, who sat trembling before them. Even the oldest harpers leant their heads upon their hands in deep attention, whilst many of them felt their eyes moistened, and their hearts beat

"My Daily Round: A Competition for All Girls Who Work with Their Hands" (Volume 18, 12 December 1896, p. 173).

COMPETITION FOR PROFESSIONAL GIRLS.—THE FIVE PRIZE ESSAYS.*

FIRST PRIZE (£2 2s.).

MY PROFESSIONAL WORK.

WELL! I am a Hospital Nurse, and such a world of meaning is contained in that short sentence, that as I have often said—had I known all I should never have had the courage to begin such a work; but no one *can* know until they themselves have gone through it, and that is why I am going to try and tell you girls a little bit about this profession.

It is no play—far from it! downright hard and earnest work. There *are* those (a shame that it is so!) who dabble in the work, but these never stay long at it, and perhaps best so for all parties concerned, so we will pass quickly over them, and if *you* want to be a nurse, do make up your minds to give up the worship of such gods as "Pleasure" and "Self" and let your high ideal henceforth be —"I was sick and ye visited Me."

Had Charles Kingsley still been with us, I think he would have thought me justified in using his words when I say it is truly the case that we

"Do noble things, not dream them all
        day long,"

though more often than not the "noble things" consist in being very common things after all, but then—"He has learnt to live well who has learnt to do common things uncommonly well."

My first impressions on entering upon my hospital duties were anything but pleasant, in fact if my home had been within walking distance my apprenticeship might have been brief, as it was I had taken good care to go out of my own town. I began work on my twenty-third birthday, and a more wretched day I have seldom spent! Instead of kind looks, and the dear familiar voices wishing me "Many happy returns of the day," I had to pass through the ordeal of being stared at as "the new pro:" and spoken to accordingly. *Now* I look upon it with different eyes, and may I never live to regret the step I took that day.

I said it was hard work for you will rarely find nurses working for less than twelve hours a day, though we do not in consequence "strike" for eight hours like many of our abler brethren! Is it because we work with the motive that all we do shall be for others, and not that we may grasp all we can get for ourselves?

So in hospital we were content to rise at 6 o'clock—no! rather must I say we were *called* at 6 o'clock, for to be honest we did not rise then: I shall not mention the correct time but shall trust to your finding ready excuse for us if our caps *were* rather crooked, and if our beds *were* only "smoothed up"— we were tired nurses! To be in time for 7 o'clock breakfast was compulsory, woe betide the one who appeared after Grace was pronounced by the "Sister" at the head of the table. Breakfast and Prayers over we began the day's routine—Patients' breakfast first and the bed-making then the medicines to be given round, and next the dusting of the wards, and the arranging of plants and flowers etc. in which one and all of us took great pride, and vied with one another as to whose should look best. All this took time, but we were supposed to have finished by 9.30, when the matron went her rounds distributing in each ward the ever welcome letters, though

to read them then was an impossibility for now we were busy with the dressings, the poultices, rubbings and what not; doctors coming and going of course "Just when we did not want them." But 1 o'clock would see us all clear again and serving out our patients' dinners amidst the usual grumbles and thanks. More routine, and then our own dinner, and I noticed we did not climb the stairs quite so easily as we had scrambled down first thing in the morning!

On alternate afternoons it was our luck to be off duty for two hours, and many were the arrangements made at the table as to what we should do, and where we should go. And here let me add that if when entering upon this life we should be willing to give up everything for it, I do not for one moment hold that we should, as it were step outside the world altogether—should give up our music and singing, our bicycling and our visiting— by no means! a girl will find in her time off duty that a run on her "bike," or an hour at the piano, and even a pleasant chat over a cosy cup of afternoon tea will all help to invigorate her, and so she will be more fitted for her evening's work, than if e.g. she had gone to her *bed*—a practice of which our wise matron highly disapproved. So *my* advice is to go on with such innocent pleasure, but just so long as you do not give it the first place in your life, tho' to do so at times is a temptation, and no very small one either, and often when I hear of others going to every concert, attending theatres and dances, well, then like the little boy in the old old poem—

"... I can't forget that I'm bereft
    Of all the pleasant sights they see."

but since they never were "promised me" I just make up my mind to submit and not to be "dull."

So the afternoon would find only half the staff on duty. During the first hour as a rule we would have nothing very special to do, though it varied: on admission days I have gone to my ward to find several new patients waiting, and if women or children this meant a good deal—if men the warders attended to them. Oh! those women! I remember one who insisted she had had a bath only that very morning. I said it mattered not for all were treated alike, unless their temperatures were much above normal, or for some other equally good reason. Poor thing! her scare upon reaching the bath was pitiable, and in her wild despair she let the cat out of the bag for alas! she had never seen such a thing before! Once in bed, and fully alive to the fact that for *this* time, at least, her life had been spared, and she had not been "drownded," she looked much happier with her now clean face, tidy hair and the orthodox red-flannel "Nightingale" across her shoulders.

At other times "urgent cases" would arrive, or an accident. Now we each had our turn for receiving these, so during our respective weeks we had always to have a bed ready in case of emergency—What lessons to be learnt by the side of some terribly mangled form, sometimes beyond human aid, and sometimes, indeed, where life was altogether extinct! Truly, "In the midst of life we are in death."

So time rarely hung heavily upon our hands, and at 4.30 the big bell would sound when we knew we might go to the kitchen for our patients' teas. By 5 o'clock we were

generally ready for ours, and needed not many little delicacies to tempt our appetites—plain bread and butter sufficed! In the evenings, besides attending to our patients, we would water our plants, tidy the lockers, (and what treasures we would find concealed therein!) and cupboards etc. for in a hospital everything must be kept as neat as a new pin; our matron would look sorely displeased if on opening a linen cupboard for visitors' inspection, she found it not up to the mark!

In the children's wards, where several nurses worked it was so arranged that every one got alternate evenings off duty, but when with the adults it depended upon our work, as to when we could get free. Sundays I confess I never liked, and would fain have taken my seat in the pew at the old church at home: the routine was similar as on other days. We got to church once a day and Evening Service was held in our chapel for all patients able to attend. And so, in spite of long hours and tired feet how short the weeks seemed, and sped past in a remarkable manner, carrying us on to Christmas and Christmas festivities, which all meant extra labour if extra pleasure. The holly to put up, the texts to choose and illuminate, and still the daily work to be got through. What wonder if our friends looked in vain for letters that week! It was at such times as these that those nurses who could play or sing were in great demand. Oh! the pleasure in getting up the "Patients' Concert"—the excitement in choosing the glees, tho' at times the weariness in singing them! I smile to think of one night when we all gave it up as a dead failure, each found fault with her neighbour for being "flat," till at length we all joined in a hearty laugh and agreed *in totum* that "Operation Day" was the wrong day on which to have a practice. So we crawled off to our beds and hoped for better success the next night!

So the time of training passed by, and though ill health will at times prevail dominant, and it was only with a struggle that I got through the last few months, yet it has not been without a feeling of regret that I have turned over the leaf to begin a fresh chapter and have joined the Private Staff, still you see in the same great work—that of nursing the sick, and still do I call myself a "Hospital Nurse," and very proud am I to hold forth my three years' certificate as testimony. But now I almost tremble to think of how Xmas will this year dawn for me, for the Private Nurse is on very different footing, often only appreciated because necessary, and after all that is not the most comfortable feeling for the poor "Necessity"! But here again the great Ideal of a nurse's life is to do for others, so I must bury such selfish thoughts, and instead shall begin to wonder what I may do in order to brighten that Day for the sick one whose lot it may be to be cast under my care, so that at night I may lay down my efforts as a birthday gift worthy for the Great Master to accept, and my Christmas will have been bright indeed, if my lot it has been to have heard His kind voice saying, "Well done! good and faithful servant,"— "She hath done what she could!"

I declare the statements in this paper to be true.

AGNES EUGENIE SMITH,
            Nursing Institute,
December, 23rd 1896.   Sunderland.

---

* *These essays are printed without correction or alteration of any kind.*—ED.

SECOND PRIZE (£1 1s.).

MY PROFESSIONAL WORK.

FOR some time back I have been engaged in Folk-Lore collecting. To me it has become most interesting, as well as being a means of making me so far independent of circumstances.

I. How I began my profession.

Having a good deal of time on hand, and seeing many things I would like to get with a little extra money; if I could only earn it at home, I began to wish I had something to do, that would be interesting, and profitable. I had learned no trade, or profession, and as my home is in an out of the way part of the country, home employment was difficult to get. Well, I was in this frame of mind about three years ago, when a person asked me if I would care to do some Folk-Lore collecting.

I asked about the terms, and the work, and whether he thought I could undertake to collect information on a subject with which I was practically unacquainted. Receiving encouragement from my friend, and making myself so far acquainted with what was wanted, and the terms offered for such work, I resolved to make a start. Although I confess I had little expectation of being successful. Indeed it was two months after that, before I summoned courage to send off my first collection of Lore; which I may say here, was a very meagre production.

II. My method.

At first I had no method. I simply talked to people about old times, who told me many stories of such things as constitute subjects of enquiry by Folk Lorists. These stories I wrote on scraps of paper in the first instance, and then when I had time, I transferred them to my collecting sheets. The penciled scraps I burnt. As time went on however, I found that I would need to take note of what I was sending, as well as what I had on hand, otherwise, I would be in danger of repeating myself. I therefore decided on the following plan. I bought some large minute books; these I paged, and indexed, and I also provided myself with a few small note books, and pencils which I gave to some of my young friends whose help I solicited, keeping one for my own use. I then took note of every item of information I could get on anything bearing on the subject in hand, and if a story, a rhyme, a legend, a riddle, or anything else was incomplete, I told my young friends, and we all did our level best to get it completed. From the note books the information was

transferred to the large minute books, with the headings written with red ink, and the page entered in the indextable This enabled me, when filling up my sheets, instead of filling them up with all sorts of scrappy information, as I had been doing at first to fill them up page after page with one, subject. It had the further advantage of giving far less trouble to the receiver, for at a glance he could see how much information he had under each heading. My sheets I paged, and joined together at the left hand corner. I numbered each item of information given in them, and where the reciters name was not to appear, I marked the top of the page with red ink. While to keep me right as to matter already sent off, I drew a blue pencil line through every page of the big book, so soon as the matter had been transferred to the sheets, as well as marking off the corresponding page in the index.

I have said nothing so far, as to the manner of dealing with those from whom information is to be got. At first I thought women would be much better versed in Folk Lore, and much more communicative than men. In that I soon found out I was mistaken. Men I found to be much more willing to tell what they knew, and they really seemed to know more. With either sex however, a F.L. collector need not expect to succeed unless she herself is interested in the subject, and has something in common with the reciter. There is no use going to a house and proceeding to pump the inmates right off. This would simply have the effect of freezing them up. The only way to succeed is to go in when you are invited; to be pleasant, kindly, and polite, and to converse with those from whom you expect to get information, as you would converse with your most intimate friend. Another thing that chokes the spring, is the presence of a note book. And this brings me to the difficulties.

III. The Difficulties of my profession.

My residence being in the Highlands, it was a great drawback to me that I knew so little of Gaelic. I could understand that language pretty well, but could hardly converse in it, and as for writing it, I could do absolutely nothing. In these circumstances, my work at the commencement of it was very much up hill. I could not use a note book in presence of my informants, for I found out from experience that if I did, it would interfere with the freedom of the conversation. My plan was to get things repeated over, and over

again, until they got fixed in the memory, after which, I took the first opportunity, to commit to my note book such information as I had obtained. The Gaelic I wrote phonetically, pending an opportunity of getting assistance from some qualified friend to have it reduced to proper form, after which I transcribed it into my large collecting Book. It will be seen that this at least was a slow process, and many a time I found that I had forgotten important points of my information, and had in these cases to go back to my informant to have it repeated, and this I had even to do in many cases, two and three times over. Such experience soon convinced me, that if I was to have any pleasure in my work, or success; I must face the learning of Gaelic, I therefore made a commencement with the result that I can now speak it wonderfully well, and am besides able to do a good deal in the way of writing it. And now I am able to tell something of my encouragements.

IV. My Encouragements.

First among my encouragements is, that I have been giving entire satisfaction, and instead of the fee at first offered, I have all along got two thirds more, and consequently I make a fair salary. Then my gaelic has improved so much that it is a great pleasure fore me to hear a story in that language, and I have seldom now to search my dictionary for any word I hear. Folk-Lore is a wide subject, and the Study of it is most educative; so that to my profession I am indebted for a great deal of my culture, and general information, as well as the ability to put my thoughts in writing. It has also shown me my ignorance. Before I began collecting I was inclined to think that book learning was the only kind of learning under the sun. Now I know that there are people who may not be able to read a line, who nevertheless have their minds stored with most useful information. They know plants, and their uses; they know the names of stars, when, and where they rise, and when, and where they set; they know how to extract dye from plants, and even from the scurff of stones, and can tell far more of how our forefathers lived than can many who profess to have studied history. All the same I think it would add much to the pleasure, and profit of my Highland friends, if they had a Gaelic G.O.P.

I declare the statements in this paper to be true.

"ST. JOHN'S WORT"
Portcharlotte.

THIRD PRIZE (£1 1s.).

MY PROFESSIONAL WORK.

I AM a musician, a sort of local celebrity in a small way, having at nineteen years of age been chosen out of ten candidates for the post of organist of a church. Before that I had been assistant-organist at the largest church in the district. Since then I have been able to spend four years at the Royal Academy of Music, where I was moderately successful as a student. I left with silver and bronze medals, and what is better, the highest award of the Academy, the Certificate of Merit. I have also gained the medal of the Society of Arts, and the gold medal of the London Academy of Music entitling me to put L.A.M. after my name, which I never do.

So much for my credentials. Now for my work. When I left the Academy I hoped to

do something as a singer, but I found that I could not get enough engagements. There are so many girls who want to be singers: it looks such a very grand thing from the outside. I fear I have not the requisite "push." But however that may be, I took the work that lay nearest and began to teach. Now it happens that the music-teaching profession is also very overcrowded. There are quite a large number of teachers within a stone's-throw of where I live. Then too we are near London, and people have a great idea of going to town for lessons. All this makes it difficult to get pupils, and also keeps fees low. Unfortunately the public does not discriminate at all between good and bad music-teachers. In the scholastic profession it is quite different; the standard is very high, and so it ought to be: but in ours, nobody seems to care whether

you know anything or not, so long as you do not charge much. The true evil is that there are a lot of bogus degrees and worthless certificates obtainable in music, and that girls rush into teaching directly they have got a certificate from anywhere and of any grade. This is a sore point with every qualified musician so I hope I may be excused the writing so much upon it. When people advertise to teach for sixpence an hour, and get pupils, there is something wrong somewhere.

My terms are two guineas for twenty-five half-hour lessons. I do not think this is at all good pay, but I frequently have to take less because if I do not I lose the pupil. I am not at all sure that it is right, but what else can one do? As a matter of fact not one of my pupils pays me my full fees. Recently a lady sent for me and offered me fifteen shillings instead of my two guineas! " That is all Miss So-and-so charges!" she said. I was aghast, but seeing I should get little it any more I said I would take her little boy for a guinea as a great favour and since he was one of my choir-boys. She held out for a long time, haggling and haggling, and I do not quite know whether to be ashamed or proud to say that I held out too, but at last she said, " Let us split the difference, Miss Pimpernel. Take seventeen-&-six."

That is the sort of thing one meets in the music profession.

As for the work, nothing can be more delightful. The hours are very irregular, because I must suit my pupils' convenience, & some of them must come at a certain time or not at all. Many of my lessons are given in the evening, and I am sorry for that, but in this district many people are engaged all day & have only the evening free. On Mondays I have little to do : two lessons, I think. On Tuesdays two lessons in the day, and lessons from six till nine in the evening. Until lately I then went out to give a lesson at half-past nine to a girl who is in a shop and cannot get home till then ; but I gave that up as I did not get home till half-past ten, & in winter I found it very trying. On Wednesdays I have a pupil at two, then I rush off as a rule to an afternoon orchestral concert given here in the winter : home to tea, then out to give two lessons from six till seven, then off to church. Service is at half-past seven. Only the boys of the choir attend that, and as we sit in the gallery out of sight, it is all I can do to keep them in order & attend to my own work as well. At half-past eight the rest of the choir comes in and we practise for an hour at least, frequently more. I play and conduct as well. It is quite easy to me now to detect faults in the singing although I am accompanying all the while, and of course I have to stop and correct them. After practice I have to write down the numbers of the hymns for the next Sunday, and give the paper to the verger for the hymn-boards. Also I must make a copy for myself, with the numbers of chants &

everything else for the service-lists. Then I have to see that the books and music are gathered up and the place left tidy. I get home between ten and half-past.

Thursday is rather an off-day with me as far as teaching goes. I usually go to London to the house of an eminent professor of singing who very kindly invites a few young teachers and students to come and discuss with him & each other the difficulties which arise in our work. It is wonderfully good of him, but he says he learns as much as we do.

On Friday I have five lessons to give, and I often have the younger boys of the choir, new ones especially, come to me for an hour for a little extra teaching. I do not do this every week, neither am I expected to do it at all, but I think it is a good thing. Choir-boys want no end of attention : indeed some organists say that you cannot make them really efficient unless there is a daily service at their church.

On Saturday mornings I begin at nine o'clock with a girl who teaches in a school all the week. She takes both pianoforte and singing lessons, and is now preparing for the Trinity College Senior Local. At the end of her hour, two little boys arrive, twins of nine years old. They are darling little fellows : both learn pianoforte, and they are also being trained for a church choir. They enjoy their lessons thoroughly and consider me their especial property. On Sundays they come to church with their parents and are very delighted if they can make me smile from my perch at the organ. After them comes the boy whose mother " split the difference," and then my head choir-boy for his singing-lesson. I give him one lesson a week for nothing, because he is a good boy and quick to learn. At two o'clock I begin again with another piano-lesson, and so on till half-past three. Then I usually write the service-lists for next day, and then I am free till five o'clock. After tea I hurry away to church for the boys' practice, which lasts until eight o'clock. We go through the next day's psalms and hymns, as well as any anthem or " service " which we have in preparation, & I usually manage, even if there is ever so much to be done, to give them a few minutes talk about

keys, time, how to produce their voices, how to manage the breath or say the words. I often think that the shorter this little interpolated lesson, is the better they remember it.

Then comes Sunday. There are only two services for me, at eleven and at half-past six. The afternoon service is merely hymns, and a young man in the Sunday-school expects & likes to play, so he is quite welcome to do so. Our services are not very ornate, since it is a Low Church, but I find quite enough to do in preparing the choir for them. We have ten boys and eight men in the choir. By the way, we sometimes use a hymn-tune of my own, & some of my chants are quite favourites. I have a nice little organ by Robson, recently renovated. It has nine stops on the great & room for a trumpet, six on the swell & room for an oboe, one pedal stop, three couplers & three composition pedals. I have given recitals for charities, got the church full & good press notices. My salary is twenty-five pounds. No extras except an occasional wedding, when as a rule the interested persons object to pay me anything, but go off & ask somebody to play —on my organ—who will do it for nothing.

Of course I get concert engagements, but the same thing is found. Cheap people can be got, so I must be cheap too. I am quite commonly offered half-a-guinea. Country engagements pay better. An oratorio engagement in the West of England last month brought me £2. 10. 0, but the expenses ran away with most of it. These are cut-throat days, and one must take what one can get. Last year I gave a Vocal Recital. Everybody called it an artistic success, but I only made about thirty shillings. However I was lucky not to lose on the venture.

Nevertheless, in spite of my grumbling I know I have a good deal to be glad about. In 1896 I made between seventy and eighty pounds, and there are many girls who work far harder for far less.

I declare the statements in this paper to be true.

" PIMPERNEL."

5th January 1897. Plumstead.

FOURTH PRIZE (£1 1s.).

I EARN my living with pen & brains ; my sister works in the same office (a publisher's), and we two have a little room all to ourselves ; it is a very ugly little room, & not very tidy, I fear : paper is dreadful stuff for getting scattered about ; when I screw up useless sheets, I always aim at throwing them into the waste paper basket, which stands by my desk, but somehow or other I but rarely succeed. On one side of our room is a large window, where my desk stands ; the window commands a not very extensive view of dirty roofs, but above them is always the sky—at which I gaze when in search of ideas. Another side of the room is almost entirely occupied by a sofa, which, even if it were not usually piled up with papers & books, would hardly be conducive to repose, for it is a very hard & uncomfortable piece of furniture ; by this sofa, in true foreign fashion, stands a table, at which my sister works, & where I work too, when I require plenty of room ; on the opposite side of the apartment is a gas-fire (horrid thing : I would far rather have a coal fire !), & in the corner a cupboard & book case combined ; against the fourth wall of the room are just three chairs which, like the sofa, are generally piled up with books & periodicals. In one corner is a typewriter on a small stand. On the walls hang a few coloured fashion-plates, a thermometer, sundry notes & reference lists, pinned up at random, a portrait of the Duke & Duchess of York, an almanac &

a picture of four chickens & three frogs playing tug of war with a poor unfortunate worm ; over the mantel-shelf hangs a card upon which is printed : ' My Work is for the King ' : that card sometimes calls me to account when I am wasting my time.

So much for our room ; on the same floor with us is a large room where four girls work at patterns, & next to that is a dining-room for those of the girls who do not go home to dinner. We are on the first floor ; below us is the shop, two offices, & a room where two more people work at patterns. Downstairs is the machine room, where 3 men work at cutting out paper patterns, packing etc. On the 2nd floor of the house is the care-taker's sitting-room, where my sister & I take our meals ; also a kitchen. On the 3rd floor are 2 bedrooms belonging to the care-taker, a store-room for books, patterns etc. & a large workroom where several girls work at patterns —cutting, stamping & folding them. On the 4th & last floor is another, still larger workroom, where a good many girls work ; I do not exactly know how many. These workrooms are all reached by a back stair-case. The three ladies who do the bulk of the editing work, do not come up to the office, except occasionally : they send their work on by post.

At home we breakfast at 8, & a few minutes after 9, my sister & I go off to business ; we have a good long omnibus ride before we get

there, but I enjoy that ; we always ride outside, so as to get as much fresh air as possible ; besides, when we ride outside, we are not tempted to read & so spoil our eyes & make ourselves sleepy. I find it exceedingly interesting to look at all that passes ; to watch how cleverly the driver dodges between all the vehicles on the road ; & to note familiar faces. At 10-o-clock we start work : my sister does various odd jobs—if I may use so inelegant an expression ; my work is to write descriptions of dresses & other garments for five monthly fashion magazines ; that is my chief work ; some of the descriptions I translate from the French ; some I write by looking at the illustrations ; but of most I have the patterns given me, which I open out separately on the table, & write from those, aided by notes & explanations which accompany each pattern. I also have to write descriptions to send abroad—lists of such being sent up to me as pleasant little surprises now & again : most often when I am very busy, seems to me. Another branch of my work is to read & correct the proofs of the magazines, before the latter are printed off ; this needs careful attention to every detail, as the printers make very funny mistakes sometimes. I also have to read all French & German papers that are sent up to me, & translate anything that I consider worth translating ; occasionally, too, I have French or German letters sent up to me to translate & answer. Sometimes I find

---

"Competition for Professional Girls: The Five Prize Essays" (Volume 18, 27 March 1897, p. 414).

myself with nothing particular to do; then I employ my time in writing stories & things that come into my head; if these be worth anything, I get paid for them, which is nice for me; my regular pay is £1 a week, but more has been promised me in the near future. We work from 10-o-clock till 1-o-clock, that is, my sister & I do; at 1-o-clock we go upstairs, where we find a hot lunch awaiting us; I generally spend the luncheon hour in reading a book or the newspaper; then at 2-o-clock we recommence work, and keep at it till 4-o-clock, when we lock up & go home —arriving there in time for tea. After tea we of course do as we please; our evenings are always pleasant, & home is all the more appreciated after a day at the dingy office— for it is dingy: there is no denying the fact. On Fridays, we do not get home until about 7 or 8-o-clock, but we do not mind that, as we have a whole holiday on Saturdays. Every Tuesday evening we have a sewing-party

(which consists of six members), from 5.30 to 7.30; why I mention this is because I wish some more girls would do the same; very likely there are many who would, if once the idea were put into their heads. We get from our clergyman the address of some poor woman who has a family to provide for; then, somewhere about October, two of us go and visit the woman, and ask permission to make clothes for her children; these we work at every Tuesday evening; when we have made one garment for each child, we take them round, & perhaps a cake or something as well; then we go on to make them something else each; we make for each child two sets of underclothes and one dress; then we leave them & go on to another family. Worked thus, I think a sewing-society is very interesting. So far, we have only been able to manage one family a year, as we stop work in the Summer; but every little helps. If all the girls who could, would !

Of course I occasionally find things to grumble at. For one thing, it is rather a bother getting up to business and going home again, when the weather is bad. It also annoys me that I cannot get my work regularly: sometimes I have ever so much to do in a very short space of time, and sometimes I have very little to do; sometimes I get through a whole day without having done anything in particular; and then, just when we are thinking of going home, something is sent up for me to do at once. Then again, it is very vexing when, through no fault of my own, I have to do the same work twice over, as sometimes happens. But there, we cannot have everything just how we like it; and these are, after all, but very minor troubles.

I declare this all to be perfectly true.

"CAULIFLOWER."
Church Road,
Jan 4th, 1897   Brixton Hill.

FIFTH PRIZE (£1 1s.).

MY PROFESSIONAL WORK.

WHEN I was fifteen I made up my mind to earn my own living: so I went to my father and said—

"Father, I want some work to do."

He smiled at me encouragingly.

"Find some," he said.

After that I went about for days turning things over and over in my mind. The result was a letter, written in my neatest style, to the village postmistress. This letter took me some hours to indite, but was very satisfactory in its result, for the answer arrived promptly by return.

My delight when it was given to me was unbounded. It was the first step toward the end I meant to achieve. I can remember the words it contained to this day—

"In answer to Miss P—'s letter, the postmistress wishes to state that she will undertake to teach all post-office duties, and telegraph instrument, for a fee of £4. 4. 0."

I carried this precious document to my father. He read it, silently laid upon it four bright sovereigns, and four shillings, then passed it back to me.

I squeezed his hand affectionately, and went away.

Those four guineas were a perfect mine of wealth in my eyes, and indeed they must have seemed almost as important to my father, for times were very hard then, and there were so many hungry mouths to fill. I was old enough to understand a little of the look of care that rested upon my mother's brow, and the money seemed to put a dreadful responsibility upon me. What if I were to fail, and so waste it all! I determined to try so hard, and all the way—as I walked to the office, with my little purse clasped tightly in my hand, for my first lesson—I was asking God, in my heart, to help me in my self-chosen career.

I was to have two hours tuition a day, and after the first week the strangeness had considerably worn off, and I found myself getting used to the duties. I remember how pleased I was, because, when I arrived exactly at 10

one morning, my teacher said "she needed no timepiece with such a punctual pupil." That was the character my father had earned. I wanted to copy him.

Of course there were difficulties to be overcome. The dots and dashes of the telegraph instrument were very bewildering, and the different rules for everything—Registered letters and parcel-post and a thousand other things puzzled me exceedingly; but I laboured —(I had almost written *manfully*) on.

In those days I slept with a penny edition of the post-office handbook under my pillow, that I might have it in readiness to study the first thing on waking, in the quiet time before the children were up. Looking back upon them now those short three months seem very bright ones, for long ere they ended my work grew full of interest to me.

I was quite sorry to leave the office, and really begin alone, although it was something delightful to bring home my first earnings. I proudly gave the money to my father. I meant to pay my four guinea debt—for it was a real debt to my thinking—as quickly as I could.

After that the way became comparatively easy. I took several holiday engagements in the country, and greatly enjoyed the novelty of seeing fresh people and places. I can safely add that I never met with anything but the greatest kindness and consideration in all my wanderings, being always treated more as a child of the home than a hired assistant.

I would like to tell you a little about my present situation, because among so many girls in business who have real grievances, it is nice, I think, to hear of those whose lines have fallen in pleasant places.

This is a small London sub office. I always thought I should hate London. Maybe it was my country up-bringing that led me to expect to find everybody in the great City rogues and "sharpers." It was not without a feeling of dread that I first took my place behind the counter here. Here—where day by day I meet with honest hearts and true as ever country villages produced, where, amid

the busy stream of men and women who hurry into the office for letter stamps, on their way to the city, in the morning, scarcely one is too busy or self-occupied to wish a pleasant "Good-day," or make some kind courteous remark, before they mingle with, and are lost in the never ending procession of toilers for daily bread. I often laugh heartily over the comical questions people put, and the strange ideas they hold. Once a lady, very aged and feeble, came to deposit the savings of her lifetime. When I gave her a bank-book with the amount entered, she looked earnestly into my face and said, "I am pleased to lend you the money, my dear, and I hope God will bless it to you."

Such confidence was certainly pleasant.

One dear old gentleman never comes to draw his monthly allowance without bringing me a nose-gay from his own tiny garden-plot, or in the winter-time from some precious indoor plant, and one hot afternoon a great basket of strawberries came. Everybody down to the smallest telegraph boy remembers what a delicious feast they were.

The hours are long. On duty from 8 A.M. to 8 P.M. without only about 15 minutes for each meal, but by the kindness of my employer I get half an hour's rest after dinner, in which time I do all my odd jobs of mending and brushing my clothes. I have to keep the accounts, and see that everything runs smoothly in the office, but I do all in my own way, and just as, and when I like. My salary is only a pound a week, but I have Sunday quite free, beside one evening. At 8 P.M. sharp I close the office, and, as I am engaged, and hope to be married before so very very many months are over, I spend the rest of my leisure time in making pretty things to adorn, what to me, at least, will I am sure be, the most wondrously beautiful little home in the whole world.

I declare the statements in this paper to be true.

"DANDELION,"
Southgate Road,
Islington, N.

"Competition for Professional Girls: The Five Prize Essays" (Volume 18, 27 March 1897, p. 415).

in disguise, for by exercising a little imagination you can make the story end as you like, and spare yourself the pain of disappointment. I rarely read a book without reflecting how much better I could have finished it myself," remarked the young lady with an assurance which evoked a smile on the officer's impassive countenance.

"You don't look much like an authoress," he said, surveying the dainty little figure approvingly, and calling up a mental picture of the spectacled and cadaverous female invariably associated with a literary career in the masculine mind. "I am afraid my imagination will hardly stand such a strain; but books are the only refuge for the destitute on a voyage, especially during the first few days, when you find yourself shut up with a herd of strangers whom you have never met before in the course of your life. There is only one thing to do under the circumstances, and that is to lie low, and speak to no one until you have found your bearings and discovered who is who. If you go about talking to strangers, you can never tell in what sort of a set you may land yourself."

"You can't, indeed! It's appalling to think of!" agreed the young lady, with a dramatic gesture of dismay which brought her little ringed hands together in emphatic emphasis. "For my own part I get on well enough," she proceeded, contradicting herself with unruffled composure, "for I can find something interesting in all of my fellow-creatures; but I feel it for my maid. The couriers and valets are so *very* exclusive that she has been snubbed more than once because of our inferior station. Naturally she feels it keenly. I observe that those people are most sensitive about their position who have the least claim to distinction; but as she does my hair better than anyone else, and is an admirable dressmaker, I am, of course, anxious to keep her happy."

The big man looked down with a suspicious glance. Through his not very keen sensibilities there had penetrated the suspicion that the small person in the white frock was daring to smile at him and amuse herself at his expense; but his suspicion died at once before the glance of infantile sweetness which met his own. Pretty little thing! there was something marvellously taking in her appearance. For one moment, as she had spoken of inferior station, he had had an uneasy fear lest he had made the acquaintance of some vulgar upstart, with whom he could not possibly associate. But no! If ever the signs of race and breeding were distinguishable in personal appearance, they were so in the case of the girl before

him. A glance at the head in its graceful setting, the delicate features, the dainty hands and feet were sufficient to settle the question in the mind of a man who prided himself on being an adept in such matters. To his own surprise he found himself floundering through a complimentary denial of her own estimate of herself, and being rescued from a breakdown by a gracious acknowledgment.

"Praise," murmured the young lady sweetly—"praise from Major Darcy is praise indeed! When 'Haughty Hector' deigns to approve——"

The big man jumped as if he had been shot, and turned a flushed, excited face upon her.

"Wh-at?" he gasped. "What do you say? You know me—you know my old home name! Who are you then? Who can you be?"

The girl rose to her feet and stood before him. The top of her smooth little head barely reached his shoulder; but she held herself with an air of dignity which gave an appearance of far greater height. For one long minute they stared at one another in silence; then she stretched out her hand and laid it frankly in his own.

"Why, I'm Peggy!" she cried. "Don't you remember me? I'm Peggy Saville!"

(To be continued.)

PHARMACY AS AN EMPLOYMENT FOR GIRLS.

THE employment of girls as dispensers becoming much more general both in hospitals and pharmacies, a few words on the subject may be useful to any who seriously contemplate adopting the occupation. In the first place, only girls of education, of average health, and who can afford to give the necessary expenditure of time and money should take up the profession of pharmacy. Lack of means at the onset has caused many girls to give up the occupation who otherwise were well adapted to a pharmaceutical career, for, unless a girl intends learning pharmacy thoroughly, taking the qualifying examination, it is unwise to enter the calling at all; because not only can the unqualified command but very low salaries, even if they obtain appointments at all, but it is positively dangerous to the public that any but experienced persons should dispense medicines.

The necessary requirements being forthcoming, a girl should turn her attention to the examinations required to be passed. Two only are essential. First, the preliminary examination of the Pharmaceutical Society, which is held four times in the year, and at the present time comprises three subjects, Latin, English, and Arithmetic (including Metric System); fee, two guineas. This examination can be worked

up alone now by any girl of average ability, but after August, 1900, will be more stringent, having the addition of Euclid, Algebra, and one modern foreign language.

Various other examinations, such as the Matriculation or Cambridge (with Latin), exempt from it, a list of which can be obtained from the Secretary of the Pharmaceutical Society, 17, Bloomsbury Square, W.C. It is distinctly advisable to pass the preliminary or its substitute before commencing apprenticeship; frequently a pupil is not accepted until this examination is passed, and under any circumstances to revert to school subjects after having commenced other studies is a great hindrance. The other essential examination is the minor or qualifying examination, which carries with it the title of "Chemist and Druggist," and admits to membership of the Pharmaceutical Society. This examination is held four times in the year; fee, five guineas (after August, 1900, ten guineas). To be admitted, candidates must have attained the age of twenty-one, and, besides having passed the preliminary or its equivalent, must furnish a form proving having been engaged three years in practical dispensing either with a registered chemist, a medical practitioner, or in the dispensary of some institution. The subjects comprise pharmacy (practical and theoretical), chemistry (practical and theoretical), materia medica, botany (including microscopy), and physics.

It is usually necessary to attend classes at some school of pharmacy. The society's school at Bloomsbury is generally recognised to give the most advanced teaching, and requires for a full course nine months' attendance; fee, thirty guineas, exclusive of books and apparatus. Girls who have worked diligently during the three years' apprenticeship,

and who have attended classes in chemistry and botany at a science school, do not always require quite so long a period of study, and frequently six months has been found to be sufficient. Very many other pharmaceutical schools, both London and provincial, receive lady pupils for long or short periods of study, the fees averaging ten guineas for three months' full time course. This qualification having been obtained enables anyone to be mistress of her own pharmacy, or to act as manager or assistant to a chemist, as head of a dispensary, and various other positions connected with chemistry and pharmacy, this being the legal qualification both to dispense and sell poisons.

These two above-mentioned examinations are necessary to be passed by every pharmacist; but two other examinations it is sometimes desirable to pass, though not essential:—

I. The major examination, which is the highest qualification obtainable in pharmacy, to pass which is a desideratum to any girl who eventually intends owning a pharmacy, and carries with it the title of "Pharmaceutical Chemist"; fee, three guineas; subjects, advanced chemistry and physics, botany and materia medica.

II. The assistants' examination of the Apothecaries' Society. Much confusion appears to exist respecting this examination, which it may be well to state has no connection with the pharmaceutical examinations. It is held four times in the year at the Apothecaries' Hall, Blackfriars, E.C.; fee, three guineas. This examination carries with it no title, nor does it qualify to sell poisons, but only to act as assistant in the compounding and dispensing of medicines.

The subjects comprise pharmacy (practical and theoretical), theoretical chemistry, and a slight knowledge of materia medica; fee, three

---

R. Kathleen Spencer, "Pharmacy as an Employment for Girls" (Volume 21, 14 October 1899, p. 19).

guineas. Very many girls take this examination on account of its not being so stringent as the minor, therefore not requiring so long a period of study, nor necessitating a three years' apprenticeship as with the latter; but, unfortunately, very many are content to remain with this qualification only, instead of using it as a stepping-stone to the minor. This qualification is, however, accepted by many of the smaller provincial hospitals, by some doctors, and is necessary to be admitted as a pupil in one of our largest provincial hospitals; but with this one exception it is advisable to have twelve or eighteen months' experience in practical pharmacy before attempting to obtain this qualification, since it is a very mistaken idea some girls hold that, after a few months' study at a pharmacy school to enable them to pass this examination, they can, without any real practical experience, obtain appointments. If they do so, by their inexperience they bring the whole question of the employment of ladies in pharmacy into disrepute.

It is then very essential to obtain practical experience, either by serving a pupilage of twelve or eighteen months in the dispensary of an institution, the fee for which averages about ten guineas, or by apprenticeship to a chemist : this latter course is the better one unless desiring a hospital career. A few ladies having pharmacies of their own receive pupils ; doubtless the number of these former will be augmented in a few years. Also, some gentlemen take lady apprentices ; the fee for a three years' apprenticeship to a chemist varies greatly according to the amount of instruction given, etc. Now for a few remarks concerning appointments available after qualification.

Hospital Appointments.—Very many of these are open to female dispensers ; and it speaks well for lady dispensers that those hospitals once opened to women invariably appoint a lady on any successive vacancy occurring. The larger institutions require the minor qualification, salaries varying from forty pounds to eighty pounds indoors and from sixty pounds to one hundred and fifty pounds outdoors. In smaller hospitals, for which the apothecaries' qualification is sometimes considered sufficient, the remuneration seldom exceeds fifty pounds outdoors.

Doctors' Dispensers.—These appointments, very many of which are open to ladies, are often the most sought after, in spite of the fact that the remuneration is usually not great. Some medical men require the minor qualification ; by others the Apothecaries' Hall certificate is accepted.

Wholesale Chemists.—A few openings present themselves in the laboratories for lady pharmacists ; also, ladies are employed in superintending female labour in the packing of drugs, perfumery, etc. : these posts are often very lucrative ; where poisons are concerned, qualification is essential, otherwise it is not so, though preferred, and these engagements usually leave the evening at one's own disposal, and afford a good opportunity for study.

Lastly, in chemists' shops, either as mistress of their own pharmacy—suitable for those possessed of business capabilities and capital— or as manager or assistant to a pharmacist. But few ladies hold either of the two latter positions : those who do, find the work congenial and fairly remunerative, and being usually well received by the public. This field is likely to further open up for really experienced women.

R. KATHLEEN SPENCER.

THE PICTURE POST-CARD CRAZE.

HINTS TO COLLECTORS.

By DORA DE BLAQUIÈRE.

PART II.

THE page of forty-three picture postcards comprises some from both England and the East, the Continent of Europe and America, and opens with one of the most lovely views in Europe, that of Chillon, as seen from Territet, with the Dent du Midi and its seven heads, as a background. On the right, too, we see one of those beautiful boats with their picturesque sails, which make a complete picture of themselves, even without their background of snowy peaks.

We have not many examples of portraiture amongst our cards, so we are naturally pleased to have the two (9 and 11) with the portraits on them, respectively of Longfellow and Lord Byron, with their several homes in the background, *i.e.*, the house at Concord and Newstead Abbey. These two form part of a set of Eminent-Writer cards, in colours ; and which comprise Dickens, Shakespeare, Tennyson, Scott, and Burns. The card between (10) is a Jubilee commemoration of 1897, a pretty, though rather garish card, with very gay colouring, and much gilding about it, and portraits of the Queen, and the Prince and Princess of Wales.

Damascus is the next (12) example, and I hope you will see that there is a cab-stand in the great square, a fact which is commented upon at once by everyone, because they have no idea that Damascus is so civilised. The sole legend imprinted on this by the sender is "Broiling," and the date was last April. Number 13 is a coloured card from Jerusalem, and represents the Jews' Wailing-place—of which you have often heard—beneath the great Wall of the Temple. This was posted at Jerusalem, and purchased there. The next three (14, 15, 16), are respectively Brighton, and the Pavilion, Guernsey, St. Peter's Port, and Oban ; all of them are specimens of the cheap printed card, this being the earliest form of card which usually appears, to be succeeded by something better later on. The next card (17) perhaps you will recognise at once as the large basin-fountain in the Pincian Gardens, under the trees. In the distance St. Peter's is seen and the Vatican. This card, like 38, the other Roman, is a collotype. The latter represents the Forum, at the back of the Capitol ; showing the whole length of the Via Sacra to the Arch of Titus, and the Colosseum in the distance. At the extreme left are the three columns of the Temple of Peace ; then comes the Arch of Septimus Severus, and then, in the centre, the range of columns of the Temple of Vespasian.

Flying over the waters to Washington (18) we reach the New World, and see on the card the Capitol, which is the most celebrated and beautiful building in America. Next to this comes (19) a view of the gardens at Baden, and then comes (20) a view of the Houses of Parliament from the Thames by moonlight, on blue-toned paper. The next (21) is more interesting, as it gives us a glimpse at Innsbruck, the capital of the Tyrol, and two of its castles, Weyerburg and Schloss Ambras. The first is associated with the Emperor Maximilian I., who lived there. Both are inhabited and are in excellent condition. Two cards (22 and 28) represent Baltimore, the capital of Maryland, one of the finest of American cities. The card shows the entrance gates of the celebrated Greenmount Cemetery, and the richly-endowed Johns Hopkins University and Hospital. In (28) we see the Battle Monument, one of those which give to Baltimore its soubriquet of "Monumental City." Baltimore derives its name from Cecil Calvert, the second Lord Baltimore. The original Baltimore is a tiny village, near Skibbereen, co. Cork, in Ireland. Baltimore received a million dollars from the famous George Peabody, and built a fine institute with it. This is also shown on the card.

Niagara Falls (23) is the next picture, a general view of it, showing the Canadian shore part of the rapids, and, lower down, the Canadian Fall only. These views are taken in summer. The Norwegian (24) "*ski*" may be seen in the next card, and as both a man and a woman are shown, you may see how the Norwegians look in winter, striding over the snow. The University at Vienna (25) comes next ; a photo-print, and a general view (26) of Naples, from Pasillipo, with the smoking cone of Vesuvius in the distance. We are still in Italy when at Brindisi (27) ; this is the point of embarkation for the P. and O. steamers ; and here Virgil died, B.C. 19. It was also the great port of embarkation for the Crusaders, in the eleventh century ; and was the chief Roman naval station in the Adriatic. Paris appears in the next (29), the column of the Place Vendôme is given ; and (30) *our* column, the Egyptian Obelisk, which we call Cleopatra's Needle, a pretty little coloured picture. Next to it is a view of the far-off land of its making, (31) Egypt, and a dromedary in the foreground. From thence we take an abrupt flight to (32), the monument on the field of Waterloo, and the Belgian lion. This card was posted on the spot, and is a photograph.

The Pyramids in the (33) distance, from the Nile, a group of date-palms and an obelisk, bring us back to Egypt again ; and the next two (34 and 35) are of Cannes and San Remo —a very frequently sketched subject is the latter. In fact, the practice of throwing arches across from house to house, in those narrow streets, make any Italian town or village look picturesque. Niagara (36) again on the Canadian side, and (37) Dresden, that beautiful Saxon capital, where so many of our compatriots reside for education and economy.

The next picture-card (39) is one that I found full of interest. It is a view of Mikveh Israel ("the Hope of Israel"), one of the among the flower-beds—gardening was her favourite occupation, and she certainly understood plant nature better than boy nature—she said it disappointed her less, and that she could see the result of her work, and maybe she was right. It was always a pleasure to see Miss Faith among her floral favourites—she looked younger and happier. I watched her now as she picked up a broken jonquil that lay in her path—of course Gordon's fox-terrier Rascal had been the sinner; she looked at it so pitifully, as though she grieved over the beautiful trodden-down thing. She had a curious idea that plants had feelings and could suffer; but I never could bring myself to believe it. For how could one ever enjoy gathering flowers and making them into posies if one were to imagine that the parent plant was wounded or lonely? It was just one of Miss Faith's pretty sentimental notions; but I have heard her maintain her point with great tenacity.

She came in presently and sat down beside me.

I could see then how flushed and tired she looked.

"How warm it is for May," she said, laying aside her cape; "but you always look so cool and comfortable. I think, after all, Berrie, that I should like to change places with you. Darning old table-cloths and thinking one's own thoughts would be ever so much nicer than visiting the old grannies of Wyngate Rise."

"That depends on one's thoughts, Miss Faith; it is easy to have busy fingers and a heavy heart"—for I never held with these complaining speeches, and change of place never helped man, woman, or child yet if a doubting, despondent heart went with them.

"To judge by appearances, your thoughts were tolerably cheerful," returned Miss Faith, for she never liked to be contradicted, and I have known her argue some trifling point, for ten minutes at a stretch, until I have given in from sheer fatigue. "Why, I even heard you singing to yourself as I came up the garden path." Then her manner changed and there was a shade of anxiety in her voice. "Do you know where Hope has gone this afternoon? I met Roberts in the lane, and he said she had just passed him."

"She has gone to the vicarage, Miss Faith—she came in to tell me so—and

very likely she will have tea there; she took——" But Miss Faith did not let me finish my sentence—she seemed very much put out.

"Hope gone to the vicarage without me! Why, Miss Ashton has just arrived, and I arranged with Hope that we would call there to-morrow. Miss Ashton will expect us, and we owe her this civility; it was an engagement, a distinct understanding, and now Hope has thrown me over."

"Oh, no, Miss Faith," I returned, as soon as I could edge in a word; "Hope has not forgotten about to-morrow; she means to call with you, but she wanted to speak to Mrs. Marland about her work."

"I shall just run across and have my chat with Daisy this afternoon," were Hope's words to me. "I don't care a jot whether Miss Ashton is there or not; to-morrow Aunt Faith and I will put on our best bibs and tuckers, and arm ourselves with our card-cases, and we will air all our fine manners." But I was not going to repeat a naughty girl's speeches, for Miss Faith's sense of humour was very small.

"It is perfectly absurd," returned Miss Faith in an annoyed voice, "and with all my knowledge of Hope's harum-scarum ways, I could not have believed in such utter want of consideration; if she thinks I will take her with me to-morrow, she is certainly mistaken. If Nina is a good girl, I shall give her the treat."

I began to feel hot—things were decidedly contrary this May afternoon.

"She has gone with Hope," I returned hurriedly. "Do look at this thin place, Miss Faith; do you think it will bear darning?" But she put the cloth aside with an irritated air.

"Do as you think best, but I am too disturbed to attend to trifles. This is rank rebellion and insubordination, Berrie"—when Miss Faith was really put out she generally used the longest words she could find, and rolled them out with unction. "Are you aware that Nina is in disgrace to-day? She was late for luncheon, and rushed in from the garden with her frock covered with sand and with dirty hands, and when I reproved her she was grossly impertinent; then she did her French parsing as badly as possible, so I gave her a French fable to translate, and told her to remain in the school-room—and now you tell me that Hope has set my authority at

defiance, and taken the child with her to the vicarage!"

Miss Faith was not softening matters certainly, but I was not going to let her run on in that fashion, for she had a knack of rolling up a grievance as boys roll a snowball, until it becomes quite formidable and too unwieldy to lift, and after all one should look at two sides of a question.

So I explained to Miss Faith that Nina had done her task perfectly, and that her sister had corrected it, and then, as the child looked pale and tired, Hope thought a good run would benefit her.

"She asked me to tell you this, Miss Faith," I finished, "and I am quite sure that she did it for the best, and had no thought of setting your authority at defiance." My tone was a little indignant, but I might as well have spoken to a rock or a mule. Miss Faith simply turned a deaf ear to me.

"Of course you take Hope's part, Berrie—you always do; in the present day the elder people are expected to apologise to the young ones"—with withering sarcasm uttered in a tremulous voice. "It is all of a piece. My wishes are disregarded, my authority set at nought. How am I to manage these headstrong young people?"—and there was real despair in her tone. "I must speak to Graham; he must judge between us; there cannot be two mistresses in one house. 'Is it to be Hope or I?'—that is what I shall ask him."

"You will do nothing of the kind," I said sharply, for I was at the end of my tether, and she was as unreasonable and aggravating as possible. "You are just tired out, and you are going to lie down, and I will make you a nice cup of tea. There is nothing like taking a nap over a worry, Miss Faith; a good sleep just irons out one's creases"—for I had a comfortable, old-fashioned belief in what mother used to call forty winks and a cup of tea, and I have never known my prescription fail. For once, however, I had reckoned without my host. "Even a worm will turn," as Gordon used to say, and Miss Faith's outraged sensibilities refused to be soothed.

"My brother must judge between us," were the only words she vouchsafed; when I took her up the tea-tray, she did not even thank me with her usual gentle courtesy as I placed it on the little table beside her.

(To be continued.)

WOMEN'S WORK IN SANITATION AND HYGIENE.

How strange our grandmothers would have thought it that ladies should actually be trained to work amongst the poor! The work of a lady inspector of nuisances is in many instances a sort of organised district visiting, and in order to accomplish the work satisfactorily a very thorough training is needed. It is to be wished that all who work amongst the poor should possess not only a sympathy for them, but a very practical knowledge of their needs and requirements. The State, nowadays, gives practical advice on important domestic matters by means of inspectors of

nuisances, and those in authority hope by these means to ensure a greater increase of cleanliness and, as natural results, better general health and a lower death-rate.

The way to the work which is being done in our time was gradually paved by the labours of Mr. Chadwick and others on the Health of Towns Commission in 1844; by such works as *Yeast* and *Alton Locke*; by the work of the late Dr. Parkes, Miss Octavia Hill, and others now dead, but whose works follow them. Thanks to Mr. Chadwick's exertions, the Public Health Act was passed in 1848;

since then other Acts have followed, all bearing on the public health, such as the Adulteration Act, Infectious Diseases Act, Factory and Workshops Act, and so on. We have not only had to learn sanitary science, but we have had to learn what sanitary science is.

Some years ago such matters as drainage, ventilation, and similar subjects were looked upon as fads quite outside practical knowledge, the study of which was considered a very suitable employment for old gentlemen with nothing better to do. We have learnt better.

Florence Sophie Davson, "Women's Work in Sanitation and Hygiene" (Volume 21, 14 October 1899, p. 29).

In 1856 a certain Dr. Roth, one of the pioneers of the health laws of to-day, succeeded in interesting a number of ladies in hygienic matters. Under his instruction they were led to see how very strongly the neglect of personal cleanliness, efficient ventilation, and effective drainage influenced the health of the community, and were responsible for the heavy death-rate. These ladies banded themselves together under the name of the "Ladies' Sanitary Association."

Their object was to encourage by all the means in their power the spread of sanitary knowledge amongst all sorts and conditions of men and women. One of the earliest works of the Society was to arm "Bible women" with materials for cleaning—soap, pails, and scrubbing-brushes; when they went to read they offered these for hire at a farthing a set, and much practical good was done in this way. It is the boast of the Society that they never lost a single implement, and that the stumps of their brooms deserved to be photographed, so worn were they! This was known as "depôt work." This branch of work is carried on no longer, as it is supposed that the appointment of inspectors has removed the need. Gradually the Society arranged lectures on sanitation, nursing, and other domestic matters for the working classes; they published an immense quantity of books and leaflets on the subject; they established *crèches* and did other good work. Canon Kingsley wrote in earnest commendation of the publications of the Society, advocating the study of them for all women, and enjoining those in any sphere of influence to enforce the matter contained in them by their own example, adding that he hoped by this system to see a large decrease in the death-rate.

Other societies gradually sprang up. The National Health Society does similar work to that of the "Ladies' Sanitary Association," and trains its own teachers as well, qualifying them to work under the County Council scheme of technical education. The fee for the course and the examination is £12 12s. Their certificate, however, does not qualify their teachers to act as factory inspectors; the certificate of the Sanitary Institute must be taken as well. The continual passing of so many Acts affecting the public health greatly increases the need for sanitary inspectors. In a few years it is to be hoped that many more appointments will be open than at present. It must be confessed that the multiplication of these measures relieves private responsibility. Whilst regretting this phase of the situation, one cannot be sufficiently thankful for the many blessings which the diffusion of sanitary science gives.

The examinations for inspector of nuisances are now open to women. There are women inspectors for boarded-out children and for idiots.

The Home Office has appointed four inspectresses, of which the lady principal is Miss Anderson. Miss Deane, another inspectress, works chiefly in connection with any special inquiries; she did admirable work in connection with the inquiry into the work in laundries made some little time ago. Miss Squire and Miss Sadler also hold appointments. The salaries attached to these appointments given by the Home Office vary from £400 to £200 a year.

Good posts are also offered under the Metropolitan Asylums Board. There are at present lady sanitary inspectors at Battersea, Kensington, Putney, Hackney, Islington, St. Pancras, and other parts, and doubtless more will be appointed before long.

The towns of Newcastle-on-Tyne, Worcester, Norwich, Rochester, Southsea, Newmarket, Harringay, and many others have each a lady inspector of nuisances.

The work of the inspector of nuisances is in all cases under the direction of the medical officer of health, who is himself appointed by the vestries. In some cases the inspectors under a particular vestry have their duties absolutely divided—as, for instance, a food inspector, a dwelling inspector, a slaughter-house inspector, and so on; whilst in other cases each of the inspectors combines all the duties. The vestries arrange all this as they think best. In all cases the inspectors take their individual orders as to where they are to go and what they are to do from the medical officer of health. Inspectors are required to visit their districts systematically, and to report to the sanitary authority on any nuisances dangerous to the public health. The "nuisance" reported may be a noxious or offensive business, a waste of water, the fouling of water with gas or filth, the sale of unwholesome food, an infectious illness, and so on.

When the houses of any district are suspected of being for some reason or other unfit for habitation, the inspector is ordered to make a house to house visitation and report to him thereon. In these cases the inspector is brought into very intimate contact with the poor of the neighbourhood, and therefore should be capable of exercising tact and discretion in the performance of what are sometimes very unpleasant duties.

The Sanitary Institute was founded in 1876, to establish an examination board for granting certificates on sanitary matters. The registrar is Sir William Guyer Hunter, and the chairman Professor Lane Notter.

Another field has been opened for women's work, a field into which none should rush too hastily or with insufficient preparation, for the amount of practical knowledge required is considerable. A little knowledge is a dangerous thing. To-day we all talk glibly of drains and drain-pipes, ventilating shafts, manholes, Tobin's tubes, damp-proof courses, and what not, too often with only the most superficial knowledge of what we are speaking about. The celebrated architect, Mr. William Henman, said recently: "Probably the greatest obstacles to the advancement of sanitary science are the popular prejudice and the unreasoning adoption of materials, means, and methods which may be good under certain circumstances and conditions, but the causes of evil when wrongly applied."

The intending student of sanitary science cannot lay these words too much to heart. The subject she is about to undertake covers a large field, for it touches on all or any of the subjects which affect the laws of health. These include nursing, disinfection, a knowledge of bacteriology, ventilation, drainage, building construction, the impurities of water, filtration by various methods, and a knowledge of the law as it stands with regard to these matters. A thorough knowledge of the vaccination question must not be overlooked. It is greatly to be wished that candidates for sanitary appointments should go deeply into the question in all its bearings, that, having done so, they may realise and may help others to realise the immense saving of life, to say nothing of the prevention of horrible disfigurement that the vaccination laws have brought about. Vaccination from one child to another is without doubt a means of spreading diseases and any hereditary ailment to which the first child may be subject; but all the principal health authorities agree that there are no dangers in vaccination from the calf when properly administered. The public vaccine stations are all under Government inspection; doubtless, in time the private vaccine stations will be also.

As all the appointments in connection with sanitary work require a certain knowledge of nursing, many trained hospital nurses wishing for a change in their labours take a certificate for sanitation. If a nurse wishes to train for sanitation, she must set aside a considerable period of time for learning her new work, after her career at the hospitals is over. It is useless to think of pursuing other work at the same time, as the training is not only done by studying, but entails a great deal of going about. Lectures on various subjects have to be attended; sewage works, dairy companies' premises, lodging-houses, knackers' yards, and other places have to be inspected, and each of these visits takes some hours, for the distances to be covered are often great. Half the training is foregone if these demonstrations arranged by the Institute are left out. The fee for the course of lectures and demonstrations at the Sanitary Institute is £2 2s. The course there covers three months. The offices and rooms of the Institute are in Margaret Street, W.

The Ladies' Sanitary Institute does not train for the work; it only sends out teachers. The latter society made a gallant attempt some time ago to start a college for hygienic training, but the scheme had to be abandoned for lack of funds.

There are other ways of making use of a knowledge of hygienic matters than by becoming inspectors of nuisances or holding any of the appointments to which I have alluded. Elementary science is now an important part of the work of all our best public elementary schools.

The Department of Science and Art at South Kensington grants certificates at the annual examinations which are held each May. These examinations do not qualify for inspectorships; but a first-class certificate will authorise the holder to teach the subject in elementary schools and would enable her to get work in private schools taking the subject. Fees obtained for such teaching vary according to the school. Under the London School Board six shillings an hour is usually given; in Church schools not quite so much. The best way to train is to take the examinations by degrees in the three years' course, instead of attempting to cram all the knowledge required to pass the honours stage into a year, or, as is sometimes done, into three months. The three stages are—

(a) Elementary.
(b) Advanced.
(c) Honours.

In the "Advanced" and "Honours" papers the student is assessed first-class or second-class according to the marks gained. In the "Elementary" there is only one stage, and she either passes or fails. All who are successful in any stage receive a certificate. To teach in any school under Government it is necessary to hold a first-class in the "Advanced" stage.

Many who have a gift for teaching employ their knowledge in coaching by correspondence those who have no opportunity of attending suitable classes.

The London County Council has in hand the clearance of insanitary areas and the building of working class dwellings in Somers Town, St. Pancras, Clare Market, Drury Lane, and other parts. To help on the work lady lecturers on sanitary work are appointed in various parts of London. A thoroughly scientific training in hygiene and sanitation is provided at Bedford College, York Place, W. This course was started about four years ago to provide a wider and more thorough course of training to that provided by the Sanitary Institute, and includes, besides sanitation and hygiene, physics, bacteriology, chemistry and physiology.

The fee for the course is twenty-seven guineas. A student starting by knowing nothing of any of these subjects would certainly require to attend the lectures and

Florence Sophie Davson, "Women's Work in Sanitation and Hygiene" (Volume 21, 14 October 1899, p. 30).

demonstrations for two sessions before she would be capable of sitting for the examination and gaining the certificate. This does not qualify for inspectors of nuisances; the certificate of the Sanitary Institute has to be taken in addition. But a change is to be made in these arrangements shortly, and the Sanitary Institute is to be superseded by a committee nominated by the Home Office which will grant certificates. The aim of the teaching at Bedford College is not only to provide sanitary inspectors, but to induce women to qualify for public voluntary work; to those who hope to work on school boards, on boards of guardians, on women's industrial committees, and so on, an opportunity is offered of gaining a scientific understanding of the dangers and difficulties that occur from insufficient sanitary arrangements.

There are many women who are not hoping for any definite appointment, but who would be glad to spend a year in obtaining organised scientific knowledge that bears on these important subjects. In an interview with Miss Ethel Hurlbatt, the principal of Bedford College, that very capable and well-informed lady expressed herself very decidedly on this subject, saying that she hoped shortly to see on every school board, on every board of guardians, women who have definite scientific training. Miss Hurlbatt also considers it just as important that women who have large properties of their own to manage should be equally well-trained.

The course of training on hygiene at Bedford College has been under the supervision of Dr. T. M. Legge until recently, but as he has lately been appointed to the important position of Medical Inspector of Factories, he will shortly retire, to the great regret of all who have had the opportunity of working under him.

In a recent number of the *Bedford College Magazine*, Dr. Legge writes: "One of the most delightful features of hygiene is that the knowledge gained from studying it enables the student to understand, and places her in a position to cope with, many of the social questions of the day. Every occupation in life exacts some toll from the individual exercising it. . . . The educational value of this course alone is high, and should appeal to those who are anxious to obtain a wide culture. A definite object, namely, the knowledge of the governing personal and public health, is kept steadily in view, and every path up to that end is conscientiously pursued."

FLORENCE SOPHIE DAVSON.

ANSWERS TO CORRESPONDENTS.

MEDICAL.

A GREAT SUFFERER.—Paralysis is in many cases but a temporary disorder. Although many forms of paralysis are both permanent and progressive, other forms last but a few days or weeks. The public is afraid of the word "paralysis," and so we have had to introduce a new word to denote minor forms of interference with motion. This word is "paresis," of which the public mind will doubtless soon become terrified, and we shall have to introduce another. Originally all forms of interference with the power of the muscles were called "palsy," the simplest and best term of all. Paralysis may vary in extent from a very slight interference with a very minute unimportant muscle, absolutely unnoticeable to the patient herself, which passes off in a few minutes, to total and permanent loss of power over every muscle in the body. So you see the word paralysis has a wide meaning, and to tell you whether your paralysis is a serious disease or not is impossible without details.

DAFFODIL.—We have discussed the subject of indigestion very many times, and a few months ago we gave a *résumé* of all that we have said about it. The most important points for you to attend to are small regular meals with little or no fluid at meal-time; avoidance of all articles likely to cause dyspepsia, and avoidance of all food, except a glass of hot milk, between six o'clock P.M. and bed-time. If you do not improve on a solid diet you will have to take to a milk diet, but do not do so unless you are compelled to, for only the severer grades of indigestion are benefited by a milk diet.

EDITH.—Try washing your head in borax and warm water, one teaspoonful of the former to a quart of the latter. Afterwards thoroughly dry your hair and use a lotion of rosemary and cantharides.

INQUIRER.—"Proud flesh" is a popular name for what in medicine we call "hypertrophied granulation tissue." It is an overgrowth of the material by which a wound is naturally closed. You know that if, for example, you chafe your heel, a raw place results; the red velvety-looking material which forms the rawness is called "granulation tissue." If this material grows too much and projects beyond the surrounding skin, it is called proud flesh. Usually proud flesh is pale and semi-transparent. It occurs in unhealthy wounds or in wounds which have been irritated or neglected.

ORCHID.—Flushing after meals is one of the commonest symptoms of dyspepsia. Of course, indigestion can exist without pain in the stomach. You must attend to your digestion, and, above all, do not run about after meals, for this is a very potent cause of "flushings." No, flushings do not permanently injure the complexion unless they have occurred constantly for years.

SAILOR GIRL.—Wearing an abdominal binder has been advised for sea-sickness already, so we are afraid that we cannot credit you with the invention of this "cure." But "cure" it certainly is not. It does sometimes prevent sea-sickness, but far more often it fails.

AN OLD MAID.—The white ring round the outer border of the iris is called the "arcus senilis." It is a ring of fatty degeneration of the cornea or transparent part of the eye. Though called "arcus senilis" (bow of old age), it does not necessarily mean that the eyes are old. Indeed, it has no special significance. It occurs usually in old persons, but may be present all through life, and we have seen it in infants. It is often hereditary, and is sometimes connected with gout. It does not interfere with the sight, nor does it tend to increase. It is not a sign of defective sight.

STUDY AND STUDIO.

AUBURN LOCKS.—Your writing is fairly good, and very clear. We should advise you to use the best ink, to keep the writing as far as possible of a uniform tint, and to *write carefully*, never letting the ends of words "trail off," and making good tails to g's and y's, also writing "and" instead of "&" in a letter. These trifles are important. We have inserted your request.

RÉVEILLÉE.—1. If we were seated beside you at the piano, we might help you by a practical illustration. But we can add nothing to what you have learned theoretically from Sir George Grove's dictionary. It certainly seems difficult to understand the sign "*f.p.*" applied to a single short note, but we can only say that you must carry out, in attacking the note, the same general idea that you indicate: the "forte" moderated by a hint of the "piano."—2. Sweeping statements of the kind you quote are rather foolish, and should not be taken too seriously. The underpaid nursery governess ought not to be expected to teach what she has not had opportunity thoroughly to study, and people who want musical training for their children included in a host of miscellaneous sundries, for a meagre yearly sum, do not, it is to be hoped, get much that is worth having. The fault in such cases lies not with the teacher, but the public. Fortunately things are improving rapidly. Did you not write to us formerly under the signature of "Persévérance?" It seems to be still applicable to you.

INTERNATIONAL CORRESPONDENCE.

ELSA WITTCHEN, Elizabeth-Ring 48, Budapesth, Hungary (sister of our earliest correspondent in this column), wishes to enter into correspondence with readers of THE GIRL'S OWN PAPER in England, Africa, Australia, America, Japan, or anywhere else in the world, in the English language.

JEAN H. ANDREW, Carmi, Hay, N.S.W., Australia, aged 21, would like to correspond and exchange stamps with girls in any Continental country, India, America (Canada especially), Africa, or any foreign land.

EVA SEARLE, aged 16, 54 Rua do Campo Pequeno, Oporto, Portugal, "would be very glad to know of a nice girl who would correspond and exchange postage stamps with her."

JOYCE MARGARET, aged 16, still at school, very fond of drawing, would like a French correspondent.

ADA J. ARUNDELL, Corner of Duke and St. Vincent Streets, Port of Spain, Trinidad, wishes to correspond with "MAY, Broadstairs," and asks for her address.

VERA would like to exchange English view post-cards for American, Russian, and Norwegian ones —especially Russian.

ELLA BAILEY, 167, Horton Lane, Bradford, Yorkshire, would like to correspond with "VALENTINA": but she is above the age mentioned by our Italian subscriber.

IVY-LEAF would like to correspond with a German young lady of her own age (16), resident in Germany and fond of music.

"MISS INQUISITIVE" wishes to correspond with "VIOLET M."

MISS EDITH LOVEJOY, Russelkonda, Ganjam District, Madras Presidency, India, would like to correspond in English with an Italian girl, who is requested to write first.

MISS V. B. ERBA, Cassera, Brianza, Italy, who has only just seen "WHITE ASTER'S" request, would like to correspond with her, and begs "White Aster" to write to her soon.

MISCELLANEOUS.

PERPLEXED.—The sacrifice of Christ was an infinite atonement for finite sin, sufficient to expiate the sins of every mortal man He created. But even were it otherwise, your debt of obedience to His laws He has an absolute right to claim; and your disobedience He has as absolute a right to pardon on any terms whatsoever that He in His mercy condescends to accept. So that, if he chose to exercise His divine prerogative in accepting the offering, say, of a flower, or any most trifling thing at His command and His divine option, who might dare to dispute His arbitrary will, or the terms on which He may extend His prerogative of mercy to His unworthy and rebellious creatures?

GITANA.—Were you in London you might take it to the shops where lace is sold, or an ordinary haberdasher's. But where you are, could you not get a notice put up in some shop-window to the effect that pillow-lace of various widths is on view within? and if the proprietor of the shop will not purchase it himself, he might dispose of it for you if allowed a small commission upon it.

POLLY.—If your hen has the habit of eating her eggs, scatter old mortar or lime rubbish about the yard. The only certain cure, however, is to blunt the point of her beak, which may be done without hurting her by burning the extreme point with a red-hot poker. Of course she should be held very tightly, as she will be frightened and struggle violently. Get a man to hold her and another to perform the operation. We can suggest no other plan, and some who have tried this report well of it.

ADELAIDE.—Your kind, appreciative letter respecting our magazine is warmly welcomed. The hair is now dressed lower than it was, and it would suit a girl of your age (17) to coil it at the back, not so low as the nape of the neck, but a little higher.

VIOLET.—Your writing is deficient in regularity. Get a set of copper-plate small-hand copy-books, and practise daily to produce the same letters and with the same slope. You should try to write a graceful, artistic, free running hand, which can only be acquired on a good foundation. Your letters lean one in one direction and another the contrary way, like old tombstones. If you wish to correspond with the "English girl 12," we must give your address —"Lydia Henderson, The Old Bank, Alcester."

G. R. H.—See our answer to "Violet" in reference to handwriting. You *can* "help saying rude things to other people." There is an old rule which you should continually bear in mind—"If you have nothing pleasant to say, say nothing"—or words to that effect. We imagine that you are too talkative. Pause and reflect before speaking.

LOUIS.—If you could procure the loan of the second vol. of THE GIRLS' OWN ANNUAL, you would find all you require to know at pp. 314-15 under the title of "Dinners in Society." Perhaps you could obtain the weekly No. for February 12th, 1881. In the same vol. you will find other articles very desirable for your instruction, *e.g.*, "The Foundation of all Good Breeding" (p. 73), and "The Art of Conversing Agreeably," as well as "The Art of Letter-Writing." In Vol. III. you would find "Etiquette for all Classes" (p. 90), "Good Breeding in Daily Converse" (p. 278), and "The Habits of Polite Society" (p. 162). In Vol. V. you will find "The Duties of Governesses" (pp. 630 and 770). All these you need. The last-named articles are in the Nos. for July 3rd and September 6th, 1884. You give no address, so no one can help you.

E. F. B.—Try syringing the trees with tobacco-juice. This we have heard recommended, and is said to do no harm to the roses.

Florence Sophie Davson, "Women's Work in Sanitation and Hygiene" (Volume 21, 14 October 1899, p. 31).

DOMESTIC SERVICE AS A PROFESSION FOR GENTLEWOMEN.

N these days of overcrowded professions, and with so many women of all classes forced to earn their own livelihood, it becomes very difficult for girls of moderate abilities to decide on a career. Although theoretically almost all professions are open to women, practically the number is very limited, especially for those who cannot afford the outlay required by a university graduation or the study of medicine. Nursing and teaching are the most popular professions for such, but the ranks of both are terribly overcrowded; and the remuneration for ninety per cent. of either nurses or teachers is decidedly small, and the number of years during which they can obtain good posts is also very limited.

The teaching of technical subjects was considered a paying occupation a few years ago, and therefore girls crowded to the training-schools and classes and obtained diplomas for laundry-work, cookery, dressmaking, and dairy-work, only to find the work extremely hard and the number of well-paid posts very small. Those who are doing this now say that it is getting worse and worse because the classes are frequently given to Board School teachers and the number of applicants for any good situation is very large. One teacher holding a good County Council position knows there are over thirty people waiting to take her post when she resigns.

On the other hand one hears everywhere the outcry for domestic servants, and mistresses say they would give anything for a good one. Whether this is literally meant in many cases is doubtful, but it certainly is a fact that the demand for good maids is very great.

There is nothing lowering in domestic work unless we make it so; it is not what we do, but what we are that constitutes our claim to be called gentlewomen; and yet how many girls consider it quite beneath their dignity to do domestic work, or if they do it prefer to be called "lady helps." Nursing was thought degrading a few years ago, but to-day even members of the Royal Family are glad to be trained as nurses that they may minister to their loved ones or help the poor and suffering. People said that the study of medicine would detract from the womanliness of women, but if the right women study, they come out better at the end, and nowhere will you find more helpful, tender women than in the medical profession.

Some years ago a quaint booklet called *Blessed be Drudgery* was published—W. Gannet, I believe, is the author—and in it the writer sought to prove that art was in every form of work, and that any man might be an artist in his own line. As examples, he mentions two shoemakers, one of whom when asked how long it took to learn his trade replied, "Twenty years, and then you must travel;" the other's answer to the same question was, "All your life." Why can we not bring this spirit into the round of household duties? And if we wish to follow Charles Kingsley's advice to

"Do the thing that's next you,
Tho' it's dull at whiles;
Helping, when you meet them,
Lame dogs over stiles!"

there are few more practical ways than by becoming really good domestic servants and helping to smooth the troubles of worried housewives.

An ardent temperance worker on hearing that a friend intended to take up cookery as a profession, talked to her seriously about throwing away her life and living among the sordidness of food and pots and pans! Was such a remark in keeping with her principles? Surely there is no system of temperance work so likely to prove successful as the providing of well-cooked food and temperance beverages. The good that might be done in this way is immense; but apart from that, as I said before, it is the spirit in which we do our work, more than the labour itself, that harms or improves us. The quaint words of the old poet, George Herbert, well express this—

"Who sweeps a room as to Thy laws,
Makes that and th' action fine."

That there is scope for the work of educated women in domestic service there is no doubt; and many of those who have tried it are proofs of the healthfulness and even pleasantness of the life. Several girls, trained as technical teachers have found that work too hard, and so have taken situations as "lady servants," and find their present positions suit them far better, and they positively enjoy the work, while the certificates they hold enable them to command good salaries.

In order to band together gentlewomen willing to engage in this work, there is a "Guild of Dames of the Household" (President, Miss Nixon, "Mona," Tivoli, Cheltenham, who will be glad to hear from ladies willing to be trained), which provides training for gentlewomen between twenty and thirty-five years of age. It is through the kindness of ladies who have large staffs of servants that this training is obtained, and cooks also attend cookery-classes. The time taken is from one to four weeks or longer. No charge is made for rooms or training, but 10s. per week is the cost of full board, or single meals are provided at a very reasonable rate.

The "dames" are also put in communication with mistresses requiring their services, and Miss Nixon says that the demand for such is far greater than the supply. Caps are not always worn, but some wear a very becoming one with a band of willow-pattern sateen supplied by the Guild. Special aprons and a Guild badge are always used.

Mistresses are required to provide separate bedrooms, give a fair amount of leisure time, and from £18 to £30 per annum. Higher salaries than those named are sometimes obtainable. One lady, known to the writer, gives £35 to her housemaid who has a laundry certificate, and although she does no washing, she is required to do starching and ironing. The same mistress gives £30 to her parlourmaid. Another lady pays especially high wages to her two maids on the understanding that if they require extra help they must pay for it, and those maids like their posts very much and find the work easy and their position a pleasant one.

In the advertisement columns of a daily paper, among vacant situations I see "Lady-cook (kitchenmaid kept), £32"; ditto, £50; lady-nurse, £30, etc.

Those who do not need training will find the fortnightly lists issued by the Central Bureau of the Women's Employment League, 60, Chancery Lane, W.C., a good medium for advertisements, and many ladies requiring gentlewomen advertise there.

In most families employing ladies, help is given with the harder and rougher kinds of work, such as scrubbing, and the maids are rarely, if ever, expected to do any washing. It has been found so much more satisfactory to have all gentlewomen in a house that it is now quite easy to get a post in such a family, the old style of lady-helps being found difficult to manage.

For nurses there is the Norland Institute, where training is given in all matters relating to the management of children, including a few months' experience in a children's hospital. The course there is one or two years, and the nurses have the additional attraction of a charming uniform!

One great advantage of domestic service as a profession is the healthfulness of it. The work offers great variety and plenty of exercise. It is not so mechanical as that of many clerks, and offers sufficient scope for intelligence to prevent one becoming dull.

Of course books and intercourse with one's equals are necessary to all, and every gentlewoman who enters this profession must take care not to allow herself to sink in her intellectual attainments. One mistress who has had a large and satisfactory experience with lady-servants says that many of her maids have been provided with introductions from their doctor, clergyman, or other friends, and have quite a little social circle of their own.

Another advantage is that training and experience in household matters are so valuable to all classes of women. Probably more than half of the trouble about domestic servants to-day is owing to the incompetence of mistresses who, not knowing what work really is, expect impossibilities, and so get less than they otherwise would do. From the lowest to the highest, every woman ought to understand how to manage a house, and a few years of domestic service would be a splendid training for future mistresses, and the "dames" will make far better wives and mothers in consequence of their experience.

ALIX JOSON.

MARQUETRY, OR COLOURED WOOD ·INLAYING.

THE old furniture was charmingly ornamented with inlays, and there can be no question that inlaid decoration is the most appropriate way of ornamenting cabinet work, as it is one of the most durable. A great revival has taken place within the last few years in this class of work, and at the annual exhibition at the Albert Hall of works made in villages under the supervision of the Home Arts Association, some quite charming effects are obtained by the use of coloured inlays.

I was much struck, too, by the use of inlays in some of the modern French furniture known as *L'Art Nouveau*.* A more naturalistic treatment was adopted by these French workers than we associate with inlays, and yet a charming decorative feeling was observed, so that the inlays did not pretend to be painted decoration, though the utmost effect was obtained by the careful disposition of the various coloured woods employed. Another feature of this French marquetry was the introduction of a sort of landscape

* Examples of this modern French work can be seen at the Bethnal Green Museum.

effect by cutting some of the inlays like trees against the sky-line, allowing the motifs to come across these landscape effects. I have endeavoured to illustrate what I mean in the two designs, but my readers must remember that what is intended to be in colour has a very different effect when translated into black and white. I have devoted a chapter in my book entitled "Art Crafts for Amateurs" to the consideration of inlays, and though my space here is very limited, I will give my readers a few practical hints which I hope will help them in their work.

The French use woods such as walnut, birch, and mahogany, which have a very decided grain, and they stain it in such a way that instead of getting the whole surface one tint, it is light in some places and dark in others. They then cut out spaces which suggest a line of trees, and by inlaying these in some dark wood obtain the effect suggested in the sketches accompanying these notes. The foliage is then taken over this. The design of the inlays should be drawn on paper full size and transferred to the wood, and then with a sharp knife—a fixed blade in a wooden handle such as can be

MARQUETRY, OR STAINED WOOD DECORATION, SUGGESTED BY L'ART NOUVEAU. *(The elder in flower is the motif.)*

Alix Joson, "Domestic Service as a Profession for Gentlewomen" (Volume 23, 8 February 1902, p. 300).

GIRLS AND THEIR EMPLOYERS.

By MARGARET BATESON (Mrs. W. E. Heitland).

NEW conditions create new difficulties. Customs change; and as they change we find that we need to modify the old rules of conduct to suit the new manner of life. The remark is made every day by somebody, that girls are now entering many employments which formerly did not exist — at all events for girls. But people do not so often pursue their reflections further, and consider the problems of behaviour which are presented to every girl who enters a world of work which is new to her.

By way of example, let us think for a moment of the case of a country clergyman's daughter who comes up to London in order to earn her living as clerk to a commercial man. In the quiet rectory life she has known only gentlefolk of her own class and villagers, and by all, as the clergyman's daughter, she has been treated with courtesy and a certain amount of deference. It has not occurred to her that she ought to be specially reserved in manner to anyone; it has not been necessary to keep people at a distance. She suddenly finds herself seated at a desk in a City office, and everything is changed. She finds herself reckoned a mere nobody. If she is one of a number of girl-clerks in the same office, she is only oppressed by a sense of her own insignificance in this new society; but if she is alone—the sole girl among a staff of men—her position is a much more embarrassing one. She realises at once, supposing her to be a girl of quick perceptions, that her happiness will depend very much upon the kind of behaviour which she adopts. But for a girl who is quite young and inexperienced, it is a far more puzzling matter to decide what is the right way to behave in circumstances so strange and foreign to her.

There are girls, I know, who think it far pleasanter to be employed by a man than a woman. There are servants who think they would be perfectly happy if they were employed in a household without a "Missis," and similarly there are girl-clerks who believe that all troubles would disappear if their employer were a man. If one listens to the complaints which girls make about their own sex as employers, I think one will learn that the grievances are somewhat as follows. Women, it will be said, as employers, are not always fair; they are prone to find fault, and lay more stress upon small errors than upon much good service. If they are painfully conscious that their own youth and best days have slipped away, they are sometimes unreasonably jealous of a young girl who may possibly prove a rival to themselves in the future. The third allegation is that they look after their employees too closely. They do not leave a girl sufficient liberty; they intrude too much upon her private affairs. They do not restrict their attention to matters of business; they inquire what their subordinates do out of office hours, and where and how they live; and (this I suspect is the worst fault of all) women employers are prone to make remarks about dress and personal appearance.

Such are the chief accusations made against women employers. Are they true? Of very many women certainly not. At the same time I will not commit the extravagance of asserting that all women are ideal persons to work under. But there is just a sufficient amount of truth in the accusations to make it worth while for girls to consider the indictment; not in order to blame their own sex, but to correct such faults in themselves as may make

them unsatisfactory employers of the young women over whom they may one day have control. Let us grant then that a disposition to inquire narrowly into each other's affairs is a fault against which girls should be on their guard. It is useless for us to try to live other people's lives for them; and it is not clear that each one of us conducts the business of existence so perfectly as to be competent to direct more lives than one. As girls come to realise how much better a thing is individual responsibility and initiative than the close imitation of other people's modes of life, one of the chief criticisms offered upon women employers will cease to be heard. Meantime, however, there are in the business world many admirable women employers—women for whom girl-workers feel the warmest affection. Such women, without forcing advice and admonition upon unwilling disciples, do genuinely befriend their girls. They set an example of conscientious work themselves, but they are observant of the health of their young people, and do not overtax the powers of those in their service. There are, I believe, in London no better employers than the matrons of some hospitals and the heads of certain typewriting offices and business firms, and their employees, by their devotion and their unwillingness to leave, show that they are of the same opinion.

I am far from wishing to imply that it is better in all cases for a girl to be employed by a woman than by a man. Girls have much to learn from men in the conduct of business. They may learn to be cool-headed, and to avoid the besetting fault of many women—"getting into a fluster" when there is a rush of work, or a decision is required in a hurry. And there are several other reasons which make it advantageous for girls to be associated with men in practical affairs. But at the same time I wish to point out that girls who choose to be employed by a man, because they think they will have more freedom and be less closely looked after, are not really gaining so many advantages as they imagine. The independence they acquire will be more apparent than real. A man will not often make observations about matters outside the business in hand, though he may do so occasionally. Supposing him to be a gentleman, he will recognise that it is hardly suitable for him to comment upon such a subject as a girl's dress. He may earnestly wish that Miss So-and-so were a little neater in her person; and for this reason (though he may not cite it) he will possibly dimiss her. A man employer will usually say less on such topics than a woman, but he will think quite as much about them, if not more. It behoves a girl therefore to remember that, though little is said, much is probably being noticed. And what will be noticed, even more than a girl's appearance, is her manner. Any familiarity or freedom of manner will certainly be observed, and will either evoke familiarity from the employer, if he is not a well-bred man, or will be remarked as an occasion for dismissal. There are men, I am aware, who will behave in an under-bred manner to a girl, however blameless she may have been in her own conduct. In such cases the only advice to be given is that a girl should leave the offending employer as soon as possible. But, in general, the rule applies equally to business relations and to society, that women are expected to show the kind of conduct which they wish to have observed towards them. In many cases where an older woman will offer guidance to a girl, at the risk of appearing intrusive, a man will say nothing and act on the assumption that a girl must look after herself. No girl is inclined to admit that she cannot look after herself, yet—reverting for a moment to the case of the country clergyman's daughter which I instanced at the beginning of this paper—a girl may know perfectly how to behave in her own home circle, but she may be quite at a loss when transported into another class of society. Those girls who feel most confidence of their ability to manage their own affairs often drift into difficulties. The difficulties may not be serious, but they are undesirable all the same. In later

Margaret Bateson, "Girls and Their Employers" (Volume 24, 1 November 1902, p. 69).

life it may not be pleasant to look back upon these little incidents.

To guard against such risks I would especially recommend girls who are coming up from sheltered country homes in order to become independent wage-earners, whether in shop or office, to try to keep their relations with their employers as much as possible on business lines. Nearly all the little awkwardnesses and disagreeablenesses that arise have their origin in the mingling of private affairs with business. It is not always possible to keep them apart, but the endeavour should be made, and especially by girls who are quite young and new to the city world. For example, a question of payment of salary may arise. It is never pleasant to press for payment of money due, but it becomes much more difficult if the girl who is owed money has been the recipient of her employer's hospitality. A girl may have the happiness to find a good friend in her employer, but she should certainly not rush into an intimacy before she has had means of learning the character of the man or woman with whom she is dealing. And if a friendship is established, let it be a friendship conducted on lines of which a girl's parents would approve. Some girls imagine that on entering an office they have left behind them all the ordinary habits of society and have come into a world with peculiar rules of its own. If this new world is governed on peculiar principles, a girl should wait until she has mastered those principles. She will not learn in a day how to live in Bohemia according to the laws of Bohemia—for even Bohemia has its laws—and on the whole she will be safer in assuming that the same social rules hold good in Threadneedle Street or Chancery Lane as those which are tacitly accepted in a country town.

Need I say that a girl should preserve a respectful bearing towards her employer? It hardly should be requisite, but there are girls who imperil their position by a tone of familiarity towards their employer which the latter will not like, though he may not care to resent it openly. An employer may often admit his or her failings quite frankly, but he will scarcely relish an equally outspoken perception of them on the part of his employee. It is a good rule that the employee should always show more deference than the employer seems to expect. This applies as much to girls who are engaged as private secretaries as to those who work in business firms. A girl does not necessarily cringe to rank because she gives a peeress her title. She only shows that she acknowledges the status of other people, as she would expect her own position to be recognised.

In short, most of the difficulties and perplexities which arise between employers and employed in their social relations with each other would disappear if the two parties would keep within their own proper limits of action. The mischief originates in the tendency of human beings to encroach upon each other; the disposition which each of us has to treat your business as though it were my business, to enlarge our borders by adding other people's affairs to our own province. If people kept to the terms of their bargains, employers would only ask that their workers should perform their duties efficiently, while the workers, on the other hand, would not feel themselves ill-used or slighted because their employers and employers' wives did not treat them as though they were private acquaintances. But in everyone the wish lurks for the "little more" which is not his rightful due; and when the wish is expressed in action, trouble comes.

THE CARE OF A GIRL'S OWN LIBRARY.

BY SUSAN M. SHEARMAN.

PART I.

" For him was lever have at his bed's head
    Twenty bookĕs, clothed in black or red,
    Of Aristotle, and his philosophy,
Than robĕs rich, or fiddle, or psalt'ry."
Chaucer.

THE title of this article perhaps sounds a rather ambitious one, and yet if you look in a dictionary, the meaning given for the word library exactly describes what I wish to write about.

A library is a collection of books; an ambiguous term which may embrace any number from six to six thousand and upwards. It also means a place where a collection of books is kept; that may either be a modest little shelf in a girl's bedroom, or it may be a large building. The subject I wish to consider is a girl's collection of books, and the place in which she keeps it. Therefore, what better word can be found for it than library?

The fact that a girl takes in THE GIRL'S OWN PAPER regularly declares that she is a lover of books; and though some may love them more intensely than others, I think all our readers must love them well enough to wish to take the best care they can of those they possess.

Books are more easily injured than thoughtless people imagine, and it is well to study their nature a little that we may be able to avoid everything that is injurious to them as far as possible. There are many things which are very

destructive to books, and which we ought to do our best to guard against. Amongst these are dust, damp, great heat, gas, rats, mice, cockroaches, bookworms, borrowers, spring-cleanings, housemaids and book-binders; a long list surely, but we need only concern ourselves particularly with those things which are likely to interfere with a girl's library.

Of all these things I think a girl often finds borrowers the most hurtful, and the most difficult to guard against. There are two kinds of borrowers: first, the one who loves books so well that she is apt to keep them altogether, and never thinks of returning them. This kind of borrower is a tiresome person who needs to be looked after and worried till you get back the book. The best precaution I ever heard of against book-keepers of this description was one adopted by the owner of a nice private library. He kept a number of blocks of wood of various sizes, and when a book was borrowed he pasted on the back of the block a paper bearing the name of the book, the name of the borrower and the date. This was slipped into the space left by the book, and remained there until the book was returned. He very rarely lost a book.

A second kind of borrower is even more to be dreaded than the first. She comes for the loan of the last volume of THE GIRL'S OWN PAPER, there is such an excellent receipt for an orange cake in it. It is a nice fresh volume just home from the binder's, and you unhesitatingly lend it. She finds the recipe, but thinks she should like to try it before taking the trouble to copy it. Down goes the book

HOUSE-DECORATION.

A NEW AND REMUNERATIVE EMPLOYMENT FOR GIRLS.

THE home being emphatically the woman's sphere, house-decoration and furnishing would seem to be a particularly appropriate profession for such as possess artistic taste, skill, energy, and business aptitude, for all these attributes are absolutely essential in order to attain any success as a house decorator. It is not easy work, and, like most things, it is fairly monotonous; it demands health, perseverance, good sense, and capability in no common degree, but, on the other hand, it offers a new field of work and the prospect of very fair remuneration.

A well-known lady decorator gives it as her opinion that "in a very few years there will be an enormous demand for women to undertake this business. It is an eminently suitable trade for them, given some taste to start with; it is pleasant, though very hard work, and it is very profitable."

HOW TO TRAIN.

In this, as in all work, training is of paramount importance. "I think," says this lady, who has established a successful business of her own, "the best method of starting would be to get a year's training in a shop. (I have great faith in this, as I had to learn by the very roundabout way of finding out my own mistakes!) After the year's training, I should not think of starting for myself, but I should then try for a post as assistant manageress in another shop, in order to see different people's methods, and to see various sides of the trade. Then if I had a connection, enough capital, say £700 to £800, and really good health, I think I should have a very good chance of success if I began by myself."

In that admirable little paper, *Women's Employment*, issued by the Central Bureau for the Employment of Women, this subject was fully dealt with about a couple of years ago. In this paper this same lady decorator urges the necessity of a knowledge of detail in all the matters connected with house decoration. "A woman in this business can hardly have too many strings to her bow; so she should be prepared not only to undertake the painting and papering of houses, but also all accessories, such as upholstery, blinds, carpets, and, if possible, furniture; and this is one of the reasons why I insist upon the necessity for training. It is impossible to have all the business details in your head, and all the papers, materials, etc., at your finger-tips, unless you have had practical experience, and have lived in an atmosphere of business for some time."

IMPORTANCE OF DETAIL.

In this trade, as in most, it is the grasp of the items which go to make up the whole, which is such an important factor in ultimate success. "I find it very difficult," she informed me, "to make people understand the importance of details in business; they all enjoy getting out paper and curtain schemes, etc., for different rooms, but when it comes to measuring the room for paper, and the windows for curtains, it is a very different matter, and they think it would be such a very much better plan to leave this part of the business to the workmen." In any case it is essential that the woman decorator should have that thorough practical knowledge of her trade which will enable her to state the approximate amounts and prices for coverings, papering, repairs, etc., as such information may be demanded a dozen times a day in the ordinary course of business.

PROSPECTS AND REMUNERATION.

"I don't think it is a very exciting trade," she said, "as sometimes there are almost weeks of comparative idleness, and then there are months when sixteen hours a day of hard work is nothing extraordinary." In fact, on this point she is insistent. "Let no one think the business is anything but hard work—drudgery would be a better word—and the monotony is appalling at first, but I think, at the worst, after a year's apprenticeship it should mean that anyone of average intelligence should be able to earn £1 a week, and in a few years about £150 per annum." The woman who has a business of her own ought reasonably to expect to make "a few hundreds a year."

Of course, certain attributes make for success in this work. "Good health and business capacity are very necessary. I am sure an amiable temper is, or the capacity to imitate one, some sort of taste, and above everything energy and perseverance."

It is the want of thoroughness in this, as in other matters, which has so often brought the average woman worker into disrepute. No one should dream of becoming a decorator unless she means to work at it with her heart and soul. "My experience is that women cannot remember that they are not amateurs, and fail to remember that business during business hours is the first, and indeed, the only consideration; that to-morrow will not do as well as to-day; that there must be no trusting to memory, but that everything must be duly entered in its proper book, and that cash-books must balance, not be 'only a shilling or two out!'"

LADY DECORATORS ON THEIR WORK.

There seems to be a general unanimity of opinion—from the expert point of view—as to the satisfactory prospects afforded by this profession for women. In Scotland there are one or two energetic and talented ladies who have gained success in this field, and who recommend others to imitate their example. One lady decorator who for years has been "a trusted consultant in all matters of house decoration and furnishing," gives it as her opinion that provided a girl has "sense, energy and taste," she is convinced "that the field is emphatically a promising one for women." Another lady, who is a well-known mural decorator, amongst other things, is certain that "if women would have less pride and more enterprise, would cease to make pleasing but unappreciated easel pictures, and make a systematic study of decoration, and prove themselves thoroughly qualified and willing workers, many of them would exchange their present penury and anxiety for lives of profitable usefulness, ease and comfort."

If a girl, possessed of genuine artistic power, would like to devote her time and talents entirely and solely to decoration as distinguished from furnishing, she could not do better than be articled for two or three years to a good architect, where she would be able to study the principle of design, both from a practical and theoretical standpoint. There is a lady in London who trains decorative artists, her course including woodwork, plaster-work, and architecture. The period of training lasts for three years, and costs £100. The student must be over nineteen years of age.

In conclusion it seems to be obvious that this work, or one of its branches, is worthy of the serious consideration of any woman who has her way to make in the world, and who possesses the necessary attributes and the requisite artistic skill. It demands undoubted talent, energy, perseverance and business qualities, but then so do most professions if success is to be attained therein; but this at least is not overstocked, and financially it presents unusually rosy prospects. "In conclusion," wrote a lady-decorator of note to me, "I must say I thoroughly believe in women going in for the work, as I have every confidence in its financial future."

And, I would urge, that it is only by taking up some work that is not overcrowded, and that demands some specialist knowledge and training, that any girl nowadays can hope to provide for her present wants and those of the future, at a time when cheap and excellent educational facilities have flooded the market with a superfluity of brains of a particular and unremunerative order.

Anon., "House-Decoration: A New and Remunerative Employment for Girls" (Volume 25, 10 October 1903, p. 24).

Independent Living

In its early years, *The Girl's Own Paper* generally assumed, in writing of home life and household management, that its readers lived either in their father's or their husband's home. Toward the end of the 1880s, however, the magazine began to feature articles on independent living. Clearly, readers who were pursuing new professions, particularly in the city, were unlikely to stay at home, so *The Girl's Own* provided advice on finding accommodation, the legal responsibilities of tenancy, and economy for the single girl, among other topics. The magazine also acknowledged that many young women might not have the option of either family or married life.

"Sixty Pounds per Annum, and How I Live Upon It" (vol. 9, 1887–88, pp. 387–88, 444, 446, 600, 602, 712, 714) is supposedly by a young gentlewoman who, on the death of her father, and without any relatives who might take her in, finds herself struggling to maintain her status on the income from her few inherited investments. It details the process of finding and engaging rooms, as well as the economies necessary on a fixed income.

S. F. A. [Sophia] Caulfeild explores other accommodation options, along with social and professional connections for women, in "Women's Clubs in London" (vol. 11, 1889–1890, pp. 598–99, 678–79). She surveys all the clubs, some of which were residential, offering city accommodations to "gentlewomen" and women professionals living in the suburbs and countryside.

The Girl's Own often offered suggestions for improving one's accommodations. "A Home-Made Shower-Bath" (vol. 14, 1892–93, pp. 516–17) shows how girls in flats without washing facilities may set up their own shower-bath.

Josepha Cranc, in "Living in Lodgings" (vol. 16, 1894–95, pp. 562–64, 677–78) provides advice on conduct and tips on safety for the single girl living alone in lodgings. She also surveys types of lodging available, with recommendations as to the most economical and sensible options.

As rooms were often cramped, *The Girl's Own* periodically ran articles on how to make the most of one's space. Bed-sitting-rooms presented a particular problem for girls who wanted their room to look as little like a bedroom as possible. "How I Furnished My Bed-Sitting-Room for Twelve Pounds" (vol. 24, 1902–03, pp. 118–19) offers some solutions.

Flora Klickmann, a successful journalist and staff-writer for *The Girl's Own* from the 1890s onward, offers hope for the middle-class girl who shrinks from having to deal with lower-class individuals in lodgings and boarding-houses with "A New Hostel for Women" (vol. 24, 1902–03, pp. 380–82). Upon Charles Peters's death in 1907, Klickmann became the editor of *The Girl's Own*.

SIXTY POUNDS PER ANNUM, AND HOW I LIVE UPON IT.

By A YOUNG GENTLEWOMAN.

SUMMER'S day in London—the precise location, Bloomsbury; *dramatis personæ*, myself—a girl of twenty-one—and my family lawyer, an elderly gentleman, and rather retiring man, of about sixty years of age. The grass plot, shaded by huge trees, on which the two large windows look, and the rather stately ancient style of the houses that surround it, have an almost monastic air, while a dull roar, like waves breaking on a distant shore, alone gives evidence of the proximity of that great London which lies close around us. I think that to the day of my death I shall remember the twitter of the sparrows, the hum of the flies, the shadows lying quietly on the sunny grass without, and the absolute stillness which reigned within the large room. Mr. Greatorex sat in the large chair facing me, and looked out with an expression of vexed and perplexed sorrow on his kindly face, while I mutely gazed at the pile of papers before me, and was silent. Then I found myself saying, "There is nothing left; and there will be nothing in the future, Mr. Greatorex!"

"No, my dear young lady, absolutely nothing. The value of the estate is quite covered by the mortgages on it and the interest on them. I much fear the shock of this recent heavy loss, through that wretched speculation of your poor father's, caused his sudden death; he had hoped so much from it, and had such faith in it and its promoters, that I suppose he had not thought it worth while to tell you of the true state of his affairs, when he hoped, by a lucky *coup*, to repair them all." Mr. Greatorex sighed, and the vexed look deepened on his face. Besides being our legal adviser for many years, he was an old friend, and naturally felt for the girl who found herself almost penniless, when, had matters been unchanged, he would have been treating with her as the heiress of a comfortable estate and fortune.

He broke the silence again by saying, interrogatively—

"You are at your aunt's?"

"No," I answered, "at Mrs. Murray's; my aunt is not in town."

"How is your grand-aunt's money invested?" he continued.

"In colonial stock and a mortgage; just as she left it four years ago. Messrs. Bertram and Kidd were her lawyers."

"Ah, yes," he said, "I remember, you have always had that, I suppose, for your dress. What does it yield?"

"About sixty pounds per annum," I answered. "Oh, if I had only been told, I might have saved something. As it is, I spent it all, though I have yet to draw my last quarter, and there are some bills to pay for mourning."

"Have you a bank account?" Mr. Greatorex asks, quietly.

"No," I answer; "you forget, I have been abroad; Mr. Bertram sent me the money."

"Who are the trustees?" is the next query.

"Mr. Bertram is one, and Uncle Tom the other."

"Where are the securities?" Mr. Greatorex continues.

"Mr. Bertram has them, I believe. He is Uncle Tom's lawyer, you know."

"It would be better for you to have a bank account. Write to Mr. Bertram, and ask him to open one for you, now you have returned to England. Do you know all the mysteries of cheques and bank books?" he asks with a kind smile.

"Oh, yes," I answer readily. "My father was very particular in showing me how to do all kinds of business. It amused him, I thought, when he was ill and lonely."

Mr. Greatorex rose from his chair, and as he shook my hand, he laid the other kindly on my shoulder.

"You must think over your future," he said, "where and how to live. When you have grasped all your troubles, write me a line, and fix a day to see me again. You may rely on me, for your father's sake, to help you with advice and counsel. Do not be cast down. Sixty pounds is not a fortune, but with forethought and care it may be a competence. It is, at least, certain that both Mr. Bertram and your uncle may be relied on, for both are excellent men of business."

I know he is trying to comfort me, to give me a safe point of rejoicing, and to brace me up to meet my future cheerfully and bravely, and I feel grateful from the depths of my soul. Even the very form this conversation has taken has cheered me, and has proved that Mr. Greatorex thinks me neither an idiot nor a careless fool. But still, as I retain the kind grasp of his hands, the sudden tears rise to my eyes; I feel forlorn and lost. My father's sudden death, added to this new trouble, is a good deal for the shoulders of twenty-one to carry. I go out into the sunlight, and find my way to Holborn, where I take an omnibus, and as Mrs. Murray lives near the Marble Arch, I make up my mind to go into the park before going home. Mrs. Murray is the kindest and most thoughtful of friends. She has been more to me than any relations, and I know will be a wise adviser; but I shrink just now from companionship, and even from sympathy; and I want to "commune with my own heart, and be still" a while, before I take any other step forwards.

In the park, under the green trees, the sun and the summer breeze comfort me. Healing seems to come with every breath I draw, and before I have been there half an hour I begin to regain my mental equipoise; my mind rights itself, and is fit for active work. I am even conscious of a feeling of elation—as of one who sees a battle before him, and longs to be a victor on the field. I have always been a passionate lover of nature, and in my greatest troubles and griefs I feel nearer to the Father in Heaven under green trees and in His sunshine than within four walls.

Then I think how thankful I am that it is summer, and not winter; sorrow's difficulties are so much less troublesome when the sun is shining; and it seems as if I have been purposely brought here to see the sparrows, so busy are they on the gravel in front of me. "I too, am one of His sparrows,"—so runs the priceless message—and though I have fallen to the ground, it has not, nor shall not, be "without my Father's" knowledge and consent.

With this peace and comfort stealing over and settling on my heart, I begin once more to think of myself and my future, and I go bravely forward. I can bear anything now—I am refreshed with the holy dew of His promises, and nothing can hurt me—all committed to Him.

Money seems always to be the first thing thought about; and that naturally comes to my mind first. As I said to Mr. Greatorex, I have not drawn my last quarter, and I have about ten pounds in my pocket. My father having died at Bonn, I did not expend much money there, and expected to get my needful mourning in town; fortunately I have only ordered one dress and a bonnet; but even that, though inexpensive, will make a hole in my ten pounds. I must have some boots and shoes, too, I think, and a few other really necessary articles; but, whatever happens, I must not touch my quarter—my precious £15—save for my actual needs of living.

The thought of living recalls me to the requirements of the moment—"how shall I live, and where? Ought I to look for some employment, or shall I be able to live on my means? Like the majority of girls of my age, I have not been brought up to do anything. I had a maid, who was half maid, half nurse, and who latterly waited much on my poor father. But I have left her at her home in Paris, and she is not going to service again. Fortunately she was a clever, notable Frenchwoman, with the thrift and ability peculiar to her nation. I know already how to make the most of everything in the household; for during the last days of my father's life, money seemed scarce, and he appeared angry when asked for it. I could make many little dishes and good coffee; and I manufactured my own bonnets and hats, not to speak of my dresses—thanks to the fact that Stephanie had always made me help her. Indeed, since my poor mother's death, ten years ago, Stephanie had been my great companion. I could speak French well, and I played fairly, and I spoke German still better than French. Of Italian I knew enough to read with facility and to speak a little.

While thus taking stock of myself and my acquirements, I felt quite determined that I would live on my income if possible, and, above all, that I would not be dependent on any one for help, if I could not live on it; neither, if possible, should my aunt have to say that I was forgetting my position as my father's daughter, *i.e.*, as a Winnington, of Winnington Moat—that dear, well-remembered old Elizabethan house in the North Countrie. I must try to live as a gentlewoman, and I felt quite sure that the people I cared for were too sensible, and loved me too well, to mind whether I lived in an ancient moated house or in a single room in London. I was mistaken in some of them, but, I am thankful to say, not in all. The majority gave me greeting for myself alone.

In these days, when one must needs appraise oneself, if they wish to be earners of money, how generally humiliating is the result of the process! Mine was no exception to the general rule, but I came speedily to the one conclusion that is forced on many a woman beside myself, *i.e.*, that all my powers towards money-saving had been cultivated. I knew how to make a pound go to its furthest extent of spreading, and I had no expensive tastes so far as I knew. During the last years of my father's life we had lived mostly on the Continent, probably for the benefit of cheap living; our life had been quiet and uneventful, and I had only occasionally come to England to pay visits to friends and relations.

But as regards making money, I was quite conscious that I should find it difficult, if not impossible. My French, German, and music were good; but I doubted that I could teach them to others, or whether I were well enough grounded myself in their elementary parts. Italian came under the same category; and though I was well read in English and foreign literature, my reading had not been directed in such a manner as to enable me to impart my knowledge to others; and as for my other arts, they were of no use to anyone but myself. I might do something in literature, but one does not begin authorship at once, and that idea was of no use either. No, I must live on my sixty pounds a year, and be happy and contented on that.

Meanwhile I am still sitting on my chair in the park, and though my meditations take some time to put on paper, they were not so slow in passing through my mind. I look back now with some wonder at myself, and the quiet way in which I took my misfortune. Perhaps, as I sometimes fancy, my experiences of the last few years of my father's life, and the knowledge that he was anxious about money matters, may have been unconsciously accepted by me as a warning for the future; and so the news was more like the confirmation of a dreaded fact than a shock wholly unexpected. I had not been conscious of any feeling of helplessness or despair, so far; and as I sat there, in the sweet pure air, I began to feel that buoyant sensation of cheerfulness that, thank God, has never deserted me since, through much trouble and anxiety. After all, when the struggle is only for one's self, it is far easier and far less anxious. One can go without things one's self, but the misery and fear of seeing those we love reduced to want, and being unable to supply their needs, would indeed be a heart-breaking trouble.

My problem now was—how to live on what I had, as a gentlewoman, and without quite losing my position in society. As I walked towards Mrs. Murray's, I began dimly to see the plan I afterwards carried out; but I also began to feel the pangs of hunger, for it was almost two o'clock, and I had been in the park nearly two hours, as I found out on passing the clock at the Marble Arch.

The door opened just as I knocked, and the kindly anxious face of my old friend appeared in the opening. With the tact born of love and pity, she only commiserated my hungry state; and with a tender kiss, she led me into the dining-room, where I found the luncheon still waiting; and, better than all food, the silver kettle boiling, ready to make me a cup of tea. I am almost ashamed to confess I enjoyed my luncheon, and felt the better for it; and when, a few minutes afterwards, we were safely ensconced in Mrs. Murray's tiny "snuggery"—as it was called in the house—before she had to time to ask a question, I said—"My journey has not been a very successful one, dear. Mr. Greatorex says there is nothing left from my father's property."

The gravity on Mrs. Murray's face deepened perceptibly as she answered: "Margaret, dear, my husband feared there was something very wrong, but as it was only a guess on his part, I did not dare to say more this morning than I did. Will the estate have to be sold?"

"Yes," I said, sorrowfully. "Everything is gone; it was all through that company of which you know my father thought so highly. There is some of my poor great-aunt's furniture left to me, with the sixty pounds a year, when she died, and that is positively all I have to live upon. Don't," I said hastily, "don't say to me anything about living with Aunt Kate, or going out a 'governessing'—like a darling, Mrs. Murray, for I will not do either. Try to help me to see how I can live as a gentlewoman in independence, and honestly, on what small means I have."

Mrs. Murray shook her head. "You are very young, Margaret."

"Yes, dear; in years, perhaps, but I feel at least fifty; and I am neither pretty nor untrustworthy, but as steady as old Time! Besides," I continued, earnestly, "I want to make some arrangement before Aunt Kate returns. You know her even better than I do, dear, and how much real assistance I shall have from her. So I want the question settled as soon as possible."

Mrs. Murray nodded. "I know," she said. "Your aunt will do nothing but discuss the 'ought to have been dones'—as Charles says—and not the 'what can be dones.'"

"That is just it," I answered, and I added quickly, "I do not feel as if I could hear my poor father discussed and blamed just yet; even though, I daresay, things might have been better arranged for me."

"Quite right," said Mrs. Murray; "I have the same feeling, and I know my husband will share it, about his old friend. Have you thought of any plan, Margaret?"

"Yes," I answered; "I want to take one or two unfurnished rooms. I think there is more than enough furniture, and I shall manage if I can get them for six or seven shillings a week. Will you mind coming to look for them to-morrow morning? I must have what service I need included in that sum, I think."

"You must not be further away from us than Paddington, or perhaps Westbourne Park," said Mrs. Murray, decidedly; "and you must have a respectable street, and a respectable landlady, who will answer the door and do the service you may need herself. How about the cooking of your food, dear? Will the landlady do that? I do not quite understand how you will manage."

"I think most of my cooking must be my own doing, dear Mrs. Murray. In this way alone shall I manage to afford two rooms, with £15 per annum."

"I think," said Mrs. Murray, "the best method of obtaining what we want will be to advertise for them, and insist on references. To-night we will talk over our plans with Charles, and get him to write an advertisement, and advise us where to insert it."

"What will Mr. Murray say?" I asked doubtfully.

"Mr. Murray is like Mrs. Murray—a mountain of sense," she answered, with a smile. "You may depend on him, Margaret. He will never discourage you, but rather aid and assist in any well-considered idea."

(*To be continued.*)

POVERTY OF BLOOD : ITS CAUSE AND CURE.

By MEDICUS.

IT is at this time of the year, more perhaps than any other, that many of my girl readers, whatever be their age or condition in life, require a little solid and useful advice, not unmixed with comfort. In the dark gloomy weather of this month in early spring, while, according to Burns,

"The moaning west extends his blast,
    And hail and rain do blaw;
Or the stormy north sends driving forth
    The blinding sleet and snaw,"

anyone if chronically ill, or in that unblissful condition called "only middling," is exceedingly apt to despond. The weather has a wondrous effect on the nerves and minds of delicate girls who are not over strong. Probably snow itself, casting its pure white mantle over all the outdoor world, is less apt to cause gloom and depression than the rain, the pelting rain rattling on the window panes, dripping from the roofs, falling from the leafless trees, and soddening all the brown leaves, that autumn left, beneath them.

A few there may be who, sitting by the window in the gloaming, and gazing out into the cheerless coming night, take a strange delight in hugging their very melancholy. Such may sometimes say with the poet—

"The tempest's howl, it soothes my soul,
    My griefs it seems to join;
The leafless trees my fancy please,
    Their fate resembles mine."

I have touched a chord in some heart, I know, and now I am going to break it, ruthlessly break it—the chord, not the heart.

I am not going to have my girls hugging their melancholy, I can assure them. Gloom sits but uneasily on that fair brow, and I would banish it. I do so by plainly telling you that romantic, even poetic as such feelings may be, they are nevertheless the result of a little dyspepsia or indigestion. I can imagine you seated by the window, the blinds not yet drawn down, the lamp not yet lit, and saying to yourself—

"I see the lights of the village,
    Gleam through the rain and the mist;
And a feeling of sadness comes o'er me
    That my soul cannot resist;

A feeling of sadness and longing,
    That is not akin to pain,
And resembles sorrow only,
    As the mist resembles the rain."

And I steal up behind you and whisper these words: "Take a Gregory's powder before breakfast to-morrow morning." Terribly unromantic of me, I confess. I can have no poetry in my soul, you say. O yes, I have; I am full of it, but I keep it diluted with a little common sense.

Now, joking apart, pleasant melancholy, delightful depression of spirits, or a feeling that the world is all wrapt in gloom, and that you prefer it like that, is one of the very first symptoms, not of dyspepsia only, but of a species of hypochondria that may end in a condition of mind and body the very reverse of pleasant; in utter wretchedness, mayhap, in weary days and sleepless nights, till life itself becomes a burden the bearer would fain lay down. I do not say that young girls are prone to this ailment, which is but a species of exaggerated *ennui* and nervousness, but I do tell them that giving way to melancholy of a causeless nature, is permitting the thin end of the wedge to find a place in the heart and brain. The ailment—for ailment it is—may take years to fully develop, but encouragement hastens it, and none of us, I should think, would like to feel like Hamlet when he says: "I have of late—but wherefore I know not—lost all my mirth, foregone all custom of exercises; and

---

A Young Gentlewoman, "Sixty Pounds per Annum, and How I Live Upon It" (Volume 9, 17 March 1888, p. 388).

A MAY SONG.

By MARY ROWLES.

O! THE Maytime, welcome Maytime,
  Of all months the sweetest comer,
  Bridal of the spring and summer,
When the earth is gay with flowers, and the air is
    sweet with song,
  Pastures deep in grass and clover,
  Honey for each wandering rover,
  Skies that laugh at tempests over
    To the emerald month belong!

O! the hawthorn, fragrant hawthorn!
  Summer snow-wreaths drifting lightly
  O'er the hedgerows, opening brightly
All its myriad, starlike blossoms to the glamour of
    the day,
  Brightening all the children's leisure,
  As they take their royal pleasure
  Gathering largess of its treasure,
    Filling hands and homes with May.

O! the bluebells, nodding bluebells,
  Tinted like the skies above them,
  Set where all may see and love them,
By the roadside, in the coppice, and the meadow-
    lands between;

Every breeze that stirs the dingle
  Sets their mimic bells a-jingle,
  All the sweets of Maytime mingle
    In their world of blue and green.

O! the fragrance of the morning,
  When the chestnut spires are lifted,
  And its clustering leaves are rifted
With the sunbeams glinting through them, opening
    out each fluted fold,
  And the wind is truant playing,
  In the lilac hedge delaying,
  And the tall laburnum swaying
    With its twinkling showers of gold.

O! the gladness of life's Maytime,
  When the common ways of duty
  Are new robed and decked with beauty,
And love hears the skylark's music every day and all
    day long.
  God is good, this witness bringing;
  Every joy from Him is springing,
  And we bless His name in singing
    In the month of flower and song!

SIXTY POUNDS PER ANNUM, AND HOW I LIVE UPON IT.

By A YOUNG GENTLEWOMAN.

CHAPTER II.

MR. MURRAY proved quite as helpful and kind as his wife had declared him to be. He listened with great sympathy to the account of my many troubles, and quite agreed with us in the idea of my trying to live on what means I had, at least until I had tried the experiment and found the feat impossible.

"If you were not the quiet, staid lassie I have always known you, Margaret, I should not agree with you," he said; "but I think you may be trusted to form your own plans in this emergency. I shall trust Lucy to look after you, and you know where you can have help if need be. For your father's sake you may depend on me always, as well as for your own."

He then aided us in the composition of an advertisement, which explained our needs clearly, *i.e.*, two rooms for a young lady, unfurnished, in a quiet and thoroughly respectable street, in Paddington or near Westbourne Grove, where the landlady could furnish references as to her character and that of her house.

This was inserted in two of the daily papers, and then we waited impatiently for some answers to it.

The next few days after our advertisement was put into the various papers we had several answers, some of which promised very well; we went to see each one in turn, but in all there was much lacking, and neither the position nor the people were what Mrs. Murray liked. Since that time I have so often thought that, if some of the money applied to building the "Peabody flats" could have been applied to building flats suitable to the purses of impecunious ladies, how good it would have been for me. It seemed nearly impossible to find what one wanted. Now I hope better days are coming, and the wants of gentlewomen who work, and gentlewomen who do not work but are also limited in means, will meet with attention. And flats are being built all over London, but in most of them, unfortunately, the rents are too high to benefit the class to which I belong. An ordinary London house, when divided out and let in unfurnished apartments, is not comfortable, because so thoroughly unfitted for the purpose. There is no privacy, and no freedom from the landlady's ever-prying eye, which even penetrates into the rooms which she does not furnish. The position is also trying, in regard to her, for her temper is rarely good, and she is often quarrelsome and *exigeante*. In fact, few women in that rank of life have the needful patience and good humour which the office of landlady requires.

Fortunately, Mrs. Murray was very anxious that I should not be in a hurry, nor make a start in my new life without finding what was needful, both in position and people. And I was not idle, for I had much also to find out as to prices and ways of getting things in London, and I wished to plan my small income so as to make the best of it. I thought £40 per annum would suffice to cover my expenses for rent, food, fire, and light, the rent to include what services I required. As

regards the fire and lighting part, I acquired much useful information from a pleasant and practical little woman, who came to Mrs. Murray as a dressmaker, and did what needle-work was needed in the house. It was through her kind offices that we ultimately found a house to suit me in every way, as the advertisements proved of no real value after all. From her I learned that the price of coal was 1s. per hundred, of coke 1s. 2d. the sack; and that I should probably find close by my new home a small coal merchant, who would send in just what I wanted. She thought I should find that the quantity above-named would last me for a fortnight during the winter for one fire. Finally she advised me, in addition to wood, to have some patent firelighters, or "wheels," at a farthing each, which would not only light my fire, but she said that in the summer one would be enough to boil my kettle, without the expense of lighting the fire at all, as they last quite twenty minutes. She also introduced to me the square blocks of coal, which are a penny each for the largest size, and three for twopence for the smaller size. They seem to be made of powdered coal formed into blocks, and are very useful for keeping in a fire. They should be put on when the fire is good, and they will burn for some hours unbroken. For instance, if put on the fire at night they will last all night, and when broken up with the poker will light the fire and serve to boil the kettle in the morning. So they prove an excellent thing for sick rooms.

In one of my chats with my wise little dressmaker, she advised me to buy one of the white glass lamps with the pearly-white shades, for my ordinary use, and added that she had seen them at 1s. 11d. in The Grove. On going in search of one, however, I found that I could only get one at 2s., but the wick was in it, and it was ready for filling and lighting. There are several kinds of oil, some more expensive than others, but I found a very good, clear, bright oil, called "safety oil," at threepence a

---

A Young Gentlewoman, "Sixty Pounds per Annum, and How I Live Upon It" (Volume 9, 7 April 1888, p. 444).

quart; and later on I paid sixpence for my quart oil-can. The quart lasted me in the winter a week, and sometimes in the summer it spun out to a fortnight. I find my lamp, trimmed and taken charge of by myself, is a perfect success always. I do not break chimneys. I have no smell from it, and no smoke; and armed with a pair of old gloves, a clean cloth, and some soft paper, I clean it without trouble.

I do not fancy that care enough is taken by ordinary servants, and that is the cause of the constant complaints about lamps, and the unpleasant smell and smoke from them. I had put down fire and light at £4 per annum, but I did not spend as much as that when I got into the way of managing my fire.

We had begun to despair of finding anything suitable through our advertisements, when one morning the maid came to me and said that Miss Dackett would be glad to speak to me. "Miss Dackett" seemed at first unknown to me, when I suddenly remembered that it was the name of my wise little dressmaker, usually called Eliza by Mrs. Murray, who had known her many years. So I hastened upstairs to find Miss Dackett and Mrs. Murray discussing some topic very eagerly, and as I entered Mrs. Murray said—

"I think Eliza has heard of the very thing you need, dear."

"Rooms?" I queried.

"Yes. Two superior servants who have left places where they have been for years, have taken a small house, and want to let three of the floors to ladies, if possible, unfurnished. They have already one lady in the dining-room, who is out all day in the City, in a typewriting office; and Eliza is very anxious we should go and look at the other two floors to-day. She is sure one of them will just suit you."

"It sounds likely," I said; "can you come with me to-day?"

"I shall be ready to go before luncheon," Mrs. Murray answered. "You may go and get ready at eleven o'clock."

"The street is a quiet and respectable one," said Eliza presently, "and the windows of the house are very nicely situated, and face the south."

Half-past eleven found us walking along one of the many rather dull but pretty streets in the Westbourne Park district. There was a general air of greenery and gardens in the place, and I was thankful that the sun shone to give us a good opinion of my new home. The house was midway up, and there was a bend of the street in front, and a cross street at the side, which made quite an open space. The landlady came in answer to our knock, and we were both agreeably impressed with her pleasant, cheery manners, which were good, respectful, and self-respecting at once. The instant we mentioned Eliza's name she seemed to know all about us, and said that Eliza's sister had been lady's-maid for years where she and her husband had lived, as indoor servant and upper housemaid. From her master and mistress they could have good references; and it was a legacy from their master's father that had enabled them to take this house. Her husband, she said, went each day to an old gentleman, on whom he waited, returning late at night.

While this conversation had been going on we had mounted the stairs and gained the second floor rooms. The house looked very clean and bright, and had been evidently newly done up for its present tenants. There were two pleasant rooms, a back and a front one, with a wide door between them. There were two windows in front and a balcony and a window at the back, with a small garden with a tree in it to look upon. The rooms were both papered with a light-grey paper, and painted the same colour, the back room being very small. This latter was 2s. 6d. a week, the front room being 4s. (without attendance, of course). There was part of a coal-cellar at my service, and I must help to carpet the stairs, the landlady paying a third, the future tenant of the first floor and myself a third each. The price of the rooms was thus £17 per annum. So, after a little consideration, I asked the landlady whether she would bring up my coals, answer the door to my visitors, keep my windows clean, and the stairs, and sweep my rooms out once a week, if I gave her 7s. 6d. a week. What little cooking I needed I meant to manage for myself. After a little time she agreed to this, first inquiring as to the probable number of visitors I should have, which I thought would not be many. I, on my part, agreed to the stair-carpet question, but said I should not like a shabby one, and I hoped she would not want one either. She quite agreed on that point with me, and said she would go and look at the carpets, and see what she could manage to procure a nice one for. I also suggested that she should have the floor of the hall and the sides of the stairs stained and varnished, to represent dark oak, which would save her time in cleaning them, and look well. The walls of the hall were hung with the usual yellow varnished hall-paper, with yellow-grained paint to match. So I begged her to get as much red as she could obtain in her carpet, and to let all the colours be rich and bright.

We arranged that Mr. Murray should draw up an agreement for a year, mentioning the service required, when the references had been seen, and Mrs. Murray gave her address, and also that of my father's lawyer. My new landlady's name was Warner, and we were both much pleased with her, though I secretly wished the rooms could have been a little larger. Fortunately I knew my grand-aunt's furniture had been extremely old-fashioned, and that it had been kept because it was of the spindle-legged kind, some of it being handsomely inlaid, and some in Dutch marqueterie. The beds and bedding had all been sold, but I knew that the linen and her plate had both been kept; and if they had once been sufficient for one single lady, they would be enough for another.

As we walked home together Mrs. Murray decided that she would write to the references at once, and get the answer with as little delay as possible, for she quite agreed with me that, if peace and happiness were to be preserved, my small mansion must be taken and furnished before my aunt returned to town.

(*To be continued.*)

ONE LITTLE VEIN OF DROSS.

By RUTH LAMB, Author of "Her Own Choice," etc.

CHAPTER XXII.

NO person was more delighted at hearing the true story of Miss Martin's diamonds than was Mr. James Smith. "It is pleasant to know for certain that the things were the young lady's own, sir," he said, when my husband told him, "though you and I could never bring ourselves to doubt that." Then, with a look of grim satisfaction, "What a pull this gives you over Mr. Fielden! It quite cheers me up when I think that if I have failed to find your property, I never made such a blunder in my judgment as he did. What you would have been drawn into if you had listened to him and got that warrant!"

My husband gave a little shudder at the thought of it, and Smith added,

"Depend on it, sir, there is something quite out of the common about that business of yours. I never was utterly at fault before, and I am certain the mystery will be explained in some very unlooked for way."

And it was.

Mr. Fielden was duly informed of the facts, which proved Miss Martin's innocence. He had been very stiff with my husband ever since the latter ventured to act in opposition to his advice. The knowledge that he had been mistaken in giving it did not tend to smooth the lawyer's ruffled plumes, though he could scarcely help a formal expression of satisfaction that the young person had all along been free from blame.

It was a bitter mortification to himself to be proved less than infallible in a professional matter, and though he was longing to know whether Mrs. Beauchamp's property had been recovered, he would not inquire. Tom—dear naughty fellow—had, I fear, a wicked pleasure in abstaining from any allusion to these diamonds. "No," thought he, "Mr. Fielden said he washed his hands of the whole affair, and I will volunteer no information. I was bound to clear Miss Martin; I am not bound to say that about the lost diamonds we are still at fault."

Though one shadow had been lifted from Ellen Martin's mind, the anxiety she still had to bear was sufficiently trying. Each day showed more plainly that Edward's condition was becoming less hopeful.

The mother never allowed herself to doubt that he would be eventually restored to health, and found her happiness in ministering to his wants. Ellen was almost thankful for the veil which yearning love threw over Mrs. Martin's eyes, and enabled her to hope against hope.

Another cause for anxiety the girl had to bear alone. There was something

---

SIXTY POUNDS PER ANNUM, AND HOW I LIVE UPON IT.

BY A YOUNG GENTLEWOMAN.

CHAPTER III.

THE references proved everything that could be wished, the former mistress of my future landlady saying that she was not only clean, honest, and respectable, but one of the kindest-hearted women possible, a fact she had proved in the course of a long family trouble and illness. So Mr. and Mrs. Murray both expressing themselves as thoroughly satisfied, Mr. Murray wrote out an agreement for a year, which was duly signed, making me the mistress of my two rooms from the 10th of the month. I was to pay monthly, as I had quite resolved to follow the ready cash principle in everything, and to manage with as little as possible; one of my great objects being to lay by a little store in case of illness or other trouble, and also because I fully intended to try to add to my small income in time, so as to enable me to look forward to a change and a little travelling some future day, as well as for extra comforts in my old age.

Now, many of my girl readers will doubtless have said, perhaps even before now, What a very odd girl! She never apparently thinks of the possibility of marriage, which might offer itself, and alter all her plans and ideas of life. And I think before I go on further, I should say that this idea of matrimony was one on which I rarely spent five minutes' thought. Perhaps if I had had the quiet home, free from anxiety, of most other girls, it would not have been so; but I had been obliged to be practical and thoughtful, both for myself and for others, at too early a period in my girlhood to have had room for much dreaming of the kind, and I felt as if matrimony would wait to be thought about some far day in the future, when only days of light-heartedness and amusement were before me, and when I could put anxiety and forethought for other matters into the past. Besides this, I had sufficiently thought out the matter to have decided against "marrying for marrying's sake" only, and to resolve to remain single, unless I found the best, the very best, that the world contained for me. This was one of the ideas my father had instilled into me, and I have thought since that he had been careful in inculcating such a lesson, because in those days he looked forward to the time when I should be in possession of the inheritance of my fathers; and he wished to guide me into making a wise choice for myself, on principle, and to defend me also from becoming the prey of fortune-hunters, who might be attracted by money alone, and not by any worthiness in me. So he had tried to form my judgment in some measure, as a rule and guide in this great event of life.

The first thing was to send for the furniture, which I have mentioned as having been left to me by my great-aunt, and find out of what it consisted, and what had to be added to it. On asking Mr. Bertram, I discovered that the furniture had been carefully stored in the house of her old servants, out at Richmond, where she had lived for so many years; and where, at my aunt's death, they had taken a house, and were letting a part of it in lodgings. They had been paid a small sum for taking care of the furniture by my trustees, and the tin box with the small articles of plate which she had also left me was in the bank; and Mr. Bertram would send it to me that very day if I wished it, and a receipt to sign, showing I had received it safely from my trustees.

That afternoon the box came, and after dinner, when Mr. and Mrs. Murray and myself were in the drawing-room, we opened it, and found a list of its contents lying on the top of the unshapely green baize bags which contained them. A coffee-pot, tea-pot, two cream ewers, a sugar basin and tongs, two salvers, a dozen each of spoons and forks, small and large, with gravy spoons and ladles; four silver candlesticks, two bedroom candlesticks, a silver box with chased designs on it, several mugs, a mustard-pot, salt-cellars, and a sugar-sifter which looked like a tall pepper-pot; besides several old-fashioned trinkets, mourning rings and lockets, and a set of cameos.

Mr. Murray looked carefully over the silver, and at last said gravely—

"Do you know anything about the value of this, Margaret?"

"No," I answered. "Nothing. It seems old."

"It is not only old but very valuable," said Mr. Murray. "The spoons and forks are all of the old 'rat-tail' sort; and the coffee and tea pot very early Georgian. There is not less than £150 worth here, I think."

I looked up without much astonishment, for I suddenly remembered that my Uncle Tom had said something of the value of my great aunt's silver to my father not long after her death, when her watch and chain had been sent out to me by my father's wishes, thinking that I might have the use of them, as I was quite old enough.

"I shall leave the box with you and Mrs. Murray, and only take the few things I need, if you will allow me."

"I was just going to say that very thing," said Mr. Murray. "In that case you will have no anxiety about your valuables."

The next day we went down to Richmond to look at the furniture. We found my aunt's two old servants much as I remembered them when a child, when I had once been with my mother to visit her. They had been respectively butler and lady's-maid in the first days of service, but latterly, when increasing age and infirmities had gained on my aunt, and she had also suffered from her nephew's losses, they had been everything to her, and any help needed had been given by a young general servant in the kitchen. My great-aunt had been nearly forty years a widow, and her husband's money had gone back at her death, of course to his family; and except what she had left to me, her namesake and god-daughter—and a pension of £80 left to her two faithful old servants so long as they lived, which would come to me at their deaths—she had nothing remaining of her own money which had come to her from her great-grand-father. The furniture had all been carefully stored in one room. The beds and bedding had been given to the two old servants, and only the best of the furniture was stored; but there seemed more than I should want, and I chose out enough for the furnishing of my two rooms from the pretty spindle-legged articles, which were all of them very valuable in the eyes of the present-day world. Some of the inlaid ones Mrs. Murray begged me to leave where they were, as being too valuable to take away. I found, however, a small wardrobe and chest of drawers, with a lovely sofa and tables and chairs, which would make my rooms look quite princely, as I thought.

Amongst the other belongings was a small-sized Turkey carpet, which I seized on with no small glee. It had not been much used, even though it was old; and its faded, delicate hues seemed quite perfect. Bennett, my great-aunt's man, was very helpful, and arranged with me to bring everything I wanted to town in a small van, and see it safely carried upstairs himself. He also promised to make the bargain, and have it done at a moderate price. I had a great deal to hear and to tell to Bennett and his wife; and so we stayed till after the sun had set, and had tea with them, returning to London and Mr. Murray to relate our afternoon's adventures, and then have dinner.

The next morning I went to my new establishment, and found my kind future landlady had cleaned the floors of the two rooms again, as I had asked her to do, and they were all ready for staining, so I turned my steps to the renowned emporium in the Grove, to purchase a quart of "Ryland's Floor Varnish," in dark oak, which costs 3s. 6d., including can and brush. This I thought would with care be all I wanted for my two rooms. The bedroom I intended to do entirely, and in the drawing-room only a border of about two feet round the edges. In a short time I was back again, and covering my dress with the apron I had brought with me, I began my work on the floor. The marking out of the border did not take very long, and I soon had the pleasure of seeing the effect of my work. The chief merit of this varnish is that it needs no sizing before use, and dries very quickly also.

The drawing-room border took me about an hour and a half to accomplish, and I was careful to work with the grain of the wood of the floor. Then I had a rest, and ate the sandwiches Mrs. Murray had given me; and when I felt quite refreshed I began on the bedroom floor, which was to be varnished all over. I was equally lucky with that, and at about five p.m. found myself quietly seated opposite my kind friend and hostess, very, very tired, but enjoying my tea, and the pleasant talk which accompanied it, after my long day's work. Thank goodness I had finished it all, and had got everything in readiness for Bennett's van and its contents to-morrow.

Mrs. Murray decidedly refused to let me go again to see about the furniture, as she was sure Bennett would do better if left to himself, and would enjoy the return to old employments, too, so I thankfully consented to rest all day at home, and wait for good old Bennett's report, when he came for the tea Mrs. Murray had promised him, after the van was emptied of its contents and sent home.

I was tired enough the next day, after my unaccustomed exertions, just as Mrs. Murray had thought I should be. Bennett arrived about five p.m., and announced that everything was quite safely housed at my new home, and that the journey from Richmond had been accomplished without any mishap; all of which I was most thankful to hear. Bennett further remarked quietly that he had taken the liberty of laying the carpet down, to save me the trouble, and that I should find it fitted very nicely indeed. For this piece of thoughtful kindness I thanked him very warmly; and his inner man having been refreshed by Mrs. Murray with some tea and a sandwich or two, Bennett departed with our good wishes, promising to send the bill for the van in a day or two.

We had our usual friendly pleasant evening, and I was already beginning to feel that the number of them was steadily lessening, and I had so enjoyed my stay with Mr. and Mrs. Murray, and their ready sympathy with me in my troubles had been such a comfort and happiness to me. I had not been much used to receiving it from anyone, and consequently I valued and enjoyed it the more.

We were always early risers at the Murrays' house, and the breakfast hour was eight o'clock, as Mr Murray went off to his office early. So the very next morning found me by nine o'clock on my way to my new home, having promised Mrs. Murray that I would return to luncheon at half-past one. As I walked along I mentally made a note of the things I wanted, and thought that a single iron bedstead, a pair of blankets, white quilt, small mattress, two pillows, a bath, and a set of bedroom crockery would be all my wants would demand for the bedroom; and I must find out the prices exactly, though I knew, approximately, what they would cost.

Pondering on all these particulars of my household arrangements, I arrived at my new abode, and was warmly welcomed by Mrs. Warner, my new landlady, who was anxious to show me the carpet she had chosen for the stairs, of which I was to pay my third share. I admired her choice very much, and she had taken a lesson from me in staining the floors, a lesson evidently well learnt. She had stained the sides of the stairs just as I had suggested, and the general effect of the wall and staircase was very good, and thus I felt that I should not be ashamed to receive anyone under my new roof.

I mounted the stairs slowly. I was tired with my walk, and the heat was becoming great in the sunshine, leaving Mrs. Warner much pleased with my praises of her choice of a stair carpet and the pretty appearance of the hall. When I arrived at my landing on the stairs and opened the door of my new sitting-room, I could not forbear an exclamation of astonishment and delight. Poor old Bennett had certainly performed miracles in the arrangement of my rooms, and the small drawing-room looked quite charming, and seemed to need nothing but an occupier. There were Venetian blinds in all the windows of the house, so one did not miss nor appear to need curtains, which, in many cases, seem to me to be mere dust-traps, especially in

London, where dust and dirt specially abound. The Turkey carpet looked beautiful, and just matched the style of the old thin-legged sofa, tables, and armchairs. Everything had an old-world look, I thought; and in my bedroom the chest of drawers, washing-stand, and chairs were neatly placed, and I made up my mind that a 3-feet bedstead would do, or even a 2 feet 10 inches, as a small bed would give me more room.

Bennett had also brought me the small chest full of my aunt's linen, which I opened, and found its contents would be amply sufficient for everything I should require, and I had only blankets, therefore, to buy. I looked at the grates in both rooms, and pondered over my plans for my own cooking, which ended in my purchasing what is known as a box of household requisites; and a spirit lamp and kettle later on. The grates were very tiny, and that in the back room had a hob, and if I needed any cookery, too considerable for my spirit lamp, I meant to use that. The subject of my experiments and contrivances in the matter of cookery I shall keep for my next and last article, as it is, perhaps, the most important of all, and needs one all to itself.

Over our afternoon tea Mrs. Murray and myself discussed the prices of beds, mattress, and blankets, and on the following morning we went out together, and I bought a small new iron bedstead, 2 feet 6 inches in width, for £1, and had it fitted with a spring lath mattress, called a "Somier," I believe, price 10s. 6d., which provides a most comfortable bed. The wool and hair mattress cost £1; and the pillows, 7s. 6d. each; while three blankets for the bed, at 4s. 6d. each, and a white quilt, 5s., finished my purchases; except a toilet set for the washstand, which cost me 7s. 6d. On my way home I bought a cheap afternoon tea-set on a tray, with six cups and saucers, teapot, sugar bowl, and cream jug. To these I added six small plates and six large ones, of the same

pattern, and a red band at the edge. Then I purchased knives, two small and two large, and I thought my investments in the household utensil kind were completed. The purchase of the afternoon tea-set gave me a tea-tray, and would also save me from using the silver too much, and having it to keep clean. If my purchases seem too extravagant, it must always be remembered that I desired to live like a gentlewoman; and, besides, I had my aunt's piercing eye to dread, and she represented to me the traditional "Mrs. Grundy." So I looked forward to having many a happy afternoon tea with my friends in spite of my narrowed means; and my expectations were not disappointed. Then I had numberless small things to buy, such as a few towels and dusters for my washing-up and household use; also a leather and a dusting-brush, a coal-scuttle and fireirons and dust-pan. All these had to be stored in the large cupboard in the sitting-room, where I intended to keep my tiny pantry and kitchen together. By the time I had completed my purchases I had spent a little over £7; not very much, when all is considered, to set up housekeeping upon.

And so the time drew on to the day when I must say farewell to my kind entertainers, and strike out into the world for myself. I did not say farewell without some tears, both on Mrs. Murray's part and my own, even though she made me promise to come and see her every two or three days without fail. Their kindness had been everything to me in my trouble, and could never be repaid; and my stay with them seemed like the last home days I was to have. However, when the day did come, I went bravely off with a little flutter of anticipation at my heart, for, after all, I was only twenty-two, and if I were rather a plain girl I had youth in my favour, and I was too new to absolute liberty not to feel some excitement as I took up life and its management for myself.

(To be concluded.)

JOSEPHINE.
A TALE OF THE VENDETTA.

CHAPTER III.

FROM the moment that Josephine knew she might any day expect the arrival of the English yacht, she could think of nothing else, for it was to bring her Dorothy—the little Dorothy, who had been the pet of the *pension*—the wilful, exacting, hot-tempered little creature, who was, nevertheless, always lovable and charming—Dorothy, who in her pretty imperious fashion had chosen her for her bosom friend, a post which had entailed many duties and responsibilities, all of which Josephine had been content to take upon herself, feeling amply repaid for any little sacrifices she might make by the knowledge that Dorothy looked up to and depended upon her as she might have done had she been a beloved elder sister. At home the rich English girl had been accustomed to the service of a maid, and seemed to have no idea of helping herself. "Of course it was hard for her to do so," Josephine thought, and many an hour was spent by her in supplying that functionary's place. It was she, too, who helped her with her studies—learning to speak English on purpose that she might do so—who shielded her from blame or punishment (often by taking it upon her own shoulders) when rules had been needlessly or wilfully transgressed. Dorothy responded to this almost maternal love with a clinging, exacting affection which was very sweet to the elder girl. Had she been allowed to do so, Josephine would now have lavished just the same kind of loving care upon her baby brother, but he was so surrounded by the attentions of nurse and

parent, that she felt almost like an outsider. A French *bonne* had arrived from Nice, who was in every way capable, and was devoted to her little charge, yet neither parent could bear that he should be left long in her care without the superintendence of his mother. Every present energy, every dream for the future, was inspired by love and anxiety for him. Josephine was no longer her parents' chief hope and occupation, but she accepted the fact as a natural and inevitable one without the slightest murmur. Her unselfishness was to be tested still more severely. Two or three days before the arrival of the Sea Nymph, Madame de Roccaserra told her daughter that her father had something of importance to tell her. The announcement was made with an anxious solemnity of manner, which prepared her for something disagreeable, and made her ask, in alarm, "Have I then done anything to displease him?"

"No, my daughter," replied her mother, tenderly, "and that makes it more difficult for us to reconcile ourselves to the alteration in your position, which your father thinks it his duty to make. But come now, he awaits you in the little *salon*." And taking her daughter's arm, she led her in silence to her father's presence.

"What is it, my father?" asked Josephine, tremblingly.

"It is simply that your mother thinks you may regret that you are no longer my sole heiress," replied her father with his usual good-natured smile, "and insists that I shall inform you of the fact, although of course you must know it."

"Is this all?" asked Josephine, in relieved tones. "I never thought about it till this moment; and, had I done so, it would make no difference. I know you will do for me what you consider right."

"But, my child——" began her mother.

"*Tiens*, Sophie! You pity the little one more than she pities herself!" interrupted her husband. "I know better my daughter's good heart than does her mother, it seems."

"Ah, Horace, you do not understand; it is through another she will feel this change," insisted his wife. "Tell her the difference it will make to Jacques!"

"To Jacques!" exclaimed Josephine, with a sudden surprised sense of uneasiness; "do you, then, think him so mercenary—so——. I shall have a *dot*, like other girls! Is it not so?"

"Listen, my daughter," returned her father, gravely. "You know what the first arrangement was. Upon your marriage Jacques was to enter into partnership with me. At my death the property would have come to you, less a certain fixed yearly income for your mother during her life. That, of course, is no longer possible—he will know that; but he may have hoped that I should still take him into partnership. Now that I have a son to succeed me, I do not intend to charge the estate with a partner. Your *dot* will be a third share of the annual proceeds of the property. Jacques will have no further interest in the matter."

"But that is much—a third," returned Josephine, quickly; "for myself I shall not use half—the rest will be his. He will know that."

THE GIPSY.

WANDERING from the busy fair,
　Free awhile from noise and bustle.
　Rests she idly in the shade;
And the softness of the air,
　And the young leaves' dreamy rustle,
　Seem to soothe the little maid.

Look of bird, half bold, half shy,
　Pretty smile, now grave, now pleasant,
　And a certain careless grace;
Dusky tresses, brilliant eye,
　Air of princess, yet of peasant—
　All bespeak her gipsy race.

She is silent as the morn,
　Yet her kindling eyes say clearly :
　" I like not your friendly stare,
Which scarce hides your kindly scorn
　For the life we love most dearly,
　Though we tramp from fair to fair.

" Nay, then, smile—if you must gaze—
　On the humble path we follow,
　While we bless you, hearth and hall :
Though they wander different ways,
　Do the tame bird and the swallow,
　They are sisters—after all !

" And, suppose we sometimes tire
　Of the tambourine and spangles,
　Of the noises and the glare;
Have you nothing to desire ?
　Has your world·no harsher jangles
　Than the music of the fair ? "

ELLIS WALTON.

SIXTY POUNDS PER ANNUM, AND HOW I LIVE UPON IT.

BY A YOUNG GENTLEWOMAN.

CHAPTER IV.

A FEW days after I was comfortably settled in my new abode, I was making rapid progress in learning how to manage my income, so that I bid fair to realise the ideal for which I was striving, i.e., to live and provide light, fire, house, and food for £40 per annum. I knew this could not be managed without great and incessant care, but still I thought it possible. It was not, however, at first that I fully arrived at my results, for I had to win my experience at every point, and I tried various modes of living before I discovered a solution for my difficulties, and adopted a settled plan that suited me. At first I began with the usual tea or coffee for breakfast, with bread and butter, but afterwards I found that wheat-meal porridge was a better substitute, with milk, for my morning's meal, and was, moreover, a decided saving. When I advanced as far as this, I also arrived at grinding my own meal in a coffee mill, for which I paid 3s. 6d., and found a considerable saving in doing so, as wheat is generally about a penny half-penny a pound, and five pounds of wheat lasted me a fortnight for my unleavened bread and my porridge. Then I discovered that I could make the latter twice a week, as it was more nutritious after keeping a day or two. When I got tired of wheatmeal porridge, I fell back on oatmeal and Indian meal instead. The last-named can also be ground in a coffee-mill, and is worth about a penny a pound.

One of the secrets of making any kind of porridge is to have the water you are about to use really boiling—bubbling up, I mean. Sprinkle the meal in with the left hand, while you stir with the right. This prevents it gathering into lumps. Oatmeal requires at least twenty minutes' brisk boiling, but wheaten meal will be cooked in ten minutes. Indian meal takes the longest time to boil of all, and will not be cooked under thirty or forty minutes. It may, however, be mixed with wheat or oatmeal with advantage. All these moist foods (I am told by a doctor) should be eaten very slowly. They may be eaten with salt or with sugar and milk, or else with "golden syrup" or a syrup made of fruit. One drawback in London is the dearness of milk. It is rarely to be depended on, save from a thoroughly good company, and costs from fourpence to fivepence a quart. Now, however, skim-milk can be got, and so can buttermilk. All the milk used should, in my opinion, be boiled before using. The unsweetened "Swiss milk" is considered by many to be the least expensive form of milk, but I did not find this the case. Perhaps I should have been more successful if I had liked it for porridge, but I did not, though it is very nice for tea or coffee; and also is preferred by many to eat with puddings, instead of cream.

I had thought a great deal over the subject of diet before I went to my new home, and I saw that I should not be able to manage on the usual diet, nor the general method of preparing the meals of the day.

In the first place, the cooking of meat was not to be thought of—even the smell and the grease alone put that entirely out of the question. So I was either thrown back on buying meat and poultry ready cooked, or on becoming in some sort a vegetarian, while retaining milk, cheese, butter and eggs in my diet. This last decision suited me best, and I felt I could manage very well on it, as I had never been a great meat-eater in my life, and did not care about it at all. I had learnt quite enough of the respective values of edibles to know that meat held a very low place, compared to the cereals, beans, peas, or lentils; the latter, indeed, contains more nutriment than can be found in any other single food. So my mind was made up. My object was to live, and to make eight shillings a week sufficient for everything, and so I went to work to arrive at my wished-for goal as soon as might be possible. The first thing after making porridge was to try to make bread.

I was rather proud, as the days went on, of my success in this way. It was unfermented, and I had learnt to like it long before in my girlish days, and everyone who tasted it enjoyed it. I had several ways of making it, either with whole wheatmeal, white flour, or a mixture of Indian-meal, ryemeal, or oatmeal, with flour or whole wheatmeal. Any of these compounds were good. The flour, whatever it be, must be mixed with boiling water till resolved into a thick dough, and then rolled out into a flat cake, which I used to bake, as the Australians do their "damper," I believe, in the frying-pan, which latter requires in the first instance a very slight greasing. Do not wet the dough too much, nor roll more than twice, if possible, for fear of making it too heavy, and doubtless I need not say to you, do not make them thick; about an inch in thickness is quite enough, if not too much. Only experience will enable you to make them well, as it is impossible to say how much flour is needed, or how much water to mix it with. I used a large white basin, and one of my cakes sometimes lasted two days. But I am not a great bread-eater. Mrs. Murray, who used to come to tea very often, thought them delicious when first made, and eaten hot, cut open and buttered. Honey is a very agreeable addition to them.

People unaccustomed to unfermented bread and cakes require to get used to it; for our tastes have become so vitiated by civilisation that we cannot get used to the primitive forms. Cornmeal bread and cakes I am particularly fond of, and they are equally good hot or cold. The following is a good and simple recipe for corn-bread.

One pint of corn-flour, one pint of ordinary flour, half a teaspoonful of cream of tartar, half a teaspoonful of soda, and a little salt. Mix the two flours together first, and rub the soda smoothly into the milk—a small quantity of milk to begin with. Mix the cream of tartar dry with the flour, then add the milk. Beat till quite smooth with a wooden spoon, and bake in a quick oven for about thirty minutes.

A Young Gentlewoman, "Sixty Pounds per Annum, and How I Live Upon It" (Volume 9, 4 August 1888, p. 712).

DERBYSHIRE SEED BREAD.

Take one pound of flour, quarter of a pound of butter, six ounces of sugar, a few caraway seeds, one egg well beaten, two teaspoonfuls of baking powder; mix the baking powder with a little cold milk; rub the butter into the flour, add the sugar and the egg, and lastly mix the whole into a light dough with a little cold milk. A few raisins will be an improvement to this very modest recipe, which costs little and will keep for days. Bake in a slow oven, forming into the shape of buns on the tin you bake in.

My small household arrangements in my new home were all gathered together in one of the large cupboards, standing about four feet high, which were fixtures on either side of the mantelpiece in the sitting-room. They were sufficiently deep and commodious to hold all my belongings, and were pantry, kitchen, and larder in one, while I used the top as my kitchen table, and had a sheet of white American cloth as a cover, which could easily be washed clean. The first summer and autumn of my living alone I did all my cooking with the aid of a spirit lamp. I have the lamp, stand, two saucepans, a frying pan, and a tea kettle. I can, I think, perform all kinds of cookery on my spirit lamp. The best of these lamps are those that have a lid, by means of which one can reduce the fire to half, and this will be found to keep the pot boiling or saucepan cooking for fully half an hour. The best saucepans are of enamelled iron, which are easily kept clean, and the frying pan should be of this also. Stewed fruit, rice milk, batter puddings, custard puddings, blancmange, stewed tomatoes, all kinds of soups; all of these are most successfully managed with the spirit lamp, and so is my wheatmeal porridge and my unfermented bread, which is baked in the frying pan.

With the advent of winter the sphere of my cookery enlarged, and I boiled my beans, peas, and lentils over the fire; and did enough of the former, and boiled enough potatoes to last some days, sometimes, indeed, quite a week. My method of cooking the beans was to soak them overnight in cold water; about half a pint of beans are enough; the small white haricots must be used. In the morning drain the beans and put them into a saucepan with plenty of cold water and a little salt. They should boil gently till they are tender, but not reduced to a pulp. Two hours is usually sufficient to cook them, then pour away nearly all the water and dredge in plenty of flour, with an ounce of butter, stirring them till they are thickened; a tablespoonful of chopped parsley is also added. Another way is to rub the butter into an ounce of flour, add half a pint of water and a tablespoonful of parsley, and when the beans are drained into a cullender, put them back into a saucepan in which the sauce has been heated. Shake them well over the fire till thoroughly mixed with it.

When cold they should be put away in a covered basin, and may be warmed up in many ways: curried, fried, mixed with Liebig's essence, and with grated cheese.

I add a few more recipes, which may be useful, if only as suggestions.

BUTTERED EGGS, OR "RUMBLED EGGS."

Break two or three eggs into a small stewpan, put in a table-spoonful of milk, a table-spoonful of butter, a little salt, and a little pepper. Set the pan over a moderate fire and stir the eggs with a spoon, being careful to keep all in motion till the eggs are set. Make a slice of toast, and pour the eggs on it, lightly pepper the top, and serve.

POTATOES "A LA MAITRE D'HOTEL."

Put a table-spoonful of butter into your pan, melt it, and mix smoothly into it a small table-spoonful of flour. Then stir in slowly a pint of milk. Stir constantly, till the milk begins to rise, when it is done. Then put in your cold potatoes, cut in slices, and add a little parsley chopped-up finely. The potatoes are ready to serve as soon as they are hot throughout.

AN EASILY MADE OMELET.

Take a small table-spoonful of flour, add enough water, or milk, to make a thin batter. Beat up two eggs very well, and add them to it, with a pinch of salt, and a little chopped up ham, or parsley. Pour the mixture into a well-greased pan, and fry to a light brown; turn and roll when done.

HAM TOAST.

Chop-up very finely the lean of a little boiled ham, beat-up the yolk and white of an egg, and mix with the ham, adding a little milk, to make a soft batter. Scald it over the fire, stirring all the time; have ready some well-buttered toast, and pour the mixture on it, and serve.

APPLE AND LEMON SAUCE.

Boil half-a-pint of water, with three-quarters of a pound of white sugar, till it becomes a rich syrup. Add the grated peel and juice of a large lemon, and a pound of apples, weighed after they have been peeled, cored, and cut small. Boil till reduced to a pulp; put into a jar. This sauce will keep for a year if needful.

CHEAP MARMALADE.

Add to twelve sweet oranges, one lemon. Squeeze out the juice, and boil the rinds till quite tender. Then cut into chips, taking out the seeds. Add to the juice, with a pound of sugar to every pound of orange peel. Boil for an hour over a slow fire, and when it begins to fasten, it is done.

MACARONI AND CHEESE.

Take two ounces of macaroni, boil for three-quarters of an hour, strain off the water; make a sauce of two table-spoonfuls of corn-flour and a little milk; put into the saucepan and boil. Then add the macaroni, and sprinkle in four table-spoonfuls of grated cheese, add a little butter and pepper, stir up well for a quarter of an hour, and serve. This may be also baked in the oven, with a little more cheese and butter on the top to make it brown, and served as "macaroni cheese."

STEWED TOMATOES.

Take a third part of the contents of a tin of tomatoes, or three or four fresh ones, cut up, put them into a saucepan on the fire, and add breadcrumbs to thicken them, a small lump of better, pepper and salt. Boil for about fifteen minutes.

TOMATO SOUP.

Take half the contents of a tin of tomatoes, put them on the fire in a small saucepan, and thicken with a table-spoonful of flour, rubbed up with a little butter. When hot, add a pint of milk, boil till thick enough, and serve. This is delicious tomato soup, and with bread, will form an appetising dinner.

SOUP WITH "LIEBIG'S EXTRACT OF MEAT."

Take a handful of the dried prepared vegetables for soup, and boil in a pint and a half of water for about half an hour; then mix enough extract in a cup with boiling water and a little salt to flavour the soup. This is generally about three-quarters of a teaspoonful.

APPLE AND RICE.

Boil three table-spoonfuls of rice. When tender, stir in two or three table-spoonfuls of stewed apples, a little piece of butter, and sugar to taste. Serve hot. Any kind of fruit many be substituted for apples in the summer, if already stewed.

FRUIT TOAST.

Make several rounds of dry toast, pour over them sufficient water to soften it. Have ready a dish of stewed fruit of any kind, with plenty of juice, and while it is boiling hot put the toast in layers in a deep dish, and pour the hot fruit over each layer of toast. The latter will absorb so large a portion of juice as to surprise you, and the dish is a most agreeable one for summer.

As I look over the various cookery books, I think there are numbers of recipes capable of adaptation to the wants of the single woman who wishes to cook for herself. I found after a time that I could reduce my labour in many ways. For instance, as I sat by my fire in the evening, I could prepare and cook the dinner for the morrow; make a little marmalade and boil my beans, peas, or potatoes; and so, when to-morrow came, my meal was soon ready. Beans and peas I considered as a meat course, and generally had some fruit for the sweet portion of the meal. Tea I never took, except at afternoon or "five o'clock tea," as I preferred a little cocoa at night, or even gruel occasionally, or a cup of Liebig, instead of a heavy meal. I am quite sure that the majority of people eat more than is at all needful, and they would be in better health with less to digest, or else with food of a lighter nature, yet more nutritious. This is the case with bread especially. The ordinary white baker's bread, or indeed the usual brown bread sold by them, are neither of them sufficiently nutritious, and people are induced to eat that which does not do them good. The real unfermented bread is so extremely solid and satisfying that one cannot eat much of it.

In addition to being a nice, pleasant woman, I found my kind landlady a most intelligent one, anxious to learn and improve herself in every way. Her admiration for my prowess in the cookery line was immense; and I soon found that she enjoyed nothing so much as a visit while my cookery was going on. Her delight over it was extraordinary, and she soon developed quite a talent for acquiring new ideas, adding to her labours the enthusiasm which I have seen manifested by a first-class *chef*, who considers his art the first in the universe! She was certainly an admirable cook, a "born" cook, such as very few are. She soon supplied herself with a small gas stove, and her husband declared her new accomplishments had "made her quite a girl again."

Her weekly cleaning of my rooms, with my daily dusting and brushing up the floor with dustpan and brush, kept everything in perfect order, and I was quite comfortable and happy. I was fortunate, too, in having the upstairs watertap close to me, on the little landing above, and consequently I could get my bath with no trouble for myself. As there happened to be no bathroom, I had been obliged to provide myself with a round sponge bath, which fortunately required but little water. When the winter came my kind landlady insisted on lighting my sitting-room fire every morning, and putting my kettle to boil before I was up. There was no use in remonstrating, for I have learnt that one can give more pleasure to people by accepting small services than by any gift you can bestow upon them.

I think I have, so far, proved that my attempt to live on my income of £60 per annum was, and has been, a successful one. At least, I have not had too many complaints or fault-findings from my aunt, who personifies "Mrs. Grundy" in my existence. She even deigns to partake of afternoon tea with me, and entertains me at dinner, without finding me too much of a "poor relation" to be presented to her friends. I have kept up my languages, and have made great progress with my painting; and Mrs. Murray has been heard to prophesy that I shall take a higher flight yet, and shall probably surprise my friends before long.

[THE END.]

WOMEN'S CLUBS IN LONDON.

PART I.

TIME was, and that even within the limits of this present century, when the idea of forming a "Women's Club" never entered into the fertile brain of the most "advanced" of our sex; although such an enormity had been suggested as a capital joke. But carried onwards by a flood of ever-augmenting difficulties — outcomes of the growth of an immense population—and with it the irresistible force of new and varied circumstances, we have had to over-rule many old-world prejudices, and content ourselves with holding the helm and steadying the ship through flood and tide beyond our power to stem.

Amongst the urgent causes necessitating social coalitions for personal improvement and mutual service amongst the several ranks of more or less educated women, more notably than others we may observe the increase of improvident marriages and those of the physically unsuitable, the many failures of financial enterprises, the deterioration of the value of land, and, most of all, the debased moral rectitude of non-paying tenantry. All these evil diseases have tended to break up the old healthy constitution of English society. Thus the daughters of the very *élite* of the untitled aristocracy are driven from home, and from private works of benevolence or recreation, to become the bread-earners for themselves and their families. Patent as this phenomenon must be to most of our readers, an article like this demands such an introduction as showing the origin of the needs-be for women's clubs. Some live in the country, and visit town for business or otherwise, and thus need such institutions. Others, though living in town or the suburbs, have no study for the pursuit of their literary, artistic, or scientific work at home; and a third party has to attend classes, and requires some more conveniently central or adjacent resting-place than home for so many days a week. Besides these cases, there are those who would prefer to take a bed at a women's club when alone to going to a hotel, if visiting town for shopping or for interviews with friends. We have at least two or three women's clubs which are residential, for the benefit of country members; of such are "The Alexandra" and "The Victoria." In addition to clubs, we also have special restaurants for women, which shall be indicated after I have dealt with the former.

I said that the mere notion of a club for the benefit of women was once in the recollection of many the most grotesque of comical ideas. But some allowance must be made for insular prejudices and slowness to accept innovations. The first step towards the appearance of women in a house of public resort for reading and entertainment was made some fifty years ago in Russia and in Germany. The system of *table d'hôtes* and the mixing of men and women took some time to become acclimatised in the brain of English folk of the upper classes, and the doleful "private dining-room" was engaged, *de rigueur*, for the benefit of the wives and daughters ostensibly out on a pleasure trip to see the world, and to acquire foreign languages by colloquial intercourse. Happily, *nous avons changé tout cela*. To return to the question of foreign clubs, though not formed for the exclusive or joint benefit of women and men, the former have been allowed introduction into them in Moscow, St. Petersburg, and in some German towns. About eighteen years ago the idea was taken up by a club in London, "The Bohemians," who had their rooms in Grafton Street, and opened their doors on Sundays to the highest class of professional singers, prima donnas, and persons of like vocations. But a grave mistake in the selection of one of these guests put an abrupt end to this first attempt. "The Bohemians" passed through several changes, and survives under the name of "The Lyric." And now, without further preamble, I invite my readers to follow me, as I seek out the various clubs for women already existing in London.

I started on my interesting quest on a lovely morning, which made the grim, black houses less unattractive in their normally most melancholy atmosphere, and I selected for my first visit of inspection what I regarded as the parent-institution of the kind. It was the first to set the example of a "mixed club," that is, one formed for the benefit of both sexes. The name will be familiar to many—viz., "The Albemarle." The house has rather an imposing frontage, as compared with the majority of its neighbours. The two drawing-rooms are lofty and spacious, and are thrown into one apartment, and the dining-room beneath in the same way. But the entrance hall robs the latter of its otherwise equal dimensions with the reception-rooms above, and can only afford sufficient accommodation for laying some forty covers at a time. This is a very inadequate number to meet the daily demand. Ascending to the bedroom storey, I found a very plainly-furnished smoking-room for gentlemen and a small dressing-room adjoining, also a library or room for writing, supplied with suitable tables (at the back), agreeably quiet and retired. Above this floor is a ladies' dressing-room, the office of the lady-secretary, and that of the housekeeping manager.

I had till now regarded the Albemarle Club as a rather fossilised institution, and drearily formal in its high and unquestionable respectability, and I was agreeably taken by surprise by the information I obtained anent the enormous proportions to which it has recently grown. Within the last four years or so it has become a great financial success, under the admirable management, I should say, of the excellent secretary and the housekeeper. The *chef* would appear to be unsurpassed amongst his fellows in other clubs, so affirm many of the gentlemen frequenters of the club, who have the credit of being good *connoisseurs* in the mysteries of the culinary art.

In view of the multitudes who have to wait in relays to be accommodated with seats at the dinner tables, for whom some four hundred covers would often prove none too many, it has been for a considerable time past acknowledged that the mansion in use is very much too small. "When and where will you have it?"—words of query in a well-known game that sometimes elicit singularly enigmatic replies—would seem, as yet, to have found no solution of objective difficulties in this case, and no response of a generally acceptable character for the many expectants.

No less than twenty-nine rules are given in their prospectus, and amongst them there is one limiting the number of members to six hundred—men and women, so far as may be possible, in about equal proportions. The entrance fee has been suspended by a resolution passed at the general meeting in 1884, but the subscription for the current year of five guineas is required from every new member on election, and the same amount thereafter, to fall due on the first of January every year. But a reduction of one guinea each is made in favour of members of one family residing together, and foreigners, colonists, and residents in India may become honorary members for one month. Members are permitted to introduce their friends to dine or otherwise use the house, provided they be above the age of sixteen. No gratuity may be offered to any servant of the club. The house is opened at 8.30 a.m., and closed at 1 a.m., no one being admitted after 12.30 a.m. This selection from the rules may suffice for the convenience of intending members, and I now take leave of this important institution, and select the nearest of its neighbours for our next consideration.

Not far to seek—on the sunny side of New Bond Street—there is a small and unpretending club, exclusively for the benefit of women, and these, without exception, must be graduates, undergraduates, and students who have passed certain examinations.

Unfortunately, there is no very apparent sign of the existence of a club to a general observer in passing. I overlooked it myself, and was moving on, when I sought again for the number specified. Yes, I was not mistaken, "31" was the number, and I only saw a tailor's shop on one side, and engravings or pictures of some sort on the other. I tried a query at the former shop, and was politely let through a side door within, and a very small brass plate indicating the locality of the club was pointed out to me—the Women's "University Club."

Before me was a narrow staircase, much in contrast with the handsome entrance of the mansion before-named; but arrived at the second floor, I was shown into a bright front room that looked comfortable and cheery, though very unpretending, and all the more suitable for study, from being raised thus far above the noisy traffic of that ever-crowded thoroughfare, New Bond Street. This pleasant room was united to one at the back, in which I noticed three or more additional writing tables, and all desirable papers and periodicals were provided. In one respect this club resembled the "Albemarle," as it is non-residential. Tea and coffee and bread and butter can be provided in the house; but were dinner, or rather luncheon, desired by the students, mutton chops, beafsteaks, cheese, or any other simple viands would be sent in on demand—not dressed, nor kept in readiness in the house.

The entrance fee is only one guinea, and the annual subscription is of the same amount, payable on the 1st of January. Members elected in April or September are only required to pay the balance of the subscription due for the current year. Persons eligible for full membership must be qualified in one of the ways of which I give a list:—

1. They must be graduates of a University.
2. Registered medical practitioners of the United Kingdom.
3. Students or lecturers who have been in residence for (at least) three terms at Girton or Newnham Colleges, Cambridge; or at Somerville or Lady Margaret Halls, Oxford.
4. Undergraduates of any University who

have passed the examination next after matriculation.

5. Students who have passed the first professional examination of any medical corporation.

The committee are empowered to invite special members to join the club, such as ladies who have taken a prominent part in the promotion of education, but who are not otherwise eligible to become members of the club. The number of these "special members" may not exceed twenty-three; the regular members at the present time comprise about 250 persons. And now I think I have given all necessary information respecting this useful little institution. No doubt it must be found not only of practical service to those needing a quiet retreat for writing or study, but also of refreshment, and a pleasant rendezvous for friends who could not arrange for private meetings elsewhere.

My next expedition was made to No. 3, Old Cavendish Street, and with this little proprietary club, entitled "The Victoria," I was much pleased. I was shown into a nicely-furnished reception or drawing-room, not very large, but lofty. On the same (first) floor there is a very nice dining-room, with several small tables; also a comfortable library. On the first bedroom floor above there were four or five bedrooms, and on the second as many more. One bedroom could accommodate three people, as it contained a double and a single bed. Seven rooms are allocated to visitors, and fourteen, or even fifteen, persons could be received. The rooms on the second bedroom floor are charged for at a somewhat less rate than those on the first. This club is a real acquisition, as it is a nice quiet place, exclusively for gentlewomen, where young ladies may be respectably lodged without a chaperon for a night or two. I heard that the young daughters of the rector of an important parish in a large provincial town were sent there without either governess or maid. I mention this with a view to the convenience of country readers, who may be at a loss for a quiet, respectable, and inexpensive refuge in visiting this great metropolis. Dinners may be had if required; otherwise, breakfasts, hot or cold luncheons, and teas are ordinarily supplied, and at very moderate charges. Ladies'-maids can be taken in. The entrance fee for members is two guineas, the annual subscription is to the same amount; and although there is a proprietress (Mrs. Goering), there are many

patronesses, amongst whom I may name the Marchioness of Abergavenny, the Countesses of Bective, Guilford, and Carnwath, and the Viscountess Strangford. Subscriptions are due in January, but ladies may join the club at any time, and be charged proportionately.

I walked on from Old Cavendish Street to the further side of Oxford Circus, until I reached No. 231, Oxford Street. A long list of names was to be seen on the side of the doorway, and amongst them I found that of "The New Somerville," "on the second floor." I went up, and found the office door open, and was received by the secretary, who was most obliging. This little office was separated from the large four-windowed general room by an iron revolving partition, which could be drawn up at will, whenever a larger room than that adjoining should be required. This, the general apartment, is pleasant, though unpretending. Two ladies were at tea in one corner, and there were others, busy or chatting and laughing together. There is a third room on the same floor, at the back, which is called "The Silent Room." Here those who have writing to do, or wish their readings and meditations to be undisturbed, can enjoy the amount of quiet they require. Above these apartments I was shown a room of considerable size, full of chairs and benches. Here the lectures, debates, and entertainments take place every week, on Tuesdays, at 8 p.m., and friends of the members are free to attend them. This apartment can be hired by the members for private receptions and entertainments. There is a lavatory on this floor.

The admission of members is by ballot—seven forms a quorum, and two blackballs exclude; but it is considered a point of honour not to blackball any candidate on account of her opinions—which, I imagine, are of a very mixed character. The club is opened at 9.30 a.m., and closed at 10.30 p.m., and on Sundays from 10 a.m. to 10 p.m. There is an entrance fee of ten shillings, and an annual subscription to the same amount. The lending library is free to all members, who now number upwards of 700, and applications from new candidates are still arriving. One special feature of this club is that a lower class, or so-called "working women," are admissible for membership. This scheme appears to have ended in failure; and, in my opinion, very necessarily so. Hereditary ideas, feelings, sympathies, and, in many cases, prejudices also, must render social intercourse on an equal

footing not only inexpedient but impossible. "Let every man abide in the same calling wherein he was called. Art thou called, being a servant, care not for it." Here there is no confounding of ranks, so far as this world is concerned; although "God hath chosen the poor (who are) rich in faith;" and they who believe are "all one in Christ Jesus, who is the Head of all," etc.

I met with much civility from the secretary of this club, who invited me to make use of either her office or "The Silent Room" for writing my notes; and when these were completed I set forth again in the now slanting sunshine, to pick up what information might be obtained in a visit to a perfectly different kind of institution.

No. 12, Grosvenor Street, Bond Street, W., is a large house occupied by an aristocratic and purely fashionable club, yclept "The Alexandra." I was shown into a comfortable room at the back, occupied by the secretary, who somewhat reluctantly supplied me with the rules and list of members. It is a residential and proprietary club, providing six bedrooms for the use of country members, and two for that of their maids. There are two drawing-rooms, dining, coffee, and reading rooms, and at the present time a new library is being constructed at the back of the house. An entrance fee of five guineas is exacted, and the annual subscriptions amount respectively to three and two guineas, the first-named for town members and the last for country ones. At the present time the number of members amounts to 726. Under no circumstances may a gentleman be introduced within the precincts of this essentially feminine resort, nor even may a woman's step profane its sacred apartments who is not introduced as a visitor by a member of the club. Only two children may be permitted to enter, and that only for a short time, "if perfectly quiet," but "little boys above seven" come under the ban of their sex.

Luncheon is served between the hours of 12.30 and 2.30 p.m., and dinners are provided on due notice. For any further details inquiry should be made of the secretary, while for a view of the apartments the curious must obtain the good offices of a private friend, if she have one, who has acquired the status of membership in this very exclusive sanctuary.

S. F. A. CAULFEILD.

(To be continued.)

VARIETIES.

A STOREHOUSE FOR GOLD.—It is much better to have true gold in the heart than in the hand.

BE PATIENT.—People are always talking of perseverance and courage and fortitude; but patience is the finest and worthiest part of fortitude, and the rarest too. I know twenty persevering girls for one patient one; but it is only that twenty-first one who can do her work out and out and enjoy it. For patience lies at the root of all pleasures and all powers. Hope herself ceases to be happiness when impatience companions her.—*Ruskin.*

WISDOM, POWER, AND RICHES.

Who is wise? She who learns from everyone.

Who is powerful? She who governs her passions.

Who is rich? She that is content.

A LOVE STORY.

"No, George," faltered the maiden, "I fear it cannot be. I admire you as a gentleman, I respect you as a friend, but——"

"Laura!" he exclaimed, "before you pass sentence, hear me out. A recent lucky stroke in business has enabled me to buy a beautiful house in Kensington, which shall be in your name. I will insure my life for ten thousand pounds, and——"

"George," calmly interposed the lovely girl, "you interrupted me. I was about to say that the sentiments of respect and esteem I feel for you, though so strong, are feeble in comparison with the deep love which—which I—which I have long——don't George, dear." For George had interrupted her again.

THE MODEST GIRL.—The truly modest girl is she who retains her modesty when she is blamed as well as when she is praised.

A PIECE OF ADVICE.

"John," said an experienced member of the Society of Friends, "I hear thou art going to be married."

"Yes," replied John, "I am."

"Well, I have one little piece of advice to give thee, and that is, never marry a woman worth more than thou art. When I married my wife I was worth just fifty shillings, and she was worth sixty-two; and whenever differences have occurred between us she has always thrown up the odd shillings."

A POPULAR BELIEF.—It is a popular belief that if there was a woman instead of a man in the moon, lunar history would no longer be a secret to us.

DO NOT QUARREL.—Is life long enough for quarrelling? Are there so many good people that they can afford to shun and avoid each other?—*Richter.*

S. F. A. Caulfeild, "Women's Clubs in London" (Volume 11, 21 June 1890, p. 599).

in another friend cost her still deeper pain. Mr. Glynne was not amongst those who traversed the five straight miles of dusty road to pay their respects to the heiress of Wyndham. Aldyth hardly expected that he would come unless invited; but when some weeks later she chanced to meet him at Mrs. Greenwood's, there was such a lack of the old friendliness in his manner as made it impossible for her to respond to his grave politeness except with a courtesy equally distant. Had anyone told John Glynne that he had spoken coldly to Aldyth Lorraine, he would have been surprised. He was conscious of an inward excitement on seeing her that forced him to exercise strong self-control. Whilst talking to others he thought only of her, and nothing that she said or did escaped his notice. But it was impossible for Aldyth to know this. She was conscious only that he remained aloof from her, and when others were paying her considerable attention, appeared indifferent to her presence. When he quitted the drawing-room without having attempted to exchange a word with her, Aldyth's heart throbbed with painful resentment.

"Why should he be different to me now?" she asked herself. "I never needed a friend more than I do at this time, and he is so wise and good; he could advise me, he could help me. There are so many things I should like to say to him, but I cannot utter a word when he looks at me in that grave, severe way. Oh, I did think I could rest on his friendship; but that, too, is slipping away from me."

(To be continued.)

WOMEN'S CLUBS IN LONDON.

PART II.

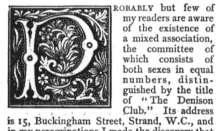

ROBABLY but few of my readers are aware of the existence of a mixed association, the committee of which consists of both sexes in equal numbers, distinguished by the title of "The Denison Club." Its address is 15, Buckingham Street, Strand, W.C., and in my peregrinations I made the discovery that the object of my search was the last house in the street, with a pleasant look-out on the gardens of the Embankment. I walked up to the first floor, and seeing no bell, I went in. A female attendant was sitting there, keeping guard alone, and in a few minutes she replaced her presence by that of the secretary. He gave me a prospectus of the society to supply all information respecting its *raison d'être,* and as there were no other apartments to be seen than three small sized rooms thrown into one, and the secretary was far from communicative, I had to content myself with the paper he gave me, and will extract the little that there is to be gleaned from it. The institution had its origin in the weekly meetings at dinner, provided in a Strand-side tavern, of from six to a dozen men, mostly workers on charity organisation committees, with a view to discuss common problems. Out of this small beginning the circle of philanthropists expanded. They were recruited by fellow-sympathisers; a club was formed, and made its first home at Toynbee Hall. The opening meeting was attended by forty or fifty members in the summer of 1885; but difficulties arose, which led to their removal to their present rooms. "A club of social workers without women was an absurd anachronism," says the hon. secretary; and so the original members joined hands with the new workers, and a mixed club was started in the spring of 1886.

My readers will inquire what this little association combined together to effect. It was "to promote friendly intercourse and frank discussion between men and women interested in social and industrial questions, and to encourage study and investigation."

Tea and coffee can be obtained by the members; writing materials and a few newspapers are provided gratis. The room is open every day (Sunday excepted) from 12 noon till 10 p.m.; but, as a rule, it is reserved for the use of men only on Wednesday evenings. To give some idea of the subjects discussed, the following may be named: "Trade Societies," "Regularity of Employment," "Poor Law and the Condition of the Poor," "How far Women's Unions can be Successful," etc. The subscription required of members is £1 annually.

I had intended to give some information respecting the "Trained Nurses' Club," to which I next paid a visit, being in the same street, at No. 15. But as the hon. secretary promised to send me the forthcoming report, I will discuss its merits by-and-by, and pass on to the "Lady Guide Association," at 16, Cockspur Street, S.W. I had not an idea when I entered the pretty, well-appointed office, just facing the equestrian figure in bronze of George III., that the club was one so comprehensive in its work, and offered so much to its members—the serving and the served—whether of the town or the country. Great taste is exhibited in the whole style of the reception, reading, and writing rooms, and although not a large house for the supply of the many requirements, it has the advantage of being residential, and can also afford accommodation for a few country members for some days if desired. There are two reception-rooms, one in which gentlemen may be received, the other for ladies only, with lavatory and a dressing-room (convenient for those too far out of town to dress for evening entertainments at home). There are two compartments screened off in the ladies' club-room, for the use of those who require privacy, whether for seeing doctors, or other persons on business. There is a very nice *salle à manger* on the entrance floor, behind the several offices, where breakfasts, dinners, luncheons, teas, and suppers are served daily, and where members may entertain their friends. The ordinary annual fee for membership is £1 1s., and, in addition to the free use of the sitting and dining rooms, a reduction is made to them in every department of the work carried on by the acting resident members. So extensive are the ramifications of business undertaken here, that I scarcely know where to begin; yet this article would be of little general use if I omitted to give a list of them. Lady guides—by the hour, day, week, or month—for London or abroad, are provided; also teachers, companions, readers, singers, artists, amanuenses, shorthand and type writers, and repairers of wardrobes. Dressmakers, milliners, and needlewomen are recommended; purchases are undertaken; arrangements made for entertainments (dinners, balls, etc.), and professional entertainers provided. Apartments are found, houses taken, rooms at hotels engaged; houses are let or sold, and their artistic decoration and furnishing arranged. Travelling tickets are procured and steam passages taken. Travellers are met at stations; arrivals, departures, and addresses are registered; tickets for places of amusement are procured; money exchanged (deposit and ready-money system); and parties of six persons are escorted for rounds of sightseeing and excursions at so much a head, inclusive of food. I need say no more. Truly we have already a good list of duties, for which this useful association makes itself responsible, under the patronage of their Graces the Duke and Duchess of Wellington. I ought not to have omitted the domestic servants' department, although the association does not supply a registry office, and servants are not to be found there in daily attendance.

On entering the outer doors, the visitor will observe a number of little arched openings on her left, in the painted screen dividing off the small offices, where orders are registered and advice is given, *in re* the several departments of business executed. Of these there are some eight or more. The whole apartment is very prettily painted in the palest tint of pea-green, and in the distance an open glass door reveals a view of the restaurant. Of course for information as to terms, the visitor should either write or make inquiries in person, when some thirteen or more printed papers will be presented to her, as they were to me. These will give the fullest particulars on all the above-named subjects, and I feel sure that the recipient will be ready, as I am, to speak favourably of all she will see, and of the politeness which she will experience from the lady who will conduct her over the premises.

"The Dorothy" is a name already well known, but in any case deserving of honourable mention. It consists of a pair of sister establishments. The first experiment was of a very charitable character, and the locality selected was in Mortimer Street, W. The object of the promoters was to meet the requirements of persons of very small pecuniary means, and to provide a good dinner or luncheon, including meat, at the trifling price of eightpence. How great a boon this has proved, and how extensively appreciated, has been demonstrated by the number of those availing themselves of it.

Students, and young women engaged in business houses, have the advantage of quick attendance, and a thoroughly good supply of food provided for them during the brief space of leisure time allotted to them. In the sister institution in Oxford Street, No. 44 (opposite North Audley Street, W.), dinners or luncheons are supplied from twelve to two o'clock, and at any cost, arranged for with the manager; and afternoon tea and coffee, ices, strawberries and cream in their season, and the meal which is supplied at eightpence included. Newspapers and writing materials are supplied free of charge. I was taken all over this institution, and found that the two kitchens and all the domestic offices and store-rooms were upstairs, so that the dining saloon and the lower premises were perfectly free from unpleasant reminders of cooking operations. The lavatory is below the tea and coffee room, and is specially well appointed, with an attendant to wait upon its visitors. There is a large central stand of marble in this brightly tiled apartment, supplied by some dozen of basins and jugs, which will prove a delightful acquisition to those who come into town from the country on hot summer days, and make "The Dorothy" a place of rendezvous and refreshment for themselves and their friends. I must here draw attention to the fact that no gentlemen-friends are eligible for enjoying the privileges of this essentially female institution; and any meetings of the "town and country cousins" of the two "opposite sexes" would have to be relegated to the rooms of the Lady Guide Association.

"The Welbeck," a home and institute in connection with the Y.W.C.A., is a very important club or association. The building is a union of two or three houses, and "returns" at the back. One of these is 101, Mortimer Street, the entrance to the restaurant; and the houses formerly known as "The Russell" or "Lotus Club" are entered from Regent Street, nearly opposite the Polytechnic. I think it took me fully an hour to walk over the institution, which is planned for the comfortable accommodation of two classes, having their respective dormitories—rooms arranged cubical fashion—and their sitting-rooms; I mean the upper or student, and the workwoman or servants' class. There are good reading and lecture rooms; the latter is capable of accommodating about three hundred persons. These Regent Street premises are now renamed "The Morley Halls," having

been acquired for the Y.W.C.A. since the winter of 1886. The list of viands that are always ready, or that may be ordered in the Welbeck Restaurant, shows a considerable variety of every description (excepting made dishes), and the prices vary from one penny to fivepence. For example, at the first-named price you have a choice of pea-soup, almost any ordinary vegetable, rice or tapioca pudding, jam roll or tart, or blancmange, or a cup of tea, coffee or cocoa, a ham sandwich, cake or bun, or a slice of bread and butter for a halfpenny extra. As the readers of the "G.O.P." are made up of all classes, I think that many amongst them will be glad to read these particulars.

Certainly, the "Young Women's Christian Association" is a wonderful club—so extensive in its grasp of ways and means, both social and religious, of benefiting all its members. Amongst their many offices in the "Morley Halls" there are those of the Continental department and International Union; for Swedes, Norwegians, Danes, Italians, French, Germans, and other foreigners are instructed, and receive advice and assistance as they may individually need. Arrangements are made for those of every nationality in the matter of emigration, or for residence abroad, as students or teachers.

Before proceeding further, I would certainly advise English girls who desire foreign situations of any kind to seek addresses and recommendations here.

It would take too much space to enter into an exhaustive account of all the departments of this really great institution. I will only add that the "Central Institute" is at 16A, Old Cavendish Street, W. In this house the "Travellers' Aid" branch is located, and lodgings for a single night are to be had. But I believe that twelve homes and restaurants exist in London under the auspices of this institution. I should not omit to name that the dining hall is used as a gymnasium in the evenings; and also that classes are held for instruction in every branch of an ordinary education, besides work—such as dress and mantle cutting and making, and shorthand writing—as well as Bible classes, choir singing, etc.

I may now pass on to the Girls' Friendly Society, of which the central office is at 3, Victoria Mansions, Victoria Street, Westminster, S.W., but there are about a dozen lodges connected with it in London, one each in Edinburgh and Dublin, and about thirty in the provinces. This association is specially designed for young working women and domestic servants, who constitute the members, all of whom must have been, and continue to be, of unblemished character—the special ground of eligibility. Ladies are desired as associates to assist in the work, the objects of the union being the advantage of mutual help, both religious and secular; the encouragement of purity of life, dutiful conduct towards parents, faithful service to employers, and thrift. The usual advantages afforded by clubs are enjoyed in the several lodges, into which I need not enter. Her Majesty the Queen is the patron.

Amongst the innumerable minor clubs inaugurated by benevolent women for the benefit of all classes of girls, we find about a dozen for general education, or special branches of the same; and besides these we have magazine societies, essay writing, musical practising, drawing and painting clubs; needlework societies, exercise and early-rising clubs, and religious unions, and "last, not least," "The Ministering Children's League," an immense and most valuable organisation; and one or two invalid clubs, associations for mutual comfort and kindly offices, exchanges of books and of other articles, and agreeable correspondence, chiefly for the benefit of the

bedridden. Most of these clubs and unions have been named, with more or less information respecting them, in the little "Directory of Girls' Clubs" (Griffith and Farran), and although some have become defunct since the publication, or their direction may have severally changed hands, yet there remain an ample number from which our readers can always make a selection.

I will now return to the "Trained Nurses' and Midwives' Institute," at 15, Buckingham Street, Strand, W.C. The present office is a very small one on the entrance floor, but the "Froebel Society" has a larger room, into which there is a door of communication, and they lend this for the meetings and other purposes of the "Nurses' Institute," until better accommodation may eventually be afforded. Here medical lectures are given once a month, and social meetings take place, from 5.30 to 10 p.m., for the refreshment and relaxation of nurses off duty for that time. About fifteen or twenty can meet together between these hours, and from thirty to seventy usually attend the monthly lectures. Medical papers are taken in, and a small lending library has been inaugurated, for which contributions of books are much desired. In a publication called the *Hospital* (of March 15th) there is an interesting account of the presentation by H.R.H. the Princess of Wales of certificates, signed by herself, to the first thousand nurses who joined the "Pension Fund." This pension is to be paid to the subscribers on their attaining the age of fifty years, according to the amount they have individually subscribed. The certificates were of an artistic character, designed by Miss Lilian C. Smith, and were greatly appreciated by the recipients. £1,400 is now being raised to bring the "Donation Bonus" Fund up to £40,000.

The last institution of the nature of a club formed for the benefit of women owes its existence to the "Ladies' Dwellings Company, Limited," having its place in Lower Sloane Street, the mansion bearing the name of "Sloane Gardens House." The annual fee for membership is only five shillings, which entitles to the daily use of the club. There are drawing, writing and reading rooms, and a very fine dining-hall will be opened shortly, to be used for all the meals. Already there are forty-eight ladies in residence, and the new block of buildings at the side, to supply sixty-eight additional rooms, was opened in May. On looking over the rules I was pleased to see an important step made in advance, ensuring much comfort for the residents. The use of musical instruments is prohibited between the hours of 10 p.m. and 8 a.m., nor can a sewing-machine be used between those hours; also dogs and cats are excluded.

In conclusion, I would observe that possibly some may say I have not restricted myself exclusively to the subject indicated in the title of these articles. Perhaps not strictly so in all cases. But there are diversities in the several characteristics of such associations. They are not all formed exactly alike in constitution, nor have they each precisely the same objects in view. But inasmuch as they are all united in one common bond of fellowship, *i.e.*, union for the benefit of women of every class, whether socially, intellectually, or religiously, or all three objects combined, I should not have felt my work complete had I left out any of the institutions I have named. Besides this view of the latitude I might fairly be allowed, there is another and weightier consideration that will fully justify the extension of my subject. By this means I am able to meet the requirements of extra thousands amongst the ever-appreciative and faithful readers of the truly invaluable GIRL'S OWN PAPER.

SOPHIA F. A. CAULFEILD.

S. F. A. Caulfeild, "Women's Clubs in London" (Volume 11, 26 July 1890, p. 679).

A HOME-MADE SHOWER-BATH.

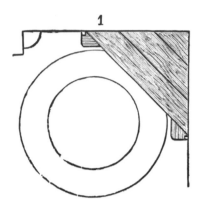

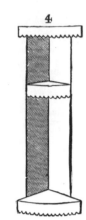

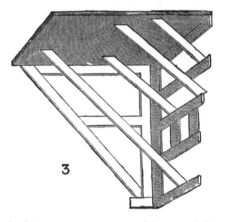

ONE of the firmest convictions of the average builder seems to be that people who live alone never wash—at least anyone who has spent days searching for a flat for one person is driven to that conclusion.

All over London there are now growing up great blocks of flats intended for the use of ladies who live alone. They are well built, prettily finished, in good situations, and with rents quite as high as the rents of six-roomed houses a little further afield; but bath-rooms are in none of them. So after two or three days spent in fruitless search early this year, I became convinced that if I wanted a bath-room I must make it myself.

My particular desire was for a cold shower-bath to follow vigorous washing in very hot water. This can be easily arranged in an ordinary bath-room; but to have it in one's bed-room, where water was not laid on, presented some difficulty.

At first I thought I should have to be contented with the ordinary cold tub, but I shrank from the idea, because I am not a very strong person; and to stand in cold water and sponge oneself is so very much colder than to stand in a dry bath and bring the water down on one in a shower. The violence with which a shower strikes the body is in itself invigorating, and the shock is much less than if one trickles single spongefuls of water over one gradually; besides, a shower-bath gives a much more complete drenching.

At last, after much study and mental debating, the spirit of contrivance fell upon me, and I began to see how the thing might be done. Among my possessions I counted a small clothes horse, which, having been broken across, was useless for its original purpose, and several small packing-cases. There is scarcely any limit to what can be done with packing-cases; these, at least, would make the framework of what I wanted.

My bedroom was so small that it would not contain both a bath and an ordinary washstand

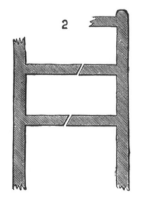

—at least, not if I was to have room to move in it; therefore the two must be combined.

The fittest place for the combined pieces of furniture was the corner between the window and the fireplace. This corner measured along the walls from the angle to the projection of the chimney, forty-four inches, and from the angle to the window forty inches. The saucer bath I already possessed was thirty-six inches in diameter, so there would be just room for the whole arrangement; and if I splashed the walls, the heat from the chimney, which was the continuation of the kitchen chimney, and the sun, which shone nearly all day through the window, would soon dry them again.

The first thing was to make a washstand. This was soon done by taking the two unbroken folds of the clothes-horse, sawing some seven inches off the feet to obtain the right height, opening it at right angles, so that it would go close into the corner, and nailing boards sawn to the right size across the top. At the corners I fitted in smaller boards shaped with a knife, so that the top of the washstand, instead of ending in a straight line, curves round anyone standing at it.

The chief part of the bath I could not make myself; this was the tank to hold the cold water. I ordered it from a tinsmith—it held about six gallons, and had a brass tap let in at

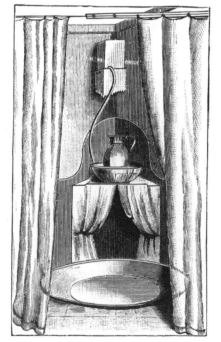

the bottom at one corner. My part of the work was to put up a bracket strong enough for it to stand upon, and sufficiently high for the water to fall from it with sufficient force.

This was no easy matter, since the wall was ill-built and so soft that ordinary nails could be pushed in or pulled out with the fingers. It was plain the weight of the full tank must be spread over as large a surface of the wall as possible.

The broken fold of the clothes-horse supplied two large and tolerably firm supports, and these were nailed flat against the wall with very long French nails, put in literally wherever I could find the space between the bricks. These French nails are very tough, but they are very slender, and bend the moment they touch on a brick. At the first sign of bending, I pulled the nail out and tried in another place. The top of the bracket was made of the small solid end of a packing-case, twelve inches by ten, just a trifle larger than the square of the bottom of the tank. I fixed the bracket so high that I should just be able to turn on the tap when standing in the bath on tiptoe.

I found that the two supports I have mentioned would not be nearly strong enough to support the weight of the tank when filled with water, but several bars of wood, left over from the remnants of the clothes-horse, sawed diagonally at both ends and fitted firmly between the transverse bars of the supports and

the bottom of the bracket made that right; indeed, before I could get the weight sufficiently diffused to be sure the whole concern —bracket, tank, and water—would not all come down on me together some day, I had put up so much woodwork that the result (Fig. 3) was decidedly unsightly. However, the unsightliness did not distress me much, as it was to be covered.

Then in the corner of the wall, made by the projection of the chimney, I fixed up a triple bracket (Fig. 4) made from two narrow boards, and three quarters cut from the lid of a round cheese-box. This was covered in red American leather, and was intended to hold a jar of fine oatmeal for softening the water, tooth-powder, glycerine, toilette vinaigre, and all the toilette necessaries or luxuries for which there was no room on so small a washstand.

Then, lest the walls should grow damp from too much splashing, I nailed red American leather round them, raising it behind the washstand—where there would be most risk of splashing—and cutting it to about three feet high along the walls. On the floor I put a square of oilcloth a little larger than the space it was intended to fill, so that the edges stood up against the walls, forming a shallow saucer.

Before the washstand was put in place the top of it was covered with red American leather, and the front draped with red and white art-muslin, a fabric that will dry quickly if wetted, but still was sufficiently opaque to hide the ugly woodwork. A red American leather valance hid the ugly woodwork of the bracket which supported the tank. Then I fitted a piece of indiarubber tubing over the mouth of the tap, and a small garden water-ing-rose to the end of the tube. It only re-mained to nail bars of wood to the projection of the chimney and to the edge of the window (this latter by means of a bracket support),

run a string along and put up curtains, and the bath was completed.

My little maid stands on a chair and fills the tank before the saucer is put in place. She says it gives her very little more trouble than the ordinary "tub."

The bather stands in the dry bath on a cork slab, washes in hot water at the stand, and then turns on the cold shower, either through the rose or straight through the tube. In either case it is less of a shock to the system than it is to go straight from a warm bed into cold water ; and, moreover, the bath can be made more delicious by a few drops of

carbolic acid (well stirred into the water), a handful of sea-salt, or the peel of an orange. This latter makes an excellent tonic for the skin, if put in the water overnight, but it must always be removed directly the tank is empty, or it will make the inside of the tank, the tap, and even the tubing slimy and un-pleasant.

The tin tank for this bath cost me 7s., the tubing 1s., and the gardening-rose 4d. The curtains, American cloth, and woodwork had all been used before, and were "waste" before I thought of utilising them in the way I have described. **V.**

VARIETIES.

A Remarkable Disappearance.

A very striking case of disappearance is told of in connection with a brother of Grimaldi, the famous clown. This brother had left his home, and gone no one knew whither for years. On one occasion, however, when playing to a crowded house, Grimaldi, while at the wings, was told that someone wanted to see him, and it turned out to be his long-lost relative.

In the very few minutes they had for conversation the brother told him that he had returned to England rich and prosperous, and resolved to roam no more.

With much evidence of affectionate emotion he made an appointment for that evening ; but he never kept it, and was never seen again.

INVENTING FAULTS.—There is such a thing as inventing faults. Trifling things said or done without the least ill-intention are ex-aggerated into serious transgressions. One would think there were enough real faults in the world to be repented of and abandoned without setting up imaginary ones that have no foundation, and can serve only to bring needless trouble, and to confuse the moral sense.

CHOOSING A HUSBAND.—A man in one of the Southern States of America asked a girl how it happened that many beautiful ladies took up with but indifferent husbands. Here is the answer she gave him. "A young friend of mine," said she, "once begged me to go into a delightful cane brake, and there get him the handsomest reed ; and I was to get it in once going through without turning. I went, and coming out brought him a reed that was as shabby a one as could be. When he asked if this was the handsomest I had seen, 'Oh, no,' I said ; 'I saw many finer ones as I went along, but I kept on in hopes of a much better until I had gotten nearly through, and then was obliged to select the best that was left.'"

GIRLS AND SINGING.—At the Milan Con-servatoire where, during the time I was his pupil, Nava was master of the girls' singing class, he was obliged to teach all those who were accepted as pupils by the directors. Privately he would not accept as a pupil, on any terms, a youth of either sex with whose musical disposition he was not thoroughly satisfied. Often he dismissed girls with advice to turn their attention to knitting stockings or other domestic work and so become useful members of society instead of wasting their time in the study of an art for which they had neither taste nor aptitude, and of which the small smattering they might acquire, instead of amusing, would only distress themselves and their friends.—*Reminiscences of Charles Santley.*

Orange Blossom.

The custom of wearing orange blossom at weddings is of comparatively recent date with us. It came to us, like most other fashions in dress, from the French, who in their turn derived it from Spain. In the latter country it had long obtained, and is said to have been originally of Moorish origin.

There is, however, an old Spanish legend which gives a different account of its intro-duction. According to this, soon after the importation of the orange tree by the Moors, one of the Spanish kings had a specimen of which he was very proud, and of which the French ambassador was extremely desirous to obtain an offshoot. The gardener's daughter was aware of this ; and in order to provide herself with the necessary dowry to enable her to marry her lover she obtained a slip, which she sold to the ambassador at a high price. On the occasion of her wedding, in recognition of her gratitude to the plant which had procured her happiness, she bound in her hair a wreath of orange blossom, and thus inaugurated the fashion which has become universal.

WOMAN'S WORLD.—The man at the head of the house can mar the pleasure of the household, but he cannot make it. That must rest with the woman, and it is her greatest privilege.—*Helps.*

Made Out of Her Own Head.

It is as well to avoid the use of phrases capable of a double meaning, as the following anecdote will show :—

A lady famed for her skill in cooking was entertaining a number of friends at tea. Everything on the table was much admired, but the excellence of the sponge cake was especially the subject of remark.

"Oh !" exclaimed one of the guests, "it is so beautifully soft and light ! Do tell me where you got the recipe ? "

"I am very glad," replied the hostess, "that you find it so soft and light. I made it out of my own head."

BE JUST.—I am afraid it is from some natural deficiency in the constitution of our sex that it is so difficult to teach us justice. It certainly was a mistake to personify that admirable virtue as a woman, and even then the allegorist seems to have found it necessary to bandage her eyes. No ; kindliness, unsel-fishness, charity, come to us by nature ; but I wish I could see more of my sisters learning and practising what is far more difficult and far less attractive—common justice, especially towards one another.—*Mrs. Oliphant.*

KEEP SILENT.—It is a good plan to say as little as possible about that of which one knows nothing.

A Deed of Heroism.

She : "I could never marry a man until he had done something brave and heroic."

He : "I'll take you at your word, dear. I ask you to be my wife."

Answer to Charade I. (p. 439).

Ser—vice—able—ness. (a)

Double Acrostic II.

Two sons highly gifted are we,
Of a beautiful isle of the sea ;
  Music, poetry, art,
    Has endowed each a part—
Guess, maidens dear, who we can be.

1. A national dish : if you buy it
You will find it an excellent diet.
  But its colour is blue,
    And 'tis decomposed through,
So you will not invite me to try it.

2. The patron of tuneful invention,
Whom the Latin mythologies mention :
  His burning darts flew
    Towards the mother he slew
And her children with vengeful intention.

3. At first I was least of the three,
But times have now altered with me ;
  My importance increased
    And, no longer the least,
I am almost the top of the tree.

4. A kingdom of old, greatly famed,
From its people a language was named
  Which, though fallen out of speech,
    Still our pedagogues teach,
And the greatest of poets have claimed.

5. A bishop was regent installed
O'er a kingdom by conquest enthralled ;
  Such rude power he held
    That the natives rebelled,
And he then to his see was recalled.

6. The most terrible thing in the world !
All the forces of earth seem unfurled :
  Rocks, water, and fire,
    Lava, tufa, and mire,
From her inmost recesses are hurled.

7. If a hindrance your path should waylay,
Overcome it you probably may
  If *this* you will do,
    And will firmly pursue
This practical, sensible way.

8. I once was the favourite town
In an isle of historic renown ;
  Now I'm almost forgot,
    Thanks to cutter and yacht,
When *élite* of the fashion come down.
               XIMENA.

(a) From the Scandinavian word "naes," a nose, which reappears as "ness," or "naze."

ALISON LAURENCE was one of the girls at Vitrie's studio.

A little, pale thing, with dark, wistful eyes, and hair that hung like a dusky cloud over a broad white brow.

No one knew much about her private life. She gave her address at 9 Ayner's Street, but she made few friends, none intimate enough to visit her.

Vitrie was always fond of her. He treated most of his pupils with a sort of contemptuous pity, and scoffed at their work in such a way, that the feeble were soon disheartened, and only the strong and persevering remained.

Vitrie's studio was a good example of the "survival of the fittest." He was apt to be hard, and sometimes almost cruel.

"You cannot paint—you will never paint," he would say briefly, to some anxious girl, who had thought she had a great gift that way. Vitrie spoke the bare unvarnished truth. But Alison he always treated with respect, and, as far as in him lay, with gentleness.

"She has genius," he would sometimes say, as he stood over her, watching her work.

Little, and delicate as she looked, she came to the studio in all weathers, and stood for hours, painting at her easel, in perfect silence: painting not only with hands and eyes, but with all her soul. Now and then, Vitrie would ask her if she were not tired, and push a chair towards her, and then she always looked at him gratefully, with her sad, dark eyes, and that little, faint shadow of a smile she kept for him alone, and said, "No, thank you."

Vitrie got into the way of seeing her home in the evenings; he said the streets through which she had to pass were not fit for a young girl to walk down alone late in the day; but he always left her at the door of No. 9; and she never asked him in.

One snowy night in December, when the short day's work was over, Vitrie was sitting at ease in his little smoking-room; he lived in rooms opening out of the studio, attended by an elderly housekeeper, who cooked, and did the housework for him.

He heard light, hurried steps coming across the studio, and a knock came at his door.

"Come in," he said, and there stood before him the little figure of his favourite pupil, her eyes fixed on him with an expression of terror and misery he could not bear to see. He threw down his cigar, and sprang up.

"Mr. Vitrie," she said in a low tone, and quickly, "I have come to say 'Good-bye.' I am leaving London to-night—for years—perhaps for always, and I could not go without seeing you again——" She broke down, and Vitrie strode towards her, and seized her hands.

"What is the reason?" he demanded roughly.

"I cannot tell—I promised"—gasped the poor girl.

"My little one," Vitrie's voice was low and pleading now. "My best pupil—you will not leave me like this—you are in trouble—I am your friend—tell me."

"No, no. Oh, Mr. Vitrie, let me go—say 'Good-bye!'"

"My darling, how can I? Don't you know—have you never known that I love you—you, yourself, apart from your work, ever since you came to the studio. I think you bewitched me with your quiet, gentle ways, and your courage and perseverance. Alison, trust me, I love you—tell me what this means."

"You love me?" she said softly, "oh, thank God—I never thought—I never dared to dream—if you love me, then let me go—if you love me."

Vitrie freed her and stood watching, as if turned to stone, as she went out into the winter's night without once glancing back.

Next morning early Vitrie called at 9 Ayner's Street, and learnt from the voluble landlady, that Miss Laurence had lived there with a drunken old father, and that last night they had both left secretly, but the week's rent had been found on the table; and the police had been inquiring after Mr. Laurence, but he had left no trace of his destination. More than this Vitrie could not find out. But he understood enough. He knew that Alison was a girl who would be likely to cleave to her father in his disgrace and misery, and fly with him, striving always to protect him, and keep him from falling lower.

Then Vitrie went back to the studio to work as usual, but there was something in his face that morning that made the usually noisy young pupils as quiet as if a sudden death had occurred amongst them. As the morning wore on, and the easel of the master's favourite pupil stood with the unfinished painting, and no little figure hard at work there, the students began to whisper amongst themselves, and Vitrie caught the words, "Miss Laurence." Then he spoke, low, but so that all could hear him. "Miss Laurence is gone," he said.

"Gone!" reiterated the students, "gone for good?"

"For good," Vitrie answered, and none durst ask another question.

He went the round of his pupils as usual, but he never once glanced at the silent easel with the unfinished painting.

Only in the evening, when all had gone, and twilight was creeping on, one of the students came back to fetch some forgotten gloves, and there saw Vitrie standing in the dim solitude, his head bent on his arms which were clasping the deserted easel.

Whereupon that student crept away in reverent silence, and in tears.

* * *

It was a December evening three years later. Work was over, the students gone, and dusky twilight lay on the studio, making the easels, and lay figures, and draperies, and quaint pots and jars look dim and strange. Vitrie sighed, as he cast a glance round the deserted studio.

He looked older and sadder than formerly, and his hair was getting very grey.

Suddenly there was a knock, and the great door opened, and he could discern in the dimness a little well-remembered figure; the pale clear face raised towards him with great, dark eyes fixed on him, half frightened, half longing.

"Mr. Vitrie," said a clear girl's voice, "I have come back to explain, but perhaps"—with a piteous break in the voice, for Vitrie gazed speechless as at a ghost, "you have forgotten about me—it is long ago, I know——"

"Forgotten!" cried the painter fiercely, and then the little figure was clasped in his arms, and nestled to his heart.

"It was my father," she said at last, "he was getting old, I could not leave him in his trouble—he had no one but me—but he did very wrong, I will tell you—but you must not be hard on him, he is dead——"

"My little one, my little lost bird, come back to me," said Vitrie, in a voice none of the students would have recognised, it was so thrilling and tender.

"You need not explain if it hurts you; I know a little, I can guess the rest, and you have come home—I am satisfied."

VANDA.

LIVING IN LODGINGS.

By JOSEPHA CRANE.

PART I.

THAT the young and unprotected female should live in lodgings by herself at first sight seems very unsuitable. Mrs. Grundy says emphatically that it can't be done, but necessity, which knows no law, is often obliged flatly to contradict her. There are very many reasons why this should be the case, though I am not prepared to enumerate all of them, simply because those reasons vary according to different circumstances. However, I will touch upon a few which determine a girl to take this course.

In these enlightened days, most girls want to work, girls at least who have any "grit," as our American cousins would say, in them, and whether it be philanthropy, art, or the purpose of earning money, which makes them take wing from the old nest, or whether they are practically alone in the world and have no nest to leave, it matters little—the result is pretty much the same. Towns, usually big ones like London, etc., are constantly the centres of attraction to them, simply because there the ways and means for attaining their desire are easy, and training in all kind of arts and crafts is to be had cheaply.

The girl who thus launches forth into the world may not be or desire to be affiliated in any way with any community of workers, under whose roof she could shelter herself. A flat may possess no charms for her, and if her purse is small, she may not be able to meet the expenses of a good boarding-house. A cheap one she shudders from, as also she does the idea of "boarding" with an impecunious family, where, if she be hungry, a second helping will be regarded as greediness, and the shifts and the contrivances to make ends meet cause her constant vexation.

Another reason—she wants liberty. This girl is by no means fast, or advanced, as to the position of women, but she wishes for freedom which cannot so well be obtained unless she live alone. By this I mean a freedom which is natural and right, and to some people a very necessity.

In a boarding-house or family, for instance, unless able to pay for a private sitting-room, it is well-nigh impossible to see friends who come to visit her and not the people with whom she is boarding. Or, she may have to see people on business connected with her work, and not be able to do so in the privacy which is desirable and sometimes absolutely necessary. Consequently for these or other reasons, the girl I have in my mind decides to take lodgings simple or grand, according to her means.

Now to this young damsel, or others who may desire to do the like, I offer a few words of advice, drawn from the wells of experience, and likely to be of use possibly to some who are either reckless and foolhardy, or nervous and timid, or—there is the third class—ignorant, and consequently, often inevitably, foolish.

As the body ranks second to the soul, I will here touch upon the moral aspect of the question, supposing my girl to live from choice or necessity alone in lodgings, I will say in or near a big town—London for example. If you are alone and desire to maintain your self-respect, and to live *sans peur et sans reproche*, you must have some common-sense and use it. The latter will guide you in the choice of rooms to secure a thoroughly respectable house. Now I do not wish to alarm you needlessly, but I do desire to warn you, and in all cases—I make no exception—you should ascertain the character of the owners, and make sure if there are many lodgers and of what kind they are. A girl ignorant of London might find herself in very objectionable quarters, did she not make due inquiries of the kind. If there are several or any gentlemen-lodgers besides yourself, it would be better for you to look for rooms where there were only ladies, or married couples, etc. Should you, however, be obliged to live in a house where there are gentlemen lodging as well, beyond a slight bow of acknowledgment if they open a door for you or render any passing act of courtesy, it is better for you to have absolutely nothing to say to them. And—though I don't want you to be prudish or silly, unless burglars are burgling, or the house is on fire, or something equally out of the common way happens—you should never go to their sitting-room or permit them to come to yours. If pretexts are made of bringing up a letter, etc., etc., you can simply and politely show that you do not encourage such attentions if they necessitate coming to your door.

Living alone you are bound to be more than ever careful even about these apparently minor matters, and not from thoughtlessness be among those whom I have classed as the ignorant and foolish. Those who are reckless and foolhardy, just take any rooms haphazard without stopping to inquire into the matters mentioned above, and the neglect of this precaution often causes them to suffer annoyance, in the long run, to say the least of it.

To the nervous and timid girl, however, with whose fears I have deep sympathy, I would say, that, given the fact that you choose your rooms carefully and are in a quiet house, there is nothing to alarm you. Take care of yourself and you will be safe, and if you are quiet and sensible you will be as much protected by your own dignity as if you were under the wing of the best Mrs. Grundy ever known as chaperon. Unless it be your relations, do not have gentlemen-visitors at all. If your business, as in some cases is likely, necessitates your having to interview men, it is better for you to go to their office or studio, and if they come to you, to ensure the visit taking place in the day-time.

Now as to the actual circumstances of your living alone. There are advantages and there are drawbacks. The advantages:—You can study better, and give yourself up to your work more fully than if you are obliged to consider others, their hours and their company.

You can—if economy is an object—economise in many ways, quite impracticable under other circumstances; you can see your friends with more facility than you could if obliged always to see them in the presence of others; for, in the natural course of things you cannot have any but your very *intimes* in your bedrooms.

The drawbacks:—Well, there are very many. But they need not dismay the timid, nor frighten the nervous. " Forewarned," as you know, is " forearmed," and as a sensible girl, you won't take a discount off the advantages of your solitary life, if I as your friend point out its snares.

In living alone you are your own mistress. True, you have to be guided by the will or caprice of the landlady who legislates for you, when it will be " handy " for her to give you your meals. And you cannot command all the attendance you would under other circumstances require. But for all that you are—really and truly—free in a way never attainable elsewhere.

So you must take care of yourself, and see that though that art or work for the sake of which you elected to live this life prospers, that it does not do so at the expense of your own higher life deteriorating. How can it do this ?

In answer to that query, I would say that in family life there are many and various means by which the individual character is perfected, if it wills to be so, be it noted, for circumstances by themselves do not alter people for the better. Often they affect them for the the worse if grace be not a handmaid.

At home, the chaff and the banter are all so much to the good for the rounding of angles, for the establishment of friendly footing, for the encouragement of a kind of spirit which discerns the playful words to mean only what they seem, and no more. All tricks vanish under fire of the close observation of quick-sighted brothers and sisters, who remark with the frankness of their kind on any such peculiarities that they observe. And these things are in themselves most valuable. For when you " see yourselves as ithers see you," you are often astounded at the amount of light this imparts to you, and you often cannot get over the humiliating fact that you were peculiar, or odd, or the victim of tricks without knowing it.

And these tricks are not got rid of quickly. There are tricks of speech, bad grammar, ugly expressions, slip-shod English, etc., which all pass unnoticed—at least unremarked upon —unless our own kith and kin are there to proclaim the fact. Then there are tricks of manner. A girl sits down in a peculiar way with her skirts drawn ungracefully tight over her knees; she winks and makes faces without being aware of so doing; she hesitates and stammers; she rubs her head or pulls her nose, or twitches her mouth, or plays a tune with her fingers, or swings her foot, or picks her fingers, or is very absent, or interrupts talkers, or laughs and talks too loudly, or slams doors, walks noisily, or does these and a hundred other things without let or hindrance when there is no one to correct her.

So, be on your guard. And be wary and not acquire one or any of the aforenamed tricks, or any of the many not here indicated.

When you live alone, unless you are careful you are very apt to get selfish. In family life there are always others to be considered, and the verbs bear and forbear to be continually conjugated. But when alone there is an absence of all this, and there is the danger of being too much concentrated on No. 1. Of course, there are the outside interests of work or study, but as far as people are concerned do not get self-contained. If, as your circumstances dictate, you are freed from the ties, iron or golden, as they may be, of home-life, yet try and be in touch with humanity, and human things. Keep your eyes open and ask Almighty God to let you have :—

> " A heart at leisure from itself,
>   To soothe and sympathise."

If you do this you will soon find something to do in the way of showing kindness and interest in your fellow-creatures. If you have no friends or acquaintances needing anything, you will, if on the look-out, find someone to be good to. Some poor child or servant—perhaps the maid-of-all-work in your own lodgings—or others to whom you can say a kind word, to whom you can do a kindly act, for Christ's sake.

Think of others as well as yourself, for in a life of solitude there is the danger of thinking self, and the interests surrounding self, of paramount importance, and letting others be, to a greater or lesser extent, forgotten.

As you have to take your meals alone you must be careful to maintain those gentle ways to which you are accustomed at home.

However poor the arrangements are, and simple your food, partake of it like a lady. Do not use your own knife in helping yourself to more butter, but use the butter-knife, even if that be not a silver, or even plated article, but a long steel knife, ground down to being short and serviceable only for butter. Sit down to your meals, and do not take them at intervals, when walking up and down the room. " Eat at your own table," says Confucius, " as if you were at the table of a king." Observe as much decorum before your simple meal as if in company, though you cannot demand as much, or any state. All these things will help you to the maintenance of that refinement which every good girl would desire to cultivate if she possess it, to acquire if she have it not. Another advantage is, that habit is not easily broken. Indeed, we all know that the old proverb, " Habit is second nature," is very hard to break. If you, in the solitude of your lodgings indulge—if it be indulgence— in untidy ways, queer tricks and slovenly manners, rest assured such will follow you when you are away. When on a visit in a pleasant, well-appointed country house, or lunching or dining with your friends in Mayfair, you will, if accustomed to untidy and queer habits in your little lodgings, feel extremely self-conscious, or—and I do not know which extreme is the worst—be ignorant of the solecisms you commit, simply from having been careless and untidy in your everyday life. As I am on the subject of food—meals rather —let me urge upon you to have good food. Not by any means costly living or extravagant dishes. But good, wholesome food, that which you know agrees with you the best, and which you can have cheaply if you are thoughtful and not wasteful.

I think it was Shirley Brooks who said that if a woman lived alone she took usually tea and ate something out of a cupboard, and that is not at all so far from the track as some people might imagine. The health of many a girl who lives alone deteriorates very much; she becomes anæmic, or has other kindred ills, the fruits of being run down, all caused, if the truth were known, of her inattention to food. Now I do not mean to advocate slavery to fixed hours, when such bondage would materially interfere with your work, but I do deprecate long fasts needlessly undergone, and the bad choice of food. If you have to be out for a great many hours, and cannot return for the meals you usually take, then make a point of having some food out. Take sandwiches with you if you like to do so, and this is important where you are uncertain about getting some small meal. If you know you can get the latter, then get it. The many new depôts all over London make such refreshments easy to obtain, and a cup of good chocolate or cocoa, coffee or tea with any light accompaniment you may select will repair the waste and give you fresh fuel for your day's labour.

It is all very well for you to tell me you can go for eight hours or more without food, but if you are working, walking, or travelling, it is bad for you, though you may not discover that fact for yourselves until you are ill and you have to pay a doctor and chemist's bill in a lump, instead of having spent that money or less in small sums for little meals very necessary, and by no means to be classed under the head of luxuries.

Another very great evil which results from not taking enough food must be touched upon here. As I have already said, insufficient nourishment brings bodily weakness in its train, neuralgia, etc. When pain comes or you are very tired and depressed perhaps, often distaste for ordinary food is the result, and then ?

Cannot you answer that question for yourselves ? If you cannot, then let me in all friendliness do it for you, and tell you that many a drunkard—yes, do not shrink from the truth—has begun the terrible path downwards leading to moral and temporal ruin by taking stimulants to allay pain which might possibly have been warded off by regular habits of simple wholesome meals, or to get the fillip that stimulants undoubtedly give in times of depression.

Now don't misunderstand me. I am not a teetotaler. So far as I know I never shall be one. I give all honour, for it is due to all those who, feeling the taking of alcohol in any shape or form to be a temptation to themselves, give it up because they cannot be temperate, and must exceed if they use at all one of God's good gifts, and I respect those who, for Christ's sake, are willing to give up what is to them no occasion of falling, but a luxury, because by so doing they can help their weak brother.

You may say there is no danger to you. I hope there is not. Only—prevention is better than cure, and if you provide yourself with good food and take it as regularly as you can, you will arm yourself against that which has been and is a temptation, nay, an occasion of ruin to hundreds and thousands of your sex.

To be on the alert and to watch against your foes only argues a possession of common sense, not by any means an inclination to side with the enemy. Then, too, if you do take stimulants, make it a rule only to do so with your meals. This is most important. When tired and depressed, if you can afford wine or stimulants of any kind, it is often to many people a temptation to take it in between meals or whenever they are " down." There are many reasons for this. One is that it is so very convenient. If you are in lodgings where there is much work and few domestics to meet it, you may in your charity not like to summon the tired servant to give you a cup of tea or coffee or make you some substitute for beef tea, such as is found in the many preparations so much advertised. Consequently you take a glass of claret and a biscuit. In your case you may never exceed moderation ; in others it is the beginning of a habit which often has fatal consequences to the health of mind, soul, and body. Another warning. Do not take stimulants to work upon. It is false strength and will do you no good. If you find them beneficial to your health, take them with your meals after your labours, whether mental or physical, are over. Then, if taken in strict moderation, they may do you good.

But if you are very busy, and as I have said you do not like ringing up the servant to give you other refreshment than that you can so easily obtain from stimulants, what are you to do ?

Take the trouble of finding out what best suits you as a fillip or restorative. Milk, soda and milk, milk with the yolk of an egg beaten up in it, is quickly prepared and can be kept in your room if that is cool. Even if kept downstairs and you have to ask for it, that is very little trouble.

If, however, you prefer tea or cocoa, or Liebig, etc., be independent and prepare it yourself. Have a small spirit-lamp and kettle for use when you have not got your sitting-room fire burning. Do not let it go downstairs at all, but keep it in your own possession and clean it yourself. A china Hobbs' tea-infuser, which costs about eighteenpence, is invaluable in lodgings, as with it a breakfast-cupful of good tea can be made with boiling water, and the necessity of a teapot be done away with. This small article consists of a perforated receptacle for a spoonful of tea, which is put in when the cup is full of boiling water. It is then covered for three minutes

with the saucer which goes with it, and when that is removed, the top containing the tea is placed upon it. This with condensed milk makes you independent of servants, and your kettle can give you water at any time for beef-tea, etc. If these things are more troublesome than stimulants, it is worth taking the trouble.

It may be said that all these warnings about stimulants could apply equally well to those who do not live alone. So they may, but they are more than ever applicable to those who are alone, because the very fact of their solitude brings with it circumstances which render the liability of abusing instead of using stimulants very much more likely.

Some people get depressed when alone, and these had better never elect to live this kind of life unless very sheer necessity obliges it. But if they are obliged to do it, then they need to be more than ever careful.

Another circumstance is that there is no one to give them a hint or to regulate the quantity they take.

Many people who live alone get to be very slovenly in dress. This is to be guarded against. If you have many visitors, or few, or none at all, be as neat and tidy as you possibly can, for untidiness, like all bad habits, is not easily broken. If your evenings are usually spent indoors, it is a good plan to keep an old dress to get into, in which you can lie down if you are tired or sit over the fire in. It will save your walking-clothes, and the change of dress will in itself be a refreshment.

Now to turn to the lodgings themselves.

The girl who wants to live alone for the purpose of work or study has usually not a very long purse, and consequently I shall bear that in mind as I offer you a few hints about choice of rooms.

Having already touched upon the question of a respectable and quiet house being strongly advisable, I will say no more on that most important subject.

Upstair rooms are more cheerful than those downstairs, and brightness of aspect is always to be aimed at, more particularly for the sitting-room. The higher up, in fact, that you go, the healthier will your rooms be, only if your sitting-room is very high up, you must remember that unless there are more servants than one that your chance of much attendance is small.

(To be concluded.)

UNIVERSITY DEGREES FOR WOMEN: THEIR HISTORY AND VALUE.

By KATHARINE St. JOHN CONWAY.

UCH has happened since 1856 when Miss White startled the great men of the London University by her application to be allowed to enter for a medical degree. We have no actual record of the scene in the Senate House, but tradition has it that it was of the stormiest kind, and that the one or two brave Senators who dared to support the application were practically compelled to recede from their position.

In the end a legal opinion was taken, and after many wigs, big and small, had met in solemn conclave, it was declared " Impossible under the Charter," and the enemies of the Higher Education for Women rested in the

fond belief that their peace was finally secured.

But in 1862, Miss Garrett, now Mrs. Garrett-Anderson, M.D., and head of the Women's Medical College in Handel Street, London, had the temerity to bring the whole matter up again by an application similar to that presented by Miss White. When she was met with a refusal on the ground of the Charter, her friends were ready with a memorial addressed to the University, praying that the Charter might be altered.

In the debate on the matter in the Senate, Mr. Grote advocated the women's claim so ably, that a resolution instructing the Senate to endeavour to gain the admission of women to the examinations was only lost by the Chancellor's casting vote.

Cambridge and Oxford were then appealed to, and, after much persuasion, sanctioned the printing of extra papers for girls in the local

examinations, which had hitherto been only open to boys. This may seem only a slight gain in itself, but it had the effect of revolutionising the education given to girls in our Middle Class Schools, and was the indirect cause of the starting of the Girls' Public Day School Company in 1871.

Following up the attack upon the two older universities, six women began to study together in a small house at Hitchin, near Cambridge, and after much trouble obtained " extra papers " for the " Previous " or " Little Go " examination, which is the first step to a degree. They were entirely dependent upon the kindness of the examiners for their knowledge of the results of their efforts, but they succeeded in the work they had undertaken, and in 1873 were allowed the use of the papers for the Tripos (or the Honours Degree) on the same lines.

By this means, in 1880, Miss Scott received

LIVING IN LODGINGS.

By JOSEPHA CRANE.

PART II.

IN engaging rooms you must remember that when you are told a price per week you would do well to inquire precisely what that sum covers.

Many a one who does not do that is filled with astonishment when the first week's bill is handed in to find many items charged, which they fancied were included in the sum named. Some of these are as follows—

Boot-cleaning, attendance, kitchen-fire, light in sitting- and bed-room, hall gas, washing of table-linen, bed-linen, blinds, curtains, etc.; cruet (meaning salt, pepper), etc.

Now if you are bent on not spending more than is really necessary, you will find it far better to arrange with the landlady for one fixed sum, to include all the above items.

As for fire in your sitting-room, that is also usually best paid for at so much per week—not so much a scuttle.

In making your bargain remember that your plans and needs must be taken into consideration. If, for example, you are out all day and your fire can be kept in with a block, you should pay less than if you were likely to be in part, if not most of the day, and desiring a cheerful fire to sit by.

If you wish for late dinners, you will nearly always be asked more rent; and in engaging rooms you should always state if you dine early or late. The former, be it known, suits nine landladies out of ten, and though you may not like it so well, you may be obliged to yield for the sake of economy. If, however, you have little money and so cannot afford to indulge your whims, yet you can make your supper really your chief meal, if you can put up with cold things accompanied by a cup of hot cocoa or something of the kind, always possible with the busiest of landladies. Another matter which affects the fire, etc., and consequently your payments, is your bath.

I hope, by the way, that you take one, not occasionally, or weekly, but daily.

It is a necessity and luxury too, for all lovers of their tub would, I think, agree with me in considering it the latter, and also say that they would sooner economise in some other respect and have that which tends to health and beauty. Yes, beauty! For to be in health means to look nice, and a skin kept in a good state by frequent cleansing looks better than the skin to which many cosmetics and lotions are applied.

But if you take a bath you had better state the fact to the landlady, ascertaining precisely if there is a bath-room in the house, and when you can use it, and if not when you can have water in your own room.

If you want hot water you must be prepared to hear that you must pay for it accordingly, as sometimes your requirements in that respect means that fire has to be kept up for that purpose, when otherwise it would be allowed to go out, and besides that, the landlady accustomed to people who do not conjugate the verb "to bathe"—and they are many—may think your request peculiar, and hesitate about the trouble it causes to her or her servants. Servant, I may say, for in small lodgings of low rent, more than one domestic is rarely kept.

However, if you take my advice, you will look upon your tub as a necessity, and deny yourself a new dress, or some small luxury so as to be able to pay for it, and also to give the servant an extra tip for whatever trouble it causes her in bringing up and taking away water.

As to the latter, you do not need such a very great deal; and if you are wise you will provide yourself with a travelling bath large enough for comfort and yet not so big that the can of hot water is lost in it.

These baths can be had very inexpensively when the cost is contrasted with the comfort they provide, and for travelling-purposes they serve instead of a trunk. If, by the way, you take your travelling-bath when away for your holiday abroad, and wish very often to use it when you are staying only one night in a place, you will find it more convenient if you have your arrangements such that the bath need not be fully unpacked. You can have a linen bag to fit the bath closely and drawn together over its contents with a running string; this can be packed and lifted out *in toto*, when you want the use of the bath, and replaced when the latter is done with.

I have known of people who had a wicker-basket made to fit the inside of the bath, and that when packed was lifted out and replaced when the bath was not wanted.

If your occupation is such as to require quiet, you must inquire in taking your rooms what noises there are; musical instruments—babies are the chief disturbers of peace. If you are delicate and not a good sleeper, inquire what noise there is at night. I write feelingly on this subject, as I have known what it was to be kept awake through most of the night with professional musicians singing and playing, or else noise caused by the members of the household coming in late and being quite regardless of the amount of noise made.

If you live in lodgings for any length of time, you can beautify even the ugliest rooms and the dingiest furniture if you have a little taste, and you can very considerably add to your own comfort by the purchase of some articles which are not at all expensive. Before however you do this, you must count the cost in this respect. Unless you make special agreement to the contrary, you can leave or be requested to do so at one week's notice, and so your tenure of lodgings is in consequence very uncertain. Very often you do not discover many disagreeable things that you cannot put up with until you are in the rooms, and you are obliged, because of them, to leave. On the other hand, you may find yourself perfectly comfortable, and like your quarters, but meanwhile your landlady, for reasons of her own, may suddenly give you notice. Though you may like her and her ways, she may not like you; she may have found some one to give her more rent, or she may have old lodgers returning to her, or some reason or other may decide her to turn you out. So that, as you may have to move often, if you accumulate the things which add to the look and comfort of your rooms, you must be prepared for the trouble, which it undeniably is, of packing and moving about with the extra luggage they entail.

If however you like beauty and comfort, and do not mind the trouble involved in extra possessions to take about with you, I can suggest a few things. I advise you as far as is possible to pack them together, and to only open the box when you know you are fairly likely to remain in the rooms.

Pretty cushions about a room are very ornamental as well as useful. These are better made of down, for though it is more expensive, it takes much less room in packing, and that is a consideration. A coloured couvre-pied thrown over an old sofa is nice, and also is comfortable when you lie down for a rest. This you can make yourself very easily with some cheap art serge roughly embroidered in crewels, or if you are not fond of needlework, you can buy what answers the purpose at a very small cost.

If you have friends to tea often, you may like to have your tea nice, and you may groan over the cups, etc., sent up by your landlady. Now you can get a few things for tea at a small cost, and if you have a Japanese tray and some of your own tea-spoons, all the better. I should advise your washing up your things yourself; your spoons at least, and thus ensuring their being taken care of. These with some worked tea-cloths will pack easily and be found very useful indeed, and with your spirit-lamp and a box of biscuits you can be, if you desire it, quite independent.

A good lamp is often not found in lodgings. If you have one, you had better keep it in order yourself, and for this purpose you had better provide yourself with a pair of housemaid's gloves as well as lamp-scissors, rags to wipe glasses, etc., with, and a brush for the chimney-glass. These said gloves you will often find very useful when you want to do something that would soil your hands. For example if your fire is going out and you want to renew it, you can often save the servant by doing it quickly yourself. It is well to keep a few bits of firewood in your cupboard so as to be able to kindle the fire soon, and a small pair of bellows are often most useful in helping you to get up a blaze.

If you like to boil your own eggs and make your own cocoa yourself, you can keep a small saucepan in your cupboard. A very nice way of doing eggs is in the little fire-proof crockery pipkins, which can be purchased now in most large shops for a few pence. You can get one just for one egg, and as a variation from a boiled egg, you will find it very nice. You place a piece of butter the size of a walnut in the little pan, with a good pinch of salt. When the butter has nearly melted—for the pan goes on the fire—break the egg into it and stir it round until it is consistent. It is eaten out of the pan itself and the egg thus cooked has a very nice flavour. If you get a larger pan, you can make yourself a very nice dish with more eggs, and if you add a little milk it is often a great improvement. One very great drawback to having your meals in your sitting-room, is the inevitable odour which seems to remain afterwards. It is always well to open the windows after a meal, and let the room be thoroughly aired. A spray atomiser is a nice thing to have, as if you spray a little eau-de-Cologne or any favourite perfume about the room, it will freshen it—after—please note this—after you have let the smell of viands, etc., out. For perfumes should not be used to cover a smell. In winter, fire, which purifies the air, removes odours very efficiently.

Photographs about a room are very nice and so are any little knick-knacks of your own which serve to give your rooms a home-like appearance. Where to place these things is often a difficulty, for in many lodgings every table and bracket and corner is crowded with gimcracks of every sort belonging to the landlady, and these are as a rule in horrible taste. It is far better to get them out of the way altogether, and this can be done without hurting the feelings of the possessor if with tact you ask for their removal on the score of wanting more room. A mantel-mat on the chimney-piece will set off your own things, and this can be made of plush or velvet in a colour that will go with most things.

If you like to provide yourself with an Oxford chair, you will often be glad of it, and if not a folding deck-chair is often useful. If you wish, you can make the latter look very pretty by covering the whole length of the canvas with any material you like, embroidered roughly in a bold pattern. The deck-chair I use has an appendage fastened with a couple of screws, which turns it into a lounge, not by any means a bad substitute for a sofa.

A folding screen is very handy. I got a cheap one slightly damaged at a sale. It was covered only with very ugly Japanese paper, and I re-covered it with coloured sateen which cost, I think, fourpence-three-farthings a yard. How useful it is I am continually discovering. It shuts out draughts and is ornamental as well, for on it are hung photographs and pictures.

Now as to the relations between yourself and the landlady, there is need for care and tact.

I will start with saying that the landlady we hear of so often in plays and read of in novels, who fleeces her lodgers, and has a permanent cat in her establishment which eats all the ends, however small or large they may be, is not always found in real life. Of course she exists, and in some lodgings the lodgers are cheated, and the landlady and family live off them in some way or other. But there are very many other lodgings where nothing of the kind ever goes on, and it is to these I trust you may be guided should you require them. Remember this however. If you are paying only a comparatively small sum for what may be classed as poor lodgings, do not expect that you can have the attendance, comforts, etc., to which you would have a right if you were in first-class rooms, paying proportionately. It is often most ludicrous to see how some people exact attendance and attention from a little overworked London slavey, which by rights they could hardly expect where a staff of efficient servants was kept. Be considerate. If you are one of several sets of lodgers and the domestics are few in number, then do not ring your bell on every small pretext, and drag the servants up and down to attend to you. Learn to wait upon yourself, and if you cannot pay much to expect but little waiting upon. An occasional tip to the servant goes a long way, and it is well to give it now and then.

To have a latch-key saves trouble, and the landlady will generally give you one. If your lot is to live in lodgings you will, as I have said before, find drawbacks and advantages. If you are good-humoured and contented, you will make the best of things where you cannot improve them, and you will learn to put up with many minor trials, all of which are in themselves part of the discipline of life. And remember ever, that it is all part of your life, and that the way in which you live, the example you set, your words, your ways, tend ever and always one way or another. By your impatience, ill-temper, exacting ways, and want of charity you may do much harm, even in the narrow circle of a life like this, and if you are true, just, gentle and good your influence will tell, and those with whom you have to deal will know for a certainty that you are living the higher life and being governed by high principles. Principles which make you considerate and thoughtful and careful for others as well as yourself. And in a house where many people live, all their homes under the one roof, consideration the one for the other is one of the Christian virtues which most tells in its effect all round.

A DREAM'S FULFILMENT.

By Mrs. L. B. WALFORD.

CHAPTER IV.

VERA lay in bed and sighed. She was better now, almost well; well in everything save ability to move without the aid of either stick or some supporting arm. But alas! her three weeks' holiday was over, and now what was to be done? The sigh brought a big, brown, motherly face to the bedside.

"Well, my dear, what ails ye now?"

"Nothing ought to ail me," said Vera, smiling back. "You have been so kind, so wonderfully kind, and I feel as if I never could thank you enough, or love you enough. As soon as the pain would let me I began at once to be happy with you; and though it was hard to give up, you know," nodding, "still I really did not feel, I did not seem to mind till —to-day." Her lip quivered, and she broke down with the word.

The Misses Claybury, aunt and niece, had departed that morning, unable to prolong their stay, and forced to the conclusion that it was equally impossible for poor Vera to go with them. They had promised that they would themselves convey to Vera's relations full intelligence of her state; and if desirable, one would accompany George to report it to her employers at the telegraph office. It was to be hoped that under the circumstances her place might be kept open, and her brother-in-law had himself volunteered a line of assurance on the subject of expenses.

Everyone had done what they could, and it was with a guilty sense of repining against a fate whose cruelty had been so tenderly mitigated in all respects, that the poor invalid yet sighed again. "My lost dream!" that was the burden of her heart.

Sometimes it seemed to her as if this check upon the very outset of its fulfilment must have been sent as a punishment for her too fixed determination to carry it out in the teeth of every obstacle. It had been too much to her—swallowed up every other thought—excluded every other sympathy.

Vera was a pious-minded girl, with perhaps a tinge of morbid introspection in her nature. She recognised the hand of Providence in her present trial, and she bowed her head in submission even while her tears flowed beneath the chastening rod; but she had something yet to learn in life. She thought she was being taught a lesson—she did not yet comprehend that an all-merciful Father has many ways of teaching His children. . . .

"But I do think, Hector, my man, that she's the bonniest, and the sweetest bit thing that has come to this house for many a day." Mrs. Macfarlane, who was not much of a writer, had never informed her son, the stalwart young owner of Invermark Farm, of the accident which had brought her a visitor during his absence; wisely considering that he would pay but little heed to it whilst away on a round of business, and that it was time enough to spring the news upon him when he would be disposed to give it its due importance. "Hector, all the fun I've had out of it, you wouldn't believe," proceeded the good old dame, with twinkling eyes. "She tells me such tales of London and its doings—but all the time it's, 'Oh, I love the country! I long for the country! I'm just daft to live in the country.' Just daft's my word, for she talks the prettiest English. And as for reading—you've brought some books with you, have you? Aye, I thought you would. I told Vera so."

"Vera? Is that her name?" At the moment Vera was heard calling from above. She had fancied the man's voice below meant that Dr. Makellar had arrived to carry her, as he had promised to do, outside into the little garden. The day was lovely; the sun warm, yet modulated in its rays; and she was eager for the treat. Was it the doctor who had come?

"Not exactly the doctor, it's—ahem! a younger man." Good Mrs. Macfarlane coughed and hesitated. "He'll carry ye better than the doctor would. He's that big and strong, and I'll tell him to be careful."

"Oh, then, tell him I'm ready." ('The doctor's assistant,' concluded the patient to herself.) And her mind being full of the change so important to an invalid, she neither raised any objection, nor felt any reluctance to accept the substitute provided. She was now able to move to an upright position, and was fully dressed; indeed, by the help of a shepherd's crook, and laying hold of different articles of furniture with the other hand, she could move about her own small chamber. Beyond that, however, she could not venture.

"Hector!" called Mrs. Macfarlane from the landing. "Hector"—on hearing his

HOW I FURNISHED MY BED-SITTING-ROOM FOR TWELVE POUNDS.

B E it ever so humble, there's no place like home." This was certainly the writer's opinion after being in apartments for some years; and she determined to have a little nest of her very own in the big, bustling city where her lot was cast. At first she thought of having a couple of rooms, but finding that two rooms meant more furniture, more rent to pay, and probably not more comfort, she decided on having one large one, and then so arranging her household affairs that the room should have a good airing. For instance, she is a firm believer in having the windows of a room open all night, as well as in the daytime; a dummy sash is easily made by placing a board, six inches deep and the width of the window, under the lower sash frame of any window. This ensures a constant supply of fresh air passing into the room without draught, and if the upper sash is lowered only an inch or so, it is sufficient to take off the foul air that always ascends to the ceiling. So this little programme was arranged: she would be dressed by seven on a fine morning, open the bed and open the window wide, then go out for half an hour's walk. Breakfast at seven-thirty, then to business until seven in the evening; after supper at nine a walk out, leaving the window open, then to bed at quarter to ten, the room smelling delightfully fresh. On a wet morning, of course a five minutes' walk in the garden with an umbrella is all that can be taken, and if the evening is spent with friends, there is no necessity for the nocturnal ramble. This point has been rather dwelt upon, because it is one of the difficulties attending the occupation of a single room.

Another difficulty is to make the room look as little like a bedroom as possible in the daytime, and yet when required for that purpose it should not be too much trouble to transform it. This second difficulty she has grappled with and overcome, though it required rather more thought than the first. For she made up her mind that there should be no bed screened round or devices of that kind in her room.

The first thing to be done was, of course, to cover the floor. As it was a good-sized room, it took twelve yards of oil-cloth two yards wide. A pattern with a little red in it of rather light design was chosen, with a view to its not showing footmarks conspicuously. Then a couple of rugs at six shillings and sixpence were bought; these were Japanese in appearance, as it was decided that as far as possible the decorations should be Japanese. The blind was fitted by a local man, and the curtain pole and rings of bamboo with curtains of reversible cretonne still further carried out the leading idea. The bed bought is known as an American camp-bed; it is six feet long and two feet three inches wide. There is a spring bed attached to it and a mattress, the whole including a roll pillow and a vallance all round, being covered with the ever-useful cretonne with a dash of red in it, and a large cushion, which is covered with turkey red and a frill round it by day, has its gay cover stripped off and is a pillow by night. Sheets, blankets, and quilt, in addition, make me a most comfortable bed, and these are kept in a shallow box underneath and hidden from public gaze by the vallance. My bed is certainly not too wide, but if the great Duke of Wellington could sleep on a couch eighteen inches wide, what need is there for my grumbling.

A secondhand set of painted drawers picked up cheaply, when they had the handles removed (white china ones), the holes filled up with putty and then nicely enamelled and little brass handles substituted—the kind one can slip the hand through—caused me to have visions of entering the furniture renovating business. They hold my things nicely, and there is one drawer to spare for my "house linen." It makes a nice sideboard with a cloth on the top, long enough to hang down at each end; at one end is a round Japanese tray, at the other a square one, while in the middle stands a round covered jar, which holds my bread, and which, treated as follows, is, I flatter myself, quite unique. It was an ordinary bread-pan costing a shilling, glazed brown inside and out, the outside covered almost completely with numerous coloured scraps, sold at every stationer's, among which Japanese ladies and gentlemen and fans, birds and flowers figure most prominently. These were stuck on with gum, and after being sized and varnished the whole presents a smooth surface, impervious to wet, and a sponge over now and then keeps it clean outside, while the inside is wiped out every day to ensure the bread being kept nice. Two ginger jars and covers, similarly treated and filled with *pot-pourri*, grace my mantelshelf, their white background forming a pleasing contrast to the brown of the bread-pan.

The next purchase of an enclosed mahogany cabinet, on which stands my lamp (on a mat to preserve its polished surface), is a most useful piece of furniture. When the top is opened, a sunk washing bowl with soap and brush-trays is revealed, and underneath, when the door is opened, is a cupboard, with a towel rail screwed on the door. The next purchase was a set of high bookshelves, which, after being scrubbed well and leather strips put along the front with fancy-headed nails at three halfpence a dozen, looked very nice. The two bottom shelves had a little curtain across them like the window curtains; this was slipped on a penny wooden rod and rested on two cup hooks screwed in the wood. The lowest shelf holds boots, and the other one any piece of work there may be on hand, and my work basket. The next purchases were an exceedingly shabby cupboard and a large old drawing-board. The cupboard, after being well scrubbed inside and out, I covered with strong Japanese paper at a shilling a yard, and a clever friend cut two pieces of brown paper to fit the panels and painted a few Japanese chrysanthemums on each with exceedingly good effect. This cupboard holds my china and glass on the top shelves and comestibles on the lower one, where are usually to be found a few tinned things, for when my friends come to see me they shall not find it in the same condition as "poor Mother Hubbard's." A scrap of paper left over from the cupboard served to cover a rather deep box, which contains my gallon oil-can, a few cloths and dusters, and hanging on nails at one side are one tea-kettle and one saucepan, for now and then I cook things on the oil-stove. The oil-cloth is carried right up to the fireplace, and the grate is hidden by a large Japanese umbrella. The box just mentioned is set in front of this, and on it is the "Beatrice" oil-stove that warms the room. It sends out a good heat and is not much trouble to keep clean, and the dust that is inseparable from a fire is avoided.

When the thermometer reaches 60° I promptly turn out the stove, and one gallon of oil, costing eightpence, serves for light and heat too for a week. The stove is particularly handy in the morning. My landlady fills the kettle overnight and puts it on the stove, and if it is lighted on rising, there is some nice warm water for washing with. Then by the time the room is aired, the water is boiling; I make coffee or cocoa and stand the pot under a cosy, and then warm up the porridge made over-night, or if I have an egg instead, I put it in a basin, fill the basin with boiling water, and cover it when I make the coffee. Then in ten minutes, by the time the table is set and the brown bread and butter cut, the egg is cooked. Sometimes I buy a little cooked beef or ham for my meals, and try to vary them as much as possible; but this subject is such a wide one that another paper could be written on it if our kind Editor will allow. Four bamboo poles at 4d. each and the drawing-board made a nice table; two sawed in equal lengths glued into holes made with a red-hot poker, and made firmer still with screws being put through, formed the four legs. Then the other two lengths cut into four and glued cross-ways between each of the legs made it stronger—this was the writing-table. Underneath stood the waste-paper basket, an old margarine basket costing twopence and painted outside and in with the enamel left over from the drawers; a yard of turkey red split in two and tied round the top, a large fussy bow being at the front. A magazine case hung over the table on the wall (and also an almanack). The case was the shape of a pair of bellows, two pieces of stiff cardboard covered with chrysanthemum cretonne, connected by strips of ribbon so that magazines could be pushed through. Three yards of art-serge in a warm brown (the colour of the drawers) only took my spare evenings for a week to transform into embroidered covers for my dining and writing-tables, and also an arrangement for the mantel-shelf. This was a straight piece a yard deep, carried up the wall above the shelf twelve inches and secured to the wall with a dozen gilt-headed nails left over from the book-shelves. The other three edges were pinked out and a little embroidery run along the front. The work on all three was chrysanthemums outlined in varying shades of golden flax thread.* In one of the corners by the fireplace I fixed my wardrobe, took the measurement and got a board and two strips of wood, to act as brackets, for a shilling. Then curtains were hung in front on the penny rod and cuphooks, as in the case of the bookshelves, a third hook put in the rod gave additional security, while a frill tacked on afterwards hid the rod. The curtains in red and brown thick art-muslin were not too heavy for the slender pole. A set of extending pegs hung on the wall behind them made a nice wardrobe for me. In passing, it may be stated that the short lengths of bamboo left from the table, made, with two pieces of wood from a box, two nice little footstools which were afterwards padded.

I will first give the cost of the various articles and then I will try to explain how the room was arranged. A once popular saying was, "Put the best side to London," and my one room required a great deal of thought before it did present the best side to my friends and to its mistress.

	£	s.	d.
American camp bedstead with spring bedding, and cretonne cover	2	0	0
Floor covering, 12 yards at 1s. 3d. . . .		15	0

* A framed bamboo mirror for 7s. 9d. hung in the middle. My two pots and a few photos make a fair show on the mantel.

	£	s.	d.
Enclosed washstand	1	10	0
Chest of drawers 12s., enamel and handles 6s. .		18	0
Bookshelves, with leather edging and nails .		7	0
Cupboard and Japanese paper for covering .		8	0
China and glass bought at an annual sale . .		6	0
Knives, forks and spoons		15	0
Beatrice stove 3s. 6d., bronze lamp with opal shade 3s. 6d.		7	0
3 sheets, 4 pillow-cases and quilt . . .		12	0
2 table-cloths, 1s. 10d., 4 serviettes 1s. 8d., 4 towels 2s. 3d.		5	9
Curtains 4s., pole and brackets 2s. 9d. . .		6	9
Blind complete		3	0
2 large rugs 6s. 6d., pillow and turkey red covers, 5s.		18	0
Shelf, curtains, and extending pegs for wardrobe		3	6
1 Pembroke table 7s. 6d., 4 bamboo rods and drawing-board		9	6
Table covers and mantel drapery . . .		3	0
1 under blanket 2s., thick Austrian ditto 5s. .		7	0
2 rush chairs 3s. each, 1 hammock chair 2s. 6d., 1 carpet chair 4s., smaller one 3s. . .		15	6
	11	10	0

This left me with a small balance apparently of 10s., out of which I bought tacks and nails for my few pictorial possessions, trays for the sideboard, and a water-jug, three little ferns in Japanese penny saucers, and one or two bits of china for mantelpiece, and my thermometer, etc. As you enter my room, along the wall behind the door (which is, so to speak, at one corner) is the Japanese cupboard. The fireplace is on the adjoining wall, with the wardrobe in the right corner, and at right angles across this, with the head to the fireplace, is the couch; the large rug here has one end at the couch, while it extends across the fireplace. The washstand is in the other fireplace corner; on the right of the window is the writing-table, and on the left (facing door) is the sideboard. The remaining wall is occupied by the bookshelves and the two rush chairs; the hammock chair and a carpet chair at the window, and the other chair at the table in the centre. Five chairs seem a good number for a lone old maid, but she is not a lonely one, for friends often drop in, and there are not too many, as it is against the laws of the Medes and Persians to sit on the couch. With a stained floor, a washstand for six shillings less, and less expenditure for cutlery, the room could have been furnished for ten pounds but I could afford to draw a little more from my nest in the ever-useful savings bank, and it is more complete and gives me more comfort by furnishing on twelve pounds.

VARIETIES.

HOW ADAM INTRODUCED HIMSELF.

What three words did Adam use when he introduced himself to Eve, which read backwards and forwards the same? "Madam, I'm Adam!"

SMILES ARE VALUABLE.—Who can tell the value of a smile? It costs the giver nothing, but is beyond price to the erring and relenting, the sad and cheerless, the lost and forsaken. It disarms malice, subdues temper, turns hatred into love, revenge into kindness, and paves the darkest paths with gems of sunlight. A smile on the brow betrays a kind heart, a pleasant friend, an affectionate brother, a dutiful son, a happy husband. It adds a charm to beauty, it decorates the face of the deformed, and makes a lovely woman resemble an angel in Paradise.

"WELL BEGUN, HALF DONE."—"When the ancients said a work well begun was half done, they meant to impress on people the importance of always trying to make a good beginning."—*Polybius.*

THE PRIMA DONNA.

Physician: "I am sorry to tell you that in five or six years you will have to abandon your profession."

Leading Singer: "You ought to have told me that before. You have cheated me out of several farewell seasons."

HOW TO BE DISAGREEABLE.—Don't develop that type of conscience that feels most keenly the sins of other people. There is little good to be attained by that style of repentance, and it is apt to make the one who practises it rather disagreeable.

THINGS NOT TO BE ASHAMED OF.—Be not ashamed to serve others for the love of Jesus Christ, nor to be esteemed poor in this world.

THE RESTLESS HEART.

A millstone and the human heart are driven ever round: If they have nothing else to grind, they must themselves be ground.

Anon., "How I Furnished My Bed-Sitting-Room for Twelve Pounds" (Volume 24, 22 November 1902, p. 119).

the sweetest of sympathetic letters, but sorry though she might be, the force of circumstances kept the two girls so far apart, that what had been the saddest time in her friend's life had seen the climax of her own gaiety. She had been dancing, and singing, and pleasure-making while Sylvia shed the bitter tears of bereavement, and in a few weeks more she would be spirited off in Esmeralda's train to another scene of gaiety. The O'Shaughnessys were by nature so light of heart that they might not care to welcome among them a black-robed figure of grief! Sylvia felt as though the whole wide world yawned between her and the old interests, and did not yet realise that this feeling of aloofness from the world and its interests is one of the invariable accompaniments of grief. She was young and not given to serious reflection, and she knew only that she was tired and miserable, that the white cliffs about which she had been accustomed to speak with patriotic fervour, looked bleak and cheerless in the light of a wet and chilly evening. June though it was, she was glad to wrap herself in her cloak, and pull her umbrella over her head as she passed down the gangway on to the stage. In Paris it had been a glorious summer day, and the change to wet and gloom seemed typical of the home-coming before her. The cloaked and mackintoshed figures on the stage seemed all black, all the same. She would not look at them lest their presence should make her realise more keenly her own loneliness; but someone came up beside her as she struggled through the crowd, and forcibly lifted the bag from her hand. She turned in alarm and saw a man's tall figure, lifted her eyes, and felt her troubles and anxieties drop from her like a cloak.

It was Jack O'Shaughnessy himself!

(To be continued.)

A NEW HOSTEL FOR WOMEN.

ONE of the most interesting features in the woman's world of to-day is the provision that is being made, on every hand, for the comfort and convenience of those who are unable to live at home, or who have not means sufficient to provide a house for themselves. In London there are tens of thousands of well-born girls and women who have to

[Photo by Burnham, Brixton.

THE LONDON HOSTEL, CROUCH HILL.

Flora Klickmann, "A New Hostel for Women" (Volume 24, 14 March 1903, p. 380).

THE DRAWING ROOM, THE LONDON HOSTEL.   [*Photo by Burnham, Brixton.*]

face the world single-handed in quest of a living, and who have possibly had to leave their homes behind them, in other parts of the country, in order to take up work in town. The majority of these cannot afford expensive rooms, and yet they shrink from the sordidness of cheap quarters and their attendant ills. Of course, there are boarding-houses as an alternative, but women have long ago discovered that cheap boarding-houses are even worse than cheap lodgings.

Moreover, in addition to the girls who are engaged in earning a livelihood, there are innumerable women, all alone in the world, who have a small private income, but not enough to enable them to live amongst people of their own station in life.

Formerly there was no other course open to such as these but to live by themselves in some out-of-the-way corner, and to endeavour to isolate themselves as much as possible from their uncongenial surroundings, dragging out a dull, uncared-for existence as best they could. The loneliness of such a life is something terrible, more especially for women, who are more nervously constituted than men.

During the last few years, however, much time, thought and money have been expended with a view to improving this state of things. It was felt that something might be done to bring such disconnected units into touch one with another. Women's "Settlements" arose, and have already proved a boon to those who were in want of some interest to occupy their lives. And now a new "Hostel" has been opened at Crouch Hill, to meet the needs of the many better-class girls and women, who shrink from the associations of second-rate boarding-houses as much as from the ordeal of living by themselves in the vast city. Take, for instance, the case of the girl who is out all day giving lessons. When her day's work is done, she is too tired to look after herself. What she requires is to come home to a thoroughly well-prepared meal, in the first place ; and then to know that there is companionship or perfect quiet, whichever she may desire. Nothing is worse for a girl, both mentally and morally, than to come home weary at night to empty rooms, with the feeling that she is a solitary figure of no account to anybody. One great aim of " The London Hostel " is to bring sympathy and friendship to those who are otherwise cut off from it in their everyday life.

A large mansion, standing in its own extensive grounds, has been appropriated for the Hostel. It is approached through lodge-gates and up an avenue of trees. Inside, the rooms are spacious and lofty ; there is a grand piano and an Estey organ in the big drawing-room, and everything has been done to make the place as artistic, and at the same time as home-like, as possible. Meals are served at the following hours :—Breakfast, 8.30 A.M. ; lunch, 1 P.M. ; tea, 5.0 P.M. ; dinner, 7.0 P.M. ; and light supper at 9.30 P.M. Family prayers are held morning and evening. The Hostel is conducted on a Christian basis, but is entirely unsectarian.

Flora Klickmann, "A New Hostel for Women" (Volume 24, 14 March 1903, p. 381).

Undoubtedly the success of the place so far is largely due to the very winning personality of Miss Helen Sarjeant, the Lady Superintendent, who gives her services to this work. Though hardly more than a girl herself, she has already had unusual experience in work of this kind, and she gives that note of brightness and cheeriness that is so much needed in such a household.

The inclusive terms for board and residence are from fifteen shillings a week, according to the bedroom. Full particulars can be obtained by sending a stamped directed envelope to The Secretary, "The London Hostel," Womersley House, Crouch Hill, N.

Would that many more such desirable homes might be established in London and other large cities and towns !

FLORA KLICKMANN.

SOME NEW MUSIC.

(VARIOUS.)

"HOME to Merry England !" What a joyful sound there is in these words to many a mother, wife, and sister's heart —faithful, anxious watchers through the war for the return of their dear ones !

> "Ah ! it's Home, sweet Home !
> O'er the laughing, leaping foam,
> And our hearts spring out to meet them
> Ere their feet can touch the shore ! "

So sings Helen Marion Burnside fervently and sweetly as is her wont ; and Myles Foster has set the verses which appeal to us to music of an easy and popular type—the pleasing swing of the refrain being especially taking (Weekes).

The names·of the same writers appear in "Crowned and Throned," one of the successful prize march songs in a neat little album of scarlet hue, published by Metzler (1s.). Both words and music are again happy, and we re-echo earnestly their purport regarding our King and our Queen that—

> "Their Crown is a Nation's love for aye,
> Their Throne is a Nation's heart."

Alicia Adelaide Needham adds to this little patriotic collection "The Seventh English Edward" in a more rugged and jovial strain—with parts for four voices. Now we are on the subject of patriotic songs, we must not omit to mention one which is of the greatest excellence—one likely to live for many a long year, we trust, namely "Land of Hope and Glory"—the words by Arthur Benson, arranged to most inspiring music by Edward Elgar. A choice of three keys is given, and the refrain will induce all our big brothers to join in it, so fine is the melody (Boosey).

For a decided contralto and a soprano, two duets by Tschaïkowsky, "Evening" and "Morning" possess very much attraction ; they are unique and poetic, and of the two "Dawn" is the easier (J. Williams). "The Meadow-Bank" is in a more every-day style with pleasant words and Frank L. Moir's equally pleasant music. This can be sung by a soprano or tenor, and a mezzo or baritone (Chappell). "Bella Napoli," by F. Boscovitz, makes a pretty duo ; it is No. 20 of Messrs. Enoch's Two-Part Song Series (6d.), a very handy one.

These are some eligible pianoforte pieces suitable for drawing-room playing when more classic ones are not required : namely, a short melodious "Berceuse," by G. Wolseley Cox (Ashdown) ; a "Wiegenlied" of W. Junker's, of the same happy type (Breitkopf and Härtel) ; Graham P. Moore's slight but elegant "Valse Novelette" (Bosworth); "Dans les Nuages," a graceful valse romantique by Tito Mattei (Chappell) ; "Le Premier Baiser," pretty and bright, by Martin Schmeling (Bosworth), and another dainty little *morceau* by G. Wolseley Cox, entitled "Bagatelle" (Ashdown). All these exact but small execution—they are so simple yet effective.

Passing from the piano to another instrument which in its really remarkably pleasing improved form is now in vogue, we see that the charming "Sérénade" of Pierné's is arranged for the zither-banjo by Alfred R. Watson, with accompaniment for second banjo (*ad lib.*) and piano ; an extra mandoline part can be added (J. Williams). A "Pavane Favourite de Louis XIV." by Brisson is arranged by the same writer for ·the same instruments, and the stately dance measure of ancient days sounds extremely well (J. Williams). Herbert J. Ellis writes a neat and very easy Mazurka for banjo and second banjo which goes glibly at no great cost of study (Allen Bros.).

Here are some new songs especially suited to girls in words, music and standard of difficulty. "The Bird and the Rose"—teaching a pretty story of contentment, by A. E. Horrocks (Boosey). "A Song of the Cruise," the words, full of courage and hope, by the American poet James Whitcombe Riley, music by F. Leoni (Chappell). Sadder ditties yet withal pointing sweet morals—such as "Birds of the City," by J. L. Molloy (admirably suitable for any "Waifs and Strays" entertainment) (Enoch) ; "The Garden of Dreams," by Hope Temple (Boosey), and Emlyn St. Maur's "Wooden Dolly" (J. Williams). "Sunbeams" is a charming one of Landon Ronald's (Enoch), and that and "A Passing Cloud" (Ashdown) treat slightly and sweetly of the tender theme. Then a soothing lullaby "Where Dreamikens Grow," by Florence Gilbert (Enoch). J. L. Roeckel's blithe "May Morning" (Hutchings and Romer), and the ingenious little songlet "Tell me," by Florence Wickins, end our list.

MARY AUGUSTA SALMOND.

Flora Klickmann, "A New Hostel for Women" (Volume 24, 14 March 1903, p. 382).

Health and Sports

The *Girl's Own Paper* presented regular articles on health. Most of these were written by Gordon Stables, a former navy doctor (a curious qualification for a writer on girls' health), under the pseudonym "Medicus." Generally the magazine promoted the notion of *mens sana in corpore sano*, or healthy body, healthy mind. Readers were encouraged to eat healthily, rest, take some exercise (usually in the form of walks), and avoid mental strain. A healthy girl was presented as a beautiful girl. *The Girl's Own* was somewhat cautious in endorsing leisure and sporting activities, for instance waiting until the Queen took up tricycle riding before endorsing bicycling. By the end of the nineteenth century, nonetheless, the volume of articles on sports and exercise had grown. In these first decades, though games for girls had yet to gain the same enthusiastic endorsement in *The Girl's Own* as games for boys had in *The Boy's Own Paper*, articles on sport still contributed to a new image of girls who were strong and fit.

Mrs. Wallace Arnold's "The Physical Education of Girls" (vol. 5, 1883–84, pp. 516–518) is one of the earliest pieces in the magazine to argue the necessity of physical education for girls, seeing physical activity as a corrective to too much time spent in study or mental activity.

The rational dress movement of the late 1880s was associated usually with the necessity of some form of divided skirt or knickerbockers to allow women more freedom of movement and safety in activities such as bicycling. It also advocated the abandonment of corsets for health reasons. Here, the Lady Dressmaker addresses "Reform in Underclothing" (vol. 9, 1887–88, pp. 19–20, 60-61).

"Ladies' Golf" (vol. 11, 1889–90, pp. 273–74), written anonymously, typifies *The Girl's Own*'s cautious adoption of new sports for girls. The article

endorses putting, but recommends leaving the "herculean 'driving'" to the men.

The Answers to Correspondents section of the magazine frequently features responses to readers complaining of nervous ailments. In "Nervous Girls" (vol. 15, 1893–94, pp. 60–61), Medicus [Gordon Stables] gives his usual bracing advice on how to regain and keep one's health. Cold baths, fresh air, walks, and avoidance of all stimulants are the key elements of his recipe.

Sir Benjamin Ward Richardson, a doctor and Fellow of the Royal Society, presents a list of approved activities for girls in "On Recreations for Girls" (vol. 15, 1894, pp. 545–47). His three main criteria are that the activities not interfere with maternal and domestic duties, that the activities not "vulgarize" women, and that the activities lead to the development of beauty.

Probably the most liberating of recreations for girls, cycling, came to hold a prominent place in *The Girl's Own*. There were numerous articles on cycling clubs, on choosing and maintaining bicycles, and even on "fancy" or trick cycling (see vol. 21, 1899–1900, pp. 728–30). Reproduced here is Dora de Blaquière's "The Dress for Bicycling" (vol. 17, 1895–96, pp. 12–14), which attempts to resolve the thorny problem of how to dress modestly yet safely when riding.

H. M. Pillans, in "Lawn-Tennis" (vol. 21, 1899–1900, pp. 305–308), addresses some of the prejudices against women tennis players and offers suggestions for their improvement.

At last, Lily Watson's "Athleticism for Girls" (vol. 24, 1902–03, pp. 61–62) summarizes the general attitude of *The Girl's Own* in this period regarding recreation for girls: it has its uses in the maintenance of a healthy body, but girls should "beware of the error of making it the chief end of their school life."

THE PHYSICAL EDUCATION OF GIRLS.

By Mrs. WALLACE ARNOLD.

FROM the number of works existing on education it might be supposed that nothing fresh, or rather of interest, remained to be said on the subject; and doubtless this is true as far as regards the mental education of girls, which in late years has taken such immense strides. But there is one branch which appears to me not to have as yet received that attention which it deserves; need I say that I allude to their physical education, concerning which, as the title of my paper suggests, I would offer a few remarks?

Firstly, then, as to its necessity. In the case of boys we have but to look around us to see in what light it is regarded. A glance at any of the numerous school-magazines, or even the ordinary daily papers with their reports of athletic meetings, and accounts of football and cricket matches, etc., so often described in what seems to us so much unintelligible jargon, will assuredly testify that physical instruction is not forgotten or neglected in scholastic life. Indeed, to some anxious parents it would seem as though mental acquirements were too often subordinated to physical superiority, and one of our leading novelists took this view of the question in a recent novel. At any rate, no school for boys now but has its athletic club, and few that are without a gymnasium.

If, then, the importance of duly training the body in conjunction with the mind is thus recognised in the cause of our boys, surely the future wives and mothers of England—for such is our girls' destiny—may lay claim to a no less share of attention in this respect.

One of the most beneficial results of a really good education is undoubtedly the equilibrium established between the respective powers, mental and physical. I might here quote that trite but ever true line of Juvenal, *Mens sana in corpore sano*, which many of our girls have doubtless read when examining with admiring eyes the silver medals of the Oxford University Athletic Club, brought home and exhibited with manly pride by their brothers, or those brothers' friends, who are ofttimes of more interest in their eyes for the time being. I could add much more as to the necessity, but I have at least made out a primary case, and must pass on to more practical considerations, and the first of these that naturally presents itself is, at what age should this physical education commence? To which I reply, it can hardly begin too early, though of course all exercise should be proportionate to age. "Let children," says Rousseau, "have substantial nourishment; let them run and play in the open air and enjoy their liberty."

In these days of higher education for women we are apt to forget that, while forcing the mental faculties to the utmost at an early age, the precious time is slipping away during which their figures are being formed, and that habits are too often engendered which in later years cannot be abandoned or remedied. Many an anxious mother must have observed with pain how many hours her daughter is compelled to sit at her studies, the greater portion of the time being occupied in writing, and that at a desk which compels an attitude that must result in a stooping form. If not engaged in writing, she is probably at the piano, where the back again, having no support, becomes weary, and sinks on one side; then to the drawing-board, where the same stooping position produces a like result, inducing too often a curvature of the spine, as many of our doctors can testify.

Moderate bodily exercise, taken under supervision, will do much to correct—nay, prevent—this mischief. Many of the subjects of the education of the day are matters which can be as well, or perhaps better and more thoroughly, acquired after the age of seventeen. Not so a naturally easy and graceful carriage. From infancy up to about the age I have mentioned our bodies are being formed, and with them our habits, gait, and deportment.

Habit is a frequent repetition of the same acts causing different modifications in the organisation. In youth habit has the privilege of modifying the original constitution, and if the habit be a bad one, of injuring it so powerfully as to render the injury thus caused incurable. How careful, then, should we be that during these few early years none but graceful, elegant, and healthy habits are acquired. Of course, I am speaking now more particularly of bodily habits, though the rule applies with equal force to all, whether physical or mental. It is useless to recommend a child already deformed to keep straight; she may endeavour to make the effort, but following the bent of the acquired organisation, she quickly resumes the position that has become habitual. These considerations bring us to the second practical object of my paper—the best means of obtaining a good physical education for our girls; and these are calesthenics, practised when possible under a qualified teacher.

Calisthenics, practised under proper super-

vision, are of incalculable benefit, not alone as a means of remedying defects already acquired, but as a preventive. Many of my readers doubtless attend some class connected with their school or independent of it, but it is not so much to these I would address my remarks as to those who, from distance or some other valid reason, are unable to avail themselves of professional instruction.

In a properly-constructed gymnasium there are, of course, a number of fixed appliances which, while of immense value in themselves, are not only out of place, but impossible to be utilised at home. There are, however, some exercises which require either no appliances at all, or else such as, not being fixtures, are easily obtainable and simple in their use.* First among these comes the chest-expander, which can be procured at any surgeon's mechanist's or indiarubber warehouse. It consists of a strip of indiarubber secured at each end to a handle; the indiarubber varies in strength, and care should be taken in choosing an expander to select one proportioned to the age and strength of the girl. In the best makes the indiarubber is concealed by a long band of goffered silk, and the handles consist of shaped flat pieces of ebony or walnut having holes pierced for the fingers. I will now proceed to describe a few of the more simple forms of its use.

The first easy exercise is as follows :—

The girl must stand with her heels together, toes turned slightly outwards, knees straight, waist drawn, chest out, head up, shoulders down, and arms straight downward in front of the body, holding the expander loose, *i.e.*, without using its elasticity, the knuckles being turned slightly inwards (fig. 1.); then slowly raise the arms until the expander, still unstretched, is on a line with the chest, in the meantime counting four (figs. 2 and 3).

2. Slowly raise the arms, counting four again, until they are over the head (fig. 4), the expander still unstretched, the arms perfectly straight, and the knuckles turned towards each other.

3. Pass the arms sideways, holding them quite stiff and straight, and bring the expander, now fully extended, behind the body until it is on a line with the shoulders (figs. 5 and 11), taking care to clear the head and back, counting as before.

---

* For young children, skipping practised backwards forms a capital exercise combined with pleasure, developing the chest, and giving full play to all the limbs.

4. Drop the arms straight down behind as far as possible, allowing the expander to contract and hang loosely, the knuckles slightly turned towards each other, and counting four, as in the previous passes (fig. 6).

Then reverse the movements, counting as before. Care must be taken that a perfectly upright position is maintained throughout the whole exercise, the chin and waist being kept well drawn in and the heels together.

This exercise should be continued for about five minutes, which will represent twenty complete repetitions of the exercise, from front to back and back to front being reckoned as one.

For a beginner this will be found sufficient during the first month's practice, as nothing is more injurious than to carry on any exercise until fatigue is experienced. After that period, when the muscles have become more strengthened and the joints more supple, the time may be increased, but in no case sufficiently to induce fatigue or a laborious habit of breathing.

When the pupil has thoroughly mastered this exercise so as to perform it easily and without effort, she may then advance to

Exercise No. 2. This is similar to No. 1, but two only are counted between each pass.

Exercise No. 3. The movements in this are also similar, but the pupil counts only one between each pass or eight to the whole exercise.

In all three care must be taken that the action is steady, uniform, and continuous, and not done in jerks or spasmodically.

Exercise No. 4. The pupil commences as in No. 1, raising the expander while counting four until it is on a line with the chest, then over the head; then pass the expander behind, lowering the right hand, and raising the left until the expander is in a diagonal line across

FIG. 7   FIG. 8

the body (figs. 7, 8, 10); now, keeping the right arm extended downward, bring the left one down sharply to the side, the thumb touching the shoulder, and the elbow close into the body (fig. 9). Repeat this action of the left arm twelve times, or less if this number is found too fatiguing, and return the expander in front, as in No. 1.

Exercise No. 5 is the same as No. 4, but in this the left arm is extended downward and the right arm worked.

As from habit the right arm is almost invariably the stronger, exercise No. 4 should be practised much oftener than No. 5, to induce as far as possible an equilibrium between the two members.

Exercise No. 6 is somewhat similar to the two preceding, but instead of bringing the expander diagonally across the body, it is stretched across the shoulders, as in No. 1, and both arms are worked into the side and out again, making the fingers touch the shoulders, and taking care to keep the expander as far as possible clear of the back (figs. 11, 12).

FIG. 9   FIG. 10   FIG. 11   FIG. 12

There are other and more complicated exercises with the expander, but those I have endeavoured to describe are the most essential, and my space warns me that I must draw these remarks to a close.

In conclusion, I would add that the exercises I have described, and which I can so confidently recommend, should be practised for ten minutes every morning, while still in the dressing-gown and slippers, before leaving the bedroom.

NEW MUSIC.

ROBERT COCKS.

Prize Day. A cantata for ladies' voices. Written by Jessie Moir. Music by Charles Marshall.—The first part is an introduction and chorus announcing the "Prize Day," when the Kaiser's prize is to be competed for by two equally successful students, who are crowned with flowers, according to an old Greek tradition. Solos for soprano and contralto, with duets for the same voices and choruses for the whole of the students, follow. There is also a pretty trio for soprano, mezzo-soprano, and contralto. The accompaniments are very good, and the cantata as a whole most enjoyable. It is printed well and clearly, although in a small-sized book.

Two Duettinos, for equal voices. Words by Theo. Marzials. Music by Ch. Gounod.— "Arithmetic" is the title of one, and "Our Letters" is another. Both are easy and of small compass.

METZLER AND CO.

Household Words. Written and composed by Cotsford Dick.—The song is written in three keys: No. 1 in D, for contralto or bass; No. 2 in F, mezzo-soprano or baritone; No. 3, soprano or tenor. Although this is by no means one of Cotsford Dick's best songs, it is smooth and pleasing.

Unbidden. Words by Jetty Vogel. Music by Alfred J. Caldicott.—This song is also written for contralto, mezzo-soprano, and soprano voices. A simple song without pretension or difficulty for singer or accompanist.

Sunshine. Words by Alice Lowthian. Music by Caroline Lowthian.—A pleasant little song, both as regards words and music. The accompaniment is light and graceful.

Sing to Me. Ballad. Words by Dowager Marchioness of Downshire. Music by Lady Arthur Hill.—The words breathe a tone of sadness and disappointment, and the music is in Lady Hill's usual style. The song is written in three keys—E flat, F, and A flat.

Lingering Fancies. Words by Robert Anthony. Music by F. Rivenhall. — The usual love song, not very original, but one easily sung and of moderate compass.

Love must Make or Mar. Written and composed by William A. Aiken.—The style is bold and sustained, with an accompaniment to suit the words.

My Heart's Beloved. Words by Mary Mark Lemon. Music by Hugh Clendon.—A pretty song for a high soprano, with an accompaniment that requires smooth and skilful playing.

Rigaudon. Par Joachim Raff. Pour piano et violin.—A good study, and one that will be appreciated by the admirers of this popular artist.

Little Treasures. A selection of popular melodies arranged as pianoforte solos. By Michael Watson.—No. 13, "Au Printemps," is an easy arrangement of Waldteufel's charming waltz, especially adapted for small fingers. We recommend it to our young girls.

Ave Maria. By Schubert. Arranged for the American organ by Louis Engel.—This talented artist has been particularly happy in the arrangement of the favourite and well-known melody before us. It is one of six from the old masters, all equally adapted to the lover of this instrument.

Three Melodious Sketches for the pianoforte. By Eugene Woycke. Morning, Noon, and Night are separately treated with musical expression. No. 1, "Morning" (*moderato cantabile* in G), is smooth and soft, as an awakening to the day's work and duties. No. 2, "Noon" (*allegretto giojoso* in A), is more stirring and brilliant, requiring good playing, but not difficult. No. 3, "Night" (*andante con moto* in D), is quiet and more restful, gradually passing from the time of activity to the time of repose. Each sketch is sold separately.

Die Fussgarde. Quick March. Composed by Alois Volkmer.—A brisk, clanking march, suitable for young pianoforte players, written in the key of C, without any unmanageable stretches or difficulties.

Pas de Pierrots. Pour le piano. By Hugh Clendon.—A very easy and pleasing little lesson for the student of the pianoforte, short and quickly learnt.

SWAN AND CO.

To a Flower. Poetry by Barry Cornwall. Music by V. H. Zavertall.—This is some of Barry Cornwall's pretty poetry set to suitable music. The accompaniment is very nice, requiring delicate playing and taste.

A Broad and Limpid Stream. From the Spanish, by J. G. Lockhart. Music by V. H. Zavertall.—A quiet song, with guitar-like accompaniment; without difficulty for either player or singer. The air is pretty.

Sunshine. Trio for soprano, mezzo-soprano, and contralto. Poetry by Mary Howitt. Music by V. H. Zavertall.—A well-arranged trio, needing good and careful singing.

Souvenir d'Helensbourg. Mazurka. By V. H. Zavertal. — A brilliant mazurka, well marked, the character of the dance kept prominently throughout.

Fantasia Scozzése. By V. H. Zavertal.—A collection of well-known Scotch airs, easily arranged and quickly acquired.

WEEKES AND CO.

Fantasia Brillante. By C. T. West.—A showy drawing-room piece in five flats, not difficult for a moderately advanced pianoforte player.

WORK FOR ALL.

CLERKS, BOOK-KEEPERS, ETC.

CLERICAL work, being in its nature quiet and sedentary, is very suitable to young women; indeed, they do it with so much satisfaction to themselves and to their employers that a tradesman who has once had the services of a thoroughly efficient female book-keeper, not only desires to retain her, or, if she marries or for other family reasons has to leave, to replace her by another girl, but recommends his friend to employ a female book-keeper, assuring him that she will be found as efficient and more generally satisfactory than the young man he can get for the same salary.

For a book-keeper, accountant, or commercial clerk the most important qualifications are trustworthiness, punctuality, and steady discharge of duty, with a quiet and self-possessed deportment. Her handwriting must be firm and legible, her figures well made and unmistakable. The value and importance of a good hand can scarcely be overrated; clerks almost invariably have to make application for a situation by letter, and the girl who writes the best letter is pretty sure to be selected—a carelessly written or ill-expressed letter being almost certainly fatal.

A clerk must be able to say what she has to say concisely and clearly: she should therefore be well practised in English composition, and accustomed to think clearly and accurately. It is a decided advantage to a clerk or book-keeper to be versed in the art of stenography, for employers not unfrequently prefer to dictate their letters, which the clerk takes down in shorthand, and copies out at leisure.

A knowledge of French and German is also a great advantage, as in many trades there is a large foreign correspondence. It will be seen from these observations that the subjects commonly taught in schools are precisely those which are most essential to the clerk or book-keeper—good arithmetic, grammatical study of language, and careful and accurate expression. In some of the middle class schools the technicalities of book-keeping are taught, and in all particular attention is given to arithmetic and English composition. It follows, then, that a girl who has successfully passed the Oxford or Cambridge local examination, or the third class College of Preceptors, is in a position to get up the technicalities of her calling without difficulty. There are excellent book-keeping classes in London at the Colleges for Working Women, 29, Queen-square, Bloomsbury, and 7, Fitzroy-street, Fitzroy-square; at the Birkbeck Institute, and in various other places; while the Society for the Employment of Women, 22, Berners-street, has for more than twenty years given a thorough and systematic training in book-keeping in all its branches, to girls who desire to seek employment as clerks or book-keepers; and when they have passed a satisfactory examination, the society does its best to find them suitable situations.

Trained women are, as a rule, quick workers, and the salaries of those who are skilled in office work average from twenty shillings to thirty shillings a week. The hours indeed are long, but as the occupation is sedentary, they are able to bear them without excessive fatigue.

The period necessary for the special study of book-keeping is from four to six months; and it is very desirable that the student should join a class, private study from a book seldom being so effectual. The learner should make her books, the items being dictated by the teacher, as they would occur in a house of business, and arranged by the student under their respective heads—an exercise of great value, as it familiarises her with the principles and minutiæ of trade, and she can hardly attain skill in this exercise if she be teaching herself from a book. A certificate from a well-known authority is of immense advantage to a book-keeper when she is first seeking employment. Our witty neighbours' *mot*: *Ce n'est que le premier pas qui coute,* is never truer of anything than of the book-keeper's start in life; a good introduction generally securing her steady and fairly remunerated employment for the rest of her business life.

Shorthand is taught at the School of Stenography, Lonsdale-chambers, Chancery-lane. Pitman's manuals, which can be procured of any bookseller, are very clearly drawn up, and it is not at all impossible for a student to acquire the art by herself; but her progress will be much more rapid if she can join a class, as the teacher will naturally explain difficulties as they occur, and will dictate distinctly at a steady rate a certain number of words a minute.

Mrs. Wallace Arnold, "The Physical Education of Girls" (Volume 5, 17 May 1884, p. 518).

Beauchamp, to my cost, a great deal too nice and attractive.

Very soon after our acquaintance began, the young man fulfilled Maud's wish by falling in love with me, and, had I been the daughter of the Queen, I could not have been approached with more respect.

Yet it is the truth that for two whole years I discouraged this young man, though I suffered a little martyrdom in thus doing violence to my own honest affection for him, and to the God-implanted feelings which gave birth to it.

Tom has often said since that no man ever had harder work to win his wife than he had, and that he should have given up in despair before half the time was over, if he had not thought it was my pride which hindered the success of his suit, and that at the bottom of my heart I did care for him.

In looking back on that time, I am inclined to think that we poor proud people are often more unreasonable and unmanageable than our rich proud neighbours.

At last Tom roundly taxed me with want of straight-forwardness, and said: "Olive, you may think it very brave and self-devoting to send me away, just because of the accidents of birth and fortune, for which I am in no way accountable. But I do not know how you will be able to answer, at the last, for having sacrificed the man who loved you, and whom I do believe you love, just to gratify your own false pride."

"Your mother does not yet know that for two years you have taken every opportunity of throwing yourself in my way, and have repeatedly asked me to be your wife," I replied.

"I ask you again now, and if you consent I will go straight to Castlemount, tell her the whole story, and seek her consent," said Tom, looking as much in earnest as the most exacting person could desire.

"Why have you never mentioned me to Mrs. Beauchamp before?" I asked, evading the real question.

"You have not replied to my proposal, Olive. You simply ask something which is beside the matter. You shall have your answer, dear, and then I shall expect to have an equally straightforward one. You ask why I have never spoken of you to my mother. How could I go to her and say, 'Mother, I have asked a Miss Stafford, a former visitor at aunt Edgecombe's and a friend of Maud Grant's to be my wife? I have repeated my proposal several times,'—and as I wish to be exact, Olive, perhaps you will tell me how many,—'and she has refused me as often.' What could my mother reply to such a communication? She would say: 'Where is the use of telling me this? If the girl will have none of you, there is an end of the matter.' I wish to take a different answer from you, but if, this time, you look me in the face and say you have no love for me, I will go my way and trouble you no more!"

I could not say it, and Tom's downright way of putting the case conquered. I felt that I could not bear the proposed alternative, and Tom left me that day in triumph. I had promised to be his wife, but, only with his mother's hearty consent, which I did not believe she would give.

"I will never creep into any family," I said; "I must have a welcome, and feel that your mother will be my mother, or I will dwell among mine own people to the end of my days."

Tom cordially agreed to this, but at the same time he showed me that weak place in his moral character which it so pained me to discover.

"There is just one thing I want you to do, Olive," he said. "My mother will take it for granted that you are connected with the Staffords of Lyndholme. Do not undeceive her. Of course I would not have you say any-thing but the truth. All I want is for you to be silent when she talks of those people, and to change the subject as quickly as possible."

I looked grave enough as Mr. Beauchamp was speaking. Then I replied: "If I were purposely to leave Mrs. Beauchamp under a false impression when I had the power to remove it, should I not be as guilty of falsehood as if I actually told one? I must tell the truth, the whole truth, and nothing but the truth."

"I do not know much of your family, myself, Olive. I have known you as the niece of Mrs. Hesketh, a lady of whose relationship no one need be ashamed, and as the friend and guest of my own cousin. I should be quite contented to know nothing, except that you are your own sweet self, and dearest of girls to me."

"That would not be sufficient even for you," I replied. "I shall tell you everything about my parents, their home, and position. When you know all, take the particulars to Mrs. Beauchamp, and abide by her decision."

"I will, should that decision prove just and reasonable. But you must remember, Olive, I am not a child, and the best mother in the world may wreck a son's happiness by the very means she takes to secure it."

"You mean that if Mrs. Beauchamp should agree with you, and give a hearty consent to your engagement, there will be no doubt as to the justice and reasonableness of her decision. I intend to abide by it whether she says yes or no."

I tried to look very much in earnest, but I am sure Tom's hopes had risen since the discovery that in one sense I was on his side, and he did not believe, as he frankly told me, that I should have courage or cruelty enough to agree with his mother in any plan to make him miserable for life.

(To be continued.)

REFORM IN UNDERCLOTHING.

By THE LADY DRESSMAKER.

PART I.

HERE is nothing in which a greater interest appears to be taken by women of all classes at present than in the alterations and reforms in their under-garments, which, inaugurated first in America, have been taken up here in a wiser and more thoughtful spirit.

The origins of dress have always been to me a subject of much interest. The chemise, now apparently a doomed garment, has been worn by women from the earliest days, much in its present simplest form, and is in very truth a garment of most unhygienic shape and form. So if it perish, it is because it has ceased to fulfil the needs of those who live in colder climes than those where its use was first adopted. The wonder seems to be that it has lasted in use so long.

The origin of drawers as a part of women's dress is quite modern, and in my opinion does not date very much before the year 1800. None of our great-grandmothers wore them (certainly as a rule), and we may guess this even from the portraits of the last century and the early part of the present one, where Reynolds and Gainsborough depict the petticoat in full play, both on little girls and their mothers and elder sisters, made long and very full, for the former to cling round the feet and supply the needful warmth to the limbs. Even for very little children the petticoat touched the ground. From an American paper I cut the following, which shows that the drawers question was a subject of dress reform seventy years ago:—

"My grandmother," says the writer, "has been telling me something about how the present styles in women's under-garments came into vogue. When she was a child no one wore any lower underclothes except stockings. After a while there came a fashion for pantalettes, which consisted simply of a broad ruffle fastened by a tight band just below the knee. Children used to have two sets—white ones for best and yellow nankeen or calico for everyday wear. She said there was a reason for the fashion for pantalettes, as there is for every decree of fashion. People had begun to think it more sensible to put short dresses on children rather than long gowns reaching below the ankles, and so the extra covering for the limbs was invented. But the presence of a tight band about the leg was objectionable, on account of its discomfort, and the remedy for this led to the next step in the evolution of the present lower under-garment. To the outside of the broad ruffle was attached the base of a long acute-angled triangle of cloth. This triangle extended up the waist, where it was buttoned to the chemise. This relieved the pressure from the band, but as the support was one-sided, it caused the ruffle to hang unevenly at times. The only remedy for this seemed to be the adoption of the present form, in which the whole of the lower portion of the body is covered. For a long time if anybody dared dream of such an innovation she dared not speak of it, and when at last the bounds were leaped by some courageous woman who donned the first drawers, there was a wonderful hue and cry, compared to which anything in the history of modern reforms is as nothing. Women wear garments like men! Women trying to get into trousers! Horror! Shame! But the reform prevailed."

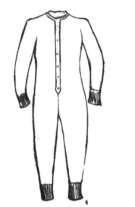

UNION OR COMBINATION GARMENT,
WOVEN OF SILK, WOOL, OR MERINO.

It seems a funny thing that the medical men of that day should have been the foremost amongst the denunciators of the new garment as "eminently unwholesome." To-day, after so many years are gone, the battle still rages over the question whether both legs shall be clothed in one garment, or each leg shall have its own to itself!

Now in the matter of dress there is nothing more difficult to cope with than custom. "We have always worn this," or "My mother wore just what I do, and considered it good," are often considered sufficient reasons to meet you when you urge the subject of some change in clothes which will tend to the health and contribute to the general wellbeing of the wearer. Next to this class of persons comes another, composed of people who read, but, having read, do not apply any new ideas they may see either to themselves or their neighbours. After this class, in somewhat wilful stupidity come the people who are afraid to do anything or adopt an improvement for fear of "what people may say." It is of no use urging with them, first, that their under-clothing is not seen, and next that, even if it were, the question is one of purely personal interest and benefit. However, the subject is so widely taken up that people are obliged to think about it, even against their will. Women who work, in particular, are earnest inquirers into the newest ideas of clothing, because in their exposure to all weathers they soon find that their usual dress is unsuitable, lacking in warmth, and restraining the natural play of their limbs. The next thing with most women is to set about reforming it, and I am glad to say these reformers exist in all classes, both of our girls and of older women. It is, therefore, to help them more especially, and the large class engaged in domestic service, that these articles are designed.

Fortunately, we have nearly outlived one bad old idea, viz., that delicacy, a constant headache, and a general look of unwholesomeness is beauty! Health and beauty go together, and generally happiness follows, forming a blessed and blessing-giving trio. For myself, I could not rely on anyone's temper if their stays were laced too tightly or their toes were pinched by pointed shoes. But, alas! in spite of our advances towards emancipation, the general health of women and girls is not too good. Many of them, though not ill, never know the "blessedness of mere living," which follows on the possession of perfect health and a quiet conscience.

One bad old idea dies a hard and lingering death, *i.e.*, the delusion that the flesh must be mortified if the spirit is to be benefited. If you impress on people the duty of the greatest personal attention to dress, diet, and comfort, you are met with the reply, "Oh, it would be selfish and wrong to think so much about myself." Those who are wise amongst us have come long since to the opinion that health is the means to a higher and more certain life of service, and that nothing is too small or puerile to claim our attention that will lead to the acquisition of that health, which will conduce to making our lives full of usefulness in our service to God and man. "Taking care of ourselves," then, so far from showing a selfish disposition, shows a thoroughly considerate and unselfish one; for how great the burden of our sickness to others, and how many the cases of sickness that might have been prevented by a little care and thought!

I must not omit to mention what Dr. Jaeger has done for us here in England, as well as on the Continent, by drawing attention to the necessity of wearing woollen underclothing, and by supplying, through his various depôts, not only the articles themselves, but copies of his valuable little book, at a moderate price, which is full of the latest sanitary information on every subject connected with the clothing of all parts of the body.

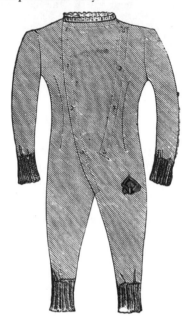

DR. JAEGER'S SANITARY COMBINATION
GARMENT, WITH DOUBLE THICKNESS IN
FRONT. UNDYED, AND WOOL ONLY.

A number of years ago a committee of ladies in Boston, consisting largely of medical women, issued a valuable series of lectures on "Dress Reform," and not only that, but did good service by proposing a series of suitable garments to take the place of those in actual wear. They were the "union under-flannel," the "chemelette," the "Emancipation suit," the "Emancipation waist and dress drawers." These are their trade names, we believe, and we give illustrations of them all, as they are useful and sensible.

(*To be concluded.*)

USEFUL HINTS.

ŒUFS A LA NEIGE.

Four whites of eggs beaten to a whip, a pint of milk kept boiling; toss a spoonful of whip into the boiling milk; take it out immediately with a strainer, and put it on a dish of custard made of the yolks of the four eggs, and pile it into graceful shapes; bonbons, mille couleurs, may be added.

FRENCH STEWED STEAK, OR OTHER MEAT.

The peculiarity of this method is that the gravy is always prepared before putting in the meat and vegetables.

Place in the stewpan two ounces of butter, and when thoroughly melted add a tablespoonful of flour, enough to absorb the butter, leaving sufficient moisture to stir easily about till it becomes of a rich brown colour: this will take fifteen minutes. If you wish for a paler gravy, for what is called a white ragoût, the mixture must be taken off the fire while it is still pale, adding three turnips sliced, two onions sliced, the steak at the top. The turnips to be laid at the bottom of the stewpan, then the onions, lastly the steak. *No water* (this is important); stew them till tender—one hour and a half or more—then take out the steak, strain the gravy from the vegetables through a seive, take off the fat; mix it in a basin with a teaspoonful of flour, add pepper and salt, mix it all well together, then add the gravy to the vegetables; give it one boil up and pour it over the steak, and put the steak in the stewpan till wanted. Be careful to shake the pan occasionally to prevent the steak burning; flavour it to your taste.

HOW TO BOIL RICE AS IN INDIA.

Two quarts of water, one pint of rice, one tablespoonful of salt.

When the water is boiling throw in a tablespoonful of salt, then the rice, after it has been well washed in cold water; let it boil twenty minutes; throw it into a colander and strain off the water. When the water is well drained off put the rice back into the same saucepan, dried by the fire, and let it stand near the fire for some minutes, till required to be dished up; thus the grains appear separately and not mashed into a pudding. Excellent with a little butter.

The Lady Dressmaker, "Reform in Underclothing" (Volume 9, 8 October 1887, p. 20).

REFORM IN UNDERCLOTHING.

By THE LADY DRESSMAKER.

PART II.

THE next garment that the Dress Reform Committee approve of is called the "chemelette" (fig. 1), now very generally known and sold in England under the name of the "com-

A GARMENT COMBINING CHEMISE AND DRAWERS IN ONE, OR IT IS MADE SEPARATE, WITH DRAWERS TO BUTTON ON, CALLED BASQUE WAIST AND DRAWERS.

bination garment" (chemise and drawers combined). This is to be the second garment worn.

The "Emancipation suit" is a variation of the chemelette, or combination. It consists of a bodice made separate, with drawers to button on—a basque bodice and drawers (fig. 2), in fact—the bodice to take the place of stays. It can also be arranged to support skirts and stockings from the shoulder, and may be made o cotton, linen, or woollen. To make it, about five yards of thirty-six inches of material is required, and it can be made either in one piece or separately, as preferred. It can be lined and made sufficiently warm to take the place of all other garments.

The "Emancipation bodice" shows the bodice made up without the drawers usually attached to it, and with buttons for fastening on the skirts or drawers.

The dress drawers are intended to be worn in place of the underskirt, for extra warmth

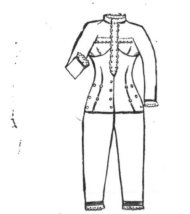

THE EMANCIPATION SUIT.

in riding or walking, and during extreme cold, in and out of doors. This article is made of coloured flannel, waterproof, or of the dress material, as may be preferred, made to fit the

ankle closely inside the boot, or with gaiters to go over the boot, and to fasten by buttons arranged for the purpose on the bodice.

Very similar garments have been long worn by ladies for riding and mountaineering.

A new magazine published in New York, called *Dress*, is conducted by Mrs. A. J. Miller.

"It assumes to become an authority on the subject of healthful, beautiful clothing for women and children. While repudiating the title of dress reformers, the leaders of the New York Association evidently advocate, as strongly as does Lady Harberton, equal distribution in the weight of garments. On the other hand, the Jenness-Miller system of dress allows the skirt of the gown or outer garment to be undivided, lets the bodice be moulded more closely to the figure, and likewise admits of concessions in the matter of ornamentation. The promoters of the association supply no less than five different articles of clothing, to each of which is given a name so suggestive as to be in itself a description. The jersey-fitting garment worn next the body is woven either in wool or silk, so as to completely cover every portion of it save the throat, hands, and feet. Over this is donned a combination cotton or linen garment, known as the 'chemelette.' This, by means of seams, fits the body smoothly but without pressure, and presents waist and drawers in one piece, free from band and binding. It is, moreover, finished both at the neck and ankles with embroidery, lace, and ribbon. Next come the leglettes—a divided garment designed to clothe each leg separately, to supersede the petticoat, and to be made in either silk, wool, or cotton. Leglettes are mounted on a yoke, which fits perfectly over the hips, and obviates the necessity of band pressure or weight upon the waist. The final garment, to which is given the name of 'gown form,' bears close affinity to a robe princesse, and, while having the upper portion shaped to the figure, is devoid of much fulness in the skirt. Upon this outline dresses of various styles of drapery and trimming can be adapted. Fashion can be followed as far as is deemed desirable, while scope is given for individual taste and fancy. A support, which is, in fact, a compromise between a bodice and a corset, but without the objectionable features attributed to the latter, provides for those women whose physical development exceeds the limits of popular taste. The use of this is only advocated until such time as the coming generation be educated to an appreciation of the beauty of fine, massive proportions and general shapeliness. The magazine promises that the dress subject will not be confined to an advocacy of the particular ideas of the editress, but will contain suggestions from all who have made the subject a study. It undertakes to draw attention to correct ideals, and to give models adapted to the means of ease and health; also to help in avoiding singularity by differing as little as possible from prevailing models."

This concise account of the newest American departure is taken from the columns of the *Queen* correspondence.

The five different articles, *i.e.*, (1) combination in stockingette, (2) woollen or cotton combination, (3) divided skirt (as we in England call it), and (4) princess robe, with no fulness, but which can be trimmed in any manner deemed suitable, have all been illustrated (except the first) in our dress articles of each month, as well as the dress bodice worn instead of stays.

There may be some, however, of our readers who desire to have a petticoat instead of the divided skirt, which would not be a difficult thing to manage, as any well-gored shape would answer. Questions on all these subjects have been asked by so many of our cor-

THE EMANCIPATION BODICE.

respondents, and it will be a pleasure to the majority, perhaps, to have all the last new ideas and all the information thereupon that can be procured.

One great change that will be brought about must not be overlooked, and that is in the work of women. Plain needlework, as applied to underclothing, will be much circumscribed in extent, and with the extinction of the chemise and drawers the demand for fine embroideries and trimmings will also be reduced.

But perhaps the greatest change of all will be in the direction of the much-abused and long-suffering washerwoman. Few of the community at the present time can wash woollens well, and it is to be hoped that the new departure will bring with it some washers of wool. But who knows that great alterations may not be expected in this department of work also? for I hear that there is no difficulty in performing the operation at home when the proper directions are followed, and aided by a small wringer to accomplish the most arduous part of it. Woollens are no longer rubbed. If very much soiled, a brush is used to aid in cleaning them. They are ironed when wet, and are carefully pulled the long way, to avoid stretching them out of shape. The first thing to do to prepare for

DRESS DRAWERS.

the washing of woollens is to cut up the soap into small pieces and boil it in water. The proportion should be about three-quarters of a pound of bar soap to six gallons of water.

The Lady Dressmaker, "Reform in Underclothing" (Volume 9, 22 October 1887, p. 60).

When all the soap is dissolved, put into a tub to cool. When ready (at about 100 deg. Fahr.), add three tablespoonfuls of liquid ammonia, or four ounces of lump ammonia. Soak the clothes for an hour, rinse twice in clean water of the same temperature as at the first washing, removing all the soap. Wring out thoroughly. Cover the clothes up when soaking, and hang them out to dry lengthwise.

But when the inner garment is always of wool, many ladies will feel it unnecessary to wear also woollen combinations, so coloured silk, cotton, batiste, and linen will all be available for the purpose of making this combination, as we in England call it, instead of the American name of chemelette. In this case trimmings of all and any kind will be available for the neck, sleeves, and legs, and the garment may be beautified to any extent. Some ladies have used it for the winter made of winsey, with a cotton lining, and consider it comfortable and useful.

The idea of the gown form or princess robe, which may be used as the invariable foundation of all the dresses required, is a very excellent one, especially for working women. In these days this is really what the highest fashion itself has arrived at—*i.e.*, that the foundation is really the skirt, the draping being added. Any style of draping may be thus adapted to the same foundation, and the wearer of the gown form may follow the fashion of the moment as nearly as she likes. A good pattern of a princess gown is really the question, and in these days of good and reliable paper patterns that is not difficult to find ; and the princess, like the polonaise, when well cut, will prove becoming and suitable to everyone.

The divided skirt has, I think, happily failed in its first intention of being the dress, and as such being visible when in movement. It is more suitable and comfortable as an under petticoat, and has been adopted and found to answer admirably by many women workers, who thankfully declare that the days of wet, miserable, draggle-tailed petticoats are over for them, and will "come again no more," and that they never have any more wearyful holding up of petticoats, which made arms and shoulders, back and sides, ache alike. How delightful to think that the days of "The Little Health of Women," as a well-known writer entitled her article in the *Nineteenth Century* magazine, are nearly over—at least so far as dress is concerned ! Of all the women I have seen for years not a quarter of them were well and warmly clad, or sufficiently covered to resist the damp and searching cold of an English winter.

NEW MUSIC.

NOVELLO, EWER AND CO.

Love and Summer. Four-part song. By John E. West.—This bright, well-written little work forms one of the latest additions to that marvellous collection of cheap and good choral music, the *Musical Times.*

Valse Caprice. Composed for the piano by Charlton T. Speer.—This musically concert piece has a most bewitching first subject in A major, and a most effective contrast later on in F major. Grace and delicacy are maintained to the finish.

METZLER AND CO.

"Alas, so long !" Words by Dante Gabriel Rossetti ; music by Mary Augusta Salmond.—A very effective setting of the words ; equally suitable for contraltos and baritones.

C. B. TREE.

The Changeless Love. Poetry by the Rev. H. C. Shuttleworth, M.A. ; music by Arthur Briscoe.—The words are beautiful, and point out the fact that whilst all things around us change,

"One changeless gift was sent below,
    The power of *selfless* love."
The melody is simple and natural.

ALPHONSE CARY.

The Millstream. Impromptu for piano. By George F. Sharpe.—A good piano piece, with the constant movement suggested by the title, but not difficult to play.

JOSEPH WILLIAMS.

Les Huguenots. One more of the operatic fantasias by E. Davidson Palmer, Mus.Bac., for violin and piano, several of which have already received notice in these pages. Mr. Palmer has arranged over a dozen favourite operas, and he always treats his subjects in an interesting manner.

Suite de Danses, Anciennes et Modernes. Par Benjamin Godard.—From a suite of six dances we select Nos. 3 to 6, viz., gigue, mazurk, polka, and valse, as the best numbers. The polka is most original.

LONDON MUSIC PUBLISHING COMPANY.

Five songs, for baritone. By Walter Frere. *Diaphenia* (words by H. Constable) is charming in its simplicity and quaintness. *A Cavalier War Song* has plenty of dash and spirit about it ; and all five songs are interesting. They are published together at a small price.

Kalékairi. Song for mezzo-soprano. By Claude Barton.—Contains a fairly difficult but most beautiful accompaniment, and is altogether a song requiring more than ordinary study. It is worth learning.

Two pieces for violin and piano. By Marie Mildred Ames. I. *Barcarolle.* 2. *Song without Words.*—Of the two the second is undoubtedly the best. Besides being free from technical errors, such as persistent and uncomfortable consecutive octaves between the bass and the violin melody, it is more spontaneous and less pretentious.

Sketches in Dance Rhythms (second series). By Erskine Allon.—The first series we know, and this second set appears to be quite equal to them in points of interest. Most charming is the slow waltz. A *Bourée* following it is curiously Swedish in character, and the *Salta-rello* bristles with life and energy.

ORSBORN AND TUCKWOOD.

Tripping through the Meadows. Published as duet or solo. By Michael Watson.

Night and Morning. Duet. By Vernon Rey.

The Mystic Melody. By Theo. Bonheur. Three compositions belonging to a harmless drawing-room class of vocal music.

Genista, Danse Royale. By Celian Kottaun. *Minuet de Napoleon.* By Jules Thérése. These are two fair specimens of the drawing-room dance piece of the present day.

STANLEY LUCAS AND CO.

My Love for You. Song. By Odoardo Barri.—Very vocal and effective.

Youthful Happiness. Jugendglück. No. 17 of a series of Liszt's songs, translated by Constance Bache. To lovers of Liszt's vocal music this edition will be welcome.

Thy Roses and *Resemblance.* Two songs. By R. B. Addison.—All that Mr. Addison writes is musician-like, and in both of these works will be found freshness of idea and wonderful novelty in harmonising.

Sonatina, No. 3 in D. By Oscar Beringer. —Having a pleasant recollection of Nos. 1 and 2, we anticipated enjoyment from the inspection of this third one, and were not disappointed. In a short compass Mr. Beringer manages to compress all the interest of a sonata, and yet the subjects are simple enough for a child to master. A concise little analysis of sonata form accompanies the copy before us, and should be read by every pupil. How many little players struggle through these classical pieces without knowing what the forms are !

Souvenir d'une Mazurka, for piano. By Glinka.

Polonaise, for piano. By César Cui.—To tell you that these two pieces are played by Rubinstein may suggest that they are beyond your powers, but that is not the case, especially in regard to the piece by Glinka, which is comparatively easy, and very nice.

J. AND J. HOPKINSON.

Mary Stuart is a cantata for ladies' voices by Gustav Ernest, on the romantic subject of the escape of Mary Queen of Scots from Loch Leven Castle.—Both Mary Seaton and the page Rolandi have parts in it, the latter as contralto.

My True Love. A setting by Ernest Birch of the oft-used lines written by Sir Philip Sidney.

Till the End of Time. Song. By Oliver King.—A ballad, above the average merit.

The Lady Dressmaker, "Reform in Underclothing" (Volume 9, 22 October 1887, p. 61).

Vol. XI.—No. 527.]   FEBRUARY 1, 1890.   [Price One Penny.

BEFORE THE STROKE.

LADIES' GOLF.

THE ancient game of golf is fast becoming a very popular pastime in England, though it may possibly be some little time before it reaches that popularity which it obtains on more northern shores, where, so great is the enthusiasm of players of all ages, and "all sorts and conditions of men," women, and children, that in such places as St. Andrews, which has long been considered its head-quarters, golfing seems to be the one absorbing subject of interest and conversation from morning to night; and even the natural beauties and historic charms of the ancient city alike appear to be of secondary interest to this engrossing pastime of our Scotch brethren.

The name of golf (pronounced "goff") apparently had its origin in the German word kolbe, or Low Dutch kolf (a club), and the game itself is considered by the best authorities to be of very ancient origin among the natives of North Britain. In the reign of James II. it had already become a popular game in Scotland, for in an Act of Parliament dated 1437, in favour of archery, it is "decreted and ordained that the weapon-schawinges be halden be the Lordes and Barronnes, Spirituel and Temporal, foure times in the zeir, and that fute-ball and golfe be utterly cryit downe and not be used."

It is, however, only of late years that ladies have—with much more becoming and feminine taste than inspires them to compete in the more masculine sports of cricket and football—taken up a game which has, especially in the modified form in which they usually play it, nothing but favourable points to recommend it, embracing as it does all the advantages of open air, healthy exercise, education of the eye, and, like most games, developing control of temper and general judgment in deciding the best method of overcoming the various obstacles and "hazards" of the links, which might well be applied to the ups and downs of life generally, with beneficial effect.

Wisely, the fair ones who of late appear apt to follow too closely the "lords of creation," are willing, except in few cases, to ignore the

AFTER THE STROKE.

Anon., "Ladies' Golf" (Volume 11, 1 February 1890, p. 273).

HOLING OUT.

sufficient, artificial holes, called bunkers, are made and mounds raised, as otherwise the game would be too simple and easy. Each hole has a flag or square piece of iron with the number of hole marked plainly on it, attached to an upright bar placed in it to show its whereabouts in the distance, and is removed when the player gets near it, until he has holed out.

The balls are made of gutta-percha, are about two inches in diameter—white in colour, or black where daisies abound, and red when snow is lying.

The game is played by two persons, or by four (two each side), which is called a "Foursome"—playing alternately. It may also be played by three or more persons, each playing his own ball. The game commences by each party playing off a ball from a place called the "Tee," which is marked on ground within a few feet of each hole on which the player, after having holed out, places it to take his first stroke for next hole.

Each hole is won by the party "holing" in the fewest strokes, and the reckoning of the game is made by the terms "odds" and "like," "one more," "two more," etc. One round of the links is reckoned a match unless otherwise stipulated. In cases where an unlimited number play, and when handicapping is introduced, the match is won by the person who does the whole round of holes in the fewest strokes.

It is usual to have an attendant, either lady or gentleman, to note down the score as the game proceeds. After the balls are struck off, the ball farthest from the hole to which the parties are playing must be played first.

As several sets of players play on the same links at the same time, the rule is, that each party wait to take their turn in playing off from any hole till those in front have "holed out" at next hole in advance, unless for any reason they allow those behind to pass them.

more energetic play of the men, with their longer links and herculean "driving," which requires greater strength of muscle than is expected in the "weaker sex," and are content with the more delicate part of the game called "putting"—(the "u" is pronounced like "u" in putty)—this requiring but one club, and dispensing with the necessity of the "caddie," who carries for the men players a bagful of clubs, known as "spoons," "brassies," "irons,"

"cleeks," "niblicks," and "putters," which their longer links and deeper bunkers, etc., necessitate for the different strokes.

The ground on which the ladies play is called the "Putting Green," and comprises (generally) eighteen holes, varying from about fifty to one hundred yards apart, arranged in an irregular circuit, commencing and finishing near the same point. It is covered with close turf, and if the natural inequalities of the ground are not

SCHOOLGIRL TROUBLES, AND HOW TO COPE WITH THEM.

By NANETTE MASON.

ON LIVING THINGS DOWN.

THERE are some girls about whom you never hear an unfavourable whisper, much less a downright bad opinion. All evil seems to keep out of their way, and by a sort of magic spell they preserve the best of characters, and never have anything to live down.

We need hardly say, however, that these are not sent into the world thirteen to the dozen. The greater number of us are wandering and wayward daughters of Eve, always doing something not just right, and making efforts more or less successful in the way of reformation.

Faults amongst this large majority are of all sorts and sizes. Agnes, if ever she turns over

a new leaf, will have to live down the unfavourable opinion of the more sensible of us, because of her frivolity; Rhoda will have the same trouble, on the score of selfishness; Sophia's weak point is vanity; and Grace will have a good deal to do before people think her anything else than changeable as the wind. By general consent Amy is a Paul Pry, worming out of everybody all that it is not her business to know. Julia has a character for doing stupid things, and it will be hard work for her to live that down, for the reputation of being a simpleton is one that pretty often sticks. It has been so with our faithful and hardworking Mary Jane, who never got credit for being anything else than "decidedly stupid,"

after the first incident that marked her going to service. She had come up from the country, as green as her native grass, and the first morning was told to put her master's boots on the tree. She literally obeyed. She hung all his boots—five pairs of them—on the tree in the garden, and it was very wet weather.

In this curious world it does not always happen that our own failings are the sole cause of trouble. Sometimes, because of one or two individuals in it, a whole family gets a bad character, and, as if living down prejudices against themselves were not enough, all connected with it are looked upon as somehow or other responsible for the doings of objectionable relations and ancestors. There used

Anon., "Ladies' Golf" (Volume 11, 1 February 1890, p. 274).

sob in her voice also. Then, so far as I could believe I heard correctly, it seemed to me that she reversed Aunt Maria's instructions, and sighed out, " Oh, Tom, stand by Perry ! ''

I thought that if my ears did not deceive me she must have uttered that injunction because our brother was so much taller and stouter, though he was in reality younger than our cousin.

But Jane, who noticed everything, pulled my sleeve to attract attention and whispered, " You heard that, Car ? Why, Sally's late snubs and slights to Perry were just a pretence."

I could not understand what reason Sally could have for pretending to snub and slight Perry, unless that girls as they grew up were bound to be affected. But I had no time to attend to the question because of the trampling and shouting overhead while the decks were being cleared for action ; at the same time there was ever so much signalling to the other ships in father's squadron to get them into position.

I have often heard father and Tom say that a naval battle is one of the most beautiful and terrible sights that are to be seen. A fight on shore is nothing to it. The ships are generally in line or in a half-crescent if they have had time to form. When the battle begins, each engages her special enemy or defends the friend who has most need of her support. In order to do so, the vessels must be sailed with as great speed as they can command and with as much skill as pieces are moved on a chessboard, so as to deliver broadsides with the utmost effect, or to escape the return fire of the enemy's guns. The ships must answer to the helm, and be brought round and sent on a new course with cunning manœuvres intended to bewilder and mislead the foe. In addition to the casualties of war on shore, the combatants at sea must be prepared for special losses. Ships founder, they are set on fire or are blown up by the explosion of their powder magazines. A sea-fight has all and more than all the features of a battle and a siege rolled into one. To conclude, all the work has to be done under the clouds of smoke which envelop the ships in action, and frequently hide the signals from the flagship and the other ships, so that the responsibility of each captain is much greater than any which can be experienced by the generals of division or the colonels of regiments belonging to an army. The naval captains have often to act on their own responsibility, an obligation which they do not dislike, as it leaves room for the exercise of individual ability and gallantry, with the reward of individual distinction. Indeed, I have heard father say that when there were captains of more genius and daring than their admirals, the captains had been known—it was so once in the case of Lord Nelson—to avoid looking out for the half-obscured signals, and to go their own way triumphantly.

But, alas, in the cock-pit, or even in the cabin we could not see the grand sight, we could only hear the hurly-burly. We sprang to our feet at the first sullen growl of a big gun, not that we were not accustomed to the sound in gun-practice and in salutes, but this meant business. And when the shock was followed by another, and yet another, louder and nearer, till the growl became a roar, and the roar was repeated every minute, because it was not single guns which were discharged but broadsides which were poured forth, even Aunt Maria, who boasted of being " gun-proof "— that is able to stand any amount of firing—began to duck her head and put her hands to her ears. And I am sure poor Jane's head was splitting with one of the nervous headaches which were so easily brought on by noise, but she would not own it, and refused at first to give way.

(*To be continued.*)

NERVOUS GIRLS.

By "MEDICUS."

I HOPE that there are not many readers of THE GIRL'S OWN PAPER who may be called nervous, yet with so large a circulation we are bound to have a few. For them this paper is written. And for girls also who are over thirty or forty, if such may be called girls at all. Indeed, it is the oldest among our readers who are the most likely to suffer from the nerves. It is they who have stood in the front ranks of the battle of life, and have borne the burden and the heat of the day ; having to fight for others as well as for themselves, and may oftentimes have had to suffer defeat, but still to hold their places in the contest.

We often hear of people's nerves having been destroyed, almost irremediably, from a sudden shock in a railway accident. Well, luckily, these cases are few and far between ; but the experience of many, alas ! will be found to confirm my statement, that a series of much smaller shocks than that which a terrible railway accident might entail, may do quite as much ultimate injury to the nervous system. The lesser shocks I refer to are, grief from loss of relatives, loss of friendships, loss of money, etc., care and worry, and oft-repeated illnesses. Some people are peculiarly resilient, and seem proof against reputed troubles. There is no withstanding nature's written laws, however—a constant drop will wear away a stone, even should that stone be granite, and ere long the strongest finds herself going down to it just a little ; finds her nerves are not so strong as they once were before this or that recent trouble, feels a kind of abiding anxiety at her heart, and that she is now more apt to worry and look at the dark side of life than formerly. Perhaps she finds herself, moreover, not so vigorous in the more mechanical portion of her system, namely, the muscular ; or finds that she catches cold more easily, or feels the cold more than she was wont to.

I may remark here, before I forget it, that this increased sensibility to cold and draughts, especially in the feet or spine, though it is a sympton that is not usually thought much of, is one of the earliest indications of deterioration in the nervous system.

The nerves, by the very old surgeons and physicians, before anatomy had become a fine art and a science, were not considered of much importance, and ailments connected with them were lightly termed " the vapours," and were supposed to be more imaginary than anything else. We know better now. The nerves are as real as the silken thread you hemmed that handkerchief with, and when strange and disagreeable feelings of pain or uneasiness call our attention to them in our own bodies, something has as assuredly gone wrong as that thread would go were you to hold it a moment in the flame of a candle.

There may be actual injury done to some of the parts or portions that are included in the words " nervous system," as from the pressure of a tumour, from the pressure of an inflamed surface, or from inflammation about the nerve itself, in which case there will, of course, be very great pain either constantly or periodically. There may be no injury to any nerve or part of a nerve that can be located easily, but only general weakness of the whole system. This is the trouble I have to consider in my present short paper, and for which I have adopted a name which may be found more euphonious than easily understood. Neurasthenia is a word derived from the Greek, and signifies want of strength in the nerves. The old-fashioned title of Nervous Debility was, perhaps, equally much to the point, and both titles are recognised by the profession more as symptoms than real disease. Perhaps in some cases of neurasthenia such should hardly be the case. When a little girl was asked how she felt when nervous, she replied that she felt " in a hurry all over." She could not have expressed it better. When one is momentarily nervous there is a positive loss for the time being of force power from almost every portion of the skin and muscles all over the body. The very heart, for the time being, feels this loss, and is sometimes said to stand still—as in cases of sudden fear or bad news. But the loss occasions a thrilling feeling throughout the body, not quite so bad as pins-and-needles in the feet, but of a somewhat similar kind. Sensations of heat and cold are also felt sometimes, and that sensation well-known as the fidgets, when you do not know what to do with your hands, and would just as soon not possess any feet. There is, for the time being, debility of the body. So great is this, often in cases of fright, that the cold perspiration covers the knees, and they feel unable to support the weight of the body.

Well, now, tiredness or weariness is but another form closely allied to this, and occurring from the same cause, the loss of vital power. Professor Michael Foster, in lecturing at Cambridge the other day upon weariness, after stating that the nervous system was a candle that could not be profitably burned at both ends, went on to prove that what we call endurance or staying power depended chiefly upon the supply of actually pure blood, and that the readiness with which the internal scavengers—the lungs, liver, kidneys, etc.— freed blood from the poisons that the muscles and other active organs poured into it was in proportion to the staying power of the worker. " The hunted hare dies,'' he says, " not because he is choked for want of breath, not because the heart stands still—its store of energy having given out—but because a poisoned blood poisons his brain and his whole body."

Now this physiological reasoning may not be quite easily understood by my younger readers, who however must admit that I seldom seek to dose them very much with "ologies" of any kind, but nearly everyone will understand the simple statement that all bodily force or vital power passes to the muscles, for example, through the nerves, just as electric force passes through the telegraph wires to work the instrument, and that if that force be not equal to the amount expended, the whole body deteriorates, and the ailment neurasthenia is the result. If in addition then to hard work day after day one has to stand up against the mental shocks caused by innumerable small worries, that seem to have a directly paralysing effect upon the nerve tissues themselves, easily may the system go to the wall, or become physically degenerated. Indeed under such a depressant it quickly deteriorates.

What are the effects of general neurasthenia? These are broad and wide, and so many and varied that while it is impossible to individualise, it is difficult even to generalise? The symptoms of the first oncoming of an attack of neurasthenia will differ greatly in different individuals. Occasional attacks of weariness and fatigue with depression of spirits are usually common to every case. The young lady thinks something is going to happen to her, there seems to be a dark cloud over all her existence. Her sky is not any longer *couleur de rose*, and life for the time being is hardly worth living. The middle-aged lady believes she is growing old, and both are nervous and dyspeptic. Alas, it is a fact that neurasthenia is a complaint which chooses its victims preferably from among the best, the cleverest, and the bravest of womenkind, and among the least selfish. Because it is they who stand in the front of the battle; they who fight in the breach, and in fighting too often fall —and all perhaps for the want of a little well-needed rest. The dull and the phlegmatic on the other hand fling down the foils on the very first signs of the enemy gaining a footing in the stronghold of life, fling down the foils and fly—perhaps to the seaside for a month for the rest and quiet which their common-sense tells them are needed to recruit the health and strength. We know which class we admire the more, but we seldom know or can appreciate the efforts of those who unselfishly and unflinchingly fight the battle of life until they droop and die. Nor do we know how much they suffer at times, especially when alone, for they cannot but see that their best efforts are certainly not overrated, the great majority caring little really for those who do the most for them. "It is their choice to be in the battle's van," says the majority to itself, "well let them; I have chosen the better part." And as with communities, so it is too often with families, the bread-winning father, who, mayhap with breaking heart and aching head, toils day after day to keep his children above want or worry is seldom a hero, seldom crowned with laurel by his sons or daughters, nor is the hard-working mother who stands by his side to assist and encourage him.

Well, I have mentioned weariness and depression as particular symptoms of nerve deterioration. But they are just those that, although probably almost diagnostic, are least attended to. If taken at once, neurasthenia would generally be curable, and the cure is rest. At least that is one portion of the cure. "But, oh," I think I hear a sufferer exclaim, "*I* have no time for rest, my work won't wait. The idea of a holiday for poor me! What would become of my family around me?"

In answer to this I should speak a parable and say: "A certain ship's captain went to sea, and all went well and gaily for a time, till at last clouds banked up in the east and a mighty storm came sweeping up over ocean and over ship. And, behold, in the midst of this storm a portion of the crew came fearfully to the captain and cried, 'Oh, master, the vessel has sprung a leak; pray repair the damage

that our lives may, peradventure, be spared!' But the captain turned to them and replied, 'Begone! I have no time to repair leaks. Am I not making a speedy voyage—a wondrous passage—so tell me not of leaks. I must hurry on.' And he did hurry on. To destruction, hurried he on."

But people may not be able to run away somewhere every time they find themselves suffering from overwork, overstrain, and weari- -ness. Nor need they. I am not convinced even till this day that, after all, the best place in which to spend a holiday isn't one's own garden with a good book. Rest should be a daily, almost an hourly, thing with every work-a-day individual. A brain worker should be like a general on the war-path. He ought to well weigh the strength of his forces and consider how he shall lead them forth and spread them out, or concentrate them to the greatest advantage. Remember this, the heart itself has its periods of rest; it rests between its own beats. The heart is seldom enough considered. It is tired when you are. Rest it therefore whenever you can, if working in your own room. You rest it by reclining. Yes, or even by putting the feet on a chair for ten minutes. You rest the mind by glancing for a few minutes at a newspaper. You rest it when you sit down to the piano—that is, if you really love music and play only the airs or pieces that touch the heart. But one can never rest either mind or body by taking a vinous stimulant or so-called cordial. A general would commit the same sort of mistake if he drew out his reserves and exhausted them before they were really required. So beware of this kind of rest, if you would not go very quickly indeed to the wall.

Rest in bed is the best rest of all. I know a hard-working literary lady who always takes a holiday in bed only for a day, but it does her good. She makes some consistent change in diet, and surrounds herself with nice books, etc., and—— Well, there she is; and if you are a friend and call, her audience-chamber for the time being is her bedroom.

But insomnia, or sleeplessness, is one of the worst symptoms of neurasthenia. It is usually a very advanced symptom too, and a symptom, moreover, that makes the disease advance, but not to a happy termination. When this comes on a cure for the complaint must be obtained whatever it costs. It is really now a matter of life and death.

Dyspepsia is a most troublesome symptom of neurasthenia, and one that not only interferes in the most marked degree with the blood-making process, but renders at times sleep almost impossible, except, perhaps, a few hours of dream-perturbed slumber toward morning, when town or country noises are making themselves audible.

Fretfulness is one of the commonest symptoms of neurasthenia. Irritability is seldom absent entirely when there is debility, and never present when the nerves are in a healthy condition and well supplied with pure food. But fretfulness is terribly distressing. More so, as a rule, to the sufferer herself than to others around her. She has every wish and desire to see everybody about her happy, but still she cannot help giving way, many times and oft perhaps, to outbursts of peevishness under scarcely any provocation at all.

There are scores of other symptoms of the ailment under consideration that I have no space even to name, but they one and all depend on the same causes, namely, on an inadequate amount of pure wholesome blood to the whole system—the supply of fuel to the human machine not being in proportion to the output of work or force.

Upon the *cause* we must found our plan of treatment.

Of course we may, by taking extra nutritious food, manage to struggle on for a little while

longer, but this is not cutting straight at the root of the trouble. I need hardly remind the reader what a terrible thing a complete breakdown is to the majority of brain-workers in these busy times, when both women and men have often to struggle side by side for bare existence. What might it not mean to your married brother for example—and I know that our readers are often as much concerned for the welfare of their relations as for their own. Well, but your brother, let us say, has not been many years married, although already two pledges have come to stay, and so the world's cares are gathering round him. He has a very pretty little house, but as it was a love marriage pure and simple—very simple, indeed—there is little behind it of worldly substance. Well, he has been working hard and has got paler and even thinner. Suppose he broke down—I don't want to frighten you— and had to take a spell of inactivity for a year. Who would fight for the children then; or get them the little comforts they and their mother have been used to? Yes, indeed, who? The world is absolutely powerless, if not pitiless.

The cure of neurasthenia should be taken in hand, therefore, from the very first week any of its symptoms made their appearance. If the sufferer cannot go for a holiday she, or he, can so regulate the life that all the rest possible may be had. While at work it is imperative that there be no driving, no distracting rushing. This it is which kills so many, or lays them on the shelf for ever and a day.

As nothing can be done without regularity some plan of treatment should be adopted and laid down in your note-book. If this be well conceived benefit may be expected from it in a week or fortnight. It is so difficult to do this. Was that what you said? And a doctor runs into expense. Well let me lay down one for you and just try if for a month.

Rise in time to have your cold sponge bath, which should if possible have a couple of handfuls of sea-salt dissolved in it. Dress as leisurely as you can. When half dressed take at least five minutes' dumb-bell exercise. Go into the open air for ten minutes before sitting down to meals. Eat leisurely. In fact you *must* learn to do everything leisurely. It will come easier by-and-by. Whatever be your duties, enter to them with all the spirit you can muster, but not hurriedly. Care killed a cat. Do you know why? Because the cat *would* hurry and would worry and so fell a victim to a fast way of living.

Do you work in the fresh air? Don't say you won't or you can't; I say you shall. Open that window of yours right up to the top and sit where you can breathe it. Three days working thus is as good as one day at the seaside. Don't be afraid of cold. If the body is well nourished it won't catch cold, *can't* catch cold. I would engage to march two hundred thousand of my girl readers to the top of Ben Nevis in the dead of winter, and they should not catch cold. But I should feed and wrap them up well. What a dinner we should all eat in the evening!

Keep out of doors as much as you can and *vary* your work if you can.

Arrange to have a nice long walk in the afternoon or evening. *Walk*, do not dawdle. Throw the chest out and keep the arms back. Walk regularly every day from three to six miles, rain or shine. Eat a solid meal in the middle of the day. Never touch tea or coffee or stimulants, but drink good milk and butter-milk whenever you can get it. Have a hot bath every Saturday night followed by a cold sponge down.

Begin to lay up for your summer holiday. If you spend your day as I tell you, you will sleep at night. But avoid worry and hurry and thinking, or anything the least disagreeable.

Medicine? No, you do not want any. Nourishing food makes good blood, and it is good pure blood you need, and nothing else.

Medicus, "Nervous Girls" (Volume 15, 28 October 1893, p. 61).

Vol. XV.—No. 753.]   JUNE 2, 1894.   [Price One Penny.

ON RECREATIONS FOR GIRLS.

By SIR BENJAMIN WARD RICHARDSON M.D., F.R.S.

THE day is fast passing away when the common belief existed that women were, by nature, consigned to the monotony of indoor life and domestic care. Hector might still declaim to his Andromache—

"No more, but hasten to thy tasks at home,
   To guide the spindle and direct the loom.
My glory summons to the martial scene ;
The field of combat is the sphere for men."

Yet I doubt if he would be quietly listened to in these days, if the enemy were at the gate, for we have now an army of women who would fight by the side of their husbands and brothers if necessity called them. Within a very short space of time, within my own re-collection, certainly, a change has been effected in respect to the cultivation of physical exercise amongst women that is historical in its character. My old and able teacher of anatomy, when I was a student, was persistent in his lesson that women were not capable of cultivation, physically, like men. He did not pretend that their ribs differed in number from those of men, indeed, from two fine skeletons, one of a woman, another of a man, he demonstrated that the sexes were alike, strictly, in respect to ribs, but in the matter of muscles he held they were not alike ; a woman could not throw a cricket-ball as a man did ; she could "chuck" it by an "underhand movement," but she could not fling it or pitch it. The muscles were not formed for the work. We know better now, for have we not a ladies' team, and does not the team do credit to the old English game ?

Of course the argument of the old-school men was based on a fundamental error. They simply witnessed the phe-nomenon of deficient development from deficient exercise, and they mistook cause for effect. Except under special circumstances women are just as able as men to take part in recreative pur-suits ; they are as much benefited by such pursuits, and, if yielding wisely

PREPARING FOR A CONSTITUTIONAL.

Sir Benjamin Ward Richardson, "On Recreations for Girls" (Volume 15, 2 June 1894, p. 545).

and judiciously to circumstances, they moderate their zeal so as not to show too competitive a spirit in any contests in which they may be engaged, they add greatly and gracefully to the science of health and to the usefulness of life, by their new efforts.

This general fact admitted, and there are, amongst scholars who have studied the subject carefully, very few, I think, who would question the matter; the points to be considered are those of detail respecting recreative exercise for women. It is to this inquiry I shall devote attention, collecting my material from the information obtained from a fairly long period of observation and experience.

Before entering into these details I would beg permission to remark that there are certain general principles relating to recreation for women which, in a degree, stand alone, that is to say, while they apply to some extent to both sexes, they especially apply to the female sex.

First and foremost, those recreations are best adapted for women which do not interfere with duties and functions especially belonging to the woman, duties and functions which cannot possibly be performed by men. One of the great dangers at the present time is that women, in their anxiety to compete in various recreative exercises, are given to forget the fact that, *nolens volens*, they are born to do what men can never do; that if the race is to progress they must some day become mothers, that they must undertake special maternal duties, and that for home to be home they must, within the sphere of home, display domestic talents, and do domestic work which comes exclusively under their control. They must remember, moreover, without thinking of giving up recreative pleasures and exercises as matters of necessity, that every attempt to pass in recreation beyond a certain bound of natural womanly duties, is to pass into a sphere with which such duties are utterly incompatible. In other words, extreme physical strength and power of resistance to natural forces, with skill to surmount great obstacles, with craft to overcome great difficulties, with courage to carry everything that may come in the way, with dispositions, in plain words, to fight and make level all that is in opposition, means a state of body and mind which could not be in harmony with those gentler traits, attributes, and affections belonging to the birth and the care of the young and feeble. Mind and body go together in action, are attuned one to the other when a mere strength of physical organisation is fully developed. The mental qualities of resolution and conflict are joined to the physical qualities which sustain strength, resolution, and conflict, and it were something worse than crushing a fly on the wheel of a locomotive, to see the representative of pure manly attributes engaged systematically in the nursery.

Secondly, those recreations are best for women which, according with the more refined spirit of the woman, do not vulgarise. All qualities that vulgarise make the woman not only objectionable generally but objectionable specifically when they unfit her for the instruction and training of children, male or female. Too often necessity makes mothers and women vulgar in their nature. Brought up in schools where rudeness and vulgarity of habit are dominant, they reflect upon young and susceptible minds their own nature, and we look with pity if we are merciful, with disgust if we are not merciful, on the mixed products of nature and imitation which follow on the rude patterns we would avoid in recreative pursuits.

Thirdly, the best recreations for women are those which cause the body to be equally developed, and to be, in development, as perfect as possible. This is another way of saying that recreations should lead to beauty, and, if I am correct in my view, every recrea-

tion should have this tendency. A man may say this without being supposed to flatter the opposite sex, for beauty is a virtue as commendable to men as to women. What is more, it is a tribute which being much sought after, is one that should render recreations for women specially agreeable to their tastes and inclinations, for women more than men love, naturally, beauty not only when they see it, but beauty as they know it in their own persons. The cynical may laugh at books of fashion, and may consider them the height of folly, but no cynic can run down the signs of beauty, or destroy that distinction which everyone recognises as between the beauty and the beast. We may call fashion the outward display of beauty, the surreptitious display if it be confined to that which is only artificial for adorning the person; but let beauty extend to the person itself, let it not only be skin deep but more than skin deep, that is, belonging to the whole frame; then the worst cynic can say nothing that the world will believe, except that "beauty unadorned is adorned the most."

There are recreations which lead to general beauty, and there are recreations which divert from general beauty. There are some recreations which add extra development of beauty to the body, and others which, being opposed to natural law and often brought into action, deform rather than beautify, and, though fitted to the recreation, is not fitted to the strength and quality of the body as a whole organisation. It is remarkable, moreover, how very little of divergence from harmony of action will throw out the animal body both in form and function. This is most conspicuous in regard to form, and those artists who are most correct and masterly in their delineations are those who are freest from defect in form. I remember a most distinguished sculptor who produced in marble a beautiful design or model of a woman; it seemed perfect when looked at in detail, but when it was glanced at from a distance, as one design, something wrong was detected in it. It ceased to be beautiful. The artist himself was conscious of some grievous fault, but did not see wherein it lay. At last a friendly anatomical eye coming fresh upon the subject lighted on the defect or deformity, if so it may be called. It was a trifling matter, but it was everything; one small section of the body on one side was enlarged, and although a very trivial erasure was required to remedy the defect, it would have been fatal if it had not been detected and removed. The removal completed the beauty of the whole design. It is the same with regard to the building up of the human body from nature. Beauty, in unity, as dependent upon recreation should ever be a first consideration. The same is the case with regard to function. It is true that the body adapts itself to various errors, to various positions, to various distortions. But that body is most perfect in which compensatory efforts to meet or conceal defects are least required, because any compensation means an unnecessary effort, and an unnecessary effort means an expenditure of bodily power—two acts, when one might be sufficient.

TYPICAL RECREATIONS.

The recreations of the English life open to women at the present time, and coinciding with the principles above narrated, is the question that now concerns us. In answering it, as briefly as possible, I shall refer to a few forms of recreation most likely to be attractive.

Walking is naturally the first exercise, and carried out correctly is, perhaps, the best of all, though it may be the most monotonous. Good walking is an art to be learned; it does not consist in moving with rapidity; neither man nor woman is destined to walk more than

four miles per hour, and the woman who achieves three and a half miles does well. The amount that should be done per day varies according to age and constitution; but even in tours six hours' walking out of the twenty-four is amply sufficient for those women who are best trained. This would limit walking exercises for recreation to a distance of twenty-four miles a day at the best. In walking, uprightness of the body is an essential aid to good development. The head should be kept erect, but some freedom of motion in the upper limbs should be permitted. The breathing should be evenly maintained, and should be always carried out by the nostrils, not by the mouth. The step should be light, elastic, and free from toe to heel. All impediments of long dresses should be laid aside, and the boot or shoe should never have a heel to it above half an inch in height. The boot should have a full-size across the fore part, so as to prevent the toes from being cramped, and the ankle should be left as free as possible. The shoe should partake, in fact, as largely as can be of the old sandal principle, which, after all, has never been surpassed.

Swimming should be cultivated not only as a recreation but as a useful practice. No recreation brings a larger number of muscles into play than swimming, and, barring accidents, I know of no exercise that more equally develops the body or gives freer play to the respiration. The dangers to be avoided in swimming are those incident to long diving, and to prolonged immersion in the water. I have seen mischief even in young women from both these sources, from long immersion especially. So soon as it is found that the body of the swimmer instead of reacting well in a warm glow on coming out of the water, is dark and cold with blue lips, goose-skin, chilliness and feebleness, the story is told that the immersion has been too long, and has done injury.

Dancing properly carried out is one of the happiest and healthiest of recreations. Unfortunately, it has of late dropped into an absurd fashion of overwork and overstrain, in late hours, and in unwholesome atmospheres. Dancing should be cultivated as an outdoor exercise as it was in the olden time, and should consist, more than it does, of individual dancing than in couples, as in the waltz. Dancing is one of those recreations which especially excites the circulation of the blood, and raises dangerously—when carried to extreme—the beat of the heart.

Lawn Tennis, which has become so essentially an English game, stands well on the roll of recreations for women, in so far as healthy movement is concerned. Without excessive fatigue it brings into play all the great groups of muscles of the body, and it has the advantage that it trains specially the sense of sight, enabling the player to measure distances with exactitude as well as to become familiar with the best mode of using muscular force with quick exactitude. The objections to it are the accidents which sometimes happen from muscular strain and the weariness that is induced from too prolonged indulgence in it as a pastime.

Cycling is unquestionably a good exercise for women, but it has its disadvantages in that it does not equalise muscular movement. Carried too far, in fact, it leads to unbalanced development of the lower limbs, and may produce a certain measure of deformity in the lower limbs. The exercise of cycling greatly increases the circulation, the heart increasing in its beat to an unnatural degree. Extreme competition even by powerful women has been shown in my experience to be detrimental to the health, and I particularly warn riders against efforts in climbing hills and against prolonged extreme efforts. I do not

Sir Benjamin Ward Richardson, "On Recreations for Girls" (Volume 15, 2 June 1894, p. 546).

consider that a woman can continue to ride safely above forty miles a day, and she must be an accomplished rider, mounted on a light machine, a bicycle, and unencumbered by unnecessary dress who can bear that effort. From ten to twenty miles of cycling exercise per day under favourable conditions of weather and on good roads is truly useful recreation, and ought to be generally encouraged but not exceeded.

Rowing in moderate degree is a good exercise for women, and the firmness with which women sit in rowing is in their favour. There are few sights more graceful than the appearance of a good oarswoman, and there is a fair amount of muscular movement in the exercise that leads to good development. But rowing is the exact opposite of cycling. In rowing, the upper limbs and upper part of the body are most brought into play. Rowing tells upon the respiration rather than on the circulation, and causes always when first carried out considerable dyspnœa or shortness of breath. This is a danger therefore which ought to be avoided. At the same time, in persons of feeble and delicate chest, good results are obtained by careful and moderate rowing from the very expansion which in time is gained from it.

Cricket is an excellent game for women; it calls into play great groups of muscles, it teaches measurement of distance, it causes precision of movement of the hands guided by sight, and it produces good active running movements of the body. The risks from it (less accidents) are overstrain, and especially overstrain from overhand bowling, which is neither graceful nor useful, nor indeed anything more than a conceit.

Skating and *rinking* are good and graceful exercises. *Hockey* is both a simple and good exercise for women, and is, I am glad to say, coming largely into fashion. *Golf,* somewhat wearisome, is a fine exercise for women advanced in life, and *archery,* good at all ages, is admirable as a trainer of the senses and a cultivator of graceful movement. *Croquet,* a gentle pastime, having great claims on our attention as a recreative pleasure, deserves considerable praise. It was the recreation which of all others was first to call women out of the drawing-room on to the lawn, and to lead to the other and more active delights of bodily movement.

I reserve to the last, *riding on horseback.* This recreation is unfortunately restricted to ladies of wealth and position, but it is a noble and splendid form of recreation when kept within legitimate bounds. I do not know that it is more healthful than cycling, but it is perhaps more exhilarating, and there is about it a touch of adventure which is by no means a contemptible part of all recreations.

"LIKE A WORM I' THE BUD."

By ANNE BEALE, Author of "The Queen o' the May," etc.

CHAPTER XI.

"A VIEUX COMPTES NOUVELLES DISPUTES."

"DO GOOD, AND THEN DO IT AGAIN."

THE next day was Saturday, the busiest of days at the work house. Mara could not get away to fetch Ivor until the afternoon, and before that came she had much to do and endure. Mr. and Mrs. Roderick considered her the cause of the unusual excitement and late hours of the previous day, and were evidently annoyed with her. Moreover, the master underwent an examination by Mr. Glyn concerning the children, and when it came out that he had flogged George, Mr. Glyn showed his displeasure more openly than was his custom.

"The boy was not to blame," he said, "he merely went in search of the foundling, and the tide came upon them unawares."

"Then Miss Vaughan was to blame, sir," said the master.

"Possibly. But you did not flog Miss Vaughan," said Mr. Glyn, dryly. "If we run the thing to ground I am to blame, who took on myself to allow her and the children the benefit of walks on the sea-shore. If you will let me therefore be the scapegoat, I will take the fault on myself also. George is a fine, brave fellow, and ought not to have been punished."

"He is very bold and impertinent, and browbeats me," said the master.

"What has he said?"

"That he would do the same again to save Ivor."

"Hum! so would I!" said Mr. Glyn; "but you would not flog me. When can George come to me?"

"After Christmas, sir."

"Then we will consider that point as settled, and I am sure you will let this little affair die a natural death. The poor foundling is saved after much danger, and nobody is the worse for it. May I see Miss Vaughan?"

"Certainly, sir," said the master, and left the board-room.

He soon returned with Mara.

"I will not keep you, Roderick," said Mr. Glyn, and the little man went away.

"Excuse me, Miss Vaughan, but as the guardians are gone, and I have a little time, I took the liberty of asking to see you, just to inquire how this affair came about. You look ill. I am afraid your generous exertions——"

"Thank you, Mr. Glyn, I am quite well. Now I have the opportunity, may I thank you from my very heart for what you did for those poor children. God will bless you. You saved his life—Ivor's. Oh! Mr. Glyn!"

"Do not name that, I am glad to have been the instrument of good. But you, Miss Vaughan! you will be more careful in future, not—not on the children's account, but on your own. Your heroism was great, but caution is the better part of valour, and—and—you understand, I am sure."

"Perfectly," said Mara, colouring. "I was careless, and oh! I have been punished enough."

"Why were the children so far away from you? and, may I ask, what brought Miss Herbert on the scene?"

"She was going over the beach, and seeing me, came and sat down by me," said Mara, with some hesitation.

"Oh, indeed! you are old friends, I fancy?"

"Yes, and true ones. Angharad never forsakes a friend."

"Perhaps she kept your attention engaged while the children strayed."

"Possibly," said Mara, shortly, remembering what the conversation had been.

"Your father was at the Board to-day, and asked me about last night," said Mr. Glyn.

"He is waiting for me now," said Mara; "I have been so engaged that I have not yet seen him."

"One word more, Miss Vaughan." This word was the one Mr. Glyn had wanted to say from the first. "You must not make a favourite of Ivor. They gossip about it."

Mr. Glyn bolted, leaving Mara in much perplexity.

No sooner was he gone than Mr. Vaughan came into the room. He kissed Mara more affectionately than usual, and she returned his embrace with unaccustomed warmth.

"Are you ill, child?" he said anxiously. "You might have lost your life in that wild walk over the cliffs."

"I am well, father. Captain Herbert saved me from danger, if there was any."

At the hated name Mr. Vaughan's temporary show of feeling was again clouded.

"I thought of you and Nanno, father, as the night came on, and I heard the sea roaring beneath me," said Mara, simply.

"Then you will avoid such adventures in future by returning to us," said Mr. Vaughan.

"I cannot, I cannot," was the reply; "I must not leave the children."

"Your anxiety about them is praiseworthy, Mara, and I am glad to hear that you do your duty by them. But your duty to your father should be first. You rarely come home now. Nanno is lonely without you, and I feel that I ought to have two daughters."

The stress on the ought roused Mara.

"You have, father. I will come at Christmas, if I may. But oh! do not ask me to leave the children."

"I am punished indeed!" said Mr.

THE DRESS FOR BICYCLING.

By DORA DE BLAQUIÈRE.

THERE can be no doubt of the interest taken in the subject of the cycle as a new form of exercise for women and girls, and this year in England it has been unquestionably quite the rage. All these things are, however, so much a matter of fashion unhappily amongst ourselves, that when next season arrives we may find the fad of this year to have become the old fashion of the next, and something else to have taken its place in the way of exercise and amusement. But behind this purely fashionable view of the matter there is the other view, that the bicycle seems to have come as a great emancipation to women, and that, when carefully learnt and used intelligently, it promises to be to her a source of pleasure beyond anything she has already had, and that it is more than probable it has "come to stay." As a means of getting about, without expense and with little fatigue, a practicable method of locomotion for everyone, youthful as well as middle-aged, it possesses advantages which appeal to all, and which will secure it a permanent acceptance as a well-beloved and useful friend. Its best

motto, where women are concerned, would be, "Use, not abuse," as all the medical profession seem to declare with one accord that the abuse only is dangerous. An American doctor, who has given much attention to the subject says, that "It ought to be a law for every woman that her bicycle ride should terminate when a distinct feeling of weariness comes over her. No ordinary woman, who rides for pleasure once or twice a week, should ride at first over ten miles at a time. This represents, perhaps, an hour's or an hour and a quarter's ride, and if at the end of it she does not feel fresh and in a glow, she may be certain that she has ridden too long. The healthy, tired feeling, which anyone can recognise after athletic exercise, can never be mistaken for that weariness which comes from too much exertion, and overstraining of the muscles and nerves." The other danger pointed out by this authority consists in that arising from a high rate of speed. This is natural enough. The machine runs so easily, perhaps, that there is a strong temptation to increase the rate of progress, and every woman

must learn to put a deliberate check on herself, to avoid dropping into it.

Yet another doctor, and this time an English one, must be heard: "Of all means of training the respiration, Dr. Fortescue Fox thinks cycling is the best. When a person first takes to cycling, he is troubled with shortness of breath, his heart beats uncomfortably, and his legs get tired, but after some training these discomforts all disappear. Why should not people liable to attacks of asthma also train their respiration by such kinds of exercise—of course, on condition of the heart and lungs being in perfect health? Cycling exercise first of all increases the depth of breathing, and that without fatigue, as the respiratory movements are automatic; at the same time it will accustom the rider instinctively to take in at each respiration the volume of air required to aerate the blood and to eliminate a fixed proportion of carbonic acid, leaving in the circulation the precise amount compatible with health."

And now that I have devoted a short space to the healthful nature of the exercise, I will turn to the doctors' opinion of the nature of the dress to be worn, so far as they have given it; but first will give an account of the dress as used in America and in France, in both of which this exercise has advanced, and been practised longer than with us, as women were using the wheel in both these countries more than two years ago.

In France it seems that women never ride, nor have ridden, in skirts. The Bloomer costume was accepted as the proper thing from the beginning; and excepting a little ridicule from the comic papers, the question of the propriety of it has never been discussed. All French women appear to agree on the subject, that the Bloomers are an advantage; but their costume seems to me to leave much to be desired on the score of beauty. In the environs of Paris, where women-bicyclists are as thick as flies, one may see fifty costumes in a morning's walk, exactly alike as to cut and pattern, and only differing in colour or in material. All wear low shoes, which are smart and well-fitting, and stockings of various colours. This summer many wore pretty-coloured silk ones, but the really smart riders are wearing the heavy English woollen ribbed-hose. Gaiters are seen in very few instances. The Bloomers come next, and are ungainly-looking articles, like full bags, from which the legs protrude, looking diminutive and out of drawing. The jacket is tight-fitting, and reaches only to the waist; this is discarded on a long trip, and its place is taken by the "sweater," which completes the ugliness of the costume, by emphasising the sharply-defined curves of the figure, which look most ungainly. Some of the Bloomers are cut after the fashion of a man's breeches, and fit tightly about the hips, then full to the knees. Others have the fulness laid in pleats over the hips, which of course increases the apparent size of the wearer. The hat worn is generally a "deer-stalker," with or without feathers on one side.

Dr. I. Championnière, of the French "Academy of Medicine," has written in the *Nouvelle Revue* an article very strongly in favour of bicycling for women, which he considers will create a great and favourable modification in women's physical condition, especially in that of French women, who, when they become wives and mothers, drop their habits of exercise to a greater extent than their sisters of England and America. In three points he considers it will benefit

women. It will insensibly cause women to train, and to modify their meals. Secondly, it will increase their habits of attention; and, thirdly, they will gain in courage and self-control.

There is no doubt of the immense mania for the bicycle in America, for the comic papers are full of jokes, the fun of which is furnished by the cycle. "How does George get along since he began bicycling?" an interested friend is reported to have asked. "On crutches," is the reply; which shows a certain amount of cruel sarcasm on undeserved misfortune. But Chicago, and her board of Aldermen, has quite exceeded everything in the ordinance recently passed, to regulate, locally at least, the dress of riders, both male and female—neither tights nor knickerbockers are allowed; whatever is worn must be baggy, from the ankles upwards. No stockings are permitted to be shown, and no gaiters to be worn; and all jackets must button up tightly to the throat. But the other day I suddenly dropped upon

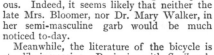

THE BLOOMER COSTUME.

the following extract from the *Chicago Tribune*, which made me think that perhaps the Board of Aldermen had had a great deal to put up with before they issued the sweeping ukase above recorded.

"One of the most notable cases of unseemly dress was that of a woman bicyclist who was seen during the week on Grand Boulevard clad in a pair of long trousers, which were evidently borrowed from her husband or brother. They fitted her rather loosely, and were held around the ankles by an ordinary pair of trouser guards, just as they are usually worn by men. The remainder of her costume consisted of a shirt waist, a lady's jacket and a man's soft felt hat. She rode a man's wheel, and, except that the coils of her hair showed plainly under her hat, would have been easily mistaken for a man.

"A pair of noticeable costumes have been frequently observed on the South Side. They are worn by a man and his wife, and are exactly alike in every detail. The two costumes are made up of handsome corduroy

knee-breeches, without any fulness at the knees, brown sweaters fitting the body closely, and brown bicycle hose and shoes. Topped off with soft brown felt hats of generous dimensions, these costumes make a very striking effect. The wheels ridden by the couple are precisely alike, and but for the masses of yellow hair and slightly smaller size of the woman, the couple could scarcely be distinguished, each from the other."

In America, as in France, the doctors are loud in praise of bicycling. In fact, in the former country, it was the wife of a leading New York physician who first learnt to ride, and became a pioneer amongst the fashionable women, and it seems remarkable that the higher ranks were also the first to adopt the cycle in England; and that London, not the country, should have been the place of its *début*. A recent writer, Lord Onslow, thinks that, in London, the craze will probably not last beyond next season, but that in the country cycling will have come to stay.

In America, too, the wheelwomen have adopted, almost with unanimity, some form of "Bloomer Costume;" but knickerbockers, the divided skirt, and short tunics and gaiters, are all adopted, as well as the tailor-made skirt. Many of the costumes seen in New York strike the onlooker as experiments, but the sincerity of all is unquestioned; for a perfect absence of self-consciousness has characterised the woman-cyclist from the first, and her strivings have been solely in the direction of simplicity and first principles. The dress, of whatever kind it is, attracts no attention, and no unkind remark; for the eyes of American spectators have long since become accustomed to costumes once thought conspicuous. Indeed, it seems likely that neither the late Mrs. Bloomer, nor Dr. Mary Walker, in her semi-masculine garb would be much noticed to-day.

Meanwhile, the literature of the bicycle is steadily increasing. Beginning with *Scribner's Magazine* in June, we find the *Nouvelle Revue*, *Engineering Magazine*, *Homiletic Review*, *Lippincott's Magazine*, and *The Idler*, all discussing the subject; and lastly, Miss Frances Willard has written a small volume, brought out under the auspices of the "Mowbray House Woman's Bicycling Association," with an introductory note by Sir Benjamin

A RATIONAL COSTUME.

Richardson. This little book is well worth reading, especially by those who are on the wrong side of fifty; and its advice, as to attempting slow progress in learning to ride being the surest and wisest plan, shows it worthy of adoption by all. First learn all the parts of your steed, and then learn how

BICYCLE COSTUME, OPENING AT THE SIDES.

Dora de Blaquière, "The Dress for Bicycling" (Volume 17, 5 October 1895, p. 13).

to mount. This last is the most difficult part of the advice to follow.

In England, as well as on the continent, the list of well-known women who have adopted the cycle is a long one, and comprises the Queen of Italy, the Duchesses of York and Connaught, Princess Maud of Wales, the Duchess of Portland, Lady Hastings, Lady Dudley, the Ladies Norreys, Wolverton, Lurgan, Yarborough, Brassey, Gerrard, and many others. It does not seem to be known who first brought Battersea Park into fashion as a retreat for cyclists, probably some well-known women who wished for a quiet place for practising the wheel. But there is no doubt that Battersea is now a rival to Hyde Park. It is farther away from crowded streets, and in its arrangements for *al fresco* meals it reminds one of a continental resort. One only wonders why we never had break-fasts under the sky long before now! The learners are there early, and at half-past ten the more expert cyclists begin to arrive, remaining in the park till nearly one o'clock. Hundreds of girls, as well as older people, are to be seen there; and one writer declares that the West End cabmen complain of fewer fares; while the livery stables also have fewer patrons, and after this "you will not be surprised to hear" (using the well-known phrase of the Tichborne trial) that an American writer opines "when cycles fall to £10, horses will go out of fashion."

In Battersea Park, as well as elsewhere, the women of position who have taken to the bicycle, have entirely held aloof from anything like masculine habiliments—knickers and gaiters, and the divided-skirt, have found no favour in their eyes. Skirts have been worn only ending above the shoes, and looking trim and neat either on or off the wheel.

During the very hot weather, skirts of serge, cloth, or *crépon*, with shirts of silk or muslin, have been universally used. When it is a little cooler, a jacket and skirt of some light material; the "sailor hat" being in very general favour; but summer hats of lace and muslin will be also constantly seen. Dainty black or brown shoes, and generally gauntlet-gloves to protect the hands and arms.

The "Rational Costume," though more seen, does not find favour in the eyes of any but people who are not of the aristocratic world, for women of high rank are much prejudiced against it. Still, a recent writer on the subject in a contemporary gives it as her opinion that the skirt is doomed, and says that nothing can exceed the ugliness of it on a windy day when it balloons-out, and the limbs are far more displayed than they would be with any form of "rational dress." Meantime, the question is a vexed one, and the apparition of a lady in "knickers" will draw a small crowd any day in Pall Mall or Piccadilly.

Country people look with unsympathetic eyes on lady-cyclists who don "knickers" and affect a mixture of masculine and feminine costume generally. Not long ago the landlady of a hotel refused to allow two of them to enter the dining-room unless they covered their nether garments with skirts, and a correspondent recently wrote to a daily paper—"I was at Dorking one afternoon, and while waiting at the railway-station noticed a lady-cyclist dressed in the latest style. She was an object of great interest to a number of natives on the platform, who looked at her with much astonishment. To a man, apparently a ploughman wearing his best clothes, who was watching the lady with staring eyes and open mouth, I whispered, 'What is that?' The countryman grinned and answered, 'I'se be hanged if I knaws, but I thinks it's an oastrich.'"

This is however a state of things that will pass away as the dwellers in the country get more used to seeing women on wheels; and we must always remember that, as an old country, we are more Conservative in our ideas and cling more to old ways than a new land like America—and things will right themselves, each woman will choose the dress that suits her fancy, or else she will abide by the wishes or the prejudices of father, brothers, or husband in her selection.

Dozens of ladies' tailors and shops in the West End are producing various descriptions of cycle costumes at all prices, many of them moderate enough to suit the most modest of purses. My own idea on the dress-question is, that there will always be those who will prefer the skirt, for one good and sufficient reason, that it is of more use when touring about, and looks better when off the wheel. In support of this opinion, I find an account of the dress adopted by a party of twelve Americans—six gentlemen and six ladies—who brought their cycles across the Atlantic this summer to use in a tour throughout England and France. The costumes were constructed by Redfern in New York. They were not uniform as to colour, but the general shape was a short coat, full in the back, and open in front, with three large buttons on each side, and short *révers* with a collar like a man's coat. A wide belt passed round the waist at the back, on the outside, and went underneath under the arms, and fastened on one side of the front. The skirts reached the ankle, and were well lined, but not stiffened. Underneath them were worn full knickerbockers to match the skirt, and gaiters were worn over the shoes; a small hat of straw trimmed simply with ribbon, and an *aigrette*, and kid gloves. The skirts worn were of washing silk, or cotton. Now, these dresses would look smart and ladylike anywhere, for walking or riding, and so would allow of the luggage being left behind or sent in advance, for some days' touring. It seems to be generally conceded that the "Eton," or short jacket to the waist, is not a becoming form of jacket for the wheel, and that some form of basque has a better effect, especially if it has a belt. The "Norfolk jacket," with box-pleats and a belt, and the skirts extending over the hips, is a popular shape; and so is a short jacket-bodice which has full basques at the back and buttons, with one button in front, over a blouse. The sleeves of this must be sufficiently ample to take in those of the blouse, without unduly crushing them.

With reference to the shape of the skirt, some are made with a broad box pleat in front in the genuine style of the Highlands. In others the skirts are shaped by gores, with the fulness at the back laid in two broad pleats, that separate when the wearer is seated.

Many skirts open, and button down the entire left side; but the best tailors button them down half way, on either side of the front, as they are easily dropped. The skirts are sometimes stiffened, and also weighted; and are always well lined. But no rule can be given about the width, as each skirt, if made by a tailor, is fitted and cut with the utmost care; just as a habit-skirt is fitted. The general width is about three yards, and the back placket-hole is always done away with, as it looks ugly, and sometimes catches on the point of the saddle. The skirt lining should be, if possible, of silk, as it steps over all other materials, and does not cling and impede movement.

The knickerbockers or "bloomers" of this year are not full, but they take the place of all under-petticoats. They are put on a yoke, which fits smoothly over the hips, and buttons at the back; expand over the knees to a

greater fulness, and are gathered just below them into a band, with buckle and strap, or else buttons and button-holes. When these are made to match the skirt, they require lining with silk or a fine sateen. If gaiters be worn, they should match the skirt and the knickers in colour.

In the *Badminton Magazine* Lord Onslow gives an account of the skirt invented by, and called after, Lady Margaret Jenkins, and thinks that it most nearly meets the exigencies of the case. This consists of a deep hem inside the skirt, which, at a sufficient distance apart (to allow of the necessary play of the knees when pedalling), is brought round each leg to fit tightly, like a garter under the skirt.

Underneath the knickerbockers a woven combination of wool, cotton, or silk and wool, should be worn, according to the season; and garters taking the shape of elastics, or any tight ligatures must be entirely dismissed in favour of the long elastic supporters, which are sewn to the edge of the corset, and fastened or tied with a loop and ribbon to the top of the stocking. Ribbed stockings are better than plain ones, and they should be of a sensible shape, with flat heels and a medium toe.

"Last but not least" you must remember that there is no gain, either in grace or beauty, in a small waist for bicycling; and an ungraceful "peg-top" look is given to the figure if the size of the hips be unduly accentuated. Whatever is worn, the long-waisted corset ought to be dismissed at once in the pursuit of any out-of-door recreation, especially cycling, where the heavily-boned stay is dangerous to health, and even to life. A pair of short riding stays is best, or else a buttoned, slightly corded, or boned under-bodice. Several modern makes of corset come up entirely to the ideal thing for wearing; and they are obtainable at any good draper's. The appearance of the tight corset on the cycle is more than ungraceful; and forms one of the eyesores in the dress of French cyclists.

Nor do I think what is known as the "sweater" (or the woven Jersey) are pretty or graceful garments for riding in, for they reveal the figure too much, and are too plain and too tight-fitting for grace or beauty. Hats must be of such a texture as to stand a shower, and the trimming should be of ribbon or velvet, in preference to feathers or lace. A wide-brimmed hat is unsuitable, but the brim should be of a sufficient width to shade the eyes. A light felt seems to be the best, on the whole, and some are both pretty and becoming. The hair should be dressed very simply, in close coils or plaits, that will not become untidy in the swift passage through the air. Nets should always be used, and veils are sometimes a great comfort. *Chiffon* and silk gauze are the most sensible, and such a length should be bought that it may be fastened securely at the back, or else the ends brought round and tied in front.

Last of all, I must mention that one of the burning questions of the hour is relative to the seats used on the cycle, and several French doctors have spoken of the danger of their producing irritation of the spine. They should be much broader and softer, and of an entirely different shape. Much discussion is taking place over the adoption of the sliding-seat, on the same principle as applied to boats. But I find that experienced wheelmen are not unanimous in their favour, and that there is much to be said against them. This subject has always been a difficult one for men, and the invasion of the fair sex makes it likely that some fresh departure will be taken, to make the present seats less objectionable.

Dora de Blaquière, "The Dress for Bicycling" (Volume 17, 5 October 1895, p. 14).

VOL. XXI.—No. 1051.]   FEBRUARY 17, 1900.   [PRICE ONE PENNY.

LAWN-TENNIS.

BY H. M. PILLANS.

THE popularity of lawn-tennis, as a game, can never be disputed. It has remained in favour now for many years, and still holds its own against golf, cycling, and many other forms of amusement which fashion decrees from time to time must be indulged in by all those who wish to be considered up-to-date.

It is true that among the many enthusiasts of the game there are few who obtain any real degree of proficiency, most girls reaching only a moderate standard, from which they find it impossible to advance.

Few games, however, can surpass it, providing, as it does, the combined advantages of healthy exercise for both body and mind, at the same time being an interesting game to watch, and affording much pleasant social intercourse.

The question has often been asked in the tennis world, "Why is the standard of the average girl's play so far below a man's?" Not implying, of course, that one ever expects to see "equality of the sexes" in this respect; but in the case of a game requiring skill rather than brute force the weaker sex should certainly be able to show to better advantage than at present.

The answers to this problem are many and various. I will first enumerate some of the reasons usually given, afterwards adding my

A LAWN-TENNIS TOURNAMENT.

H. M. Pillans, "Lawn-Tennis" (Volume 21, 17 February 1900, p. 305).

FIG. I.

personal opinion as a player of more than ten years' standing.

1. That a girl is not physically strong enough to make a powerful player.

2. That the sex are naturally unoriginal and incapable of working out the theory of the game for themselves.

3. That a woman's dress greatly impedes her movements and handicaps her in more ways than one.

4. It is also said that a girl cannot run, and on a tennis-court so often stands upon her heels, thus rendering it an impossibility to move quickly. Surely this is more their misfortune than their fault? A woman has always been accustomed from her childhood to wear more or less high-heeled shoes. In tennis the rules of the games deny her this support, at the same time telling her to stand upon her toes. Observation shows, however, that she usually stands upon her heels, or strains the muscles at the back of her foot, which are unaccustomed to being stretched in this way. Doubtless this is one of the many reasons why a girl tires so easily, because this strain must act indirectly upon the spine, and soon gives a feeling of exhaustion.

My personal opinion is as follows :—

1. I agree that although the average girl is very persevering, she will not apply any theory to the game. She simply clings to the idea that "practice makes perfect"; this I can tell her from bitter experience is a fallacy. Unless she is going the right way to work, she may play for half a century with practically no result. There is always a right and a wrong way to do everything; and unfortunately the girl's natural way of playing lawn-tennis is usually the wrong way.

2. Sporting women are practically a new creation. Until recent years it was never considered necessary for them to use either their brains or their muscles, which consequently have remained undeveloped for generations. Therefore it is not to be wondered at that the girl of the present day labours under many disadvantages.

3. They are too often handicapped by the problem of £ s. d. Girls and boys should be treated alike in this respect; with the former, however, it usually means an appeal to a parent or guardian, who is often willing to

lavish money upon the boys, but begrudges every sovereign asked for by a girl. This takes the spirit out of her at the very commencement, for to become a first-class player cannot be considered a cheap amusement.

4. On the vexed subject of dress there is a great deal of nonsense talked. A girl with any common-sense never wears a long or heavy skirt for tennis, or, in fact, any garment in which she does not feel perfectly free and comfortable. Although I am an advocate for reform in many ways, I do not like to see dress made a handle for excuses. The faults much more often lie in the girl herself than in her dress. This does not take into account the frivolous individual with an eighteen-inch waist and a large hat who poses upon a tennis-court. Doubtless her dress considerably impedes her movements, but happily this type of player is now almost as extinct as the dodo. In the matter of shoes, if a girl feels the want of support previously alluded to, and is inclined to stand upon her heels, it is a good plan to have shoes made with a half-inch cork elevator fastened inside. The upper leather of the shoes, of course, must be cut proportionately higher to allow for this heel.

Lessons.—On the subject of lessons in lawn-tennis there is much to be said. Not only is it beneficial for a beginner or bad player to receive tuition from a competent teacher, but undoubtedly it is an absolute necessity for all those who desire to become good players. Almost without exception is instruction needed before proficiency can be acquired in any accomplishment or sport. Therefore why not in lawn-tennis, which is acknowledged to be one of the most difficult of ball games? True, there are few professionals who teach the art, those at Queen's Club, West Kensington, FitzWilliam Club, Dublin, and at the covered court, Llandudno, being the only ones of any note; but if the demand for their services became greater, doubtless it would create a supply.

In these days when one hears so much about distressed ladies, I feel confident that if a few would turn their attention to "training the young idea," they would find it a remunerative and healthy employment. I seriously recommend it to their notice.

Verbal instructions, with practical demonstrations, are always much easier to grasp than book theories. Many girls also are too bashful to have tennis lessons from a man.

A book, recently published, entitled *Lessons in Lawn-Tennis*, by Eustace M. Miles, however, gives a great deal of useful information, with diagrams of good positions and angles, and would be a great help to many. But it must not be supposed that people can be made good players all at once. The process requires great patience and perseverance, the would-be reformer remembering that it is much harder to unlearn a bad habit than to learn a good one. This recalls the incident of an impetuous young Irishman taking lessons from a professional. On being asked how he was progressing, replied—

"I seem to have unlearnt all the strokes I used to score by, and still find myself unable to hit the ball as I am told. Therefore my last state is considerably worse than my first."

Like many other deluded mortals, he thought the strokes looked so easy, and imagined he would be able to put the whole system into practice in two days.

This same professional mortally wounded the feelings of a poor damsel by telling her she did not possess a back-hand stroke. Poor girl! To be told this after many years of patient but blind practice, was indeed mortifying. I notice, however, that this same lady is since considered to have improved her games more than fifteen, and she now plays in the matches for her county, besides blossoming as a first-class player in the open tournaments.

Positions.—The following remarks, let it be clearly understood, are in no way original, but simply a repetition of "counsel's opinion."

In recent years it will be seen that the general style of play has been altered considerably. Fig. I shows an example of the old-fashioned laborious style. This meant hitting the ball when quite near the ground, the striker standing directly facing the net. Needless to say, this was a lifting and most tiring stroke. Note the grip of the racket, with the wrist facing outwards, the position of the body, the right foot being foremost, also where the ball touches the racket. The striker is evidently looking towards the spot where the ball is intended to go to. Now look at Fig. 2; imagine this player standing in exactly the same place; compare the grip and position of the racket, the angle of the body which is turned nearly sideways to the net, left foot foremost, the eyes being fixed on the ball, which is almost at the top of the bounce. Fig. 3 shows the position of the racket, as it should appear at the finish of the stroke. The ball is now travelling across the net, into the far corner of the opposite court.

Advice to beginners.—Stand in front of a cheval-glass, holding the illustration in your left hand, so that you see the reflection of it in the glass. (This enables you to see the figure facing the same way as yourself.) First put yourself into the position of Fig. 1, afterwards into the position of Fig. 2, and remember that the one is up-to-date, and the other is out of date.

The Fore-Hand Stroke.—Again take up your position in front of a long glass, standing in the attitude of Fig. 2. Describe a semicircle (slightly behind) with the racket, so as to get a swing, at the same time bringing the weight of the body on to the front foot at the moment the racket touches the (imaginary) ball, bending the front knee a little, and carrying on the racket now until it is in the position of Fig. 3.

After the stroke is finished, bring the feet back level with each other, and stand straight facing the net, weight equally divided upon both feet, the body leaning slightly forward, the racket horizontal, supported near the head with the left hand.

The Back-Hand Stroke.—Fig. 4 shows the old style of a back-hand stroke. Notice the ball has already past the striker, consequently

FIG. 2.

FIG. 3.

all power over it has been lost. The head of the racket is very much below the level of the wrist, the left (instead of the right) foot being in front.

It will be found that this stroke requires a superhuman amount of strength, and even then seldom reaches the top of the net. Fig. 5 shows the correct back-hand stroke—the weight of the body well on the front foot; right foot foremost, knee slightly bent, the head of the racket slightly above the level of the wrist, which is rigid as soon as it comes in contact with the ball.

The Volley.—This is a most difficult stroke for the average girl-player. The chief features to remember are, to always strike the ball when it is in front of you, and in the case of an over-head volley, reach well up to the ball (as if you were anxious to hit it as soon as possible). Turn a little to the side the ball is coming, whether right or left. The pace depends much on the swing of the body. Point the toe of the front foot, and bend the knee slightly, bringing the weight of the body from the back foot on to the front, as the racket meets the ball.

It is curious to note how many men break down at an overhead volley, if they have to step back for it. It is so much easier to move forward a step than to move back one. Anyone who can carry out all these instructions has become a good player. It is easier said than done, and, as previously stated, it is much simpler to have the positions shown you than to acquire them from printed instructions.

General Instructions.—1. Every ball must be hit when in front of the striker.

2. Always rest on your toes, and stand where you think the ball would fall at the second bounce.

3. Every stroke should be deliberate. The racket should meet the ball (never jerk it). The pace is regulated by the correct body-swing in conjunction with the arm.

4. Keep your eyes always fixed on the ball.

5. The racket (when not in action) should be held in a horizontal position, supported by the left hand. Never head downwards.

6. Cultivate independence, always remembering your own handicap; score in games and points. Umpires are not immaculate!

The Service.—It is important to cultivate a good service. Whether it is an over-hand or an under-hand stroke, the chief object in view should be to impart the maximum of strength, expending only the minimum of force.

The over-hand service is undoubtedly the best style, and all should try to acquire it, but it is well also to cultivate an under-hand stroke, as variation has many advantages. For instance in a mixed double, the man is often puzzled by a cut, low-bouncing, under-hand service. On the other hand the girl often fails to make a good return from an over-hand stroke. Therefore suit your service to your opponent, and try to place it as much as possible.

Many girls have no idea where to stand to receive a service. The rule, as previously stated, is quite simple. Always stand where you think the ball would fall at the second bounce. Example. When waiting to receive a man's really hard service, your position should be about three feet outside the back line; but if it should be a screwed or twisted service, it will sometimes be necessary to stand almost parallel with the ball as it bounces, as if prepared to take it back-handed, but in

FIG. 4.

reality it will bound right over to your forehand. It must be a very twisted service, however, that bounces at right angles instead of straight ahead. If you carefully watch your opponent's racket, you can always see whether it will be a cut or straight service.

Cutting the ball.—This is a very usual fault with girls, and is a most difficult habit to get out of. Some say it is incurable when every ball is cut. This, of course, is not the case, but patience and perseverance will be required in considerable quantities before the fault can be eradicated. It is caused by the wrist being turned back at the moment the ball is hit; this again turns the face of the racket slightly upwards, and the ball is sliced rather than hit. The great disadvantage of this stroke is that it takes the pace off the ball and allows your opponent plenty of time to get to it, however well placed. On occasions, of course, it is useful to be able to cut a ball "short" over the net, but as a rule the habit is to be discouraged.

Imitation is the highest form of flattery.—The next suggestion for the struggling amateur is to go as a spectator to a large "Open Tournament." Select a court where a first-class player (with notably good style) is in action. Set yourself to watch *not the game* but his positions, attitudes, on what strokes he succeeds best, where he fails, and the reason why. I am assuming that a man is taken for the model, because a girl's dress and other loose draperies tend to distract the eye. Now keep your eyes fixed on the model, watch closely how high he throws the ball before serving, the swing of the racket preparatory to striking the ball; then again watch the fore-hand stroke off the ground, where the model stands, the position of the feet, the angle and swing of the body, the position of the racket when the stroke is finished, likewise the back-hand, the volley, and in fact all the different strokes. This will provide you a much more instructive afternoon than commenting on the personal attractions and beauty of the players. *Handsome is as handsome does!*

Having made mental notes of all these positions, retire to a private court, get some charitable friend to send you easy balls, and see how far you can carry out the lessons you have learnt.

I remember at a tournament watching a model for two days, and at the end being called upon to play a single myself. A bystander in the crowd was heard to remark to his friend, "Dear me, how much that girl's style is like Mr. ——!" This is proof that the suggestion is a practical one.

Health and Training.—Health and strength are undoubtedly the backbone of all sport. Without it none can ever hope to succeed; therefore it is a most important item in the career of a tennis player. Those who already possess these necessary and excellent attributes are to be envied, but the usual cry is, "*I am not strong enough.*" To which my reply is, "Then *make yourself strong enough,*" providing you have not a weak heart or infirmities of that nature.

People are very much what they make themselves. It is sad to see the individual who is content to believe that she is strong enough for all her requirements; one cannot help feeling that this contented person would be a better person in every way by remembering the fact that there is room for improvement in everyone, and that by developing the muscles of the body there

FIG. 5.

H. M. Pillans, *"Lawn-Tennis" (Volume 21, 17 February 1900, p. 307).*

would ensue consequent enlargement of the mind. It is a well-known fact that physical development not only endows the individual with health and strength, but improves the character and disposition. A well-known authority says, " It is one of the pleasantest features of to-day to see so many girls and women realise, and are encouraged to participate in, what was once regarded only as man's domain, viz., the world of sport." Some of the leading physicians now state that bicycling has cured half of the nervous and imaginary ailments due to inactivity of the mind and body. May it be said in future years that sport and honest work have cured the other half.

This training, however, will require patience, for people cannot be made " Samsons " in a week. Regular and consistent practice, night and morning, with dumb-bells, etc., even if only for ten minutes, will soon show a good result. A book entitled *Strength and How to Obtain It*, by Sandow, is most useful in showing the amateur how to go to work.

Fencing and gymnastics of all kinds are very beneficial for all those who have time and inclination to indulge in them. Hockey is also to be recommended for teaching a girl to turn quickly, and run well.

Nerves are also a great source of trouble to many. Those suffering from this malady are much to be pitied; but pity without relief is like mustard without beef. Any speedy cure for this evil will be welcomed as a blessing to many.

Drugs and other strong remedies are sometimes resorted to, but as a rule they are to be avoided.

Singles.—The game of singles soon shows a girl the real necessity of training, good lasting powers being of decidedly more value than short-lived brilliancy. The great point of weakness, however, in this game lies in the back-hand stroke, scarcely one girl in six possessing even a moderate back-hand, and consequently adopting the most fatal mistake of running round all balls placed to her left side, endeavouring to take every ball fore-handed.

The disadvantages of this plan will be seen at a glance and, moreover, will be forcibly impressed on the memory, when a girl employing these tactics comes against a first-class player, who never hesitates to take full advantage of this weakness.

The correct position to stand for a single is somewhere on an imaginary line drawn straight down the centre of the court (except, of course, when serving or receiving a service). It therefore stands to reason that if a ball is placed to your left side, and you run round and take it fore-handed, you find yourself either tucked up in a corner, or considerably beyond the side-line. This is exactly what your opponent wants, for she has now the whole court vacant to place the ball where she pleases. If the beginner will adopt this suicidal plan, she simply kills herself by madly rushing from side to side of the court, instead of remaining more or less stationary. The best players, when they find themselves out of position, invariably lob the ball. This gains time and enables them to get back into position before the ball is returned.

Advice.—It is well to determine, " come what may," never to run round a ball. At first, be content with passing it carefully but gently back, placing it as near as possible to your opponent's back line, as good length is indispensable in singles.

When the beginner has succeeded so far, it will be time enough to increase the pace. The player who can volley has a great advantage, being able to run in and kill any short balls.

Ladies' Doubles.—The definition of a ladies' double has been given as follows : " A court with four ladies, viz., one at each corner, all having an unswerving devotion for the back line, and who are all much too tender-hearted to kill a ball."

This is the unkind criticism of a cynic. It is not to be disputed, however, that this event in a tournament is seldom wildly exciting for the on-lookers. Neither is it renowned for great head-work and punishing strokes, but nevertheless the ladies enjoy it ; this in the meantime is a very good reason for supporting the ladies' doubles.

A committee of wicked men occasionally try to deprive the ladies of their doubles, on account of the great length of time they take ; but every girl should take up the cudgels against the perpetrators of such wilful injustice. They cannot do without the support of the " fair sex," therefore why treat them so badly ? Page 305 shows a good study in positions.

Notice the lady champion in the far corner has no intention of losing her balance, the racket is held horizontally and she is standing well on her toes. Note also the exaggerated body-swing of the player administering justice upon the ball. Apparently she is a heartless young woman, trying to prove herself an exception to the rule by killing a ball !

Mixed Doubles.—The players who are most successful in mixed doubles are those who can hit hard (not necessarily always into court, for the opposing man will usually try to volley any ball not going more than a few feet out). This, combined with some consistent lobbing, makes an ideal mixed player.

What to do with a bad partner is a question much disputed. A new idea is to ask a really weak girl player to remain stationary near the side line and only about three feet from the net, with instructions only to take balls within easy reach. This plan has proved successful on several occasions, but means that the man must do the majority of the work. If the lady is new to this position, it causes much confusion and irritation to the opposite side, as she invariably hit the balls all round the wood of the racket, which consequently fall where least expected.

Others will say a weak partner is best from five to fifty yards outside the court, only coming near the line to serve. Some men even boast of winning in this way, against indifferent opponents, but " weak woman " will not always be down-trodden, and now often asserts her right to a portion of the court. The " lords of creation," however, do not as a rule like their partners to come up to the net and volley. It is a comparatively recent innovation, but time will prove whether it makes a successful combination. At present no doubt it often leads to confusion even among the best players.

" Gallant man " is always most profuse in his praise, often applauding very bad strokes, so long as they go over the net, but at the same time often complains that his good strokes pass unnoticed. Possibly a little more equal division of praise would be better.

> " Women have many faults,
>   Men have but two,
> Nothing right they say,
>   And nothing right they do."

MR. AND MRS. SWEET AND THEIR SLAVE.

By MAY CROMMELIN.

CHAPTER III.

A FORTNIGHT of sunny spring weather had passed away since the Sweet couple ended house-building. The nest itself had only taken some two days of loving labour, thanks to the excellent supply of materials with which the slave had supplied her owners.

" Yah! Yah! Lazybodies ! " jeered the sparrows that used to hop on the window-sill and stare in with vulgar curiosity. " We are free ! We fly about and search for our straws and stuff in the streets and squares ; we pillage and rob these giant humans. They never lock us up in prisons as they do you. No ! Our armies are too mighty. They dare not ill-treat any of us or we should descend in a horde upon them and peck all the oppressors to death. Your children will never be hatched in that stuffy cavern, you'll see. Or if they are, they will be all kinds of horrid colours—blue and green and red, like so many parrots."

" Wretches! Beggars! Robbers ! " shrieked Mr. Sweet in a rage. " You are all no better than so many vagrants. How dare you prate of your nests to us—you who steal straws from each other, and quarrel and scold all day long in the most shocking manner ! Listen to me ! I and my wife are a king and queen of small birds. These men and women are our loyal subjects, and they serve us in our palace and bring us humbly all we want. Search for our own moss and wool indeed ! What an idea ! No, no, no ! Golden birds like us are too rare and precious. The humans obey us, but they scorn your brown brood. We have subdued them by our song. You, who are of no use at all, they only suffer as scavengers ; but when your houses choke their rain-pipes, how they sweep them down into the street—young ones and eggs and homes. Ha ! I know. I have heard your hoarse out-cries and gibbering rage. Such an outrage would have stirred me to a song that would thrill the hearts of my foes. . . . Oh, our nestlings will be ugly, will they ? "

All the while he had never paused for breath, but poured out his wrath and scorn in a burst of melody.

" How those squeaking sparrows do excite him," remarked Violet Jenkins, pausing an instant from her never-ending sewing to listen.

" Tweet ! tweet ! Let them say what they please, dear," chirped Mrs. Sweet languidly from where she sat patiently on her nest, that was guarded by a curtain from prying eyes. " I have been dozing a little until this row woke me up. Please give me some food. I am rather hungry."

" Certainly, my love ! I beg your pardon for neglecting you. These common birds are so annoying, they made me almost forget my duty for a little while. . . . Have some hard-boiled hen-meat ? I have kept you the biggest and best piece, really ! " And Mr. Sweet, who was saying the strict truth—and thought himself a very noble fellow for being so unselfish—nimbly hopped down to search the larder for the best tit-bits to bring his spouse.

" Well, you are good to me," said Mrs. Sweet. And, being a dear little soul, she forgot how her lord used to tyrannise over her at other times.

" I am, I am," twittered Mr. Sweet. " In our exalted position we have to set a good example, you see, to the outside world, my mutual understanding and tenderness, which is the sweetest bond in family life. Then Florence took up her flowers and went back to the house to write her letter, whilst the father looked after her with a world of love in his eyes, suddenly exclaiming—

"Bless my soul, Lilian, our little girl has grown into a woman, how, I don't know! Suppose some bold youngster dares to fall in love with her whilst she is away yonder! However should we put up with such a thing?"

Father and mother exchanged glances. The idea was not quite so new to the mother as to him. She smiled tenderly, sweetly, yet half sadly.

"If such a thing were to happen, and it were to be for her best happiness, I trust we should be able to rejoice with her. And we must comfort ourselves with the wisdom of the old saw—

"'A son is a son till he gets him a wife,
But a daughter's a daughter the whole of her life.'"

(*To be continued.*)

ATHLETICISM FOR GIRLS.

THIS combination of words has a distinctly modern sound.

Let us, to emphasise the contrast between the former days and these, glance at a girls' school of deservedly high reputation, in the neighbourhood of London, some sixty years ago.

It is after breakfast on a summer's day. Two and two, the pupils, fifty in number, are pacing through the house! On they go, round dining-hall, music-room, school-rooms, and so on, till the allotted time has been completed for the dreary indoor exercise.

Eleven o'clock strikes, and an exodus takes place into the garden. This at least is a sensible arrangement! But no sound of merry voices, no running and scampering, no semblance of a game, breaks the decorous monotony of two and two. On they file, through the gravel walks, among the ordered beds and trim lawns, till recalled to their lessons within.

The chief exercise of the day takes place a little later, and this time the long procession of two and two issues without the precincts. Decorously the girls travel on their way, through the leafy outskirts of suburban London. There is no stint as to the extent of this walk; it is protracted, and for the most part along green and airy thoroughfares. But as the sole outdoor amusement, how dull and stiff and dreary the parade must have appeared! It is sad to learn that an occasional furtive ring at the gate-bell of some solemnly respectable house in Camberwell Grove served as a safety-valve for high and frolicsome young spirits!

The evening comes, but no "games" come with it. It is darkly whispered that once upon a time a requisition was sent to the Principals that dancing might be permitted among the girls in the hour of relaxation. The reply was a refusal.

Nothing but crochet and conversation may be the entertainment after the day's work.

Such was the programme of recreation at one of the most enlightened "Establishments for Young Ladies" in the days of our grandmothers.

A generation later things had improved. At a similar school of high standing which we take as an illustration, dancing was allowed and encouraged among the girls in the evening. The mid-day walk was supplemented in suitable weather by a rule ordering each girl to traverse a certain distance between landmarks in the garden, after breakfast, so many times. As the girls were just then in a hurry to prepare for school, they would run backwards and forwards at full speed! Croquet was permitted, and excursions into the country were sometimes arranged. But still (and we write of the sixties of last century) there were no games involving bodily exercise.

In boys' schools the case was even then very different.

And Herbert Spencer, in his well-known essay on Education, pleads the cause of girls. After contrasting boarding-schools for girls and boys, he asks—

"Why this astonishing difference? Is it that a girl has none of the promptings to vociferous play by which boys are impelled? Or is it that, while in boys these promptings are to be regarded as stimuli to a bodily activity without which there cannot be adequate development, to their sisters Nature has given them for no purpose whatever—unless it be for the vexation of schoolmistresses? Perhaps, however, we mistake the aim of those who train the gentler sex. We have a vague suspicion that to produce a robust *physique* is thought undesirable; that rude health and abundant vigour are considered somewhat plebeian; that a certain delicacy, a strength not competent to more than a mile or two's walk, an appetite fastidious and easily satisfied, joined with that timidity which commonly accompanies feebleness, are held more ladylike."

Times have indeed changed, and we have changed with them!

In selecting a boarding-school for her daughters, the first question of many a matron is now, "Do they play hockey? Are the games good?" To ensure the variety and efficiency of games is one chief care of the Principal, and she frequently has to provide a "Games Mistress." Hockey and cricket, as well as tennis, are encouraged to the full. Hockey especially seems fast growing in favour. The afternoons in many schools are devoted to these outdoor games; they are a *sine quâ non*. Even day schools have their "playing field," and keen is the emulation between school and school. It is unnecessary to enlarge upon this side of the question, as every girl who reads our paper will be able to fill in details from her own experience or that of her comrades.

Apart from games, strictly so-called, the modern girl "goes in" for riding, rowing, swimming, gymnastics, shooting, skating, bicycling and so forth, even as her brothers do. But as the first three of these pursuits, even in the days of the limited training described, were allowed to the girl who was emancipated from lessons, they scarcely enter into our subject, as do the games that form part of the modern school curriculum. It is in this prominence given to physical training as such—a prominence rapidly increasing—that the great difference lies between "Then" and "Now."

It is scarcely necessary to express satisfaction at the disappearance of all false notions as to the charm of the anæmic complexion, wasp-like waist, and tendency to swoon on the slightest provocation! We are wise now in understanding that the "sound mind" must dwell in the "sound body," and modern schoolgirls reap the benefit of this enlightenment.

The public mind is so keenly alive to this aspect of the question that it is superfluous to say anything in praise of the new wisdom.

Rather is it necessary, as we think, to say a word of caution as to rushing to extremes in its pursuit!

In progress, there is always a danger of going too far in one direction. The zigzag Alpine path climbs the height

Lily Watson, "Athleticism for Girls" (Volume 24, 25 October 1902, p. 61).

by going first to one side, then to the other. The pendulum swings in the same way. But the path must not run too far to the right or to the left, or ground will be lost in the ascent ; if the pendulum swings too far, the balance will be destroyed.

Some have been known to lament the exaggerated glorification of games, even in boys' schools. There has been much excitement of late with regard to Rudyard Kipling's "flannelled fool at the wicket ; muddied oaf at the goal." Without attempting to enter into the question raised by that remarkable poem, it is easy to see that it is possible to attach too much importance even to the handling of a ball ! The incidental advantages of the playing-field are, of course, beyond doubt, and English boys will never, it is to be hoped, cease to excel in athletic sports. But every lad who, through—it may be—delicacy of health, is unable to distinguish himself at cricket or football, is not necessarily a fool or a coward. The conviction that he is, and must be, has embittered the childhood of more than one man of genius. It is a brutal and a stupid notion.

We well recollect a certain Saturday evening when we were visiting the Head Master of a well-known school. Terrible gloom prevailed. One culprit there was, pointed out for universal execration. What had he done ? He was a University man, one of the masters, young, athletic, with a pleasant bearing, and a face that would have been bright and open had it not been overcast by remorse.

Of what crime had he been guilty to overshadow his countenance, to destroy his influence with the boys, and possibly to blight a promising career at the outset ?

There had been a cricket match that afternoon, and he had missed a catch.

It was, frankly, a great pity. But we could not help feeling that the scornful wrath on the one hand, the despair on the other, were exaggerated. That man was intensely to be commiserated, in good earnest ; all the more so as this one slip would destroy his prestige to a disproportionate extent. No scholarship, no intellectual feat, would make up for it.

It is not our business, however, even if we were competent, to enter into the matter as it concerns boys' schools ; but we do say that it will be a great misfortune if this conviction of the supreme importance of games above everything else enters into the education of girls ; and this we say while heartily approving of outdoor amusement in moderation.

To hear some modern schoolgirls, and even modern mothers, talk, one would suppose that hockey was the chief end of all education ! The tone of the school—the intellectual training—these come in the second place. Tennis, cricket, but above all, hockey ! These are the allurements to such and such a school, the pride, occupation, and distinction of the pupils when they get there !

One hears, for instance, of a girls' hockey team travelling, during the school term, five hundred miles to play a match with another school. A thousand miles' railway journey in all would be involved !

Well, if the parents like it, and the girls enjoy it, why not ? someone may say. And we may be accused of lack of the sporting instinct !

It would be quite out of place to criticise individual instances, which may be perfectly justified by circumstances. But such journeys and such importance assigned to games do show in which way the tendency is going ; and we declare that there is a danger in it all.

The reasons for this opinion are threefold.

First, the violent exercise which is good for boys is not always, and to the same extent, good for girls. They develop more quickly than boys. It is impossible, as Herbert Spencer points out, to get more vital energy from the body than it possesses at any given moment ; growth, digestion, and intellectual effort also make heavy demands upon this vital energy. Then if excessive energy is flung into any one direction, some one of the other processes must suffer. The girl who is *too* violent and vigorous in her daily hockey or cricket, for example, may find a corresponding decrease in her mental power, or the overstrain

will affect her development in some other way ; although, of course, games in moderation are good for her. It is therefore a mistake to infer that the more violent tearing and racing, and physical effort, and rushing about a girl indulges in, the better it is for her " all round."

Secondly, there is a danger of the decrease of womanly grace. But oh, how difficult it is to guard such an assertion as this, lest we be accused of worshipping the old-fashioned ideal of sentimental weakness !

The girl with supple form, vigorous tread, health showing itself in the clear complexion, bright eye, and cheerful energy of the whole personality, ready to row a boat or climb a mountain, is the girl we admire. But it is possible for a girl to possess perfect health and vigour without the undue development of muscle, the rough ways, the coarseness of grain, that mark the " athletic girl."

Let us stop and weigh the phrase. Everybody admires the " athletic " man ; the ideal is felt directly to be a true and fitting one. But is there the same feeling with regard to the quality " athletic " as applied to women ? Does it not raise an instinctive wonder, a feeling of incongruity, suggesting a development in one direction that has cost something in another ?

To quote Herbert Spencer once again, he says, in regard to the sports for which he wisely pleads, that there is no fear of their making girls rough and boisterous, for womanly instincts will in time put an efficient restraint upon any such manifestations. The excessive worship of such sports does, however, tend to produce the effect mentioned by the philosopher. Loud voices, loosened hair, rough words and gestures, the contemptuous application of the term " crock " to any girl who is not skilled in athletic games ; these are a few of the demonstrations we have noted, and they are not beautiful ; neither are big, reddened hands, large feet, to be admired.

Thirdly, the making of games the chief object in school life tends to give a wrong ideal of life as a whole.

There is already no small danger of modern young people regarding pleasure as the chief object of their existence ! Girls know perfectly well that games are, after all, amusement ; it is to their elders that the incidental physical advantages on their behalf chiefly appeal. Then to make these things, the hockey match, the cricket match, of such importance that time is constantly devoted to practice, to long journeys, in which money is spent, the kingdom scoured, on their account, is to encourage a selfish conviction that pleasure is supreme. After all, study is one chief end of school discipline ! And all this modern tendency towards exalting physical exercise and the playing of games before everything else is in the way of encouraging a wrong ideal of life. Recreation is made the first duty, rather than re-creation.

There is another way of looking at it. The English boy, whose devotion to games is known the world over, is, after his University life, called to a career, a profession. The playing of games, which has helped to make him what he is, now falls into the background, becoming merely a resource for leisure hours. The middle-class English girl, with nothing particular to do, and parents to support her in comfort, may, and occasionally does, carry her school training to the legitimate issue of regarding these games as a suitable life-occupation. Her days are filled with golf, for example. For a recreation this is excellent ; for an engrossing pursuit it is scarcely the life-work of a rational human being, with a reason for her existence to render to her Creator. And the girl who does nothing else but play this or some other vigorous game, rising to eminence, stalking over the land playing matches, contemptuously styling her less distinguished sisters " crocks," is likely to view her life entirely out of its true proportion.

Of course, this protest is not universally applicable. But is it unnecessary ? We fear not, and urge " our girls," while they enjoy recreation to the full, to beware of the error of making it the chief end of their school life. Do not let them elevate " the ball " in one size or material or another, into the tutelary genius of their existence, or they will find it a hard, unintelligent, and featureless idol.

LILY WATSON.

Lily Watson, "Athleticism for Girls" (Volume 24, 25 October 1902, p. 62).